AREA HANDBOOK
for the
PHILIPPINES

Coauthors

Nena Vreeland

Geoffrey B. Hurwitz
Peter Just
Philip W. Moeller
R. S. Shinn

Research completed January 1976

Second Edition

Published 1976

(This handbook supersedes DA Pam 550–72, February 1969)

DA Pam 550–72

Library of Congress Cataloging in Publication Data

Vreeland, Nena, 1934-

Area handbook for the Philippines.
"DA pam 550-72."
"One of a series of handbooks prepared by Foreign Area Studies (FAS) of the American University."
Supersedes 1969 ed. prepared by F. H. Chaffee et al.
Bibliography: p. 393.
Includes index.
1. Philippine Islands. I. Chaffee, Frederic H. Area handbook for the Philippines. II. American University, Washington, D. C. Foreign Area Studies. III. Title.

Library of Congress Cataloging in Publication Data

DS655.V73   1976   959.9'04   76-22732

For sale by the Superintendent of Documents, U.S. Government Printing Office
Washington, D.C. 20402 - Price $6.90

FOREWORD

This volume is one of a series of handbooks prepared by Foreign Area Studies (FAS) of The American University, designed to be useful to military and other personnel who need a convenient compilation of basic facts about the social, economic, political, and military institutions and practices of various countries. The emphasis is on objective description of the nation's present society and the kinds of possible or probable changes that might be expected in the future. The handbook seeks to present as full and as balanced an integrated exposition as limitations on space and research time permit. It was compiled from information available in openly published material. An extensive bibliography is provided to permit recourse to other published sources for more detailed information. There has been no attempt to express any specific point of view or to make policy recommendations. The contents of the handbook represent the work of the authors and FAS and do not represent the official view of the United States government.

An effort has been made to make the handbook as comprehensive as possible. It can be expected, however, that the material, interpretations, and conclusions are subject to modification in the light of new information and developments. Such corrections, additions, and suggestions for factual, interpretive, or other change as readers may have will be welcomed for use in future revisions. Comments may be addressed to:

The Director
Foreign Area Studies
The American University
5010 Wisconsin Avenue, N.W.
Washington, D.C. 20016

PREFACE

Since 1969, when the last *Area Handbook for the Philippines* was published, the country has undergone significant changes. In 1972 the incumbent president, Ferdinand E. Marcos, imposed martial law, and at a stroke the former democratic institutions of the country ceased to function. The country experienced other changes as well, including an outbreak of insurgency, the expiration of an agreement that had long governed United States-Philippines economic relations, and shifts in international power relationships within the Asian region. The possibility of further change was suggested by Marcos' call for the creation of a New Society in the Philippines. His determination to impose a consensus on a country of great and persisting inequalities was perhaps his most formidable task as the second half of the decade began. The year 1975 was thus an appropriate point for reconsidering the course of Philippine society.

The purpose of this handbook is to provide a concise, balanced, and objective description and analysis of dominant social, political, military, and economic aspects of Philippine society. It seeks to identify dynamic forces and major trends and to give the reader an understanding of the aims and values of Filipinos. Interpretations are offered on a tentative basis as befits research undertaken without field study in a nation undergoing change and without the previous advantage of a completely free Philippine press.

The 1969 edition of the handbook was the product of a team composed of George E. Aurell, Helen A. Barth, Elinor C. Betters, Ann S. Cort, John H. Dombrowski, Vincent J. Fasano, and John O. Weaver under the chairmanship of Frederic H. Chaffee. In the present edition, particularly the chapters dealing with geography, history, religion, and social structure, use has been made of materials from the 1969 edition and of some updated materials prepared in 1972 by John E. MacDonald, Kenneth Martindale, Jeffrey Record, and Charles Townsend.

The present edition results from the combined efforts of a multidisciplinary team of researchers assisted by the staff of Foreign Area Studies. The team was chaired by Nena Vreeland, who wrote chapters 1, 3, and 8 and coordinated the contributions of the other authors. Geoffrey B. Hurwitz wrote chapters 12, 14, and 15; Peter Just wrote chapters 4, 5, and 13; Philip W. Moeller wrote chapters 2, 6, and 7; and R. S. Shinn wrote chapters 9, 10, and 11. The authors express their thanks to Richard E. Snyder, who wrote chapters 16 and 17. The authors also acknowledge with gratitude—and without associating them in any way with the contents of the present edition—the assistance of both private individuals and persons in various agencies of the United States government who gave their time, documents, and special knowledge to provide information and perspective.

Spellings of place-names used in the handbook conform generally to official standard names approved by the United States Board on Geographic Names. In instances where information is expressed in weights and measures not employed in the United States the equivalent is provided. Tons are metric unless otherwise specified. The reader may refer to the glossary for United States dollar-peso equivalents and for other frequently used terms.

COUNTRY SUMMARY

1. COUNTRY: Republic of the Philippines. Colony of Spain for over 300 years and territory of the United States for almost fifty years. Became independent in 1946. Capital: Quezon City. Largest city: Manila.

2. PHYSICAL ENVIRONMENT: Archipelago of over 7,000 islands extending 1,000 miles from north to south separating the South China Sea from the Philippine Sea and the Pacific Ocean beyond. Total land area of about 115,700 square miles, of which the two largest islands, Luzon and Mindanao, make up about 65 percent. Mountainous topography creating narrow coastal plains and interior valleys and plains. Tropical climate with mean average temperature of 80°F in the lowlands. Two seasons, wet and dry, determined by monsoon conditions. Frequent typhoons.

3. POPULATION: Estimated at over 42 million in early 1975. Average annual rate of growth between 1960 and 1970 was 3 percent. More than 60 percent of population in 1970 under age of twenty-five. Luzon contained over 45 percent and the Visayan Islands approximately 35 percent of total population. Except for small minority of ethnic Chinese, population composed of common racial stock. Ethnic differentiation on the basis of language. Conflicts have existed between majority and three minority groups—Muslim Filipinos (Moros), small pagan groups of the interior, and ethnic Chinese.

4. LANGUAGES: English, Pilipino (a form of Tagalog), and Spanish are official languages; Pilipino is national language, spoken by over 55 percent. English widely used in government, business, and as medium of instruction in most levels of schooling. Of the numerous native languages spoken, eight are major, including Tagalog.

5. HEALTH: Public and private medical and health services concentrated in urban areas and reached about two-thirds of population. Pure water systems and sewage disposal being upgraded but remained inadequate. Crowded housing in urban areas and lack of access to medical personnel in rural areas slowed improvement of living conditions. Communicable diseases remained major health problem and were cause of 42 percent of all deaths in early 1970s. Pneumonia and tuberculosis were among major causes of death. Malaria prevalent in Luzon and in Mindanao.

6. EDUCATION: Literacy estimated at about 80 percent in early 1970s. Complete system of public and private education from elementary to university level offering general, vocational, and specialized training.

Heavy reliance on private sector for secondary and higher education. Various educational reforms initiated in 1972.

7. RELIGION: Over 90 percent of population Christian, mostly Roman Catholic. Roughly 5 percent Muslim. Religious fiestas play important social role, especially in rural areas and small towns.

8. MASS COMMUNICATIONS: Long tradition of free press and public information altered along with other mass media as result of government efforts in 1970s to control information. Urban areas served by daily newspapers, periodicals, and television; rural areas served by radio. Limited book publication. High concentration of all media in Manila.

9. GOVERNMENT AND POLITICS: Martial law declared in September 1972. Government legitimized and operating under mixture of 1935 Constitution, 1973 Constitution, and series of proclamations and decrees issued under presidential emergency powers. At end of 1975 still in transition from presidential to parliamentary form of government. President Ferdinand E. Marcos continued to exercise extremely broad range of powers in absence of a national legislature. Indefinite moratorium on partisan politics and elections. Unlike situation before 1972, military elements played significant role.

10. ADMINISTRATIVE DIVISIONS: Country divided into provinces, municipalities (counties), chartered cities, and *barangays* (formerly *barrios* or villages). Greater metropolitan area of Manila had special status. For administrative coordination, provinces grouped into eleven regions. Certain cities held special status.

11. JUSTICE: Legal and court system influenced by Spanish and American legal philosophy and experience. Court hierarchy included Supreme Court, Court of Appeals, courts of first instance in provinces, municipal courts in chartered cities, and city courts in municipalities and municipal districts. No trials by jury. After September 1972 military courts assumed prominent role in adjudicating certain cases.

12. ECONOMY: Private enterprise economy. Predominantly agricultural. Government plan attempting to remedy traditional problems of high unemployment, disparities in distribution of wealth, heavy reliance on imports of raw materials, and high inflation. Fiscal year from July 1 through June 30; starting in 1977 fiscal year to run from January 1 through December 31. Foreign capital inflows greatly increased after 1972. Industrialization policy after World War II favored investment in large, capital-intensive industrial plant; after 1972 increased interest in investment in agriculture and infrastructure. Targeted growth in gross national product (GNP) for 1974–77 period was 7 percent; actual performance for 1974 and 1975 was under 6 percent.

13. AGRICULTURE: Provides over 50 percent of employment and 70 percent of export earnings. Commercial crops for export include coconut, sugarcane, and abaca; food crops include rice, corn (maize), and fruits.

Land tenure characterized by tenancy, especially on rice and corn lands; land reform program of modest effectiveness.

14. INDUSTRY: Third largest sector in economy after agriculture and services. Manufacturing accounted for over two-thirds of all industrial activity. Production geared toward domestic market. After 1970 government emphasis on production for export. Rich natural resources. Major manufacturing industries: food and beverages, chemicals, and textiles.

15. LABOR: Labor force estimated at about 14 million in 1974; about one-half engaged in agriculture, forestry, and fishing. About 30 percent of labor force estimated to be unemployed or underemployed in 1973.

16. FOREIGN TRADE: Major exports include forest products, sugar, copper ore, copra, coconut oil, and abaca. Principal markets are United States, Japan, Netherlands, and Federal Republic of Germany (West Germany). Chief imports are machinery, base metals, mineral fuels, transport equipment, and foodstuffs. Major suppliers are United States, Japan, West Germany, Australia, and Saudi Arabia. Imports exceed exports. International economic relationships being revised to reflect expiration of Laurel-Langley Agreement with United States, expanding economic ties with Japan, opening of trade with communist countries, and rising importance of oil-producing countries.

17. FINANCE: Philippine peso ₱7.50 equaled US$1 at end of 1975) divided into 100 centavos. Strong inflationary pressures in mid-1970s. Financial system governed by Monetary Board and Central Bank. Both private and government-owned banks operate.

18. TRANSPORTATION: In 1974 country lacked widespread infrastructure to support movement of goods and services necessary for economic development. Major islands have highways, most surfaced with earth or gravel. Panay and Luzon partly serviced by railroad. Fleet of vessels provided interisland sea transport. Good international air communication and domestic service.

19. INTERNATIONAL MEMBERSHIPS AND AGREEMENTS: Member of most international organizations and active participant in regional cooperative schemes of Southeast Asia. Maintained security ties with the United States through a mutual defense treaty signed in 1951 and agreements covering military bases and military assistance signed in 1947.

20. NATIONAL DEFENSE: Armed Forces of the Philippines under Department of National Defense included army, navy, air force, and police. Regular forces in 1975 estimated at about 67,000 almost twice force level at time of declaration of martial law in 1972. Army largest of three military branches. Reserve forces and conscripted trainees also increasing.

21. INTERNAL SECURITY: In 1975 local police placed under com-

mand of national Philippine Constabulary to form Integrated National Police under Department of National Defense. High crime rates of 1960s sharply reduced during initial stages of martial law. Regular military forces augment police in maintaining internal security. Active Muslim insurgency in southern islands. Domestic security also troubled by communist insurgents on Luzon.

THE PHILIPPINES

TABLE OF CONTENTS

LIST OF ILLUSTRATIONS

LIST OF TABLES

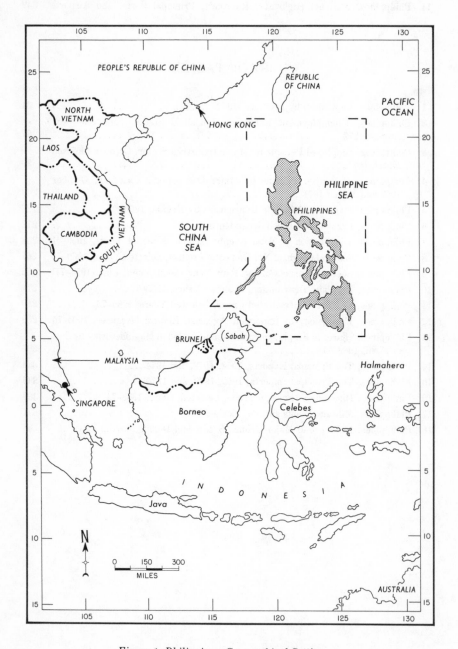

Figure 1. Philippines, Geographical Setting

SECTION I. SOCIAL

CHAPTER 1

GENERAL CHARACTER OF THE SOCIETY

The Republic of the Philippines entered the decade of the 1970s amid warnings of impending crisis. The country's political, social, and economic system seemed in rapid decline or at least under great pressures and tensions. Crime rates soared, and political violence intensified. Social and economic inequities had become more conspicuous as did the lavish style of living of a privileged minority. Unemployment and underemployment in 1971 was estimated at between one-quarter and one-third of the labor force. Some Filipinos apparently sought a solution to problems of impoverishment, unemployment, and insecurity through support for radical communist movements; others no longer could identify a ready cure for their difficulties; still others found solace in one of the many religious revitalization movements whose memberships were again on the increase in the 1960s. In Manila students broke abruptly with past behavior patterns and in 1970 took to the streets to demand change and reform. Political cynicism was evident everywhere. In the southermost islands the hostility of the Muslim minority, which had simmered for over 300 years, once again erupted in conflict. Adding to the country's woes was a series of unusually destructive typhoons in the summer of 1972.

It was evident to many observers that the Philippines in 1970 stood at a crossroads in its history and that the various pressures and tensions in the society allowed little time to pause there. But five years later, at the end of 1975, it was equally evident that the country had indeed managed to buy time. With the exception of the Muslim insurgency comparative calm prevailed in the mid-1970s, and the explosive national crisis anticipated from clear social, economic, and political trends did not materialize despite a slowness of fundamental social and economic reforms.

The nation's apparent resiliency could be attributed partly to political and economic expedients and partly to more basic features of the country and its society. The most important of the political expedients was the declaration of martial law in September 1972 by the incumbent president, Ferdinand E. Marcos. Terming his martial law regime one of "constitutional authoritarianism" rather than dictatorship, Marcos ruled by decree without the former hindrance of a legislature. He continued to do so at the end of 1975; no immediate prospect was held out for an end to martial law or the reestablishment of a regular government under the new Constitution adopted in 1973. The institutions of a legislature, political parties, and popular elections with which the Philippines had embarked upon its independence in 1946 ceased to function (see ch. 9; ch. 10).

A number of interpretations have been offered for Marcos' move. Some saw it simply as an effort to remain in power in the face of the scheduled constitutional change and growing political opposition. Others interpreted it as a vindication of rational, modernizing, and urban elements in the society against a conservative, oligarchical elite who had long dominated the nation and whose outlook was supposedly regional, traditional, and rural. Another contrary explanation saw in martial law an effort to suppress new moves toward fundamental reforms, in the interests of foreign investors and the nation's elite in whose hands were concentrated most of the country's industrial assets. Still others interpreted martial law as a final authoritarian stage of a long-term decline in the autonomy of local leadership in favor of the concentration of political power at the center. In 1975 Marcos and other political leaders enjoyed greater power than ever before, further buttressed by the use—new to the Philippines—of such modern forms of domestic control as a politicized military, a centralized national police, and an obedient mass media (see ch. 7; ch. 16; ch. 17).

Marcos himself initially explained martial law as a response to widespread lawlessness, violence, disorder, and active communist and Muslim insurgency. In the first months he decreed a number of beneficial measures, some of which had been urged for years, and took successful steps to curb crime and disorder—much to the relief of Filipino citizens. In addition Marcos justified martial law as an opportunity to create a New Society to replace the old system that had led to the country's difficulties and to galvanize Filipinos toward eventually overcoming these difficulties. These goals constituted a formidable task, one that would require the skillful use of all the resources of the country and its people.

The Philippines consists of a group of about 7,100 tropical islands— about 700 of them inhabited—situated roughly 600 miles southeast of mainland Asia. The archipelago extends generally north to south for some 1,000 miles and east to west for about 400 miles at its widest part. Most of the islands are mountainous; the population is concentrated in a few lowland areas and interior plains, including the large and densely settled central plain of Luzon, the country's largest island. At the foot of this plain is the country's primate city, Manila, situated on one of the world's best natural harbors (see ch. 2).

In 1975 the population numbered over 42 million and has been growing rapidly. Although the urban population increased, especially in Manila, the population remained predominantly rural. Population pressure on scarce arable land was very high despite continued migration to towns and cities. During the two decades after World War II most economically exploitable land was brought under cultivation. Although estimates of the amount of arable land under cultivation vary, the land frontier available for development appears to have been closed. Increased agricultural production has come mainly from higher yields rather than expanded acreage. As a consequence the ability of agriculture to absorb labor is declining (see ch. 13). The Philippines, however, has not yet been burdened by the acute overpopulation problems afflicting some other regions in Asia. The country, moreover, enjoys the advantages of a high literacy rate, a relative abundance of other natural and mineral resources except for petroleum, and considerable economic diversity from one region or island to the next.

In tackling the creation of the New Society Filipinos enjoyed another distinct advantage. Although the population was made up of a number of linguistic groups, including eight major ones, and although the country had important regional differences, the Philippines was a nation without acute communal cleavages along ethnic, economic, or religious lines—with the major exception of the Muslim minority, numbering about 5 percent of the population (see ch. 4; ch. 8). The country is united by a set of shared experiences, including more than 300 years of Spanish rule and another fifty years of American control. The overwhelming majority are Roman Catholic. Language barriers are to a great extent overcome by a knowledge of English or the national language, Pilipino (a form of Tagalog). The linking together of the island nation through a centralized governmental bureaucracy and a system of public education was largely accomplished before independence. A sense of nationhood was further supported by the extension of the franchise and enthusiastic participation in elections before 1972.

Nevertheless the Philippines is not one but a cluster of societies, each organized along vertical ties between patrons and clients, superiors and subordinates, rather than along lateral ties within social classes or occupational groups. The principal cleavages in the society are vertical rather than horizontal. Within and between vertically integrated social hierarchies rivalry among clients for patrons seems to have intensified over the years as a rapidly growing population competed for scarce resources and jobs and discouraged the emergence of interest group cooperation except at the lowest, most parochial level. The family is the key social unit and object of intense individual loyalty, followed in rural areas by the principal unit of residence, the *barrio* (village). Family loyalties often transcend occupational or income status; tenants are very often related to their landlords (see ch. 5).

The national elite served to integrate this fragmented social system at the top. The core of this elite consisted of a few families whose prominence could be traced well back into the eighteenth century and to regional strongholds based initially on landholdings. Its membership overlapped that of the country's political and economic leadership. By the 1960s mobility into this elite, although not impossible, seemed to have slowed.

These social characteristics influenced the actual political behavior that took place within the nominal institutions of a democracy before 1972 (see ch. 10). Family ties, personalities, and patron-client links took precedence over issues or ideologies during elections. By and large voters easily shifted their allegiance between the two major political parties according to mutually beneficial ties with a patron or a political broker linked to a candidate. Thus voting was more reminiscent of the machine politics of some American cities than of choices made according to class, occupational, or even regional interests. Corrupt or irregular practices were also prevalent, reflecting both the irresistible influence of family ties and the expectation of a quid pro quo for political loyalty. Such practices occurred at all levels in the society; the pattern of alternating power between the two major parties held out the hope that loss in one election would be compensated by a windfall in the next. This alternation ended with the declaration of martial law. Marcos thereby assumed the role of the ultimate patron of the entire society. As he himself was the first to admit, the ultimate test of his government would be its ability to furnish jobs and adequate incomes to all.

Studies made of the Philippines during the 1960s, mainly on Luzon, indicated that some major changes had occurred or were occurring in these social and political systems. The consequences of these changes were just beginning to work themselves out before martial law was declared, and it was difficult to evaluate their implications for the New Society. One of these changes, which had been taking place over several decades, was the loss of leadership and resources at the local level of the municipality—roughly equivalent to an American county—and their accumulation in Manila. Underlying this shift in the balance between local areas and the center was the erosion of traditional patron-client relations between landlords and tenants in a way that increased the leverage of the former and reduced the bargaining power of the latter. The landlords often departed for the city or large towns, draining off profits to invest in an urban life-style or industrial and commercial ventures and leaving the tenants without their former security, leadership, and resources. In some provinces of Luzon this development was already far advanced before World War II. In these areas the bereft peasantry tended to respond warmly to radical political movements, including most recently the Maoist New People's Army (NPA).

Governmental centralization also weakened local autonomy and potential leadership, as did the migration to the cities of young, better educated, and ambitious men and women. The decline of traditional loyalties, leadership, and resources at the local level was indirectly reflected in the emergence of the *lider* (political broker), who gathered a bloc of votes for a candidate in exchange for tangible benefits for supporters, including cash. Given the expansion in the size of the electorate this development undoubtedly contributed to the soaring election costs that periodically drained the public treasury during the 1960s. These costs in turn further discouraged able individuals from running for public office and further encouraged local dependence on the political center for resources.

Another very different response to the decline of traditional institutions was the nascent development at the local level of interest groups composed of farmers and workers whose influence was beginning to be felt in the legislature in the early 1970s. Little information was available on this novel development after the declaration of martial law; the government seemed to regard such groups with suspicion or sought to co-opt their leadership.

It was mainly the *liders* and local authorities—mayors and councillors—who appeared most likely to find a place in the new political system created under martial law, mainly as agents of the central government. A new political system apparently designed to reestablish ties between the population and the national elite was still being constructed at the end of 1975, and uncertainty was evident at all levels over matters of political power and authority. A particularly knotty problem seemed to be the relationship between authorities at the local and intermediate levels and military and police commanders with direct ties to the center. The granting of political and economic powers to the military under martial law and the establishment of military courts that circumvented the established judiciary were new experiences for Filipinos and for the military itself. Marcos decreed a new organization, the *barangay* (citizens' assembly), to replace the *barrio* and ward administrations at the local level and to serve as a forum for the expression of popular views. A hierarchy of related organizations was being formed; these incorporated existing authorities at each level. They were based on a form of indirect elections tightly controlled from the center and were required to reflect four sectoral groups—capital, professional, industrial labor, and agricultural labor. The government's creation of new institutions reflected a tendency toward evolutionary, moderate, bureaucratic, and integrative solutions based on an enforced consensus. The government remained suspicious of groups that represented potential social conflict or radical change. The extent to which these new organizations filled the void in local leadership and met the expectations of a highly politicized population could not be determined at the end of 1975.

The importance of local leadership and initiative as essential to overcoming basic economic problems was emphasized in an International Labor Office report of a survey made in 1973. These economic problems stemmed from the structure of the economy. The Philippine economy is

5

usually described as dualistic in structure, having a largely agricultural rural sector and an urban industrial sector joined to each other and to the world through foreign trade. The rural sector produced food and exported commodities to pay for imports of capital goods and materials needed by the industrial sector (see ch. 12).

At least until the late 1960s the rural sector remained traditional and was continually drained of investment resources. As the population doubled and then doubled again between 1900 and 1970, the problem of farm tenancy became acute. Numerous reform measures were adopted, but their implementation was invariably blocked or qualified by landlord interests. Introduction in the late 1960s of the so-called miracle rice seeds and related inputs of fertilizer and pesticides for the first time broke the pattern of low farm productivity; without land reform, however, the principal beneficiaries continued to be landowners, not tenants. With martial law Marcos described land reform as a key element in his New Society program. Observers agreed that more progress in this direction was made in the early 1970s than under any previous administration. By the end of 1975, however, even these efforts had slowed, and they excluded large numbers of tenants altogether (see ch. 13). Little if any improvement in rural income distribution had occurred. By 1970, moreover, the agrarian problem was compounded by the emergence of a large force of agricultural laborers—without even a tenant's access to land—for whom land reform was irrelevant.

The urban industrial sector also displayed structural characteristics that contributed to the problems confronting the Philippines in the 1970s. Until World War II the industrial sector was comparatively small. With government encouragement substantial development in manufacturing took place beginning in 1950. This development, however, was of a self-limiting kind, and one of its most remarkable features was the tenacity with which it was pursued long after its drawbacks had become evident. Thus industrial development was capital intensive, providing relatively few employment opportunities for a rapidly growing labor force. It was inefficient, depending heavily on various kinds of government subsidies and supports. Directed almost exclusively to a limited domestic market, the manufacturing industry continued to depend on the rural export sector for foreign exchange with which to import capital equipment and materials. Ownership became increasingly concentrated in the hands of elite families, whose social and political position gave them preferred access to government favors; small- and medium-scale entrepreneurs found it increasingly difficult to enter the industrial field. Similar tendencies were apparent in construction and mineral development. Industrial activity was, moreover, concentrated in Manila and its environs.

One major consequence of these structural characteristics was that income distribution, already very unequal, became even more so during the 1950s and 1960s. Particularly hard hit were the poorest households, accounting for the lowest 20 percent of family incomes, and especially the rural poor. The small middle-income group, largely urban wage earners, might also have had difficulty in maintaining income levels and were undoubtedly seriously hurt by the very high rate of inflation in the mid-1970s. Meanwhile both excess rural labor and migrants to the cities swelled the ranks of those who barely made ends meet through a variety of low-paying jobs or self-employment in services (see ch. 6).

The principal task set by Marcos for his New Society was a more equitable distribution of income through a restructuring of the economy, including the development and dispersal of medium-and small-scale labor-intensive industries, a greater emphasis on export industries, and a revitalization of the rural sector. Some initial progress in this direction had been made by the end of 1975, although there still remained a tendency for private investment to flow into capital-intensive enterprises as well as real estate and speculative ventures. The government proved singularly successful in attracting private foreign investment and obtaining development assistance from international agencies. Under the development plan in effect in late 1975 government investment was to be directed mainly to the rural sector and especially to the development of roads, bridges, irrigation, and other infrastructure. A full marshaling of resources for development, however, was handicapped by other obligations, including an increase in military expenditures to over 15 percent of the national budget for fiscal year (FY) 1976.

The armed forces, which include the national police, grew substantially in the first half of the 1970s to meet the requirements of martial law and especially to deal with active insurgency in areas of Luzon and the Muslim regions of the southern islands of Mindanao and the Sulu Archipelago. The regular forces of the army, navy, and air force together with the police numbered an estimated 100,000, not including reserve elements; military force levels were roughly double those in 1972. During 1975 an estimated 35,000 to 50,000 government forces were engaged in Muslim areas. In the same period the police were reorganized into an integrated national force, and various improvements were made in military and police capabilities, including advances in communications facilities. The increased military requirements also reflected a basic change in mission to one stressing a more self-reliant military posture (see ch. 16; ch. 17).

The United States withdrawal from Vietnam also prompted a sudden concern over the nature of Philippine foreign relations, but a basic continuity in policy was subsequently reestablished. This traumatic event, however, together with the overall reevaluation of national goals implied by the New Society encouraged a new framework of external political and economic relations stressing flexibility and adaptation in a world of uncertain change. New guidelines aimed at the establishment of diplomatic relations with socialist states, including the People's Republic of China

(PRC) and the Soviet Union, and closer identification with countries of the third world. A new basis for continued relations with the United States, long a matter of particular concern and great sensitivity to Filipinos, was also being sought. In 1974 a 1946 agreement providing among other things for certain economic privileges for Americans in the Philippines expired. Even as discussions were initiated regarding this and the matter of American base rights in the Philippines, the continuation of sizable trade with the United States and growing American investment in the Philippines suggested a basic continuity in the pattern of relations between the two countries (see ch. 11).

CHAPTER 2

PHYSICAL ENVIRONMENT AND POPULATION

The Philippine archipelago contains about 7,100 islands and extends over 1,000 miles from north to south (see fig. 1). Only 154 of these islands, however, exceed five square miles in area. The two largest islands, Luzon in the north and Mindanao in the south, comprise about 65 percent of the total land area of the archipelago. The very complex and volcanic origin of most of the islands is visible in their varied and rugged terrain. Mountain ranges divide the island surfaces into narrow coastal strips and shallow interior plains or valleys; no point on land is more than twenty-five miles either from the coast or from a mountain range. The sea and mountain barriers have been constant factors shaping the historical, cultural, and demographic development of the nation.

The sea has been both a barrier and a bridge and correspondingly both a source of isolation and a means of communication. It was the sea that isolated the archipelago from the mainstream of Asian history. As a result the islands never experienced the cycles of conquest and collapse of suzerain empires known in the rest of Asia. The sea also, however, brought the migrants who became the ancestors of the majority of the nation's population, important contacts with Chinese and Arab traders, and eventually the Spanish. The proximity of the islands and the calmness of the interisland seas, straits, and other waterways, however, did not encourage development of the skills required for long, open sea voyages, and the Philippines has not become an important seafaring nation. Early migrants settled in narrow communities strung along the coast and established a settlement pattern still evident today. Among some groups arrival in the same boat or at the same time became a basis for identification and social organization. Fishing and interisland transport have remained important occupations; fish continues to provide a major portion of protein in the Filipino diet.

The climate is generally tropical throughout the archipelago, but the sea and mountains determine variations. Only a narrow range of temperature variance occurs between the country's northern and southern limits. Except for diurnal variations, the greatest extremes in temperature are the result of differences in altitude. Seasonal variations in rainfall are also modified by such local features as mountain barriers and altitude. Climate differences in turn influence a wide spectrum of living patterns ranging from agriculture to seasonally migratory labor.

Most of the Philippine Islands are situated in a region of considerable geological instability and extreme climatic phenomena. The unusually complex origin of the archipelago—still not fully understood—continues to be expressed in minor earthquakes and occasionally in a major eruption. A major fault line extends along the eastern part of the archipelago roughly paralleling the very deep Philippine Trench and—like Japan to the far north and Indonesia to the southwest—most of the Philippines is considered part of the volcanically active regions of the western Pacific. In addition the northern islands are especially affected by typhoons that, although mainly seasonal, bring destructive winds and flooding rains.

This geological complexity and climatic activity nevertheless formed a relatively rich resource pattern. Ancient uptilting has exposed many sites rich in minerals; volcanic activity has enriched arable soils; seasonal rainfall and local rainfall variations support a diversified agriculture.

Most of the larger islands have exceptionally narrow coastal shelves. Population clusters have generally been restricted to the more irregular, wider, western coastal regions. The north-south mountain barriers have generally hindered the development of east-west passage. The road system follows the same north-south pattern, and neither Luzon nor Mindanao has a completely circumferential highway (see ch. 15).

Economic development generally has followed the pattern of population settlement. The fertile lands of the Central Luzon Plain have supported one of the major agricultural areas. The attractiveness of the region resulted in overcrowding and the highest rate of land tenancy in the country. The southern end of the plain opens onto one of the world's best natural harbors, and the location of the city of Manila on this bay made the city a center of economic activity. Established under Spanish rule as the capital, Manila evolved into the principal city of the Philippines. It is the country's political, commercial, and cultural heart; the cosmopolitan residence of the country's elite, and the goal of aspiring migrants. Its commanding position was not offset by the designation of nearby Quezon City (subsequently absorbed into the greater Manila metropolitan area) as the official capital in 1948.

Manila also has played a central role in the social and cultural evolution of the country. The extent of Hispanic influence, including conversion to Christianity, was in proportion to the accessibility of a region to Manila. The remoteness of the Moros (Muslim Filipinos) in the southwest and of mountain peoples on Luzon and Mindanao enabled their culturally distinct development (see ch. 4). In an extreme case the Tasaday of Mindanao were untouched by outside contact until the early 1970s.

The effects of rapid population growth have become increasingly apparent since World War II. The real per capita share of increase in the gross national product (GNP) was being seriously eroded by population increases during the 1960s and early 1970s. Projections in the mid-1970s indicated a dangerously high consumption of national resources in order to support the mushrooming population. Although it has been difficult to establish a government-supported population control program in a society where religious life is dominated by the Roman Catholic Church, by 1975 such a program had been implemented and was being expanded; the effectiveness of the program, however, was difficult to assess.

An increasing concentration of the population in urban areas strained service facilities and exacerbated the already complex and interwoven problems of urban unemployment and underemployment. The high rate of urbanization was largely the result of migration from rural areas, motivated by the search for improved employment opportunities and a higher living standard. Most of the migrants lacked technical skills and could only enter the poorly paid service sector. Dissatisfaction over the gap between urban and rural standards and the even sharper differences in living standards noticeable within urban areas represented potential threats to national stability that could be overcome only by the outlay of considerable national resources (see ch. 6).

GEOGRAPHIC REGIONS

The territory of the Philippines can be conveniently divided into several geographic regions, three of which—Luzon, the Visayan Islands, and Mindanao—are based on geographic proximity of islands rather than any physical, social, or economic homogeneity. Separate from these regions are Mindoro Island and the islands of the Palawan group, which together form an island bridge stretching southwest from Luzon to Sabah (on the island of Borneo and part of the Federation of Malaysia), and the Sulu Archipelago, which extends similarly from western Mindanao to near Sabah (see fig. 2).

The Luzon Region

The Luzon region consists of Luzon Island, many much smaller adjacent islands, and the small island groups of Batan and Babuyan lying to the north. The island of Luzon has an area of 40,420 square miles, or more than one-third of the country's total area. In shape it resembles an upright rectangle with an irregular southeastern peninsular handle. The main part of the island is roughly 250 miles in length and has a width generally between seventy-five and 100 miles, although the widest point is 138 miles.

The portion of Luzon that lies north of Lingayen Gulf is very mountainous; its highest peak, Mount Pulog, rises to 9,626 feet. The island has three mountain ranges that run roughly parallel in a north-south direction. A range in the east, the Sierra Madre, runs so close to the island's eastern shore that there is barely any coastal lowland. The valley of the north-flowing Cagayan River separates this eastern range from a large mountain complex to the west, the Cordillera Central; the Cagayan Valley, about 140 miles long and averaging about forty miles

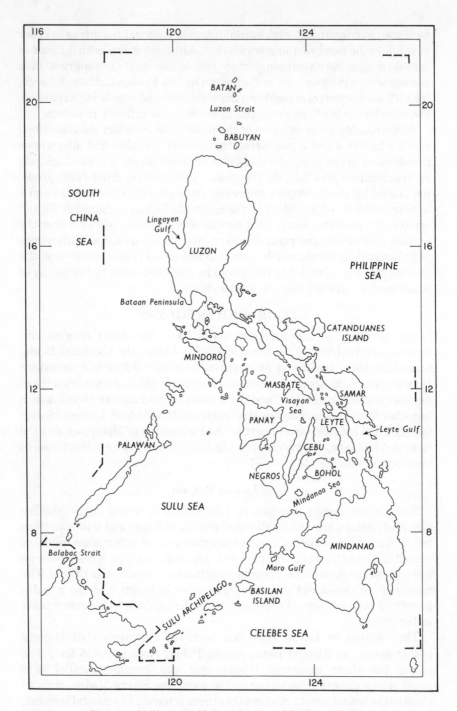

Figure 2. Philippines, Major Islands and Bodies of Water

in width, is an area of rich soil and is an important agricultural region. The valley is separated from the Central Luzon Plain by a cross flow of volcanic origin between the Sierra Madre and the southern extension of the Cordillera Central (see fig. 3).

The rugged central mountain complex of the Cordillera Central covers most of the northern part of the island but affords a productive narrow coastal strip to the west. Below it lies the Central Luzon Plain, which extends south to Manila Bay. This plain, one of the country's most important agricultural areas, is approximately 100 miles long and roughly fifty miles wide (see ch. 13). Its altitude is not much above sea level, and the plain includes a number of extensive swampy stretches.

The Central Luzon Plain is bordered on both sides by rugged coastal ranges. On the west the third range, the Zambales Mountains, extends from the Lingayen Gulf southward through the Bataan Peninsula and terminates at Manila Bay. The range crowds the shore and leaves only a narrow coastal lowland but is economically important because of its extensive mineral deposits. The mountains to the east, an extension of the Sierra Madre, drop off sharply to the Pacific Ocean and leave little accessible level terrain and no protective harbors against the heavy Pacific surf.

At the southern end of the central plain a large, natural, ample harbor is provided by Manila Bay. The city of Manila is located on the bay's eastern shore. Lying to the southeast of the bay and joined to it by the short Pasig River is the largest freshwater lake in the Philippines, Laguna de Bay, which at one time was probably an arm or extension of Manila Bay. It has a water surface of 356 square miles. A few miles to the southwest of Laguna de Bay lies lake Taal. This lake has an active volcano in its center that erupted in 1965, causing several deaths.

Southeastern Luzon consists of a large convoluted peninsula that accounts for one-third of the island's overall length. A mountainous volcanic area, it contains the periodically active 7,941-foot Mount Mayon volcano, one of the world's most symmetrical large volcanic cones. Although the peninsula's terrain is extremely rugged, the fertility of the volcanic soil and heavy rainfall make over one-half of the area agriculturally productive. In addition there are many good, sheltered harbors available for interisland shipping.

The Visayan Islands

The Visayan Islands are grouped in a roughly circular pattern around the Visayan Sea. They include seven large, populated islands that range in size from Masbate, which is 1,262 square miles in area, to Samar, 5,050 square miles. The others are Bohol (1,492 square miles), Cebu (1,707 square miles), Leyte (2,785 square miles), Panay (4,446 square miles), and Negros (4,905 square miles). Including a myriad of islets, the group comprises over half the total number of islands that make up the country.

The seven larger islands have a combined land surface area of over

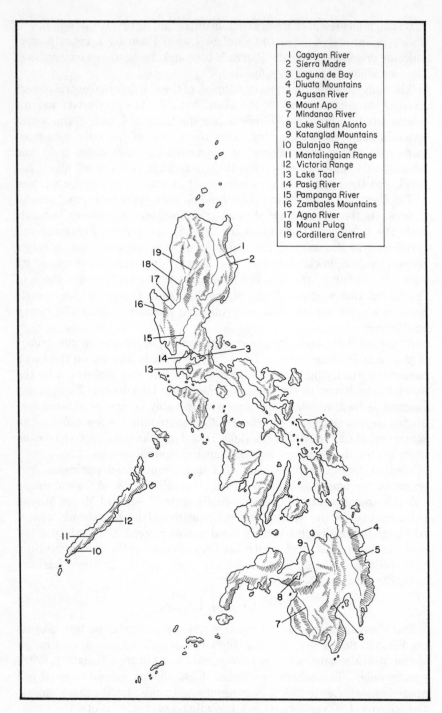

1 Cagayan River
2 Sierra Madre
3 Laguna de Bay
4 Diuata Mountains
5 Agusan River
6 Mount Apo
7 Mindanao River
8 Lake Sultan Alonto
9 Katanglad Mountains
10 Bulanjao Range
11 Mantalingaian Range
12 Victoria Range
13 Lake Taal
14 Pasig River
15 Pampanga River
16 Zambales Mountains
17 Agno River
18 Mount Pulog
19 Cordillera Central

Figure 3. Philippines, Physical Features

14

21,600 square miles, representing about 19 percent of the national total. Most of the Visayan Islands have mountainous interiors, and in general lowlands are few and small, usually confined to the coastal strips of the larger islands. There are, however, three sizable lowland areas: the Leyte Valley, the Iloilo Plain on Panay, and the plains of western and northern Negros.

Samar and Leyte, the easternmost islands, act as a buffer for the other islands against the full force of storms and occasional typhoons originating from the Pacific Ocean. Samar's interior has rugged mountains, but elevations are generally below 1,000 feet; these mountains are covered with commercially exploitable forests.

Leyte is separated from Samar by a narrow strait and is actually a detached peninsula of Samar. A central mountain range running north and south divides the northern part of the island. To the east of the range is the fertile, alluvium-filled Leyte Valley, and to the west is a comparatively flat highland. Both are used for agriculture; the principal crops are rice, corn, abaca, and coconuts.

Cebu, Negros, and Panay are important agriculturally and also form the commercial center of the region; their ports contribute significantly to both interisland and overseas shipping. The long narrow island of Cebu is one of the most distinctive of the Visayan Islands. In 1970 it had the highest population density of all of the Philippine Islands. It is the center of corn cultivation, accounting for a quarter of all the country's acreage devoted to the crop. The island is the site of the country's largest copper mine and also produces low-grade coal and limestone for cement. Cebu has long been one of the most prosperous of the islands.

West of Cebu, Negros and Panay are roughly similar in area and population. Both islands have sizable lowland plains that permit intensive agriculture. Negros is an important producer of both sugarcane and corn; cultivation of rice is dominant on Panay.

The two smallest islands—Bohol and Masbate—are both under 1,500 square miles in area. Masbate is extremely productive, yielding rice, corn, and hemp. Bohol is covered mostly with secondary forest but has extensive rice cultivation on the coastal lowlands.

The Mindanao Region

The Mindanao region consists of the island of Mindanao and numerous small offshore islands, including a mineral-rich group off the northeastern coast. Mindanao, the second largest of the Philippine Islands, has an area of 36,537 square miles. Its very irregular shape is characterized by a number of sizable gulfs and bays and several large peninsulas that give it an extremely long coastline. It has five major mountain systems, some formed by volcanic action, and a varied and complex topography that includes numerous rivers and a number of lakes.

The eastern edge of Mindanao is highly mountainous. This mountainous area, which is a southward continuation of the mountain range in

Leyte, is heavily wooded. It shelters the interior from most of the storms of the Pacific but leaves almost no coastal lowlands. The northern part, known as the Diuata Mountains, contains several elevations above 6,000 feet, and the southern section rises to over 7,000 feet, reaching a high point of 9,200 feet.

West of this eastern range is an extensive longitudinal lowland plain area known as the Davao-Agusan Trough, through which the Agusan River flows south to north for almost its entire extent. The valley, over 100 miles long and twelve to thirty-seven miles wide, has an excellent agricultural potential; however, its development has been slowed because of the scarcity of roads and the distance of markets. A large-scale influx of homesteaders into this frontier region occurred in the 1960s. The port of Davao, the country's third largest city, is at the southern end of the trough and is the island's principal city.

On the west the trough is bordered by a broad mass of rugged mountain ranges, one of which bisects the island from north to south. This range contains 9,692-foot Mount Apo, the highest peak in the country, which overlooks Davao Gulf. Between these highlands and a southwestern coastal range lies another broad lowland area, the Cotabato Lowland, which covers over 2,500 square miles. The most extensive part of the lowland is the Cotabato Valley, which is drained by the Mindanao River. The valley has large swampy stretches but comprises a region of great agricultural potential. Areas in and around the Cotabato Lowland were the scene of bloody conflicts in the early 1970s between elements of the traditional Muslim population and government forces (see ch. 17).

The central mountain complex extends into the northwest corner of the main body of the island, terminating in the Bukidnon-Lanao Highlands. An undulating expanse of plateau formations at approximately 2,000 feet in elevation, the highlands are interspersed with a number of extinct volcanic peaks—some rising to heights of 9,500 feet. Roughly centered in these highlands is Lake Sultan Alonto (formerly Lake Lanao), 134 square miles in area and the second largest lake in the country. This area and the northern coastal province of Misamis Oriental have been extensively colonized by immigrants from the Visayan Islands. The plateau is the site of a number of large cattle ranches, and pineapples are grown there commercially.

Just west of the lake the island narrows to an isthmus ten miles wide, from which the long Zamboanga Peninsula protrudes to the southwest for some 170 miles. The peninsula is covered largely with mountains and possesses limited coastal lowlands. Soils in some of the lowlands and floodplains of the small rivers, however, are fertile. The peninsula has a number of rubber plantations, coconuts and abaca are grown commercially, and there are forests of commercial importance. The city of Zamboanga, the second largest city on Mindanao, is located on the southern tip of the peninsula, between the Moro Gulf and the Sulu Sea.

16

Mindoro, Palawan, and the Sulu Archipelago

Just south of Luzon lies Mindoro, the country's seventh largest island, having an area of 3,758 square miles. The island is largely mountainous and has high peaks rising above 8,000 feet. Much of the island is covered with secondary forest, apparently the result of earlier destruction of the original forest by slash-and-burn cultivation. A moderately wide coastal lowland lies to the east and northeast of the mountain zone, and there is some agricultural exploitation of this area. The lowland contains Lake Naujan, one of the country's larger lakes.

Extending southwestward from Mindoro is Palawan, fifth in size among the Philippine Islands. It has a length of over 275 miles, a width varying from five to thirty miles, and an area of 4,500 square miles; it is surrounded by well over 1,100 smaller islands and islets. A ridge of rugged mountains that run its entire length is bordered by narrow coastal strips. A good part of the island is covered with forests, which include some important commercial species. Agricultural development has been limited. In 1970 Palawan had the lowest population density of any of the major islands. Both Mindoro and Palawan are considered essentially as pioneer areas.

Southwest of the Zamboanga Peninsula of Mindanao is the Sulu Archipelago, a string of smaller islands of volcanic and coral origin protruding from a submarine ridge that joins Mindanao to Sabah in Malaysia. A chain some 200 miles long, it has over 800 islands, including some 500 unnamed ones; its total area is about 1,600 square miles. The three principal islands are Basilan, directly offshore from Zamboanga; Jolo, containing the capital city of the same name; and Tawitawi, near Sabah, which has one of the best fleet anchorages in the world—used during World War II by a large part of the Japanese fleet. Fishing is a major industry. Although most of the islands are heavily forested, local agriculture generally supports the population.

THE LAND

Climate

The climate is tropical, and generally hot and humid conditions prevail at all times of the year. Temperatures are exceptionally uniform for a land area extending over 1,000 miles—a function for the most part of the insular nature of the country. The mean annual temperature is about 80°F in the lowlands, and only about a 1°F variation occurs between the extreme northern and southern parts of the archipelago. Differences in altitude, however, result in marked temperature variations. Baguio, situated over 4,800 feet high in the Cordillera Central, some 130 miles north of Manila, has mean monthly temperatures that are 15°F to 16°F lower than those registered in Manila. At sea level absolute temperatures almost never drop below 60°F, but at Baguio absolute lows of around 48°F have been recorded.

The seasonal variation between the hottest and coolest months is generally less than 8°F, the greatest differences occurring in the higher latitudes of Luzon. Davao on Mindanao has a difference in average mean monthly temperature between its hottest and coolest months of only 2.5°F, whereas Aparri on the northern coast of Luzon shows a variation of about 7.7°F. The most noticeable variations in temperature are diurnal. For example, Manila, which is typical, experiences a daily variation of around 16°F during the dry season. At that time a daily minimum reading of approximately 75°F is recorded shortly before sunrise. The temperature then rises to a maximum of about 91°F in the early afternoon, after which it begins to drop.

About 60 percent of the Philippines receives between seventy and 120 inches of rainfall annually, a quantity usually sufficient to permit rice culture without irrigation; another 10 percent of land receives less than seventy inches, and about 30 percent has a rainfall in excess of 120 inches. Rainfall throughout the islands is mainly seasonal and is associated with major air movements originating in the Indian Ocean (southwest monsoon), the Asian landmass (northeast monsoon), and the South Pacific and North Pacific. Locally mountain barriers play a considerable part in the amount of precipitation deposited.

Most of the country, except along the east coast, has a summer season during April, May, and early June when it is hot and dry and the sky is clear. The season of heavy rains occurs in these parts of the country from late June to October; it is caused by the southwest monsoon from the Indian Ocean—a warm and very moist air mass that flows constantly across the islands.

During November and December an air movement comes from the northeast, off the cold North Pacific; at the lower levels it carries limited moisture, which is deposited as rain along the east coast. In the south another air mass coming from the South Pacific strikes Mindanao from the southeast, depositing substantial rainfall.

From January to March the predominant air movement is the cold northeast monsoon that originates in Siberia. Part of it moves across the landmass of China and is cold and dry, whereas another part, which crosses the Sea of Japan and the Pacific Ocean, picks up humidity. The former part strikes northern Luzon, and the area above Manila experiences cool and rather dry weather during these months. The latter, more humid movement causes some precipitation on southern Luzon, the Visayan Islands, and Mindanao.

The seasonal pattern in eastern Luzon, the eastern Visayan Islands, and northeastern and eastern Mindanao is characterized by heavy winter rains and only a comparatively short, irregular dry period during the summer and autumn. Rainfall is actually year round, and the area does not have the period of drought experienced by most other parts of the archipelago during their dry season. The mean annual rainfall is uaually 100 inches or more, and the mountainous east coast section receives more than 120 inches. The heavy rains along the coast and the possibility of typhoon damage have hindered agricultural development there.

A few places, mostly sheltered valleys, receive seventy inches or less of rain a year. They include the Cagayan Valley in northern Luzon, the Cotabato Valley, and an area around Davao on Mindanao. The central part of the Visayan Islands also is sheltered from the full effect of the rain-bearing air masses and receives less precipitation. The smaller amount of rainfall has been responsible in part for the extensive cultivation of corn—which needs less rainfall than lowland rice—in these spots.

Superimposed on the periodic mass air movements over the Philippines are frequent cyclonic storms known as typhoons. These originate in the area of the Caroline Islands or the Marshall Islands in the western Pacific and approach the Philippines from the east. Although such storms have been recorded during every month of the year, they are rare between January and May; their greatest frequency is in August.

A study of cyclonic activity from 1948 to 1970 made by the Climatological Division of the Weather Bureau indicated that an average of 19.7 typhoons struck the Philippines each year during this period (they ranged from a low of twelve in 1951 to a high of thirty-two in 1964). Over ten of these brought, at the least, heavy rainfall; and five or six struck with destructive winds and torrential rains. A particularly violent typhoon in mid-1972 brought heavy rains that lasted for over a month, causing floods that resulted in widespread damage especially to rice-growing areas of the Central Luzon Plain. Early in the season storms usually hit northern Luzon, whereas later ones strike not only that island but also the eastern part of the Visayan Islands, which generally are hit by typhoons in October or November. Typhoons rarely strike Mindanao, Palawan, or the Sulus.

Soils and Vegetation

A wide range of soils is found in the Philippines. These soils are relatively more fertile than many found in other tropical areas in large measure because of the extensive occurrence of coralline limestone and materials of volcanic origin, which served as parent materials.

The most fertile soils are alluvial. They occupy about 15 percent of the land surface and are found in the principal lowland areas on the major islands. Some alluvial soils are of fine texture and retain water. This kind is used for lowland wet rice cultivation and constitutes the main soil in the Central Luzon Plain, the Iloilo Basin on Panay, and the Leyte Valley. Alluvial soils of a coarser nature and with better drainage characteristics are used for sugarcane culture and for growing corn. Coarser alluvial soils are important in the Visayan Islands where they form the best corn-growing soils of the Philippines.

Soils developed directly on underlying limestone cover about 13 percent of the land area and occur from northern Luzon to southern Mindanao. They are prevalent in much of the Visayan Islands, being widespread on Bohol, Cebu, Negros, and Samar. The porous nature of these soils makes them unsuitable for wet rice cultivation; however, they are generally well adapted to growing corn and coconuts, and some are also suitable for banana and citrus fruit cultivation.

Shale and some sandstone are parent materials for soils covering about 15 percent of the country. Soils developed on shale are generally of a clay-like texture, are difficult to manage, and usually have poor agricultural yields. On Cebu and Bohol islands soils that developed on calcareous shales are somewhat better and are used to cultivate sugarcane, corn, and other crops.

Soils originating from the hard andesites, basalts, and agglomerates cover about 21 percent of the country. They occur usually in upland areas and are often quite deep. Their fertility varies, but some of the most common of these soils are well suited to growing sugarcane, upland rice, and coconuts. Another soil is derived from volcanic tuff, the product of recent volcanic eruption. This soil chiefly occurs in a large area of southwestern Luzon where it is used for growing upland rice, sugarcane, vegetables, and fruit. Some of the alluvial soils on Luzon are also derived from tuff. These soils have a higher clay content than those that formed in situ. They retain water, making them excellent for wet rice cultivation.

Although the Philippines is comparatively well endowed with good soils, erosion and the resultant depletion have become a national problem of serious proportions. In many regions farmland yields are significantly lower than they were many years ago. Land use and soil management practices continue unchanged from traditional patterns, and soil-exhausting crops are planted year after year with little regard to rotation or fertilization (see ch. 13).

The Philippines has generally lush tropical vegetation, which includes a great variety of plant forms; more than 10,000 different species of flowering plants and ferns have been identified. Because of the slight variation in temperatures between the northern and southern parts of the country, however, the vegetation throughout the islands is much the same. The principal differences are related chiefly to altitude and to rainfall.

Two main kinds of forest grow at lower altitudes. Their tree associations differ substantially, the result of major differences in the amount of rainfall and length of wet and dry seasons. One variety, the evergreen rain forest, is found in areas of relatively consistent and heavy rainfall. Such forests occur ordinarily in lowland areas and on the lower slopes of mountains up to about 2,000 feet. They are dominated by the so-called Philippine mahoganies, of which the lauans constitute the most numerous species.

The primary evergreen rain forests are three tiered. They have an upper level that reaches over 200 feet, tree diameters being from three to six feet or more. Trees of the second layer grow to between 125 and 150 feet; both layers consist chiefly of lauans. A lower third level consists of a variety of smaller trees that reach heights of thirty to forty feet. Of great commercial importance these lauan forests were estimated to constitute about 57 percent of the total forest area in the 1960s.

The other main kind of forest is the so-called molave forest, named after the molave tree, a member of the teak family. These forests are also found at lower altitudes but in areas in which distinct wet and dry seasons occur. Trees of the molave forest are generally deciduous. The larger trees are scattered and are usually under 100 feet in height; they have maximum diameters of about four feet. The molave occurs only rarely in pure stands, but its wood and that of some other associated species are highly sought because of their hardness and great strength. The relative accessibility of these low-lying forests and the great value accorded to the wood have resulted in the destruction of many of the molave forests.

Between elevations of about 2,000 and 3,000 feet the larger islands have a dense forest cover consisting of a variety of tree species. These trees have no general commercial value but serve an important role in the protection they afford to watersheds. In certain areas of northern Luzon at elevations above 3,000 feet pine forests occur. These trees usually are found in pure stands as groves in grassland areas. Pines also grow naturally in the higher elevations of Mindoro.

Mangrove swamps line many coastal regions and cover about 1 percent of the total land area. Because mangrove trees are used as a source of firewood, mangrove forests near more densely settled areas have been extensively destroyed.

Coarse wild grasslands, known as *cogonales* because of the dominant cogon grasses that cover them, are found throughout the islands in all kinds of terrain, from mountain summits to flat lowlands. Although some grasslands appear to be of natural origin, they are mostly the result of slash-and-burn agriculture and repeated burning. The cogon grasses reach five to seven feet in height and have widths of up to one-half inch. It has been virtually impossible to reconvert the soil on which they grow into productive farmland.

Drainage

For the most part the country's mountainous terrain causes drainage systems characterized by short violent streams. The larger rivers are not navigable except for short distances. Most main streams and their tributaries are subject to extensive damaging floods during the heavy rainfall of the monsoon and typhoon seasons.

The largest river in Luzon is the Cagayan River, which drains the Cagayan Valley. Over 200 miles in length, it flows northward and empties into the sea at Aparri. The low-lying Central Luzon Plain is interlaced by a network of rivers and streams. Two of the plain's more important rivers are the Agno, which flows northward into Lingayen Gulf, and the Pampanga, which empties into Manila Bay. The Pasig River flows through Manila and, although relatively short, is one of the country's most important rivers commercially.

Two large rivers, both over 200 miles long, are found on Mindanao. The Agusan River flows northward through the Agusan Valley into the Mindanao Sea. The Mindanao River and its tributaries drain the Cotabato Lowland. This river empties into Moro Gulf northwest of the city of Cotabato.

Minerals

The country's known mineral resources are extensive, and broad areas are still relatively unexplored. The principal metallic minerals are gold, chromite, copper, iron, and mercury. Others include silver, manganese, lead, and zinc. Cadmium, platinum, and palladium are obtained as by-products in the processing of other metallic ores.

Nonmetallic minerals include asbestos, diatomite, feldspar, gypsum, limestone, dolomite, marble, perlite, quartz, and talc. Clays are found throughout the islands. Sulfur deposits are found on Luzon, and a large sulfur deposit of volcanic origin—estimated to contain 30 million tons of ore—is located in Negros Oriental Province.

Gold has been mined since before the Spanish era and is found in many scattered locations on various islands from Luzon to Mindanao. In the early 1970s the Philippines was among the top ten gold producers in the world. The major locations known were in the mountains of northern Luzon.

At the beginning of the 1970s there were estimated reserves of over 500 million tons of copper ore. Copper production in the Philippines was the largest in the Far East. The largest mine, located at Toledo on Cebu Island, was worked both through underground tunnels and open-pit excavation. Other sizable copper mines were located in Laguna and Mountain provinces on Luzon and on the islands of Negros and Samar. Copper was the country's most important mineral in the mid-1970s.

The chief deposits of chromite, in Zambales Province in western Luzon, have reserves estimated at over 10 million tons of refractory grade ore and over 3 million tons of metallurgical ore. Iron ore deposits are found throughout the islands; some of the major concentrations are on Luzon and Mindanao, and deposits also occur in the Visayan Islands. In the mid-1970s iron ore ranked after copper and gold in economic importance. Nickel occurs in low-grade laterites in Surigao del Norte Province in northeastern Mindanao. Ore reserves in the area were estimated to be over 100 million tons, containing about 1.45 percent nickel.

Coal deposits are found from Mindoro to Mindanao; some are also located in southeastern Luzon. At the beginning of the 1970s, however, commercially significant mining was carried on only in Cebu. Although there has been extensive exploration, as of 1975 petroleum had not been found in commercial quantities.

Wildlife

There are about 760 different species of birds on the islands, but over 100 of these are migratory visitors. Larger animals are few in number and variety, consisting mainly of monkeys, small deer, wild pigs, and a few members of the cat and civet families. Rodents are numerous, including more than fifty known species of bats. A species of wild water buffalo, the tamarau, is found only in Mindoro. Crocodiles, once widespread, are found mainly in Mindanao. Although several varieties of poisonous snakes exist, only three are widespread—the coral snake, pit viper, and a kind of small cobra. Large pythons are also found. Saltwater fish are abundant; over 750 species are used for food. Mollusks, many of which are edible, occur in large numbers. Pearl oysters abound.

ADMINISTRATIVE DIVISIONS AND INTERNATIONAL BOUNDARIES

At the time of the 1970 census the country was divided into sixty-six provinces and fifty-eight chartered cities; the city of Manila was also considered a province. By mid-1975 the total number of provinces had been increased to seventy-two and the number of chartered cities to sixty-one (see fig. 4). The provinces in turn were divided into municipalities and municipal districts, similar to counties, of which there were about 1,594 in mid-1975; at the end of 1975 thirteen municipalities in the metropolitan Manila area were combined into a single administrative unit. The lowest level of administration was the *barrio*, a subdivision of a municipality, municipal district, or chartered city; the *barrio* was renamed *barangay* in mid-1974 (see ch. 9).

The country's international borders are all water boundaries established by specific treaties. The Treaty of Paris, signed on December 10, 1898, between the United States and Spain and a further treaty between the two countries signed on November 7, 1900, set the major boundaries; the treaty signed between Great Britain and the United States on January 2, 1930, determined the final western borders. In general boundary questions have not been the cause of serious disputes with neighbors, but there have been exceptions. In 1963 the Philippines laid formal claim to certain areas of Sabah on the island of Borneo, which is part of the Federation of Malaysia. This dispute led to a temporary disruption of diplomatic relations between the two countries, but by the mid-1970s relations had been normalized (see ch. 11).

In 1961 the Philippine government passed an act defining the base lines of its territory according to the so-called archipelago principle. It identified eighty straight base lines surrounding the landmass areas of the islands. Based on this act, still in force in 1972, the Philippines considered all waters within the base lines to be internal waters. (Waters within the so-called treaty limits of the Philippines were considered territorial seas.) This act resulted in a considerably greater area of open sea being brought under Philippine jurisdiction than is usually recognized under international law. Upon publication of the act in May 1961, the United States government entered a protest, declaring that it could not regard claims based on the legislation as binding. Along this same line Article I of the 1973 Constitution declared that all waters around, between, and connecting the islands of the archipelago, irrespective of their dimensions, formed part of the internal waters of the Philippines.

SETTLEMENT PATTERNS

The country's principal pattern of settlement derived from the original Malay village, called a *barangay*, which consisted of a group of dwellings usually along a waterway. In addition there were isolated houses and *sitios* (small clusters of houses) scattered over the countryside. To facilitate their rule the Spanish established *poblaciones* (stylized towns), built around a plaza; they usually included a church, a government building, and the residences of the leading citizens. These settlements became centers of religious, social, political and—to a more limited extent—commercial activity under the Spanish. Patterns of interaction emerged that differed significantly from rural areas.

Over the years the different kinds of settlements grew, and some fused with others. The *sitios* expanded along roads or trails until in many places they became almost continuous. Simultaneously the *barangays* also expanded and absorbed many *sitios* in the process. Thus enlarged they constituted what were known as *barrios*, a term also used to denote the lowest administrative unit, renamed *barangays* in mid-1974. These were the country's principal settlement form and were often made up of long lines of houses only two or three deep, stretching along both sides of a road or stream or along the seashore.

The country's urban development generally conformed to traditional patterns, the major cities evolving either from ports, at historic crossroads, or from administrative centers. Because of the insular structure of the Philippines, this development has been based almost exclusively on settlements around ports or harbors. Virtually all of the larger cities are terminals for sea lane traffic or interisland communication. Manila, in addition to being a major port, has also been a political center since the time of the Spanish occupation. Western influence is clearly evident in the development of the larger cities, which follow a European design of grid-patterned streets with public buildings, parks, department stores, and hotels fronting on broad, tree-lined boulevards.

POPULATION AND NATIONAL DEVELOPMENT

The beginning of the twentieth century marked the start of a race between economic development and population growth in the Philippines. Although dislocations resulting from World War II gave a

PROVINCES	CAPITALS	PROVINCES	CAPITALS
1 Batanes	Basco	37 Aklan	Kalibo
2 Ilocos Norte	Laoag (c.c.)	38 Samar	Catbalogan
3 Cagayan	Tuguegarao	39 Eastern Samar	Borongan
4 Abra	Bangued	40 Capiz	Roxas (c.c.)
5 Kalinga-Apayao	Tabuk	41 Antique	San Jose de Buenavista
6 Ilocos Sur	Vigan	42 Iloilo	Iloilo (c.c.)
7 Mountain	Bontoc	43 Leyte	Tacloban (c.c.)
8 Isabela	Ilagan	44 Cebu	Cebu (c.c.)
9 Ifugao	Lagawe	45 Southern Leyte	Maasin
10 La Union	San Fernando	46 Negros Occidental	Bacolod (c.c.)
11 Benguet	La Trinidad	47 Bohol	Tagbilaran (c.c.)
12 Nueva Vizcaya	Bayombong	48 Surigao del Norte	Surigao (c.c.)
13 Quirino	Cabarroquis	49 Palawan	Puerto Princesa (c.c.)
14 Pangasinan	Lingayen	50 Negros Oriental	Dumaguete (c.c.)
15 Nueva Ecija	Palayan (c.c.)	51 Siquijor	Siquijor
16 Quezon	Lucena (c.c.)	52 Agusan del Norte	Butuan (c.c.)
17 Zambales	Iba	53 Camiguin	Mambajao
18 Tarlac	Tarlac	54 Surigao del Sur	Tandag
19 Pampanga	San Fernando	55 Misamis Oriental	Cagayan de Oro (c.c.)
20 Bulacan	Malolos	56 Zamboanga del Norte	Dipolog (c.c.)
21 Bataan	Balanga	57 Misamis Occidental	Oroquieta (c.c.)
22 Rizal	Pasig	58 Bukidnon	Malaybalay
23 Cavite	Trece Matires (c.c.)	59 Agusan del Sur	Prosperidad
24 Laguna	Santa Cruz	60 Zamboanga del Sur	Pagadian (c.c.)
25 Camarines Norte	Daet	61 Lanao del Norte	Iligan (c.c.)
26 Batangas	Batangas (c.c.)	62 Lanao del Sur	Marawi (c.c.)
27 Camarines Sur	Naga (c.c.)	63 Davao	Tagum
28 Catanduanes	Virac	64 Davao Oriental	Mati
29 Mindoro Occidental	Mamburao	65 Maguindanao	Maganoy
30 Mindoro Oriental	Calapan	66 North Cotabato	Kidapawan
31 Marinduque	Boac	67 Basilan	Isabela
32 Albay	Legazpi (c.c.)	68 Sultan Kudarat	Isulan
33 Romblon	Romblon	69 Davao del Sur	Digos
34 Sorsogon	Sorsogon	70 South Cotabato	Koronadal
35 Masbate	Masbate	71 Sulu	Jolo
36 Northern Samar	Catarman	72 Tawitawi	Balimbing

Note-- (c.c.) indicates chartered city.

Figure 4. Philippines, Provinces and Provincial Capitals, 1975

foretaste of the emerging confrontation, not until the 1960s did the competition become sufficiently intense to cause concern. By that time much of the progress achieved through development planning was being eroded by population growth. As a result the annual per capita increase in gross national product (GNP) was reduced to only 1 or 2 percent.

The structure and dynamics of the country's population have become critical factors in the efficient utilization of human and natural resources and all phases of planning for national development. Population statistics are important clues to contemporary problems, and they are vital to predicting future needs. Forecasting spending and savings patterns, estimating the level of government expenditures necessary to provide qualitative improvements in education, health, and other social services, and calculating agricultural production requirements—all depend upon population information.

An accurate appraisal of the situation was complicated in the 1960s and remained complicated in the 1970s by inadequate statistical materials; demography remained a young field in the country. Serious defects in the national vital registration system have been recognized; in certain years as high as 40 percent of all births and deaths have gone unregistered. The percentage of underreporting has varied from year to year, complicating efforts to adjust discrepancies. Surveys by such groups as the Population Institute of the University of the Philippines, various private research groups, and certain government agencies have been used to evaluate national vital rates published by the Bureau of the Census and Statistics. Although these are useful indicators of inconsistencies or errors in the official national figures, they are neither broad enough nor frequent enough to replace the data provided by the national registration system. In the early 1970s the bureau established a dual registration system under which the existing registration process was checked against periodic household samples. This verification process was checked against periodic household samples. This verification process encountered difficulties that had not been resolved sufficiently to improve the accuracy of official vital rates by mid-1975.

Various attempts have been made to estimate vital rates on the basis of projections from the six national censuses, the most recent of which was taken in 1975. Major reliance had to be placed on the information contained in the 1970 census. The final census report was not available in mid-1975, but a preliminary summary based on a 5-percent sample of the total enumeration was available. Analysis of the sample indicated that the accuracy of the overall age and sex structure and particularly the data for those under the age of ten was questionable. Although not definitive, the available information nevertheless provided a general illustration of the population problems facing the Philippines.

POPULATION STRUCTURE AND DYNAMICS

The 1970 census reported a total population of about 36.6 million, compared to the 1960 census total of about 27 million. According to a preliminary count of the 1975 census, the estimated population slightly exceeded 42 million in that year. The average annual rate of population increase for the decade ending in 1970 was 3 percent. This average rate was estimated to have continued through the early 1970s; there was some indication that the rate may have declined slightly in the mid-1970s, but, without subsequent declines, the reduction was not expected to have a significant effect on the population pressure to be faced by the country in the next decades.

The 3-percent average annual growth rate for the decade of the 1960s, one of the world's highest rates, increased the population by almost 10 million. Continuation of this rate would double the population in almost two decades and yield a population of over 100 million by the year 2000. Projections based on a rapid decline in age-specific fertility rates to 80 percent of the 1970 level by 1975 and to 60 percent of the 1970 level by the year 2000, at which point the growth rate would have fallen to 2.2 percent, would yield a population of over 60 million in the next two decades and about 79 million by the year 2000. In order to reach the lower rate, over 25 million births would have to be averted, and the birthrate would have to decline from forty births annually per 1,000 of the population in 1970 to about thirty.

There were about 777 Filipinos per square mile of arable land in 1970, a ratio that compared favorably with the Republic of China (Nationalist China (3,885 people) and Japan (over 4,600 people). The rapid growth of the population, however, had brought about serious pressures on the land, and each person was dependent on about four-fifths of an acre of agricultural land—an area considered inadequate in view of the crop yield and of the stage of development of agricultural technology in the Philippines. Moreover the country no longer had new frontiers providing an abundance of land to distribute (see ch. 13). Official government sources estimated in 1971 that what little new land remained to be opened for settlement would be exhausted by 1976.

Age and Sex Distribution

According to the 1970 census the country had a high proportion of young people: over 43 percent of the population in 1970 was under fifteen years of age, and more than 62 percent was under twenty-five (see fig. 5). Some 34 percent was in the twenty-five to sixty-four age bracket, and 3.5 percent was reported as being over the age of sixty-five.

The 1970 census showed a ratio of 98.8 males to every 100 females. This contrasted with a ratio of not quite 100 males to 98.3 females in the 1960 census. The low ratio for the fifteen to nineteen age group of 91.2 males per 100 females, compared with the sex structure of the same group in the 1960 census, could only result if there had been very low male and very high female survival rates. Both rates were in general questionable.

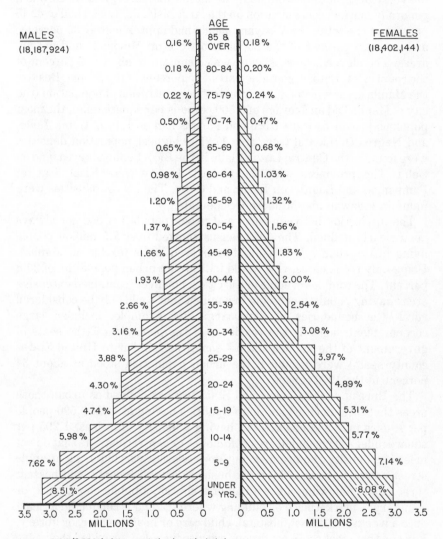

MALES
(18,187,924)

FEMALES
(18,402,144)

	AGE	
0.16%	85 & OVER	0.18%
0.18%	80-84	0.20%
0.22%	75-79	0.24%
0.50%	70-74	0.47%
0.65%	65-69	0.68%
0.98%	60-64	1.03%
1.20%	55-59	1.32%
1.37%	50-54	1.56%
1.66%	45-49	1.83%
1.93%	40-44	2.00%
2.66%	35-39	2.54%
3.16%	30-34	3.08%
3.88%	25-29	3.97%
4.30%	20-24	4.89%
4.74%	15-19	5.31%
5.98%	10-14	5.77%
7.62%	5-9	7.14%
8.51%	UNDER 5 YRS.	8.08%

3.5 3.0 2.5 2.0 1.5 1.0 0.5 0   0 0.5 1.0 1.5 2.0 2.5 3.0 3.5
MILLIONS   MILLIONS

Note -- 6,419 (0.02%) of the population is not included.

Source: Based on information from Philippines, Department of Commerce and Industry, Bureau of the Census and Statistics, *1970 Census of Population and Housing: National Summary, Philippines: Advance Report*, Manila, 1972, table A–2, NS–3.

Figure 5. Philippines, Population by Age and Sex, 1970

Regional and Rural-Urban Distribution

The average population density in 1970 was 317 persons per square mile, compared with 234 per square mile in 1960. The population was unevenly distributed throughout the nation, however, and there was a generally marked concentration on the larger islands. Luzon had over 45 percent of the total; the Visayan Islands had approximately 35 percent; and some 20 percent of the population were on Mindanao and nearby areas. The eleven largest islands, which constitute almost 95 percent of the country's territory, contained about 95 percent of the people. Besides the Manila area, which had the greatest concentration of population (the city of Manila had an average of 9,500 persons per square mile), the most populous provinces were Rizal and Pangasinan on Luzon, Cebu, Iloilo, and Negros Occidental (see table 1). The highest population densities were found in the Central Luzon Plain, in the Bicol Peninsula area, and on Cebu. The provinces with the highest density were Rizal, Cavite, Pampanga, and Laguna on Luzon and Cebu. The lowest densities were found in Palawan and Mindoro Occidental.

The distinction between rural and urban population has not always been clearly defined. The 1970 census showed over 7.5 million people living in the country's fifty-eight chartered cities (excluding Manila). Using only those cities, this would indicate an urban population of 20.8 percent. The confines of some of the cities, however, contained extensive areas having populations living in a milieu that could only be considered rural—the boundaries of Zamboanga, for example, included large coconut plantations. If the residents of the *poblaciones* (the seats of government of the municipalities—somewhat similar to United States county seats) were included, the urban population stood at about 34 percent in the 1970 census.

The Bureau of the Census and Statistics has defined as urban those areas that include cities and municipalities having at least 2,590 people per square mile and *poblaciones* having a density of at least 1,295 per square mile. Also included are *poblaciones* or central districts that do not meet the density requirement but do possess a parallel or right-angle street network, have at least six business establishments, and possess three of the following: a town hall or a church; a public plaza, park, or cemetery; a marketplace or building where trading is conducted at least once a week; or a school, hospital, child care or health center, or library. *Barrios* that meet these conditions are also included, provided they have at least 2,590 inhabitants whose occupations are predominantly nonfarming or fishing. All other areas are classified as rural. Applying these criteria the 1970 census classified about 31.8 percent of the population as urban.

Migration

Although the urge to migrate has not been a traditionally dominant

Table 1. Philippines, Population by Province, 1970

Province	Population	Province	Population
Abra	145,508	Lanao del Sur	455,508
Agusan del Norte	278,053	La Union	373,682
Agusan del Sur	174,682	Leyte	1,110,626
Aklan	263,358	Manila	1,330,788
Albay	673,981	Marinduque	144,109
Antique	289,172	Masbate	492,908
Bataan	216,210	Mindoro Occidental	144,032
Batanes	11,398	Mindoro Oriental	328,364
Batangas	926,308	Misamis Occidental	319,855
Benguet	263,550	Misamis Oriental	472,756
Bohol	683,297	Mountain Province	93,112
Bukidnon	414,762	Negros Occidental	1,503,782
Bulacan	836,431	Negros Oriental	715,240
Cagayan	581,237	Northern Samar	306,114
Camarines Norte	262,207	Nueva Ecija	851,294
Camarines Sur	948,436	Nueva Vizcaya	221,965
Camiguin	53,913	Palawan	236,635
Capiz	394,041	Pampanga	907,275
Catanduanes	162,302	Pangasinan	1,386,143
Cavite	520,180	Quezon	983,324
Cebu	1,634,182	Rizal	2,844,689
Cotabato	1,136,007	Romblon	167,082
Davao del Norte	442,543	Sorsogon	427,047
Davao del Sur	785,398	South Cotabato	466,110
Davao Oriental	247,995	Southern Leyte	251,425
Eastern Samar	271,000	Sulu	425,617
Ifugao	92,487	Surigao del Norte	238,714
Ilocos Norte	343,427	Surigao del Sur	258,680
Ilocos Sur	385,139	Tarlac	559,708
Iloilo	1,167,973	Western Samar	442,244
Isabela	648,123	Zambales	343,034
Kalinga-Apayao	136,249	Zamboanga del Norte	409,379
Laguna	699,736	Zamboanga del Sur	1,034,018
Lanao del Norte	349,942		

Source: Based on information from Philippines, Department of Commerce and Industry, Bureau of the Census and Statistics, *1970 Census of Population and Housing: National Summary, Philippines: Advance Report*, Manila, 1972, pp. 36, 486, 684.

trait among Filipinos and close family ties and community interests have generally discouraged large-scale movement of the population, two significant internal migrations of a permanent character have occurred since World War II. The first was a trend to the cities, particularly to the Manila metropolitan area, and this movement showed few signs of slowing in the mid-1970s. For example, in the ten-year period between 1960 and 1970 the urban population increased from 14 to 20 percent of the total population. While the nation's population was increasing at an estimated 3 percent per year, the urban population increased at 6.7 percent annually during the ten-year period. The greatest growth occurred in both the number and population of cities of 100,000 or more.

Many of the migrants to urban areas have moved to escape their subsistence life in rural areas. Their only hope of employment, however, is usually in the low-paid, unskilled sector of the labor market. The high cost of housing in urban areas forces most of these migrants to reside in shantytown communities; living conditions in these districts are usually worse than those the migrants had known in rural areas, but they seldom return to their home provinces. In the mid-1970s about 30 percent of the population of metropolitan Manila, including both suburbs and the central city, lived in such shantytowns (see ch. 6).

Although the population of the city of Manila, estimated at about 1.3 million in 1970, had increased by 17 percent since 1960, population pressure had been relieved by a secondary migration from the central city to suburbs in the metropolitan area. When compared to overall population growth, the central city of Manila has had a net loss of population. The population of Rizal Province, containing the major suburban receiving areas for secondary migration, nearly doubled during the same ten-year period. Real estate developments and the relocation of industry to suburban areas have facilitated the shift in population.

The migration to Rizal as well as to Mindanao reflected the second major migration pattern, consisting of resettlement from the more densely to the less densely populated regions. Rates of population change between 1960 and 1970 exceeding 50 percent were observed in seventeen provinces, but the most significant increases along with Rizal included: Bukidnon, 113 percent; Davao Oriental, 87 percent; Agusan del Sur, 86 percent; and Mindoro Occidental, 71 percent.

Internal migrations of a temporary nature also occur periodically. In the central Luzon provinces of Rizal and Laguna and to an extent in Batangas and Cavite, many farmers go to the cities to seek employment during the dry season from January through May when construction activity in urban areas is at its maximum. They then return home to their wet season rice crop. From Pangasinan, south of the Lingayen Gulf, many men go to the northern Luzon mountains to work in the mines but return if possible to help with the rice. From western Panay temporary workers migrate to the Iloilo area or to Negros during the sugar-harvesting season but return to their homes to take part in rice cultivating or corn planting. Other relatively small-scale seasonal displacements of a similar nature take place throughout most of the major islands.

External migration in the early 1970s represented about 6 percent of the annual increase in population. Overseas migration was principally to the continental United States and Hawaii, about 20,000 immigrant visas being granted annually during the early 1970s. Other smaller numbers migrated on either a permanent or a temporary basis to Canada, Australia, and Spain. Filipinos also have migrated to Sabah.

FAMILY PLANNING

The country's rapidly expanding population became a serious problem in the 1960s as pressures on available resources and the shrinking availability of land occurred. Traditionally, large families were considered desirable—a concept encouraged by the government. Although a few private clinics offered maternal care, their activity was largely limited to prenatal examinations. The Roman Catholic Church disapproved of birth control through contraceptive techniques, and the topic was considered a subject not to be discussed in polite society.

The gravity of the situation, however, brought about a change in official attitude in the late 1960s, and the need for a program to limit the size of families was debated openly. In 1968 the government and the United States Agency for International Development (AID) signed an agreement for an initial family planning project. Because of the subject's still sensitive nature, however, no government funding was provided, and direct participation by government staff was avoided.

In February 1969 President Ferdinand E. Marcos created by executive order the ad hoc Commission on Population, composed of over twenty national leaders, to study the matter. In December of that year the president approved a statement on national population policy and progress prepared by the commission that in essence committed the government to adopt quantitative population goals, promote family planning education, modify existing restrictions relating to family planning, and cooperate with private and international organizations concerned with population control. An existing ban on importing contraceptives was lifted, although abortion continued to be illegal unless deemed necessary to save the life of the mother.

In June 1971 the Congress passed legislation that formally established the national Population Commission (POPCOM) to replace the earlier ad hoc body. The measure also authorized government funds to implement a national family planning policy, the long-term objective of which was to provide family planning services within a reasonably accessible distance to a minimum of 90 percent of the population.

By mid-1974 the number of family planning service outlets or clinics was over 2,100, as compared to seventy-eight in mid-1969. The hours these were open ranged from full time to half a day a week. Over twenty-five different organizations were involved in the operation of the service, but 70 percent were under the Department of Health, the Institute of Maternal and Child Health, and the Family Planning Organization of the Philippines.

The central task facing POPCOM was the coordination and direction of the various facilities in operation as well as expansion of the overall program. POPCOM had direct representation in the National Economic and Development Authority and a central staff under its director. Regional offices, however, were not established until 1974. The assumption of control by POPCOM was still in a transitional stage in 1975, and it was premature to forecast the effect the new offices would have in increasing the ability of the commission to coordinate the national family planning program beyond the policy planning level.

Financing of the family planning program has been largely through foreign aid; although the national budget for fiscal year (FY) 1974 included about US$6 million for family planning, the government expenditure in FY 1970 had been insignificant. Contributions by AID, which had reached about US$25 million by 1973 and were expected to reach US$34 million by 1976, represented the largest share. The second principal contributor was the United Nations Development Program, which planned to spend US$9.3 million on population control activities in the Philippines between 1972 and 1977. Various international private organizations also were active, including the International Planned Parenthood Federation, the Population Council, the Ford Foundation, the Pathfinder Fund, Church World Services, the Rockefeller Foundation, and a number of other interested overseas agencies. Funding had also been sought from the International Bank for Reconstruction and Development (IBRD, commonly known as the World Bank) and the Japanese government.

The number of new accepters of some form of family planning, an accepter being defined as a person who had visited a family planning clinic at least once, grew rapidly from about 96,000 in FY 1969 to 440,800 in FY 1973. The percentage of women who knew of at least one contraceptive method by specific name rose from 4 percent in 1968 to 86 percent in 1972, and the percentage of women who had practiced contraception at one time or another rose from 19 to 32 percent.

The composite conclusions of various surveys taken between 1970 and 1974 of accepters in the family planning programs indicate that the program has been only moderately successful, however. Only about 50 percent of the new accepters were likely to continue for as long as one year using the birth control method they first adopted. About 33 percent stopped using contraceptive techniques of any kind, and about 20 percent of the women became pregnant before the end of one year.

The intrauterine device (IUD) was found to have the highest rate of continuation. The use of the IUD indicates a high degree of motivation; women who discontinued using it usually turned to other methods of birth control. Only 20 percent of the women in the program, however, elected using the IUD. About 60 percent selected birth control pills. The use of the pill offered the next best continuation rate, but pregnancy among users was higher. Most women who terminated the use of the pill did so for medical reasons or because of side effects.

A common theme in most studies of the family planning program indicated the importance of accepter motivation. Various efforts have been made by the government to stimulate national motivation for family planning. Income tax and labor laws have been modified to encourage small families. All government agencies have been instructed to support national efforts to reduce the rate of population growth. Other efforts have included special education programs, such as conferences designed to enlist the support of labor unions and management in promoting family planning.

There has been a disproportionate participation of women in urban areas in the family planning program. About 40 percent of all new accepters have been residents of chartered cities and represented only 20 percent of the target group. As a group, women in urban areas are more open to new ideas and are more accessible to family planning facilities and information programs. Urban life makes the benefits of family planning more evident. Women in rural areas, especially in Muslim and undeveloped regions, are more closely tied to traditional values, such as large families and the desire for male children. Future efforts of the family planning program to obtain new accepters will undoubtedly meet increased resistance. A special program for rural areas combining personal contact, radiobroadcasts, and newspapers and other printed media has been initiated. Family planning services will be offered at an increasing number of rural health centers. The ability of these efforts to motivate rural families to accept and continue family planning techniques will be crucial to the success of the population program.

The role of religious beliefs in delaying the acceptance of family planning is difficult to assess. It is generally felt that both Islamic and Roman Catholic beliefs have been principal deterrents in the past. In 1962 a Roman Catholic bishops' conference issued a statement endorsing the government's exploration of the need for a population policy and called for a Filipino-planned program. The conference approved only the rhythm method of birth control, but disapproval of other forms of contraception remained muted. In 1975 the administrative council of the bishops' conference pledged its support of the government's policy of supporting all family planning methods if the choice of method were left to the conscience of the user. Controversy over the display and sale of contraceptive kits occurred but was settled by compromise. The influence of religious beliefs was expected to decline in subsequent years to the point of being but one of the factors influencing the acceptance or rejection of family planning services.

LABOR

Based on a nationwide sample survey of households conducted in March 1971 by the Bureau of the Census and Statistics, it was estimated that almost 12.3 million individuals were in the active labor force. They constituted 48.6 percent of the estimated 25.3 million people ten years of age or older (the potential labor force was officially defined to include all individuals ten years old and above). This young age reflected the high rate of early school leavers (see ch. 7). The 51.4 percent who were not in the active labor force consisted largely of students and persons engaged in housekeeping. The remainder comprised mainly disabled and retired persons and seasonal workers who were not working and not looking for work.

Since 1960 the rate of open unemployment has ranged between 5 and 10 percent. In the early 1970s the rate fluctuated above and below 6 percent, and there seemed to be some evidence of a slight downward trend. Breakdowns by age, sex, and region, which have been maintained since 1965, have also been relatively stable. Most of those who are unemployed are new labor force entrants and young workers under twenty-five years of age (see table 2). The rate of unemployment is higher for young males in urban areas. Most individuals remained unemployed for only short periods of time; more than 50 percent had been looking for work for less than six weeks, and only 3 percent had been without work for more than six months.

A more significant problem was presented by underemployment, based largely on the inability of a worker to obtain a position commensurate with acquired training or skills. There are no fixed means of measuring underemployment, and estimates ranged from 12 to almost 30 percent of the labor force in the early 1970s. An estimate provided by a study mission of the International Labor Office indicated total unemployment and underemployment to be about 25 percent.

The annual rate of growth of the labor force in the 1960s was estimated at 2.9 percent. This was considerably below the 3.4-percent annual growth rate estimated for the working-age population during the same period. The drop in participation in the active labor force was pronounced in the ten- to twenty-four-year age-group. This downward trend continued into the mid-1970s. In October 1966 some 52.3 percent of the fifteen- to nineteen-year age-group was in the active labor force. The proportion had dropped to 40.6 percent by March 1971. Similarly participation by the twenty-to twenty-four-year age-group declined in the same period from 68.3 to 57.5 percent. The chief explanation advanced for the decline was the continuance in school of a larger proportion of individuals in that age-group. A reduction in the demand for jobs resulted, but the increased number of students who will finish their schooling in the 1970s can be expected to have an important impact on labor market developments as the 1970 decade progresses.

In the early 1970s about 800,000 students or trainees annually completed their formal educations and became eligible for employment. This figure was expected to grow during the 1970s and to exceed 1 million by 1980. Annual withdrawals from the labor force totaled about 300,000. At least 80 percent of the annual net increase would be actively seeking employment. In order to find positions for these new entrants and also meaningfully reduce unemployment, the economy would need to generate nearly 450,000 new jobs annually. This figure was at least 30,000 more than the number being provided in the early 1970s.

As early as 1962 the government established the Emergency Employment Administration to oversee the development of short-term employ-

Table 2. *Philippines, Unemployment Rates by Household Status, Age, and Sex, August 1972*
(in percent of labor force)

	Heads of Household	Other	Age of Unemployed		Total Unemployment
			15-24 Years	25 Years and Over	
Urban					
Male	5.2	24.1	26.9	7.8	12.4
Female	2.2	8.8	13.0	5.5	8.3
Total Urban	4.0	14.7	19.8	7.0	10.8
Rural					
Male	0.9	6.6	7.2	1.4	3.1
Female	0.8	6.7	13.2	3.4	6.2
Total Rural	0.9	6.6	8.9	2.0	4.0
Total Male	2.1	11.4	12.0	3.4	5.7
Total Female	1.3	7.5	13.1	4.2	7.0
Total Unemployment	2.1	9.3	12.4	3.6	6.1

Source: Based on information from International Labour Organization, *Sharing in Development: A Programme of Employment, Equity, and Growth for the Philippines,* Geneva, 1974, p. 6.

ment programs. Since the mid-1960s a wide variety of programs have been discussed. Those selected for implementation usually have been administered through the Department of Public Works, Transportation, and Communications. A special committee was appointed in late 1972 to study kinds of infrastructure development that could best provide labor intensive projects. One of the pilot projects developed by the committee was a river control project to repair damage to levees and dikes resulting from the summer floods of 1972; the area chosen for the project, however, did not have a significant unemployment level. Most other short-term projects were equally experimental and offered only marginal contributions to short-term unemployment or underemployment.

Of the 11.6 million people actually employed in March 1971, 48.5 percent were engaged in the agriculture, forestry, hunting, and fishing sector. In the nonagricultural sector the chief subsectors were manufacturing, which accounted for 12.3 percent; commerce, 12.0 percent; and govermental and other services, excluding personal and domestic services, 10.1 percent (see table 3).

Most of the occupational opportunities in the country's still underdeveloped economy continued to be in rural areas, and persons engaged in farming—as either operators or farm employees—together with loggers, hunters, fishermen, constituted almost half of all employed persons in 1971 (see table 4). The trend, however, was for fewer persons to be employed in such occupations.

In contrast, in the period from October 1967 to March 1971 professional, technical, and related workers increased from slightly over 4 to 6 percent of employed persons. The increase was actually greater than indicated because an unknown number of individuals classed as athletes, sportsmen, photographers, and related workers had been included in this category in 1967 but were excluded from the category in 1971. A significant increase also occurred during the same period in the number of skilled workers engaged in the processing or production of goods and in construction work—from 1.35 million to almost 1.6 million. This represented a rise from 12.4 percent of all employed persons to 13.7 percent. Reflecting the increasing importance of transportation and communications, the proportion of individuals engaged in this area rose from 2.6 percent of all employed workers to 4.4 percent.

Wage and salary workers in the 1971 survey constituted 41.3 percent of the persons employed. Another 40.4 percent were self-employed, and unpaid family workers made up almost all the remaining workers. There was a substantial number of self-employed persons in the manufacturing sector (35.8 percent). Almost 60 percent of those engaged in commerce were also self-employed. Many of them were operators of small retail shops and *sari-sari* (see Glossary) shops. Others in this same category included vendors in markets, street vendors, and peddlers and hawkers. Almost 39 percent of the individuals providing personal services (other than domestic) also were self-employed.

Table 3. *Philippines, Employed Persons by Major Industrial Sector, October 1967 and March 1971*
(in thousands and percent)

Major Industrial Sector	October 1967		March 1971	
	Number	Percent	Number	Percent
Agriculture, forestry, hunting, and fishing	6,330	58.3	5,635	48.5
Mining and quarrying	45	0.4	49	0.4
Manufacturing	1,223	11.3	1,483	12.3
Electricity, gas, water, and sanitary services	30	0.3	55	0.5
Construction	276	2.5	419	3.6
Commerce	1,078	9.9	1,400	12.0
Transport, storage, and communication	375	3.4	532	4.6
Government, community, business, and recreational services	769	7.1	1,170	10.1
Domestic services	502	4.6	630	5.4
Personal services other than domestic	229	2.1	251	2.2
Industry not reported	10	0.1	54	0.5
TOTAL	10,867	100.0	11,627*	100.0*

*Figures do not add to total because of rounding.

Source: Based on information from Philippines, Department of Commerce and Industry, Bureau of the Census and Statistics, "Labor Force," *The BCS Survey of Households Bulletin*, Series No. 28, Manila, March 1971, p. xxviii.

Table 4. *Philippines, Employed Persons by Major Occupational Category, October 1967 and March 1971* (in thousands and percent)

Major Occupational Category	October 1967		March 1971	
	Number	Percent	Number	Percent
Professional, technical, and related workers[1]	441	4.1	692	6.0
Administrative, executive, and managerial workers[2]	393	3.6	112	1.0
Clerical workers	357	3.3	433	3.7
Sales workers[2]	695	6.4	1,334	11.5
Farmers, farm laborers, fishermen, hunters, loggers, and related workers	6,299	58.0	5,565	47.9
Miners, quarrymen, and related workers	34	0.3	25	0.2
Workers in transport and communication occupations	159	2.6	516	4.4
Craftsmen, production-process workers, and related workers	1,351	12.4	1,598	13.7
Manual workers and laborers (not elsewhere counted)	281	1.5	203	1.7
Service, sports, and related workers[1]	847	7.8	1,101	9.5
Occupation not reported	10	0.1	48	0.4
TOTAL	10,867	100.0[3]	11,627	100.0

[1] In 1967 athletes, sportsmen, photographers, and related workers are included in professional, technical, and related workers. In 1971 they are included in service, sports, and related workers.
[2] *Sari-sari* store operators are included in administrative, executive, and managerial workers in 1967 and in sales workers in 1971.
[3] Figures do not add to 100.0 because of rounding.

Source: Based on information from Philippines, Department of Commerce and Industry, Bureau of the Census and Statistics, "Labor Force," *The BCS Survey of Households Bulletin*, Series No. 28, Manila, March 1971, p. xxix.

40

The Philippines has suffered a loss of professional and skilled persons through emigration. Economic considerations appear to be a main underlying factor. Individuals in the professions cited low salaries, the lack of professional opportunities, and inadequate facilities as the main reasons for seeking residence outside the country. Most migrants in the early 1970s went to the United States. An estimated one-third of this group were engineers and engineering technicians. Among professional and technical personnel emigrating to Canada and Australia, nurses and teachers reportedly predominated.

In May 1974 a new labor code was enacted by presidential decree. Preparation of the new regulations was begun by the Department of Labor in the mid-1960s. A transition period of six months was planned for implementation of the new code, which was seen as a flexible document open to amendment. The document reaffirmed the principles set out in the 1973 Constitution promoting full employment, equality of employment opportunity, and the regulation of relations between workers and employers. The code introduced many changes in existing legislation. Innovations included employment exchange services—which, with the exception of urban areas, are undeveloped—a new social security system, regulations concerning unemployment, and guidelines for labor union activities pending the lifting of martial law and the restoration of the right to strike.

CHAPTER 3

HISTORICAL SETTING

The Republic of the Philippines became independent in 1946 after nearly four centuries of colonial rule, first by Spain from 1565 to 1898 and then by the United States after Spain ceded the islands as a consequence of defeat in the Spanish-American War. The achievement of Philippine sovereignty climaxed almost three-quarters of a century of growing nationalism, a nationalism that continued in the 1970s to exercise strong influences on the republic's economic development and foreign relations policies.

The establishment of Spanish authority in the sixteenth century had been relatively rapid owing to the absence of organized resistance by the locally autonomous communities of the dominant lowland population (see ch. 4). Opposition to the Spanish, however, continued for over three centuries by the Muslim Filipinos (Moros) in the southern islands. Colonization of the Philippines was originally undertaken by Spain for both economic and Christian missionary purposes; the economic objective was not realized, as spices and precious metals were not found, and the colony became an essentially missionary endeavor.

For over 300 years the Roman Catholic Church and the Spanish state imposed—although superficially—their Western concepts and organizations on the indigenous structure. The lowland peoples adapted Spanish forms and ideas but retained many of their own cultural values. The original two classes of chiefs and dependents maintained their identities and relative positions while adjusting to Spanish innovations of private ownership of land and to administrative responsibilities at the lower levels of government.

Elements of the population remained unassimilated into the society that evolved under Spanish influence. The Igorots in the mountains of northern Luzon and the Muslims in the extreme south—whose expansion northward was blocked by the Spanish conquest—retained their individual cultures (see ch. 4).

Exposure to nineteenth-century European liberal thought brought into being a modern nationalist movement in opposition to Spanish colonialism; that opposition in modified form was later directed against American administration. American innovations abetted this development, especially the introduction of popular education and the opportunities offered by the American system of politics, at which the Filipinos quickly became adept. The widespread teaching of English and increased literacy in a common language acted as a national unifying force.

Unlike most former colonial territories, the Philippines achieved independence after World War II without a political struggle against a colonial power. The new state was challenged nearly successfully, however, by an internal communist insurgency against a government weakened by fiscal irresponsibility and a serious decline in public morality. In the postwar period, with few exceptions, political change took place within boundaries set by the national elite, which represented both traditional landed interests and those of newly established large industries and businesses. The elite successfully limited the effective implementation of various economic and agrarian reforms. By the 1960s the country also faced serious problems arising from a lagging economy and rapid population growth.

EARLY HISTORY

Negrito, Proto-Malay, and Malay peoples were the principal contributors to the population of the Philippine archipelago. The Negritos are believed to have migrated by land bridges 30,000 years ago during the last glacial period. Later migrations were by water and took place over several thousand years in repeated movements before and after the start of the Christian Era (see ch. 4).

Even before the Christian Era important cultural differences had developed, illustrated by the contrast between the seafarers of the Sulu Islands and the rice farmers of central and northern Luzon, who were sedentary village dwellers cultivating land in irrigated terraces. Among the various settlement patterns that evolved, a common one was a village in a protected coastal site, its inhabitants using the sea for fishing and the forested hinterland for shifting cultivation. Later arrivals brought more complex technologies and introduced crops native to mainland Southeast Asia.

The social and political organization of the population in the widely scattered islands evolved into a generally common pattern. There was only a vaguely developed concept of territoriality other than among the permanent field rice farmers of northern Luzon. The basic unit of social structure was the *barangay* (Malay word for boat, which also came to be used for village), originally a kinship group headed by a *datu* (chief). Within the *barangay* the broad social divisions were those of nobles, which included the chiefs; freemen; and a group described in terms of the Philippine social organization before the Spanish period as dependents. Dependents included a number of categories with differing degrees of dependency: landless agricultural workers; those who had lost freeman status because of indebtedness or as punishment for crime; and slaves, most of whom appear to have been captives of war. The nonslave dependents were liable for certain services, such as labor and delivery of commodities to the nobles (see ch. 5). Social relations were influenced by

44

customary modes of achieving consensus, saving face, and avoiding hostility among members of the community.

The practice of slash-and-burn agriculture using relatively simple implements did not involve any concept of individual landownership. Even in areas of settled cultivation, control of the land and the use of land under cultivation were communal. Some settlements grew to considerable size—incorporating the development of various craft skills and conducting widespread trade—even though political organization did not develop beyond an extension of kinship ties. In general, however, settlements were widely dispersed and economically self-sufficient, resulting in separatism and some hostility among groups.

Trade relations between the Philippines and both mainland Asia and the islands to the south started early in the Christian Era; they first centered mainly in the Sulu region, reaching the northern islands later. The earliest foreign traders were Hindus, Indonesians, and possibly Arabs. By the tenth century the Chinese were engaged in trade with the Philippines, and they were joined in the fifteenth century by the Japanese who, like the Chinese, established resident trading communities. Before the fifteenth century the Philippines felt the repercussions of political events in the Indonesian archipelago. The rise and fall of kingdoms to the south resulted in a series of refugee movements to the Philippine area. For a brief period in the fourteenth century the southern half of the Philippines was drawn into the trade and tributary boundaries of one of these kingdoms.

Islam, brought to the Philippines by traders and proselytizers from the Indonesian islands, often with armed force, had a far stronger and more lasting impact. By 1500 Islam was established in the Sulu Islands and spread from there to Mindanao; it reached the Manila area by 1565. Muslim immigrants introduced a political concept of territorial states ruled by rajas or sultans, who exercised suzerainty over greater or lesser native *datus*. Neither the political state concept of the Muslim rulers nor the limited territorial concept of the sedentary rice farmers of Luzon, however, spread beyond their original boundaries. When the Spanish arrived in the sixteenth century, the majority of the estimated 500,000 people on the islands lived in *barangay* settlements.

A written literature in several local languages—including Tagalog— had developed by then. Although this early written literature has largely been lost, a picture of various tribal societies survives in epics that have been transmitted orally from generation to generation (see ch. 7).

SPANISH COLONIAL PERIOD (1521–1898)

The Philippine Islands were ruled by Spain for over 300 years. Yet the impact of the Spanish on the islands was comparatively limited and shallow with the possible exception of the spread of Roman Catholicism, which effectively halted the earlier penetration of Islam from the south. Historians have described the first 200 years of the colonial period as inert. Although social and economic changes were taking place—one of the most significant being the emergence of a dynamic Filipino-Chinese mestizo element—the pace of change was slow until the late eighteenth century. The colony itself was largely isolated from the mother country, and contact was maintained not directly but through Mexico. Within the Philippines the Manila-based Spanish community of officials, traders, and assorted soldiers of fortune—never very large—was insulated from the indigenous population except through Catholic friar intermediaries. Nowhere was isolation more complete than in local village communities, sealed off from outside economic and social contact at the insistence of the friars. This isolation was quite effective: the form of priestly and indirect rule adopted by colonial authorities left the traditional village relatively autonomous, and Filipinos were spared most of the economic exploitation and social degradation apparent in other colonial areas. Isolation also, however, tended to encourage local aberrations, idiosyncracies, and considerable syncretism in the adaptation of Spanish Catholicism and legal forms to weakened traditional institutions (see ch. 8).

Successive Spanish governors, mainly concerned with making their fortune and keeping their health before returning to Spain, found their authority limited by lethargic and corrupt Spanish petty bureaucrats and, most important, by rich, powerful, landed, and administratively indispensable friars. The colony's financial means were chronically meager. Commercial energies were wholly absorbed in the galleon trade, for which Manila served as an entrepôt rather than a source of products. Consequently efforts to exploit the natural resources of the islands were minor and sporadic.

In marked contrast the late eighteenth century witnessed the first of many changes that, accelerating in the early 1800s, worked a major transformation in the archipelago. The decade of the 1820s is considered a watershed in Philippine history, and the six decades that followed saw the emergence and consolidation of major social and economic features that still broadly characterized Philippine society in the 1970s. Of these changes, the most important was the establishment of a truly national elite transcending local or ethnic origin, whose interests were identified with the country as a whole and who served to fuse Hispanic and indigenous elements into a Filipino culture. In fact during this period the term *Filipino*, once used to denote a Spaniard born in the Philippines, came to acquire its Philippine national meaning.

The Establishment of Spanish Rule

The European discovery of the Philippines took place on March 16, 1521, during Ferdinand Magellan's historic circumnavigation of the globe, when he landed on Cebu and claimed the land for Charles I of Spain. A month later Magellan was killed by a local chief. The Spanish crown sent several expeditions to the archipelago during the next decades. Permanent settlement was finally established in 1565 when

Miguel López de Legazpi, the first royal governor, arrived in Cebu from Mexico to found a Spanish settlement. Eight years later he moved to Manila, a location that offered the excellent harbor sites of Manila Bay, a large population, and proximity to the ample food supplies of the central Luzon ricelands. Manila remained the center of Spanish civil, military, religious, and commercial activity in the islands. The islands were given their name in 1543 in honor of Philip II of Spain.

Spanish policy toward the Philippines, Spain's only colony in the Far East, had three objectives: acquisition of a share in the spice trade; development of contacts with China and Japan in order to further Christian missionary efforts there; and conversion of the Filipinos to Christianity. Only the third objective was eventually realized, and this not completely because of the active resistance of the Muslims in the south and the Igorots in the north. The attainment of the other objectives was blocked by warfare with the Dutch, Portuguese, and British, which was in part an extension of wars in Europe, and by disputes among religious orders over missionary territory.

Philip II explicitly ordered that Spanish pacification of the Philippines be bloodless, avoiding a repetition of Spain's sanguinary conquests on the American mainland. The ideal was not completely attained, but the Spanish occupation of the islands, essentially a missionary rather than a military enterprise, was accomplished with relatively little bloodshed. The achievement was facilitated by the absence of initial armed resistance by most of the population except by the Muslims, who were well established in the south.

Church and state were inseparably linked in carrying out Spanish policy. The state assumed administrative responsibility for the new Church of the Indies—expenditures and selection of personnel—and in turn assigned responsibility for conversion of the natives to the several religious orders, the members of which were known as friars. There was, however, frequent disagreement over means to reach the common goal both between church and state and among elements of each. The most acrimonious of the disagreements within the church was between the friars and the church administration under the bishop of Manila, who claimed the power of visitation of parish work. The friars rejected the bishop's authority over them in their capacity as parish priests, recognizing only the supervision of their own orders.

Rule over the Spanish colonies was vested nominally in the person of the king, but authority over all aspects of colonial activities was delegated to the royal Council of the Indies in Madrid. Responsibility for the actual execution of colonial policy was fragmented. In the Philippines there were the governor, responsible to the viceroy of New Spain in Mexico; the Audiencia, the highest court of justice; the church authorities, both local clergy under the bishop and friars of the missionary orders; and the autonomous fiscal authorities. All possessed considerable power and autonomy in spite of the nominal centralization of authority in the governor. The result was constant disagreement and a slow-moving and inefficient colonial bureaucracy, which did, however, maintain Spanish authority without major dependence on military force.

The colonial administrative organization was small relative to the scope of the political, economic, and social changes envisioned by Spanish policy. The degree of success achieved in a comparatively short time resulted in part from the favorable response of most Filipinos to Spanish administrative innovations, a response characterized by enthusiasm, rapidity, and an acute perception of their own self-interest.

At the lower levels of their decentralized administration, the Spanish built on traditional village organization, thereby co-opting and confirming the status of traditional leaders over their followers and dependents. The *barangay* (renamed the *visita* and later the *barrio*) was kept as the lowest administrative unit; the position of *datu* was retained and renamed the *cabeza de barangay* (headman) and initially made hereditary. The next highest level was that of the *pueblo*, the forerunner of the municipality, made up of several *barangays* and incorporating a principal town where the parish church was located. Through a semielective procedure a *pueblo* magistrate was selected, known as the *gobernadorcillo* (petty governor); the local church and Spanish authorities also had considerable say in his appointment. The *gobernadorcillo* was the highest political office that could be held by a Filipino. At a higher level was the province, governed by an *alcalde mayor*, a Spanish official reporting directly to Manila and responsible for all administrative, military, and judicial affairs in his region.

This system of indirect rule helped create in rural areas a Filipino upper class, referred to as the *principalía* or the *principales* (principal ones). This group came to combine local wealth, high status and prestige, certain privileges such as exemption from taxes and lesser roles in the parish church, and appointment to local offices. Somewhat enlarged from the preconquest nobility, the *principalía* succeeded in creating and perpetuating an oligarchic system of local control.

Religion played an intimate part in Spanish relations with, and attitudes toward, the indigenous population. The Spaniards considered conversion through baptism a symbol of allegiance to their authority. Although they were interested in gaining a profit from the colony, the Spanish recognized a responsibility to protect the property and personal rights of these new Christians.

The church's work of conversion of Filipinos was facilitated by the absence of other organized religions, except for Islam in the south. The missionaries had their greatest success among women and children, although the pageantry of the church had wide appeal. Its appeal was reinforced by the incorporation of Filipino social customs into religious observances, for example in the fiestas celebrating the patron saint of a *barrio* (see ch. 8). The eventual outcome was a new cultural community of the main Malay lowland population from which the Muslims and the mountain peoples of Luzon remained detached and alienated.

The *encomienda* system, which had originated in the New World, was introduced as a way to secure a material return and to protect those who had been converted. The population of the colony was divided and apportioned into *encomiendas* for the collection of tribute in the form of labor, goods, and cash. This tribute was considered recognition, in part, of the services provided by the Spanish administration. *Encomiendas* were both retained by the crown and allotted to *encomenderos* (private individuals), primarily as pensions to military personnel. In return for the grant the *encomenderos* were supposed to prepare for baptism and attend to the spiritual welfare of those from whom they were collecting labor, goods, or money; in practice, however, many *encomenderos* were concerned only with what they could exact, and the system was abused. Around 1621 when the private *encomiendas* reached their height, there were nearly 100,000 such grants awarded to some of the Filipino nobility and to pensioned soldiers and Spanish officials.

The *encomienda* system in the Philippines differed from that in the Spanish colonies of the New World with respect to ownership of land. The *encomenderos*, who had been awarded the right to tribute, did not automatically attain ownership of their *encomiendas*, as the crown refused to grant them succession in perpetuity. The *encomiendas* were to revert to the state after a stipulated period of succession. Various subterfuges allowed longer retention, but by the late 1700s the number of private *encomiendas* had been reduced from around 100,000 to about 18,000. The church's holdings, although extensive and concentrated in the Luzon area, were only a minor part of the cultivated land; Filipinos and Chinese mestizos kept or acquired possession of the bulk of agricultural land.

The Spanish found neither spices nor exploitable precious metals in the Philippines. The ecology of the islands was little changed by Spanish importations and technical innovations with the exception of corn cultivation and some extension of irrigation in order to increase rice supplies for the growing urban population. Other imported plants that assumed some importance were tobacco (promoted by the colony for monopoly profits), sweet potatoes, manioc (cassava), peanuts, pineapples, avocados, guavas, and cacao. The colony was not, however, profitable. The long war with the Dutch from 1609 to 1648 and intermittent conflict with the Moros nearly bankrupted the colonial treasury. Annual deficits were made up by a subsidy from Mexico. Colonial income derived mainly from entrepôt trade: the "Manila galleons" sailing from Acapulco brought shipments of silver bullion and minted coin that were exchanged for return cargoes of Chinese goods, mainly silk textiles. Failure to exploit indigenous natural resources and investment of virtually all official, private, and church capital in the galleons or Chinese junks en route to Manila constituted a financial disaster for the colony.

The entrepôt trade quickly attracted growing numbers of Chinese to Manila. The Chinese, in addition to managing trade transactions, assumed necessary functions in provisioning and servicing the capital. The Spanish regarded them with a mixture of distrust and acknowledgement of their indispensable role. During the first decades of Spanish rule the Chinese in Manila became more numerous than the Spanish, who tried to control them by residence restrictions, periodic deportations, and actual or threatened violence sometimes degenerating into riots and massacres during the period between 1603 and 1762. From the 1750s to the 1840s the Spanish apparently succeeded in limiting the Chinese community to perhaps 5,000, compared with its much larger earlier size.

While the size of the Chinese population thus tended to vary, a mestizo element of Chinese and Filipino parentage continued to increase. There were few women in the Chinese immigrant population, and intermarriage between Chinese men and Philippine women was common; descendants of such unions continued to be classified officially as mestizo until the late 1800s, even after several generations of intermarriage. The Chinese mestizos (as they are usually called) were much more numerous than so-called Spanish mestizos and other Eurasians. By the early 1800s they numbered about 120,000, roughly 5 percent of the total population and a much higher percentage in Manila; in the late 1800s their number was estimated at about 250,000.

The Chinese mestizos were a forceful influence in a society in which various elements were mutually isolated. They came to dominate trade in areas closed to the Chinese and became landholders through outright purchase, lease of church property, and moneylending to small farmers. Converted to Christianity, they contributed to the development of an urban Hispanic-Philippine culture that was "more Spanish than the Spanish." They set the fashion and a standard of luxurious indulgence for members of the *principalía*, with whom they merged and from whom they eventually became indistinguishable through intermarriage and shared interests.

Among the most significant and enduring changes under Spanish rule was the replacement of the Filipino idea of the communal use and ownership of land with the concept of private, individual ownership. The Filipinos gradually adopted the principle of individual landownership, which in practice meant that local *datus* acquired titles. The crown retained title to land not presumed to be under any form of ownership before the arrival of the Spanish. When such land was assigned to Filipino settlers, their titles were not in fee simple (as were those of *datus*) but were entailed, which meant the property could be transmitted to heirs but could not be sold without the government's concurrence. The substitution of a system of private landownership resulted in a legal landlord class initially composed of the traditional Filipino nobility and later including Chinese mestizos. Those who had been of the dependent class were perpetuated in their position as sharecroppers or as peons through debt servitude.

The labor of the Filipino was essential to accomplish Spanish objectives, to build churches, roads, or ships, and in general to provide the means of profit for the colonists. Labor service was an important objective of the *encomienda* system, but abuses led to its abolishment in 1595 through commutation of the tribute labor obligation to payment in cash or kind.

The economic strains of the 1609–48 war with the Dutch caused the government to undertake two measures of ruthless exploitation of labor for such war needs as shipbuilding. The first, known as *polo*, was a system of direct draft labor in which the laborers were virtually unpaid. The second, *vandala* (Tagalog for purchase), was a system of compulsory sales of local products to the authorities, who set quotas of products for *poblaciones* and *barrios*. Because little or no payment was made except by promissory notes issued by a colonial treasury unable to make good on them, the individuals producing the goods were not compensated for their labor.

The measures taken during this period caused serious suffering in the Luzon provinces in both loss of population through deaths caused by hardship and loss to their economies. Pampanga Province, adjacent to Manila, was the most seriously affected. As economic conditions improved after the end of the war, the government relaxed some of its onerous measures: for example, it abolished the assessment of rice levied on villages for distribution to *polo* workers.

The colonial government created a judicial organization designed to enable Filipinos to seek redress by legal process. As in Spanish colonial practice elsewhere, local customary law was recognized and applied in civil actions in which it was not counter to Spanish precepts of morality. In 1599 the Audiencia made applicable Tagalog customary law, which had been codified by a Spanish priest. The principles of Spanish law—derived from Roman concepts—were applied in all criminal actions and in civil cases in which customary law provided no guidance. The lowest level of the formal judicial organization was established in the municipalities. In a hierarchy extending upward to the Audiencia, responsibility for original jurisdiction and appeal varied according to the kind of action and the amount of money involved. The royal Council of the Indies in Madrid was the court of final appeal for cases originating in the Philippines.

The population of the Philippines remained overwhelmingly rural during the Spanish colonial period. The few Spanish officials outside Manila lived in the towns, and the average Filipino had no contact with Spaniards except for the local friar or priest, who spoke the local language and often used it rather than Latin in church services. Members of the Spanish-speaking Filipino nobility who could afford it also lived in the towns; there were few Spanish mestizos except in Manila. Spanish policy did not provide for instruction in the Spanish language and, when the policy was changed in the mid-nineteenth century, there was very little response. The consequence was that after more than 300 years of Spanish administration Spanish was spoken by less than 10 percent of the population.

The Spanish were obliged to use Filipino manpower to supplement their small military forces in operations against the Muslims, defense against the Dutch and British, and putting down local rebellions. A Filipino constabulary was established as a separate army modeled on Spanish organization; it proved reliable against both domestic and foreign enemies. Local resistance to Spanish authority resulted in five major uprisings before 1762 that were eventually suppressed by a few Spanish soldiers and a much larger force of Filipinos who were drawn from provinces or islands different from those of the rebels. In the 1637–38 campaign against the sultan of Jolo in the Sulu Archipelago, which culminated in the capture of Jolo, the Spanish general's force consisted of some 1,000 Filipinos and 600 Spaniards.

Social and Economic Change in the Nineteenth Century

The 1800s witnessed an economic and social transformation in the Philippines. On the one hand, the isolation of the colony was broken, and it moved from a subsistence to an export crop economy, leading at last to the internal development of the colony. On the other hand, the Spanish never succeeded in developing a consistent policy or set of attitudes that would enable them to participate positively in these changes. In fact the Spanish did not prosper from the new economic developments, and they watched with envy and frustration as new opportunities were seized by others. The Spanish community was troubled by internal dissension. Increasingly insecure, yet unable to respond constructively to the accelerating pace of change, the Spanish—in particular the powerful friars—continued practices that were inflexible, repressive, and discriminatory. In such circumstances their greatest fear—that social and economic change would lead to revolution—became a self-fulfilling prophecy.

The changes were even more momentous for Filipinos in that they provided the vehicle for the emergence of a fairly cohesive Filipino national elite, which in turn helped create and popularize Filipino nationalism. The origins of this elite are to be found mostly in the Chinese mestizo group and partly in the *principalía* and its core of hereditary leadership. The majority appeared to be Chinese mestizo families, but the group also included landowning *principalía* families, Spanish mestizos, and even creoles (Spaniards born in the Philippines) who identified themselves with archipelago interests. Although including members of the *principalía*, the new elite in effect replaced the latter. The source of the elite's preeminence was the ability of certain families to prosper from the new forms of wealth created by the development of export crops and derived from landholding. In the process status came to be equated first and foremost with wealth—land and money—rather than with descent from the traditional nobility and associated ethnic or localized considerations. The new elite was described by the Spanish as "brutes laden with gold" and has sometimes been referred to as a "third class."

With wealth came new cultural opportunities, including travel and education. The expansion of higher educational facilities in Manila, the increase of Filipino travel to Europe after the opening of the Suez Canal, and association with American and British and other European entrepreneurs in the Philippines created at the apex of the new elite a group that embodied a broad, cosmopolitan Western outlook. Known as the *ilustrados* (enlightened ones), members of this relatively close-knit group were by the mid-1800s also active in medicine, law, and other professions. Their view transcended purely local interests, and they had many interprovincial ties. Toward the end of the century they formed the vanguard of the nationalist movement.

Spanish administration of the Philippines suffered from the general decline of the fortunes of the Spanish empire. A major blow had been the British occupation of Manila in 1762; although the archipelago was returned to Spanish control two years later, Spanish authority had been weakened and the colonial treasury exhausted. The subsequent effort to develop local resources to make the Philippines self-supporting accelerated after the collapse of the Spanish empire in Latin America, the loss of Mexico in 1820, and the end of the galleon trade. Foreigners rather than the Spanish merchants, however, played the major role in the economic development of the islands. From the time of the opening of the first non-Spanish commercial house in 1809, the restrictions on access to the islands by foreigners were consistently eased. The trade with new markets for Philippine hemp, sugar, copra, and coffee resulted in a wave of prosperity for Filipino landowners.

Economic requirements also led to the lifting of restrictions on Chinese immigration and residence after 1839. The number of Chinese increased dramatically, with two major consequences. These full-blooded Chinese quickly recaptured from the Chinese mestizos their former dominance in domestic trade and also became intermediaries in the new export trade, thus hastening the movement of Chinese mestizos out of commerce and into landholding. Moreover the very presence of Chinese in such large numbers pointed out the ambiguous ethnic and cultural position of the Chinese mestizos, whose search for a secure identity greatly contributed to the emerging concept of being Filipino. This process of identification was virtually completed when the Spanish authorities eliminated the distinct legal and taxation status of Chinese mestizos in the 1880s. Along with the indigenous inhabitants of the islands they became Filipinos, except for those who chose reintegration into the Chinese community.

Social tensions arising from economic change were further exacerbated by changes in colonial policy. The conflict between liberals and conservatives in Spain was mirrored in the Spanish community in Manila. With the collapse of the Spanish empire a great number of Spaniards expelled from Latin America moved to the Philippines; anticlerical reforms in Spain drove additional clergy to the more congenial islands; and direct contact was opened between Spain and the Philippines, encouraging increased Spanish settlement in the islands. The newcomers disdained locally born Spaniards and Spanish mestizos, further polarizing colonial society. Many arrived armed with patronage from one of the rapidly changing governments in Madrid and swelled the ranks of the colonial bureaucracy, which became almost wholly characterized by personal greed, corrupt practices, and disregard for the interests of the islands.

Despite occasional efforts at reforms, usually decreed in Madrid and disregarded in Manila, the overall response to these conditions of uncertainty and change was the rallying of the conservative Spanish community to the defense of the status quo. Colonial policies became increasingly discriminatory. In the mid-1800s laws were adopted designed to stratify society in a rigid mold and prevent further social change; the present-day style of a loose, open-necked shirt derives from one such law allowing only Spaniards to wear ties.

The role of the friars surfaced as a major issue on which advocates and opponents of change focused their attention. The close entanglement yet mutual tension between church and state in the Philippines made the position of the friars more than a purely religious matter. The friars were an important arm of colonial government at the municipal and local levels; at the same time they retained a high degree of jealously guarded independence from governmental authority. So powerful were the friars that the Philippines in the nineteenth century has been described as a "friarocracy."

The issue was complicated by the struggle within the Roman Catholic Church between the religious orders of the friars and the diocesan hierarchy of priests and bishops over control of parishes. Efforts to assert diocesan control over parishes initially converted by the friars had led in the late 1700s to an experiment in appointing Filipinos as priests in the hope that their willingness to serve in remote rural areas would help to curb the power of the friars. The experiment failed, few Filipinos having been given the necessary training. By the early 1800s the friars, who admitted no Filipinos into their religious orders, were again dominant. With the emergence of a Filipino elite and especially of the educated and westernized ilustrados, however, the question of clerical discrimination and parish control reemerged in a potentially more explosive form. In addition the religious orders owned large areas of farmland that, although amounting to only a small percentage of all land under cultivation, were concentrated in the Tagalog region around Manila, where the pace of social and economic change was most rapid. Rarely operated as plantations, they were customarily leased to Filipinos—

usually mestizos—who worked the land with tenant sharecroppers. These landholdings became another source of controversy in the conflict between *ilustrados* and friars.

For the largely rural population the changes during the nineteenth century appeared to have had relatively little immediate impact. The few histories of rural society suggest that, despite a spate of peasant disturbances following the weakening of Spanish authority in 1762, the development of a new landholding Filipino elite left the peasants in much the same economically inequitable but socially secure position they had held since the imposition of Spanish rule. For some the opening of new areas to cultivation meant migration to new villages and towns and such new economic relationships as wage labor (see ch. 13).

For the vast majority, however, their lives continued to be governed by the spiritual guidance of a Spanish friar and the economic guidance of a landlord who maintained a mutually satisfactory patron-client relationship with his tenants. This latter relationship, together with the closeness of family ties and associated values and behavior patterns, was basic to the social, economic, and political life of Filipinos. The landlord, although customarily taking about half the harvest, provided his tenants with various forms of security—cash loans, rations to tide the family over the preharvest shortage, assistance in family crises, financing the education of a promising child, or assuming the important social role of godparent; in exchange the tenant offered a variety of personal services as well as political and economic loyalty.

As the 1800s drew to a close, however, there were signs of impending change. Under the pressures of a cash crop economy, informal landlord-tenant agreements were replaced by more impersonal and elaborate contracts. The economic gap between landlord and tenant widened, and a similar gulf developed in cultural and social orientations (see ch. 7). Already landlords maintained residences in town as well as their haciendas; the wealthiest had homes in Manila.

The Philippine Revolution

The creation of a Philippine nationalist movement is usually dated from a mutiny of garrison troops and workers at the Cavite arsenal across the bay from Manila in 1872. The grievances of the mutineers were modest ones, mostly relating to pay, and the uprising was quickly suppressed. The Spanish authorities, however, took the occasion to remove other irritants to the status quo. They arrested three Filipino priests, leaders in the drive for clerical equality; a number of *ilustrados* were arrested or deported, and others fled into exile. The priests were subsequently executed, an event watched by some 40,000 people. They became martyrs of the nationlist cause, and the events of 1872 effectively politicized many prominent *ilustrados*.

A number of young *ilustrados*, including José B. Rizal, Marcelo del Pilar, and Graciano López Jaena, adopted a common cause of working for independence through their writings, chiefly done in Europe, where they were influenced by liberal ideals and Spanish freemasonry. Rizal is considered the most gifted, and two of his most important works, *Noli Me Tangere* (The Social Cancer) and *El Filibusterismo* (The Reign of Greed), helped greatly to crystallize Philippine nationalism. This émigré movement, known as the Propaganda Movement, produced an influential biweekly newspaper, *La Solaridad* (Solidarity), first published in Barcelona in 1889.

Upon his return in 1892 Rizal was instrumental in organizing the Philippine League in Manila as a vehicle for a peaceful campaign for various evolutionary reforms and social improvement. His almost immediate arrest and imprisonment in Mindanao after formation of the organization meant to many of his associates that it was necessary to prepare for an armed struggle against the Spanish. A revolutionary secret society, known by its Tagalog acronym, Katipunan, was formed the same year to carry out Rizal's ideas, unite the people in the fight for independence, and overthrow the colonial regime.

Under the leadership of Andrés Bonifacio, a clerk in Manila, the Katipunan, drawing its membership from lower and middle classes in the Manila area, had grown considerably by 1896, when its existence was discovered by the Spanish. Enough of its leaders escaped arrest to organize a rebellion in the Luzon region, and the call to revolution came on August 26, 1896. Rizal dissociated himself from the radical goals of the revolt, but he was charged with complicity in the uprising; a military court found him guilty, and he was executed on December 30, 1896. Rizal remains the martyr of the Philippine Revolution and the country's national hero.

Rizal's martyrdom did not fully succeed in animating prominent *ilustrados* to join the revolution; most were put off by Bonifacio's radical social goals. Yet *ilustrado* support was essential in bringing to the rebellion their interprovincial connections and great prestige to supplement Bonifacio's localized support and limited education. Several *ilustrados* did serve the revolution in one capacity or another, but their position and loyalty vacillated throughout its course.

The Philippine Revolution lasted from August 1896 to February 1899, when it was transformed into the Philippine Insurrection or the Philippine-American War (depending on an American or Filipino perspective), which officially ended in 1902 but dragged on with rapidly ebbing intensity until around 1907. The events of this period form a complicated picture of ambitious personalities, shifting military fortunes, changing political alliances, chance occurrences, and—according to United States President William McKinley—the intervention of the Almighty.

Militarily the revolution initially ended in a stalemate. Bonifacio, who proved to be a poor general, was replaced by Emilio Aguinaldo and was killed by the latter's followers in 1897. Reinforced Spanish troops drove

Aguinaldo and his forces into the mountains where, in the small town of Biak na Bato, a constitution for a Philippine republic was declared in November. Under increasing military pressure, however, Aguinaldo entered into negotiations with the Spanish, who were anxious to avoid repeating the costly campaign going on in Cuba. In December 1897 an agreement was reached providing for Aguinaldo's exile in exchange for a general amnesty and a cash payment by the Spanish. Although the agreement was not fully honored on either side and sporadic incidents broke out in early 1898, the outcome of the Philippine Revolution remained in doubt until May 1, 1898, when Commodore George Dewey sailed into Manila Bay and wiped out the Spanish fleet.

The American presence immediately altered the power balance. Dewey permitted Aguinaldo to return from exile, and within a month Aguinaldo had reorganized the revolutionary forces but with significant differences. He actively courted the *ilustrados* who, perceiving the collapse of Spanish power and Aguinaldo's willingness to abandon the radical goals of the Katipunan, joined the revolutionary movement. National independence was proclaimed on June 12, 1898, the date that Filipinos celebrate as Independence Day. By August the revolutionary forces controlled the countryside except for the heavily fortified Manila area, and they established a capital at Malolos. Aguinaldo continued to maintain his fragile agreement with the *ilustrados* by ceding political decisions. Thus the constitution of the republic promulgated at Malolos in January 1899 favored a strong legislature through which the *ilustrados* could expect to maintain their dominance in a new government. Aguinaldo was elected president of the young republic.

As the revolutionary government was establishing itself, the first intimation of future events appeared in the reinforcement of American forces in July 1898. In August, after a token battle, the Spanish surrendered by prearrangement to American rather than Filipino forces, and the latter were refused entry into Manila. Aguinaldo was denied representation at the Paris peace conference. After weeks of mounting tension Spain formally ceded the Philippines to the United States by the Treaty of Paris, signed December 10, 1898, ending the Spanish-American War.

The United States Congress proved to be unenthusiastic over the new acquisition. While arguments raged in Washington, tensions mounted along the perimeter around Manila. On February 4, 1899, in still disputed circumstances, armed conflict broke out between American occupation forces and Filipino republican forces. On February 6 the United States Senate ratified the treaty by a margin of a single vote. The fighting expanded into bitter but localized warfare, with revolutionary activity concentrated in the Tagalog regions of Luzon. Although Aguinaldo was captured in 1901, sporadic fighting continued for several years, local economies were disrupted, and many communities suffered the depredations of passing military formations and roving bandits.

AMERICAN COLONIAL PERIOD (1898–1946)

The questions of colonial policy and continued administration of the Philippine Islands remained issues in American politics for nearly half a century. From the beginning American political leaders appeared disposed to rid the United States of the embarrassments and costs of being a colonial power, although the intensity with which this view was expressed varied greatly with changing circumstances. It was generally agreed that the occupation should last only as long as it took the people to prepare for self-government; envisioned was a gradual evolution toward informed democratic participation and efficient government based on expanded education as well as political and administrative experience. The achievement of such a goal would probably have taken considerably longer than a generation. By the end of the colonial period the United States had succeeded in implanting governmental and political models familiar to most Americans but with very little of the substance.

Decisions made at the beginning of American rule fixed the pattern of political development very early. The various changes introduced with the aim of self-government were in practice adapted and molded to fit the Filipino social system that had already evolved in the 1800s; its major features remained remarkably stable as late as the 1970s. The social and economic oligarchy of the late 1800s thus became the political oligarchy as well. And the basic patron-client relationship of the rural Philippines was enlarged and elaborated into a national patronage system through the institutions of government administration and political parties.

In effect the American occupation authorities and Filipino *ilustrados* cooperated in the development of government. The Americans sought *ilustrado* collaboration as a means of ending the bitter warfare, drawing educated Filipinos into administration, and obtaining through their status and cooperation the acquiescence of the population in the goals of colonial rule. The *ilustrados* in turn participated in the joint venture because it provided them the long-denied political hegemony they believed they had earned by virtue of their status and historic role as creators of Philippine nationalism. Political power would help fix the social and economic preeminence they had already achieved. They believed that their participation was in the best interests of the country. In particular they believed that the future of the islands should not be left in the hands of a Bonifacio. They correctly told the Americans—for whom they served as a major source of information—that those Filipinos who were continuing the insurrection or declaring that the islands were ready for self-rule were middle class, poorly educated, made up largely of military leaders and petty government employees, and not representative of the majority of the population. The American interest in accommodation was expressed immediately and clearly. And, as the harried Aguinaldo retreated from one position to the next, *ilustrados* abandoned his camp for Manila.

The costs of accommodation were quickly understood by the Americans: in extending political power to the *ilustrados*, they had also accepted the social and economic system that supported the Filipino elite. William Howard Taft, the first commissioner (later governor general) of the American civilian administration that began on July 4, 1901, expressed in 1908 his concern that colonial policy might simply serve "to await the organization of a Philippine oligarchy or aristocracy competent to administer the government and then turn the islands over to it." American policy was, however, pragmatic. Moreover Taft was willing to draw *ilustrados* into the government despite his view that with few exceptions they lacked "moral character" and political integrity. An additional consequence was the high degree of leverage provided the *ilustrados*. In the years between 1898 and 1935 even the matter of the timing of independence became a football in Filipino politics.

In many respects, therefore, the history of the American colonial period is the history of the successes and failures of the Filipino elite to adapt new structures to conform to their interests. They were partly aided and partly handicapped by other important changes that took place under American rule.

These changes were many. The temporal power of the church was greatly reduced, and the Philippines became a secular state. Government administration was soon strengthened and centralized; roads and public services were improved; and educational facilities, although never reaching the extent and scope of the American ideal, were greatly expanded (see ch. 7). Partly as a consequence the degree of urbanization increased, and the size of the middle class grew to include greater numbers of civil servants, teachers, social and welfare workers, and small-scale entrepreneurs. Mostly of very modest income, they emulated the elite in dress, manners, and even in the acquisition of a small parcel of land. The size of the population, which had already grown rapidly during the 1800s, almost tripled from an estimated 6.6 million in 1896 to 19 million in 1948. Few basic economic changes took place, however, American rule serving mainly to reinforce the dependence on a cash crop export economy.

Underlying all these developments was a change of even greater moment to the overwhelming majority of the population that remained rural. The landlord-tenant relationship, even while its essential functions of patron-client exchange were being applied on a national scale, was weakening at the local level. The landlord's interest in his tenants' welfare was waning; important landlord services ceased; surpluses were being withdrawn to support the landlord's urban style of living or for investment in other kinds of enterprises; and the security of peasant families was being undermined. The little information available regarding this change suggests that the situation varied from place to place. Even as late as the 1970s areas remained where the landlord-tenant relationship continued to be close, direct, and mutually supportive. But the underlying trend was in the opposite direction (see ch. 13).

It appears, moreover, that several events in the 1920s and 1930s represented peasant responses to this basic change in their lives. There was a spate of peasant strikes, arson, and legal disputes between landlords and tenants. Increasing tenant insecurity and unrest concentrated in Luzon eventually supported organized forms of insurgency. In other cases the response was not directed against the landlord but against the entire process of modernization and urbanization that had produced the change; various millenarian or quasi-religious movements sought mainly to restore a simple, comprehensible, and idealized past.

American Administration to 1935

United States control over the Philippines had to be established initially by military force, the first such major operation by United States military forces acting alone. During the hostilities a survey mission was sent to the Philippines and subsequently recommended the establishment, under overall American control, of a national legislative body and provincial and municipal administrations; the early replacement of military rule by a civilian government; the development of natural resources; and the setting up of a comprehensive system of public education. In 1901 control was passed to a civilian administration under Taft, who was to play a major role in United States policy in the Philippines as the first commissioner, then as the American secretary of war, and finally as president of the United States. He vigorously carried out the recommendations of the survey mission and made a concerted effort to enlist Filipino support.

Some 440 laws were adopted to initiate the process of modernizing the Philippines, applying American principles of government to achieve the rule of law and the freedom of the individual. Filipino habits, customs, and traditions, however, were taken into account; an example was the retention of Spanish civil law. New laws included codes for local and provincial administration by elected officials. Public service and functional bureaus were established, such as those for agriculture, water and forests, printing, customs, and public health. The judicial system was reorganized into a hierarchy headed by the Supreme Court of the Philippines, the chief justice of which was a Filipino.

Once law and order had been restored—with the help of the newly recruited Philippine Constabulary—and cholera and other epidemic diseases checked, the administration gave priority to education. Six hundred American schoolteachers were recruited for a new countrywide system of free education, the eventual result being an increase in literacy and the spread of English as a second language (see ch. 4).

Although the initial American program did not provide a national legislature or include such rights as trial by jury or permission to bear arms, this was changed significantly by the Philippine Organic Act passed by the United States Congress in 1902. The act disestablished the

Roman Catholic Church, extended the franchise, and provided for Filipino participation in the legislative process by authorizing an elected assembly. The first assembly was elected in 1907 and established the position of governor general as the chief executive authority.

The new legislative system offered an enlarged arena of political activity for Filipinos. Although the system remained under the effective control of the traditional elite, a new generation rose to prominence. Manuel Quezon and Sergio Osmeña were outstanding figures among those who found that politics as a profession was a congenial occupation under the new system and were highly adept in its practice; the two men dominated politics for the next forty years.

Filipino autonomy was further extended in 1916 by a second organic act—commonly referred to as the Jones Act—that explicitly stated the intent to grant Philippine independence as soon as a stable government was established. By this act the Philippine legislature was made bicameral. Its actions were, however, subject to veto by the governor general. It was not empowered to pass legislation affecting the rights of United States citizens, nor could it affect the right of Spanish citizens residing in the Philippines to retain allegiance to the Spanish crown as stipulated in the 1898 treaty.

The Jones Act remained the basic legislation for the administration of the Philippines until the United States Congress passed new legislation in 1934 establishing the Commonwealth of the Philippines. Its provisions were differently interpreted, however, by the governors general. Under Francis B. Harrison, who was governor general until 1921, the assignment of positions in the civil service to Filipinos was very rapid, and the Philippine legislature was rarely challenged by his use of the veto power. His successor, General Leonard Wood (governor general from 1921 to 1927), was convinced that American withdrawal from the Philippines would be as disastrous for the Filipinos as it would be for the interests of the United States in the Far East. He aroused the intense opposition of Filipino nationalists by the use of the veto power 126 times in his six years in office. The opposition created a political deadlock when ranking Filipino officials resigned in 1923 and remained out of office until Wood's term ended with his death in 1927. Although Wood's successors reversed his policies and reestablished effective working relations with Filipino politicians, nationalist leaders were strengthened in their determination to attain independence, and Quezon seized upon the issue to emerge as the dominant national figure.

Early in its administration the United States directly addressed the problems of friar landholdings and clerical political influence and administrative power in various activities of local governments. Filipino public opinion was nearly unanimous in demanding reduction of church control. In 1904 the administration bought for US$7.24 million the major part of the friars' holdings of some 430,000 acres (of which one-half was in the vicinity of Manila). The land was eventually resold to Filipinos, some of them tenants but the majority estate owners.

Another effort at land reform in 1903, modeled on the United States Homestead Act, proved a disappointment because of complex procedures and the inadequacy of rural credit facilities. Although the area under cultivation increased markedly during the period of American administration—owing to the growth of both population and foreign trade—only a small percentage of the new cultivators were the owners of the land (see ch. 13). Tenancy rates were especially high and rural poverty particularly noticeable in central Luzon.

Beginning in 1913 the American authorities also undertook the enormous task of registering landownership through a cadastral survey. The procedures adopted, even though they served to reduce title conflicts in the long term, led in the short term to numerous cases of litigation. The registration of titles also led to a further strengthening of the landlords' position and a weakening of tenants' rights.

The economy of the islands was profoundly affected by access to the American market under the free trade provisions of United States law. This trade provided impetus for economic growth, especially expanding production of the principal agricultural exports of the islands. The United States, moreover, furnished a source of capital, technology, and training. Roadbuilding and port construction were undertaken, mainly in the heavily populated areas. As population increased, settlement patterns were altered; new sites of settlement appeared, often along the highways and roads.

As the economic pace quickened, Chinese migration to the Philippines increased. The Chinese continued to dominate the retail trade as they had toward the end of the Spanish period. They also handled a large share of the rice and timber trade and were prominent in banking and various small industrial enterprises. Japanese immigrated to the Philippines, mostly to northern Luzon and Mindanao; they were farmers, fishermen, artisans, and traders. Both the Chinese and Japanese were resented by Filipinos because of the extent of control they exercised over the economy, and both were explicit targets of popular movements.

Internal reform of the Roman Catholic Church in the Philippines had been an important objective of Filipino nationalists in the late nineteenth century. In response to the initial failure of reform efforts, in 1902 (the same year in which the Roman Catholic Church was disestablished by United States law), a Filipino priest, Father Gregorio Aglipay, presided over the organization of the breakaway Philippine Independent Church, whose members are often referred to as Aglipayans. By 1918 the new church had 1.4 million adherents. The Aglipay movement was followed by the rise of the Church of Christ, another indigenous religious group, which had enough members by 1914 to register with the government. The admission of Protestant missionaries immediately after the United States acquisition of the Philippines introduced further complexity into

Philippine religious life, although there were relatively few converts to Protestant denominations.

When the United States substituted civilian for military administration in 1901, it created the Philippine Constabulary as a national law enforcement agency. Filipinos took command of the constabulary in 1914. American officers continued to serve in the organization, and Americans served as chiefs during the 1927-34 period. The United States retained responsibility for defense of the islands and for that purpose maintained American army, navy, and air units at a number of military installations. No Filipino military organization was established.

Although the Philippine assembly annually passed unanimously a resolution reiterating their desire and capacity for independence, it was not until the late 1920s and early 1930s that American sentiment began increasingly to favor Philippine independence largely because of considerations having to do with American farm and labor interests. Some eleven proposals for Philippine independence were unsuccessfully introduced in the United States Congress before passage of the Hare-Hawes-Cutting Act in 1932. Submission of the 1932 act to the Philippine assembly for approval caused a split between Quezon and Osmeña. Quezon succeeded in maneuvering rejection of the act, claiming opposition to its provision for retention of American military and other reservations in the Philippines. There was also opposition to its provision for a ten-year transition period, continuance of certain American trade preferences, and restriction of Filipino immigration to the United States.

After rejection of the Hare-Hawes-Cutting Act, Quezon succeeded in negotiating a somewhat more favorable law, the Philippine Independence Act of 1934 (Tydings-McDuffie Act), passed by the United States Congress in 1934 and approved by the Philippine assembly. The most important difference in the new law was its provision for retention only of naval reservations and fueling stations. It authorized the president of the United States to approve or veto amendments to the Philippine constitution and required approval of matters involving finance. The provisions on trade and immigration remained the same.

The Commonwealth of the Philippines

After a constitution had been drafted by the Filipinos under the provisions of the Tydings-McDuffie Act and approved by the United States president, the Commonwealth of the Philippines was established on November 15, 1935. Quezon and Osmeña became the first president and vice president respectively, and United States Governor General Frank Murphy became the first United States high commissioner to the commonwealth. Preparations for the new commonwealth had begun inauspiciously. In May 1935 a brief but bloody peasant uprising occurred in the provinces near Manila. Organized by a group known as the Sakdal, the uprising was quickly put down. Ostensibly directed against establishment of the commonwealth and motivated by the belief that immediate independence was necessary to bring material relief to the countryside, the uprising also revealed the potentially explosive nature of social schisms in the countryside.

The first act passed by the new National Assembly on December 31, 1935, provided for a system of national defense in which military service was obligatory for all male citizens. The commonwealth had renounced war as an instrument of national policy, and the new capability was accordingly envisaged for defensive use only. President Quezon obtained the services of General Douglas MacArthur, who had retired from the United States Army; MacArthur was made field marshal of the Philippine Army to plan the organization. He developed a ten-year plan for a regular force of 10,000 men including the Philippine Constabulary, which was deactivated and most of its men transferred to the new army. The plan provided for an eventual trained reserve of 400,000 men. Financial difficulties made achievement of these goals impossible; thus at the time of the Japanese attack in December 1941 the strength of the regular army was about 4,000, and there were 132,000 in the reserves (see ch. 16).

President Quezon's government addressed itself to a wide range of political, administrative, social, and economic problems. It improved the quality of administration through a strengthened civil service and attempted to combat popular discontent by setting minimum wages, limiting rents, and expropriating and dividing large estates. The president's program, which he called Social Justice and which may have been partly a response to the Sakdal uprising, achieved only meager results. There were insufficient funds to carry it out, and implementation was blocked or postponed at the provincial and municipal levels.

The Tydings-McDuffie Act provided for the termination at independence in 1946 of existing trade preferences for Philippine exports to the United States. This matter caused considerable Filipino concern, and it was taken up in 1937 by a joint committee whose recommendations for amendment of certain trade preferences in the 1941–46 period was adopted in the Tydings-Koscialkowski Act of 1939 and approved by the Philippine assembly and by a plebscite. The recommendations dealing with the post-1946 period were not acted on. In 1938 the United States high commissioner proposed reconsideration of the economic provisions of the Tydings-McDuffie Act that would have resulted in indefinite retention by the United States of controls over Philippine public finance, tariffs, and immigration. This was to Filipino politicians an unacceptable compromise of full independence and was also not acted upon, leaving the trade preference question unresolved at the outbreak of World War II.

World War II

The Japanese attack on the Philippines started on December 8, 1941, ten hours after the attack on Pearl Harbor. Initial aerial bombardment was followed by landings of ground troops both north and south of Manila. The defending Filipino and American troops were under the command of

General MacArthur, who had been recalled to active duty in the United States Army earlier in the year and designated commander of the United States armed forces in the Far East. The aircraft in his command were destroyed, the naval forces were ordered to leave and, because of the circumstances in the Pacific region, reinforcement and resupply of his ground forces were impossible. Under the pressure of superior numbers, the defending forces withdrew to the Bataan Peninsula and to the island of Corregidor at the entrance to Manila Bay. Manila, declared an open city to prevent its destruction, was occupied by the Japanese on January 2, 1942.

Defense continued for five months until the final surrender of the besieged forces. President Quezon and Vice President Osmeña accompanied the troops to Corregidor and later left for the United States where they set up a government-in-exile. General MacArthur was ordered to Australia, where he started to plan for a return to the Philippines.

The Japanese military authorities immediately began organizing a new government structure in the Philippines. Although the Japanese after occupation had promised independence for the islands, they initially organized the Council of State, through which they directed civil affairs until October 1943, when they declared the Philippines an independent republic.

The Philippine elite, with a few notable exceptions, accommodated to the Japanese occupation. Collaboration in Japanese-sponsored political institutions—which later became a major domestic political issue—was motivated by several considerations. Among them was the effort to protect the people from the harshness of Japanese rule (an effort that Quezon himself had advocated); protection of family and personal interests; and for some a belief that Philippine nationalism would be advanced by solidarity with fellow Asians. Not a few used the device of collaboration to gather information for the Allies. The Japanese-sponsored republic headed by José P. Laurel proved to be unpopular.

Japanese occupation of the Philippines was opposed by increasingly effective underground and guerrilla activity that ultimately reached large-scale proportions; postwar investigations showed that about 260,000 men were in guerrilla organizations and that members of the anti-Japanese underground were even more numerous. Their effectiveness was such that by the end of the war Japanese control extended to only twelve of the forty-eight provinces. The major element of resistance in central Luzon was furnished by the People's Anti-Japanese Army (Hukbalahap, commonly called Huks—see Glossary), organized in early 1942 and led by Luis Taruc, a Communist since 1939. The Huks came to arm some 30,000 men and extended their control over much of Luzon, where they also organized soviets, redistributed land, and set up cooperatives.

General MacArthur's forces landed on Leyte on October 20, 1944, accompanied by Osmeña, who had succeeded to the presidency on the death of Quezon on August 1, 1944. Japanese resistance in the Philippines lasted until Japan's surrender on September 3, 1945, after which the Japanese commander in the Philippines, General Tomoyuki Yamashita, also surrendered. The Philippines had suffered great loss of life and tremendous physical destruction by the time the war was over. An estimated 1 million Filipinos had been killed, a large proportion during the last months. The final fighting for Manila left the city one of the most extensively damaged as the result of World War II.

The national elections, which according to the constitution would have been held in November 1945, were postponed to the following April because of the chaos of immediate postwar conditions. In the interim a split occurred in the Partido Nacionalista (Nationalist Party) of President Osmeña, brought on in part by disagreement over the issue of collaboration, which deeply divided the country. President Osmeña on his return to the Philippines in 1944 had expressed understanding of the position of officials who had remained at their posts during the occupation. Others, including some American officials, favored action against collaborators and succeeded in having a bill passed by the Philippine Congress in August 1945 under which President Osmeña established a people's court to try traitors. Manuel Roxas, who had been close to Quezon, had served under Laurel, and had opposed strong measures in general against reputed collaborationists, broke away and founded the Liberal Party. He was supported by MacArthur and drew on powerful support from the elite. The Liberals won, Roxas was inaugurated president of the commonwealth, and on July 4, 1946, he became the first president of the Republic of the Philippines. In 1948 he declared an amnesty for arrested collaborators, only one of whom had been indicted. The resiliency of the prewar elite, although remarkable, nevertheless left a bitter residue in the popular mind. The collaboration issue lingered as late as 1969 when, in the presidential election of that year, Ferdinand E. Marcos, a much decorated guerrilla leader, defeated an opponent who was tainted by accusations of World War II collaboration.

REPUBLIC OF THE PHILIPPINES

Upon independence Filipinos inherited a country that in all important respects was a nation in which the majority of the people identified themselves with the concept of nationalism and its symbols. It was, however, a nation afflicted by serious domestic problems. In the first twenty-five years of the independent Philippine state, the dominant themes were the inability of the elite to remedy these underlying problems and the results of this failure in eroding both the national consensus and the effectiveness of the very mechanisms by which the elite ensured its status. Among the most pressing of these problems was the growth in population—from 19 million in 1948 to 27 million in 1960 and almost 37 million in 1970; by 1970 almost a third of the population was concentrated in Manila and nine adjoining provinces on Luzon. This growth, in lagging economic conditions, overwhelmed employment opportunities (see ch. 2). Serious analysts and casual observers alike commented on the general deterioration in the quality of life and the increasing gap between rich and poor (see ch. 6).

The centralization of administrative and political power before and after World War II enabled the elite—the descendants of the *ilustrados* of the revolutionary period—finally to achieve national power. In addition many abandoned their primary reliance on estate agriculture to engage in industrialization programs inaugurated after World War II, especially in manufacturing (see ch. 14). With some exceptions members of this elite acquired a wholly national orientation focused on Manila. Their position came to depend on their close association with the central government rather than on the loyalty of their former clients at municipal and *barrio* levels.

At least until 1969 political change represented contests within the confines of this elite. Although two presidents, Ramón Magsaysay and Diosdado Macapagal, were of humble, nonelite backgrounds, their programs were handicapped by an elite-controlled legislature. National leaders had enormous patronage powers and in some instances opportunities for self-enrichment; but they had very little ability to implement changes, much less to galvanize the country toward fundamental reform and progress. On the one hand, patterns of political activity remained those of the prewar years in that power was shared through a political party system in which individual politicians easily shifted their allegiance for immediate advantage. On the other hand, until 1969 there was a succession of one-term presidents, each of whom yielded office to the next incumbent through constitutional means. This transfer, although usually marked by election violence and illegalities, always held out the hope that the new leader would somehow manage to tackle the problems confronting the republic (see ch. 10).

As the elite consolidated itself at the national level, the functions of patron-client exchange were almost entirely transferred to the institutions of government—the administration and the political parties—which came to operate an elaborate patronage system of nationwide scope. The influence of traditional personal loyalty and kinship ties, the Spanish model of self-interest, and the centralization of administration during United States rule had already set the character of the Philippine bureaucracy. These characteristics continued after independence. It appeared, moreover, that much of the middle class of the Philippines was largely contained within this system, serving important functions as administrators and political brokers at lower levels and tending to look outside their localities for the sources of their own social position. Many observers have noted, however, that this patronage system served partly to redistribute income through the use of public money for favors and obligations to kin and supporters. Even a lowly tenant otherwise lacking security could find some modest benefit, if only cash for his vote.

Nevertheless, by the late 1960s this elaborate system was faltering partly because there were not enough public resources and partly because of the demands placed upon it.

Another major theme of the post-World War II years was the increase rather than the abatement in nationalist sentiment after independence. This sentiment focused on what Filipinos perceived as inequalities in the provisions of major treaties governing relations with the United States. Although several of the most acute irritants to Filipino national pride were removed through agreements made in the late 1950s and 1960s, the perception of remnants of colonial status continued to plague Philippine-American relations and to motivate domestic political unrest (see ch. 11).

Economic, social, and political confusion characterized the Philippines when the republic assumed sovereignty in 1946. The most pressing problem was rehabilitation or reconstruction of the economy, which was ravaged by war losses ranging from sugar mills to farmers' carabaos. Food was scarce, inflation was severe, and malaria, previously almost eradicated, had returned. The United States Army and later the United Nations Relief and Rehabilitation Agency furnished emergency relief.

In 1946, shortly before Philippine independence, the United States Congress enacted two laws embodying United States policy on economic arrangements with the Philippines. The Philippine Trade Act of 1946 (Bell Act) provided for the gradual elimination of preferential treatment of Philippine trade over a period ending in 1974; set quotas on imports from the Philippines; placed restrictions on Philippine authority in financial actions; and, most important, included a "parity" clause stipulating that Americans were to have equal economic rights with Filipinos, for example in exploitation of natural resources. The Philippine Rehabilitation Act of 1946 provided for the payment of war damages conditioned upon the Philippines' acceptance of the parity clause and other provisions of the Bell Act. These conditions to Philippine independence and American aid, coming on top of the war sacrifices, were a blow to the Filipinos.

Acceptance required amendment of the Philippine constitution; it was passed by the Philippine Congress after ten opposing members were barred from their seats and was confirmed in a plebiscite in March 1947. The imposition of this requirement nevertheless hurt Filipino pride. One explanation of their acquiescence was that the sugar interests of the islands regarded duty-free access to the American market as a vital means of rehabilitating the sugar industry. Parity rights subsequently became a sore point in relations between the two countries.

President Roxas organized the Philippine Rehabilitation Finance Corporation as a means for the reconstruction and encouragement of new industry. Other measures were taken to create a central bank and to extend credit to small businesses and farmers. The economy recovered and expanded in the immediate postwar period; by 1949 production was

91 percent of the 1937 level compared with 40 percent in 1946, and national income was rising. The foreign exchange situation of the country deteriorated, however. Exports were slow to recover, and there was a large balance-of-payments deficit. When special postwar dollar receipts from the United States declined sharply, the Philippines quickly lost a large part of its foreign exchange reserves. A foreign exchange crisis in December 1949 was followed by the imposition of exchange controls but not by devaluation of the peso, which was greatly overvalued at the rate of ₱2 (for value of the peso—see Glossary) to US$1.

The republic entered into two defense-related agreements with the United States in 1947. One granted the United States a ninety-nine-year lease on military bases—in 1944 the United States Congress had passed a joint resolution providing that the United States would retain military, naval, and air bases for the mutual protection of the United States and the Philippines and the maintenance of peace in the Pacific after Philippine independence. The second agreement provided for training and logistical assistance to the new Philippine military establishment. The Philippine Constabulary was first reorganized into the armed forces Military Police Command but was soon reincorporated into the army ground forces under its original name. In 1950 the constabulary became a separate major command element of the armed forces (see ch. 16).

Postwar negotiations with the Huk leaders failed to result in their surrender of arms. In 1947 after Huk leader Taruc had been deprived of his seat in the Congress (he was one of the ten legislators expelled in the dispute over the parity clause amendment), violence continued, and eventually the Huks openly rebelled. Their rebellion was aided by unrest in the countryside, which a 1946 law had attempted to reduce by providing that the customary equal shares of crop to landlord and tenant be changed to 70 percent to the tenant and 30 percent to the landlord; however, the law was generally violated. The Roxas government was unable to suppress the Huks who, despite their inability to break out of a localized, rural base, came to control large areas around Manila.

Upon Roxas' sudden death in office, Elpidio Quirino succeeded to the presidency in April 1948. Quirino was elected in 1949 in a contest marked by intimidation and fraud. The delay in government action in bringing an end to the Huk rebellion, as in the failure of other social and economic measures undertaken during this time, has generally been attributed to government reluctance to undertake needed fiscal reforms and to a decline in public morality. Coming on top of the bitter divisiveness and self-interest that emerged during World War II under the Japanese, the outcome was a loss of faith by Filipinos in the integrity of their government. World War II collaboration in particular remained an issue in the groupings and decisions of the younger generation of leaders who emerged from the guerrilla and resistance movements.

Restoration of the education system after 1945 was severely hampered by wartime destruction of buildings and loss of books and equipment. As a result the quality of education declined. Filipino nationalists criticized continuation of the requirement for instruction in English, although the republic added to the curriculum the teaching of both the local vernacular and Pilipino, a modified form of Tagalog adopted in 1939 as the national language (see ch. 4).

Philippine policy toward the outside world was defined by President Roxas in his first address on July 4, 1946: close association with the United States; sympathy for the aspirations of all dependent countries, particularly those of Asia; and close cooperation with the United Nations (UN), of which the Commonwealth of the Philippines had been a founding member. In the immediate postwar period of the cold war, Roxas placed the Philippines unequivocally in opposition to communism as a matter of both foreign and domestic policy.

In 1950 the Huk leadership was captured and their forces defeated, ending their armed challenge to the government. The government's success resulted from the efforts of the secretary of defense, Magsaysay, to reorganize the armed forces and to obtain popular support for the government. Many former Huks were resettled in Mindanao, although some remnants of the movement persisted as essentially bandit groups in the mountains of Luzon. In the same year the Philippines appealed to the United States for financial assistance, which was provided on the basis of the Foster-Quirino agreement stipulating Philippine action on taxes, exchange controls, and a minimum wage law. In 1951 a United States economic aid mission was established. In the same year a mutual defense treaty with the United States was signed, which was ratified in 1952.

Magsaysay, of relatively humble background, a World War II guerrilla leader, and enormously popular, was elected to the presidency by a large majority in the election of 1953 in which he was the candidate of the Partido Nacionalista in opposition to Quirino. He did not live to complete his full term, dying in an airplane crash in March 1957. His conduct in office was marked by a new style of administration in which he attempted a direct relationship with the *tao*, the common man. Magsaysay created novel institutions for the purpose of handling complaints and grievances; he sought to improve agrarian conditions, extended self-government to the *barrio* level, and encouraged the unionization of labor.

Magsaysay was the first president not of the elite class, and his practical application of the concept that sovereignty resided in the people was a departure from the previously elitist character of Philippine politics. His leadership and constant tours of the provinces won him tremendous popularity. Magsaysay was not, however, able fully to carry out his reform programs partly because of his own political inexperience and temperament and partly because of opposition from the elite. For example, his land reform program was diluted, and sufficient funds were not made available for aspects of the reform calling for purchase or appropriation of large estates for redistribution to the landless.

In 1954 Manila was the site of the conference that resulted in the formation of the Southeast Asia Treaty Organization (SEATO). Philippine interest in regional defense arrangements had already been demonstrated by the sending of an army battalion to Korea in 1951 as a component of UN forces there. In 1956 diplomatic relations were resumed with Japan after Japan had agreed to pay over a twenty-year period the equivalent of US$800 million as reparation for war damages.

Negotiations were conducted with the United States in 1955 on economic problems and in 1956 on problems relating to military bases. Agreement was reached on economic questions, but those relating to the military bases were not resolved. The Revised United States-Philippine Trade Agreement of 1955 (Laurel-Langley Agreement) was negotiated as an overall instrument to govern commercial relations between the two countries for twenty years, modifying the Philippine Trade Act of 1946. The new agreement abolished the authority of the United States to control the exchange rate of the peso; made parity rights reciprocal; extended the Philippine sugar quota; and extended the time period for reductions of other quotas and for the progressive application of customs duties on Philippine imports into the United States.

Magsaysay's vice president, Carlos P. Garcia, succeeded to the presidency at the time of Magsaysay's death in 1957 and was shortly thereafter elected to the office. Garcia emphasized the nationalist themes of "Filipino first" and attainment of "respectable independence," especially economic independence. Further discussions with the United States took place in 1959 on the question of the military bases. Early agreement was reached on one of the issues under consideration, the American relinquishment of large land areas initially reserved for bases but no longer required; as a result the United States turned over to Philippine administration the town of Olongapo on Subic Bay north of Manila, which previously had been under the jurisdiction of the United States Navy. The settlement of other issues relating to the 1947 base agreement, as well as to various Philippine claims for World War II salaries and services, was postponed.

The national independence trend during Garcia's administration was reflected in part also in Philippine association with Malaya and Thailand in the Association of Southeast Asia (ASA) in 1961, in the foundation of which Garcia was instrumental. The organization, however, was soon inoperative because of a diplomatic crisis between the Philippines and the new state of Malaysia over conflicting claims to areas on the island of Borneo.

The growing numbers of Chinese aroused official Philippine concern in the late 1950s after investigation showed that many Chinese residents had entered the country illegally or, having entered legally as visitors, refused to leave. In 1959 Philippine government repatriation negotiations with the government of the Republic of China (Nationalist China) were unsuccessful because that government refused to accept those whom the Philippines proposed to deport. A token repatriation, however, was agreed to after the Philippines temporarily banned the entry of all Chinese, but the problem of the overstaying Chinese was not settled to Filipino satisfaction.

The 1957 election had resulted, for the first time, in a vice president from a party different from that of the president. The new vice president, Macapagal, resembled Magsaysay in that he did not belong to the elite. He ran as the candidate of the Liberal Party, which followers of Magsaysay had joined after unsuccessful efforts to form an effective third party. By the time of the 1961 presidential election, the revived Liberal Party had built enough of a following to win the presidency for Macapagal. In this election the returns from each polling place were reported by observers (who had been placed there by newspapers) as soon as the votes were counted. This system, known as "Operation Quick Count," was designed to prevent fraud.

Macapagal's announced objectives were restoration of economic stability, the alleviation of the plight of the common man, and the establishment of a dynamic basis for future growth. He immediately eliminated some economic controls, those on imports being abolished between 1960 and 1962; the peso was freed from its rate of ₱2 to US$1, which resulted in the disappearance of the black market in dollars and a new exchange rate of about ₱4 to US$1. The nationalist trend in Filipino attitudes was demonstrated further during Macapagal's term by his issuance of an executive order in 1962 changing Philippine Independence Day from July 4 to June 12, the day in 1898 when Aguinaldo had read the declaration of independence.

Macapagal's program included the enactment of the Reform Code of 1963, which sought to promote an agricultural leasehold system as a step toward the eventual abolition of sharecropping tenancy (see ch. 13). The president designated certain areas, starting in central Luzon, for initial implementation of the program. The first results were encouraging, but the extent of the area affected at the end of Macapagal's term in 1966 was insignificant; it amounted to some 72,000 acres out of about 1 million acres of rice and corn cultivated by sharecropping tenants.

Philippine foreign policy under Macapagal turned to closer relations with Asian peoples. He took the initiative in an effort to bring the Malay peoples together in an organization called MAPHILINDO, which would be a regional consultative organization consisting of Malaya, the Philippines, and Indonesia. The arrangement failed after Malaysia was formed in 1963 because both Indonesia and the Philippines disputed the territorial claims of the new state to Sabah on the island of Borneo; the Philippines had formally laid claim to Sabah in 1962.

The issue of jurisdiction over United States servicemen in the Philippines—which had not been fully settled after the 1959 discussions—continued to be a problem in relations between the two countries. A series of incidents in the first half of the 1960s, chiefly associated with Clark Air Base, aroused considerable anti-American feeling and demonstrations. Negotiations took place and resulted in August 1965 in adoption of provisions similar to the status-of-forces agreement of the North Atlantic Treaty Organization (NATO). In the next four years agreements were reached on several other matters relating to the bases, including in 1966 a shortening of the duration of the 1947 base agreement from ninety-nine to twenty-five years. Despite these various alterations the 1947 base agreement remained a source of controversy. This controversy appeared to be fueled by a combination of factors, including strongly emotional Filipino sensitivity to any matters that appeared to detract from the independent authority of the Philippine government, especially in relations with the United States; an unfulfilled search for equality and dignity; press exaggeration; occasional incidents; and the changing foreign policy environment (see ch. 11).

In the elections of 1965 Macapagal lost to Marcos. Macapagal's reforms had not achieved their goals, and once again the electorate expressed dissatisfaction with official corruption and high prices. The election of Marcos, a very able politician with an attractive record of political invincibility, inaugurated a new stage in political development. The events of his first term suggested that, like his predecessors, he learned that patronage would not be a sufficient technique to assure reelection in the face of insistent and increasingly acute economic problems, aggravated by growing lawlessness and violent crime. Unlike his predecessors, however, he apparently refused to accept this limitation on his political career. In the period between 1966 and 1969 his administration tackled, not entirely successfully, the serious problems of smuggling and crime. Considerably more successful were two impact programs. The first was the substantial support given to the dissemination of new "miracle rice" varieties developed by the International Rice Research Institute (IRRI) in the Philippines as a means of overcoming popular dissatisfaction with the availability and cost of rice (see ch. 13). The second was a massive public works program—roads, bridges, schools, health centers, irrigation facilities, and urban beautification projects; Marcos' personal delivery of public works checks to *barrio* captains— allocations that helped drain the treasury—reportedly contributed to his reelection in 1969. His early admission that "we are in crisis" and his theme of "the New Filipino" directly addressed popular cynicism and discouragement. Using his patronage powers to the fullest, he also appointed able technocrats to the government.

Foreign policies responded to increasing nationalist sentiment and to changes in the regional environment following the statement of the Nixon Doctrine in mid-1969 of a reduced United States military presence in Asia. In 1966, after heated debate, the Philippine legislature had provided for the commitment of a 2,000-man civic action group to the Republic of Vietnam (South Vietnam), the first contingent being sent in August of that year. In 1969, shortly after Marcos' reelection, withdrawal of the Philippine unit was announced. Marcos also espoused greater national independence in foreign policy and closer ties with other Asian countries. Diplomatic relations with Malaysia, which had broken off in 1968 as a consequence of the on-again, off-again dispute over Sabah, were restored in 1969 (see ch. 11).

The reelection of Marcos in November 1969 was unprecedented in several respects, the most significant being that he became the first president since independence to achieve a second term. In breaking with the established pattern of alternating political power and the benefits of office, Marcos thereby took on a major political challenge—how to treat his opposition, which would, as in the past, tend to rally disaffected elements and critics in the legislature in anticipation of the next election. Insofar as the alternation of office was an important factor in maintaining political stability in an environment of great social and economic inequalities, this challenge was all the greater. Moreover Marcos assumed his second term against a background of continuing tension and malaise. The political power of the elite was being challenged, and violent student demonstrations erupted in Manila in early 1970. A bill authorizing a constitutional convention had been adopted in 1967, and in 1970 delegates to the convention were elected; some hopes were placed in a new national charter. The early 1970s would bring renegotiation of several agreements governing relations with the United States. How Marcos approached these challenges, as well as the almost insurmountable social and economic problems of the country, were the major questions as the 1970s began (see ch. 9; ch. 11; ch. 12).

CHAPTER 4

ETHNIC GROUPS AND LANGUAGES

The Philippines, a nation of islands inhabited by a population speaking different and mutually unintelligible languages, has many of the components necessary for cultural pluralism like that of Indonesia. Yet the Philippines has entered the last quarter of the twentieth century as a remarkably homogeneous society with a strong sense of national cultural unity. The eight major indigenous languages spoken—Cebuano, Tagalog, Ilokano, Ilongo, Bikolano, Waray-Waray, Pampangan, and Pangasinan, in order of number of speakers—are the native languages of roughly 90 percent of the population. Stemming from a common racial stock (as do all Filipinos except a small minority of ethnic Chinese), the members of these eight groups also share a common culture history and a common belief in Roman Catholicism that has reduced their cultural differences to a point where they are more than counterbalanced by cultural similarities. Each of these eight groups, known collectively as the Lowland Christian groups, has preserved a sense of distinctness and group pride that is expressed more often in the form of chauvinism, group stereotypes, and intergroup rivalry than in intergroup hostility or hatred. The racial homogeneity of the population has precluded serious racism; individuals from different Filipino groups are not racially distinguishable.

In contrast to the homogeneity of the vast majority of Filipinos, however, has been the development of serious conflicts between the majority and three minority groups—Moros (Muslim Filipinos), the small pagan groups of the interior, and the ethnic Chinese. Although racially the same as the Lowland Christians, the Moros of southern Mindanao, Palawan, and the Sulu Archipelago have rejected Catholicism in favor of Islam, the religion and way of life to which they have been committed since before the arrival of the Spanish. Strongly resenting the incursion of Christian settlers into their territory, the Moros have continuously resisted outside authority since the fifteenth century, and five centuries later this resistance once again erupted in a militant separatist movement. Common opposition to outsiders has historically created solidarity among the different Moro cultural-linguistic groups.

The interior pagan groups have evinced far less unity than the Moros and, having far greater differences in culture and degree of acculturation with the majority groups, have been generally unable to protect themselves from the frequently hostile and violent contacts they have had with the outside world. The Chinese have historically found themselves in an ambiguous position in Filipino society. Chinese who have married Filipinos and have accepted Filipino culture have experienced little or no resentment; many Filipinos are the offspring of Chinese-Filipino marriages. But unassimilated Chinese are mistrusted by the general population and have been the objects of restrictive and discriminatory legislation.

Each group has a recognized core region and, although these regions are generally not restricted to single islands, they are often demarcated by features of physical geography. There is, however, a fair degree of interspersion among groups, and individuals of some groups are found throughout the islands. Intergroup contact occurs most frequently in urban areas. Areas inhabited by more than one of the eight major Christian groups tend to be without distinct residential segregation by cultural origin and, although Ilokano expansion into Pangasinan and Pampangan regions has resulted in some resentment, group boundaries tend to be relatively fuzzy. Intermarriage among the majority groups is frequent and unremarkable. The existence of two lingua francas, Pilipino and English, has been a crucial aid in intergroup communication. English, the language of instruction in all but the first two grades of school, is generally the language of formal communication in government, business, and other endeavors; it is spoken by roughly 45 percent of the population. Pilipino, a form of Tagalog, has been established as the national language; it is spoken by about 55 percent of the population.

CULTURAL DIFFERENCES AND INTERGROUP RELATIONS

The principal source of cultural differentiation among the vast majority of Filipinos is language rather than race, religion, or social and economic organization. Nine out of every ten Filipinos are Christians—virtually all of whom are Roman Catholics—and live on lowland coasts and in valleys. Although they are divided into groups that speak a number of mutually incomprehensible languages and exhibit some differences of diet, dress, and custom, the Lowland Christians (as these groups are generally called) are remarkably homogeneous in culture and society and have had a long history of harmonious interrelations. As a whole, they form a picture of cultural variety within a framework of national homogeneity. Clearly distinguished from the Lowland Christian groups are two other groups, numerically small but politically and commercially important: the Moros (Muslim Filipinos) and the unassimilated Chinese. The Moros are principally located in the coastal lowlands of southern Mindanao, the Sulu Archipelago, and the southern end of Palawan; unassimilated Chinese live almost entirely in the major urban centers of the republic (see fig. 6). Only the unassimilated Chinese are racially distinct from other Filipinos or speak a language unrelated to Philippine languages.

Relatively cut off from the mainstream of Philippine life—although fascinating to anthropologists—are a variety of pagan tribes known

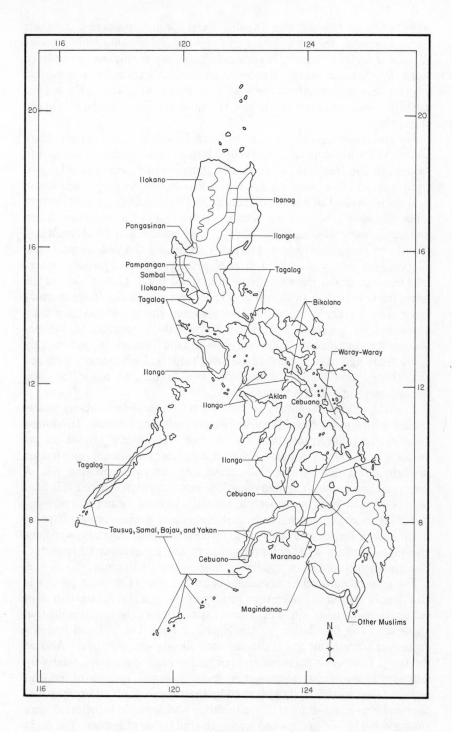

Figure 6. Philippines, Cultural-Linguistic Map

collectively as Igorots, the Tagalog word for mountaineers. As their name suggests, they are located in the rugged mountainous interior regions of northern Luzon, Mindanao (where they are known by the Moro word for mountaineers, Manobo), and other generally inaccessible interior regions throughout the islands. Also scattered among the islands are tiny remnants of Negrito tribes, the earliest known inhabitants of the archipelago.

The racial homogeneity of all but a few Filipinos is rooted in the culture history of the archipelago. The earliest human inhabitants are thought to have been the Negritos, a people of pygmy stature, who had migrated from mainland Southeast Asia as far back as 30,000 years ago, when land bridges between the mainland the islands existed. In the centuries that followed, small groups of migrants from throughout the Southeast Asian mainland, generally of Proto-Malay (Indonesian) and Deutero-Malay (Southern Mongoloid) stock, gradually increased the population of the islands, completely absorbing most Negrito groups and pushing others into the highlands. Pure Negritos numbered fewer than 25,000 in the latter part of the twentieth century. This version of Philippine prehistory contradicts earlier postulations that assumed the islands to have been populated by successive waves of large-scale migration, the Proto-Malays arriving roughly 5,500 years ago and the Deutero-Malays roughly 2,300 years ago. Asian scholars such as Frank N. LeBar have discarded this theory as "overly mechanistic" and failing "to allow for local development of cultural forms."

From the eleventh century onward small numbers of non-Malay people traded with and colonized the archipelago, including Chinese, Hinduized Indonesians, and Arabs; the last two had a significant impact on the cultures of the Malay peoples. Spanish, and later American, colonization brought small numbers of Caucasians into the racial melting pot. A continual process of intermarriage has in most cases blurred the lines between Proto-Malays and Deutero-Malays beyond meaningful recognition. Intermarriage has extended to Chinese and Arabs as well; offspring of Chinese-Filipino marriages are known as mestizos, and those who have chosen to identify with Philippine culture are generally well accepted. Racism as such does not appear to exist in the Philippines.

The general cultural homogeneity of the Lowland Christian groups is also deeply rooted in the culture history of the islands. A fair degree of cultural homogeneity appears to have existed before the Christianization of most of the population by the Spanish. Both lowland and interior groups exhibited cultural traits common throughout Southeast Asia at the time. Residence patterns and political organization were relatively diffuse, depending on *barangays* (usually small groups of related families) that were loosely governed by individuals of noted bravery and personal charisma—a form of organization still found in its original form among some Igorot groups and among the hill tribes of Borneo. The term *barangay* has been adopted for a contemporary political institution under the martial law administration of President Ferdinand E. Marcos (see ch. 3; ch. 9). Presumably the looseness of this form of social and political organization permitted the fairly rapid and thorough penetration of external influences that later swept through the islands. The most important of these influences was the introduction of wet-rice agriculture, an innovation that revolutionized residence patterns and the relationship of man to the land and created a new order of economic and political relationships. It is believed that wet-rice cultivation was first practiced around 2,000 years ago in central and northern Luzon, although at what time it became generally established is not known.

Interisland relationships and the further cultural leveling that accompanied them were first cemented under the influence of the Indianized kingdoms of Java and Sumatra in the eighth century A.D. The economic expansion of their coherent sociopolitical system into the Philippine archipelago not only brought the lowland coastal peoples into contact with some of the cultural patterns of insular Southeast Asia but also established trade routes and marketing patterns that brought the indigenous peoples together with one another. Contact with Chinese traders in the tenth century served much the same purpose and gave rise to the first communities of unassimilated Chinese in the population centers that came into being in response to trade. Although general similarities in culture and society had begun to characterize differing groups, there were no overarching political, economic, or religious institutions serving as an integrating base.

Just such an institutional base was provided by the Spanish, whose advent also prevented the rise of Islam in insular Southeast Asia from completely dominating the archipelago. The indigenous population accepted Spanish culture and the Roman Catholic faith with remarkable rapidity but almost always adapted them in ways that were congruent with their own culture; the economic and political system that evolved under Spanish rule maintained the power of the precolonial elites, and the folk Catholicism of the Philippines has many non-Christian elements. The resulting amalgam and the all-encompassing institutions of government and church gave Filipino culture considerable continuity and unity. The Moros, however, proved impervious to Christian proselytization and Spanish control and, along with the inaccessible mountain peoples, were cut off from the mainstream of the emerging national culture. This contributed to an enmity between the Moros and the Christian Filipinos that has constituted the most serious problem in intergroup relations.

The growing sense of cultural unity was augmented by the rise in intergroup contact that accompanied the diffusion of a cash economy, urban centers, literacy, and other factors contributing to communications among and within the islands. Inevitably the growth of cultural unity gave birth to a sense of nationhood, and the anticolonial movements that ensued under the Spanish, Americans, and Japanese both fueled and were fueled by sentiments of cultural homogeneity.

What cultural diversity and conflict exists in the modern Philippine nation can be attributed in large part to the failure of the Spanish to bring the entire population under control. The steadfast adherence of the Moros to Islam has clearly distinguished them from the Filipino majority for more than four centuries. Although they constituted only 5 percent of the national population in the early 1970s, their geographical concentration and resentment of Christian encroachment into their traditional heartland has alienated them from the national society to an extent sufficient for the maintenance of a militant separatist movement (see ch. 17).

The pagan mountain tribes that live in the interior regions of Luzon, Mindanao, and other islands form an only partially integrated minority that hs often been the victim of its isolation. Regarded by many Filipinos as merely primitive savages, they have often been the losers in conflicts with expanding logging enterprises and Christian settlers. With relatively few exceptions, however, they have never been entirely cut off from lowland culture and society, and a gradual process of integration appears to be under way. Several government agencies, including the Commission on National Integration and the Presidential Arm for National Minorities (PANAMIN), have been established to aid and protect these peoples. The historic experience of the small minority of ethnic Chinese in the Philippines has characteristically been ambivalent. On the one hand, ethnic Chinese choosing to identify with Filipino culture have intermarried with Filipinos in large numbers and have experienced virtually no barriers to acceptance; a high proportion of the national elite have been mestizos. On the other hand, ethnic Chinese have experienced greater difficulties in securing citizenship in the Philippines than have the Chinese minorities elsewhere in Southeast Asia.

Although cultural differences within the Lowland Christian majority do not begin to approach the differences between the majority and the Moro, pagan, and Chinese minorities, there exists a fair amount of generally friendly intergroup rivalry. Aside from the more obvious differences of language, dress, diet, and custom, distinctions within the majority groups most often take the form of generally held cultural or regional sterotypes. Although these sterotypes cannot be considered a scientific description of cultural traits, they do give an indication of the ways in which Filipinos of differing origin perceive each other.

Tagalogs are typified as voluble, boastful, and proud, especially with regard to other Filipinos, and are considered to be fussier about their food than others are. They are strongly attached to their families and land and are noted for holding strong political convictions. Tagalogs of the southern part of central Luzon are thought to be especially strong willed and pugnacious. The Visayans (Cebuanos, Ilongos, and Waray-Waray) are usually grouped together and have indeed been known for a degree of regional solidarity—at least when confronting Tagalogs. They are renowned for their bravery; most Filipino boxers hail from the Visayan

Islands, particularly Cebu. They have a considerable reputation as bon vivants, are characterized as flashy dressers, and are thought of by Tagalogs as ostentatious—something of which they often accuse Tagalogs. In contrast, the Ilokanos are noted for their thrift, industry, and austerity and have been known as the "Yankees of the Pacific" for their similarity to an American cultural stereotype. Their industry is admired by other Filipinos, but their austerity is often ridiculed. The Pampangans are characterized as independent and self-centered as well as brave and combative. They have shown a degree of intragroup solidarity perhaps greater than any other Christian group and have been strong supporters of militant agrarian movements in central Luzon (see ch. 13). Both the Pangasinan and Bikolano groups have a reputation for conservatism and unaggressiveness. They rarely leave their home areas. Pangasinans are known to have a high proportion of mestizos in their numbers.

Most intergroup contact takes place in an urban context. A 1974 study by the American geographer Daniel F. Doeppers confirmed the essential homogeneity of Filipino culture. In contrast to Indonesian cities, where cultural minorities tend to settle in exclusivistic neighborhoods, Lowland Christians in Filipino cities and towns are evenly dispersed, and the overall parameters of neighborhood formation tend to be socioeconomic rather than linguistic or denominational (as between Catholics and Protestants). The profusion of Filipino languages and dialects is apparently overcome by the relatively great extent of multilingualism and the use of two lingua francas, Pilipino and English. In general the language of the locality is used for most communication, and Pilipino (in non-Tagalog areas) or English is used as a supplement. In newer cities with a high proportion of migrants—such as those found in parts of Mindanao—the language of the majority of migrants is used as a lingua franca. Cebuano and Ilokano may also be used for general communication in the Visayan Islands and northern Luzon respectively. The native language of a minority is often preserved in the home. Associations of migrants sharing a common language exist but have usually been inactive aside from providing politicians from the home region with a forum for electioneering in pre-martial law times. Doeppers remarked upon the considerable readiness of individuals to "shift language use to a new urban social situation." Language and cultural differences appear to form no barrier to intermarriage between people of different groups. Such marriages are considered entirely unremarkable; the cultural affiliation of the offspring is usually determined by the language used in the home, although the matter is not considered very important by most.

A study by C. Neal Tate, an American political scientist, indicated that "a candidate [for national political office] would do well in those provinces with a high proportion of voters who share his ethnolinguistic status, and poorly in those provinces whose voters do not share his status." Presumably this is a result of several factors, including a sense of ethnic solidarity among the voters and greater facility for the candidate in establishing personal political ties with local leaders if they speak the same mother tongue. These personal ties, so crucial a part of Philippine political dynamics, are cemented by marriage, however, and it is difficult to determine to what extent they are aided by bonds of ethnic solidarity and to what extent they are made with the help of kinship connections (see ch. 10). Moreover it is not impossible for political ties to be made across intergroup barriers; Philippine presidents have been drawn from virtually all of the eight major Christian groups.

In contrast to the Lowland Christian groups, Moros and some Chinese have a greater tendency to group themselves together. For the Moros, Islam serves as a means of identifying themselves with each other as against other Filipinos. Moreover parts of a city with a high concentration of Moros are often subdivided into neighborhoods determined by linguistic and cultural differences within the Moro community. Moros are not, however, totally unintegrated with their Christian neighbors. Insofar as petty commerce is a common Moro occupation, Moros learn and use local languages; intermarriage with Christians is not rare, although it is contingent on the conversion of the prospective spouse— usually a woman—to Islam. Neighborhoods of ethnic Chinese, once concentrated in the commercial districts of the larger cities, have begun to dissolve; Doeppers' study of three provincial capitals showed that only one-third of the ethnic Chinese continued to live at their shops.

THE LOWLAND CHRISTIAN GROUPS

Eight major cultural linguistic groups, known collectively as the Lowland Christians, constitute roughly 90 percent of the population. Bonded together by a common culture history, these eight groups make up the fiber of Filipino society and culture. Distinguished from each other principally by the related though mutually incomprehensible languages they speak, these eight groups share a sense of common identity as the core of the Philippine nation; a number of similar social and cultural traits can be ascribed to all of them, including forms of ecological adaptation, settlement patterns, kinship systems, sociopolitical organization, and social values (see ch. 5).

Like other Filipino languages, theirs belong to the Malayo-Polynesian language family of the more general Austronesian grouping; they are related to Malay, Indonesian, and other Southeast Asian languages. None of the eight major languages is internally homogeneous. Each has a number of dialects, Bikolano and Cebuano having the greatest number with ten and eight respectively; some dialects of the same language are reportedly mutually unintelligible. All eight languages have extensive literatures, Tagalog being the oldest and richest (see ch. 7). The richness of Tagalog literature and its smaller number of dialects compared to the more widely spoken Cebuano were important considerations in its selection as the national language. The languages were written using a seventeen-symbol syllabary of Indic origin that was later replaced by the Roman alphabet, introduced by the Spanish. These languages have acquired a number of loanwords, mostly Spanish but including some English terms as well. Several pidgin languages have also evolved, including Chabakano (Spanish-Cebuano) and Caviteño (Spanish-Tagalog).

The eight major languages of the Lowland Christian groups fall into two natural subdivisions based on linguistic affinity. Ilokano and Pangasinan are grouped together as Northern Luzon languages, and the remainder are classed as Central Philippine languages. These subdivisions are a determinant in multilingualism; a Pangasinan speaker will find it easier to learn Ilokano than Tagalog (Pilipino), and in northern Luzon Ilokano is frequently used for intergroup communication. Similarly, among the Central Philippine languages there is a close affinity among the Visayan languages (Cebuano, Ilongo, and Waray-Waray), and speakers of these three languages find it relatively easy to communicate with each other; it has been suggested, though not substantiated, that the Visayan languages are dialects of a single language. However, English and Pilipino (for non-Tagalogs) remain the most important second languages and, while Pilipino has grown considerably in distribution and prestige, English has remained the most useful language for formal communication in education, government, and business.

Size and Distribution of the Lowland Christian Groups

Tagalogs

The Tagalogs are generally considered the most prominent cultural-linguistic group. Their prominence is largely a result of the fortuitous placement of their home region in the Central Luzon Plain, including the capital city of Manila. The 1970 census counted roughly 9 million individuals as native speakers of Tagalog. Although they easily constitute the largest single group in Manila, they are primarily agriculturalists, as are most Filipinos. A disproportionate number of Tagalogs have achieved positions of national power and importance.

Cebuanos

Cebuanos (also Sugbunanon or Cebuan) numbered roughly 9 million in 1970. They are the dominant group in Cebu, Bohol, Siquijor, eastern Negros, and western and southern Leyte. They are the most prominent among the Visayan groups.

Ilokanos

The Ilokanos (also Ilokans, Ilokos, Ilocos, and occasionally Samtoys) are the third largest group with about 4 million speakers in 1970. Their home region is located along the western coast of Luzon north of the

Lingayen Gulf, but they are also found in large numbers in the Central Luzon Plain. Expansion of the Ilokanos into parts of the plain inhabited by Tagalogs, Pampangans, and Pangasinans has reportedly resulted in some friction among the groups. Ilokanos have actively participated in migration to southern Mindanao. Although not approaching Tagalogs in this respect, the Ilokanos have also contributed heavily to national leadership; President Marcos is an Ilokano.

Ilongos

Second to the Cebuanos among the Visayan groups, speakers of Ilongo (also Hiligaynon or Panayan—among which are included some minor Christian groups) numbered roughly 3.5 million in 1970. Their home region is found on most of Panay, western Negros, the southern end of Mindoro, and the smaller islands between Panay and Mindoro. Their region is an important center of sugarcane cultivation.

Bikolanos

The Bikolanos (also Bikols, Bicols, or Vicols) inhabit the Bicol Peninsula of southeastern Luzon, Catanduanes, Burias, Ticao, and adjacent parts of Masbate. They numbered approximately 2.5 million in 1970. Unlike Tagalogs, Cebuanos, and Ilokanos, the Bikolanos have tended to remain in their home region. Only a few towns in "Bikolandia" have populations in excess of 20,000; most Bikolanos are peasants, growing abaca, rice, and coconuts.

Waray-Waray

The third of the Visayan groups is the Waray-Waray (also Samarans, Samarons, Samarenno, Samar-Leyte, or Warai), numbering 1.7 million in 1970. They inhabit Samar and eastern Leyte.

Pampangans and Pangasinans

The Pampangans (also Kapampangans and Pampangos) and the Pangasinans (also Pangalato) are the two smallest of the major Lowland Christian groups, numbering about 1.2 million and 837,000 respectively in 1970. They share the Central Luzon Plain between Subic Bay and the Lingayen Gulf and are interspersed with Tagalogs and Ilokanos. Although outnumbered by the surrounding Ilokanos and Tagalogs, they have proved tenacious in preserving their languages. Pangasinan is reportedly difficult to learn for other Filipinos, and there is presumably a high rate of multilingualism among Pangasinans. Much Ilokano expansion has taken place in areas formerly dominated by Pangasinans, and their home region is smaller than it once was. Pampangans make up a disproportionate number of the Manila population, largely because of their proximity to the city. Both groups have intermarried heavily with ethnic Chinese.

Minor Christian Groups

In addition to the eight major Christian groups, there are twelve minor groups. They inhabit generally isolated territories—small islands or coastal strips separated from the interior by mountains. Although this isolation has tended to preserve some aspects of their cultures, greater contact with the major Christian groups has resulted in increasing integration with the national culture and society. In particular, the minor Christian groups in the Visayan Islands have come to resemble the Ilongos in culture.

Of the twelve groups, four—the Ibanag, Sambal, Gaddang, and Isinay—are located on Luzon. The Ivatan are located in the Batan Islands north of Luzon. The Aklan and the Hantik are found in the Visayan Islands—mostly on Panay—as are the Banton. The Kalamian, Kuyonon, and Agutaynon inhabit the Calimianes Group, and the Isamal are found on Samal Island in Davao Gulf, off Mindanao.

MUSLIM FILIPINOS

Muslim Filipinos, commonly known as Moros, constitute the single most important exception to the general pattern of cultural homogeneity. Once extending as far north as Manila Bay, Muslim influence in modern times has been restricted to parts of southern Mindanao, Palawan, and the Sulu Archipelago. The Moros are racially and linguistically indistinguishable from other Filipinos, but their religion and way of life have set them apart since the beginnings of the Hispanization that brought the Lowland Christian groups together, and they have jealously guarded their cultural independence to the present day.

Moros are divided into at least ten groups, differing in language and degree of Muslim orthodoxy. The four most important groups are the Magindanao (also Maguindanao) and Maranao of the Illana Bay area of southern Mindanao and the Tausug (also Tau Sug and Taw Sug) and Samal of the Sulu Archipelago and the Zamboanga Peninsula of Mindanao. Other groups include the Ilanon and Sangir on Mindanao; the Yakan and Bajau (also Bajao) of the Sulu Archipelago and Zamboanga Peninsula; the Melabuganon (also Melabugnan) of southern Palawan; and a tiny group known as the Jama Mapun on the Cagayan Islands in the Sulu Sea. Together they numbered approximately 1.6 million in the 1970 census.

Moro languages are classed with the Visayan and southern Luzon languages as a part of the Central Philippine linguistic subdivision. Some of them, such as Maranao and Maguindanao, are mutually intelligible. Some Moro groups are more orthodox in their practice of Islam than others. Generally speaking, the more recently Islamized groups such as the Yakan and the Bajau have preserved some pagan elements in their religious practices and are relatively lax in their observation of the Islamic proscriptions against eating pork or drinking alcoholic beverages. As the first group to adopt Islam, the Tausug are generally considered the most orthodox and are accorded considerable prestige among Moros for this distinction. They treat the Samal, with whom they share the Sulu Archipelago as a home region, somewhat contemptuously and consider the Maranao and Magindanao uncouth.

Despite differences amont the various groups, Moros as a whole have demonstrated considerable solidarity when confronted with a perceived threat from the outside. To a large extent this solidarity stems from a fear that Christian outsiders—the Spanish at first and the Philippine government later—wanted to deprive them of their religion and way of life. But Moro solidarity is also rooted in a history of indigenous political organization that antedates the Hispanic period and an orientation toward other Islamic peoples of Southeast Asia and the world at large rather than toward the rest of the Philippine nation. Enmity between Christian and Muslim Filipinos in the twentieth century has often been fueled by the movement of large numbers of land-hungry Cebuanos, Ilokanos, and other Filipinos into parts of Mindanao that the Moros have considered their own. Moro separatism, which dates from the earliest Spanish attempts to subjugate them, remained a smoldering issue for years thereafter and erupted into full-scale guerrilla warfare in 1972. By mid-1975 the government attempts at negotiation with Moro separatists had remained inconclusive, as had the status of Moro autonomy (see ch. 9; ch. 10; ch. 17).

Historical Background

In the late thirteenth century Islam swept through the Malay Peninsula and insular Southeast Asia, gaining large numbers of converts through the agency of Arab traders. Although the Sulu Archipelago and Mindanao initially served as havens for refugees from the militant spread of Islam in Indonesia during most of the fourteenth century, by 1500 the Sulu Archipelago was firmly Muslim, and by 1565 Muslim trading outposts were to be found as far north as Manila Bay. Those who resisted Islam were eventually driven into the mountains and remained pagan; in Mindanao they constitute the Manobos, who are to the Moros what the Igorots are to the Christians of Luzon. Muslim expansion sought and achieved three objectives—the establishment of trade bases, the spread of their religion, and the increase of the personal power of Muslim leaders. The Muslims were aided in their conquest by the possession of firearms and an Arabic heritage of warfare and brought with them a superior alphabet and the science and art associated with Arabic culture. Although initially accompanied by military conquest, the spread of Islam was not always accomplished through bloodshed, and Muslim proselytizers were considerably more tolerant of local customs than were the Catholic missionaries in the north. As a result local differences among the Moros have persisted, and there is greater cultural heterogeneity among the Moros than among Christian Filipinos.

In Luzon and the Visayan Islands the Spanish encountered relatively little difficulty in replacing Muslim influence with Catholicism and Spanish political and economic institutions. Attempting to extend their dominance into southern Mindanao and the Sulu Archipelago, however, the Spanish encountered still and well-organized resistance, as the formerly feuding sultanates of that region banded together in opposition to the Spanish. Spanish attempts to establish control over Moro regions continued as long as the Spanish held control of the Philippines; gradually they were able to establish Christian enclaves on Palawan and parts of the Zamboanga Peninsula; the sultan of Sulu capitulated to the Spanish late in the nineteenth century, but Spanish control over the Moros was never complete; Spanish education was not extended to many areas, and the people's way of life, including the practices of polyamy and slavery, continued.

Destructive and often brutal raids on settlements by each side characterized Christian-Moro relations for three centuries. Moros frequently raided the Visayan Islands to take slaves, and even in modern times the Moro word for slave is *bisaya*. To the Moros the Filipino Christians were agents of the enemy who wished to rule them and destroy their religion and thus their way of life. A fierce pride in their culture and independence largely motivated Moro resistance to Christian authority. To the Christians the Moros represented a danger and an alien way of life. As the Christian Filipinos looked increasingly to the West, the Moros turned to their Muslim neighbors to the south and west for communication and identity.

The United States inherited the struggle to subjugate the Moro groups when it took over control of the Philippines from Spain and, like the Spanish, encountered stiff resistance. Pursuing a policy that combined military and diplomatic offensives, the Americans ended organized Moro opposition by 1915. Although the Moros respected American military power and appreciated American policies of noninterference with the people's religion and a concern for the preservation of their culture and the confidence of their leaders, Moro acceptance of American authority did not extend to Christian Filipino officials in the colonial government. Attempting to cope with this lack of acceptance after achieving indepenence, the Philippine government designated Sulu, Lanao, and Cotabato as special provinces without elected provincial or national officials. The rule of Christian Filipino governors was resented by the Moros, and in 1950 the special province category was abolished. Conflict continued, however, because of strong cultural conservatism, a feeling of alienation and neglect, and long-standing ties with the Muslims of Borneo, Sulawesi (the Celebes), and other parts of Indonesia.

By far the most serious source of animosity between Moros and Christians, however, was the growing influx of Christian migrants into Mindanao. The creation of economic patterns based on sedentary agriculture led to rapidly increasing population densities in Luzon and the Visayan Islands in areas of fertile land. Government attempts to resettle migrants from densely populated areas began under American colonial rule as early as 1913 and continued after independence. Large-scale internal migration, however, began only after 1948, the migrants being drawn principally from overcrowded regions of the Ilokano, Bikolano, and Visayan peoples. Mindanao was the principal target of migration. Considerable conflict has been generated over questions of landownership, the Moros claiming ownership on the basis of initial settlement, and the Christians, reinforced by a public law declaring all lands within Moro territories not specifically occupied to be in the public domain, also claiming ownership.

Government attempts to ameliorate relations between Christians and Moros have been largely ineffective. Moro resistance to government authority, formerly limited to simple banditry and smuggling, took the form of an armed guerrilla struggle after 1972 and reportedly received support from other Muslim countries. According to a June 1975 interview with Abdul Khayr Alonto, vice chairman of the Moro National Liberation Front—reportedly the guiding power behind the insurgency—separatist ideology was "Islamic and democratic. We do not intend to return to the old sultanates. We want independence, and we are for a democratic federated republic because we recognize the fact that not all people in Mindanao are Muslims. [We are willing to accept the] establishment of an autonomous Bangsa Moro state out of the islands of Mindanao, Sulu, Basilan, and Palawan within the context of Philippine sovereignty."

Shared Characteristics

The various Filipino groups that are now Muslim had cultural differences before their conversion, and they maintain those differences. In addition to these cultural differences, characteristics that are directly related to their Islamization, which thus set them apart from the Christian Filipinos, are shared.

Political Organization

A kind of political organization functioning in Malaya and Indonesia arrived with the Islamic religion to influence the organization of the converted groups. Independent principalities ruled by sultans were established. These principalities ranged in size from units comprising a few villages to the sultanate of Sulu, which included the Sulu Archipelago and parts of Borneo, southern Palawan, and Mindanao.

The sultan was both the secular and the ecclesiastical leader, and his authority was sanctioned by the Koran. Political and religious activities were in fact combined. Taxes were considered religious tithes, and fines were imposed for breach of both religious and customary law. Important officials under the sultan were religious advisers (kadis) and teacher-priests (imams).

In terms of political dynamics the most important figures were the *datus* (local leaders; sing., *datu*). The *datus* used personal prestige, wealth, and the force of power to gather and keep followers. Protection was traditionally the primary obligation of leadership, and leaders have always tried to ally themselves with more powerful leaders. The traditional role of the *datu* was to extract tribute and labor while providing emergency aid, food for festivals, and protection from other *datus* through a system of courts (called *agama* courts), which resembled clan councils. Theoretically anyone who could acquire wealth and influence could become a *datu*, although most were drawn from a hereditary upper class.

The pacification of Moro areas and the imposition of a new political structure have destroyed the power, if not always the prestige, of the sultans. *Datus*, however, remain powerful and continue to enforce customary law through *agama* courts. They have important religious and traditional sanctions, the wealth to provide aid, and the influence to provide jobs. People still relate their personal fortunes with that of their *datu* and display a strong loyalty. *Datus* can no longer extend their power through raids; so they seek to increase their wealth and gain political office. Although they are loyal to their *datu*, people can, and do, shift allegiance if he fails to provide protection and aid, and the continuous maneuvering among *datus* to build up their political machinery characterizes the dynamics of power in Moro communities. The *datu* does not occupy a nationally recognized political office; his actual power is such, however, that government agencies work best if they work through the local *datus*, and conflicts arise when *datus* are disregarded.

Customs and Values

A number of customs and social values held by Moro groups create virtually irreconcilable cultural differences between the Moros and Christain Filipinos. Polygamy, slavery, and the concept of *maratabat*, or "face," are among important of these differences; all are rooted in Islamic tradition.

Polygamy, to the extent of having four wives, is authorized by Muslim law and is present, although rare, among Moros. Because it requires the expense of high bride-prices, the consent of the bride's parents, the ability to support several wives and their children, and the agreement to treat all wives equally, polygamy is practiced only by a small minority of wealthy men. A survey in the city of Marawi among the very conservative Maranao revealed an estimated 2 percent of Muslim husbands to have more than one wife. It is possible that the percentage is higher in more remote rural areas. The Philippine government generally does not interfere with this practice.

Traditionally slaves were acquired through raids on Christian settlements, rulings of the *agama* courts, buying them from others, the progeny of slaves, and through people in debt who sold themselves to the wealthy. In the hierarchical society slaves belonged to the hereditary aristocracy, who were the sultans and wealthy *datus*. Slaves ranked below farmers and artisans, but they shared a similar status with servants. Slaves received no pay, however, and they could be severely punished for attempting to escape. It was possible to marry or buy oneself out of slavery.

In 1968 slavery was outlawed in the Philippines, and most Muslim leaders take as adamant a stand against it as do Christians. It still exists, especially in the more remote and conservative regions of Lanao but to a far lesser degree than in the past. Raids for slaves do not occur, but debtors may work without pay for people to whom they are in debt. On rare occasions an *agama* court may sentence someone to slavery; people in this position may be sold, and their children are considered to be of the same status as their parents.

Maratabat is associated with fierce pride in one's honor and in that of one's kin group. Injury to one's *maratabat* demands revenge, most appropriately in the form of killing. Within Moro society one is expected to be very sensitive to possible injury to his *maratabat*, but Moros who are working or studying in a Christian social setting feel less need to consider *maratabat* in their interpersonal dealings.

IGOROTS AND OTHER PAGAN GROUPS

Although they may be considered interesting survivals of prehistoric Philippine cultures, the numerous small communities of pagan peoples that inhabit isolated regions are of little social, political, economic, or cultural consequence to the mainstream of the society. The groups inhabiting the mountainous regions of northern Luzon are generally called Igorots, after the Tagalog word for mountaineer. Similarly the interior pagans of Mindanao are sometimes lumped together under the name Manobos, after the Moro word for mountaineer. Although they are generally classified together and do not appear to depart significantly from the basic racial and linguistic relatedness of all Filipinos, the Igorots, Manobos, and other pagan groups exhibit great variation in culture, degree of technological advancement, and integration with the national culture. Relative sophistication ranges from the Bontoc and Ifugao of the southwestern mountain region in northern Luzon—famous for their spectacular feats of engineering in the construction of rice terraces on steep hillsides without the use of mortar—to the Tasaday, a tiny cave-dwelling group in Mindanao whose first contact with the outside world came in the early 1970s. Moreover, the groups often exhibit considerable cultural variation within themselves, inasmuch as the village is generally the largest unit of social or political organization, and the greater the distances between villages the greater the differences in culture.

Certain generalizations, however, can be made. Four major Igorot groups (Ifugao, Bontoc, Kankanai, and Ibaloi) are distinguished by their sedentary, terraced, wet-rice agriculture from several other groups (Apayao, Tinggian, Kalinga, and non-Christian Gaddang) who practice shifting swidden cultivation of dry rice. The first four groups are characterized by a more complex form of social and religious organization. Of the Igorots in general, it can be said that social relations and obligations are determined almost entirely by the bonds of kinship, which are reckoned bilaterally to at least third cousins. The individual can rely upon this body of kindred for succor and protection and to avenge him should he fall afoul of people from other villages. Revenge in such instances often took the form of headhunting, which carried with it considerable prestige. Cycles of murder and revenge often grew into vendettas between neighboring villages, although opportunities for intergroup trade have developed since the nineteenth century and some groups have established peace pacts among themselves and with other groups to encourage trading. Since then headhunting has declined considerably, although it has presumably not disappeared altogether. Political power is usually vested in those individuals able to accumulate sufficient wealth and prestige. Religious activity is generally centered on the propitiation of the numerous malevolent spirits—ghosts of ancestors and animist beings—that are the cause of misfortune and disease. Frequently elaborate rituals and taboos are observed to this end.

Increasing contact with frequently hostile Christian settlers and loggers has provided many Igorots with a motive for intergroup solidarity. Western beliefs, institutions, and ways of life are increasing among most Igorot people through a generally selective process. Igorot groups do not regard the present-day national leadership with the same hostility that was shown to the rulers before the twentieth century, and government policies are geared more toward introducing educational, economic, and health facilities than toward a direct imposition of drastic change. A breakdown of isolationist sentiment among small groups has produced a wider sense of ethnic identity and pride. Growing numbers of Igorots have learned English, Ilokano, and Pilipino; in many areas the speakers of these languages outnumber the speakers of any one Igorot language. Nevertheless Christian Filipinos intent on exploiting the rich natural resources of the mountainous interior often regard Igorot people as mere savages; attacks by Christians have sometimes been returned by Igorots and, despite the efforts of some Christian Filipino leaders to protect and organize Igorots, relations between Christian Filipinos and Igorots are frequently violent.

Interior pagan groups in Mindanao have likewise been exploited and harassed by both Christians and Moros. They are generally more dependent on Lowland Christian and Muslim peoples for supplies of metal, salt, and other necessities than are the Igorots. While many groups have moved further into the interior in response to hostile contacts with Christian and Moros, others have become more acculturated, those in northern Mindanao accepting Christian languages and ways; those in southern Mindanao and on Palawan have accepted Islam and the *datu* pattern of social organization.

CHINESE

In the early 1970s it was estimated that there were 600,000 ethnic Chinese living in the Philippines; alien Chinese—ethnic Chinese without Philippine citizenship—were estimated to number somewhat less than 100,000. Ethnic Chinese, particularly those without Philippine citizenship, hold an ambiguous position within the society. Chinese mestizos— the offspring of Chinese-Filipino marriages—have always been willingly accepted into the national society. Intermarriage between the two groups, most often between Chinese men and Philippine women, has been frequent throughout the long history of Chinese presence in the Philippines. Unmixed and unassimilated Chinese, however, have experienced considerable difficulties with respect to citizenship and are frequently the object of prejudice and discrimination.

Chinese trade relations in the Sulu Archipelago occurred at least 1,000 years ago, and by the twelfth century merchant colonies had been established on islands now a part of the Philippine nation. Such items as porcelain, pottery, silk, bronze, gongs, and jade were traded by the Chinese for raw cotton, hardwoods, rattan, placer gold, pearls, tortoiseshell, and edible birds' nests. When the Spanish arrived in 1565, the Chinese population was small, but trade was active.

Manila became the center for the Spanish-Chinese galleon trade, and the Manila Bay area was quickly established as the focal point of Chinese population incursions. The Chinese dominated financing and the retail and wholesale trade, and they were also valuable as the bearers of agricultural innovations and technological handicrafts. They became the shoemakers, silversmiths, masons, painters, tailors, and weavers. As Manila developed into a true urban community, it was the Chinese, not the local population, who had the experience necessary to take advantage of the new commercial opportunities. More than the Spanish, the Chinese intermarried with the local population and introduced a significant new ethnic element.

Spanish policies toward the Chinese varied. Chinese agricultural pursuits, such as growing tobacco for export, and their technological and commercial skills were valued. The Spanish, however, felt a threat in Chinese success. In 1571 about 150 Chinese were in Manila. Until 1603 the Chinese population increased by approximately 1,000 a year. In that year the Spanish vented their antagonism toward the Chinese in a massacre that took over 20,000 lives. The vacillation between acceptance and attack continued throughout the Spanish period. The Chinese population has slowly increased, but it was not until the last decades of Spanish rule that a marked increase occurred. The estimated Chinese population of Manila in 1896 was 100,000.

The United States applied the Exclusion Act of 1894 to the Philippines, limiting Chinese immigration to those who were teachers, students, clergy, traders and, most significantly, dependents of residents. The last category precluded any stemming of Chinese immigration, and during the first six years of American rule the Chinese population in the Philippines tripled. Concomitant with increasing nationalism, legal strictures against Chinese steadily increased, causing many to enter illegally and to fail to register as aliens.

Although comprising an alien ethnic minority, the Chinese population is segmented along lines determined by lineage, language, and native region. Those sharing these features are bound into groups in which preferential treatment is given co-members. Related to them are voluntary associations having elected officers and prescribed duties. These groups and associations have implicit functions as well as explicit duties. They help maintain Chinese culture and govern themselves by Chinese laws, philosophy, and customs; members are given aid, and internal disputes are settled.

A primary function of Chinese associations in the Philippines is to act as mediators and middlemen between the local government officials and the Chinese community. Possibly as a result of this function leadership in Chinese communities, whether in a village or a city, is based almost exclusively on wealth. In the Philippines these leaders must deal with officials enforcing stringent antialien laws and requirements for naturalization. As an alien minority that has achieved conspicuous economic success, the Chinese experienced restrictions on their economic activities. The use of their resources to attempt to gain more favorable treatment has characterized Chinese relations with Filipino officials.

Traditional Chinese marriage and family patterns are characterized by marriages arranged by parents and, especially in the Fukien and Kwangtung areas, extended families having households composed of three generations including perhaps several married brothers and their families. The Chinese in the Philippines tend toward more freedom in choosing a spouse and a preference for nuclear family households. Traditional features have importance, however, and kinship solidarity is especially prominent. People with the same surname, even if they do not have a known common ancestor, think and act as a social unit.

The majority of Chinese retain their traditional religious and ethical codes—Buddhism, Taoism, and Confucianism. There is, however, a substantial Chinese Catholic population, partly because of the arrival of Chinese Catholics from the mainland after the communist takeover. For example, in 1955 the former bishop of Amoy was commissioned by the Vatican to assume direction of the Chinese Catholic community in the Philippines. Proximity to a predominantly Catholic population has also produced some conversions.

Actions of the Philippine government in regard to the Chinese have been generally restrictive. Legislation limiting foreign commercial enterprises aimed mainly at the Chinese has been implemented, and pressures to increase restrictions continue; even though Chinese dominance in domestic trade has become largely a thing of the past, the popular stereotype of clever and unscrupulous Chinese merchants keeping a stranglehold on domestic trade persists. The issue of citizenship for Chinese who had not been born in the Philippines remained clouded in the mid-1970s. A presidential decree in April 1974 required the registration not only of "all aliens living in the country for more than six months" but also of all former aliens, together with their children fifteen years and older, who had been naturalized since independence. This move was clearly aimed at the Chinese, who constitute the overwhelming proportion of both aliens and naturalized citizens in the country, and prompted considerable concern on the part of the Chinese Filipinos.

In 1975 a special state committee on naturalization was created to accept applications, and permanent residence was granted to a number of aliens "for humanitarian reasons." Although the process of naturalization was complicated and involved a difficult literacy test in Pilipino and a requirement for a sizable annual income, over 19,000 applications for citizenship had been filed by mid-1975; it was estimated that these applications would cover about 60 percent of the alien Chinese population. Since the declaration of martial law in 1972 efforts have been made by the government ot "Filipinize" the more than 130 Chinese schools in the country (see ch. 7).

LANGUAGE POLICY

Language is the principal source of cultural differentiation among the vast majority of the population that constitutes the Lowland Christian groups. However, multilingualism is the rule rather than the exception, and the boundaries created by language differences are frequently bridged—even in areas where there is relatively little intergroup contact. The makers of language policy in the Philippines have sought to expand the use of two languages, Pilipino (a form of Tagalog) and English, as a means of facilitating communications and enhancing national solidarity. Spanish has been retained as the third official language, partly in recognition of the impact it has had on indigenous languages and partly because of its popularity among a small but influential segment of the landed and commercial elite. Of the three languages, only Pilipino is the national language.

While the Philippines was a colony of Spain, the official language of administration was Spanish. Although Spanish contributed a large number of loanwords to the vernaculars of indigenous languages, it was never widely distributed. It remains an official language but is rarely used, even for official purposes. Acts of congress are only occasionally translated and published in Spanish. Spanish is considered the most important, but by no means the most expedient, language by a small segment of the elite who prefer Spanish culture and conscientiously foster the continuation of Spanish traditions. Spanish was not a required subject in most Filipino universities until 1952, when a law was passed making twelve units of Spanish mandatory for the completion of an undergraduate degree. In 1957, under pressure from the advocates of Spanish, the Spanish requirement was doubled, thus making the total required language courses equal to half of the courses needed for a degree. Despite constant and vociferous protest on the part of parents and students, the law was not repealed for ten years, when a new law reduced the requirement to a single unit devoted to the Spanish writings of Filipino patriots and men of letters.

When the United States assumed control of the Philippines, the focus of language policy became the school system. President William McKinley had wanted primary education to be given in native languages, but the lack of books and teaching materials in Philippine languages made this impossible. The school system, patterned after the American system, thereafter used English as the sole language of instruction; literacy in Spanish or English, but not an indigenous language, was made a prerequisite for officeholders when the Philippines was granted a degree of autonomy in 1916.

The impact of English as the language of instruction has been enormous. It is the universal language of government, commerce, and mass communications, as well as education. English runs a close second to Pilipino as a lingua franca; according to the 1970 census some 45 percent of the population were able to speak English, compared to about 55 percent who were able to speak the national language. In several provinces the number of people able to speak English exceeds the number able to speak Pilipino. The English language is distributed fairly evenly among the Lowland Christians and to a lesser extent among the Igorots; it is less well distributed among the Moros. Neither English nor Pilipino (in non-Tagalog areas) has replaced the native vernacular, however, and local vernaculars continue to be used between native speakers and in the home. Debates in congress are usually conducted in English, and most laws are framed in that language, later to be translated into Pilipino by the Institute of National Language.

Some Filipinos believe that the quality of education suffers because of the use of English as the language of instruction. This view is based not only on nationalist sentiments but on the fact that virtually all children are forced to receive their education in a foreign language that must be mastered as they are learning other subjects as well. On the one hand, it is felt that those students going on to a university have the enormous advantage of knowing the most important international language well; on the other hand, the vast majority of students, who do not proceed to higher education, are more limited in the education they do receive because of the language problem. It is felt that Pilipino might serve as a better language of instruction, because it can be more easily learned by non-Tagalog students.

The question of language policy was one of the first matters addressed by Manuel Quezon when he became the first president of the Commonwealth of the Philippines (see ch. 3). Upon his recommendation the Institute of National Language was created in 1936, charged with the task of "developing a national language based on one of the native dialects." The institute, composed of representatives from all of the major language groups, deliberated for slightly more than one year and recommended the use of Tagalog as the basis for a national language. The recommendation was accepted, and by 1940 a dictionary and grammar had been composed and published. That same year an act was passed making Tagalog the national language, effective on the day the Philippines was to achieve independence. In 1959 the secretary of education ordered the name of the national language changed to Pilipino, presumably as a gesture of national solidarity in overcoming the regional and cultural connotations of the term *Tagalog*. There were several reasons for choosing Tagalog rather than Cebuano, which had more native speakers. Tagalog was already relatively widespread throughout the islands; it had the most venerable and richest literature of any indigenous language; it was the language of the earlier movements for national independence; and, probably most important, it was the language of the capital city and of central Luzon and as such carried considerably more prestige than other Philippine languages.

After its adoption as the national language, Pilipino spread rapidly. In 1939 only 25.4 percent of the population spoke Pilipino, scarcely more than the number of native speakers of Tagalog. The following year Pilipino became a mandatory subject in all schools, and by 1948 the number of Filipinos able to speak their national language reached 37.1 percent of the population—a number roughly equal to the number of English speakers. By 1960 the number of Pilipino speakers exceeded the number of English speakers, and by 1970 over 55 percent of the population spoke Pilipino.

The spread of Pilipino has been mainly the result of its being taught at every grade level, including university. Since 1957 the local vernacular has been used as an auxiliary language of intruction in the fifth and sixth grades of primary school. Spanish is available as an optional subject in secondary school and as a required subject, along with English and Pilipino, in higher education. Some graduate degrees require French or German. Although a majority of publications still appear in English, the growing number of newspapers, magazines, comic books, and the like that have been published in Pilipino has also greatly aided in the spread of that language, as has its increased use in the electronic media. Improvements in transportation between central Luzon and the other parts of the country have also been instrumental in promoting its use.

Any distinction between Pilipino and Tagalog is largely academic; Pilipino can be thought of as a more formal or "pure" version, Tagalog as a vernacular. Considerable controversy has been generated over the maintenance of the "purity" of Pilipino, largely over questions of orthography and the treatment of loanwords. The Pilipino *abakada* (alphabet) consists of twenty letters and excludes the letters c, f, j, q, v, x, and z, although the excluded letters are often used in the spelling of proper names. The diphthong *ng* has been added to the alphabet. The antipurist school holds that loanwords should be adopted freely and spelled as they are in the lending language rather than according to Pilipino orthography (for example, *molecule* rather than *molikiyul*). The more extreme purists hold that loanwords should be rejected altogether in favor of old Tagalog words or Tagalog translations. Those in an intermediate position hold that loanwords should be adopted but spelled according to Pilipino orthography unless the Pilpino spelling "looks funny," as in *diyep* for jeep. The general reading public seems to prefer the more vernacular form, as evidenced by the increased circulation of *Tabila*, the largest Tagalog daily in Manila, after it changed its editorial style to include widely understood English and other foreign phrases.

CHAPTER 5

SOCIAL STRUCTURE

Philippine society appears to have overcome the centrifugal forces of regionalism, linguistic and ethnic differences, and difficulties of physical communication to a degree sufficient for the creation of a national society. Certain groups, however, notably the Muslim Filipinos (Moros) of southern Mindanao, the unassimilated Chinese, and the pagan hill tribes, have remained outside the mainstream of the national society, and confrontations between them and the Filipino majority have often been violent (see ch. 4). But the great majority of the population is bound together by commonalities of religion, education, values, and government. Moreover social organization generally follows a common pattern throughout the majority of the population, although there are variations on the common theme based on differences of ecological adaptation, economic base, and local tradition.

Despite this degree of cultural homogeneity social organization can be characterized as segmented and shows an overwhelming tendency toward a vertical rather than a horizontal form of social integration. Thus individuals are integrated in localized, hierarchical structures based between superiors and inferiors—patrons and clients—rather than on the basis of such common attributes as class, occupation, or ideological interest. These hierarchical structures can be seen as being linked together at the top by the Manila-based and closely knit national elite, whereas at their base the elements of these hierarchies are mutually isolated, localized, and particularistic. Among the long-term changes taking place in the Philippines perhaps the most significant is the apparent erosion of the hierarchical system of social organization and the tentative emergence of new mechanisms of integration, new social relationships, and new local leadership.

Peasant families tend not to look to other peasant groups outside the local community. Nor will they turn to institutional means of obtaining a job, advancing a promising child's education, dealing with government bureaucracy, obtaining use rights to land, or securing a loan; institutions serving these needs are by and large absent in the Philippines. Instead the peasant family will turn to the landowner—a *cacique, hacendero,* or middle-class *proprietario*—on whose land they are tenants or to some other individual of recognized wealth, power, or influence to serve these needs. The difference in wealth, status, and power between these men of influence and the peasant is striking and immutable and dramatically reflects the gap between rich and poor, between landlord and tenant, and between town and country. The individuals of local influence in turn are personally linked to other individuals of influence at the higher provincial and national levels, forming conduits from Manila all the way to the village. In the Philippine system of political dynamics before the declaration of martial law in 1972 they served as the crucial linkage between national politicians and the voters (see ch. 10).

These relationships have been characterized as dyadic, taking place personally rather than institutionally, between two individuals of unequal status. They were supported by feelings of personal loyalty and obligation and predicated on the expectation of mutual benefit. Thus the tenant farmer would look to his landlord as a patron who could provide him not merely with land to work but with loans of rice or cash in times of need and personal assistance at other times in exchange for deference, loyalty, personal service, votes, and so on. In many parts of the country this form of dyadic patron-client relationship has been weakened by absentee landlordism and mere exploitation of the peasantry—a factor partly responsible for peasant unrest and the hesitant formation of peasant organizations based on common interest that took place before martial law. Similarly the increased demand for immediate and tangible rewards for votes appeared to have replaced the traditional loyalties. Nonetheless influential families continued to hold a virtual monopoly on rural elite status, wealth, and power even though they might not be personally involved in municipal or provincial political activity.

Philippine society in the 1970s remained highly stratified, as it had been in the past. The uppermost elite, frequently described as an oligarchy, held a virtual monopoly on wealth, power, and status. A few members of the oligarchy could trace their ancestry to the local leaders of precolonial times; most had their origins in the development of regional and national elites in the course of the 1800s (see ch. 3). American rule opened a new opportunity for upward mobility through the extension of education and the expansion of government institutions but also afforded the oligarchy the opportunity to consolidate its position of power and expand into commerce and, since World War II, industry and urban real estate ventures. Wealth and education became principal means of acquiring superior status, but ownership of land retained a great deal of its popular force as the only "real" form of wealth. An urban middle class, composed of government officials, teachers, educated professionals, and technocrats, had been firmly established by the mid-1970s but remained relatively small. Observers have noted that education continued to provide opportunities for admission to the middle or upper classes but that competition for these opportunities was becoming increasingly intense. Status as an officer in the armed forces or the constabulary, relatively insignificant before martial law, became more important as an avenue for mobility.

National integration was further supported by several national institutions. The Roman Catholic Church, to which some 83 percent of the population adheres, provides one form of commonality for the population. The relatively high rate of literacy has also permitted Filipinos to participate, at least vicariously, in national events, and the broad diffusion of English and Tagalog (Pilipino) has enabled Filipinos of differing ethnic origins to communicate. Before the declaration of martial law a system of electoral politics also served as a basis for national integration and provided a system of patronage that reached from the national treasury to the village voter. It was apparent, however, in the last days before martial law, that this system had become overburdened and could no longer provide the redistributive functions it had formerly served.

Most observers, however, noted the relative lack of social organization based on a recognition of common interests. The institution that provides the greatest cohesive force in the life of the individual has been the family. Through his family the individual has established virtually automatic social relationships with a large number of people related to both of his parents and, after marriage, to his wife's parents. Relationships within the circle of kin can be expanded and elaborated at the discretion of the individuals involved, but the individual is always assured of support from his most immediate kin. The individual can also rely on the support of his close neighbors and a number of persons brought into a familylike relationship through the institution of godparenthood.

These relationships are cemented by a system of obligations that can be created and discharged in a variety of ways but cannot be ignored. These ties of obligation exist not only between kin but between any two individuals where one has performed a service for or given a gift to the other. Traditionally such ties partly bound landlords and their tenants together, but this relationship has changed considerably in those parts of the country where absentee landlordism or extreme exploitation have become prevalent (see ch. 13). Similar relationships also formerly existed between local political leaders and their constituents, but this system too has been changed. In those sections of the country where they have remained prevalent, however, these relationships continue to serve as a powerful integrative force.

RURAL SOCIAL ORGANIZATION

For most nuclear family households that make up the rural majority of the population, the place of residence is the *sitio*, the cluster of households usually composed of kin and close neighbors, which is a component of the *barrio*—the lowest administrative district in the Philippines (see ch. 2). The *sitio* and *barrio* are the most important units of rural social organization besides the family itself, forming the basis for interhousehold cooperation, educational opportunities, political organization, social control, and most religious activity.

Most *barrios* consist of between fifty and 200 households divided among several *sitios* of between fifteen and thirty households; a somewhat larger cluster, including a small school providing four years of elementary education, a general store, and perhaps a small chapel, may form the center of the *barrio*. A *población*, the administrative seat of the municipality comprising several *barrios*, is larger and will usually contain a church, the area high school, the weekly market, and the homes of the local elite.

Most *sitios* are composed primarily of kinsmen—a single household having grown into a *sitio* within a few generations. Related and unrelated households may choose to move into the *sitio* if a quarrel or some other form of dissatisfaction has made such a move desirable. Because the *sitio* as a unit of residence generally conforms to kinship ties, the dynamics of family relations take precedence over any other form of social organization. Relatives generally working together may include a group of siblings cultivating their fields in common either together or alternately; or relatives may hold common ownership of a fishing vessel or some other capital investment too large to be borne by a single household.

Several work groups cut across lines of kinship and are based on proximity of residence. The obligation to help one's neighbors is almost as important as properly discharging one's obligations to relatives, and the necessity of helping neighbors in need is a value frequently pointed out to children. The most frequent kind of cooperative work is the *tagnawa*, or work bee, where a group of men composed of both relatives and neighbors helps a member of the group for a day in a particularly difficult task, such as the building of a house or the clearing of land. The man for whom the work is performed provides tools and, in the afternoon, a feast. Such groups are voluntary and operate without specified leadership; the afternoon meal is a festive occasion much looked forward to by the participants. Membership in a *tagnawa* may remain active even after a member has moved away. Similarly a man's brothers are expected to join in a *tagnawa* given for him, even though their homes may be at some distance. Because of the increased availability of cash in the countryside, *tagnawas* have begun to be replaced by hired contract labor. Contract groups are sometimes composed of the same individuals who had made up the *tagnawa* group or may be composed of a semipermanent group under the leadership of a carpenter or some other skilled worker. Contract labor may be preferred to *tagnawa* labor because the expense is not significantly greater, and the inconvenience to the entire family of preparing a large feast can be avoided.

Residence in the same *sitio* carries with it considerable obligation for mutual support in times of need, even when individuals are not related. These obligations include assistance with small tasks, attendance at festive occasions, or loans of money. The obligations of neighborliness are such that obligations to distantly related kin in the same *sitio* may be more important than obligations to more closely related kin living elsewhere.

More structured and formal working associations also exist within the community. The *kompang* serves as a permanent agricultural *tagnawa*, composed of six to ten men under the leadership of one of them. They engage in a day-by-day pattern of rotating work in each other's fields; clearing and plowing land or repairing flood damage to dikes or irrigation facilities are frequent *kompang* tasks. The leader is known as the *bastenero* (literally, cane wielder) and acts as a foreman, directing work and making decisions; in return for his leadership he receives additional help on his fields or is required to do less. Fines—usually one day's work—are assessed for failure to attend, but the provision of a draft animal earns extra credit.

Within the *barrio* free labor is expected for community purposes. This may include work on religious fiestas, school repairs, and bridge and road mending. Increasingly, however, peasants have come to expect such tasks to be performed by the municipal or central government, and the institution appears to be a dying one.

A fairly distinct social line divides the *barrio* from the *población*. Although the centers of larger *barrios* may house members of the middle class—such as teachers or lawyers—those who have managed to move up the social scale by dint of hard work, luck, and education will most often move to the *población*. Upward social mobility beyond the *barrio* most frequently takes place through the school as a young person moves through the secondary school in the *población* and from there to a vocational school or college.

Teachers and school officials command considerable prestige in the community and often serve in other capacities, such as election officials. Like other members of the middle class of the *población*, including municipal officers, policemen, and small entrepreneurs in various services, teachers are often owners of land tenanted by peasants (often relatives) that is held mainly for reasons of social status rather than as an investment. The *población* may include the residences of larger landowners who represent the traditionally prominent area families. The largest landowners in an area, including the traditional *cacique* families who acquired numerous scattered plots during the 1800s and the *hacenderos* who own extensive single estates, had most often moved to the regional city or Manila by the 1960s and managed their lands through agents and overseers (see ch. 13).

The most important links between the peasant and the national society were once expressed through close ties with a paternalistic landlord who also sponsored various community activities and programs that helped enrich the lives of his tenants. By the 1960s the links had been severed in many areas because of the departure of the landlord and the acquisition of small plots by members of the middle class. The ties appeared to have

103

been replaced by those of a largely political nature through a *lider*, an individual of higher than average education and status who acted in much the same way as the ward boss of American machine politics. Formerly able to deliver the votes of all or part of the *barrio*, the *lider* was the principal focus of pre-martial law political dynamics at the lowest level of a system of patronage that ramified throughout the entire society. Although loyalty to municipal-level *liders* was once *utang no loob* (a matter of obligation), peasants have come to demand tangible benefits of works projects, jobs, and money as a quid pro quo for political support (see Social Values, this ch.). The *liders* themselves have also come to expect immediate and tangible benefits in exchange for their bloc of votes. It is unclear to what extent the introduction of martial law in 1972 has altered the role of the *lider*, but there are some indications that many former *liders* have been integrated into the functioning of the *barangays*, the new *barrio* political and administrative organizations, and that their position of influence and ability to provide patronage has remained at least partly intact (see ch. 9; ch. 10).

Disputes and misbehavior are preferably handled by the parents within the nuclear family. The *sitio* also tries to handle internal disputes autonomously, and it is considered shameful for the existence of such disputes to become common knowledge; disputes within the *sitio* are handled informally in the spirit of *pakikisama* (getting along) (see Social Values, this ch.). The threat of ostracism is the heaviest sanction available to the *sitio* in exercising social control but, given the intense feelings of mutual dependence on the kin-neighbor group, it is usually sufficient to contain all but the most intractable of problems. The *barrio* captain usually has little effective political power but may be resorted to as a mediator in disputes that cannot be settled within the group. Only in the most bitter disputes will peasants resort to the legal channel constituted by the municipal justice of the peace. The ensuing litigation occasioned by such action is usually too expensive for the average peasant and is avoided when possible.

Class distinctions in rural areas come into clear focus only in the *población*. An elite of wealthy landowners may make their homes in the *población*, although a general shift of large landowners to the cities has been under way since at least the end of World War II. An identifiable rural middle class of professionals and successful merchants is also evident in the *población*. The basic class division in rural areas, expressed by differences in social status, economic conditions, and virtually no intermarriage, is that between the wealthy landowners and the farmers and laborers. Traditionally this was based on a paternalistic relationship between landlord and tenant in which each had obligations and mutually supportive roles. The formerly stable structure characterized by the landlord-tenant system has been altered because of several twentieth-century developments. The paternalistic relationship was drastically affected by the movement of landlords to the city and the resultant system of absentee landlordism. The former highly personalized relationship has become an economic one between tenant and hired manager.

A sense of deprivation has developed among the rural lower class, both tenants and small farmowners, aggravated by rising population pressures threatening their subsistence level and by improved means of transportation and communication that increase their awareness of standards of living inaccessible to them because of their economic position. This sense of loss and resentment has fueled dissident rural movements that have included the takeover of rural land and crops without regard for the landlords. Militant movements of dissatisfied peasants have continued into the 1970s (see ch. 17).

In the mid-1950s such peasant organizations as the Federation of Free Farmers began to achieve some success in creating common interest groups but were divided and emasculated after the declaration of martial law. The creation of local agricultural cooperative units, Samahong Nayons, under provisions of the agrarian reform program may provide a form of common interest organization, but their effectiveness was undetermined in the mid-1970s (see ch. 13).

URBAN SOCIAL ORGANIZATION

The social structure of the cities provides a much greater variety of factors that determine social rank than does the social structure of rural areas. More opportunities for wealth, education, and prestigious occupation exist; and greater mobility is possible. To the extent that a middle class exists it is a largely urban phenomenon. Although an identifiable stratification exists, it is more open and more subject to change than is that in rural areas.

An upper class made up of absentee landlords, top political figures, and successful businessmen constitutes about 3 percent of the population. This group wields great social power and controls a very high percentage of the nation's wealth. One segment of the upper class is made up of foreigners—including a great many American and Spanish citizens—who retain ties with their native countries and are important in the Philippines in such roles as bankers, financial experts, businessmen, manufacturers, industrialists, and importers and exporters.

A second segment of the upper class is composed of those Philippine-born Spaniards and Spanish mestizos who are oriented toward Spanish culture and who are wealthy landowners and shipping magnates whose families have amassed and retained their wealth. Many are descendants of the elite class that developed under Spanish rule, and they generally emphasize their Spanish identification. They are involved primarily in commercial, rather than educational or political, activities, except in the use of their wealth to support special interests. They generally enjoy close social relations with the foreign elite and have a well-developed sense of social exclusiveness.

Finally the Filipino segment of the upper class, including Chinese mestizos, wields political power and enjoys the high social prestige given to high educational levels and to certain occupations. This component of the upper class is the most accessible to those striving upward. Some of the members of this group emphasize their upper class status by the traditional means of landownership. Others stress their ties with the common man. Political figures, intellectuals, and educators most often express both a strong nationalism and the desire to make Philippine society egalitarian rather than hierarchical.

Entrepreneurship offers some opportunity for gaining and much opportunity for sustaining high economic status and membership in the upper class. Most successful entrepreneurs come from Manila and its adjacent provinces and are well educated. Opportunities for upward economic mobility from the lower and middle economic classes were best before 1950. Since then, because of increased governmental control of industry and the need for larger initial capital investment in order to become an industrialist, entrepreneurial mobility from the lower economic classes has decreased. Entrepreneurship has permitted the traditional landowning elite and the new industrial elite to solidify and enforce their upper class position.

Education offers opportunities for upward mobility, partly because a university degree is prestigious in itself and partly because occupations requiring higher education carry much prestige. A small middle class developed because of educational, business, and political opportunities along with increasing social mobility. It represented about 10 percent of the urban population in the late 1960s and is composed mainly of writers, civil servants, teachers, clerical workers, merchants, mechanics, tradesmen, small businessmen, and small property owners. This middle class is neither as culturally conspicuous nor as cohesive as the elite. Many of its members tend to identify with either the upper or lower class, largely on the basis of their familial or racial background. A few developed systems of social relationships unite them into a social entity with similar values, goals, and life-styles. Chambers of commerce (including Jaycees), such service organizations as Rotarians, and various Roman Catholic and Protestant lay groups provide opportunities for middle-class interaction and sometimes exercise vigorous community leadership in municipal towns and cities. The imposition of martial law in 1972 considerably improved the wealth and position of the military, particularly the officer corps, which is largely composed of individuals of a middle-class background.

The majority of urbanites belong to the lower class. These people have such occupations as domestic servants, peddlers, laborers, drivers, and minor clerks and own virtually no residential properties. They can be divided into two major subgroups: those who have lived all their lives in the city and occupy a familiar economic and social position and those provincials recently arrived from rural areas. Every major city has a squatter population made up mainly of provincials. The Tondo district of Manila in particular reflected in its high crime rate the poverty, erosion of social controls, and difficulties of adjusting to urban life that prevail within the migrant population (see ch. 6; ch. 17).

KINSHIP AND THE LIFE CYCLE

The paramount importance of the nuclear and bilaterally extended family as the principal focus of social, economic, religious, and—to a large extent—political activity makes kinship relations the most significant and influential set of relations in the life of a Filipino. The social status of the individual is in large measure linked to the wealth and power of his family. Traditionally the average Filipino has evinced a loyalty to his or her family that virtually precludes loyalty to any nonfamily institution, such as the *barrio*, the church, trade unions, political parties, or the government, and has turned to the family for both emotional and material support rather than to institutional forms of social service. Social, economic, and political relationships that reach beyond the circle of kinship are usually based on an alliance of families founded on common interest and generally dominated by the leadership of the most powerful and prestigious of the families involved. The importance of kinship relations even beyond the strict bounds of relatedness and the pervasiveness and force of social values dictating the solidarity and preservation of the family circle are considered extremely important factors contributing to the generally fragmentary character of Philippine society at large. There are indications, however, that mutual interest groups of peasants and workers not based solely on family ties had begun to develop in the latter half of the twentieth century.

The paramountcy of family relations is reflected in the 1953 Civil Code of the Philippines, which recognizes the family as "a basic social institution which public policy cherishes and protects." Similarly the 1973 Constitution affirms that "the State shall strengthen the family as a basic social institution." As formulated by the code, all presumptions in legal proceedings "favor the solidarity of the family" and "lean toward the validity of marriage, the indissolubility of the marriage bonds, the legitimacy of children, the community of property during the marriage, the authority of parents over their children, and the validity of defense for any member of the family in case of unlawful aggression."

Family ties are reckoned bilaterally, that is, equally on both parents' sides of the family. The extent to which ties of kinship are recognized and considered important is much greater in the Philippines than, for example, in the United States; third cousins—who share a common great-great-grandparent—are often included in the effective range of kinship. A Filipino may consider as many as 100 or more individuals to be his relatives, although the relative intimacy of the relationship is subject to a number of factors and will not be the same for all those he considers his relatives. Although this broadly extended family is of considerable importance in determining the obligations and sources of support an individual has, the nuclear family of parents and their children (and occasionally one or two aged grandparents) is the principal unit of residence and serves as the basic building block of the extended family.

As the language of the code implies, familial loyalty and solidarity are social imperatives of the highest degree. This loyalty and solidarity are expressed in several ways: through the linking of individual status to family status—and vice versa; through the extension of both emotional and physical protection to family members against attack from outsiders; and through the extension of financial assistance, employment, and other forms of support by more fortunate individuals to less fortunate relatives. Throughout all of these expressions of loyalty and solidarity, indeed in every aspect of life, the interests of the individual are subordinated to the interests of the family. A person's social standing is identical with the position of his or her family, and his or her occupation, political affiliations, and choice of spouse are inseparable from family connections. Upward social mobility—especially through education, the acquisition of land, or government service—is often made possible with the aid of family connections and in turn enhances the status of the entire family circle, who will legitimately expect to share in the benefits of such mobility.

If upward social mobility reflects favorably upon the status of the entire family, the converse is equally true, and antisocial or disreputable activities on the part of one family member bring discredit to every other member of the family. This serves as a powerful mechanism of social control, inhibiting antisocial or unsanctioned behavior. The same feelings of family solidarity, however, also work to protect the individual from outside threats, even when he or she has brought discredit upon the family. A threat to one family member is perceived as a threat to all, even if the threatened member has committed a crime; concern for family welfare and honor usually outweights concern for legal mechanisms. The protective aspects of Filipino family relations extend to emotional as well as physical threats; to insult one member of a family is to insult the entire family and thus earn their enmity—an important factor in the politeness cultivated by most Filipinos (see Social Values, this ch.).

The solidarity of the family is expressed economically as well. Even among the very wealthy, property is considered as belonging to the family rather than to the individual. As a matter of loyalty and familial solidarity a person who achieves wealth, even in very moderate degree, is expected to share that wealth with less fortunate relatives, an attitude that produces a significant redistributive effect on accumulated wealth. The extended family acts as a complete source of social insurance; the mutual protection of family members is both a duty and a sanctioned right. Relatives can be depended upon for aid in times of sickness and misfortune, in the education of a promising child, in the establishment of a new household, and the like. No family can honorably ignore the plight of a member in need, and orphanages and institutional homes for the aged have proved to be fairly superfluous in the Philippines. This expression of family solidarity extends to the use of influence as well; a person in a position to grant a job or to use influence in the acquisition of a job or some special favor will almost invariably favor a kinsman. Nepotism is all pervasive and is tacitly approved throughout the society, from the *barrio* to the highest levels of national government.

The extension of family support may involve a poorer member of the extended family taking up residence in a more fortunate relative's household. In return he or she will work, often performing menial tasks as a servant. In other instances a poor household may become tenants on a wealthier relative's land. This practice is particularly prevalent among the Ilokanos in northern Luzon, where such an arrangement is known as *kaysugpon*. The feelings of obligation and loyalty created by such arrangements have made the implementation of agrarian reform measures a matter of considerable ambivalence, insofar as landlord and tenant are also related to each other and feelings of family loyalty may preclude the tenant from asserting rights guaranteed him by legislation or decree.

The web of interpersonal relations created by the extended family system is held together by a set of mutually reinforcing obligations. Just as it is incumbent on an individual to aid his or her kinsmen when possible, so is it incumbent on those receiving aid to return loyalty and, in some respects, obedience. Before the declaration of martial law in 1972 political dynamics were largely based on the reciprocity of familial obligations. An individual in a position to deliver patronage or to provide financial aid to his relatives could in turn deliver the votes of an entire extended family at election time—often as much as one-third or one-half of a *barrio* population. Other extended families might choose to ally themselves with the family of such an influential individual—often cementing the alliance through marriage—and thus increase both the flow of patronage and influence downward and the flow of votes and political support upward.

The system of obligation for mutual support operates with considerable flexibility when the relationship between individuals is a distant one. Two distantly related individuals may choose to strengthen and elaborate the bond by working together, requesting or offering assistance, and so on. An individual who achieves particularly notable wealth or influence may find numerous distant relatives eager to establish and revitalize the relationship; he or she may choose not to enter into these relationships but will often accede inasmuch as doing so earns prestige and broadens influence.

Relationships with relatives outside the household are important, but other factors besides kinship, such as frequency of meetings and similar concerns and interests, tend to determine the degree of their importance.

Relatives living in the same village form a closely knit social unit, but relatives of the same degree who live far away are not thought of as intimates. When, however, someone goes to another town or city where relatives live, he or she will visit them and expect to be welcomed. Persons with political ambitions maintain ties with all members of their kindred group, constantly reinforcing sentiments of mutual obligation and solidarity.

Nonrelatives are brought into a kinshiplike relationship through the Philippine version of the Christian institution of godparenthood. Individuals are usually sponsored by godfathers *(padrinos)* and godmothers *(madrinas)* at baptism, confirmation, and marriage, but only some of the mechanisms and results of the practice are directly related to Roman Catholic Canon Law.

From a functional rather than religious point of view the important aspect of godparenthood is that it makes the sponsors coparents, along with the real parents, of the individual. The man becomes a *compadre* (cofather) with the individual's parents, and the woman a *comadre* (comother). The rituals that make them godparents thus tie them into a kindred relationship with the child's parents. As kinship provides the basic organizational principle of the Philippines, this system of ritual coparenthoood, termed *compadrazgo*, brings nonrelatives into a social unit characterized by the same obligations and emotional ties as those of actual kinship.

Usually close friends, neighbors, or relatives are chosen to be godparents for one's child, and the new ties produced by this coparenthood situation are fraternal. If, as sometimes occurs, a person asks his landlord or employer to be godparent to his child, the godparent has a paternal relationship with his godchild's parents. In either case the relationship is understood as one of kinship and is lifelong.

Although the godparent system functions primarily to unite adults, the relationship between godparents and their godchildren is also important. Godparents are expected to see that their godchildren receive proper religious training; to give them gifts on such occasions as Christmas and the child's name day; and, if wealthier than the real parents, to aid the child in times of financial need and perhaps defray educational expenses. Godchildren are expected always to express deference and respect toward their godparents.

Within the nuclear family household most authority is vested in the father, although the mother exercises considerable authority because she generally maintains control over family finances. The relationship between siblings is considered particularly important and usually remains close and affectionate even after they have married and established separate households. The relationship between grandparents and grandchildren is generally featured by great affection and indulgence, and both sets of grandparents compete for the opportunity to look after their grandchildren. Familial authority is largely founded on a respect for age that calls for considerable deference to be paid to older individuals of both sexes. Family decisions are most often arrived at only after a consensus has been reached, after which the decision will be adhered to by all.

Procreation is considered the natural and desired outcome of marriage, and childless couples are pitied. Methods of birth control are not widely known and when known are not often used (see ch. 3). There is no special preference for children of either sex; the progeny of both daughters and sons carry on the family line. Most couples probably prefer to have children of both sexes. When children, especially girls, are young they perform useful functions at home, and older children, especially boys, help support their aged parents.

Children may be baptized in the parish church when they are a week or two old, but more often they are baptized along with the other infants in the community at the time of the local fiesta honoring the town's patron saint. Having the baptism at that time avoids the inconvenience of repeating the preparations for the festival and having relatives make another visit to the community. In many rural areas infants are conditionally baptized before baptism by a priest. This method is supposed to be resorted to only in emergencies, but in some communities it has become a routine procedure.

Before the baptism takes place parents must choose a Christian name for the infant and must select the godparents. Almost all children are named for the saint on whose feast day they were born or baptized or for a relative, parent, or friend. Having a child named after one is considered an honor. The godparent who is of the same sex as the child usually pays for the baptism, and both godparents give gifts to their godchild.

Until weaning, at approximately two and one-half years, the infant is master of the household and is constantly in the care of and being indulged by a parent, older child, or grandparent. Infants are not expected to be able to distinguish between proper and improper behavior.

After weaning, a child becomes subject to discipline and may very well have had its center-stage place taken over by a new baby. Children's substitues for the mother's attention are older brothers and sisters and neighbor-kin children or adults. Children become dependent on the neighbor-kin group for most of their social needs and activities.

In games and in school children generally subordinate competition to cooperation, especially among their relatives and neighborhood playmates. The rivalry that does occur is between groups recognizing different loyalties. Aggressive behavior, especially within the kindred group, is condemned. Even the children who are better dressed and fed and whose families are able to let them finish at least high school are not expected to manifest their better economic and social position by dominating others. Individuals, whether youths or adults, who put their own welfare over that of their kindred group are criticized.

Usually between the ages of five and eight children are confirmed by a bishop during his annual visit to the community, generally at the time of the town fiesta. As in baptism, the child gets new godparents, who act as sponsors during the ceremony, thus extending the familial social alliances of the parents. At about age seven children receive First Holy Communion. This follows a period of religious instruction, usually by the child's grandmother and often by someone at the local church. While recognized as having great religious importance, the event does not involve godparents or the broadening of social affiliations.

Individuals who conscientiously bear their familial responsibilities are respected even if unsuccessful in their economic pursuits, and children learn early that they have tasks to perform and a responsibility to their family to perform them. The primary responsibility of schoolchildren, both boys and girls, is often child care. Babies are watched or held while games are played. A division in training and duties eventually occurs; rural boys learn agricultural activities, and all girls learn household chores. Responsible behavior is rewarded by a child's being given more serious responsibilities and thus closer ties with the desired adult world.

The development of self-reliance in children is not considered necessary, as children are taught to be both dependent upon and responsible to their kindred group. The desire for solitude is not considered normal; personalities characterized by gregariousness are favored. During early adolescence youths develop strong friendships with one or two youths of the same sex. The friends work and play together in close and continual companionship. These friendships emphasize division between the sexes and enforce tendencies toward mutual dependence.

The process and time for becoming an adult varies. A rural youth in his or her late teens does the work of an adult and, if definite plans have been made for marriage, the person may be considered an adult. Those in school are usually not thought of as adults despite their age, unless married or clearly past school age. University students retain their nonadult status longer than do their age peers who are out of school. The most common and expected way to be accepted as an adult is to marry and begin raising a family.

Children are expected to establish their own households at marriage, although residence is ideally taken up close to the bridegroom's family. Households may be established near the bride's family if, for example, the bride has no brothers and her parents have land she will inherit or if her family can help to provide a job or is located near job opportunities. Couples sometimes establish their households near neither's parents if job opportunities are lacking or if one of the couple—usually the bride—wishes to escape the sometimes too watchful eye of her in-laws. Most marriages, however, tend to take place between couples from the same *barrio*, and the question of where to establish residence usually comes down to which *sitio* is preferable.

In arranging marriages important consideration has traditionally been given to the interests and welfare of the families, rather than the individuals, to be united. Until a generation or two ago virtually all marriages were arranged by parents, and in both rural and urban areas parents still continue to exert strong influence in the choice of a mate. Discussions between family heads and exchanges of gifts usually occur before plans are made final. Given the importance of kinship, marriage forms a social alliance between groups, and the economic and social status of potential in-laws is an important consideration.

Every Filipino is expected to marry and begin a family as soon as possible. The birth of a child cements the ties between the parental families more than does the marriage ceremony. Children, unlike either of their parents, are equally related to the kin groups of both parents.

Traditionally the potential son-in-law lived in his fiancée's house and did work for her parents. Either along with or instead of this the bridegroom's family supplied money, land, or work animals to the bride's parents. One or the other of these customs still occurs in the more remote areas, but generally the obligation of the bridegroom and his family is to pay for the ceremony and wedding feast.

Roman Catholics have marriage ceremonies performed by a priest in the town church or the *barrio* chapel. The few civil ceremonies that occur take place in the cities or in the rare cases of elopement, when a simple church ceremony usually follows the civil marriage.

In rural areas and among many people in the cities the bridegroom's parents, their *compadres* and *comadres*, and all their nearby kin begin preparations a few days before the wedding. Food is prepared, and visiting relatives are housed and entertained. The couple gets the wedding license from the town hall and visits the parish priest for final formalities.

The bride is escorted to the church by her attendants and parents. Her father gives her away, and the wedding ceremony takes place followed by a mass. The couple is sponsored by a godfather and a godmother who become tied to the couple's parents in the coparenthood system. After the mass a photograph of the wedding party, including the priest, is taken, and all proceed to the bride's house. The couple then leaves, at which time the bride is formally separated from her natal home and goes to the bridegroom's house for a less elaborate feast. The last to leave this final celebration, after giving the couple their blessing and wedding gift, are the godparents. When the couple retires to their room within the bridegroom's house or to their own house, they find an envelope with money, all or most of which is provided by the bridegroom's parents.

A good marriage is one in which the parents' functions complement each other and the husband exerts authority but not dominance. Traditional and legal codes specify that any property the wife takes into the marriage remains hers, thus supporting equality between the sexes. Economic security is the primary aim and function of both parents. Parents who provide their children with the opportunity for an education, who provide the necessities for ceremonial occasions, and who have acquired some money or land to pass to their children are considered to be functioning successfully.

Each spouse's relationship with his or her kin group is expected to remain as strong after marriage as before. Neither the responsibilities nor the emotional ties toward one's family are lessened by marriage, and in-laws are not expected to remain aloof from conflicts between the couple. In ideal marriages conflicts are minimized and quickly resolved so that antagonisms do not develop between the two family groups. The fact that children are of equal concern to both families enforces the view that their welfare should be of paramount concern to the parents.

Except among Muslims and some unassimilated groups divorce is not recognized in the Philippines, and even among non-Christians strong sanctions exist against the divorce of couples with children. The legal code does allow separation. It is permitted in cases of adultery on the part of the wife or concubinage on the part of the husband or when one spouse attempts to take the life of the other. The mechanisms for obtaining a legal separation and the adverse publicity involved in doing so keep most people who might otherwise separate from taking the legal steps. Informal separation, after which the husband may establish another union without legal sanction and set up a new household, appears to be quite common.

SOCIAL VALUES

The system of social values adhered to by Filipinos of all walks of life emphasizes a strong sense of personal honor, dignity, and pride. Filipinos feel an intense need to maintain their sense of personal pride by recognizing and discharging their obligations and are extremely sensitive to imputations that they have not done so. In response to the imperatives of the social value system, Filipinos have a deep sense of indebtedness, a high sensitivity to insults, and a great reluctance to act in any way that might offend or insult others. George M. Guthrie, among others, has identified four principal values as the primary expression of this system of social values. The most important of these in terms of interpersonal behavior is *utang na loob*, which in many ways serves as the principal cohesive force in Philippine society. More directly related to the individual's perception of himself and others are the values of *amor proprio* (self-esteem) and *hiya* (sense of shame). The desire to avoid placing others in a stressful or unpleasant position results in *pakikisama*.

Utang na loob denotes a primary debt, which functions within a system of reciprocal obligations. The finest compliment one can pay an individual is to say he is exceptionally faithful in fulfilling obligations, and conversely the strongest indictment is to label someone extremely ungrateful. A less strong but still serious charge is having a weak sense of obligation and a reluctance to honor obligations. To achieve the maximum acceptance a person must not only fulfill sanctioned obligations but also want to fulfill them; it is an unfavorable judgment to say an individual avoids and dislikes being obligated to members of his group.

The system of reciprocal obligation begins with a gift given by the free will of the giver and with no agreed upon form of repayment. Acceptance of the gift denotes recognition of one's membership in a specific group with all the rights and responsibilities involved, agreement to be obligated to the donor, and willingness to make repayment with an item or service of greater value than the initial gift. The initial gift is nearly always made to a person already or potentially within the donor's in-group. Rejection of the gift means the rejector denies membership in the group or wishes to sever his ties with the group. It is impossible to reject a freely offered gift and maintain ties with the giver and his associates.

Repayment should be more valuable than the original gift but is a social rather than a commercial enterprise and cannot be transacted with money. Repayment, by its nature, redirects the obligation; the original donor becomes the debtor. The new debtor has the same reciprocity obligation as the original. On the one hand *utang na loob* acts as a system for exchanging services and resources within a never-ending context of social obligation; on the other hand it serves the social functions of providing a mechanism for maintaining social relationships and reinforcing membership in a group composed of specific individuals.

Whereas most of the individuals within any group that share *utang na loob* obligations are socially equal, the condition may exist between superiors and subordinates. The person with limited means is not expected to reciprocate with items of equal or greater value than those he receives from the superordinate person; but he is expected to acknowledge his debts, make repayment in the form of items that have value to him and, most important, maintain the attitude of indebtedness. By fulfilling his obligations according to his means, the tenant or poor relative, for example, is perfectly justified in expecting and asking for items and services according to his needs.

It is permissible to ask for repayment but only when the person asking has a known need and the person being asked has a surplus. Ideally one never asks for repayment unless he is absolutely certain his debtor can repay. Thus if a person does not repay a debt when asked, he faces the serious charge of being ungrateful and socially irresponsible.

A person in need can solicit aid by approaching someone already in his debt or by making an unsolicited gift to one who has a surplus of the needed item or can help him. Giving unsolicited aid to someone in need is not considered proper behavior. It is believed to embarrass the person by exposing a need he may not have acknowledged, and it places on the person an obligation to reciprocate that may increase rather than alleviate his needy position. Therefore needs are satisfied, if possible, by asking a member of one's group, and the asking is not in the form of asking a favor but rather an approved part of the *utang na loob* reciprocal system.

Utang na loob serves to distribute services and surpluses within a defined group, to maintain beneficial relationships between specific people of different social rank, and to provide effective sentiments to reinforce family closeness. To an extent it may also function to personalize relationships with such professionals as doctors, lawyers, bankers, and government officials. Service from government officials is often considered as creating *utang na loob*, largely because the concept of depersonalized bureaucratic service is not well developed. It is considered proper to give a gift to a helpful official to show that one recognizes one's obligations to be grateful. This kind of repayment, however, does not include reaching an agreement before the service is made and then providing payment. This would be a contractual rather than an *utang na loob* form of reciprocity and would be considered immoral in such a situation.

Under the political system before martial law, politicians and their constituents frequently entered into an *utang na loob* relationship wherein the delivery of votes to the politician created indebtedness in him and benefits delivered by the politician created a debt of personal loyalty on the part of his constituents. In the late 1950s and the 1960s, however, these exchanges of debt had begun to rely more and more heavily on the provision of tangible and immediate benefits for the voters.

Utang na loob reciprocity is sanctioned by beliefs concerning the nature of society and by personal values. Obligations not only require continual social relations but also offer the most effective means for severing social ties through the violation of obligations. An emphasis is therefore placed on the value of recognizing and fulfilling obligations; any other attitude would threaten the cohesion of social units. Because the world of men outside the cohesive group and the world of nature are seen as essentially hostile, social cohesion is the prime mechanism for interdependence among people who recognize ties to each other and the need for protection against potential dangers.

Utang na loob contrasts with contractual forms of reciprocity in which people provide an item or a service with the explicit agreement that an equal item or service will be repaid and the contract will thus be ended. It is also different from quasi-contractual reciprocity where no repayment is agreed upon but custom determines the kind of item or service that satisfies the requirement of repayment.

The primary personal sanction of correct social behavior is the awareness that guilt and shame are associated with the violation of social values. This condition is referred to as *hiya*. Having *hiya* is having a sense of social propriety. It regulates behavior in *utang na loob* situations and in other interpersonal contexts. A strong insult is to charge a person with not having *hiya*, essentially meaning either that he does not know the difference between right and wrong or that he does not feel the proper sense of shame when in a socially unacceptable position.

Incorrect behavior is felt to be not only inexpedient but also shameful. The feelings of shame and guilt are sentiments to be avoided in themselves and because the conditions producing them threaten social acceptance. Every value important to the Filipino is related to his place in a social setting. His primary concern is to be accepted and approved by his peers and by recognized authority figures. This approval and acceptance is naturally due him only by his proper behavior according to his station in life.

Filipinos are taught as children to behave in a way that will meet approval and appreciation within the community, because what neighbors think and say about each member of the family is important. Tradition should be followed, especially the traditional authority of age and of family heads. Innovations, persons, or ideas that challenge the authority structure of the family threaten the extremely important value places on emotional and material security within the family. To prevent such threats the authority figure must be followed even if one's feelings are ambivalent toward specific demands.

It is important to maintain the approval of authorities outside the family. Such people should be respected and obeyed, unless they grossly overstep their dominant position. Escape from or retaliation against severe treatment is permissible. Otherwise one suppresses unfavorable opinions about those in direct authority over one unless they lose their authority.

One advantage of seeking the approval of those in authority is that such people can be of help in obtaining a job and other benefits. It is seen as permissible and wise to establish good relations with people in high position, as benefits are seen to come primarily as gifts and by way of patronage.

Filipinos place a premium on social acceptance and are extremely sensitive to attacks on their personal honor. A strong sense of *amor proprio* helps to maintain acquired acceptance and to refute the questioning of one's basic qualities. Potential threats are somewhat determined by the person's place in society. For example, a farmer may not feel his *amor proprio* threatened by aspersions on his lack of education but will be highly sensitive to remarks about his role as a husband and father.

Whereas a high value is placed upon the emotional closeness and security within the kinship group, relationships with non-kin tend to be more delicate and uncertain. Because social relationships are based upon the mutual understanding of obligations, relations with outsiders are on a strictly formal basis. Because both acceptance and interdependence are strongest within the kin group, individuals expect their kin to be active allies in any dispute. The social, political, and economic functioning of a community can be disrupted by such factional disputes.

Because of sensitivity to real or presumed attacks on one's *amor proprio* much importance is placed on smoothness of relations with non-kin. The ability to get along with other people and to avoid any outward signs of conflict at almost any cost is cultivated. A part of this attitude is referred to as *pakikisama*—going along with the will of a leader of the majority, at least nominally. This often manifests itself in agreeing with another person's views and stating the opinion one believes another person holds, even if a real disagreement exists.

Another manifestation of the value placed on smooth social dealings is the use of euphemistic and indirect speech. When it is necessary to state an unpleasant truth or an opposing opinion or to make a request of a non-kin, it is done in as pleasant a manner as possible. Tone of voice is as important as the words; a harsh tone implies ill-feelings. Insulting speech is highly condemned and feared. Frank and direct speech in many situations may correctly be used only between intimate friends or sworn enemies.

To minimize the potential tensions in certain situations it is common to use a go-between. Third parties are employed both to avoid possible friction and to heal disputes. They can make requests that might otherwise be embarassing, introduces strangers, voice complaints, and relay decisions. The party being approached by the go-between is as protected as the party who sends the go-between, because he can be more direct in his response. A long tradition exists of using the go-between especially to heal social disruptions.

A high value has always been placed on striving for the economic security of the family. Both husband and wife, and children when they are old enough, are expected to do whatever work and make whatever sacrifices are necessary to aid family security. This has generally promoted an economic conservatism in the use of family capital for entrepreneurship and a resistance to new agricultural techniques that may be considered risky.

CHAPTER 6

LIVING CONDITIONS

Living conditions in the Philippines reflect a marked distortion in income distribution favoring a relatively small number of wealthy families and an equally noticeable distinction between rural and urban areas in living standards and access to health, welfare, and related services. According to President Ferdinand E. Marcos, one of the primary reasons for his declaration of martial law in 1972 was a concern for the living conditions of the Philippine peoples. For the purpose of generating a more equitable distribution of the country's goods and services, Marcos called for the creation of a New Society.

Income was generally the most important determinant and index of a family's standard of living, although education and geographic factors were also influential. The greatest comforts were found among the wealthy in urban areas. Sections within cities varied widely, however, and conditions in squatter communities were often worse than those generally known in rural areas.

Although studies indicate that in the decade before the declaration of martial law the number of Philippine families enjoying a median level of living had grown, the distance between the extremes continued to increase. Rapid population growth placed continuing pressure on sanitation services, housing facilities, and employment opportunities. The effectiveness of governmental efforts to counter these problems was restricted by periodic budgetary constraints and remained uncertain at the end of 1975 (see ch. 12).

President Marcos cited growing dissatisfaction with living conditions as one of the fundamental causes of civil strife and crime, which would have led to anarchy had martial law not been declared. Immediately after the declaration of martial law, security in urban areas improved significantly. By 1974 the continued inflationary increases in the costs of food and other commodities were believed to be among the causes of increased rates of theft and larceny. The president called on the military to survey the situation and to take any measures necessary to prevent crimes resulting from "hardships in life."

Achievement of the ideals of the New Society envisioned by Marcos would require considerable reconstruction of the old society. Clearly the most important challenge faced by the government in the transition to the New Society in the mid-1970s was to improve living conditions sufficiently to justify the loss of certain political and civil freedoms. The complexity and breadth of the problems involved made the fulfillment of this challenge a formidable task.

EFFECTS OF URBANIZATION

Disparities in living conditions have come about largely because developmental activities have been concentrated in urban areas and the profits of this development have been shared by comparatively few. Most commercial and industrial concerns have been situated in urban areas. Such operations have provided the tax base necessary for provision of such municipal services as sewage treatment and electric power. Urban areas have exerted greater influence than rural areas on governmental decisions concerning the construction of facilities ranging from hospitals to recreation centers. Urban areas have had both private donors and commercial credit facilities to make possible the construction of private and charitable facilities.

The extent to which the benefits of national development have filtered down to the level of the *barrio* (village) is largely a function of the access of a rural area to urban centers and the relative sizes of these centers. The major centers of national development are on Luzon, especially metropolitan Manila, although such cities as Cebu and Cagayan de Oro provide similar levels of development. Access of any area to these centers depends both on geography and on communication facilities.

In addition to the inferior health, sanitation, and recreational services and facilities in rural areas, educational and employment opportunities were limited, offering rural residents fewer chances for economic and social mobility. Although free from such concerns as congested living conditions and pollution hazards, residents of rural areas had fewer hopes of improving their lot than did urban dwellers.

After World War II, as the disparities between urban and rural living conditions and employment opportunities not only increased but also became more visible, migration to urban areas increased. Between 1960 and 1970 the urban fraction of the population increased from 14 percent of the total population to 20 percent. The annual urban growth rate exceeded twice the annual growth in the total population throughout the decade (see ch. 2). Larger cities attracted the largest proportion of emigrants from rural areas.

The influx of people into urban areas has severely strained the very urban services that stimulated migration. New arrivals are usually willing, however, to accept conditions inferior to those they knew in rural areas in the belief that they will eventually be able to improve their situations. The search for better conditions and opportunities often results in migration from one urban area to another, Manila usually being the eventual target.

Residential patterns based on economic class are readily discernible in larger cities, especially in Manila. The quality of housing, the extent of sanitation facilities and services, and the amount of floorspace per person is higher in such middle-income districts as Ermita, which is the most modernized residential area in Manila proper, than in such working-class neighborhoods as Tondo. Less than 30 percent of all occupied dwellings in certain lower income sections of Manila near the harbor have flush toilets; in most other sections of the city 60 to 90 percent of such structures have flush toilets. Suburban areas often offer the best average levels of facilities.

A major consequence of the urban congestion caused by migration since World War II has been the development of squatter communities on marshy lowlands, empty lots, or unused agricultural land close to urban centers. Housing in these areas is substandard and often constructed of salvaged materials, including cardboard and scrap sheet metal. Water for cooking and drinking must be carried long distances from communal faucets. Many units use kerosine for lighting and fuel, and strings of extension cords sometimes provide hazardous electrical connections. Garbage and human waste are usually wrapped and placed in heaps or disposed of in nearby bays or rivers. The erection of squatter structures over or too close to drainage ditches and riverbanks in Manila seriously complicates flood control.

In the mid-1970s there were efforts to ameliorate the results of rapid urbanization. Among these efforts were government-financed programs and self-help programs with private or minimal governmental funding. There was a critical need for integrated national planning and coordination of these programs. The first steps in this direction had been taken in 1968 by the establishment of pilot urban development planning programs in five cities, of which Baguio was one. These were to serve as guides in overall national planning, but several observers expressed concern over a history of only partial implementation of urban plans.

Progress had been made, however, toward creation of a unified administrative system for metropolitan Manila. Five different proposals detailing boundaries and areas of jurisdiction were still under consideration in 1975, although in the interim President Marcos provided for the integration of essential public services in municipal corporations by means of an executive letter of instruction. The office of general manager for the integrated system and a special committee to determine integrated policy areas were established. In late 1975 Imelda Romualdez Marcos, the president's wife, was declared governor of the new administrative system of Manila.

The squatters had resisted relocation to new areas. Cost analysis in social and monetary terms of such relocation, moreover, indicated that the most efficacious approach might be transformation of these areas rather than their elimination. Most squatters wanted to remain in the houses they had built; they needed help in improving these structures, obtaining city services, and being able to buy the land on which their houses had been built. Such an approach could never provide high-quality housing and would retain indiscriminate mixes of land use, but it could substantially upgrade living conditions.

The government also sought to revitalize the inner city of Manila, an effort that it was hoped would bring higher income families back from the suburbs and upgrade the tax base. Squatter housing had been removed from certain sections of the old Spanish walled city, almost completely destroyed during World War II, and gardens and civic facilities had been established. The area had become a popular tourist attraction.

Efforts designed to stem migration to urban areas included projects to improve conditions in rural areas and the creation of new regional centers to attract future migrants. Secondary or tertiary centers outside metropolitan Manila had been suggested by the Office of the President. Business was being encouraged to situate new facilities outside existing urban areas. Small towns were eligible for special fiscal help under the Village Development Program and were being offered special planning guidance under a pilot project of the National Economic Development Authority. Most of these efforts were newly established and experimental, and in the mid-1970s it was impossible to determine their long-term effect.

HOUSING

The growing scarcity of adequate housing constituted one of the most serious problems faced by the country in the mid-1970s. Official statistics indicated a shortage of about 3.8 million housing units in 1974, and projections indicated that the shortage would increase by almost 500,000 units by the end of 1975. Efforts to combat the situation included both private and governmental programs; in the meantime obtaining adequate housing was beyond the budget of most families. Housing built from such traditional materials as bamboo and various plant fibers, however, although neither durable nor adequate protection in high winds, was inexpensive and quickly constructed.

The total number of housing units reflected in the 1970 census after certain adjustments stood at about 5.6 million. Of these about 37 percent were well constructed. About 83 percent were in rural areas. Comparison with 1960 data shows that the annual growth rate of urban housing units was 4.5 percent and that of rural housing units only 1.0 percent. The amount of well-constructed housing in rural areas had increased from 6 to 28 percent, and construction of comparable quality in urban areas had increased from 40 to 60 percent. Some of the worst housing in rural areas had been replaced, whereas in urban centers housing of the worst quality had increased as a result of migration to urban areas.

The housing situation reflects difficulties in the construction industry as a whole. Although construction technology in the Philippines is ahead of that in many other developing countries in Asia, the construction industry had the lowest growth rate of all industries in the Philippines and was one of the least developed in Asia (see ch. 14). The cost of high-quality construction largely restricted its use to public buildings and the homes of the more affluent in urban areas. Common defects in housing involved faulty corner supports, roof anchors, window and door frames, and wall- and roof-bearing supports. In response to widespread damage to housing caused by typhoons in the early 1970s, special studies were under way in the mid-1970s on design criteria for low-rise housing resistant to wind damage. Funds for these studies were made possible in part by the United States Agency for International Development and the United States National Bureau of Standards.

Social and cultural considerations played a role in housing construction. Certain sites—especially on higher ground and along the banks of waterways—were considered lucky. The orientation of windows and doors in relation to sunlight and wind as well as to open spaces was also believed to bring luck or misfortune. Stairways had to have odd numbers of steps. Interiors were usually open spaces, with curtains to provide minimal levels of privacy. Certain periods of the year were considered luckier than others for beginning a building, and traditional rituals were performed before occupancy.

Home construction in rural areas often followed these practices even in the mid-1970s, and newly arrived migrants often brought to the city traditional concepts regarding housing. This was reflected in both squatter communities and low-income housing. For example, one post-World War II development project of orderly, white-painted, one-level, two-family houses had been transformed radically by their owners into an unorganized community of highly individualized if shabby houses. Although original walls were usually retained to ensure luck, second stories or wings had been added without consideration of building codes but in accordance with traditional preferences. Owners in the project, as is true of most residents in squatter areas, took great pride in the individuality of their houses and would not exchange them for new, modern, better built government housing.

Governmental efforts to provide low-cost housing were limited by budgetary and administrative considerations. Such governmental agencies and offices as the People's Homesite and Housing Corporation (PHHC), the Presidential Assistant on Housing and Resettlement Agency (PAHRA), the Tondo Foreshore Development Authority (TFDA), the Central Institute for the Training and Relocation of Urban Squatters (CITRUS), and the National Housing Corporation (NHC) were involved in various programs. In July 1975 President Marcos created the National Housing Authority by decree in order to coordinate all national housing programs, and the other agencies were dissolved.

Typically, governmental programs involved small-scale projects providing either low-priced land without structures or both land and structures. Increasing interest was shown in stimulating privately supported programs. Firms were offered low-interest-rate loans through the Government Service Insurance System and the Social Security System to finance company housing. The construction of new towns near new sources of employment was also supported. Typical of such efforts was the opening of housing for 122 families in early 1975 at the Kalingagan Relocation Site in Misamis Oriental Province near a new industrial park of firms ranging from a steel mill to cottage industries. The government also sought to stimulate foreign investment in the construction industry. In September 1974 a joint venture with a Japanese firm was established for the production of prefabricated housing units. Materials and equipment were to come from the domestic market. Initial production was scheduled for 2,000 units annually, but subsequent expansion to 4,000 units was projected.

INCOME AND PRICES

Analysis of family incomes in 1971, the most recent year for which comparable statistical information was available in 1975, indicated wide differences in income. The average family income for the country as a whole was ₱3,736 (for value of the peso—see Glossary); the average in urban areas was ₱5,867 and that in rural areas ₱2,818. Metropolitan Manila had the largest average income, ₱7,785, as well as the highest median family income, ₱5,202; the national median was ₱2,454. Other urban areas reported a median income of ₱3,972 compared to ₱1,954 in rural areas. The lowest median family incomes in rural areas were in the eastern Visayan Islands, the Bicol Peninsula, and the Cagayan Valley.

Although national figures for wages were not available, statistics for laborers in industrial establishments in Manila and its suburbs indicated that between 1965 and 1971 wages increased by about 40 percent for skilled labor and about 45 percent for unskilled labor; wages in 1973 compared to 1965 indicated increases of about 55 percent for skilled labor and 68 percent for unskilled labor.

Wage increases in the first half of the 1970s were outpaced by a sudden rise in inflation (see ch. 12). The consumer price index showed an increase of 94 percent by 1973 over 1965 prices, compared to an increase of only 14 percent by 1969 over 1965 prices. Prices in Manila had risen by 88 percent of the 1965 price level. The highest rates of inflation affected the prices of food and clothing. For the first nine months of 1974 prices were 36 percent higher than for the same period in 1973.

When adjustments are made for inflation, real income during the ten years following the mid-1960s declined for many families. Although wages in metropolitan Manila, for example, increased between 1965 and 1973, real income, computed on the basis of consumer price indexes, fell during that same period by about 17 percent and 10 percent for skilled and certain unskilled workers, respectively. When computed on the basis of wholesale price indexes, real income fell by about 29 percent and 23 percent for these groups. Unless wages increased substantially, further erosion of real income was indicated by the differences between the indexes.

The fall in real income was most pronounced in urban areas among middle-income group and unskilled workers, especially those working in unorganized industries and small-scale operations. The self-employed were also vulnerable to erosion of real income. The rural poor who were most affected were those in areas dependent upon one-crop cultivation.

Accompanying the erosion of real income was increased inequality of income distribution during the two decades after the mid-1950s. The median income of the poorest segment of the population failed to rise as fast as the national median. The share of national income obtained by the lowest 20 percent of families fell significantly; an even more noticeable drop took place in the share of the lowest 60 percent of the rural poor (see ch. 12).

The government first established minimum wages by legislation in 1951. Separate rates were set for agricultural and nonagricultural workers, and additional categories were later established. Periodic increases brought the minimum daily wages in 1970 to ₱8 for nonagricultural workers working in companies employing more than five workers and for employees of the central government, ₱6 for workers in establishments employing five or fewer workers, ₱5 for provincial and local government employees, and ₱4.75 for agricultural workers. A more complicated minimum wage system based on differential rates according to industry was subsequently adopted, bringing the minimum for some categories to as high as ₱12. Only one-third of the labor force, however, was employed in jobs with wage structures to which the legislation applied; enforcement was effective in only a few sectors and then generally only in larger companies. Wage ceilings were also established in 1974 for certain categories of employment.

Before 1970 authority to control prices was restricted to temporary action in time of emergencies, such as typhoons, floods, or earthquakes. In an effort to curb inflation, however, the national Price Control Council was established and empowered to prevent hoarding and speculation by fixing the prices of certain essential commodities. The life of the council was extended periodically and in 1975 was further extended until 1977. In 1975 eighteen items were covered, including rice, corn, wheat, and flour; certain cuts of meat; sugar; cooking oil; milk; inexpensive clothing of certain fabrics; kerosine and oil products; soap; basic building supplies, such as plywood and galvanized metal sheets; and school supplies.

FOOD AND NUTRITION

Malnutrition is the most serious health problem among the young and the major contributing cause of illness among the population as a whole. Eating habits, traditional practices in feeding infants, agricultural techniques, food processing, and food costs all contribute to malnutrition.

Practices such as eating with the fingers without previously washing also contribute to such health problems as intestinal parasites.

The Food and Nutrition Research Center of the Philippines recommends daily per capita consumption of about 2,000 calories, including 50 grams of protein and 50 grams of fat. Excluding food exports, such as coconuts and sugar, the country does not produce enough food to meet these levels. Average per capita consumption was estimated in 1970 to be 1,683 calories, including about 47 grams of protein and 22 grams of fat. These figures constitute declines from previous estimates of consumption in the 1960s. About 70 percent of the population lived on the food they produced at subsistence levels.

Surveys conducted in the 1960s by the Food and Nutrition Research Center indicated regional differences in levels of nutrition (see table 5). The highest average caloric intake was in metropolitan Manila, where the average was 90 percent of the recommended daily average; the lowest was in the eastern Visayan Islands region. Although statistics concerning national differences by income level were not available, more affluent families not only were able to buy more food but to some extent purchased different commodities.

The traditional diet relied heavily on wild vegetables, small game, fish, and various forms of waterlife caught in fresh or salt water. The shift from gathering to cultivation, increasing population, and socioeconomic changes during the Spanish and American colonial periods brought an increasing incidence of malnuturition (see ch. 3). By 1900 average caloric and protein consumption had deteriorated to levels little better than those existing in the 1970s, and imports of food, especially rice, were necessary to feed the population. Governmental efforts in the mid-1970s to remedy the problem included projected increases in international donations, local production, and food imports, which, if successful, might achieve the recommended daily average by 1985. In the meantime the

Table 5. Philippines, Protein and Calorie Deficiencies by Region, 1960s

Region	Daily Average Intake (in percent of RDA)*		Households with Less than 70 Percent of RDA* (in percent of households)	
	Calories	Protein	Calories	Protein
Manila and suburbs	90	92	30	20
Southern Tagalog.....................	79	81	28	30
Ilocos and Mountain provinces	88	97	16	15
Cagayan Valley and Batanes Province	81	87	26	21
Eastern Visayan Islands	68	80	47	24
Western Visayan Islands	75	88	38	20
Southwestern Mindanao	74	86	40	16

*Recommended daily average.

126

government was considering such programs as food stamp plans to help redistribute food to the most poorly nourished.

Since World War II the diet has changed in much the same way as it has changed elsewhere. There is growing demand for and consumption of wheat breadstuffs, dairy products, fruits and vegetables, and modern confections. There is, as well, a growing preference for highly polished rather than unmilled or lightly milled rice, for white sugar and white flour instead of brown sugar and whole wheat or rye flour, and for other overprocessed foods that have lost much of their nutritional value.

More than 70 percent of all Filipinos depend on rice for their daily diet, but there are regional variations in food staples and in complementary vegetables and fruit. People in the Visayan Islands, where the soil is less suited to rice cultivation, depend on corn, prepared in much the same way as rice, and migrants from that area have carried their taste for corn to the parts of northern Mindanao where they have settled. The sweet potato and other root crops are the staple foods for people in the mountainous and isolated areas of northern Luzon and are planted and eaten in other areas when rice is scarce.

The main source of protein for most people is fish, and the daily diet is supplemented by a variety of vegetables—eggplant and green beans being the most common—and many kinds of tropical fruit. The diet is generally lacking in nutrients other than carbohydrates, with particular deficiencies in fats and proteins, vitamins A and B$_1$, riboflavin, calcium, and ascorbic acid, which is plentiful in the ordinary raw fruits and vegetables but much of which is lost during food preparation.

In areas where the daily diet consists almost entirely of highly polished rice, during the processing of which the vitamin B$_1$ is destroyed, the incidence of beriberi (a vitamin B$_1$ deficiency disease) is high, not because more nutritious foods are unavailable but because ignorance of basic nutrition prevails. People in ricegrowing areas consider corn and root crops low-status foods and will not eat them, although on the whole they cost less than rice and are more nutritious.

Severe deficiency of vitamin A often results in an eye disease called xerophthalmia. About 27 percent of those afflicted are left blind, and about 59 percent are permanently left with greatly reduced vision. Vitamin A deficiency also affects resistance to disease and protein metabolism and is closely associated with high mortality rates among children.

Feeding habits for infants vary from region to region but often reflect ignorance concerning nutrition. Many mothers stop breast feeding a baby who has diarrhea and give it water remaining from boiling rice, which has almost no nutritional value. Some mothers dilute canned milk with as many as twelve parts of water. Newly weaned children are fed a rice gruel rather than solid foods, such as meat, vegetables, and fruit, in the belief that such foods would give children worms.

Both the Chinese and the Spanish and, to a lesser extent, the Americans and the Japanese have influenced native Filipino ways of preparing food. Everyday meals are quite simply prepared and consist of boiled rice or *bihon* (rice noodles), fried fish, and a kind of vegetable stew, with fruit for dessert. *Sinigang* is a popular way of preparing various kinds of fish or meat by boiling with vegetables and spices.

For special occasions the fare is more elaborate. *Lechon*, the national fiesta dish, is a pig stuffed with banana leaves, tamarind leaves, or boiled rice, roasted whole on a bamboo spit over charcoal, and basted with water. It is served with a sauce made of pig's liver, garlic, onion, and stock. *Adobo* is a chicken or pork dish, often cooked with garlic and bay leaves in vinegar, soy sauce, and cooking oil. *Sugpo* (giant shrimp) and *alimango* (river crab) are boiled in salted water and eaten with a vinegar and garlic sauce.

Patis (fish sauce) and *atchara* (pickled fruit or vegetables) complement many foods. A variety of desserts and snacks, called *kakanin*, are made with rice dough. The most popular of these is *bibingka*, sometimes sweetened with sugar and topped with grated eggs, native cheese, or coconut. *Suman* is a native cake made of glutinous rice, sugar, and coconut milk and cooked in banana leaves, which impart their flavor to the cake.

Native alcoholic beverages include *tuba* (fermented coconut juice), *basi* (fermented sugarcane juice), and the very potent *lambanog* (distilled from fermented rice). Despite the availablility of alcoholic beverages, the incidence of alcoholism is low.

CLOTHING

In most areas men and women wear lightweight, Western-style clothing. Everyday clothing for the working man is usually shorts or loose trousers and a T-shirt for manual labor and slacks and a shirt for less strenuous activities. Women wear either Western-style dresses or, in more rural areas, near-ankle-length wraparound straight skirts and blouses. Very young boys may wear simply T-shirts for protection from the sun, and girls may wear T-shirts and pants or dresses. Clothing is often made at home or by a local dressmaker, although ready-made clothing is available in the cities and is becoming increasingly popular.

The national costume for men is the *barong tagalog*, an elaborately embroidered shirt that hangs outside the pants; for women it is the *mestiza* dress, or *terno*, with its distinctive scooped neckline and butterfly sleeves. This is usually worn for more formal affairs in the cities.

The regional costumes of non-Christian peoples are somewhat different, reflecting different cultural influences (see ch. 4). The Muslim Tausug men may wear skintight trousers, said to be of Hindu origin, whereas the women wear loose, colorful trousers, more Chinese in character. The Maranao Muslims usually wear the *malong*, a large oblong cloth wrapped around the body to serve as a dress for women or a kind of skirt for men. Muslims who have made a pilgrimage to Mecca are distinguished by the white turbans they wear. Some Igorot, Negrito, and Mangyan (Mindoro) wear loincloths, and the women wear lengths of cloth wrapped as dresses or skirts.

HEALTH AND MEDICAL SERVICES

During the nineteenth century smallpox and cholera reached epidemic proportions several times because of increased contact with mainland Asia. The colonial government sought to control these epidemics and was somewhat successful in controlling smallpox. Environmental sanitation, sewer construction, and sanitary water supply systems were also undertaken. The limited health measures introduced by the Spanish in the seventeenth and eighteenth centuries were accessible to only a small minority of the population.

The establishment of the United States presence in the Philippines coincided with the time when great advances in public health were being made in the West, and the Philippines was to share in these advances. Rapid improvements were effected, especially in environmental sanitation and the control of epidemics. The Americans augmented the work of the Spaniards by building more hospitals, sewers, and waterworks and by expanding medical education. Special attention was given to maternal and child care.

The United States introduced into the formal governmental structure an administrative apparatus for improving health standards. It also instituted laws and regulations for health protection, including a sanitation code, pure food and drugs legislation, and laws and regulations governing the teaching and practice of medicine, nursing, dentistry, and pharmacy.

Mass inoculation campaigns were undertaken against a variety of diseases; these campaigns, along with improved environmental sanitation, served to suppress bubonic plague, smallpox, and cholera, although outbreaks still occasionally occurred. Measures were undertaken to improve the dietary habits of the people and to check nutritional disorders, such as beriberi, and such diseases as dysentery, leprosy, and tuberculosis, although all of these remained problems in the 1970s.

In the mid-1970s medical and health services were provided by the Department of Health, the Philippine Medical Care Commission, the chartered cities, and the private sector. Services in urban areas were provided mainly by the private sector and the chartered city authorities. Medical facilities were largely concentrated in urban areas. Rural areas were served largely by the Department of Health and the more recently established Philippine Medical Care Commission. Medical facilities were concentrated in urban areas and reached only about two-thirds of the population.

Traditional Attitudes and Practices

Filipinos have been receptive to modern medical programs and practices without necessarily abandoning their traditional theories of disease and health practices. Provincial immigrants to the cities often maintain certain rural ways of life that are inappropriate in an urban setting. To some extent traditional beliefs persist even among the wealthier, more westernized urban dwellers. Such persons often bring servants to the cities from the provinces who may transmit their traditional beliefs to the children of their employers. Except in the more remote rural areas, however, traditional beliefs and practices were being eroded in the 1970s.

These traditional beliefs frequently hinder the efforts of public health workers, particularly preventive efforts. If people feel well, they see no need to go to clinics for vaccinations or examinations; a dentist may not be consulted until a person has an intense toothache and the tooth must be extracted. When epidemics were a clear and present danger, implementation of public health measures was perhaps easier than in the 1970s, when the emphasis was on prevention, particularly of diseases that people can tolerate, such as malaria, goiter, schistosomiasis, and others that may not even be considered diseases in areas where they afflict almost everyone. People want to be healthy but only in the framework of their own beliefs, and they often hold prescientific concepts regarding disease.

The belief that certain malevolent spirits, departed ancestors, and witches cause sickness and death is widespread, as are precautions taken to ward off such spirits. For example, people hang peppers or herbs outside the house during an epidemic or wear talismans when they travel outside a familiar area. Belief in such outside agents encourages a fatalistic outlook and discourages development of the concept that the individual can change his environment.

If sickness should strike, there are various traditional prescriptions. The patient may be whipped with leafy twigs or subjected to a smoke treatment; various means may be tried to trick the supernatural being into ridding the patient of the sickness. A shaman, or medicine man, who is believed to be in communication with the spirit world, may be called in, although relations with him are colored with fear because his powers are considered dangerous. The shaman's practices are similar in most ways to those used by the people to cure minor ills. Some people treat sickness by sacrificing chickens, pigs, or carabaos.

Pregnancy is thought to be a time of potential danger for the woman but, because the danger is thought to come primarily from supernatural forces, precautions take the form of avoiding contact with the spirits. Certain foods are proscribed during pregnancy for fear that they may cause miscarriage or deformity in the child, but a woman may work in the fields almost until the birth occurs.

A traditional midwife, who has learned her trade by watching someone skilled in its practice, is usually in attendance at the birth of a child, although what she does may be less important than the reassurance she gives the mother. Usually more care is given to the health of both mother and child after birth than before, a fact that may account for the high rate of miscarriage but relatively low rate of postnatal complications in some areas.

Common ills, such as colds and stomachaches, are not attributed to the supernatural. They are treated in various ways: by the family using local plants, by an herbalist who prescribes a variety of herbs for medication, or by a masseur who uses the native technique of massaging or smudging with curative substances. Some traditional cures have been found to be truly effective. These have not been extensively studied in the Philippines; but simple, traditional treatments for indigestion, intestinal worms in children, and minor wounds appear to be useful.

Public health programs that do not require value changes have met with greater success than those that do; for example, the installation of water pipes and drainage systems requires little cooperation on the part of the people, but it often results in a decrease in water-related diseases, such as cholera, typhoid, and malaria. Innovations that complement the traditional system also meet with acceptance; for example, maternity and child care services have spread rapidly and effectively in the Philippines. Modern medical treatment in the form of injections, as opposed to pills, powders, and liquids that require strict adherence to directions, has also met with acceptance, although this acceptance may be compromised by a number of traditional beliefs. For example, if an individual receives the first in a series of inoculations, he may simply regard it as an internal talisman and not bother to complete the necessary series. Another common belief is that good medicine will cure immediately. As a result patients may simply abandon a long-term treatment or one that alleviates the symptoms of a chronic disease.

Interpersonal contact is of the utmost importance to most Filipinos. Many recent immigrants to Manila will forgo the services available at free public clinics and pay cash to herbalists and masseurs in the belief that folk practitioners take more personal interest in their problems. Rural health workers often report that their success begins only after close social ties have been established. Rural Filipinos are loyal not to causes but to persons, which means that any personnel changes in a rural health program may put the program in jeopardy, at least until the newcomer establishes his own personal ties. Most rural health innovators, however, work in the *poblaciones* (the central towns of municipalities); residents of the more isolated *barrios* may seek their services only after all other efforts, including those of the traditional healers, have failed and the patient's condition is serious.

The public school system, which reaches most *barrios*, has been a major agent of change (see ch. 7). The community school program launched in 1949 has undertaken improvement projects in food preparation, child care, hygiene, toilet construction, garbage disposal, drinking water facilities, and others. Most *barrio* improvement projects are connected in some way with the public schools.

Teachers are expected to set examples for others to follow; for example, they are sometimes required to use mosquito netting and to have at least a sanitary outhouse for their use. The communities hold teachers in high esteem and are often moved to copy their actions for reasons of prestige. Educational campaigns against folk medical practices will probably become more effective as modern medical facilities become more widely distributed and accessible.

Organization and Policies

Responsibility for all national health services is vested in the Department of Health. The department was reorganized in 1973 into sixteen divisions under the secretary, who is aided by an under secretary. Among the divisions were the Malaria Eradication Service, the Office of Health Education and Personnel Training, and the Bureau of Quarantine. Three divisions provided administrative services. Other divisions were the Food and Drug Administration, the National Family Planning Office, and the National Nutrition Program. Departmental administration was directed through eleven regional offices headed by regional health directors. Each region contained several provinces, each of which had a health officer under whom there were a number of municipal health officers.

The Bureau of Health and Medical Science was a special division of the department responsible for licensing and standardization of hospitals and all other health facilities including the rural health units (often referred to as RHU), which were the facilities sought out by the majority of the population for medical attention. Initially department policy differentiated between curative services in hospital facilities and preventive programs in local clinics, such as the rural health units. In practice most services were curative rather than preventive.

The total central government expenditure for health services for fiscal year (FY) 1972 was ₱274 million. Although this was somewhat more than twice the allocation for FY 1967, annual expenditures from 1967 to 1972 averaged about 5 percent of total budgetary outlay. In 1972 about 93 percent of the expenditure was for current expenses, and the remainder was for capital expenses. The preponderance of current expenses had also been characteristic of previous years, although the exact percentage for capital costs varied from year to year.

Medical Facilities and Personnel

In the mid-1970s most modern health facilities were operated by the government. Government facilities consisted of hospitals and rural health units. The service operated through a two-way patient referral system. Patients first went to the rural health unit for diagnosis. If a patient required further treatment beyond the capabilities of the local unit, he was referred to a nearby emergency hospital, a provincial hospital, a regional hospital, or one of the national medical centers. Once inpatient care was completed, the patient was referred back to the local rural health unit for outpatient care.

In the operation of this referral system several difficulties were encountered that severely limited the ability of the system to serve the needs of patients. Many of these difficulties were related to the administration of the system. Personnel either failed or were unable to enforce regulations, and many patients claimed difficulties in dealing with referral slips and other paperwork. High-risk patients were not always sent to adequate facilities. Patients released from hospitals tended to return to the hospital outpatient services rather than to the local rural health units.

A sample of patients treated in Rizal Province indicated the existence of various other problems in the health services provided by the government, which reflect to varying degrees problems found throughout the country. Patients cited the long distances and cost of transportation as major deterrents to visiting health facilities before an illness had reached an advanced stage. In addition to perceiving a shortage of personnel, hospital beds, and free medical supplies, patients claimed that the hours facilities were open were selected to serve the preferences of staff members rather than the needs of patients; scheduled hours were irregularly met.

The sample suggested a highly negative attitude toward government health services. Most people felt that private facilities—which only the more affluent could afford—offered far better services. They felt that there were shorter waiting times in private facilities and that greater interest existed in the welfare of patients. Many believed that they received inferior medications at government facilities even though they paid relatively high prices for them.

In 1972 there were 525 hospitals under the Department of Health, thirty-seven hospitals under other government agencies, and 449 private hospitals. These services provided an overall ratio of about 1.5 hospital beds per 1,000 people. The government estimated in 1974 that increases in the number of hospitals since the declaration of martial law had brought the ratio up to 1.7 beds per 1,000 people. It estimated that 22 percent of all hospital facilities, including the largest, were situated in Manila.

In 1972, of the 525 hospitals directly under the department, 239 were classified as general hospitals. Sixteen of these had between 101 and 200 beds, and five had more than 200 beds. About 60 percent had twenty-five or fewer beds. There were eight regional hospitals, to which three hospitals were to be added to provide each of the new administrative regions with such a facility during the mid-1970s. Remaining facilities included eight leprosariums.

Rural health units were first established in 1953. The staff composition of each unit was determined by the size of the municipality in which it was located. Eight different categories were delineated. The lowest category, for municipalities with populations of less than 2,000, was authorized one midwife. The top category, for municipalities with populations of 50,000 and over, was authorized two doctors, four nurses, and four midwives. About 70 percent of the 1,500 units in 1972 were in categories serving populations of between 10,000 and 50,000.

The services actually provided by each unit had not yet met specified requirements by mid-1975. One-third of all units were situated in government-owned buildings; the others were in municipal buildings, multipurpose halls, and a variety of other rented structures. Most were not able to provide full clinical services. About 23 percent of all posts to be filled by doctors and 46 percent of all positions to be filled by nurses were vacant. In order to qualify for local funds, however, the units had more midwives than specified by the central government.

Revision of the categories and modification of personnel levels were proposed by the department in 1973. It was suggested that the number of categories be reduced, that each unit be headed by a physician, and that the staff provided to municipalities with populations of more than 50,000 be increased. An incentive system for health personnel in remote areas was also under consideration, as was a requirement that every medical student spend some time in a rural area before being granted a professional license. Implementation of these proposals was under way but had not been completed by 1975. Suggestions for future consideration included placing workers on the staff of each rural health unit and the establishment of *barrio* health stations.

According to government estimates there were about 13,000 doctors and 20,000 nurses in the country in the mid-1970s. This was a ratio of one doctor per 3,000 people and one nurse per 2,000 people. According to the Department of Health 37 percent of all doctors and 46 percent of all nurses were in Manila. This would indicate one doctor for every 600 people in Manila but only one doctor for every 9,000 people in the provinces. The department maintained that the major problem was maldistribution rather than supply, and it expressed only limited concern about the migration of Filipino medical workers abroad.

Health services in the mid-1970s and proposals for future expansion of medical facilities depended on extensive use of midwives. Training was being provided at more than thirty schools supported by the government and private sources. All schools were under the jurisdiction of the department and were required to be associated with hospital facilities having at least fifty beds. Training followed secondary education and lasted for eighteen months. There were no reliable estimates of the total number of midwives in the Philippines in the mid-1970s. About 3,500 midwives worked for the department, and approximately 1,000 worked for the private sector. Roughly 5,500 women had been trained in midwifery but either were not working or were working in positions for which such education was not a requirement. Projected government expansion of medical facilities would require an additional 2,600 midwives by 1980.

Disease Control and Sanitation

Many diseases that were prevalent in the mid-1970s could best be controlled and eradicated by improved nutrition and environmental sanitation. Accordingly the Department of Health, in conjunction with other public and private agencies, concentrated its efforts on preventive measures. The Long Range Environmental Sanitation Program, begun in 1959, is a concerted effort of many public and private agencies, including the Department of Health, to encourage and help carry out such tasks as the construction of sanitary toilets, the improvement of water supplies and garbage disposal methods, and the inspection of food in public places.

For many years quarantinable diseases were absent from the islands, having been virtually eliminated in the earlier years of the twentieth century, but an epidemic of cholera broke out in September 1961. The Muslim people around Lake Lanao (present-day Lake Sultan Alanto) were most affected by the disease, in part because they refused to stop drinking water from contaminated lakes and rivers and in part because they balked at being inoculated by government health workers, whom they distrusted. The epidemic was further complicated by the reluctance of the administration to admit the seriousness of the outbreak. Mass immunization programs during the middle and late 1960s were initiated, however, and the disease was believed to be largely under control in the mid-1970s.

Communicable diseases remained the major health problem, although the percentage of deaths caused by communicable diseases had declined from about 77 percent in 1923 to about 42 percent in 1972. Four of the ten leading causes of death were communicable forms of pneumonia, tuberculosis, gastroenteritis, and bronchitis. The other leading causes included heart and vascular disease, undiagnosed disease among infants, and malignancies.

Three basic categories of communicable disease were respiratory, gastrointestinal, and viral. Respiratory disease was responsible for about 31 percent of all deaths and about 74 percent of all deaths from communicable diseases; pneumonia alone accounted for about 17 percent of all deaths and 28 percent of all infant deaths. Gastrointestinal diseases were the cause of about 7 percent of all deaths and about 16 percent of all deaths by communicable diseases, including 9 percent of all diagnosed infant deaths. Viral diseases accounted for 2.2 percent of all deaths and 5.2 percent of all deaths caused by communicable disease.

Regional variations in morbidity existed. Malaria was a major disease on Luzon and Mindanao; it was a minor problem on the Visayan Islands.

Filariasis, a parasitic disease transmitted by biting insects, was found in certain provinces such as Laguna, Northern Samar, and Agusan del Sur.

In the mid-1970s modern waste disposal methods, toilet facilities, and safe water supplies were not available to the majority of the population, particularly in rural areas. Most dwelling units obtained water from force pumps, open wells, springs, rivers, or lakes. Only about half the population had access to safe drinking water. Slightly more than one-half of the dwelling units were believed to have toilet facilities. Spitting and urinating by both adults and children whenever and wherever convenient was common even in cities.

The most modern water and waste disposal systems are concentrated in Manila and the surrounding provinces and, to a lesser extent, in provincial capital and the *poblaciones*, but these systems are plagued by severe maintenance problems. For example, in the Tondo district of Manila, a center for low-income rural migrants, most people have access to piped water but, because leaky pipes are rarely repaired, the water is sometimes contaminated, particularly when the pressure is low during the dry season. The migrants do not appreciate the value of maintenance, because in the rural areas it is not considered worthwhile to repair damaged buildings; they are simply replaced. Many of the migrants come from areas on rivers or by the sea where waste and sewage are carried away by currents or tides; in the city they throw rubbish into the streets and run sink drains onto the sidewalks. Thus the migrants' habits, inappropriate to the urban context, result in sanitation problems and promote the spread of diseases.

In the mid-1970s there was growing concern for environmental issues ranging from industrial pollution to the use of agricultural lands for urban development. Manila Bay and nearby rivers were becoming increasingly polluted. Pollution and congestion from motor vehicles were growing problems, especially in Manila, where half of all such vehicles in the country were registered.

PUBLIC WELFARE

Responsibility for the welfare of people unable to take care of themselves has traditionally belonged to the family, ritual kin, or landlord(see ch. 5). Although family consciousness tends to encourage favoritism, particularly on the part of government officials, it relieves the government of a responsibility that it cannot afford. Welfare problems are increasing, however, particularly in cities, where traditional values and obligations are breaking down. Public and private agencies, with the help of international organizations, are taking over some of the welfare responsibility, particularly for industrial and governmental workers and indigents; however, most of these agencies are handicapped by the lack of funds necessary for large-scale programs. Although their programs are, for the most part, restricted to Manila and the nearby provinces, efforts are being made to extend the programs to other areas.

The Social Welfare Administration, established in 1915 as the Public

Welfare Board, provides both emergency relief in the wake of natural disasters and services for the needy. Most of these are aimed at providing people with the tools for self-care. Other programs included services for widows, abandoned wives and their children, and children with a variety of social and medical problems. Rehabilitation programs for the handicapped were also maintained. In addition to regular government programs, a special agency was created in 1974 to alleviate conditions in the Filipino Muslim areas. Government programs often involved cooperation with private relief agencies, such as the Catholic Relief Services of America and the Cooperative for American Relief Everywhere (CARE).

The Social Security System of the Philippines was authorized by law in 1954 and began operations in 1957. The goal of the system was universal coverage. Legally the system covered all wage and salary workers between the ages of fifteen and sixty; a separate system—the Philippine Government Service Insurance System—was maintained for government workers. Although more than 80 percent of the wage and salary workers were nominally registered in the system, wage and salary workers constituted less than 15 percent of the work force. Those not covered were primarily tenant farmers, itinerant workers, domestics, self-employed persons, and professionals. Those covered were mainly industrial and government workers and their families, who received benefits for death, disability, sickness, and retirement at old age and could be granted housing, salary, and educational loans.

Revenue for the system was based on a payroll tax levied jointly on employees and employers. The employer pays a decreasing percentage of the tax as the employee moves up the salary scale. During 1974 the system earned ₱173.3 million, an increase of 35 percent over the previous year, and paid benefits of ₱130.6 million, an increase of 44 percent over the previous year. Projections indicated that the system would need government subsidy unless modified.

In 1969 the Philippine Medical Care Act was passed, and the first phase of the Philippine Medicare System was implemented. Immediately affected were all employees under the Social Security System and the Government Service Insurance System, covering in 1973 about 3.8 million workers. On January 1, 1973, medical coverage was also extended to legal dependents of these workers, bringing total coverage to almost half of the population. Coverage of the program included hospitalization and surgical expenses as well as limited periods of medical confinement. Not covered were dental services, cosmetic surgery, optometric services, psychiatric care, normal obstetrical services, and simple diagnostic services. Members contributed to the system on the basis of income. After a claim was filed, separate checks were remitted to the hospital, attending physician, and pharmaceutical outlet involved in caring for a patient.

LEISURE ACTIVITIES

The most important religious and social occasion for most people is the annual fiesta held on the feast day of the town's patron, usually the saint after whom the town's church is named (see ch. 8). The fiesta is usually held sometime after the harvest, when people are relatively well off, and not during either the rainy season or Holy Week when it would be difficult to celebrate with appropriate festivity. The days and weeks preceding the fiesta are spent cleaning, repairing, and making other preparations. Houses and yards are decorated with garlands of flowers, streamers of paper, and swags of brightly colored cloth. It is the season for reestablishing community and kin ties and a time when the status and prestige of the whole community and individuals within the community are demonstrated and reinforced. Hostesses pride themselves on displays of food and gracious acts of hospitality. Relatives from other parts of the islands are drawn to the town for the fiesta.

Fiestas alternate joyous celebration and religious rituals. Activities often commence with novenas, rosaries, and litanies. The ringing of bells and shooting of firecrackers often follow. The image of the patron saint, which usually is kept in a special niche in the parish church, is carried on the shoulders of townsmen followed by devotees through the streets and back to the church. The procession consists of barges or small boats if the town is near a river or other body of water. A fiesta queen is selected from local nominees through a contest that may begin several weeks before the fiesta and may cost a good deal of money. On the night selected for the coronation of the queen an all-night dance is held.

Although festivities are more in evidence during the fiesta period, the religious side of the celebration is essential. Thus during times of misfortune—as in the wake of a destructive typhoon or flood—the festivities are eliminated, but the religious ritual is kept intact. Festive occasions are also associated with baptisms, confirmations, and weddings.

Other more strictly traditional Christian holidays are solemnized or celebrated throughout the year. The Christmas season begins on December 16 with the first of a series of early morning masses and processions representing the search of Mary and Joseph for a place to stay, which continue until December 24. On Christmas Day people visit relatives and celebrate in a quiet but festive manner. One sees in virtually every home at Christmas an elaborate paper lantern (farol) shaped like a star, bell, flower, or miniature structure. January 6, the traditional Feast of the Three Kings, marks the end of the Christmas season.

The Easter season begins with special services in Lent. Ash Wednesday is solemnized by fasting and prayers. On Palm Sunday palm fronds woven in intricate patterns and tied with colored paper and flowers are blessed by priests and hung by parishoners over windows and doors. Holy Week is also solemnized, although church authorities disapprove of the penitential scourging that flagellants sometimes perform throughout the week. In many villages passion plays are performed on Good Friday, and special services commemorate the seven last words of Christ. On

Easter almost everyone goes to church, as they do during fiestas and the Christmas season.

Muslim communities celebrate the new year on the first day of the tenth month of the Islamic lunar calendar. It is preceded by Ramadan, a thirty-day period of fasting. Gifts, cards, and special greetings are exchanged, but much of the day is devoted to sports and games. In the evening there is either a musical performance or a literary reading. On the tenth day of the twelfth month of the Islamic calendar, Muslims who have made the pilgrimage to Mecca celebrate by praying in the mosque, visiting friends, and eating special delicacies. The first or second week of June is celebrated to mark the birthday of the prophet Muhammad. Religious processions, feasting, professional dance performances, and sports events are part of the festivities.

National holidays are becoming increasingly popular, especially in Manila and the surrounding provinces, and they are usually noted in public schools. The most important are Rizal Day (December 30), National Heroes' Day (November 30), Bataan Day (April 9), and Independence Day (June 12), which commemorates the day the Philippines declared independence from Spain in 1898. July 4, the day of independence from the United States in 1946, is commemorated as Philippine-American Friendship Day. Parades are often held in honor of these occasions.

Tourism has become a new pastime for the more affluent. Sights in Manila and Baguio are most popular, but battlegrounds from World War II are also visited. Many families enjoy spending their leisure time with relatives and neighbors or going to motion pictures. Men attend cockfights, gamble with friends, or play volleyball or basketball, favorite sports throughout the islands. Playing tennis, visiting museums and art galleries, and involvement in various social and professional organizations and charity groups are also pastimes of the middle and upper classes, especially in urban areas, as is going to nightclubs, intimate bars, and restaurants.

CHAPTER 7

EDUCATION, MASS COMMUNICATIONS, AND THE ARTS

In defense of his declaration of martial law on September 21, 1972, President Ferdinand E. Marcos advanced the concept of a democratic revolution for the Philippines designed to save the republic from subversion and to rectify the ills of society. Plans for the New Society envisioned by the president included modification of the political, economic, and social systems of the country. Various social and economic programs were included under the Four Year Development Plan (1974–77) (see ch. 12; ch. 13). The creation of the New Society, however, continued in 1975 to await the formation of a national culture in which all Filipinos could participate and with which all Filipinos could identify. The development of a new national culture and associated attitudes, skills, and forms of expression is a process that in most societies takes several generations. Compressing the process into one decade, even if possible, would make heavy demands on Philippine national resources.

Responsibility for the formulation of this culture and its attitudes and skills fell to a diverse group of individuals ranging from government officials to members of the artistic community. For some the process represented part of a concerted effort guided by governmental policies; others contributed in a less coordinated way through individual leadership in the search for national identity. These efforts did not always reflect a consensus. The facilities, programs, and activities with which these individuals were associated were generally in urban areas, especially in Manila, and they usually held positions making them an elite segment of society. The ability and motivation of such an urban elite to create a meaningful national culture for the majority of the population which was rural, was thus restricted. A similar urban-rural division was reflected in the educational system.

State support for cultural expression, for which specific provision was made in the 1973 Constitution, ranged from the construction of cultural facilities to funds for the performing arts and cultural festivals. National cultural policy included both the preservation and the development of cultural expression. Revitalization of traditional forms and themes rather than alienation from traditional cultures was implied. Although the traditional cultures contained many similarities, their incorporation into a new national culture was complicated by regional difference such as language and especially by discontinuities between urban and rural life.

The educational system was designated the institution primarily responsible for instruction in the ideology and skills necessary for the New Society. Reform of the system under way in the mid-1970s gave increased emphasis to technical and vocational training, the promotion of desired cultural values, and the development of national consciousness. The professed goal was promoting an accelerating rate of economic development and social progress as well as maximizing participation by all of society in the benefits of this growth and progress.

The role of the mass media in the New Society was restricted on several accounts. Although geography and linguistic variations had tended to limit the growth of a national press or broadcasting system, before the institution of martial law the Manila press had become a vibrant force containing both respected editorial and sensational elements. Government restrictions imposed in 1972 reduced the role of the press as a critic of the New Society and led to immoderate praise of government activities and policies. As a result the government felt that the press had become too laudatory and sought more balanced coverage, although still within a framework of self-imposed censorship.

The dissemination of printed information was facilitated by a relatively high rate of literacy, somewhat qualified by the multiplicity of languages (see ch. 4). English had been the language of the Philippines while it was under United States political control. Pilipino, a language based on Tagalog, was declared the national language in 1939; English, however, remained the principal language of the press, radio, government, trade, and commerce. The multiplicity of languages has been a source of difficulty for the educational system. Instruction during the first two years of primary education is in the local vernacular; students are required to study both English and Pilipino, which are taught as formal courses during the first two years. Beginning in the third grade instruction is given in English, and the local vernacular sometimes is used as an auxiliary. After independence there appeared to be increasing popular pressure to make Pilipino the language of instruction, and this goal was incorporated into official educational policy in the early 1970s.

ARTISTIC EXPRESSION

Arts and Society

Artistic expression in the Philippines in the mid-1970s contained a diversity of form and content reflecting indigenous innovations as well as contact with external cultures. Artistic traditions were not an assimilated whole but more a layering of cultural contributions. The process was sometimes dysfunctional, especially the inclusion of certain Western forms, or internally contradictory. Discontinuities existed between different regions—especially between Muslim and Christian areas, between rural and urban areas, and between different social classes. The vitality of the arts both as a reflection of, and as a means of increasing, national identity was considerably weakened by these discontinuities.

Artistic expression as it evolved among the earliest peoples who occupied the archipelago was still reflected in the iconography of groups living in the more remote mountainous areas (see ch. 4). These people and their culture were largely displaced by the arrival of later migrants from Southeast Asia whose Hinduized culture provided the base from which pre-Hispanic culture on the islands evolved (see ch. 3).

Artistic expression in the culture founded by these chiefly Malay migrants served both aesthetic and functional social needs. The survival of certain forms and themes from this period into the twentieth century occurred as a result of their close association with the social fabric and practical needs of everyday life. Most vital and enduring were the performing arts, including dance, music, and oral literature, which were used to pass sacred beliefs and myths from generation to generation. Children were thus instructed in the norms of the community, and all members of society were given guides for behavior and interaction. Artistic expression to some extent also served to delineate and define sexual roles. The performing arts communicated ideal sexual attributes and approved kinds of behavior. Certain rituals for courting of maintaining family honor were found among artistic forms. Men and women had specialized roles in the production of certain crafts, and some forms of ritual music were performed only by one sex.

Varying degrees of sophistication developed in techniques used to make pottery, fabrics, jewelry, and metal; glassmaking and iron smelting were established as early as the first century A.D. Some of these crafts along with raw materials were traded with Chinese and other merchants who plied the western coastlines. The cultural consequences of this trade were only poorly understood by historians.

The sociopolitical order of the pre-Hispanic period, however, did not follow the Hindu tradition of a centralized state having a major cultural center. Each *barangay* (see Glossary) consisted of thirty to 100 families and was largely self-sufficient and usually isolated from the next village. This pattern and dependence on a subsistence economy created neither need or time for the construction of monumental structures of stone nor the evolution of visual art forms to decorate such structures. This pattern in conjunction with geography also provided for regional variations that diverged from the basic model brought by the Malay migrants.

During the sixteenth century artistic expression was modified on certain southern islands in the archipelago by the effective establishment of Islam. The Islamic prohibition of graphic representation of animate objects, an emphasis on both written and oral forms of religious scripture and related mythological accounts, and new musical traditions were introduced. These new approaches, although they did not eradicate the traditional cultural base, did create a distinctive character of artistic expression in Islamic areas.

The sixteenth century also marked the arrival and establishment of the

Spanish in the archipelago. Although they did not attempt to transform the traditional culture, their demands for labor and food initially disrupted the preexisting sociopolitical order. Certain traditional forms of artistic expression lost their meaning and disappeared; others lost their vitality and deteriorated.

New forms and themes were provided by the Spanish clergy in their attempts to convert the people to Christianity. Roman Catholicism, however, was not directly assimilated by the people but was merged with indigenous beliefs and practices to form a syncretic system (see ch. 8). Thus the observance of holy days and saints' days became occasions for fiestas and frivolity into which traditional forms and themes were incorporated along with those introduced by the church. Localized differences and village isolation from the center of Hispanic culture in Madrid were intensified because the Spanish clergy served as the agents of the colonial government and were the only contact the local population had with Europeans. On the basis of their Latin American experiences, the clergy sought to isolate the population from economic penetration by the Spanish in Manila. They served as principal censors of artistic expression in rural areas. As a result the majority of the population had little opportunity to experience European culture, and the development of a transitional culture was blocked.

By the end of the nineteenth century an indigenous elite had developed in provincial towns. Ties between this elite and the land they held in rural areas provided a potential means of building a transitional culture between varied traditional cultures and the Spanish culture of Manila and other growing urban areas. Families belonging to the elite began to sponsor brass bands, art exhibitions, and literary activities, and a knowledge of European artistic expression became a symbol of status and social mobility.

After 1910 the economic interests of the provincial elite increasingly began to shift to urban areas, especially Manila. Their residential patterns also began to shift to Manila and other urban areas, Western forms of artistic expression and related cultural and educational facilities became concentrated primarily in Manila, and the transition between rural and urban culture was disrupted. Western art forms became associated with progress and modernization. Competitiveness in the arts became a point of national pride among the elite. The resulting discontinuity between urban and rural areas and between upper and lower classes remained an obstacle to the creation of a national culture in the mid-1970s.

In the early 1970s the vitality and sensitivity of artistic creativity and performance in Manila had become internationally recognized. Supported and patronized by Imelda Romualdez Marcos, wife of the president, new facilities for the arts were constructed, and appreciation of the arts, including revitalized traditional and rural forms, was encouraged. These activities were still largely concentrated in urban areas, notably Manila, where attendance at various cultural functions and exhibitions seemed to be incumbent on those who sought to demonstrate their support for the new order. It appeared in the mid-1970s that such cultural expression continued to suffer from the lack of a broadly based national audience. Within the urban framework itself there was an absence of salutary criticism.

Literature

By the time the Spanish arrived in the sixteenth century, the Filipinos had an alphabet and were writing on bark and polished bamboo. The written literature that has survived contains descriptions of religious rites, lists of animals, various business dealings, and two legal codes. The Maragatas Code is thought to have been written about A.D. 1250 by King Maragatas, and the Kalantiaw Code by King Kalantiaw is dated 1433.

The oral literature of pre-Hispanic times consisted of a large body of folktales, mythology, and epic poems that were passed on in the local dialects from generation to generation; many continue to be popular. Although a few folktale cycles are indigenous to the Philippines, most oral literature draws from Hindu, Malayan, Muslim, and Chinese literature. Folktales relating the adventures of the ape and tortoise, for example, originating in Indonesia, are widespread in Mindanao and Luzon.

The *hudhud* and the *alim* are epic poems chanted at ceremonies for the dead or for rice harvests by poets of the Ifugao people of the northern Luzon mountains. The narration may take several nights, for it may cover the origin of the Ifugao, their religious beliefs, and tales of the lives of their mythical heroes. The Maranao Muslims on Mindanao have the *darangen*, an epic song believed to have existed before the spread of Islam to the Philippines. It relates the origins of the Maranao, how their enchanted city sank into the sea, how a princess was abducted and fought for, and various other legends. Some chapters, thought to be the oldest, are full of archaic words. Others, containing Islamic words and ideas, Arab words, and a reference to the Castilians, show that the *darangen* has been growing for over 1,000 years. Other non-Christian peoples who have preserved their ancient narrative poems are the Sulu Muslims, the Subanum of Mindanao, and the Tagbanuwa of Palawan. Some Christianized peoples also have epics, notably the people of Panay, Ilocos, and Bicol Peninsula.

Some regional differences are apparent in the folklore. The mountain tribes of northern Luzon have myths about the repopulation of the world after a flood but none about the origin of the world. The Mandaya of Mindanao tell similar myths, but the survivors of the flood differ from those of the Luzon myths. The creation of man is pictured in different way; for example, in Tagalog myths man and woman originate miraculously from a hollow bamboo stalk or an egg; certain non-Muslim groups of Mindanao tell of a creator using various materials, such as earth, wax, or grass, to create man and woman.

Written literature was stimulated by the arrival of the Spanish and their efforts to convert the Filipinos to Christianity. The Spanish introduced printing and wrote works mainly of a religious nature in indigenous languages and Spanish. By the beginning of the seventeenth century a limited number of Filipinos had been educated sufficiently by the Spanish to engage in scholarship. Most of their works concerned linguistics.

Until the nineteenth century the most popular works written by Filipinos usually followed one of the two kinds of metrical romances introduced by the Spanish, the *corrido* and the *awit*. The *corrido* was used in Mexico to recount current events, but in the Philippines it became associated with the fantasies and legends of European origin; the *awit* was a similar work. Most of the metrical romances were secular, although a few dealt with the lives of the saints.

Toward the middle of the nineteenth century a new kind of literature evolved as a reflection of profound social changes, the deepening Filipino frustration over Spanish oppression and discrimination, and the growing demand for clerical and political equality (see ch. 3). These trends were epitomized in the views of a new group of educated, westernized Filipinos, the *ilustrados* (enlightened ones). Their feelings were first expressed in poetic form. One of the earliest poems, patterned on Spanish metric models, was *Florante at Laura*, written in 1838 by Francisco Balagtas. It is considered the foremost Filipino epic for its expression through political satire of the national desire for political freedom. Another example is *Filipinas*, a lyric poem that was written by José Palma and later became the national anthem.

One of the most gifted and highly revered writers of the late nineteenth-century reform movement was José B. Rizal. He had personally experienced the abuses and injustices perpetrated by Spanish religious and civil authorities. While studying philosophy and medicine in Madrid he started his first political novel, *Noli Me Tangere* (translated into English as *The Social Cancer* but known to all Filipinos as the *Noli*). He had hoped to rally the sympathies of Filipino nationalists in Spain to collaborate on a symposium describing conditions throughout the islands but, failing this, he decided instead to write a satirical novel. Through it and its sequel, *El Filibusterismo* (The Reign of Greed), known as the *Fili*, Rizal attempted to open the eyes of the Spanish to the mistakes and injustices being committed in their name in the Philippines and the eyes of the Filipinos to their real condition.

The publication of the *Noli* in 1887 had a dramatic effect; Rizal was immediately recognized by the Spanish and his fellow countrymen, both at home and in Spain, as the leader of a nationalist movement for reform. The openly anticlerical tone of the book stirred the Filipinos' resentment

146

toward the friars, already keenly felt; and the ridicule of the governing officials angered the Spanish, so that in the year of its publication the *Noli* was declared heretical and subversive by a jury of the University of Santo Tomas.

Subsequently a government board of censorship recommended that the *Noli* be banned in the Philippines. Persons found to have a copy of the book were considered disloyal to Spain. Rizal was forced to leave the country, but he continued his reform efforts abroad while encouraging scholarship in Philippine history and culture. Upon his return in 1892 he was banished to Mindanao, where he spent years under constant surveillance, practicing medicine and teaching. When the Philippine Revolution broke out in 1896, Rizal was accused of inspiring it and was publicly executed on December 30. He became a national hero, and his works, which have been translated into many languages, have become required reading in the education system.

Spanish, Tagalog, Cebuano, and Ilokano remained the principal literary languages during the early years of the American occupation, although for business, government, and education English was spoken. For a time patriotic essays and poems dominated the literary output of Filipino writers, but by 1900 the novel, in Tagalog, was beginning to appear serialized in periodicals. Novels in the Ilokano and Pampangan languages preempted the popularity of the earlier essays and poetry and dominated the scene for ten years.

Despite heroic attempts to sustain it, however, the novel gradually declined in importance and was succeeded by the short story. As early as 1910 short stories in English appeared in locally published periodicals, many of which offered prize money for literary contributions. At the same time short stories in Spanish, Tagalog, the languages of the Visayan Islands, and other languages were widely published and read. For the first two decades of the American occupation short stories in English suffered from a stilted style but, after Philippine authors mastered the language, this handicap was overcome.

By the 1930s a large group of distinguished Filipino writers was active in poetry, the essay, the short story, and an attempt to revive the novel. Literature in Spanish had declined as English usage became more widespread, and except for a small group of writers producing in Tagalog the vernaculars were seldom used for literary expression. The flowering of Philippine letters in the late 1930s was cut off, however, by World War II and the Japanese invasion.

During the Japanese occupation (1942–45) three Filipino writers commanded attention in the United States. José Garcia Villa, who had become famous in the 1930s for his short stories, was the greatest of the Filipino writers in English. His book of poetry, *Have Come, Am Here*, was published in New York in 1942 and received warm praise from American and British critics. Carlos P. Romulo, who served his apprenticeship writing English from 1910 to 1920, produced a series of novels based on wartime experiences. Carlos Bulosan wrote short stories in English that were later collected in *The Laughter on My Father*.

The two best known postwar writers were Nick Joaquin and N.V.M. Gonzalez, both of whose stories and poetry have been published in England and the United States, winning substantial praise from critics. Joaquin in particular writes deeply moving stories, sometimes touching on the supernatural, that make the reader feel as if he were experiencing the incidents. Joaquin was considered the foremost of contemporary writers in the 1960s and as such was something of a model for younger postwar writers, such as Andrés Cristobal Cruz and Pacifico N. Aprieto. Both pupils of Gonzalez when he was teaching at the University of the Philippines in 1961, Cruz and Aprieto collaborated on a collection of stories about the Tondo district of Manila. They show a life of grueling poverty and sadness, relieved by moments of tenderness among the characters and insights into their personalities.

By the beginning of the 1970s Philippine literature possessed a social vitality that sought to comment on the meaning of concrete realities in Philippine society. Although the declaration of martial law in 1972 did not affect the quantity of literature produced in the country, it did seem to affect both its quality and its focus. Themes shifted from social comment to a search for self-awareness and personal identification. Associated themes included the discernment of appearance from reality and the glorification and romanticization of the countryside. The picture represented in these works was an abstraction rather than a reflection of contemporary Philippine society. Alienation from, rather than leadership in the creation of the New Society was characteristic of the mood of these works.

Drama

Before the arrival of the Spanish there was no independent dramatic tradition. Short representations of everyday life or scenes from mythology, however, were frequently incorporated in performances of dance, music, and song. In an effort to convert the population to Christianity the Spanish introduced miracle plays in which Bible stories were acted out to music. These proved very popular and became the basis of dramatic forms still preserved.

The most popular religious dramatic form is the *sinakulo*, performed during Lent either by local amateurs or by touring groups of professionals. These plays are not restricted to depictions of the Passion and often include scenes going back to the Creation. Rehearsals start at the beginning of Lent, and the play is shown during Holy Week. A stage is usually set up in a prominent place in the *barrio;* the actors wear costumes, and the dialogue is sung and spoken in verse. In the wealthier *barrios* and rural towns professional groups may present the *sinakulo*. These actors may assume the same roles each year and often are succeeded by their sons and daughters, whom they have trained to carry on the tradition. The stage and costumes are as elegant as the townspeople can afford, for the *sinakulo* is a community project, and the expenses are shared.

The *pabasa ng pasiyon*, frequently shortened to *pabasa*, is the chanting of the Passion in rhymed verse. Each major linguistic group has its own *pabasa*. In Tagalog the most famous was written by Mariano Pilapil, a secular priest and teacher early in the nineteenth century. His *pabasa*, entitled *Kasaysayan ng Pasiyong ni Hesukristong Panginoon natin* (History of the Sacred Passion of Jesus Christ Our Lord), is about 300 pages long and encompasses the Creation, the life of Christ, and the crowning of Mary as queen of heaven. The *pabasa* is chanted before a richly decorated altar, usually by women, some of whom are famous locally for their singing ability. It may take place in the *barrio* chapel or in a private home and may be spread out over a week or last only forty-eight hours.

Two other dramatic forms to evolve under the Spanish were the more secular *moro-moro* and the *zarzuela*. Both are informal, performed by local groups or traveling amateurs, and still very popular, though somewhat changed. The *moro-moro* tells a love story against a background of the Christian-Moorish struggle in which the Christians always win. The *zarzuela* is a kind of folk opera in three acts and has a special style of delivery called *indayog* in which the actors pitch their voices higher than ordinary speech. The higher pitch and a conventionalized rising and falling intonation accentuate the rhythm. The *zarzuela* popularized the *kundiman*, a Tagalog love song, for folk songs and dances are used to enliven the drama.

The young playwrights of the late nineteenth and early twentieth centuries attempted to do away with the *moro-moro*, which they considered obsolete, bombastic, and vulgar. Their efforts were opposed by *moro-moro* troupes and popular opinion. The form remained popular in the 1970s and has been adopted for motion pictures in Tagalog and as an advertising device for commercial firms.

An interesting change took place in the *zarzuela*, brought about by the Philippine Revolution and the beginning of the American administration. It gradually became a vehicle for public opinion in which young playwrights presented their views on current topics, such as divorce, marriage between Filipinos and Americans, and separatism in Mindanao. Songs from the *zarzuelas* of the 1920s are still sometimes heard.

After World War II, when radio and television became popular, the old *moro-moro* and *zarzuela* dramas became the source of various popular operettas and plays. Radio drama in particular centered almost entirely on soap opera, although occasionally serious plays were tried. The age-old themes were given a few modern touches in order to sell the sponsor's product, but in essence they remained the same: the poor people were the good and noble-hearted, and the rich were grasping and greedy; in the conflicts between them, the poor, good people always won.

Since this formula was eminently pleasing to both the audience and the sponsor, more sophisticated kinds of drama were not given serious attention.

In addition to the popular preference for comedy or melodrama, the development of serious, formal theater was inhibited by inadequate facilities and training programs, a low economic return to playwrights for their work, and the existence of a thriving domestic motion picture industry. The first step toward the establishment of legitimate theater occurred in 1954 when the Dramatic Philippines, a comic theater company, split, and the Barangay Theater Guild was established. This company produced both radio and stage plays by Filipino writers as well as popular versions of English-language classics.

During the late 1960s interest in formal theatrical forms increased considerably. A high point in the support for theater occurred in late 1969 when the stage facilities of the new Cultural Center of the Philippines opened. Productions offered in the first years of operation included both traditional Philippine and Western theatrical forms and contemporary experimental theater. Popularization of the theater as an art form was initiated in conjunction with the Philippine Educational Theater Association.

The declaration of martial law had a marked effect on the theater. Reflecting the reaction of the literary field as a whole, theater turned to an obsessive search for national identity. The search for roots and cultural heritage took the theater back to traditional Philippine forms. Works dating from the beginning of the twentieth century revived. Some controversy arose over the meaningfulness of the revival of these forms. Some critics saw their vitality as tied to the social setting in which they had been created and that no longer existed; they suggested that their transformation into the contemporary social setting might alter their original character.

Music and Dance

Self-expression through music and dance is an integral part of Philippine social life. The ability to improvise and harmonize are highly valued. Musical forms include folk traditions and Western classical forms. The most popular and pervasive are eclectic. Music is played and sung as accompaniment to all kinds of work and leisure activities and is not limited to professional musicians, for nearly all young people can play some instrument and sing.

As in literature, music rooted in the pre-Hispanic period shows the influences of other cultures, particularly Indonesian and Malaysian. There is a wide variety of musical instruments, including stringed, wind, and percussion, that are played separately or in combinations. The nose flute, which is played by blowing through the nostrils, has such a delicate sound that it is ideal for serenading. It is used during courting by some of the peoples of northern Luzon. Conventional flutes of bamboo and mouth harps of bamboo or brass are similar to instruments believed to have developed first in Malaysia. In Jolo and to the south two kinds of flute are played—a flute with six holes and a double-reed flute that also has six holes. Other instruments include gongs and bells, rattles, and a variety of stringed instruments.

In some areas music is bound by ritual. The Ibaloi of Luzon play imported brass or bronze gongs, handmade drums, and *kolas* (two pieces of iron struck together) at ceremonies. For leisure playing the Ibaloi like the *kambatong* (a coconut-shell guitar), the bamboo flute, and the *kading* (a brass mouth harp). The women play a bamboo sounder while walking to and from the fields. Songs are classified by the Ibaloi as sacred songs *(mang-ay-yang)*, drinking songs for men, funeral dirges, or songs often sung around the house for pleasure. Although the words are extemporaneous and recount experiences in the singers' lives, each of the four kinds of song must be sung only on the appropriate occasion. Sacred songs must be sung at a certain point in the ritual by a specific number of people and may not be sung at any other time.

Folk songs are usually group songs, and many originated as dances or as accompaniments to dances, such as the *kumintang* of the Tagalog. Each ethnolinguistic group has its own folk songs, some of which were written by known composers; some are ascribed to various composers, and some were originally family property and have been handed down. A few modern love songs have acquired a permanent place in folk music.

Vocal music originating in the pre-Hispanic period is divided into at least six styles: love and courtship songs, work songs, ceremonial songs, sacred songs, joking songs, and funeral dirges. The joking song of the Samal in the Sulu Islands is called *tenis-tenis*. It is improvised by the singer or singers, usually joking about the people present but sometimes simply telling a story. It is sung in consecutively rhyming four-line verses. The singers are usually accompanied by a *gabbang* (xylophone) made of bamboo, metal, or wood and having fourteen to twenty notes.

The *kundiman*, or Tagalog serenade, is a Christian Filipino love song that became part of the comic theater introduced by the Spanish late in the nineteenth century. The first part of the *kundiman*, plaintive and in a minor key, is followed by a second part that is lilting and gay. The Visayan serenade, called the *balitaw*, is like the *kundiman*. In Negros Occidental Province the serenade is a poem recited to a guitar accompaniment and is called a *balak*. English or Spanish love songs are also used for the serenade in all the lowland areas of the Philippines.

A wide variety of dance forms exists. Dancers often accompany themselves in song or with drums, bells, or gongs, or they may be accompanied by a *musikong bumbong* (a bamboo band consisting of string, wind, and percussion instruments made of bamboo). Aspects of daily life are acted out in dance, such as rice planting and harvesting, sowing, winnowing, and threshing.

The principal pre-Spanish foreign influences on the dance were East

Indian, especially noticeable in Mindanao. A Muslin wedding dance, the *kandingan*, for example, displays these influences in the bent knees turned outward and the fingers held stiffly together except for the thumb. In the *sua-sua* a couple holds an open fan in each hand while dancing. Other Indian influences can be traced in north-central Mindanao, where bells are attached to the dancers' knees or ankles and provide the only musical accompaniment, and in Cotabato Province, where the hand movements are stiff and formal. Such East Indian influences are limited mostly to Mindanao and Sulu. The dances of Luzon and many of the mimetic dances throughout the islands are apparently basically indigenous.

The movements of the Philippine rail, a small wading bird related to the crane family, as it runs between grass stems along riverbanks and swampy areas are pantomimed in a dance called the *tinikling*. The *tinikling* is an especially fascinating and popular dance in which a couple holds a pair of bamboo poles parallel and close to the ground. As they strike the poles together in rhythm to accompanying music or tap them on wooden crosspieces, another couple dances between and beside them, faster and faster, trying not to let the poles catch their ankles, which causes great merriment.

The indigenous body of music and dance was enriched by the introduction of Christianity and the music of the church, but probably the secular music and dance of the West had a greater impact. The Filipinos accepted with delight new musical instruments (such as the Spanish guitar), European scales and harmonies, the courtly dances and, later, Western popular music and dance.

Over the years a brass band contest has become traditional in the *barrios* and towns at fiesta time. For this occasion the townspeople invite two groups of musicians from different *barrios* to attend the festival. When they are in position opposite each other in the plaza, one band begins to play; when it stops, the other one begins. Throughout the festival, which may last from three to seven days, the bands alternate, trying to outdo each other in volume, brilliance, and repertoire. Everything is played from memory—selections from Italian opera, Hungarian rhapsodies, and the most pyrotechnic Italian overtures. The winner is the band still able to play when the festival ends. The result, however, is usually a tie, as no band will admit to being second in variety of selections, dazzling technique, or wind.

In the early twentieth century popular songs and dances from the United States and Latin America threatened to obscure the folk music of the islands, particularly when the amplifier, record player, and motion picture came. The record player and amplifier, to the dismay of many band and orchestra musicians, became widely used for social and school functions and provided music in dance halls. In 1934 a committee from the University of the Philippines toured the islands, filming and recording some of the folk music and dance before they completely disappeared. The exhibition that they gave the following year was so enthusiastically received by the public that folk songs and dances were then included in concerts and festivals. The *kundiman* is often played as an encore at classical concerts in Manila.

Although performances of classical Western music have been an integral part of cultural life in Manila and certain other urban areas, support for symphonic music rested on a narrow base. The theory of Western music was taught in elementary schools, but few children in rural areas had an occasion to hear classical works performed except on radiobroadcasts. A few Filipino composers were modeling works on contemporary Western forms, and the repertoire of the Philippine National Symphony Orchestra was largely Western.

Spanish dances and European ballet were quickly assimilated; some were taken into the repertoire without change, and others became the basis for new dances. The *pandango sa ilaw* (candle dance) is a variation on a Spanish fandango in which a female dancer performs with a lighted oil-filled glass on her head and one on each outstretched hand, which she holds palms down. The tempo of the music increases, and the dancer makes patterns with the oil lights as she moves. This takes skill as the rhythm of the fandango is complex and the tempo quick. Philippine variations on the fandango have been the addition of the lights and its alteration from a dance for a couple to a solo. Steps from the polka, the schottische, and the mazurka have been incorporated into local folk dances. The mazurka lent itself especially well to Philippine folk dance, since some steps are improvised as the four or eight couples go along.

The first ballet school in the islands was founded in the late 1920s. At first ballet was a fad among the well-to-do, but by 1932 interest was great enough to promote the establishment of a second school. The Ballet Moderne, founded at the end of the decade, presented classical and modern European ballet. In 1941 native folk dance was incorporated into the choreography, and interest in ballet began to spread from Manila's well-to-do families to a wider audience. National dance groups made tours abroad and won international fame during the 1960s; ballet was an established aspect of cultural life in Manila in the mid-1970s.

Visual and Plastic Arts

The visual and plastic arts were overshadowed in pre-Hispanic society by the performing arts because they usually represented items for use in everyday life or for ritual ceremonies. Not valued essentially for their aesthetic merits, they have been displaced in large part by forms from abroad. Less complex forms have survived in crafts, which the government is encouraging under a program supporting the development of cottage industry (see ch. 14). Wooden objects inlaid with shell and other decorative items, metal filigree, embroidered bags and clothing, and

153

carved plagues and figures of wood are included in this category.

The best surviving examples of indigenous art are found among the Ifugao of northern Luzon and the Muslims of Mindanao. The Ifugao carve human and animal figures on the handles of their spoons and on their pipes. Effigies of their gods and ancestors are carved in wood and are used in religious ceremonies or as village guardians. Representations of plants and fish are confined to the carving on religious utensils and may not be represented on domestic utensils because the taste and smell of certain foods are thought to be offensive to the gods.

Although Muslims may not use animal and human figures and thus have evolved a purely ornamental art based on geometric designs of varying intricacy and conventionalized representations of buds, leaves, and flowers, some Filipino Muslims have flouted the taboo against animal representation. The open jaws of the crocodile are symbolized by an angular cut in the ends of house beams, on boats, and on musical instruments. In weaving cloth the artisans frequently put in designs that are recognizable as fern leaves, serpent skins, or carabao horns. One pattern, which may be pre-Islamic, is clearly a stylized rooster.

Western techniques of painting and sculpture were introduced by the Spanish. During most of the Spanish period the visual and plastic arts were of a religious nature. In the early nineteenth century, however, Damian Domingo founded the first art school in the country. The first Filipino artists to become widely known appeared in the last half of the century and preferred classical Greek and roman subjects. They studied and worked in such European cities as Madrid, Barcelona, and Paris and with other Filipinos formed colonies of artists, writers, and scholars.

Filipino artists showed an early preference for painting instead of sculpture. Technical skills were firmly established by the beginning of the twentieth century, but the subjects selected were conservative and related to realistic representations of Filipino life, such as rice planting and harvesting or landscapes. By World War II Filipino artists had begun to show an interest in abstractionism, expressing themselves in color, line, and spatial relationships.

For several generations the number of sculptors producing works has been small. Favorite materials include metal, marble, clay, plaster, and coral. Wood carving is especially popular and includes both religious subjects and variations of traditional sculpture designed for export or the tourist trade.

In the mid-1970s there was a high demand for painting and sculpture. There were over 130 one-man or group shows in Manila in a single season. Attendance at these shows and the purchase of art was regarded as an index of social prestige, a sign of personal taste, and one of the best investments in inflationary times. Art sales had become big business, and the more popular artists had long lists of commissions. Some critics expressed concern over the quality of the works being produced in such a demand market.

EDUCATION

Education and Society

The educational system served to provide productive skills necessary for economic development and to inculcate values and attitudes supporting national cohesion and identity. The system also played an important role as a means of social mobility, and educational attainment had long been considered an important determinant of social status. The educational system was, in the 1970s, viewed as a crucial mechanism in the forging of the New Society envisioned by President Marcos.

The educational system of the Philippines evolved over a period of some 400 years. Under Spanish, formal education beyond basic literacy was available primarily to children of the Spaniards. Emphasis at all levels was given to literary and religious training. Two universities were founded in the seventeenth century, and by the early 1800s higher education was offered in law, theology, medicine, and military arts. Special schools for girls were established to prepare them for married life raising children. Instruction in all the schools was given in Spanish, and discipline was strict.

For the majority of the Filipinos before the mid-1800s education was mainly a process of Christianization by the priests and curates. All instruction was in the dialect of the locale, and most children attended only until they could recite the catechism from memory and were prepared to make their confessions and receive communion. Boys who were especially bright were taught some Spanish. Rigid as the educational system was, it enabled many Filipinos to read and write and to raise themselves in their communities. Those who learned Spanish were especially fortunate, and many became clerks, printers, and government officials.

The Educational Decree of 1863 provided for expansion of the educational system and the establishment of free, compulsory education for all children seven to twelve years old; this goal, however, was not attained until the twentieth century. A limited number of secondary and higher educational facilities for Filipinos, including the University of Santo Tomas in Manila, were eventually established by the Spanish colonial government; most facilities beyond the primary level were private schools with religious affiliation, a characteristic that survived into the 1970s. Spanish was the language of instruction at all levels.

The decree brought about some important changes. Filipinos who graduated from the newly established normal schools were respected and influential in their native communities and were given social and political advantages. Primary schools increased in number from twenty-five in 1867 with an enrollment of 1,940, to 2,167 in 1898 with an enrollment of about 200,000. All these schools were government supported and run by parish priests. The discontent of the people during the last part of the nineteenth century was partly caused by their unsatisfied demands for

155

the expansion of educational opportunities.

Under the American colonial administration a centralized system of public education was introduced on the primary level. The language of instruction was changed to English, and religious instruction became optional. Teacher training and vocational training programs were introduced. Secondary and higher education remained largely in private hands.

After World War II various efforts were made to increase participation in the educational system. One of the most effective was the *Barrio* Education Movement, which was a self-help program designed to maximize the use of existing facilities and personnel in rural areas. As the result of continued efforts into the 1960s school enrollment reached levels second only to the United States and Canada and included virtually all primary-school-age children.

A high regard for education evolved as a means of both personal and family advancement. Families make every effort to educate at least one child for as long as they are financially able. He in turn is expected to help with the education of his brothers and sisters when he starts earning a salary. The possession of a certificate of higher education is important as a means of material advance and has resulted in a proliferation of private secondary and higher education facilities, some of dubious quality.

The most actively sought professions are medicine and law. A person with a degree in law or medicine can either practice his profession or go into politics, for education with or without wealth is important for a man seeking public office. A political career opens the way to higher social status. Those who cannot study medicine or law frequently go into the civil service, which carries both influence and tangible rewards. Engineering, pharmacy, dentistry, accounting, and architecture are also popular fields. In general the white-collar and professional positions are most esteemed. Vestiges of the old disdain for manual labor still exist. Often young men and women whose training does not prepare them for white-collar jobs depend on their parents for support rather than take blue-collar or agricultural positions.

Quantitative development of the educational system by the mid-1970s was not fully matched by qualitative achievements. Although graduates of certain higher educational facilities were eminently qualified in their fields, others held degrees for which they had not been adequately trained. The best training in many cases was offered by private schools where high tuition charges restricted attendance to members of the elite, thus limiting social mobility for the less privileged. Children from low-income families gravitated toward less expensive preparation in education, commerce, and business; children from high-income families entered programs in medicine, science, engineering, and the arts.

Discontinuities also existed between educational facilities and programs in rural and urban areas, reflecting and reinforcing the rural-urban gap in all aspects of national culture. Rural children often had access only to four-year programs, as opposed to six years in urban areas. The quality of instruction and facilities provided by those four years, moreover, has not been commensurate with that of four years in urban schools. Completion rates were higher in urban areas. In some areas of Mindanao about half of those engaged in agriculture had received no schooling at all.

The urban concentration of educational facilities beyond the primary level, especially of higher educational facilities, not only restricted access to the educational system but also encouraged migration to urban areas. The graduates of the many small colleges and institutes in Manila showed little inclination to return to rural areas, because of both the lack of employment opportunities there and the preference for urban life.

The concentration of educational facilities in urban areas has also increased the potential threat to the government posed by student activists engaged in the expression of popular dissent, the first significant instances of which developed in the mid-1960s. Although not all students were involved in such activities, the potential for sizable disruption existed, since the twelve university campuses in Manila had a total enrollment of about 200,000 students in the early 1970s. Student demonstrations contributed to the increasingly unstable climate before the imposition of martial law (see ch. 3; ch. 10).

Attempts to improve the quality of the educational system were directly tied to the rate of population growth and associated enrollment rates. Projections for the remainder of the twentieth century varied in absolute terms, but all indicated declining rates of increase for both categories. Improvements in educational quality would nevertheless be restricted by the needs of quantitative expansion. Progress was expected to require restructuring the educational system and redefining its social and economic goals.

Educational Reform

After the declaration of martial law in 1972 the government formulated a ten-year development plan for education enacted as the Educational Development Decree of 1972. The decree specified the broad national development goals toward which the educational system was expected to contribute. It also enumerated the direct tasks of developing a national consciousness; raising the skills, values, and sense of responsibility of all citizens; increasing equality of opportunity; and increasing participation in economic development and provision of social services. Extensive reform of the educational system included modifications in the philosophical, curricular, moral, pedagogical, and administrative structure of the system.

Much of the proposed plan for educational reform was based on the findings of a 1970 report of a presidential commission that had resulted in the formulation of a four-year development plan initiated in 1971. The educational system represented one of the most surveyed systems in the world, and reforms instituted on the basis of such surveys in the past had encountered numerous problems as a result of the decentralized structure of educational planning and ineffective administrative controls by the government over private facilities. Much of the success of the overall proposed reforms would be determined by modifications in these areas.

The basic guide to educational reform was an emphasis on educational relevance. Curriculum changes were designed to include such subjects as population planning, nutrition, consumer education, and civic action projects. Other policy changes announced in the early 1970s included the use of Pilipino along with English as a language of instruction; the use of Arabic as a language of instruction was to be allowed in certain areas of Mindanao.

Increased emphasis on relevant education included vocational training. Various studies indicated, however, that in shifting to technical training there were dangers that did not take into account the rapidly changing structure of the labor market. Additional research was necessary to determine the extent to which technicians and skilled workers were in short supply; industry was critical of the relevance of existing vocational training. Various studies made in the early 1970s suggested that the basic reading, reasoning, and mathematical skills offered by elementary and secondary education seemed the most valuable goal of educational reform.

In a major effort to upgrade the quality of higher education and to control college admission the National College Entrance Examination was initiated in 1973 on a nationwide basis for all high school seniors. About 75 percent of all those who took the examination were allowed entrance to four-year facilities offering higher education. In 1974 the cutoff point was raised from 25 to 30 percent, and about 70 percent were considered to have received passing scores. The system was not binding on educational institutions, each of which could determine its own cutoff point and administer its own entrance tests. Effective application of the examination depended upon further testing, study, and refinement.

The findings of the first two administrations of the entrance examination indicated that the upper 50 percent of the passing students came from highly urbanized areas and from families of high-income levels. They were also enrolled in prestigious schools and in college entrance curricula. These findings substantiated those of earlier surveys. Efforts were undertaken in the 1975 administration to offset in part the urban bias.

Institutional accreditation was being expanded by the Philippine Accrediting Association of Schools, Colleges, and Universities, a private professional group that was the only nationally recognized private accreditation association in the Philippines and also had the official recognition of the government. The association first began college-level accreditation in the late 1950s. Accreditation of secondary schools was begun in 1955 and of elementary schools in 1971. Teacher education programs were included in 1973, and the accreditation of nursing and agricultural programs was under discussion in 1975.

Administration and Financing of Education

After the declaration of martial law the Department of Education was reorganized as the Department of Education and Culture in an effort to coordinate the development and implementation of education programs and to make these programs more responsive to the needs of national development and the creation of the New Society. The formulation of general educational objectives and policies and long-term plans for educational development remained the responsibility of the National Board of Education, which was attached to the department, and the Board of Higher Education was created to assist and advise in the formulation of objectives, policies, and programs pertaining to post-secondary education.

Internal reorganization of the department involved a major revision of the structure of authority and the operation of departmental divisions. Each division or unit previously operated almost independently of all others. Separate jurisdictions existed for public, private, and vocational schools. Under the new structure jurisdiction was to be divided on the basis of separate bureaus for elementary, secondary, and higher education. Additional units were to provide auxiliary services ranging from finance to information.

The reorganization reflected in part an effort to improve governmental control over the educational system, including its oversight of private school operations. The large number of private schools, mainly at the secondary and higher educational levels, included sectarian and charitable institutions, Chinese and other foreign schools, and a number of schools operated as commercial enterprises. Their quality varied; they ranged from highly reputable institutions to diploma mills. A few received modest government financial support. In general the private schools reflected a response to the strong demand, especially within the middle classes and in urban areas of the country, for the advantages of social mobility and individual opportunity afforded by secondary or higher education. In the early 1970s this demand confronted the government's efforts to curb the proliferation of redundant schools and to improve the quality of secondary and higher education in both the academic and vocational fields.

The operation of private schools was subject to rules and procedures, including some curriculum standards, established by the Department of Education and Culture. Schools and colleges received official departmental recognition and theoretically were permitted to operate only after inspection and the posting of a bond, the size of which was determined by the office of the secretary of the department. Subsequent control and supervision by the department was very loose until the early 1970s. As part of the government's reforms, private schools (with the exception of charitable and sectarian institutions) were then subject to a tax on net income, allowance being made for outlays to improve the quality of school facilities. Steps toward accreditation, the adoption of new standards for government grants-in-aid, and the introduction of a system of college entrance examinations were also expected to encourage private schools to improve the quality of their programs.

While efforts were being made to consolidate educational planning, the department was also being decentralized. The plan called for the establishment of eleven regional offices under which provincial and city educational offices were to be placed. These offices were to be structured along the same lines as the department and would constitute its operating arms. The regional offices were intended to play a special role in coordinating operational activities of the department within each region.

Under the new reorganization the department was to play a special role in national integration and the development of national culture for the New Society. In all areas relating to the educational and cultural development of minorities the department was to coordinate closely with the Commission on National Integration. The department was to be aided in the task of cultural development by other agencies, including the Institute of National Language, the National Library, the National Museum, the National Historical Institute, and the National Institute of Arts and Letters.

Total national expenditure in fiscal year (FY) 1972 on all kinds of formal education was estimated at the equivalent of about US$381 million, or roughly 4.6 percent of the expected gross national product (GNP—see Glossary) for the same period. Of this amount the national government contributed about 55 percent, which represented about 26 percent of the national budget. About 85 percent of the national allocation to education was devoted to primary education, 3 percent was expended for secondary education, and 12 percent was allocated for higher education. Private schools were eligible for certain kinds of government aid.

Local governments, using provincial, municipal, and city budgets, contributed about 11 percent of the total expenditure on education. They bore responsibility for the majority of government support for secondary education. Their funds were in part generated by personal property taxes but were heavily dependent upon transfers from the national government.

About one-third of the total national expenditure on education came from student fees. Fees were charged by all secondary and higher education facilities and by private elementary schools; public elementary schools were free.

Recurrent expenditures represented the vast majority of the total spent on education. The amounts allocated to capital expenses, such as textbooks and teaching equipment, were not adequate in the early 1970s, which eroded efforts to improve the quality of the educational system. Projections based on present trends indicated that the total expenditure on primary education by 1980 was likely to be double the 1972 figure. Government expenditures on education would have to increase to 28 percent of the national budget to maintain the proportional allocations to the other two levels of education; significant improvement in secondary, vocational, and higher education was questionable under such conditions.

Structure of the Educational System

In the early 1970s there were almost 10 million students enrolled in the school system, about 25 percent of the total population. The majority were elementary-age children enrolled in public schools. There was a high dropout rate throughout the system, resulting in incomplete education cycles, and grade repetition throughout was widespread. The quality of education was seriously handicapped by a shortage of textbooks. School libraries were generally inadequate. School facilities needed expansion and upgrading and were generally in need of repair. There was a serious lack of equipment for classes in science, industrial arts, home economics, and business education.

Although preschool education was not required for entrance to elementary school, many parents were eager to offer their children this experience. In 1972 there were an estimated 58,000 children enrolled in programs for three- to four-year olds in nursery schools or for five- to six-year-old children in kindergartens. These schools were almost exclusively private facilities for which the parents paid enrollment fees.

Although the national literacy rate was estimated in the early 1970s at about 80 percent, various adult education programs were in operation. Out-of-school youth were included in these programs, the two major divisions of which included functional literacy and continuing education. Functional literacy focused on reading and writing, mathematics, citizenship, and health and sanitation. Continuing education provided cultural or personal enrichment programs, vocational development, practical handicrafts, and health and safety education. Other programs covered homemaking, civic education, women's education, and worker education.

Elementary Education

Elementary education generally consisted of six years of instruction (see fig. 7). The Elementary Education Act of 1953 authorized the addition of a seventh year but, except for a few schools, financial considerations prevented the implementation of this provision. In certain rural areas schools offered only four years of elementary education. Official estimates, however, reported that virtually all primary-age students were enrolled in educational facilities; even taking into account the inclusion of overaged pupils in this estimate, elementary school enrollment was in the upper 90-percent bracket.

Children entered elementary school at the age of seven. Instruction was in either the local vernacular or Pilipino. Pilipino and English were

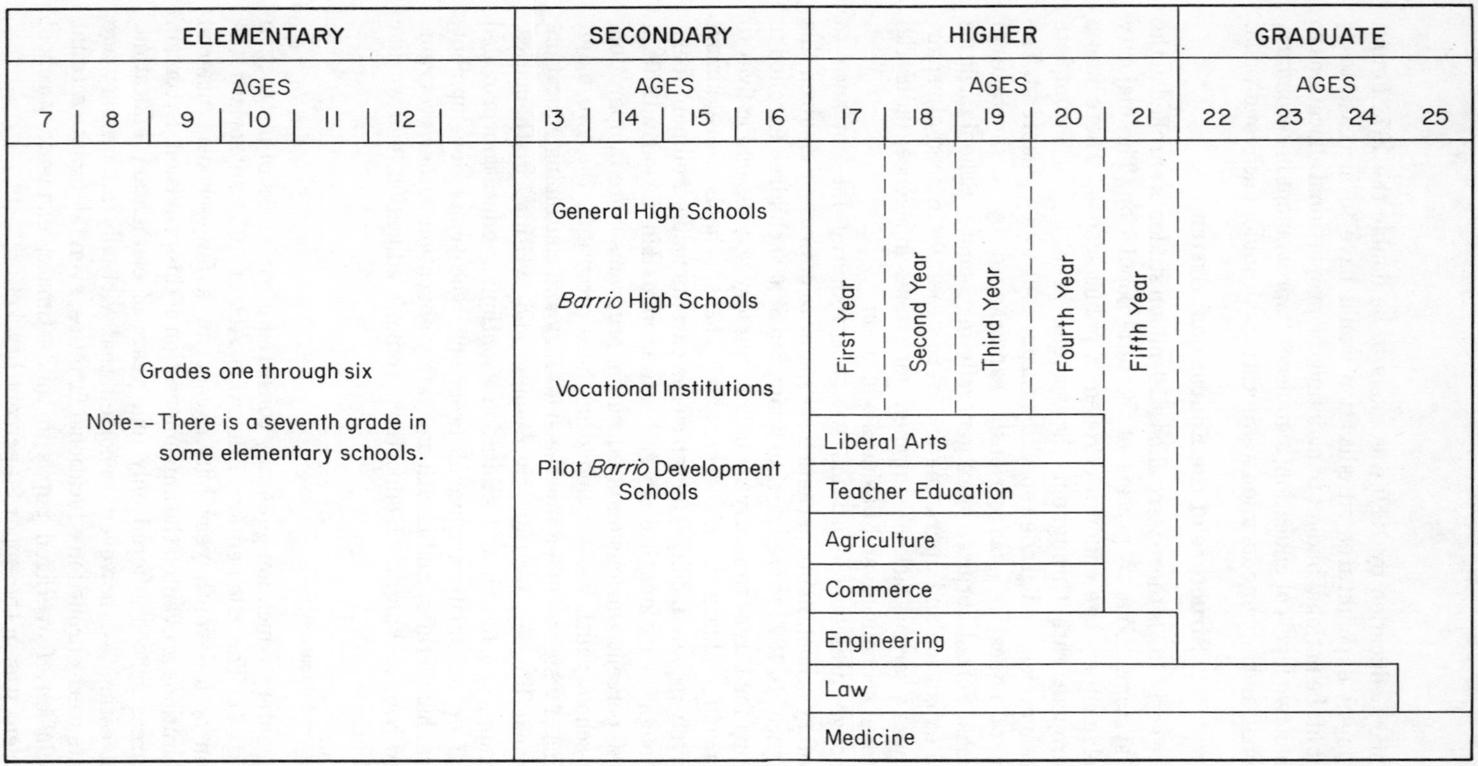

ELEMENTARY | SECONDARY | HIGHER | GRADUATE

AGES: 7 8 9 10 11 12 | 13 14 15 16 | AGES 17 18 19 20 21 | AGES 22 23 24 25

Grades one through six

Note-- There is a seventh grade in some elementary schools.

General High Schools

Barrio High Schools

Vocational Institutions

Pilot Barrio Development Schools

First Year
Second Year
Third Year
Fourth Year
Fifth Year

Liberal Arts
Teacher Education
Agriculture
Commerce
Engineering
Law
Medicine

Figure 7. Philippines, Structure of the Educational System, 1973

162

taught as formal subjects until the third year, when English became the medium of instruction. Because in certain areas language instruction created difficulties that limited classroom instruction in other subjects, improved methods of language instruction were under study.

In the early 1970s somewhat over 7 million students were enrolled in elementary schools. Of these about 95 percent were in public schools. About 96 percent of all public school teachers were graduates of either four-year college programs or two-year teacher training programs and were considered fully qualified to teach at the elementary level. The pupil-teacher ratio was approximately thirty to one, and the ratio of boys to girls was nearly equal, as it was throughout most levels of the system.

According to the findings of the presidential commission, elementary education was deficient in several aspects. The curriculum not only was excessively factually oriented but also relied on rote learning as a teaching method. Standardization of achievement tests was inadequate, audiovisual materials were in short supply, and educational guidance programs were virtually nonexistent. The pupil to textbook ratio ranged from four to one to as high as seventeen to one in certain poor regions; reduction of this ratio would represent a major step toward improving the quality of elementary education, even at the cost of increasing the student-teacher ratio.

Secondary Education

Secondary education consisted of a four-year program offering different combinations of general and vocational training. The three major kinds of institutions were general high schools, *barrio* high schools, and vocational institutions. During the 1960s the Department of Education sought to introduce a curriculum program into all general high schools under which two years of general education were to be followed by two years of either academic or vocational education. The lack of funds for constructing new workshops and buying the necessary equipment for the vocational stream restricted full implementation of this program to about 5 percent of all general high schools. The other schools usually were able to all general high schools. The other schools usually were able to supplement the academic education they offered with only one vocational course a year.

The earlier shortage of secondary schools in many rural areas resulted in the establishment of *barrio* high schools in the mid-1960s. These schools were overseen by village councils and were to be supported by student fees that students were to earn through work projects, most of which were in agriculture. These schools rapidly became popular, but the work-oriented aspects were gradually eroded by a concern for preparation for higher education.

Vocational high schools theoretically specialized in providing work skills and were to be terminal programs for students before they entered the work force. Most secondary students, however, sought entrance to higher education and regarded vocational schools or vocational tracks as an alternative way to enter college. In the late 1960s about 82 percent of those who finished the vocational track in general high schools and 37 percent of those graduating from vocational schools later enrolled in college.

In the early 1970s there were almost 2 million students enrolled in secondary schools, representing about 71 percent of the secondary school age-group. About 150,000 of the total were enrolled in vocational high schools. Of the total enrollment in secondary schools about 67 percent were attending private schools. There was a surplus of teachers in most areas except the sciences, and about 94 percent of all teachers were believed to be fully qualified. The student-teacher ratio was thirty-six to one.

The quality of secondary education was the weakest of the three educational levels and, despite the high continuation rate to higher education, there was a dropout rate of 25 percent. The greatest deficiencies were in the areas of English, science, and mathematics. Instruction in the sciences was hindered by a lack of facilities, which restricted not only participation by students but demonstrations by teachers as well. Instruction in the social sciences often was not keyed to the realities of Philippine history, geography, or society.

The quality of vocational training offered at the secondary level was similarly inadequate. Most vocational courses were taught by teachers who had little or no industrial experience. Vocational training was twice as expensive to provide as academic training, and the facilities were usually poor and outdated. Craft skills were often the substance of vocational courses because they were easier and less expensive to teach. Vocational training seldom provided adequate preparation for employment in the industrial sector.

In addition to the three major kinds of secondary institutions there were such other schools as agricultural and fishery high schools and experimental *barrio* development schools. These represented a small number of institutions, and most had marginal levels of teaching materials and poorly trained staffs. Shorter training programs in such fields as animal husbandry and mechanization also existed.

Higher Education

In the early 1970s there were over 650 institutions offering higher education ranging from four-year programs in the liberal arts to eight- or nine-year programs in law and medicine. Of these about 60 percent offered teacher training programs. About 86 percent of the total were privately operated. Total enrollment was estimated at about 800,000, or roughly 25 percent of the college-age population. About 35 percent of all students were studying education, and just under 25 percent were studying the social sciences. There were also over 100 schools of arts and trades not included under the general category of higher education facilities. Leading institutions of higher education in terms of size and reputation included the University of Santo Tomas and the University of the Philippines.

Higher education is largely concentrated in Manila. Just under half of the forty-two major universities and about 40 percent of all students enrolled in higher education were in Manila. Students in higher education were generally dependent upon family support for their expenses, and most came from families with higher than average or median incomes.

Higher education was obtained with little thought for the needs of the economy or employment potential. Although there was an excessive surplus of teachers in general, there was a scarcity of teachers in certain technically oriented professions. Degrees in agriculture and forestry were below national requirements. The total number of graduates produced in almost every field was second only to the United States and Canada. Although most graduates were eventually able to find employment, their positions were not always directly related to their preparation.

Higher education suffered from several qualitative inadequacies. Economic factors took precedence over academic criteria in decision-making and program planning. The qualification of most faculty members was no more advanced than the degree for which the students were studying. Only 24 percent of the faculty had master's degrees, and 3 percent had doctorates. Faculty tenure was not an established system. Although a new system of college admission on the basis of examination was being implemented, most students in the mid-1970s were still able to obtain entrance to a school of higher education if they had the ability to pay the required fees.

SCIENCE

A basis for scientific inquiry was laid before the end of the Spanish colonial period, but the greatest impetus to the growth of scientific research did not occur until the assumption of colonial administration by the United States. In 1901 the Bureau of Government Laboratories was established. Three years later it was absorbed by the newly created Bureau of Science. Government facilities continued to expand and be reorganized, and in 1933 the National Research Council of the Philippines was created. By this time numerous scientific publications, such as the *Philippine Journal of Science* and the *Natural and Applied Science Bulletin*, were being published, and such societies as the Philippine Islands Medical Association and the Philippine Scientific Society had been established.

In 1958 the National Science Development Board was created to serve as a national coordinating agency for the promotion of science in the Philippines. The National Institute of Science and Technology and the Philippine Atomic Energy Commission were created at the same time and placed under the supervision of the board. Various other agencies were subsequently placed under the board's supervision, including the Philippine Textile Research Institute, the National Water and Air Pollution Control Commission, the Metals Industry Development Center, and the Forest Products Research and Industries Development Commission.

In 1968 the Special Science Fund was established under the aegis of the board to provide funds for research projects in science and technology. The number of projects covered by the program had expanded to over 300 by 1973 when the funding was to expire; the success of the first five-year fund led President Marcos to extend the program until 1982. Major progress was made in areas of technology relating to agriculture.

Highly regarded by agriculturists throughout the world, and particularly in Southeast Asia, was the International Rice Research Institute, an independent research facility based in the Philippines. The most significant contribution of the institute was the development of various strains of "miracle rice" (see ch. 13). Lesser known independent research facilities existed, some of which operated in conjunction with private institutions of higher education.

Under a grant from the United States the Philippines constructed a nuclear reactor from which the first nuclear-fission chain reaction was produced in 1963. The reactor was used for training, the production of radioisotopes, and research studies in the fields of agriculture, biology, medicine, chemistry, and physics. Technical assistance was obtained from various sources, including the United States Agency for International Development, the International Atomic Energy Agency (IAEA), and the Colombo Plan for Cooperative Economic Development in South and Southeast Asia, and through bilateral agreements with other nations.

In early 1972 the government successfully launched its first rocket, which was christened "Bong-Bong II" after the son of President Marcos. This projectile was eight inches in diameter and several feet in length. It was developed as a consequence of experimentation with liquid rocket fuel used for powering windmills when the wind velocity was insufficient to operate pumps in irrigation projects. Applications of the rocket to peaceful uses were discussed but had not been implemented by 1975.

MASS COMMUNICATIONS

Patterns of Communications

Among Southeast Asian nations the Philippines has one of the longest and best established traditions in the fields of the press and public information. Facilities destroyed during World War II were replaced by new and modern equipment, and other media, such as radio and television, were subsequently developed. In the mid-1970s the country was served by a daily press and by periodicals, a complex of radio stations that blanketed the islands, expanding television facilities that provided service to Manila and to various other major urban areas, and an active and increasingly significant cinema industry. There was also some book publishing, although the number of titles published each year was small, as was the size of each edition. There were only a few public libraries or reading centers available to the general public.

Factors limiting the dissemination of public information included the insular nature of the nation and the general poverty of the majority of the population, especially in rural areas. Because of the geography of the islands it was difficult, except by radio. to communicate information rapidly and cheaply to potential audiences; moreover, once materials had been distributed, few residents could afford the cost, whether of a newspaper, periodical, book, or theater ticket. The cost factor also cut down the influence of radio-disseminated information because the cost of batteries for transistor receivers was also beyond the means of many residents.

The greatest factor limiting the impact of the public information system, especially of the printed media, was the high concentration of public information facilities in Manila. Over 80 percent of all publishing facilities and the majority of the daily newspapers and periodicals were located in the city. It was also the location of a disproportionate number of radio and television broadcasting stations and the center of the cinema and book publishing industries.

The upper class elite in the capital owned most information media and were the molders of national opinion. Although there were numerous daily newspapers, they were largely grouped under the ownership of a few large corporations, many of which were family enterprises and some of which also owned magazines and broadcasting stations.

The efficacy of the various media differed according to whether the audience was urban or rural. In the cities people had access to all media but seemed to rely on the daily newspapers and the weekly news-magazines for information. Radio and television were extremely popular but were looked upon primarily for entertainment rather than information. Professional journalists, for example, tended to have a low opinion of the quality of news disseminated over the electronic media.

The role of provincial newspapers in information dissemination remained limited. Many of these newspapers inserted vernacular news-sheets as a means of expanding their circulation among non-English readers. Projections in the early 1970s indicated, however, that the circulation of the urban press in provincial areas exceeded that of local newspapers by 50 percent. Analysis by observers of the content of provincial newspapers suggested that they were not effectively serving national development; they neither created popular sympathy for the development effort nor contributed to the achievement of new skills and attitudes related to that effort. Their major function was to report local events independent of analysis.

In rural areas few people received information directly from a primary source. Most could not afford to subscribe to a newspaper or periodical or to purchase a radio receiver, even an inexpensive transistor. Television was not available outside the cities. The major sources of information in rural areas, therefore, were *barrio* leaders, teachers, priests, or the more affluent residents who could afford a publication or radio and who shared the information they received. Apart from this word-of-mouth method, rural residents who could find access to other media preferred the radio and weekly newsmagazine to the daily newspaper or other printed matter. They also appeared to believe what they heard on the radio more readily than what they read in any publication. Motion pictures, including documentaries, however, were the most popular and effective medium of all.

The Media in the New Society

The evolution of the Philippine press after World War II into one of the most vital and free national presses in Asia in the 1960s was a process in which Filipinos took pride; other media were also demonstrating signs of growing independence. Various bills designed to protect sources of information used by the media, to open government files to the public, and to provide specific definitions of libel were passed or seriously considered during the decade. The media, particularly the press, did not at all times show an enlightened vision of their responsibility—and in fact often tended toward exaggeration and sensationalism—although occasional efforts to police themselves were undertaken through such organizations as the Philippine Press Institute.

Every government since independence protested against the mass media, but it was not until the Marcos administration that such protests were translated into policy. No government official could hope to escape the critical eye of the press, and few public figures took legal action against what they claimed were false reports for fear of the notoriety that might be associated with such action. The general attitude of most critics of the press was that an excessive press was better than a controlled one.

Efforts by the Marcos administration to bring the media under control preceded the declaration of martial law. Beginning in the late 1960s government information services were placed more directly under the office of the president and significantly expanded in an effort to absorb an increasing number of journalists into direct government and to control some of the commercially operated mass media. Journalists were appointed to important administrative positions. Attacks against the media increased and included criticism of facilities owned by members of the political faction opposing Marcos.

Although certain actions attributed to efforts by the government and supporters of Marcos to manipulate the media caused concern both within the country and abroad, selected arrests and deportations throughout 1971 were sufficient to increase the exercise of cautious self-restraint by some editors in their criticism of the government. The declaration of martial law in September 1972 ultimately brought strict curbs on press freedom and marked a milestone in the long journalistic tradition of the Philippines. A number of media operations were closed, in some cases permanently, and certain journalists were arrested or detained. Subsequent resumption of operations was permitted only with operating permits and supervision by government representatives. All government media operations were merged under the Department of Public Information, created at that time from the former Presidential Press Office. The new department issued decrees detailing guidelines for journalists and procedures for censorship and control. Implementation and operation of these decrees was initially handled by a military office, but in November 1972 they were transferred to the newly created Mass Media Council. Censorship of news agencies was lifted, and editorials were permitted the following month. Efforts to ease controls somewhat included the establishment in May 1973 of the more representative Media Advisory Council to replace the Mass Media Council and the separation of the council in November 1974 into two self-regulating groups, one for the press and one for broadcasting.

The stated intention of the Marcos government in controlling the media was to ensure positive support in the creation of the New Society. The media ceased to function as an institution for social and political criticism. Uncertain of the degree of free expression permissible under the phase of liberalized control introduced in 1974, the media have tended to avoid the controversial. The copy devoted to politics has been reduced and that given to sports and culture increased. Nonetheless, various unapproved forms of printed media expressing opposition views have been circulated since the first days of martial law, including short newspapers, newsletters, chain letters, reports, documents, and literature from abroad. Although the possession of such material was punishable by six months' imprisonment, there was little evidence that the government actively sought to eliminate operation of the underground press.

The media in late 1975 remained in a depressed state. Unemployment among former newspapermen and broadcasting personnel as a result of martial law remained high; the ownership and control of commercial media continued to change hands. Such organizations as the Press Council, the Philippine Press Institute, and the National Press Club were moribund or operated only under direct and indirect government control. These effects appeared to be greater than desired by the government in its efforts to create the New Society, and in the mid-1970s the government faced the difficulties of revitalizing an institution that it had weakened by its own efforts.

Martial law brought not only the imposition of controls but also the restructuring of the press. The only newspapers initially allowed to continue publication in 1972 were the *Daily Express*, the *Evening Express*, and the *Pilipino Express*. None of these was more than one year old. The major established newspapers, such as the *Manila Times*, the *Manila Chronicle*, the *Philippine Herald, Mabuhay*, and the *Manila Daily Bulletin*, were closed, and in some cases their publishers or editors were detained. The combined circulation of the *Daily Express* chain reached 400,000. Competition was introduced by allowing publication of a new newspaper, the *Times Journal*, and the reopening of the *Manila Daily Bulletin*. The *Manila Daily Bulletin*, which had had the second largest circulation before martial law, changed its masthead to *Bulletin Today* and had climbed to a circulation of over 200,000 by 1974. The *Times Journal* and the *Daily Express* became the second and third largest daily newspapers.

Although reports conflicted, it appeared that by late 1974 there were sixteen major weekly newspapers. One of these specialized in economics and three in sports. There were about fifty minor provincial newspapers and seventeen lesser weekly publications. About seventy magazines were published monthly; some eighty other publications were published less frequently.

The national news service was reconstituted after 1972 as the Philippine News Agency. The agency provided copious amounts of news copy on daily events to both the printed and the broadcasting media. Copy was also sent abroad to the news services of embassies and consulates of the Philippines. The agency also provided services to foreign correspondents in the Philippines, who had been freed from censorship or controls in 1973. The agency maintained correspondents in major Philippine cities and in Jakarta and Tokyo. News exchange services existed with several Asian press agencies; offices of Reuters, United Press International (UPI), and Agence France Presse were located in Manila.

After the declaration of martial law only the official radio stations, operated by the Philippine Broadcasting Service, and one of the original seven television channels were allowed to operate. By mid-1974, however, some 220 radio stations and the pre-martial law television stations had resumed broadcasting. The quality of news coverage by the broadcasting media had reportedly declined. There was little news commentary, and the presentation was undramatic. Television programming featured such entertainment as motion pictures, musicals, and skits. Broadcasting time was back to the usual amounts, from early morning to after midnight, depending on the day of the week. A few programs sought to exploit the potential of television for educational purposes.

CHAPTER 8

RELIGION

Approximately 83 percent of the population of the country is Roman Catholic. Indigenous Christian cults, most of them traceable to the antifriar agitation that played such a prominent role in the war for independence from Spain, account for about 6 percent of the population (see ch. 3). Two of these cults, the Philippine Independent Church and the Iglesia ni Kristo (Tagalog for Church of Christ), have significant followings.

Islam, introduced into the southern islands in the fourteenth and early fifteenth centuries—two centuries before Christianity—remains confined primarily to Mindanao and the Sulu Archipelago. The Muslim community, at odds with the Christian majority for several centuries, is only 5 percent of the population. In recent decades the pressures of a growing Christian settler population in areas of traditional Muslim dominance have aggravated the historic animosities.

Protestant Christianity was divided into over 200 denominations, some of which depend heavily on churches in the United States for economic support and missionary personnel. About 3 percent of the Filipino population was affiliated with these groups.

Another 2 percent of the Filipinos—concentrated in the mountainous areas of northern Luzon—continued to adhere to indigenous beliefs and practices that had prevailed before the introduction of Western culture and its influence on national life.

The Roman Catholic Church, dominant since 1600, declined in the late nineteenth and early twentieth centuries because of its association with the Spanish colonial regime. The conversion of one out of every four Catholics to the nationalistic Aglipayan movement in the early decades of the 1900s, the influx into the islands of hundreds of Protestant missionaries after the beginning of United States rule, and the legal disestablishment of the church in 1902 forced Philippine Catholicism into a major although temporary retreat. By the early 1930s, however, having eliminated most of the grievances of the disaffected segments of the population through a process of internal renewal and a new stress on education, the church recovered most of its traditional prestige and appeal. In the late 1940s Roman Catholicism was further strengthened by a reaction against Japanese occupation policies and also by a weakening of the Protestantism that was closely identified with the United States.

The principle of the separation of church and state is recognized in the 1973 Constitution, which also exempts religious activities from taxation and specifically forbids the use of public resources by religious institutions with minor exceptions. Article XV of the Constitution, however, provides that—at the option of the parents and without cost to them or the government—religious instruction may be given in the public schools. The use of public facilities and teachers for religious education had been supported by the severely undermanned Roman Catholic Church.

The predominance of the church continued to exert an influence on secular life. Its precepts regarding marriage and divorce were still reflected in late 1975 in the Civil Code, although the possibility of a change in the divorce law was periodically discussed. Perhaps the most controversial issue involving the church was that of population control. The church was slow to acknowledge the population problem confronting the Philippines and remained opposed to all forms of birth control except the rhythm method. Nevertheless, confronted with criticism of the church's stance among the laity and younger priests and by the government's adoption of a family planning program incorporating all contraceptive methods, church officials expressed agreement with the government's policy of leaving the method of birth control to the individual.

In general the Roman Catholic Church remained a conservative bulwark in Philippine society. Nevertheless it has not been immune from the pressures for both internal reform and amelioration of social and economic problems that have affected the church in other countries, particularly after the Second Vatican Council, which began in 1962. Elements within the church as well as some Protestant groups became deeply involved in efforts to mitigate conditions of poverty, urban growth, farm tenancy, and labor in the Philippines. With the imposition of martial law in 1972 these activities brought individuals and social action groups into conflict with the government, and a number of priests, nuns, missionaries, and laymen were detained.

Religion, although it provides for the individual an emotional bond and a source of cultural identity, is highly syncretic. There is general agreement among scholars of Philippine culture that centuries of exposure to a variety of organized religions have not resulted in displacement of earlier forms of worship and superstition that predate Islam's introduction to the islands. The average peasant, although nominally a Roman Catholic, continues to adhere to ancient rituals indigenous to his locale. Moreover he has demonstrated a remarkable ability to blend these beliefs and practices with the demands of the organized major world faiths that have been superimposed upon them.

The religious experience of the Philippines includes the phenomenon of periodic movements of an intensely revivalist nature—merging Christian and indigenous elements—characterized by mysticism or supernaturalism and led by authoritarian, charismatic figures. One student of these religious movements in the Philippines, David R. Sturtevant, has suggested that the underlying cause is cultural alienation within broad sections of the population, both rural and urban; it may represent rebellion against social change or efforts to grapple with historical trends that have undermined individual security and traditional values and led to chronic stress. A number of such movements appeared in the early twentieth century; they subsided between 1932 and 1952, when peasants were organized into such secular movements as the Sakdal group and the Huks (see Glossary). With the collapse of these organizations millenarian movements reemerged, and by 1960 a large number had been established in Luzon and the Visayan Islands. In 1967 a bloody confrontation erupted in the center of Manila between the members of one such religious movement and a surprised constabulary.

ROMAN CATHOLICISM

Christianization of the Philippines

However tenuous allegiance to Roman Catholicism may be for many Filipinos, it is a focal point of their distinction from pagan mountain tribes on the one hand and the Filipino Muslims (Moros) on the other. As a primary factor of national culture, Roman Catholicism is also intimately associated with folklore in various aspects. The rich pageantry of most holidays and various aspects of family life are closely associated with the Roman Catholic liturgy.

Before the arrival of the Spaniards most Filipinos practiced a polytheistic religion in which gods, spirits, and men were under the rule of a supreme being. Prayers and sacrifices were offered routinely to the numerous lesser deities and to ancestor spirits, considered benevolent or malevolent depending on whether they came from one's own or an enemy's tribe. Many rituals had the curing of illnesses as their principal purpose. Ritual drinking to the point of drunkenness was prevalent. The sun, moon, rainbows, rivers, mountains, plants, caves, trees, and certain animals were objects of worship. Carved idols used in religious ceremonies were representations of ancestor spirts who were intermediaries between man and the supernatural. Reward or torment after death, depending on behavior in this life, was a dominant belief. Filipinos commonly resorted to magical practices. The priestly class, where it existed, was composed predominantly of elderly women (see ch. 4).

Serious efforts to Christianize the Philippines began in 1565 with the arrival of the Miguel López de Legazpi expedition from Mexico. Muslim influence was already spreading northward from Indonesia but was firmly established only in Mindanao and the Sulu Archipelago. Muslim communities in Luzon and Cebu were quickly expelled by the Spaniards (see ch. 3; ch. 4).

Legazpi had been instructed by King Philip II of Spain to fight only in self-defense and to explain to the natives "the law of Jesus Christ by which they will be saved" and under which they would be protected and live in peace and friendship with their conquerors. The Spaniards believed they were liberating the Filipinos from enslavement by the devil. They perceived their conquest of the islands as a mutually beneficial arrangement whereby the natives swore their fealty to the king of Spain in return for religious instruction, for the administration of Spanish law, and for military protection from depredations by their enemies—the Japanese, Chinese, and Muslim pirates and their unconverted neighbors. The conquest itself and the conversion of most Filipinos were accomplished with little violence. Although repeated local uprisings and occasional sustained insurrections testified to the intensity of Filipino resistance, native opposition was never a serious challenge to Spanish authority in the islands except in Mindanao and northern Luzon, where Muslims and Igorots successfully defied the Spanish writ until the end of the nineteenth century.

The relationship between the state and the Roman Catholic Church was defined by royal patronage, described in a series of papal decrees issued between 1493 and 1508. The Spanish crown assumed responsibility for the financial support of the church and in return was granted the right to collect tithes and to propose candidates for the office of bishop.

Because of unsettled conditions and the difficulty of communicating with Spain—it took between three and four years to get a reply—the crown depended on members of the religious orders, mainly the Augustinians, Franciscans, Jesuits, and Dominicans, to carry out the work of Christianizing the islands. Unlike the secular clergy, religious clergy were directly subordinate to the superior of their order rather than to the local bishop. It was expected that eventually they would be replaced in parish duties by secular parish priests, but opposition on the part of all the religious orders prevented the change. Although the religious clergy took perpetual vows of poverty, the wealth and influence of the religious orders grew until the end of the nineteenth century. They also played a major role in economic and political life. This self-serving accumulation of power and a distinctly racist attitude toward Filipinos, combined with occasional lapses in probity and with other abuses encouraged by the decentralized organization and lax discipline in all of the orders except the Jesuits, generated widespread resentment. This sentiment was effectively exploited by those agitating for independence from Spain.

Rivalry and Renewal

Within a century after the conquest the religious boundaries within the Philippines had become fairly stabilized. The Sulu Archipelago and much of Mindanao, primarily the shores of Lake Lanao and the Cotabato River basin, remained Muslim strongholds. The most mountainous parts of

Luzon became the last refuge of native religions. Everywhere else Roman Catholicism, combined in most cases with many elements of non-Christian origin, was dominant. Before 1898 the only challenge to the power and prestige of the Roman Catholic Church in Christian areas came from the Spanish Orient Lodge of Freemasonry, which rapidly gained in strength and influence during the second half of the nineteenth century. Many independence leaders were Masons.

Large numbers of Protestant missionaries from the United States began arriving in 1899 at a time when the prestige and influence of the Roman Catholic Church was at a low ebb. Many priests and bishops had been forced to flee their dioceses by insurgent forces. Anti-Spanish nationalism was at its height. Moreover many of the Filipinos and Americans in charge of the local government administration and the public school system were militantly anti-Roman Catholic.

Reform of the church began with the arrival of a personal representative of Pope Leo XIII in November 1902 with a new apostolic constitution for Philippine Roman Catholicism. The document suppressed most of the privileges of the religious orders, established new dioceses, and called for a better educated clergy as well as the establishment of parochial primary schools for both boys and girls.

In 1907 Pope Pius X appointed a Benedictine monk as papal delegate to preside over the Philippine Provincial Council. The council, held in Manila during 1907 and 1908, set in motion a counterreformation in response to the challenges of Aglipayanism, Protestantism, and the trend toward the secularization of Philippine society. It was modeled after the Plenary Council of Latin America, which had been held in Rome in 1899. All of the decrees of the council were adopted almost verbatim "due to similar conditions obtaining in our countries." A large number of decrees were restated to deal with specific Philippine problems. Seventeen decrees dealt directly with the Aglipayan schism, and the decrees were indirectly related to many others.

Largely as a result of these changes Philippine Roman Catholicism required greater vigor and more unity than it had had at any previous time. Priests were forbidden to accept government positions. For the first time Roman Catholic education was made available to the majority of Filipino children of both sexes in more than 1,200 schools. In 1927 there were more than 1,000 boys and men preparing for the priesthood. By the early 1930s a major portion of those who had joined the Aglipayan movement had returned to Roman Catholicism.

Anti-Spanish nationalism, the major source of strength for the Aglipayans, was not directed against Roman Catholicism as such but rather against a church dominated by foreigners. By 1910, however, most of the Spanish friars and bishops had returned to Spain. Nationalist sentiment began to focus upon the United States and, by association, Protestantism.

Celebrations and Devotions

Such external aspects of Roman Catholicism as publicly performed rituals and religious festivals play a major role in the life of the Filipino Roman Catholic. The major feast days and liturgical seasons are essentially the same as those observed by Roman Catholics elsewhere, but the manner of observance is uniquely Filipino. Each town and *barrio* has a patron saint, whose day is celebrated as a local feast day, reflecting diverse customs and traditions.

In contrast to other countries with Hispanic cultural traditions the Philippines celebrates Christmas rather than Easter as the most important event of the year. Festivities commence on December 16, when the majority of rural Filipinos begin attending a nine-day series of daybreak masses, which may be accompanied in some areas by daily processions. The financial burden of the celebrations is borne by nine of the wealthier families of the parish chosen by a parish committee in consultation with the parish priests. Although there is no binding obligation on the part of the families selected, the nomination is considered a sign of social distinction and is seldom rejected.

In all households everything is cleaned, waxed, decorated, or painted. Chinese lanterns and paper decorations are hung throughout the neighborhood or village; paper Christmas trees are also common. The celebration begins about 3:00 A.M. on December 16 with the ringing of church bells, band processions, and fireworks. Mass begins between 4:00 A.M. and 5:00 A.M. After mass, youths gather in groups at a traditional spot. Christmas and Easter are the only seasons when large numbers of young men attend mass, many of them because of social rather than religious motives. In very small communities, where no mass is held because there is no priest, there is a sung rosary, followed by a community breakfast at the home of the sponsor of the day's feast.

Throughout the nine-day period groups of children carol throughout the community. The festivities increase in intensity until midnight on December 24, when a child dressed as the infant Jesus appears at the church. In some areas there is also a dramatic representation of the angels appearing to the shepherds in which all the roles are played by children. Processions usually take place after sundown and involve either statues of Mary and Joseph or persons representing them. The procession stops at various predetermined houses where a request for shelter is sung. The sung reply always states that there is no room. In some communities there is an invitation to come in for refreshments. These processions may take place on each of the nine days or only on December 24.

The Christmas season is also the time for family reunions. Many people who have moved to other areas return for midnight mass on Christmas Eve or arrive for the main meal on Christmas Day.

The Feast of the Purification of the Virgin Mary occurs on February 2. On this day candles are brought to mass to be blessed. These candles are lit during thunderstorms and during earthquakes, fires, sickness, or death. In some areas rice seed is blessed after mass, and some towns have an annual procession at this time.

Penance and self-denial during Lent very often involve staying away from motion pictures, cockfights, gambling tables, and other forms of entertainment. Frequent reception of the sacraments is encouraged, although the acute shortage of priests in the Philippines precludes the administration of the sacraments in many areas. More severe forms of penance, such as walking on one's knees or public flagellation, are still practiced in a few areas. More widely observed Holy Week customs are the washing of the feet of the "apostles" and *pasos*, a procession of floats depicting scenes from the events that took place shortly before the Crucifixion.

Other folk celebrations or observances of a religious nature occur nearly every month of the year. The most important are the Flowers of May celebrations in honor of the Virgin Mary, which last the entire month; the observance of the Finding of the Holy Cross, also in May; the feasts of Corpus Christi, the Sacred Heart, and Saint John the Baptist, all observed during June; and All Saints' Day and All Souls' Day, at the beginning of November. The feast of All Souls' Day has incorporated many elements similar to Filipino folk and Chinese customs honoring ancestors.

Roman Catholicism and the Life Cycle

A Filipino child is often baptized on the feast day of the saint whose name he bears or the patron saint of his town. In a large town where there is at least one church, several thousand children may be baptized on the day of the town festival; however, in many remote *barrios* the church permits certain elderly women to baptize newborn infants. Most children undergo a formal ceremony performed by the parish priest or one of his assistants. Present at this ceremony will be at least two godparents, one of each sex, who enter into a lifelong relationship with the child and his parents that involves many mutual obligations.

Children are confirmed between the ages of five and eight; in many cases this is done much later but occasionally at the time of baptism. At the age of seven a child receives First Holy Communion after a verbal examination testing his knowledge of his faith. His first religious instruction ordinarily is given by his grandparents, especially the grandmother. This is often complemented by formal lessons from the parish catechist in the local church or chapel. The child goes to confession for the first time just before he receives the Eucharist. The occasion of First Holy Communion is surrounded by considerable solemnity and little folk ceremony. Boys usually wear long white trousers and a white shirt, and girls are dressed in a white outfit similar to that of a bride. After the ceremony all the children usually eat breakfast at the rectory, and a picture-taking session follows.

In contrast to these childhood religious rituals, customs and observances surrounding marriage are elaborate and colored by local customs.
The priest places a ring on the ring finger of the bridegroom's left hand;
the bridegroom then places a second ring on the bride's finger. In
each instance the priest gives a blessing. The priest then drops thirteen
silver coins into the cupped hands of the groom, who in turn lets them
drop into the bride's hands, cupped below his own, saying "My wife, I
give you this ring and these coins as a sign of our marriage." She replies,
"I accept them." This act is said to symbolize the pledge of support on the
part of the husband. During the Nuptial Mass that follows a cord is placed
around the couple tying them together. They are also both covered by a
single veil at the end of the mass.

Reception of extreme Unction, the last rites of the Roman Catholic
Church, is not widely observed, partly because of the scarcity of priests
and partly because of the dominant belief that death will shortly follow
the reception of the sacrament as an inevitable consequence. Almost
every village and neighborhood, however, has at least one man and one
woman who specialize in providing the consolations of the religion to the
dying adherents of that faith.

A dying person usually is surrounded by his immediate family and close
relatives, including minor children. The church bells are rung to inform
the people that someone is dying in order to solicit everyone's prayers.
When word reaches the church that the person has died, the death knell is
sounded and is repeated at regular intervals until the time of burial. Like
marriage the burial ceremony is accompanied by much folk ceremony and
many traditional customs.

Roman Catholic Church as an Organization

In early 1975 the church had ten archdioceses, twenty-eight dioceses,
twelve prelatures nullius, four apostolic vicariates, and 1,741 parishes.
These were under the care of one cardinal (a second cardinal, the first
Philippine cardinal to be chosen, died in 1972); nine archbishops; fifty
bishops; and 4,511 priests. There were also about 1,900 seminarians,
more than 3,000 male members of religious orders, and almost 7,000
nuns.

The greatest organizational weakness of the church in the Philippines
was the shortage of priests. In early 1975 there were an estimated 7,000
Roman Catholics for every priest in the islands—more than three times
the minimum ratio deemed necessary by the church to fulfill its basic
educational and sacramental functions. In some parishes the high ratio of
communicants to clerics denied any sustained contact between the two.
As late as 1967 in Tondo Parish, which covers a major protion of Manila's
slums, three priests ministered to over 150,000 Roman Catholics. The
more than 1,600 Roman Catholic schools at various levels, including
colleges that accommodated over 500,000 students in 1974, added to the
burdens on the church's manpower resources (see ch. 7).

The small number of clerics in the Philippines was the result of several factors. Unlike families in other countries heavily influenced by Hispanic culture, the Filipino family has no tradition of sending at least one male offspring into the service of the church. Moreover the church's controversial role in Philippine history, the hierarchy's long association with conservative and regressive elements of society, and the persistent domination of the religious orders by foreigners during most of the church's history in the Philippines combined to make the priesthood an unattractive career. By 1975, however, most of the secular clergy—including most bishops and the country's cardinal—were Filipinos, and at least the older religious orders were largely Filipino and administered by Filipinos.

In the mid-1970s the church was characterized by several conflicting tendencies that appeared to reflect trends within the church worldwide and within specific locales in the Philippines. During the 1960s a number of so-called progressive groups, both clergy and laity, challenged not only the church's stand on several substantive issues but also the hierarchy's reluctance to tolerate dissent, which it regarded as sowing confusion among the faithful. To some extent the historic roles of religious and secular clergy were reversed. The formally conservative orders—notably the Jesuits—became actively involved in social action and reform. Dioceses came under attack for their conservatism and the wealth that they—unlike the orders—had retained after the end of Spanish rule; several dioceses, however, also maintained social action programs. Questions directly addressing conditions after the imposition of martial law were raised by the Association of Major Religious Superiors in the Philippines. Members of the diocesan hierarchy similarly questioned, although with greater circumspection, certain aspects of martial law through the usually conservative Bishops' Conference, pastoral letters, and statements by individual bishops, including the archibishop of Manila. During the 1973-75 period churchmen called attention to the dangers to human rights under martial law and the "climate of fear" in the country and deplored the indefinite detention of political prisoners and government efforts to regulate or suppress church involvement in labor causes.

INDIGENOUS CHRISTIAN CULTS

Nationalism and Rebellion

The Propaganda Movement of the late nineteenth century, headed by José B. Rizal, was the source of Philippine nationalism. Heavily influenced by the Spanish Orient Lodge of Freemasonry, many propagandists gradually became openly anti-Roman Catholic as well as anti-Spanish (see ch. 3). After armed rebellion against Spanish authorities broke out in 1896, Emilio Aguinaldo, formal head of the insurrectionary forces, appointed a Filipino priest, Gregorio Aglipay, as

"Spiritual Head of the Nation under Arms" with the title of military vicar. Because of their Spanish nationality all bishops were declared deposed; most fled, and others were arrested. Parish priests who remained loyal to the bishops were also relieved of their responsibilities.

The clergy was informed by manifesto that they had to follow the leadership of Aglipay against the hierarchy of the Spanish-dominated church. Those who did were united and organized under Aglipay; Filipinos still loyal to the Spanish hierarchy of the Roman Catholic Church were labeled traitors to their country. The desertion to Aglipay's movement of one out of every sixteen diocesan priests and over 25 percent of the Roman Catholics in the Philippines testified to the magnitude of popular disaffection with the church in the early twentieth century.

In the four decades that followed, numerous indigenous churches sprang up. Most were little more than personal followings of a man or a woman with messianic pretensions. Some were intensely nationalistic and formally deified or canonized Rizal and other revolutionary heroes, adopting the precedent of the Anglipayans—which in 1902 formally declared Rizal and three other Filipino patriots to be saints. Common among most of these national Christian religions was a tendency to consider Filipinos chosen people of God and the only true Christians in existence.

The Aglipayan movement and that of the Iglesia ni Kristo belong to the category of nationalistic, personalistic, and politicoreligious movements that are of national rather than just local significance. They are noteworthy because of their phenomenal success in recruiting new members. The Aglipayan movement grew to more than 1 million adherents within the first two years of its formal existence, and the Iglesia ni Kristo has been the most rapidly growing sect in the islands since World War II. The Aglipayan movement is unusual to the extent that its two principal leaders have been greatly influenced from abroad. They received considerable advice, money, and public relations support from both Spanish and American freemasonry and at different times from the Unitarian and Episcopal churches in the United States.

Aglipayanism and the Philippine Independent Church

At its zenith in 1904 the Philippine Independent Church was reliably estimated to have had a membership of between one-quarter and one-third of the Christian population. Since then, however, this proportion has declined markedly, although in 1970 the church remained the largest indigenous Christian group.

The movement's principal basis was the intense nationalism that accompanied the war for independence and the strong anti-Spanish and antifriar sentiments directed against a church that was dominated by a foreign clergy. In the first decade of the twentieth century the movement

180

received support from Masons in Spain and the United States and from a majority of Protestant missionaries from the United States.

In 1899, after United States armed forces intervened against Spain and later against Aguinaldo's insurgents, Aglipay became the leader of a guerrilla band that harassed the Americans until the band formally surrendered in 1900. In April 1901 two priests representing the dissenting Filipino clergy went to Rome to ask the pope to agree to recognize the actions of Aguinaldo and Aglipay and to commit himself to appointing only Filipinos as bishops, except where appointment of a foreigner received the approval of a majority of Filipino priests.

This request was supported by a similar petition drawn up in Madrid by a Philippine committee headed by Isabelo de los Reyes, a Filipino newspaperman and pamphleteer who had been imprisoned for complicity in an anti-Spanish conspiracy and sent to Madrid, where he was released. In August 1902 de los Reyes launched the Aglipayan movement by proclaiming—in a Manila newspaper—the establishment of a new church under Aglipay. To head the executive committee of laymen he appointed Governor General William Howard Taft, an American; General Aguinaldo; and Trinidad Pardo de Tavera, a Filipino member of the governing commission under Taft. Pardo de Tavera, however, publicly denied having any connection with the movement, as did a majority of the priests mentioned by de los Reyes as leading the Philippine Independent Church.

After attempts at reconciliation failed, Aglipay broke with the Roman Catholic Church. On September 27, 1902, he informed both Governor General Taft and the church authorities of his demand that the cathedral of Manila be turned over to him as head of the Philippine Independent Church. Although rebuffed this gesture was the beginning of a five-year campaign that resulted in the acquisition of nearly one-half of the Roman Catholic Church's properties in the Philippines by Aglipay's followers. In many cases force was used, and considerable bloodshed resulted. Many churches were burned, and several priests were killed. At the height of the movement, in 1904, Aglipay asserted that half the population of the islands belonged to his church. His claim, however, proved premature. In 1906 the conservative Philippine Supreme Court ruled that all the buildings of the Roman Catholic Church that had been occupied by Aglipay's followers had to be returned to the church. Forced to move to makeshift quarters the movement faced financial difficulties and a rapid decline in membership.

De los Reyes created a distinct doctrine, liturgy, and organization for the Philippine Independent Church. Although he was never a Mason, he drew his concepts of theology and worship from the Masonic Code and much of his support and inspiration from Miguel Morayta, the grand master of the Spanish Orient Lodge of Freemasonry in Madrid. According to this doctrine, which was approved formally by Aglipay, their church was founded principally to worship the one true God and to liberate the human conscience from "all anti-scientific error, exaggeration and scruple." They rejected the doctrine of the Trinity as well as the possibility of miracles, including those mentioned in the New Testament. A new version of the Gospel was produced based exclusively on that of Saint Mark; the other evangelists were considered apocryphal. In this version angels, devils, miracles, and other manifestations of the supernatural do not exist. Revelation and prophecy are denied.

The Aglipayan creed states that God is a universal and intelligent force, the principle of all life and movement. Satisfaction of human needs is achieved through work rather than prayer. All reward and punishment for virtuous or evil behavior occur in this life. The origin of the universe is explained as development and not creation because matter has no beginning.

At the time of the break with Rome in 1902 Aglipay had claimed that the doctrine and ritual of his church were identical to those of Roman Catholicism. Although new doctrine and ritual were proclaimed officially, for several decades most Aglipayan priests continued to teach Roman Catholic doctrine and to follow Roman Catholic ritual. They continued to say Mass, venerate the saints, and perform all customary acts of devotion, even though the acts were opposed to official doctrine. As a result of doctrinal disintegration a schism developed even before the death of Aglipay in 1940. In the meantime de los Reyes had reverted to Roman Catholicism.

Early official books, while denying the Trinity, recognized the divinity of Christ, but by 1919 the revised plan for studies contained instructions for "discarding . . . what is said about Christ's divinity, a doctrine which we accepted in the beginning only out of compulsion." Christ is said to have taught the more grave errors. There is an emphasis on science as the source for all religious truths. Morality is highly relativistic. The Ten Commandments are said to be pure myth.

The closer Aglipay brought his church toward unitarian teachings the greater the tension within it became. Many of his ministers complained that they had to continue the traditional practices and rituals at the risk of losing their income and most of their followers. During the 1920s two of Aglipay's ministers formed their own splinter groups. Angel Flor Mata called his branch the Philippine Reformed Church (Iglesia Filipina Reformada), and in 1924 Ciriaco de las Llagas founded the Independent Philippine Evangelical Church (Iglesia Filipina Evangélica Independiente).

In 1928 an open battle erupted within the Philippine Independent Church over the doctrine of the divinity of Christ and other traditional dogma, which was to result a decade later in a major split in the movement. Servando Castro, the Aglipayan bishop of Ilocos, and five other founding members of the Aglipayan movement publicly protested the unitarian doctrines that de los Reyes and Aglipay had introduced, without the approval of the Supreme Council of Bishops. They asserted that the rank-and-file Aglipayans held to the traditional teachings, that immutability is a characteristic quality of religious truths, and further that the new doctrines were contrary to the faith that the leaders of the Aglipayan church publicly swore to preserve.

In April 1938 a group known as the Trinitarian faction, under the leadership of Isabelo de los Reyes, Jr., broke away. After the death of Aglipay both the Unitarian and Trinitarian groups maintained that they were the true Philippine Independent Church. Finally in 1955 the courts awarded the right to that name and possession of Aglipayan church property to the Trinitarian faction. The Unitarian faction continued to insist that it represented the true form of Aglipayanism. Since 1948 the dominant Trinitarian faction has been associated with the Protestant Episcopal Church of the United States, which consecrated three of its bishops. In turn these bishops consecrated the other bishops of the Philippine Independent Church. In 1961 this faction, having a total membership of just over 200,000, entered into a Concordat of Full Communion with the Protestant Episcopal Church of the United States.

Iglesia ni Kristo

The decline of the Aglipayans was closely connected with the rise of the Iglesia ni Kristo (Church of Christ), by far the fastest growing, most dynamic, most disciplined, and most unified of all religions in the Philippines. The church membership was estimated at between 250,000 and 500,000 in the late 1960s, although church leaders claimed a following of 4 million. Virulently anti-Catholic, the church was founded in 1913 by Felix Manalo Ysagun and claims to be "the only continuation of the Church of Christ in Jerusalem." Moreover, unlike other churches on the islands, the church possesses a highly political orientation and played a direct and formidable role in Philippine electoral politics before martial law.

Ysagun was born in the village of Tipan on Laguna de Bay in 1886. In 1911 he decided to start his own church. Although baptized a Roman Catholic, at the age of thirteen he had joined the Methodist Episcopal Church but soon transferred to a Presbyterian school. After studying the doctrines of both the Disciples of Christ and the Seventh-Day Adventists, he struck out on his own in Manila. By 1914 he had a sufficiently large group of followers to register the Iglesia ni Kristo with the government.

Highly charismatic, Felix Manalo (he dropped Ysagun at the time he began his church) believed he was the fifth angel of the apocalypse and insisted that his cult was the only legitimate Christian church in existence after a lapse of some nineteen centuries during which no true church existed. In 1940 he published a 122-page pamphlet in Tagalog, translated as *The Torch to Throw Light upon the True Nature of the Roman Catholic Apostolic Church*. Largely a polemic against Roman Catholicism, the work also stated his messianic pretensions. His church strictly denies the divinity of Christ, who is nevertheless recognized as the sole mediator between God and man. He is also the redeemer through whom salvation is possible if one becomes a member of his mystical body which, according to Manalo, is the Iglesia ni Kristo. He stated that outside his church there was no salvation; nevertheless he denied the immortality of the soul. Manalo died in 1963.

As an organization the Iglesia ni Kristo is highly authoritarian. Headed by an executive minister who possesses an absolute monopoly of power within the church, the Iglesia ni Kristo seeks to regulate virtually every aspect of the lives of its followers. Attendance is required at twice-weekly religious services (Sundays and Thursdays) where armed guards keep out nonmembers and also tally names of latecomers and absentees. Sermons in Tagalog or a local dialect are standardized throughout the country, and dues based on the ability to pay are mandatory. Adherents of the faith must also meet rigid standards of personal behavior imposed on them by the church or else face expulsion. Proscribed activities include gambling, excessive drinking, apostasy, marriage outside the church, and membership in labor unions (forbidden on the grounds that labor-management disputes violate the Christian concept of brotherly love).

In addition the Iglesia ni Kristo instructed its members on how to vote, and the church constituted one of the few disciplined electoral blocs in the Philippines. Its ability to deliver the votes of its members accounted for the unusually solicitous attention it received from almost all candidates for office at the national level before martial law.

The Iglesia ni Kristo invests most of its resources in caring for its members. In addition to socioeconomic welfare programs and a massive campaign to eradicate illiteracy among its followers, the church secures jobs for its adherents and has embarked on a number of entrepreneurial ventures. It has established an agricultural development project in Nueva Ecija Province to accommodate tenants from neighboring provinces who were ejected from their lands by local landlords. The growing antagonism of the Roman Catholic Church, the Huks, and the New People's Army toward the church stems in large part from the competition among all four organizations for followers.

The Iglesia ni Kristo gains new converts primarily through large public rallies. Resembling American fundamentalist revival meetings, the rallies are held upon the request of local church ministers. Appeals are usually simple and designed to arouse racial and national pride. Strident denunciations of the Roman Catholic Church are common. The effectiveness of the rally as a vehicle for recruitment is reflected in the spectacular growth of the church, which during the 1960s registered from 15,000 to 20,000 new converts each year.

Minor Groups

The diversity of the Philippine religious environment is most apparent

184

in the numerous minor groups that developed at the beginning of the twentieth century and subsided and reemerged in the decades thereafter. Most of the groups in the 1960s and early 1970s revolved around the worship of national heroes, principally Rizal. These groups, extremely varied in style and mutually competitive, tended to concentrate in impoverished rural and urban settlements. Most borrowed to one degree or another elements of Roman Catholic hierarchy and ritual.

A complete listing of these religious movements was not possible, many of them tending to spin off even smaller splinter groups. Among the larger groups in the 1960s were the Lapiang Malaya (translated as Independence Party); Sambahang Rizal (Rizal Church); Iglesiang Pilipina (Philippine Church), known also as Adarnistas; Bathalismo (Godism); Iglesia Sagrada Filipina (Sacred Philippine Church); Iglesia Sagrada ng Lahi (Sacred Church of the Race); Iglesia Filipino Apostolico Catolica (Philippine Apostolic Catholic Church); and the Iglesia Watawat ng Lahi (Pride of the Race Church), perhaps the largest of the various sects with a claimed membership of 125,000 in the late 1960s.

ISLAM

Islam was originally introduced into the Philippine Islands nearly 200 years before Christianity. Arab traders and adventurers and Malayan and Indonesian missionaries came to the Sulu Archipelago during the middle of the fourteenth century. From there Islam spread to the southern coast of Mindanao. A century later firmly established Muslim political organizations began a somewhat systematic effort at religious conversion of the natives of the island. Along with their religion. the Muslims introduced a superior alphabet and more developed forms of art and science.

The arrival of the Spaniards ended the intermittent warfare among the major Muslim groups and united them in a jihad against the Spanish intruders that was to last almost 300 years. It was not until 1879 that the sultan of Sulu signed a peace treaty with the Spaniards and agreed to become a subject of Spain. Under the terms of this treaty the religion and customs of the Sulu Muslims were to be respected, but Christian missionaries were to be allowed full freedom to spread the Gospel. The Muslims on Mindanao, however, remained hostile to the government in Manila until they were finally subdued by the United States Army by around 1915. In a like manner they did not make peace until they promised that they would be undisturbed in the practice of their religion.

Unlike Muslims in most of the rest of the world, those in the Philippines knew very little about their religion. They were devoted to Islam to the point of fanaticism because they considered it the focal point of their identity and the source of their way of life. The degree of orthodoxy varied among ethnic groups; generally, however, except for the religious advisers to local sultans, Filipino Muslims were unfamiliar with the Koran and observed very few of the rituals and prohibitions it prescribed.

The recital of the prescribed prayers five times a day and the pilgrimage to Mecca also were largely unknown before the twentieth century. There were very few mosques.

As a result of centuries of fighting for the survival of their customs and way of life, Filipino Muslims developed an extraordinary rigidity and a conservatism in social, political, and religious matters. This conservatism has diminished greatly in most areas since World War II, however, owing to the influence of Muslim missionaries from Egypt, Saudi Arabia, Pakistan, and Indonesia. For example, only after observing that Muslims from other countries wore Western-style clothing did Filipino Muslims begin to do so in any significant numbers; if a Muslim moved to the city and adopted the form of dress of Christian Filipinos, it was assumed he had given up his way of life and his religion.

Before the twentieth century Islam was largely a veneer under which Filipino Muslims preserved most of the original values and cultural institutions that had existed before the arrival of the Spaniards. Islam was a source of unity among various groups, and it left life within these groups very largely as it had been before. Nevertheless Islam had a great influence on legal and political organization; in the early 1970s law was still largely administered through religious courts in Muslim areas, and the decisions rendered were based on a combination of Koranic and customary law.

In essence political organization in Muslim areas was theocratic. Obedience to a sultan was obedience to Allah. Every sultan had as the source of his authority either the claim that he was a descendant of the Prophet Muhammad and therefore his representative or that he was authorized to rule by the caliph of Constantinople. Under the system religious and political authority in any given area was vested in the same individual. Numerous attempts by the government to eliminate slavery, polygyny, and divorce in Muslim areas have been unsuccessful because such institutions have the double sanction of custom and religion. As a rule only those changes that can be deduced from the Koran or from customary law are acceptable. For this reason Muslim missionaries have succeeded in introducing change where other outsiders have failed.

The resurgence of Islam in other countries after World War II had a profound effect upon Islam in the Philippines. New mosques were built in Muslim areas, and additional religious schools teaching the Koran, the Arabic language, and principles of Muslim morality were established. Some were staffed by teachers who had studied in or were from Egypt and Saudi Arabia. Pilgrimages to Mecca became more numerous. Religious literature is being published in larger quantities and is widely distributed. Many Islamic societies for social and religious purposes also have been established.

Muslim prohibitions against pork and against ballroom dancing are more widely observed, but the prohibition against alcoholic beverages does not appear to have made a significant impact. Orthodox rituals accompanying circumcision, marriage, and burial are followed. The annual fast of Ramadan and the festivities that follow it, as well as other holy days and liturgical seasons, have been introduced successfully in many areas, but the custom of the five daily prayers has not generally been accepted.

Consciousness of religious and cultural distinctiveness was heightened by an influx of Christian Filipino settlers, farmers, and loggers, particularly in the post-World War II period. This migration, mainly from the Visayan Islands, increased to the extent that in several traditionally Muslim areas Muslims were greatly outnumbered by Christians. Disputes over landrights, especially in rich farming regions on the island of Mindanao, erupted in the late 1960s into open communal warfare, apparently aggravated by disputes between Muslims themselves, reflecting broad social divisions similar to those elsewhere in the Philippines. Although the conflicts in Mindanao and the Sulu Archipelago appeared to be largely territorial, economic, and political, Muslims understandably perceived them to represent one more chapter in a centuries-old struggle to preserve their way of life in a nation dominated by what appeared to them to be a hostile Christian majority.

PROTESTANT CHRISTIANITY

Whereas Spain introduced Roman Catholicism to the Philippines, Protestant religions accompanied the arrival of the United States as Spain's colonial successor in the islands. Two months after the outbreak of the Spanish-American War representatives of various American Protestant denominations met in New York to make plans for converting the Philippines. The Presbyterians arrived in the islands in 1899; Methodists and Baptists in 1900; Episcopalians, United Brethren, and Disciples of Christ in 1901; and Congregationalists in 1902. Several other church groups followed. After World War II a variety of evangelical and pentacostal missions were introduced, and in the early 1970s there were some seventy-five pentacostal groups alone. Within the Philippines some older churches and newer missions underwent schisms reflecting both personality clashes and doctrinal divisions, partly offsetting an opposing tendency toward cooperation and ecumenism.

Of all the Protestant denominations arriving during the first three decades of the twentieth century, only Episcopalians did not proselytize among Filipino Roman Catholics, because they considered Roman Catholics to be genuine Christians. In order to prevent duplication of effort and mutual antagonism, Protestant groups initially reached a comity agreement among themselves regarding territorial division of the islands for purposes of missionary work; Manila was declared common ground for all denominations. With increased population migration and the multiplication and fragmentation of Protestant groups after World War II, however, this division has tended to blur.

The public school system introduced by the Americans and staffed by several hundred American volunteers was also an important vehicle for conversion of Filipinos to Protestantism. Many teachers were ministers or former ministers; most were hostile to Roman Catholicism.

There were more than 200 Protestant Christian denominations in the islands. In 1948 three churches and church unions, including the Presbyterians, Congregationalists, and United Brethren, formed an organized union in the United Church of Christ in the Philippines, the largest Protestant Church in the early 1970s. Other numerically significant groups included the United Methodist Church, the Methodist Evangelical Church in the Philippines (Iglesia Evangelica Metodista en las Islas Filipinas), Seventh-Day Adventists, Convention of Philippines Baptist Churches, Southern Baptist Convention, Churches of Christ Philippine Mission, Philippine Episcopal Church, Jehovah's Witnesses, Assemblies of God, and the Christian and Missionary Alliance. At least in the first decades of Protestantism in the islands, early converts demonstrated considerable upward social mobility—from relatively poor to middle-class status—perhaps as a result of the educational activities of Protestant missionaries. The Protestant churches yielded a disproportionate number of prominent regional and national figures. By the early 1970s, with some notable exceptions, Protestant churches drew their members mainly from the middle class.

Eight churches—including the major United Church of Christ in the Philippines, the two large Methodist organizations, and the Philippine Independent Church—were members of the National Council of Churches in the Philippines, inaugurated in 1963. Most other denominations were somewhat antagonistic to the council because they considered it to be dominated by members and affiliates whose theological positions were too liberal and contrary to Holy Scripture.

Schisms also have occurred in the Protestant churches. In the Baliwag Revolt of 1905, for example, a large group under Manuel Aurora broke away from the Methodist church. His group, called the Philippine Evangelical Religion of the Living Christians (Religion Evangélica Filipina de los Cristianos Vivos), split in 1910, when a group of its members formed the Philippine National Church (Iglesia Nacional Filipina). In the meantime the Methodist church suffered another, more serious schism, launched in 1909 by Nicholas Zamora, who formed the Methodist Evangelical Church in the Philippines. This sect later underwent two schisms of its own, producing the Christian Trinitarian Church (Iglesia Cristiana Trinitaria) and the Church of God (Iglesia de Dios).

Most of these early schisms resulted at least in part from nationalist sentiments and racial sensitivities. Filipinos tended to resent the fact that control of their churches was in the hands of foreigners and that Filipinos could not aspire to rise in the church hierarchy. Since World War II, however, Filipinos have risen to the highest levels within most churches in the islands. The control exercised by the parent bodies in the United States, which provided the bulk of the financial support necessary to keep the churches going, had loosened considerably by the early 1970s. The dependence of Protestant churches in the Philippines on American money and manpower, which was a source of irritation for many Filipinos in an era of increasing nationalism, had also been reduced. With the exception of the small Lutheran church, for example, all the members of the National Council of Churches in the Philippines were led and controlled by Filipino churchmen.

In addition to preaching and ministering to their own congregations, the principal efforts of major Protestant groups have been in the fields of education and medicine. Much of this work was supported by funds from the United States. The Association of Christian Schools and Colleges oversees more than fifty affiliated schools that provide instruction on all levels from elementary grades through graduate study. Silliman University, Central Philippine University, Philippine Christian College, Philippine Wesleyan College, Dansalan Junior College, and Southern Christian College were all members of the association. There are also a number of Protestant hospitals and clinics under religious auspices. Protestant groups were also active in organizing cooperatives and credit unions.

SECTION II. POLITICAL

CHAPTER 9

THE GOVERNMENTAL SYSTEM

In a proclamation signed on September 21, 1972, and announced two days later, President Ferdinand E. Marcos placed the archipelago nation under martial law, citing as a principal reason the danger of a violent overthrow of the government by communist rebels. The proclamation was issued under a constitutional provision that gave the president emergency powers in the event of invasion, insurrection, or rebellion.

At the end of 1975 Marcos was using his nearly absolute powers to implement a wide range of reforms in the social, political, and economic fields. As officially envisaged, these reforms—if successful—would result in the establishment of a so-called New Society, a society that would be no longer beset with corruption, inequities, and injustices as was "the old society." Efforts to build the New Society were being undertaken in accordance with what Marcos called "constitutional authoritarianism," a form of rule he described as less totalitarian than democratic since the ultimate aim of the martial law regime was to be "the reinstatement of individual and national freedom." Marcos insisted that rule by martial law was intended to be only "an interlude to a new society, that is, in sum, a Cromwellian phase in our quest for a good and just society. Certainly, the enterprise is worth a little sacrifice."

After a new constitution was ratified and put into effect in January 1973, replacing the 1935 Constitution, the governmental structure underwent gradual and selective reorganization, a process that was still continuing in the mid-1970s. The 1973 Constitution, in breaking with a quarter-century of tradition, provides for a parliamentary rather than a presidential form of government. Under the new setup the unicameral National Assembly was to elect from among its members a prime minister as the chief executive or head of the government; the assembly was also to elect a symbolic or ceremonial president as head of state—both officers for a term of six years. The prime minister, who was also to be the commander in chief of the armed forces, would form a cabinet. As under the 1935 Constitution the judicial power was vested in the independent Supreme Court.

Actually the Philippines had yet to have the parliamentary system of government. In the mid-1970s it was still under the old presidential system and was expected to remain so until Marcos pronounced that the country was ready for the new system after a period of transition. During this period Marcos was authorized, under transitory provisions in Article XVII of the 1973 charter, to rule, combining the executive powers as vested in both the 1935 and 1973 constitutions.

The institutionalization of martial law government in September 1972 marked a major turning point in the evolution of Philippine government and politics (see ch. 10). Until then the governing powers of the state were divided into executive, legislative, and judicial branches, each exercising checks and balances against the others. No single branch or personality had been able to dominate the others as completely and absolutely as President Marcos and his executive establishment were able to do in the years after 1972. Before martial law the government had been accountable to the public through periodic elections; partisan politics and elections had assured a degree of popular participation in political processes. After 1972 the decisionmaking process was removed from the vagaries of parliamentary politics and came to be identified increasingly with a select few around President Marcos. Politics and government became steadily personalized.

In the scheme of the governmental system the central government continued to enjoy preeminence over the local counterpart. Under the Spanish the central authority had seldom extended outside major population centers, the rest of the country being in the hands of feudal powers. The advent of American rule at the beginning of the twentieth century changed this picture as local areas were steadily brought under central control. This penetration from Manila continued unabated in postindependence years (see ch. 3).

THE CONSTITUTIONAL FRAMEWORK

The ultimate legal basis for the organization and operation of the government was Article XVII, entitled Transitory Provisions, of the 1973 Constitution. As a practical matter the legality of government operation rested on what Article XVII calls "all proclamations, orders, decrees, instructions, and acts promulgated, issued, or done by the incumbent president." The presidential actions would have the force of the law of the land and were to be valid "even after lifting of martial law" unless modified or repealed by the regular National Assembly in some indefinite future.

Background

The country's first constitution was framed by a constituent assembly formed in 1934. Approved by plebiscite in May 1935, this document laid down the basis for the country's ten-year transition period of self-government under American tutelage (see ch. 3). The Philippines became an independent republic in July 1946, at which time the 1935 Constitution, as amended in 1939 and again in 1940, was retained in toto; it remained in effect until replaced by a new one in January 1973.

The 1935 charter drew heavily upon the United States Constitution, providing as it did for an elaborate scheme of checks and balances among the three separate but equal branches of government—the legislative, executive, and judicial. The government was presidential in form but was organized as a unitary rather than a federal system, meaning that the powers of the central government extended to all political subdivisions in the country without being divided into federal and state jurisdictions.

The 1935 Constitution was amended three times. The first change occurred in 1939, when discriminatory trade restrictions imposed on the Philippines by the United States Congress were removed, if only partially. The second modification was made in 1940, adding a senate to what had until then been a single-house legislature; it also enabled the president and the vice president to run a second term of four years in lieu of the previous nonrenewable, single term of six years.

The third and final amendment was in 1947, when American citizens were granted equal rights with Filipinos not only in the exploitation, disposition, utilization, and development of natural resources but in the operation of public utilities. This provision was to be valid until July 1974 (see ch. 11; ch. 15).

Under that constitution and as actually practiced, the presidential mandate was renewed every four years through fiercely contested partisan elections. Politics revolved around the president, who was the head of state, chief executive, commander in chief of the armed forces, and by convention leader of the dominant political party. The constitution limited presidential tenure to two consecutive terms of four years each, or a maximum of eight years.

The constitution provided for the separation of state and church, acknowledging at the same time the supremacy of Divine Providence over the state. Sovereignty was to emanate from the people and to be exercised by the popularly chosen instrument of a republican state. The government was directed to promote the social justice, well-being, and economic security of all the people rather than of a privileged class. Suffrage was granted at first only to male citizens twenty years of age and older, but women, too, were enfranchised in 1937.

A bill of rights, as familiar to the American people, was incorporated into the constitution. The 1935 document guaranteed an array of fundamental rights, such as the sanctity of homes and private property; freedom from unreasonable searches and seizure except on probable cause; the privileges of the writ of habeas corpus (except in cases of invasion, insurrection, or rebellion); freedom of abode and movement; and privacy of correspondence. Among other constitutional safeguards were the freedom of speech and the press, the freedom of assembly, the right to petition the authorities for redress of grievances, the freedom of religious worship, and the right to form associations.

Economically a free enterprise system was constitutionally sanctioned, but at the same time its operation was to be qualified by provisions authorizing government intervention when warranted in the interest of general welfare or national defense or both. All natural resources were declared as belonging to the state, and the constitution spelled out in detail the conditions under which these were to be developed and utilized.

The 1973 Constitution

In the years after independence in 1946 the constitutional order as laid down in 1935 was tested by numerous events, bearing witness to a democratic experiment introduced initially by the Americans but continued by the Filipinos. The 1973 Constitution was in a sense the outgrowth of this experiment, which had been punctuated by intermittent voices for the "Filipinization" of political processes.

The move to reexamine the 1935 Constitution and frame a new one to be consistent with the nation's dignity as full-fledged independent state received its first official blessing in March 1967, when a bill was enacted to establish a nonpartisan constitutional convention at a later date. The delegates were elected in November 1970, and the convention, attended by 312 delegates, opened its inaugural session in June 1971. In his speech to that session President Marcos urged the delegates to prepare a new charter, one that would reflect Filipino aspirations to "a Filipino progress, built upon Filipino energies, opportunities, and resources."

The convention grappled with its formidable task amid a general sentiment in favor of delimiting presidential powers and of replacing the presidential structure of government with a parliamentary one similar to that of Great Britain. Among other proposals were those relating to the independence and integrity of the judiciary, the strengthening of local governments, the emphasis on human over property rights, and electoral reforms.

The draft constitution, for the most part embodying these proposed changes, was formally approved by the Constitutional Convention in November 1972. It was declared ratified on January 17, 1973, by "an overwhelming majority" of the members of *barangays* (citizens' assemblies), which were formed as popular organs of consultation under Presidential Decree 86, dated December 31, 1972 (see ch. 10). Marcos explained that the haste with which the *barangays* were formed was compelled by secessionist plans of Muslim rebels in the southern islands (see ch. 17). It was said to be necessary, therefore, to dispense with a secret or written ballot and more time for popular discussion on the pros and cons of the draft constitution. Marcos characterized the plebiscite as a "legal and constitutional gamble" and added, "no matter how much it was questioned by a few, the result of the plebiscite achieved the purpose I had envisioned. The secessionist plan was upset."

The 1973 Constitution became effective on the same day it was declared ratified. Apart from the preamble, its seventeen articles deal with the national territory, declaration of principles and state policies,

194

citizenship, Bill of Rights, duties and obligations of citizens, suffrage, the president, the National Assembly, the prime minister and the cabinet, the judiciary, local government, the constitutional commissions, accountability of public officers, the national economy and the patrimony of the nation, general provisions, amendments, and transitory provisions.

The document retained many of the old provisions relating to the Bill of Rights, and the directive principles of government. Among the new provisions were those dealing with the redefinition of the presidency and other public offices that was made necessary because of the change from presidential to parliamentary form of government. Also new were stipulations governing the accountability of public servants and the institution of local self-government. The 1973 Constitution also expressly affirmed the supremacy of civilian authority over the military and in addition directed the state to provide for social services so that the people could have a "decent standard of living." In a similar vein Section 6 of Article II empowered the state to take a more active role than was the case under the old constitution in the promotion of social and economic justice (see ch. 6; ch. 12).

The question of citizenship was clarified in Article III. Under this provision citizens were defined as those who were citizens of the Philippines at the time of the adoption of the 1973 Constitution; those whose fathers or mothers were citizens of the Philippines; those who elected Philippine citizenship pursuant to the provisions of the 1935 Constitution; and those who were naturalized in accordance with law. Additionally the article stated that a female citizen who married an alien would retain her Philippine citizenship unless by her act or omission she was deemed, under the law, to have renounced her status. A natural-born citizen was defined as one who was a citizen of the country from birth without having to perform any act to acquire or perfect his Philippine citizenship. As a practical matter this definition of a natural-born citizen applied for the most part to the Chinese community in the country (see ch. 4).

Authority to interpret the articles of the Constitution was vested in the Supreme Court. All cases involving the constitutionality of a treaty, executive agreement, or law had to be heard and decided by the full bench of the Supreme Court. Judgment required the concurrence of at least ten justices. The procedure for amending or revising the constitution required initiatory action either by the National Assembly or by a constitutional convention; in the latter case the assembly was empowered either to call the convention by a vote of two-thirds of its members or, by a majority vote of its members, to refer the question of calling such a convention to the electorate. An amendment would be considered valid when ratified by a majority of the votes cast in a plebiscite, which was to be held not later than three months after the proposed amendment was approved.

Transitory Provisions

Article XVII outlines the general procedures under which the parliamentary system of government would eventually come into being. It provides for, among other things, an interim national assembly, which was to come into existence automatically upon the ratification of the 1973 Constitution and which was to continue until the regular National Assembly was chosen through an election called by the interim legislature. The interim body was to have as its members the incumbent president and vice president, those members of the existing bicameral Congress who opted to serve therein, and those delegates of the Constitutional Convention who had voted affirmatively for Article XVII.

The 1973 Constitution was proclaimed on January 17, 1973. At the same time Marcos proclaimed that the interim assembly, the inaugural session of which was to have been called by the president after the adoption of the Constitution, would not be convened at that time; he had not convened the assembly as of late 1975 (see ch. 10). According to Section 5 of Article XVII the assembly was to have given "priority to measures for the orderly transition from the presidential to the parliamentary system, the reorganization of the Government, the eradication of graft and corruption, the effective maintenance of peace and order, the implementation of declared agrarian reforms, the standardization of compensation of government employees, and such other measures as shall bridge the gap between the rich and the poor."

Continuity in national leadership was assured under Section 3 (1) of the same article, which stipulated that the incumbent president should:

Continue to exercise his powers and prerogatives under the nineteen hundred and thirty-five Constitution and the powers vested in the President and the Prime Minister under this Constitution until he calls upon the *interim* National Assembly to elect the *interim* President and the *interim* Prime Minister, who shall then exercise their respective powers vested by this Constitution.

This continuity was also legitimized under Section 3 (2) of the article, which stated:

All proclamations, orders, decrees, instructions, and acts promulgated, issued, or done by the incumbent President shall be part of the law of the land, and shall remain valid, legal, binding, and effective even after lifting of martial law or the ratification of this Constitution, unless modified, revoked, or superseded by subsequent proclamations, orders, decrees, instructions, or other acts of the incumbent President, or unless expressly and explicitly modified or repealed by the regular National Assembly.

Article XVII further stated that "all treaties, executive agreements, and contracts entered into by the Government . . . are hereby recognized as legal, valid, and binding." It also authorized the president to review "all contracts, concessions, permits, or other forms of privileges for the exploration, development, exploitation, or utilization of natural resources entered into, granted, issued, or acquired before the ratification of this Constitution." The rights and privileges granted to citizens of the

United States or to corporations or associations owned or controlled by such citizens in 1947 would automatically terminate on July 3, 1974, under the terms of this article. After the declaration of martial law, however, several measures helped alleviate the problem faced by Americans holding land in the Philippines and eased the divestment process (see ch. 15).

CENTRAL GOVERNMENT

As of late 1975 the martial law administration continued unchallenged under Marcos's firm executive and legislative control. Indications were that his "constitutional authoritarianism" would remain unchanged as long as he felt that the Philippines was faced with what he called "the grave danger of complacency of old habits that refuse to die, the claim of ancient legacy, the exacting demands of daily and routinary living and survival in a world crushed by crisis and emergency."

The President and the Executive Branch

The presidency continued to be the most powerful institution (see fig. 8). The range of powers at the disposal of this office was extremely broad. The powers enjoyed by Marcos were those originally provided for under the 1935 Constitution, which were declared retained by the incumbent president under the transitory provisions of the 1973 Constitution. These powers enabled him to control the executive domain and the military establishment as well. The presidential prerogatives with respect to policymaking, execution, appointment, and dismissal of senior officials and the issues of war and peace were exercised and implemented through decrees that had the force of the law of the land. In addition the president had at his disposal broad emergency powers, including the authority to place the country under martial law wholly or in part.

The chief executive was aided by a number of staff units, the most important of these being the Office of the President under the charge of a cabinet-rank presidential executive assistant, who had been called executive secretary before November 1975. As part of a personnel shakeup and organizational change announced at that time, Executive Secretary Alejandro Melchor, Jr., was removed along with a deputy executive secretary and assistant executive secretary; and the powers and functions previously exercised by Melchor were transferred to Presidential Executive Assistant Jacobo C. Clave, who was concurrently chairman of the Civil Service Commission. In line with the announced intention of providing the presidential office with efficient staff assistance in clearly delineated functional areas, President Marcos created new positions for five presidential assistants respectively in charge of legal affairs, economic and development affairs, financial and monetary affairs, budget and fiscal affairs, and general government matters.

A dozen or so units within the office performed administrative, coordinating, and other support functions, including the drafting of policy

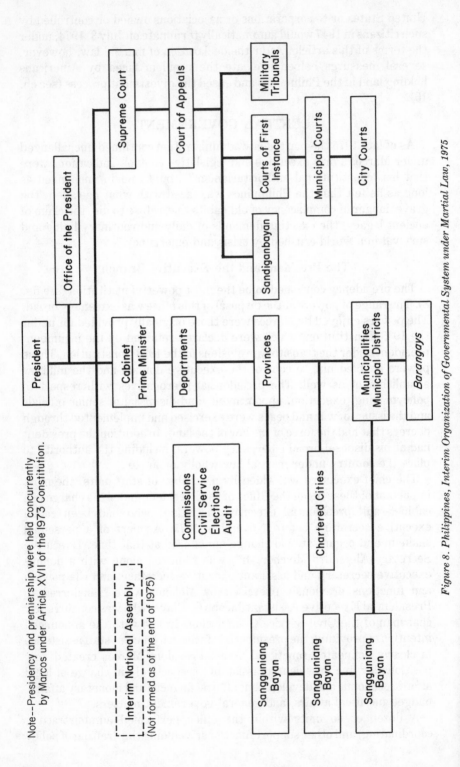

Note--Presidency and premiership were held concurrently
by Marcos under Article XVII of the 1973 Constitution.

Figure 8. Philippines, Interim Organization of Governmental System under Martial Law, 1975

President

Office of the President

Supreme Court

Court of Appeals

Military Tribunals

Courts of First Instance

Municipal Courts

City Courts

Sandiganbayan

Cabinet Prime Minister

Departments

Provinces

Municipalities Municipal Districts

Barangays

Commissions
Civil Service
Elections
Audit

Chartered Cities

Interim National Assembly
(Not formed as of the end of 1975)

Sangguniang Bayan

Sangguniang Bayan

Sangguniang Bayan

guidelines and legislative proposals, the monitoring of both central and local government activities, and the preparation of reports based on fact-finding or investigative work. Under the Office of the President were also a number of commissions, committees, and boards created for ad hoc purposes. The trend in the mid-1970s was to reduce the number of these bodies sharply either by integrating several functions into a single body or by delegating more administrative matters requiring presidential attention to individual cabinet-level departments.

The cabinet was the principal advisory and deliberative forum for the president. It was composed of the president, the vice president, the heads or secretaries of all executive departments, and other cabinet-level officials, including the presidential executive assistant, the budget commissioner, the chairman of the National Economic and Development Authority, the chairman of the National Science Development Board, the chairman of the Civil Service Commission, the governor of the Central Bank of the Philippines, and the presidential press secretary. Its weekly meeting was chaired by the president and discussed a wide range of national issues. Although the cabinet members' deliberations had a policymaking impact, they were only recommendatory and not binding on the president.

For years the government departments varied in number and in composition, depending on the needs of the day. As of late 1975 there were nineteen departments (called ministries in the 1973 Constitution) headed by presidentially appointed secretaries. The departmental portfolios included: agrarian reform; agriculture; cultural minorities; education and culture; finance; foreign affairs; health; industry; justice; labor; local government and community development; national defense; natural resources; public highways; public information; public works, transportation, and communications; social welfare; tourism; and trade.

Under the parliamentary system of government provided for in the 1973 Constitution, the choice of a chief executive (the prime minister) would be decided by a majority of the members of the National Assembly from among themselves. Until the convening of the interim National Assembly, there were no constitutional restrictions on Marcos' tenure. During the period of transition the issue of succession also remained unclear. In September 1974 Marcos stated that he did not anticipate any succession crisis since there was a special arrangement to which he and a dozen or so top military officers had concurred shortly before the proclamation of martial law in September 1972 (see ch. 10). He said that under this still-secret arrangement he would be succeeded, in the event of his disability, by a collective leadership. This civilian-led caretaker group would have to seek a new mandate through a referendum. In June 1975 it was reported that a collective group, identified as the executive cabinet committee, would attend to the affairs of state while the president was away on a foreign visit.

The Legislature

Until 1972 the Philippines had a legislative branch called the Congress, which was bicameral and operated in the context of an open, very spirited bipartisan political competition (see ch. 10). Its upper house members, or senators, were elected to a term of six years, one-third of them being elected every two years to ensure parliamentary continuity. The lower house representatives were chosen every four years. The last general election for the lower house was held in 1969 and the last mid-term election for the senate in 1971.

The Congress was renamed the National Assembly and was made a single house under the 1973 Constitution. Its members were to be elected to a term of six years. During the transitional period the members of the old Congress were to continue in office as members of the interim National Assembly. In January 1973, however, President Marcos proclaimed that the interim assembly, which was to have come into existence when the Constitution went into effect, would not be convened at that time.

In 1973 President Marcos continued to express his distaste for old-style parliamentary politics, which he argued was discredited by corruption and the prohibitive cost of electioneering. In August 1975 the president stated, for example, that the Congress had to be done away with because it was "the cause or principal reason for anarchy and injustice and the inequities perpetuated in the name of democracy."

The Judiciary

Under martial law certain offenses previously under the jurisdiction of civilian courts were transferred to military tribunals. These included: crimes against national security and the law of the land; violation of antisubversion laws; espionage; crimes against public order; violation of laws on firearms and explosives; crimes against personal liberty; and rumormongering and spreading false information. Besides, criminal and civil cases involving "graft and corrupt practices and such other offenses committed by public officers and employees, including those in government-owned or controlled corporations" were transferred to a newly created special court called Sandiganbayan. Otherwise the regular civilian court system continued to function without substantive change.

The Philippines had a long experience in legal principles and practices, derived for the most part from Spanish and United States precedents. Many of the civil code procedures adopted under the Spanish were blended with the practices under common and statutory law introduced by the United States. Spanish influence was evident, for example, in the absence of jury trial, although there was a wholesale incorporation of United States court procedures. The Spanish heritage was particularly pronounced in the domain of the civil code pertaining to family and property. The bulk of the country's important statutes, however, were of

American derivation, as in matters of trade and commerce, labor relations, taxation, banking and currency, and governmental operations in general.

At the top of the judicial system was the Supreme Court, which had administrative supervision over some 2,000 judges and 17,000 employees of all inferior courts; before 1973 this supervisory function had been under the Department of Justice. Accordingly the court had the power to discipline judges of inferior courts and order their dismissal, but under the 1973 Constitution power to define, prescribe, and apportion the jurisdiction of these courts was vested in the National Assembly.

The Supreme Court had a chief justice and fourteen associate justices. All justices and judges of the subordinate courts held their offices during good behavior until they reached the age of sixty-five, but the transitory provisions of the Constitution exempted from this age requirement those judges in office at the time the new charter was ratified in January 1973. The justices and judges were to be appointed by the prime minister under the new Constitution; this meant that during the transition period President Marcos would exercise this constitutional prerogative.

The Supreme Court had original jurisdiction over cases affecting ambassadors, other public ministers, and consuls and over petitions relating to injunctions and writs of habeas corpus. In addition it had appellate jurisdiction over cases relating to the constitutionality of a treaty, law, ordinance, or executive order; cases involving the legality of any tax, impost, assessment, or toll; cases in which the jurisdiction of any inferior court was at issue; criminal cases in which the penalty of death or life imprisonment was involved; and all cases in which only an error or question of law was involved. The Supreme Court could also order a change of venue to avoid a miscarriage of justice.

Most appellate cases, other than those reserved for the Supreme Court, were heard by the eighteen-member Court of Appeals, which was below the Supreme Court but above the courts of first instance at the provincial level. The appellate court met either in full body or in six divisions of three justices each. Every province had at least one court of first instance, presided over by a district judge. Below the provincial level were municipal courts in chartered cities and city courts (formerly justices of the peace) in municipalities (counties) and municipal districts. These courts had exclusive original jurisdiction over minor criminal and civil offenses, and appeals from the decisions of these courts were referred to the courts of first instance.

The Constitutional Commissions

The 1973 Constitution listed three government agencies as independent constitutional commissions: the Civil Service Commission, the Commission on Elections, and the Commission on Audit. Each of these would be headed by a chairman and would include a varying number of commissioners, who were to be appointed by the prime minister, that is,

President Marcos during the transition period. The appointment was for a single, nonrenewable term of seven years. In order to ensure their integrity and impartiality, the chairmen and commissioners were forbidden to engage in any other employment, public or private, directly or indirectly, while they held office.

The Civil Service Commission was responsible for the recruitment, training, appointment, and discipline of all career civil servants in the executive, legislative, and judicial branches. Its scope extended to all political subdivisions down to the municipality and chartered city levels as well as to corporations owned or controlled by the government (see Civil Service, this ch.) The Commission on Elections (usually abbreviated as COMELEC) was empowered to enforce and administer all laws relative to the conduct of elections, including plebiscites (see The Electoral System, this ch.).

The function of ensuring the fiscal integrity of the government, national and local, was assigned to the Commission on Audit, formerly known as the General Auditing Office. This commission audited the financial condition and operation of all government agencies and submitted its findings to the prime minister, that is, the president during the current transition period. Its report would also be sent to the National Assembly when and if the legislative body came into existence.

LOCAL GOVERNMENT

For nearly two decades after independence the central government sought to improve the performance of local government units by delegating more power to the local subdivisions and by encouraging local initiative and participation in community affairs. More often than not this effort proved unproductive, however, as the affairs of local government were subjected to conflicting pressures emanating on one side from the proponents of a strong centralized government and on the other from the supporters of decentralization. Moreover the situation was complicated by the general paucity of funds available to local authorities.

The continuing effort to provide for more local autonomy culminated in the establishment, in November 1972, of the cabinet-level Department of Local Government and Community Development. The need for local self-rule was also given the first constitutional recognition in the 1973 charter, which contained a separate article on the subject.

The way and the extent to which the various local bodies actually enjoyed self-rule were not fully clear in the mid-1970s. The situation was at best as fluid and transitional—and uncertain—as it was at the national level. President Marcos had to reconcile the need for effective control from the center with the equally pressing requirement for broad grass-roots support of and participation in his reform measures of the New Society. As far as could be ascertained, local autonomy varied considerably from region to region. On the whole the weight of central authority was felt more heavily in those areas infested with insurgency.

As of mid-1975 the country had a three-tiered structure of political subdivisions, with seventy-two provinces at the top, sixty-one cities and 1,594 municipalities in the middle, and more than 40,000 *barangays* that replaced the *barrios* at the bottom. The provinces were grouped into eleven regions based on such factors as historical association, cultural affinity, and economic interdependence. The region was created to help national and local government agencies pool their resources and coordinate their regional developmental activities more efficiently with a minimum of duplication.

Inadequate financial resources were in the past nearly always singled out as the principal cause of lackluster local government performance. The local units, including the *barangays* had some limited power to raise their own revenues, but receipts were scarcely enough to meet local needs. They invariably had to depend heavily on the national treasury, obliging the national government to intervene in local affairs, especially in matters of development activities, such as public works projects and the construction of schools, housing, and roads.

The taxing power of local governments was given formal recognition in the 1973 Constitution, subject to certain statutory limitations. A new local tax code was promulgated in an attempt to improve the local financial position. In July 1975 President Marcos also authorized the provincial, city, and municipal governments to borrow funds from certain lending institutions to finance priority projects or to meet budgetary needs (see ch. 12). It was the expectation of the national government that this additional measure would help spur the economic development of the rural areas.

The province was the largest administrative unit of the local government system. It was headed by a governor, whose status was changed in 1975 from elective to appointive. The incumbent governor in mid-1975 had been elected directly for a term of four years in the midterm election held in November 1971. President Marcos used his discretionary power to retain or dismiss all elected local officials before their terms expired on December 31, 1975. The elected local officials had been those holding positions as governors, vice governors, and members of provincial boards and as mayors, vice mayors, and councillors in chartered cities as well as in municipalities.

In November 1975 local legislative bodies at the provincial, city, and municipal levels were all renamed the Sangguniang Bayan; and the membership of these bodies was enlarged to include representatives of *barangays* and of other unspecified sectors of the population. The announced purpose of this expansion was to give the people a greater voice in the administration of their local affairs and to keep them better informed of local needs and problems.

The guidelines for forming the Sangguniang Bayans were radically different from those governing the formation of representative bodies before 1972. Under a presidential decree issued on November 14, 1975, the incumbent members of the provincial, city, and municipal Sangguniang Bayans were to remain in their posts and were to be joined by additional members. Specifically the new members of the provincial Sangguniang Bayan were to include one representative from each of the municipalities under its jurisdiction as well as the head of the *barangay* association of the province concerned. The representative of each municipality was to be chosen by, and from among, the members of the municipal Sangguniang Bayan.

The municipal and city Sangguniang Bayans would consist of, apart from incumbent authorities, as many *barangay* captains and representatives from other sectors of the community as there were incumbent members. The so-called sector representatives—those speaking for professions, business executives, agricultural and industrial labor, and the like—were to be appointed by the president based on the recommendation of the secretary of the Department of Local Government and Community Development. The secretary was to select these representatives from a list of nominees and alternates submitted by the *barangays*.

The governor was not only the provincial chief executive but also the principal agent of the national government. He was assisted by a number of officials concerned with finance, tax collection, auditing, public works, agricultural services, public health, and schools. These officials and their assistants were nominally under the supervision of the governor but were actually controlled by and reported directly to their respective departments in the capital. They were paid wholly or partly out of national funds, but the salaries of those minor employees appointed locally by the governor came from provincial funds. Through the early 1970s at least 50 percent of provincial revenues had come from internal revenue allotments and national subsidies; the balance had been met by local revenues from real estates taxes, fees and licenses, and proceeds from the sale or rental of provincial property (see ch. 12). In some cases the level of national funding had reportedly been in direct proportion to the effectiveness of the governor in delivering votes on election day.

Among the more notable developments in local government under martial law was the administrative restructuring in late 1975 of the metropolitan Manila region, the hub of national politics, economic power, and cultural activity. The new government of the Manila area had under its jurisdiction four cities and thirteen municipalities with a total of 1,830 *barangays*—or a combined population of nearly 5 million inhabitants. The provincial-level metropolitan government was placed under the first governorship of Imelda Romualdez Marcos, the wife of the president.

Physically within a province but administratively independent of the provincial government was the chartered city. The power and structure of a city government varied according to local peculiarities. The city had generally more and broader taxing powers than other local subdivisions. Many of the cities were previously municipalities, which could be elevated to cities when they met the minimal self-governing potentials.

The city was headed by a mayor. The pattern of national representation through departmental officials at the provincial level was also common at the city level. The mayor, however, had discretionary powers of appointment relative to positions dealing with engineering and public works, finance and assessment, public health, and schools.

The municipality, unlike the chartered city, was controlled by the provincial government and hence had less autonomy than the chartered city. It was governed under a uniform municipality law applicable throughout the country. The government of the municipality, under a mayor and situated in a central town called a *población*, was responsible for law and order and operated the public market but, as in the provincial government, agricultural services, health, education, and public works were under the national government.

Apart from the municipality the president was authorized to create a municipal district, usually in an area inhabited for the most part by non-Christians. The district could be raised to a regular municipality when it was considered to have attained the certain minimal level of revenues and what a Filipino scholar called "the degree of culture needed for self-government."

The lowest and the most numerous subdivision was the *barangay* (*barrio* until mid-1974), which varied greatly in size but was typically rural and inhabited by about 200 people or about thirty-five families (see ch. 2; ch. 5). The *barangay* was located in the municipality, municipal district, or even in a highly urbanized city. It had limited tax powers and the authority to enact ordinances, and its qualified voters had, until 1973, the right to elect their own local government. Originally, under Republic Act 3590, otherwise known as the *Barrio* Charter Law, the *barrio* government was run by a *barrio* council, the head of which was called the *barrio* captain. Assisting the captain were several *barrio* councilmen. These officials were accountable to a *barrio* assembly, which was made up of all eligible voters who were eighteen years of age and older. The presidential decree issued in 1974 changed the name of *barrio* to *barangay*.

The primary functions of the *barangay* government were to maintain law and order and to provide limited support services to the national government's community development projects by putting up matching funds or by offering labor and local materials. Minor village disputes were settled by the *barangay* government, as they were previously under the *barrio* setup.

CIVIL SERVICE

The civil service system dates back to the start of American rule in the first decade of the twentieth century (see ch. 3). In its early days the American-inspired system was independent of partisan influences, as recruitment and appointment were based on objective, nonpolitical standards fixed by rules and regulations. This independence was gradually undermined, however, if only because the bureaucracy could not function in isolation, divorced from the sociopolitical reality of the islands.

Government service was for many decades, and continues to be, considered the most desirable and prestigious occupation for college graduates; it offered more opportunities for financial security and social mobility than other pursuits. Competition for civil service jobs was intense, and too many well-qualified applicants for a limited number of positions meant that political connections rather than merit more often determined who got into the service. Once admitted to the system through these connections, civil servants would be expected to return favors to their sponsors or patrons under the traditional Filipino pattern of reciprocal social obligations (see ch. 5). The result was the susceptibility of these recruits to graft and corruption (see ch. 10).

The rhetoric of civil service integrity figured prominently in election campaigns every two years, but expressions of concern on the part of politicians faded almost as soon as the election was over. Successive governments found it difficult—and unwise—to effect any substantive change in the civil service structure simply because a drastic reform would have had disturbing effects on the existing system of political patronage.

The civil service embraced all branches and agencies of national and local government down to the chartered cities and municipalities; also subject to its administrative control were public corporations owned or controlled by the government. Public officials were classified into two main categories: competitive and noncompetitive. Roughly one-third of the civil service was competitive, meaning that civil servants were recruited through competitive examination. The remaining two-thirds were appointed by the president at his own discretion or by the heads of local government. Some of these appointees were said to be protégés of national and local politicians, the immediate beneficiaries of the deeply rooted system of political patronage.

Well-intentioned efforts to improve the government service continued throughout the 1960s. The situation was to take a dramatic turn upon the declaration of martial law in September 1972. President Marcos ordered all central and local government agencies to weed out "undesirable" bureaucrats in both civilian and military establishments. By the end of the year more than 6,000 officials were dismissed.

In addition, as part of his efforts to improve morale, efficiency, and integrity in the civil service on a more enduring basis, President Marcos in September 1972 adopted a plan to create a career executive service, to be composed of officers assigned to the positions of under secretary, assistant secretary, bureau director, assistant bureau director, regional director, assistant regional director, chief of department services, and positions of equivalent rank. There were at that time about 800 officers in these positions.

These officers were to undergo special advanced study and training under the Career Executive Service Development Program, which was to be prepared by the Development Academy of the Philippines, a public corporation created in June 1973. The academy was designed also to provide advanced training to top- and middle-level executives in business and industry. The first ten-week residential training program started in November 1973, focusing on the academic and applied aspects of such issues as "New Society perspectives," communications and human relations in organizations, theories and strategies of development, contemporary sociocultural change, recent reforms and innovations in Philippine government, and development management.

About 300 government officials had completed the training program by mid-1975. At that time President Marcos expressed the hope of graduating at least 1,000 by increasing the yearly output to 500. He also stated that this program had become the "all important critical program of government" at a time when his administration was "in the process of rectifying past mistakes in a graceful manner."

Evidently, however, old habits had not yielded to the process of rectification as readily as President Marcos would have wished. In acknowledging the growing popular desire for reinstatement of the dedication and discipline that had been displayed in the early days of martial law, President Marcos in March 1975 ordered certain classes of government officials, civilian and military, national and local, to declare their financial assets as of December 31, 1974; Additionally they were ordered to reveal their assets as of December 31, 1965, or as of the date on which they entered the government service, whichever date was later. Official efforts to weed out corrupt and incompetent elements from civil and military establishments were still continuing at the end of 1975 (see ch. 10).

THE ELECTORAL SYSTEM

The last time the Filipinos had cast their secret ballot in a national election was in November 1971, when eligible voters aged twenty-one and above elected one-third of the senate membership and the officials of local government. When and if elections were resumed, they would be conducted under the charge of the Commission on Elections. The 1973 Constitution empowered the commission to administer and enforce all election laws and to serve as the sole judge of all disputes growing out of national as well as local elections. The commission was authorized to deputize, with the consent or at the instance of the prime minister, law enforcement agencies and the armed forces to ensure free, orderly, and honest elections; to register and accredit political parties subject to law; and to recommend to the National Assembly effective measures designed "to minimize election expenses and prohibit all forms of election frauds and malpractices, political opportunism, guest or nuisance candidacy, or other similar acts."

Under the parliamentary form of government envisaged in the 1973 Constitution, the election of the National Assembly would have to be considered the most important, since the political party or a coalition of parties commanding a comfortable majority in the assembly would almost certainly choose the prime minister, the center of power. A qualified candidate for the assembly would have to be a natural-born citizen, at least twenty-five years old, able to read and write, and a resident of the electoral district concerned for at least a year. The assembly election was to be held on the second Monday of May every six years; presumably local elections would be held on the same day.

The voting age under the 1973 Constitution was eighteen as compared to twenty-one under the old constitution. The presidential proclamation establishing the *barangays* in January 1973, however, lowered the voting age to fifteen, a move that President Marcos said was consistent with the ancient Filipino custom in which the fifteen-year-olds were called upon to protect the village and stay on guard while the older men engaged in combat. Voting was compulsory, and absence from the polls except for "justifiable reasons" was subject to imprisonment ranging from one to six months. The number of qualified voters in these referenda ranged from 20 to 22 million.

CHAPTER 10

POLITICAL DYNAMICS AND VALUES

In the mid-1970s the Philippines was undergoing an arduous test of political transition under the martial law government of President Ferdinand E. Marcos. At issue was whether a political structure long accustomed to a laissez-faire interplay of competing interests and pressures could be galvanized by fiat into a new system laying heavy stress on authoritarian control, discipline, and austerity. The transition was set in motion in September 1972 when Marcos declared martial law and proclaimed his intention of establishing a New Society by effecting a number of sorely needed reforms throughout the society.

The official rationale for a new political order was based on the view that seventy-five years of experimentation in classical Western democratic forms had failed to meet the Filipino need for progress and modernization. The political system before 1972 failed "disastrously," according to an official explanation, because it was grafted on a society still feudal in many respects, a society that lacked both an egalitarian base and the "required minimum of affluence in a broad segment of the population." Moreover the pre-1972 system was said to be incompatible with Filipino political traditions and was therefore abused and misused.

The politics of the New Society was markedly different from that of the old society. Gone were free-for-all partisan activities waged through a loosely structured two-party system; a free press; elections held every two years both as a check against abuses of public offices and as a device for expressing the popular mandate; and the sharing of power, with attendant checks and balances, between the two principal focuses of power, the presidency and the Congress.

Under martial law the business of bringing the people closer to the government—and vice versa—was to be undertaken by a government-sponsored institution, the *barangay* (citizens' assembly). Public officials, in the absence of elections, were accountable solely to Marcos, who held broad discretionary powers of appointment and removal. Political power was concentrated for all practical purposes in the hands of Marcos alone. Significantly, the military establishment emerged as the principal instrument of power in the New Society. Steadily politicized, the military appeared destined to play a key role in national affairs even in the unlikely event of martial law's being lifted.

Changes notwithstanding, the New Society retained a number of traditional qualities. In government, business, and every other sector of the society familyloyalty and patron-client relationships remained practically unaffected as a quid pro quo basis for sociopolitical interaction. The distinction between public and private interests in government was more apparent than real, and President Marcos was obliged to purge erring public officials by the hundreds. Politicians were gone but not the old economic oligarchs or families, who bore the initial brunt of Marcos' assault on "the sick old society" but quickly demonstrated their resilience and capacity for survival. The old oligarchs were joined by others whose access to economic power was a product of the New Society.

The New Society was intended to be a community of equals who would benefit from the democratization of wealth and property. Marcos stressed that the egalitarian principle required a "reconstruction of our political values." Although still accepting the importance of personal freedom, individualism, and private initiative as hallmarks of a free society, Marcos sought to impress on the people the need for discipline and order under what he called constitutional authoritarianism. The extent to which Marcos' viewpoint was internalized in the mid-1970s was difficult to ascertain. In any case, on the third anniversary of martial law in September 1975 President Marcos stated with candor that the task of transition from the old to the New Society was complex and arduous.

At the end of 1975 Marcos reiterated his intent to hasten the process of transition to parliamentary government but added that transitional steps would be taken with due care. He maintained that hasty action would hamper rather than help the efforts of his "crisis government" to restructure the political order and stamp out what he called "illicit, illegal political agitation."

As part of this politics of transition, Marcos initiated measures to constitute organs of popular representation that had until 1971 been directly elected through partisan competition. Indications were that these organs, known as Sangguinang Bayans, would be formed through a combination of indirect, government-controlled elections and presidential appointment—and without the open competition of party politics (see ch. 9).

POLITICAL PATTERNS BEFORE 1972

The old political order, legitimized by the 1935 Constitution and buttressed by convention drawn from American precedents, was fashioned by an evolutionary process of trial and error spanning over half a century. The American-introduced democratic system of managing public affairs had been continued after independence with very little structural modification. The system endured the initial period of uncertainty and a myriad of social pressures, and its apparent success gave the Philippines a reputation as "the showcase of democracy in Asia."

In the pre-1972 Philippines, powers were divided among and exercised by the three branches of government: executive, legislative, and judicial. These branches generally maintained their independence by adhering to constitutional stipulations of checks and balances. In the presidential system of government the leaders were accountable to the electorate through direct elections held every four years. To forestall the possibility of an incumbent president's remaining in power indefinitely, the 1935 Constitution limited presidential tenure to two consecutive terms of four years each (see ch. 9).

Political power was contested openly through the framework of a two-party system. Party politics were colorful and intense, especially during election campaigns. Coups and countercoups were unheard of, and the military was subordinate to civil authority. Although elections were customarily accompanied by irregularities and sometimes intense disorders, the transfer of power from one group to another through the constitutional means of elections was accepted.

Political power was centralized in the Manila area, but the way it was exercised from the presidential palace—the Malacañang—was democratic. The presidency and the Congress—the two centers of power—jealously guarded their respective domains from encroachment by the other. This countervailing balance between the two institutions, coupled with the general lack of discipline and solidarity within the country's two major parties, tended to neutralize the possibility of dictatorial one-man rule.

The mass media constituted practically a fourth branch of government; the press was a fierce critic of public affairs and helped preserve democratic norms (see ch. 7). Filipinos were highly literate and shared a general consensus that political leadership should be regularly checked against excesses through electoral means. Voter participation in national and local elections was consistently high. In political attitudes Filipinos were pragmatic and flexible.

It is probable that the pre-1972 system endured for as long as it did because it had been tempered by and adapted to indigenous patterns of resolving sociopolitical conflicts. The system was distinctly Western in form but overlaid the traditional pattern in such a way that the old and new could coexist and in fact complement each other. The old patterns were rewoven into such Western-inspired institutions as political parties, civic organizations, and occupational interest organizations. Aspirants to elective offices had to compete for popular votes under the banners of major national parties.

Party Politics

Party politics were introduced in 1900 when, with American encouragement, a group of prominent, wealthy Filipinos formed the Federal Party to evoke grass-roots support for American rule. In the first Philippine elections, held in 1907, this party was defeated by the Partido Nacionalista (Nationalist Party), which called for immediate national independence. Organized shortly before the elections and led by two powerful yet competing figures, Manuel L. Quezon and Sergio Osmeña, the Nacionalistas continued to dominate the political scene before independence. Opposition was fragmented and weak, except during the 1917–31 period, when a third group, the Partido Democrata (Democratic Party), demonstrated a modicum of electoral strength.

Factional rivalry between Quezon and Osmeña, endemic from the very beginning, led to a permanent split after Quezon died in 1944. Osmeña renamed his wing of the party the Nacionalista Party; Manuel A. Roxas, a prominent prewar Nacionalista leader, formed the Liberal Party with former Quezon supporters as its nucleus. In the years after independence until party politics were proscribed in 1972, the Nacionalista Party and the Liberal Party were the backbone of a two-party system that had evolved since the beginning of the twentieth century. The two parties held power alternately at the national level, providing the executive and legislative leadership necessary to the operation of a presidential form of government under the 1935 Constitution (see table 6).

The party system had some notable aspects. It was marked by a two-party dominance; minor parties built around one or two personalities and narrow issues or ideologies were seldom able to elicit mass followings. The high costs of elections made it difficult for parties having limited resources to reach out for popular support, especially in a country like the Philippines, where most voters used their ballots for some immediate personal gain. This meant that political candidates with major party identification had decided advantages because the overwhelming majority of successful politicians gained their access to patronage and the pork barrel through the two-party channel of competition. The boards of election inspectors, which could frequently "make or break honest elections" in the Philippines, tended to be prejudiced against minor parties or independent candidates; in most cases these boards were dominated by representatives of the two major parties.

Table 6. *Philippines, Presidents since Independence*

Term	President	Year Elected	Party Affiliation
1946–48	Manuel A. Roxas	1946	Liberal
1948–49	Elpidio Quirino	...[1]	Do.
1949–53	---do---	1949	Do.
1953–57	Ramón Magsaysay	1953	Nacionalista
1957	Carlos P. Garcia	...[2]	Do.
1957–61	---do---	1957	Do.
1961–65	Diosdado Macapagal	1961	Liberal
1965–69	Ferdinand E. Marcos	1965	Nacionalista
1969-[3]	---do---	1969	Do.

[1] As vice president succeeded to the presidency upon Roxas' death in April 1948 and was elected to a full term in 1949.

[2] As vice president assumed presidential powers upon Magsaysay's death in March 1957; elected to a full term in November 1957.

[3] Ineligible for a third term under the 1935 Constitution, Marcos remained in power beyond the terminal year of 1973 under a new constitution ratified and promulgated in January 1973, under martial law; there were no elections in November 1973.

The Nacionalistas and Liberals were broadly based mass parties supported by all social strata and regions. They were virtually identical in policies and modes of operations. Issues or policies advocated by either or both assumed little importance at the grass-roots level. Electoral success for a major party did not necessarily mean the triumph of a party platform, nor for that matter was the platform viewed by the public as binding on the incumbent administration. The concept of a responsible party government as the term is viewed in the West was remote, reflecting an enduring pattern of political expectations in which the human factor usually outweighed Western emphasis on institutionalism.

Philippine parties were loosely banded together, as R. Stephen Milne put it, "by loyalties to *persons*—to party leaders, to friends, to *compadres*, to relatives, and not to party platforms or ideologies." Common action based on platforms or intraparty discipline was neither a condition of survival nor a virtue to be upheld. Most Filipinos joined or looked upon parties less as instruments of sociopolitical change than as vehicles through which their personal comfort and economic gain could be maximized. Political parties offered a useful outlet through which individual aspirations and demands could be articulated to those who were believed to have the best qualifications and who promised most in terms of rewards to their constituents. Party philosophies, issues, or policies meant little.

The highly pragmatic way in which most Filipinos related to the political community made for a fairly fluid structure of party loyalty. Loyalty could be permanent when based on strong kinship ties. It could also be temporary, because there was no social or political stigma attached to a shift in party identification. Ramón Magsaysay switched allegiance from the Liberal Party to the opposing Nacionalista Party shortly before the elections of 1953 in which he won the presidency. In like manner, shortly before the elections of 1965, Marcos left the Liberal Party to realize his presidential aspirations through the Nacionalista Party.

Personal loyalties were translated into the political process through what Carl H. Landé calls "vertical chains of dyadic patron-client relationships" extending from the provincial elite down to lesser figures in the towns and *barrios* (smallest administrative divisions, renamed *barangays* in 1974) and thence to the voters. It was this informal system of mutual-aid relationships, not the formal organization of party commit-tees, that constituted the real backbone of individualistic partisan politics in the Philippines. It was through this informal mechanism that local factions or personal followings articulated their interests directly to their patrons parading under the banners of various parties.

The dyadic ties served as a fairly accessible means for the expression of grass-roots aspirations and needs. As such they were an indispensable part of the country's politics. In a society like the Philippines where the free-for-all, laissez-faire pattern of partisan competition could easily

213

fractionate the political scene and engender destabilizing pressures, the dyadic relationships performed integrative and what might be called safety-valve functions. By and large this indigenous pattern helped successive governments maintain an open and stable society that was otherwise marked by great social and economic inequalities.

The dyadic pattern was in effect a form of voluntary contract between patrons and clients. Success or failure was essentially a personal affair. When patrons failed to honor their electoral promises for one reason or another, the voters or their middlemen could always switch their allegiance and find new accommodations. Political parties with which they were associated were not necessarily blamed, and in any case the voters were fully aware that they were supporting party politicians as individuals and not the parties. Although the dyadic pattern worked to the satisfaction of many, there was no firm assurance that it would continue to be effective. For one thing, the electorate, especially rural voters, were becoming increasingly politicized—a trend evident since the Magsaysay years of the early 1950s. For another, the monetization of the rural economy and the attendant erosion of the traditional basis of landlord-tenant relations meant that landlords could no longer take for granted the loyalty of those dependent on them.

In general the behavior of public officials, high and low, was marked by a strong, enduring tendency to exercise power in a personal and reciprocal way. Technically all public servants were expected to uphold the integrity of their offices and discharge their functions according to rules and regulations. But in the Philippines, as in many other transitional societies, human relations were not perceived in terms of a strict differentiation between public and private spheres. According to Jean Grossholtz, "Filipinos do not distinguish between the man and his job . . . Filipinos expect that personal obligations and desires will dominate the behavior of everyone" including those in important positions of public trust.

What Onofre D. Corpuz calls "privatization" of public offices was essential if these officials were to promote their own interests and those of their families and to fulfill the personal obligations inherent in the dyadic relationships. Although publicly maligned, corruption was widely viewed as unavoidable; the popular assumption was that corruption could be curbed or contained but never eliminated.

The ubiquity of personalism tended to discourage the evolution of intermediary sociopolitical institutions. The Philippines was not lacking in these institutions, as evidenced by the abundance of business and economic groups, professional groups, labor and agricultural associations, and church related social action organizations. But interest groups also suffered from a lack of effective political leadership, group solidarity, and continuity; they had only a weak role in a political system in which politicians found it necessary to appeal to nearly all social segments.

Elections

Until 1971 elections played a significant part in fostering democratic norms and in providing the citizens with a forum in which they could participate in the vicissitudes of partisan politics and most of all in which they could use their power of vote for a quid pro quo. The electoral system was thus central to politics before 1972, serving as the main channel for access to power and influence at the national, provincial, and municipal levels.

Because of the increase in the number of voters and the growing Filipino inclination to exchange votes for material rewards, the cost of elections soared sharply over the years. This condition not only financially wrecked those who were defeated but also discouraged competent men from seeking public office. As a result campaign spending was limited by law to not more than the total amount of the emolument for one year attached to the office sought, but this stipulation was more honored in the breach than in the observance. The high cost of elections not only gave a distinct advantage to wealthy candidates but, according to E. R. Kiunisala, was "one of the main causes of graft, corruption and mis-government."

The expense of elections was attributable to a combination of causes. Kiunisala explains that to a degree the voters could be blamed for this situation because they would "ask the candidates to contribute to all sorts of civic projects; they demand handouts, food, drink, transportation, and cash during the campaign." Another contributing factor was the "spend now and recover later" tactic used by parties and candidates; once elected, public officials would use their offices, in the words of Vicente Albano Pacis, as "bases for piratical operation" partly to recover the expenses partly to finance the next election. Still another factor was what Sotero H. Laurel calls the "fierce competition" within the power elite to maximize their positions at the expense of others; the ruthlessness of this competition was responsible in part for "reckless, illegal, immoral, and ultimately, undemocratic practices."

The bulk of election expenses was for dispensation of pork barrel and vote buying; a considerable sum was also spent on transportation and communication. The rise in election costs could also be ascribed to such objective factors as the steady increase in the number of eligible voters and the necessity to raise the ante in those areas where traditional loyalties based on kinship and landlord-tenant ties were weakened and could no longer be relied on (see ch. 5).

Invariably each election was described as the most scandalously expensive, only to be outdone by the next. The elections of 1961 were once described as "the most expensive in Philippine history"; the total expenditure incurred by all candidates in that year was estimated at a sum equal to about 8 percent of the annual national budget. During the election campaign of 1969 President Marcos' Nacionalista Party alone

215

reportedly spent a sum equal to about one-third of the national budget for that fiscal year. As described by Teodoro M. Locsin, this overspending contributed to "a cruel inflation of prices of commodities and the bleakest Christmas that many could remember."

Before 1972 electoral practices were, not surprisingly, a major object of reform. A growing number of concerned citizens within the government and outside it came to recognize that, unless something was done to remedy electoral practices, the democratic institutions of the country would be irreparably undermined. Occasionally there were vocal demands for clean government through electoral reform—such as that spearheaded by Raul S. Manglapus—but the electoral system was so enmeshed with the dyadic pattern of politics that it seemed impossible to alter it short of a total repudiation of the pre-1972 system of representative government. Meanwhile corruption remained a favorite issue during all election campaigns; an opposition candidate would elaborate at length on the corruption of an incumbent, only to indulge in the same practices once elected.

The Political Elite

Before 1972 the political elite consisted of some 200 top government officials, both elected and appointed. The top figures included the president, vice president, cabinet members, presidential assistants, leading senators, some congressmen, and a few important provincial governors. Some owed their prominence to personal merit and skill, some to their ties to the president, some to their independent wealth, and some to the economically powerful families for whom they rendered services as clients.

Below the top level were local elites at the provincial and municipal levels. In most instances local political leaders were those who held elective office as provincial governors, provincial board members, and municipal mayors as well as those who held no government positions but were influential locally because of their wealth or their capacity to sustain the personal loyalties of the local population. Together these local elites constituted the vital links between national politicians and their grassroots constituents. As political middlemen they helped their patrons at the national level by delivering local votes or by raising political funds.

There was considerable validity in the observation that the political and economic life of the Philippines was unduly dominated by a privileged minority composed, as one source put it, of "at most 400 families." These economically powerful families, or oligarchs as they were often called, controlled the major commercial and banking houses, industrial enterprises, real estate holdings, and sugar plantations. Their economic power overlapped political power more often than not. A considerable number of top public officials were drawn from these wealthy families and served their family interests; some others of these officials were clients of, and protected by, powerful oligarchs. In several instances the interests of politicians were protected by "private armies" that were beyond the reach of local civil authorities and a source of growing public concern before 1972.

Institutionally, important constitutional powers were vested in the presidency and Congress, but the real roots of power were not in these bodies but in the geographically dispersed political and economic fiefdoms of powerful families. Principles of egalitarianism and general welfare as a basis for government policies and actions were not disputed by these vested interests, but any change that would basically alter the status quo was fiercely resisted for many years. As a result reforms were painfully slow in coming. Technocrats and revisionist politicians alike suffered at the hands of powerful oligarchs.

The political system before 1972, built around a ramified structure of dyadic relationships and topped by a minority of powerful families, was at least nominally democratic but clearly confronted pressures that threatened its viability. Most Filipinos could participate in the ritual of democratic politics as a means of access to material reward and as an outlet for the release of grass-roots tensions. The consequences of this participation—victory or defeat at the polls—were generally accepted with equanimity, and the system of representative government and the assumptions underlying it were not brought into question. The pre-1972 pattern of party politics, electoral competition, and leadership recruitment proved remarkably stable.

The stability was purchased at an increasingly high price, not only in terms of staggering election costs. Not all issues or grievances in a society of great inequality could be resolved through the prevailing framework. In some cases the aggrieved parties opted for extralegal channels for the satisfaction of their demands. These instances were relatively few and localized but nonetheless had serious consequences, as seen in the persistence of popular sympathy for communist groups in parts of Luzon and in the Muslim rebellion in the southern islands (see ch. 17). Moreover stability meant resistance to reform and implied social rigidity. Although political activity continued to revolve around personalities rather than issues and programs, social and economic developments were taking place in such a way that this stability tended to favor the privilege of a few against the welfare of the majority. As it turned out, the resulting tensions had by the late 1960s undercut the democratic intent and structures of the pre-1972 political system.

POLITICS UNDER MARTIAL LAW

President Marcos, the architect of the New Society reform program and the single most powerful figure after 1972, was a product and a beneficiary of the old political order. Born in 1917 in Ilocos Norte Province and educated in law at the University of the Philippines, he became the most decorated Filipino guerrilla leader in World War II. First elected to the House of Representatives in 1949 as a member of the

Liberal Party, Marcos quickly gained recognition as an able lawmaker and served as the minority leader in the lower house before winning a Senate seat in 1959. A minority leader in the Senate, Marcos served as its president from 1963 to 1965. He first won the national presidency in the November 1965 elections under his newly acquired label as a Nacionalista. Unprecedentedly he won the mandate again in 1969, and his second four-year term would have expired at the end of 1973 if politics had been allowed to take the usual course under the 1935 Constitution.

Background

In the 1969 presidential election Marcos handily defeated Senator Sergio Osmeña, Jr., the nominee of the Liberal Party, garnering nearly 60 percent of the popular votes. A substantial number of Nacionalista candidates were also returned to the Senate and the House of Representatives. The landslide victory greatly enhanced Marcos' personal stature, solidified his position within the Congress and, most of all, assured the continuity that his party said was essential to achieve the sloganized election pledges: "Marcos means more rice, Marcos means more roads, Marcos means more schoolhouses, Marcos means more progress!"

The 1969 mandate gave Marcos a free hand in dealing with affairs of state. He was freed, so to speak, from the customary constraints on presidential aspirants seeking a second term. Since he was constitutionally barred from a third term he need, as the *Far Eastern Economic Review* observed in November 1969, "no longer worry about keeping the party bosses and associated financial interests sweet." Whether he could have exercised that freedom of action to initiate innovative policies within the old political framework is open to question. It was always difficult for a winning president to mobilize congressional support behind a legislative program, given the weakness of political party discipline and the traditional conflict of power between the presidency and the legislature.

Marcos appealed for a renewal of his mandate on the strength of his impressive achievements in popular impact programs during the late 1960s. This appeal was further buttressed by an enormous campaign chest drawn from both government and private sources. Osmeña challenged Marcos by focusing on the president's alleged failure to restore law and order, contain soaring consumer prices, check rampant corruption, and minimize poverty and unemployment. The 1969 contest was more acrimonious and violent than any other campaign and resulted in 107 people killed and 117 wounded in election-related violence—in 1965 thirty-four died, and thirty were injured.

In 1970 the Philippines faced what Robert O. Tilman called "another of its recurring postelection financial crises"—amid mounting signs of tension brought on by lawlessness, corruption, unemployment, and the widening gap between affluence and poverty. Evidently the tension was more acute among the informed and vocal residents of Manila and its

218

suburbs than among the rural inhabitants. In January the tension erupted into violence in Manila, where thousands of students took to the street and clashed with police in bloody confrontations. Their protest was focused on campus reform and political issues and included demands for the end of bureaucratic inertia, the purge of corrupt officials, and the formation of a constitutional convention as a nonpartisan body. At the height of the rioting the students attempted to extract a written pledge from Marcos that he would not seek a third term through subterfuge.

Student activism, which was confined mostly to the Manila area, was more reformist than revolutionary, except for the radical wing represented by the Patriotic Youth (Kabataang Makabayan—KM) (see ch. 17). This moderate thrust was also true of nonstudent organizations seeking to evoke popular response to their demands—oriented to issues and ideology—for broad-gauged social reforms. Notable among these organizations were the Christian Socialist Movement of former Senator Manglapus, the Movement for a Democratic Philippines, and the Socialist Party of the Philippines.

During 1971 politics were punctuated by several foreboding developments. In January Fernando Lopez, vice president since 1965, publicly broke with Marcos, who retaliated with a virtual declaration of war against the oligarchs in general and the powerful "Lopez interests" in particular. The Lopez affair was followed by the defection of José B. Laurel, another powerful figure, and the resignation of the influential and often critical Senator José W. Diokno from the Nacionalista Party. These events evidently weakened the ruling party and appeared to signal a growing crisis of confidence in the Marcos administration.

In August Filipinos, long accustomed to election violence, were shocked by two explosions of fragmentation grenades at a Liberal Party election rally being held at Plaza Miranda in Manila. The explosions killed ten people and wounded or maimed ninety others, including several top Liberal Party leaders. The culprits were never apprehended; President Marcos blamed communist factions. Senators Diokno and Benigno S. Aquino, Jr., accused the president of using scare tactics to perpetuate himself in power. Marcos charged that Aquino, who was popular and widely regarded as the most likely to supplant Marcos, was a Communist.

In the off-year elections of November 1971 the Liberal Party captured six of the eight senatorial seats that were at stake. Some observers speculated that the Liberal triumph was a clear case of popular rejection of the Marcos administration. Although reportedly accompanied by less blatant electoral fraud, that election also took a heavy toll, with over 200 killed and somewhat more than that number wounded.

Violence struck on another front during 1971. The long-simmering tensions between Muslims and Christians in the southern frontier island of Mindanao flared up in communal clashes; more than 1,000 lives were reported taken from late 1970 to September 1971. In part exploited by their own leaders and in part seeing their rights to land and their customary way of life threatened by Christian settlers, the Muslims took up arms and rebelled against local security forces (see ch. 8; ch. 17). The gravity of the situation was underscored by the fact that the Muslim rebellion increasingly took on characteristics of a separatist or secessionist movement.

In early 1972 the economy, still reeling from financial problems caused in no small part by the 1969 election spending, was dealt a severe blow by devastating typhoon floods that inundated much of central Luzon in June and July and by an equally disastrous summer drought in the Visayan Islands and Mindanao. Resulting crop failures were severe enough to affect trade patterns.

During 1972 pressures came from other sources as well. The Muslim rebellion showed no sign of abating. There was a resurgence of communist guerrilla activity, led by the Maoist-oriented New People's Army (NPA), the military arm of the outlawed Communist Party of the Philippines (Partido Komunista ng Pilipinas—PKP) (see ch. 17). Other sources of aggravation were growing lawlessness in Manila and elsewhere. Charges and countercharges between the administration and critics painted a grim picture of ineffective national leadership, corruption, and irresponsible oppositon for the sake of oppositon.

From mid-1972 the government claim of a communist menace figured rather prominently in partisan exchanges. In July Marcos disclosed "the first clear evidence of any foreign vessel landing supplies in support of communist subversion." He was referring to a 100-ton cargo ship, the *Karagatan*, of Philippine registry, that was alleged—and since then officially accepted—to have landed arms and supplies to NPA rebels in Northern Luzon. Critics of the government contended that the "mystery boat" incident was staged by supporters of Marcos to prepare the ground for martial law.

The "*Karagatan* affair," highly publicized amid official reports of full-scale military action against the NPA insurgents in parts of Isabela Province, was followed by sixteen mysterious bombings in the Manila area. In blaming the NPA for the violence, the government again spotlighted a growing "Communist menace." Senator Aquino argued that the communist threat was exaggerated. Whatever the case, Alejandro Melchor, the chief presidential assistant and the foremost government technocrat, reportedly told the president that the growing domestic insecurity would result in a lower economic growth rate than had been projected.

In September the imminence of martial law was widely rumored in Manila, fueled in part by President Marcos' hint on September 12 that emergency powers might be invoked if necessary. The next day Aquino, citing unnamed ranking military officers as the source of his information, disclosed the existence of a contingency plan that would place Manila and the strategic provinces of Rizal and Bulacan under military control. On September 16, Marcos accused the Liberal Party of conspiring with the

220

NPA in order to launch a possible united action against the government. On September 21 he charged more specifically that Aquino had secretly met with NPA leader José Maria Sison as part of this conspiracy.

Martial Law

On September 23 President Marcos went on the air to make a formal proclamation of martial law throughout the country. For better or worse it marked an end to an era and the beginning of a "New Society." The decree, officially named Proclamation 1081, was dated September 21, but the executive order enabling its implementation was signed on the evening of September 22. Within hours after the signing and before the proclamation was made public, about twenty persons were arrested. Among those taken into custody were senators Aquino, Diokno, Ramon V. Mitra, and nearly all prominent newspapermen. Others included were several congressmen and provincial governors—some of them closely associated with President Marcos—detained because of their involvement in smuggling, gunrunning, and other illegal activities, as well as some minor figures involved in communist front organizations. All newspapers and radio and television stations were seized and closed down except for one progovernment daily newspaper, one television station, and four radio stations (two of them government owned).

The president said that martial law was declared in accordance with the powers vested in him by the 1935 Constitution in the event the republic was threatened with lawlessness, violence, invasion, insurrection, or rebellion. There was said to be "throughout the land a state of anarchy and lawlessness, chaos and disorder, turmoil and destruction of a magnitude equivalent to an actual war between the forces of our duly constituted government and the New People's Army and their satellite organizations." According to President Marcos the danger of a violent overthrow of government had become graver and rebellion had worsened during 1972, paralyzing the functions of government, severely affecting the productive sectors of the economy, forcing the closure of many schools, and undermining the effective administration of justice (see ch. 17). In light of these conditions he emphasized two objectives: the restoration of law and order and a sweeping reform of the social, economic, and political institutions of the country. At the same time he stressed that the imposition of martial law as not a military takeover; all public officials were told to discharge their duties as before but in a manner compatible with the spirit of "a new and reformed society."

After the proclamation all schools were offered temporarily closed; tight control was imposed on mass media; carrying firearms outside private residences was banned; a crackdown on illegal possession of firearms was begun; a curfew from midnight to 4:00 A.M. was enforced; all public rallies, demonstrations, and strikes in public utilities were forbidden; and partisan politics was suspended. Within days the private armies of political warlords were disarmed, thousands of illegal weapons were voluntarily surrendered, some price controls were imposed on basic food items, and the government took over airlines, railroads, public utilities, and privately owned aircraft and watercraft. An extensive purge of corrupt and inefficient bureaucrats and judges was swiftly undertaken, affecting about 6,000 officials by the end of 1972. Steps were also initiated to change tax procedures, banking laws, and sugar and rice marketing organizations—objects of long-frustrated reform efforts. The government then announced a sweeping nationwide land reform program for small tenant farmers; when fully implemented the program was to improve the lot of up to 65 percent of Filipinos engaged in agriculture. In underlining the importance of this program the government pointed out that the New Society would probably stand or fall on the success or failure of land reform, which had long been frustrated by landlord opposition (see ch. 13).

The dramatic martial law measures were generally popular, despite a wait-and-see attitude. There was no bloodshed; Manila was calm and displayed few menacing signs of soldiers or tanks. The president's intention of establishing the New Society by removing the social inequities of what he called the "old sick society" was greeted by a feeling of relief if only because of a general eagerness for long-delayed, genuine reforms. Specifically, as enunciated in mid-November 1972, the New Society program focused on major changes in seven areas: law and order, land tenure, labor, education, the economy, social services, and politics and government.

Within weeks crime was sharply reduced, criminal syndicates were forced off the streets, tax collection improved, corruption in public offices was considerably contained, and the economy showed signs of renewed vigor. Martial law, however, had the opposite effect on the Muslim population in southern Philippines; very few arms were turned in to the authorities, and the Muslim uprising actually intensifed (see ch. 17).

The Politics of Legitimization and the Barangays

In the mood of expectancy in Manila during the first weeks of martial law, few Filipinos bemoaned the sudden disappearance of partisan politics. Political attention, if any, was centered on the Constitutional Convention that was in its final stage of drafting a new constitution. With little publicity on October 20, 1972, the convention—dominated by forces loyal to Marcos—adopted an article covering the transition from the old presidential system to a new parliamentary system of government. To ensure a smooth transition the article provided that all presidential orders and decrees issued under martial law would become part of the law of the land, to be valid even after the lifting of martial law; another stipulation was that, during the period of transition, the incumbent president would continue to rule by combining the powers vested in him under the 1935 Constitution and the executive powers vested in the office of prime minister under the newly drafted constitution (see ch. 9). The transitory provisions also stated that the interim National Assembly under the new constitution would have as its members, among other persons, those delegates to the convention who voted affirmatively on the new constitution.

On November 29, 1972, the draft constitution was approved in its entirety by the convention; three days later President Marcos announced that the draft would be submitted to a popular referendum on January 15, 1973, for formal ratification. At that time he indicated that, even if the constitution failed to win popular endorsement, he would go ahead with the reforms initiated since martial law. In order to enable the people freely to discuss and debate the new constitution, on December 20 he ordered a partial relaxation of martial law. On December 23, however, the plebiscite was declared postponed on the ground that more time was needed for the debate.

On December 31 President Marcos ordered the formation of *barangays* in each *barrio* in municipalities, in each district in chartered cities, and in each ward in major cities having no *barrios*. Each *barangay* was to consist of those persons resident in a given area for at least six months who were fifteen years of age and older. According to Marcos the *barangay* system was "necessary to broaden the base of citizen participation in the democratic process and to afford ample opportunities for the citizenry to express their views on important national issues." In his book *The Democratic Revolution in the Philippines*, published in 1974, the president described the *barangay* as "a modern rendering of the effective *barangays* of a primitive democratic age" and stated, "now they are an indispensable feature of our democracy."

On January 7, 1973, in his nationwide address concerning the achievements of the first 100 days of martial law, President Marcos called on citizens fifteen years old and above to participate in the formation of the *barangays* and take an active part in "national consultation" on critical issues to be conducted through these bodies between January 10 and January 15. He said that popular cooperation would help to establish "a real basis of a working, direct, participatory Filipino democracy with a base unequaled in its magnitude and without precedent in the history of modern democracy."

In the same speech, however, he expressed concern that Filipinos were indulging in their habit of *ningas-cogen*—a habit, in his words, "marked by a short, sudden spurt of enthusiasm, followed by a slowing down of one's efforts, then a slipping back to the old habits." He felt constrained to urge the people to subordinate their personal interests to "the higher interests of the state and government" and "desist from asking politicians, public officials, the industrialists, relatives, and men of affluence for their intercession to obtain favors and concessions, but to reply merely on the merits of their own case." He appealed to the people to go back to the discipline and enthusiasm of "the first few weeks of martial law."

The president also sounded a note of concern that enemies of the state were taking advantage of relaxed martial law to foment anxiety, confusion, discord, and subversion. In light of this situation he said that he was reinstating the full force of martial law and that the plebiscite on the draft constitution would be postponed to a date to be decided on after a national consultation of *barangays*.

President Marcos asked the *barangays* to debate certain questions: whether or not they approved of the New Society program, the reform measures initiated under martial law, the convening of the interim National Assembly, and the holding of a plebiscite on the draft constitution. Additionally the government-formulated questions dealt with whether or not the *barangays* would approve of the way President Marcos ran the country, the continuation of martial law, the holding of regularly scheduled national elections in November 1973, and the adoption of the draft constitution.

On January 17 Marcos declared the draft constitution ratified, inasmuch as an overwhelming majority of *barangay* members, voting by a show of hands, had not only endorsed the new charter but also expressed the view that their vote should be considered an act of ratification in a plebiscite. In accordance with what he called "the wishes of our people expressed so forcefully, so unanimously, so overwhelmingly," he also signed a proclamation for continuation of martial law and another providing that the interim National Assembly should not be convened at that time (see ch. 9). In the plebiscite the *barangays* had also voted that elections in November 1973 under the 1935 Constitution would not be held and that other elections would be suspended for the next seven years. Marcos did not specifically address the matter of elections in his January proclamations.

In a televised interview with foreign correspondents on January 20, 1973, Marcos said that his regime could be characterized as "constitutional authoritarianism" but not dictatorial. He let it be known that each January, or whenever necessary, the *barangays* would be called on to voice their views on important national issues.

A second *barangay* referendum was held on July 27–28, 1973, to test popular reaction to the government-posed question of whether or not the people wanted Marcos to continue in office beyond December 30, 1973, to press forward his New Society reform. Official results showed 90 percent in favor of a continued mandate for the president.

On February 27, 1975, Marcos again went to the *barangays* on the issue of whether the electorate approved of the way he had exercised martial law powers and, if so, whether they wished him to continue to use the same powers. For the residents of the greater Manila area an additional referendum question was whether they would let the president reconstitute Manila and its outlying areas into a reorganized, integrated system of local government. A major issue for voters outside the Manila area was whether the four-year (1971–75) terms of all local officials elected in 1971 should be renewed through elections or by presidential appointment. On election day Marcos warned that he would step down from the presidency if the people rejected his mandate. Results were reported as overwhelmingly in favor of Marcos. On local questions the majority of voters in the Manila area wanted an integrated local government; those outside Manila wanted presidential appointment rather than elections.

By the end of 1975 it had become clear that the *barangays* constituted a force in Marcos' attempts to popularize his New Society program, instill discipline in the people, and gauge grass-roots sentiments and attitudes toward his martial law administration. From mid-1973 efforts were under way in earnest to strengthen these bodies as an integral part of the political structure. In mid-1974, under a presidential decree, the *barangays* replaced the more than 40,000 *barrios* as the lowest political subdivisions. In November 1975 a measure was announced by the government to broaden the membership of the provincial, city, and municipal boards or councils—to be known henceforth as Sangguniang Bayans—to include *barangay* representatives (see ch. 9).

THE NEW SOCIETY IN THE MID-1970s

At the end of 1975 the process of institutionalizing the ideals and policies of the New Society was still in progress under martial law. The political structure was characterized by bureaucratic dominance with heavy emphasis on discipline and stability; the army continued to have a low-profile, but nonetheless powerful, impact on the political process. Indications were that "constitutional authoritarianism" would remain the basis for political actions as long as, in Marcos' view, the country was threatened by sources of destabilization, actual and potential.

The political scene was generally calm, the notable exception being in the southern Philippines where Muslim rebels continued to tie down three-fourths of the army's combat battalions. The rebellion seemed to have been weakened, however, as a result of government measures to redress Muslim grievances by improving their economic conditions and by granting more autonomy to the Muslim population. A number of defections from the insurgent ranks were reported during 1975, although apparently few leaders of the rebellion came down from the hills to accept government offers of amnesty (see ch. 17).

In the New Society there were virtually no legitimate outlets through which opposition forces could rally and mount an effective challenge against the Marcos leadership. Some former party politicians, militant students, religious leaders, intellectuals, and labor groups agreed that civil liberties and democratic institutions should be restored; but they had no political machines with which to campaign for popular backing and in any case had been forbidden to hold public rallies since September

1972. In addition they were unable to air their views and alternatives through the mass media, which were under strict self-censorship (see ch. 7).

The Roman Catholic Church was potentially the only mass-based source of challenge to the Marcos regime, but the church was not united as to whether it should be involved in social and political action. A number of young, liberal priests and nuns and a few bishops expressed concern about authoritarianism and about the plight of the country's poor and underprivileged. Often referred to in government statements as "the Christian left," these militant members of the clergy were in a minority. For the most part the church leadership stressed prayer and noninvolvement in political affairs (see ch. 7).

Opposition not only was fragmented but lacked a viable symbol of unity. In early 1976 former Senator Aquino, described by one observer as the politician most feared by Marcos because of Aguino's acumen and ambition, was languishing in jail in his fourth year of detention. In August 1973 he was first ordered to appear before a military court to hear government charges of crimes allegedly committed before the imposition of martial law and for which he was never indicted. Aquino refused to be tried on any charges leveled against him by what he said was an unconstitutional regime.

In late 1975 opposition activities continued to be sporadic. In September 1975 a group calling itself the Civil Liberties Union of the Philippines publicly appealed to Marcos to restore democratic rule. In the following month a group of 133 Filipinos including former party politicians, educators, lawyers, religious leaders, and students issued a manifesto calling on Marcos to dismantle his one-man rule in favor of a democratic system of government based on the separation of powers. The manifesto, delivered to the presidential palace by the former senator Jovito Salonga, expressed concern that, after three years of martial law, the country was still beset with "the same old ills plus all the evils and injustices of one-man rule." Popular reaction to these appeals could not be readily ascertained.

The important political actors of the New Society were mostly bureaucrats; top-ranking army and constabulary officers, a small number of technocrats advising Marcos on economic issues, and some senior civil servants in key departmental posts. The dominant group was the military (including the Philippine Constabulary), generally recognized as the main power base of President Marcos. Also influential but less so than before 1972 were a number of economic oligarchs who, with the notable exception of the Lopez empire, survived the political change and were joined by those who acquired economic sinecures after martial law. Most of these old and new elements were close supporters of Marcos.

The Marcos administration was civilian led but depended largely on the military to enforce presidential decrees. Although traditionally nonpartisan and under strict civilian authority, the military was steadily politicized under martial law. In the initial weeks of martial law the military was asked to restore and maintain order so that civilian offices could function more effectively. The broadly defined internal security role of the military resulted in a widening circle of direct and indirect involvement in civil functions previously under the charge of provincial governors and municipal mayors (see ch. 16). The tendency, apparent since early 1972, continued of appointing to key military commands officers from the Ilocos region of northern Luzon, Marcos' own home area.

Amid growing speculation at home and abroad that the military would eventually assume power in the Philippines, Marcos stated in September 1974 that such a takeover would never take place. He disclosed that he and twelve top defense and military officials had agreed, shortly before the proclamation of martial law, on a system of presidential succession to be put into effect in the event he was disabled. These officials were said to have pledged support of a civilian president at all times. The contents of the succession arrangement were yet to be made public at the end of 1975.

Among those often mentioned as likely to succeed Marcos was the first lady, Imelda Romualdez Marcos. Wealthy and widely respected for her political acumen, she was appointed in November 1975 as the governor of the newly integrated metropolitan government of the greater Manila area. Relatives of both Marcos and his wife held prominent positions in government and business. This phenomenon was essentially in accord with the Filipino tradition whereby family loyalty is considered an overriding social value and, according to Corpuz, "the key to Filipino political behavior." Nepotism was technically frowned on in the Philippines but was in practice expected and encouraged because of the ingrained view of the family as a defense against the potentially hostile world (see ch. 5).

After three years of martial law President Marcos sounded both satisfied and sober in his appraisal of the New Society. In September 1975 in an address to the nation Marcos said that the economy was vigorous and resilient in the face of crisis, that there was order where there used to be none, that anarchy was "only a memory of the past," and that the rights and liberties of citizens were "on the whole much better secured today than they were before the intervention of constitutional authoritarianism." He also maintained that "Filipino farmers have been and will continue to be the main beneficiaries of the major government program launched over the first one thousand days of martial law and the New Society. . . . Our administration has succeeded through deliberate policy and action in helping the Filipino farmer rediscover himself, attain a new dignity and secure true freedom" (see ch. 13).

The president stated that "all hostilities in Mindanao, in central Luzon, and all over the Philippines" might be terminated "in the immediate future." In foreign affairs he said that, since the fall of Vietnam, his government was reassessing its security arrangements with the United

States in accordance with the principle of national self-reliance. The establishment of diplomatic relations with the People's Republic of China (PRC) in June 1975 was singled out as a major foreign policy achievement (see ch. 11).

Marcos pinned high hopes on the *barangay* as the viable and dynamic institution through which the people and their community-level politics could be brought closer to national decisionmaking. The *barangay* was said to be in effect a replacement for the old electoral processes—a new forum in which the individual could make his voice heard on public issues.

In underscoring the continued importance of discipline and order in the days ahead, Marcos referred to what he called "the dangers of decay" not only in government but in other sectors of society. He said:

> Sadly, we note, the dramatic gains of the past three years . . . have ironically intensified natural appetites for finery and show, for lavish parties, flashy cars, mansions, big homes, expensive travel and other counterproductive activities that dissipate the ethic of work, sacrifice and discipline that is the meaning of the New Society. Because Manila is the hub of economic and international life in the country, it is not difficult to find the simplest amenities of life among the rich increasingly feeding on the bitterness, the frustrations and exploitation of the very poor.

In stressing the need for "a new climate of confidence and hope, a passionate renewal of faith and devotion, "Marcos acknowledged that the general signs of national strength and progress somehow had not completely translated into realities sufficiently relevant to the ordinary individual. He noted that the facade of popular enthusiasm for reform was belied by a number of disturbing phenomena:

> I raise my voice in alarm today for we are in fact a nation divided against itself—divided between urban and rural, rich and poor, majorities and minorities, privileged and underprivileged. Among some of the poor there is still the nagging fear that they have, again, been left behind, and that we have liquidated an oligarchy only to set up a new oligarchy.

Marcos defended the institutions, policies, and programs of the New Society as vigorous and successful but was not sanguine about the human factor of government—men of power, wealth, and high government position who were said to have failed popular expectations. He called on the people to join him in a new war against graft and corruption within the government service and against men who were misusing their government positions not only for personal enrichment but for the sake of their business colleagues, relatives, and friends.

As an initial remedy Marcos announced the dismissal of 2,000 "undesirables" from the civil service; he promised a broader sweep later in various parts of the government, including the judiciary and military organizations. In the first two weeks of November 1975 there were reports of an imminent purge among top military officers, but Secretary of National Defense Juan Ponce Enrile denied the reports, adding that since September 1972 the military establishment had purged its own ranks of about 2,000 officers and men and that the same process of weeding out "misfits and undesirables" would continue unabated. In late November the *Christian Science Monitor* reported from Manila that "the subject of everyday conversation among educated Filipinos" in a number of provinces was alleged corruption and abuses in military ranks.

The government's anticorruption drive took another turn in late November 1975 when Melchor, President Marcos' chief development planner and right-hand man since 1970, was himself removed as executive secretary. The official explanation was that his removal—and the abolition of the post of executive secretary—was part of an effort to increase flexibility and efficiency (see ch. 9). As the top official in charge of preparing the purge list, however, he appeared to have aroused the displeasure of powerful groups in the government.

POLITICAL VALUES

In the years after national independence most Filipinos formed political opinions and attitudes and made political choices—consciously and unconsciously—according to a set of values combining both indigenous and foreign influences. In the mid-1970s these values, along with the political institutions with which they were associated, were objects of reform in order that they might contribute more effectively to the admittedly difficult task of establishing the New Society.

The value system before the imposition of martial law in 1972 showed two salient features. On the one hand politics and government were highly personalized affairs; such political symbols as authority, power, government, and nation-state were perceived primarily in terms of their practical relevance to family welfare and individual rewards. Technically the public sphere of life was to be governed by impersonal rules and regulations, but in practice the rules of procedure were bent or modified to suit varying situational needs dictated by family loyalty and obligations or by the dyadic patterns of mutual assistance between patrons and clients. Few Filipinos could ignore these time-honored patterns of conduct (see ch. 5).

On the other hand Filipino political values were tempered by the ideals or norms associated with a Western democratic political framework, notably that of the American model. The notions of popular representation, partisan politics, personal freedom, private initiative, free enterprise economy, and free speech were readily identifiable, if not deeply rooted, parts of the value system. American influence was ascribable to a half-century of free public education based on textbooks drawn from those used in the United States, and Filipino teachers were initially American trained. Even after indepedence in 1946 the effects of the political socialization of preindependence endured.

The values extolled through formal education were focused, among other things, on loyalty to the nation-state, public service to the community, voting as a civic duty, loyal opposition, cooperation with the government of the majority popularly expressed, and respect for law enacted by the popular instruments of government. As noted by Grossholtz, however, these exhortations had "no relevance to the bargaining behavior required of the Filipino for the simplest of his daily relationships." To most Filipinos the dominant political preoccupation was to use public channels of competition and public office to satisfy personal needs. Values stressing the higher imperative of public interest continued to be ritualized in schools and public institutions, but few failed to recognize the incongruity of formal ideals with the Filipino reality accentuating parochial interests.

Among the foremost critics of the pre-1972 democratic values was President Marcos, who argued that, although these values had inherent merits, they had been corrupted by the intervention of wealth and in any case were not in accord with Philippine traditions. He contended that the mere possession of political rights or legislated equality was not a meaningful criterion of political democracy; the critical test was whether or not these rights were effectively enjoyed by the majority. Marcos stated that, in this critical regard, the old institutions and values failed because they tended to favor what he called "oligarchic values" or "oligarchic democracy." He asserted that the pre-1972 political order was essentially an "oligarchic order" accentuating the privileges of wealth, the rights of property, and the protection of special interests.

The political ideals of the New Society centered on discipline, sacrifice, austerity, hard work, faith in national reformation, and participation in the *barangays*, which a Philippine source described as "the real democratic practices" that Filipino ancestors had used to best advantage in securing the welfare and satisfying the needs of the entire community. Government sources were replete with promises that the New Society would usher in a truly representative system if these values were scrupulously honored as a basis for political commitment and action.

Official publicity was increasingly focused on the need for popular support of and participation in the *barangays*. Marcos sought to convince the people that the *barangays* provided them with "a ready access to political authority"—an access that in the past was said to have been confined to "the oligarchy pulling the strings in the background." The *barangays* were in effect visualized as the institution best suited to satisfy the democratic aspirations of the people—an institution of popular rule through which power could be returned to the people. Government spokesmen were quick to admit, however, that the process of obliterating "deeply rooted evil political habits"—including the task of creating "a new soul" for the Philippines—was at best a long-range undertaking. Difficulties were anticipated in light of human weaknesses and failings that could not only dampen the spirit of reform but also undermine the implementation of even the best laid plans.

CHAPTER 11

FOREIGN RELATIONS

Flexibility, adaptation, and revision were the dominant themes in the mid-1970s as the Philippines attempted to work out a new framework of external relations. New ground rules often referred to in Manila as "the new foreign policy" came about through a growing Filipino realization that the old foreign policy should be adapted to a world of rapid and uncertain change.

The old foreign policy was anchored in the special relations that the Philippines had with the United States. It had its origin in the early period of independence after nearly half a century of American colonial administration. In the post-World War II years the United States was the only power upon which the Philippines could depend for its economic and security needs. In 1947 the Philippines signed a series of agreements with the United States under which the latter pledged both economic and military assistance. As the country gained self-confidence as an independent state, however, a growing number of Filipinos voiced the nationalistic sentiment that the terms of their security and economic ties with the United States contained what they called inequalities and ambiguities. They felt that this relationship should be reassessed in keeping with their dignity as a sovereign republic.

As the 1970s opened, domestic pressure for a reassessment of Philippine-American relations grew stronger. This development was precipitated initially by the United States decision, announced in Guam by President Richard M. Nixon in mid-1969, to redefine its military role in Asia; the announcement occasioned growing anxiety in Manila that the United States might eventually terminate its military involvement in Asia. The dramatic unfolding of Sino-American détente in early 1971 added a further note of uncertainty, compelling the Philippine government to revise its cold war assumptions and adopt a new set of rules by which to reorient its foreign relations.

At the heart of the foreign policy perceptions was the belief that the critical choice facing the Philippines had less to do with cold war confrontation than with the need for functional collaboration among nations regardless of ideological differences. Growing stress on diversification resulted in the opening of diplomatic and economic ties with communist countries in 1972. The fall of United States-backed governments in early 1975 in the Khmer Republic (Cambodia) and the Republic of Vietnam (South Vietnam) to communist-led forces gave an added sense of urgency to President Marcos' search for a new foreign policy. As stated by President Marcos at that time, the new guidelines included the establishment of diplomatic relations with socialist states in general and the People's Republic of China (PRC) and the Soviet Union in particular, a closer identification with third world countries, broadened relations with neighboring nations, continued beneficial relations with Japan, and finally a new basis for continued relations with the United States.

Although the emphasis on identification with third world countries was relatively new, the Philippines had been moving for several years to establish relations with socialist states and to seek a new formulation of its ties with the United States. Also, the importance of Philippine commercial ties with Japan and the Philippine desire to strengthen bilateral and multilateral relations with Southeast Asian states had become established tenets of Philippine policy. Thus there was evolution rather than dramatic change in President Marcos' call for self-reliance, and at the end of 1975 Philippine leaders continued to emphasize that their search for new friends would not be at the expense of old friends.

THE EVOLUTION OF PHILIPPINE FOREIGN POLICY

Since independence Philippine foreign policy makers have taken into account two major considerations—the country's Western orientation in external affairs as evidenced by its initial dependence on the United States and the country's Asian background. Both factors contributed to the Filipino view that the archipelago republic represented something of a bridge between Asia and the West; but they were also a source of ambiguity in the eyes of the country's Asian neighbors. Because of the country's half-century of association with the United States, many Asians and others elsewhere in the world tended to look upon the Philippines as a "little brother" of the United States. Many Filipinos concluded, therefore, that their country needed to build a more independent image through the pursuit of what they called self-reliant foreign policy.

For pragmatic reasons each successive Philippine government sought to strengthen economic and security relations with the United States while promoting regional cooperation in Southeast Asia. As a practical matter, however, this two-pronged orientation was tilted heavily toward the United States. Thus in the mid-1970s efforts were under way to improve relations with Philippine neighbors substantially.

Direct Philippine involvement in world affairs actually predated independence. During World War II its leaders were included in the Pacific War Council and participated in other international meetings. In 1945 its delegation, headed by Carlos P. Romulo, attended the Conference on International Organization at San Francisco that resulted in the creation of the United Nations (UN). After independence the Philippines at a regional conference held at Baguio in 1947 advocated a Marshall Plan for Asia on the grounds that Asia was as important as Western Europe to world peace. In 1949, at a regional conference in New Delhi, the government of President Elpidio Quirino stressed the need for an Asian union based on cultural, economic, political, and military bonds. In the same year it also proposed a Pacific pact as a vehicle for common defense against communism in Asia. In May 1950 the Philippines was host to a conference attended by Australia, Ceylon (present-day Sri Lanka), India, Indonesia, Pakistan, and Thailand; the participants discussed the possibility of establishing an organization for mutual cooperation.

Because of the intensification of the cold war climate after World War II and the Communist Chinese victory in 1949, much of the Philippine interest in Asia was focused on security. Initial anxiety was put to rest in 1947 when Philippines signed two military agreements with the United States; but nonetheless a perceived threat from communism from within as well as from without became a principal factor in the shaping of Manila's foreign policy. In September 1950, shortly after the outbreak of the Korean War, the Philippines sent one combat infantry battalion to the Republic of Korea (South Korea) as part of the forces under the United Nations Command. Subsequently, after the French defeat at Dien Bien Phu in Vietnam in early 1954, the Philippines joined a group of anticommunist nations to sign in Manila the Southeast Asia Collective Defense Treaty. The Manila Pact, as it came to be called, created the Southeast Asia Treaty Organization (SEATO), comprising Australia, France, New Zealand, Pakistan, the Philippines, Thailand, the United Kingdom, and the United States.

The first tangible achievement in regional cooperation in the nonmilitary field of economic and cultural matters was registered in 1961 when the Philippines, Malaya, and Thailand agreed to establish the Association of Southeast Asia (ASA). ASA remained, however, a paper organization because its member states not only were economically weak but also had political differences. Moreover other countries in the region were not inclined to associate themselves with ASA since the Philippines and Thailand were members of SEATO.

Nonetheless, growing emphasis on nonmilitary approaches was evident in the Philippine reaction to, and involvement in, the Vietnam conflict. As the Vietnamese communist insurgency gradually escalated in the early 1960s, the Philippine government expressed concern over the situation. It welcomed the United States policy of actively supporting the government of South Vietnam against the insurgents but showed its own reluctance to become directly involved in combat operations in Vietnam. In the fall of 1964 the government of President Diosdado Macapagal started discussions with the United States regarding a Philippine military contribution; these discussions resulted in the Philippine decision to send civic action teams—doctors, nurses, construction engineers, and security forces—under the name of the Philippine Civic Action Group (PHILCAG). At that time Marcos, then an opposition senator, actively opposed the sending of any forces to South Vietnam.

When he was elected president at the end of 1965 and assumed the office in 1966, Marcos modified his earlier opposition. Later that year about 2,000 Filipino noncombatants were dispatched to South Vietnam—a move widely supported in the country at that time.

The quest for nomilitary cooperation did not, however, entail any relaxation of anticommunist posture externally. This was shown in Philippine participation in a new regional body, the Asian and Pacific Council (ASPAC), formed in 1966 under the main initiative of South Korea. The purpose of ASPAC was to promote greater mutual assistance and solidarity among the noncommunist nations of Asia in their common efforts to remain independent in the face of the communist threat. The members of the organization included Australia, Japan, Malaysia, the Republic of China (Nationalist China), New Zealand, the Philippines, South Korea, South Vietnam, and Thailand.

Meanwhile a series of developments involving Indonesia and Malaysia in the 1965–66 period infused a new note of optimism for an improved regional political climate. In Indonesia a new locus of power emerged in the figure of General Suharto in the wake of the ill-fated Indonesian communist coup on September 30, 1965; this dramatic turn of events removed a major obstacle to regional cooperation—the confrontation between Indonesia and Malaysia. The resumption of normal relations in late 1966 between the two countries gave impetus to the formation of a new regional arrangement, the Association of Southeast Asian Nations (ASEAN), of which the Philippines became a leading member.

ASEAN was formed in August 1967 with a view to promoting mutual cooperation in food production, commerce and industry, civil aviation, tourism, communications, meteorology, and shipping. Its members were Indonesia, Malaysia, the Philippines, Singapore, and Thailand. In effect ASEAN replaced ASA, which had failed to show much vigor. In an effort to bring about broader regional solidarity Burma, Cambodia, and Ceylon were asked to join in 1967, but none of them chose to join the new grouping.

The effects of increasing efforts to develop self-reliance were felt in another initially low-keyed though significant foreign policy direction. In March 1968 the Philippine government hinted at the possibility of establishing trade relations with the Soviet Union and other communist countries as early as practicable, and fact-finding missions were dispatched to the Soviet Union and Eastern Europe in March and October of that year.

The year 1969 was marked by growing Filipino unease about the future of security in Southeast Asia in general and in the Philippines in particular. An early portent of Filipino concern appeared toward the end of 1968 when President Marcos expressed the view that the United States might eventually remove its military presence from Asia and therefore appropriate countermeasures should be taken. In the eyes of the Filipinos such a view was confirmed at least in part in July 1969 when

President Nixon enunciated his new Asian policy, commonly known as the Nixon Doctrine (see Relations with the United States, this ch.). In mid-1970 the United States government formally announced that it would withdraw 6,000 troops from the Philippines by mid-1971.

Philippine foreign policy showed signs of increasing maturation in 1971. In his annual message in January of that year President Marcos proclaimed the intention of establishing diplomatic relations with the communist countries "in the near future," adding that this step was dictated by the need for new markets. In line with this policy the long-standing posture of hostility toward the communist-bloc countries was formally repudiated in November 1971, thus paving the way for the first diplomatic ties—with Romania and Yugoslavia, both in March 1972.

The dramatic opening of contacts between the United States and the PRC in the spring of 1971 further accelerated the Philippine search for new policy options. In this situation Manila was receptive to the concept of a Southeast Asian zone of "peace, neutrality, and freedom," an idea first suggested by Malaysia in September 1970. In July 1971 and November 1971 the Philippines stated its support for the Malaysian concept, which it linked to President Marcos' own favorite idea of convening an Asian summit conference.

President Marcos' concerted efforts to build a new image for the Philippines continued apace under martial law, which he imposed in September 1972. They were given additional impetus with the approaching end of the war in South Vietnam. After January 1973, when a cease-fire agreement was signed in Paris to end the war and restore peace in Indochina, the Philippines accelerated its quest for a niche in post-Vietnam Asia.

RELATIONS WITH THE UNITED STATES

In the years after independence in 1946 Filipinos of all walks of life believed that their preindependence ties with the United States should be continued if only for pragmatic reasons—but with proper modifications to fit the new circumstance of Philippine independence. Close cooperation with the United States was considered by successive Philippine governments essential for at least three reasons. Politically the Filipinos inherited a set of democratic institutions and practices of government that in essential respects were patterned after those of the United States (see ch. 9). Economically the Philippines had provided the American market with sugar, coconut products, and hemp, and the retention of this export trade was considered necessary to economic recovery after World War II. Militarily the United States was the only Pacific power that could be relied upon to safeguard the republic from external threat.

Unquestionably the United States was the dominant factor in Manila's external affairs for more than two decades after independence. In 1946 it pledged US$620 million to help the Philippines recover from war damages to private and public property; this was in keeping with President Franklin D. Roosevelt's wartime statement that the Philippines would be aided in the "full repair" of the ravages wrought by the war. The Filipinos argued, however, that the aid for repair would be closer to US$1 billion (see ch. 15).

Also in 1946 the United States Congress passed the Philippine Trade Act (also known as the Bell Act) to provide for continued duty-free trade with the United States until 1955; beginning in 1956 tariff preferences were to be gradually phased out. The bill also contained, among other provisions, a stipulation that American citizens residing in the Philippines would have the same or "parity" rights as the Filipinos in the exercise of economic rights. A companion bill on war rehabilitation, under which the United States was to assist the Philippines, was passed by the United States Congress and provided that the Philippine Trade Act had to be ratified by the Philippine Congress if the United States were to honor individual Filipino war damage claims in excess of US$500. Given this condition the Philippines endorsed the trade act and granted parity rights to Americans through a constitutional amendment in 1947. Filipinos found the situation somewhat unpalatable, however. For one thing, the Filipinos residing in the United States were not granted the same parity rights. For another, the circumstances surrounding the passage of the two bills were viewed as something of a unilateral imposition on the hapless Filipinos.

The parity issue left a residue of misunderstanding or irritants, as the Filipinos would say, between the two countries. Filipinos tended to regard their economic ties, however important these were to their economic recovery, as inequitable and humiliating. They argued for the rectification of the situation to fit the new circumstances of their independence as a sovereign republic. In 1954 the two countries negotiated a new trade accord as a revision of the 1946 trade act; in the following year the revised version became official as the Revised United States-Philippine Trade Agreement of 1955 (Laurel-Langley Agreement). Under the new arrangement Filipino citizens residing in the United States received reciprocal parity rights equal to those enjoyed by American investments made before 1974 would be protected in accordance with the 1935 Constitution. Discussions aimed at continuing a exports to the United States were extended with some adjustments (see ch. 15).

The 1955 agreement became the basis for substantial economic exchanges between the two nations. Through the end of 1973 the United States was the Philippines' top trading partner. And as of September 1972 investments by American citizens accounted for 76 percent of total foreign investments in the Philippines; the bulk of the American share was in the manufacturing, chemical, and processing industries (see ch. 14).

The Laurel-Langley Agreement expired on July 3, 1974; previously

236

the United States had indicated—as early as 1965—that it did not wish to exercise parity rights after July 1974. It had also expressed the hope that American investments made before 1974 would be protected in accordance with the 1935 Constitution. Discussions aimed at continuing a stable and mutually beneficial framework for economic relations had been initiated a number of years before the Laurel-Langley Agreement expired. Although no formal bilateral agreements had been reached as of late 1975, the two countries continued to enjoy close trade relations. As of mid-1975 American equity investments in the Philippines were estimated to be close to US$2 billion in market value (see ch. 15).

Foreign aid was also a key factor in Philippine-American relations. Between 1946 and 1973 the United States provided a total of US$2.7 billion, including about US$1.6 billion for economic assistance and US$709 million in military assistance. The balance was accounted for by long-term loans from the United States Export-Import Bank, war damage and rehabilitation payments, and flood relief contributions.

Relations with the United States were as conspicuous militarily as they were economically. The fluid and uncertain regional situation in Asia in the years after World War II and the inability of the Philippines to defend itself culminated in United States military presence on Philippine soil. Security ties were based on three arrangements: the Military Bases Agreement of 1947, the Military Assistance Agreement of the same year, and the Mutual Defense Treaty of 1951 (see ch. 16). The first of these provided for the retention of base rights by the United States and for use of these facilities to promote mutual security for a period of ninety-nine years; these bases were to be located away from population centers as the Filipinos desired. The second agreement, superseded by a new one in 1953, became the basis for American military aid, including the provision of weapons and training. In the Mutual Defense Treaty the two countries recognized that "an armed attack in the Pacific Area on either of the Parties would be dangerous to its own peace and safety" and that they would act to meet the common dangers in accordance with their respective "constitutional processes."

The cordiality and mutual benefits so characteristic of Philippine-American relations were, however, as often as not clouded by the unresolved question of court jurisdiction over civil and criminal cases involving American military personnel and Filipinos. The Filipino grievance was focused particularly on the Military Bases Agreement, which they viewed as an affront to their national pride and dignity.

At issue was the Filipino contention that the United States was exercising extraterritorial jurisdiction by virtue of the bases agreement and that the agreement had not provided an equitable clause dealing with original jurisdiction over offenses by Americans or Filipinos on or off the base while on duty. Bilateral efforts to resolve the question were begun in earnest in 1956, and by 1959 the two countries had agreed to delimit American base areas, to return certain bases to Philippine jurisdiction, to establish a mutual defense board, and eventually to reduce the lease on American bases from ninety-nine to twenty-five years. The thorny issue of criminal jurisdiction remained unresolved, however, and was the subject of intermittent bilateral discussion in subsequent years.

Filipino sensibilities were calmed somewhat in August 1965 when the United States authorities made certain concessions on the question of criminal jurisdiction and consented to put into effect the 1959 agreement on shortening the base lease to twenty-five years (see ch. 16). Nevertheless the military base issue remained an irritant as far as the Philippines was concerned, and in fact the Filipinos singled it out as the major problem to be resolved if the two countries were to continue their relations on terms of mutual respect.

The subject of military bases was at the heart of Filipino nationalist agitation for a new framework of relations with the United States. The Philippine leadership insisted that the base agreement be renegotiated to make it more comparable with the agreements that the United States signed with other foreign governments.

In July 1969 President Nixon paid a brief visit to Manila and told the Filipinos that the old special relationship would be terminated in order to build a new relationship based on mutuality of interest and mutual respect. This statement was generally welcomed, as was his pledge that the United States would remain a Pacific power and would honor its commitments to its Asian allies. The Nixon message, known as the Nixon Doctrine, was a reiteration of what he had enunciated in Guam shortly before his arrival in Manila. The Filipinos had cause to be concerned, however, since President Nixon also set forth the United States intention of lowering its military profile in Asia in due course—hence the concern in Manila over the prospect of a power vacuum in Asia. At that time Nixon made it clear that the United States would not get involved directly in internal subversion problems and that it would expect its Asian allies to assume more responsibility for their own defense.

The Nixon statement, interpreted at that time in Manila as a harbinger of eventual American military disengagement from Asia, tended to reinforce President Marcos' resolve to chart a more independent and diversified course in foreign affairs. It became increasingly clear that the Philippines' search for a new foreign policy was inseparable from, and integrally linked to, its demands for a revised security relationship with the United States.

In 1971 the two countries started a series of low-keyed, unpublicized discussions regarding the military base issue—without much substantive result. The issue catapulted to the fore as a subject of intense self-searching in Manila after the capitulation of Cambodia and South Vietnam to communist-led forces in the spring of 1975. President Marcos almost immediately questioned the value of the existing military ties with the United States and even declared the readiness of his government to "discard" the Mutual Defense Treaty with the United States and to take over American military bases if in the national interest. "Let no man, friend or foe," he said, "think in terms other than the national interest." He ordered an acceleration of the Philippines' self-reliance defense program, coupled with a sweeping review of all security pacts with the United States in the light of what he called "new realities" in Asia.

The Philippine reaction was based in part on the apparent belief that the Nixon Doctrine could not be taken on faith in light of what had happened to South Vietnam and Cambodia. In late May 1975 Secretary of Foreign Affairs Romulo echoed the concern of his government: "We are inescapably led to the conclusion that the mutual defense treaty is far from being mutual and that it exists solely for the protection of the United States forces stationed in the Philippines." This was a pointed reference to the belief of many Filipinos that the provisions of the Mutual Defense Treaty did not guarantee as automatic or as rapid an American response to an external attack on the Philippines as was provided to the member countries of the North Atlantic Treaty Organization (NATO) by the language of the NATO treaty.

The reaction in Manila was tempered by pragmatism, however, Despite President Marcos' announced intention to "put an end to the practice of extraterritoriality in our country" and "to assume control of all these bases," he made it clear in the summer of 1975 that the Philippines would extend to the United States the use of all facilities on the bases so that the United States could remain a Pacific power and maintain peace in the region. But Marcos declared, "Let it be understood that the Philippines and the Filipinos are offering these facilities voluntarily and as an independent, dignified country and people."

RELATIONS WITH JAPAN

In the immediate postwar years fear and mistrust complicated Philippine relations with Japan. The legacy of bitterness stemming from the Japanese occupation of the archipelago during World War II could not be easily forgotten. But the passage of time, coupled with pragmatism, gradually healed the wounds of the past, and eventually the two countries developed close relations, especially in the field of economic exchange and cooperation. Japan not only became a principal source of loans for Philippine industrialization but also in 1975, replaced the United States as the Philippines' foremost trading partner (see ch. 15).

Philippine policy toward Japan was initially devoted to ensuring that Japan would never again pose a military threat, that it would evolve into a peace-loving and democratic nation, and that equitable and sufficient war reparations would be obtained. As a first step the Philippines (along with forty-seven other allied nations) signed a peace treaty with Japan at San Francisco in 1951. In that year it also initiated negotiations for reparations.

The negotiations were complicated because among other reasons the Philippine claim had to be balanced against Japan's ability to pay. The

Phipippine government, like other claimants, wanted to see Japan recover economically so that it could perform a self-sufficient and constructive role in Asia. Thus its initial demand for US$8 billion was scaled down in the face of Japan's offer of US$250 million. Several years of intermittent and hard bargaining resulted in the signing of a reparations agreement in 1956 under which Japan pledged a total of US$800 million in compensation. Of this total, US$500 million was to be paid in capital goods and US$250 million in private loans for economic development over a period of twenty years ending in July 1976 (see ch. 15).

Diplomatic relations were established in July 1956 almost immediately after the reparations settlement. Later that year the Philippines cosponsored a resolution for Japan's admission to the UN, and slowly but steadily relations with Japan grew cordial. This improvement was most noticeable in the sharp increase in trade, despite Japan's having to carry on trade under certain restrictions (see ch. 15).

The restrictions were imposed for protectionist reasons. They reflected the lingering Filipino apprehension that without built-in safeguards the Philippines might become economically subservient to Japan. Such a suspicion was also the underlying reason for the refusal of the Philippine legislature to ratify the Treaty of Friendship, Commerce, and Navigation with Japan that President Carlos P. Garcia had signed in December 1960. Nevertheless in 1966 President Marcos all but lifted the existing trade restrictions in the belief that the country's goal of economic development would be better served by open trade. During 1967 the two countries for the first time undertook joint ventures and established civil air links between Manila and Tokyo. These measures paved the way for a substantial inflow of Japanese investments, technology, and tourists in subsequent years.

In early 1969 Japan pledged a loan of US$30 million to help finance the construction of a pan-Philippine highway from northern Luzon to southern Mindanao; this was the first of many Japanese contributions toward the development of the Philippine economic infrastructure. Meanwhile the question of ratifying the Treaty of Friendship, Commerce, and Navigation was annually debated in the Philippine Congress. In 1972, as in previous years, the Congress again refused to endorse it, the argument being that the draft treaty lacked sufficient protectionist clauses and that President Marcos showed an insufficiently nationalistic posture concerning the ratification issue. At that time a number of Japanese firms operating in Manila also came under sharp rebuke for alleged economic aggression.

The treaty was finally ratified in December 1973 by President Marcos himself under broad emergency powers granted him under the new 1973 Constitution (see ch. 9). The president no longer had to contend with the legislature, which had been dissolved after the country was placed under martial law in September 1972 (see ch. 10). The instrument of ratification was exchanged in December, and the treaty went into effect in January 1974.

President Marcos was able to discuss a wide range of issues with Japanese Prime Minister Kakuei Tanaka when the latter paid a state visit to Manila in January 1974. The two leaders exchanged views on ways of expanding economic relations, including possible Japanese participation in oil exploration, steel mill, and shipbuilding ventures; a Philippine request for Japanese fertilizers; and mutual cooperation in food production. At that time Marcos' chief foreign policy spokesman, Romulo, also called upon Japan to launch a Marshall Plan for Asia to help rehabilitate Southeast Asia in the same way the United States had helped Western Europe after World War II. He maintained that there could be no development of the region without Japan's playing a principal role. On the question of regional security, however, he did not believe that Japan or any other single power should be allowed to fill the power vacuum that might be created in the event the United States withdrew from the region.

For his part Prime Minister Tanaka assured the Philippine leaders that Japan had no intention of seeking economic domination anywhere in Asia and promised to take necessary action against Japanese firms suspected of unethical and aggressive business activities in the Philippines. The Japanese leader also sought to enhance mutual understanding and trust by proposing a cultural exchange program designed to enable Southeast Asian youths to visit Japan.

RELATIONS WITH NEIGHBORING COUNTRIES

In the mid-1970s the Philippines had close and friendly ties with a number of countries in Southeast Asia. The ideological factor, once a key criterion of Philippine foreign relations, was gradually receding into the background. As a parallel trend the government sought to downgrade the once overriding consideration of a military alliance for the region.

Broadly stated, relations with neighbors were closest with Indonesia, Malaysia, and Thailand. Before Indonesia gained full independence in 1949, the Philippines had played an important role in the promotion of the Indonesian cause. During the 1950s and through the mid-1960s, however, the two countries more often than not differed in their basic approaches to the question of the East-West ideological confrontation. Philippine alignment with the United States was not warmly viewed in Jakarta. As early as January 1961 Indonesian President Sukarno, while on a visit to Manila, indirectly criticized the Filipinos for their Western orientation in foreign policy and called on them to return to their oriental heritage. Philippine reaction was predictably hostile.

Nonetheless the two countries sought a common ground for close mutual association. This effort was to culminate in an agreement reached by the Philippines, Indonesia, and Malaya in August 1963 to take initial steps toward the establishment of MAPHILINDO (Malaya, the Philippines, and Indonesia). The purpose of this loose nonpolitical federation of the three countries was to seek solutions to common problems through mutual consultation and assistance. MAPHILINDO, heralded in Manila as the Philippines' "greatest achievement of 1963," was stillborn, however, because in the following month Malaya announced the formation of the Federation of Malaysia. Consisting of Malaya, Singapore, and two of the states of northern Borneo (Sabah and Sarawak), this federation was denounced by Indonesia as a vehicle for perpetuating British military bases and colonialism in Southeast Asia (see fig. 1). Sukarno almost immediately launched the so-called Crush Malaysia campaign; this and his steady drift toward the PRC in foreign policy made it difficult for the Philippines to maintain warm relations with Indonesia.

The situation took a dramatic turn in the 1965–66 period, during which Sukarno fell from power in Jakarta and his anti-Malaysian confrontation policy was ended. The resumption of diplomatic ties between Indonesia and Malaysia in August 1966 portended the participation of these countries in the newly formed ASEAN in August 1967. Relations with Indonesia steadily improved. In 1974 the Philippines and Indonesia signed a series of agreements on mutual cooperation in the fields of economic, technical, and scientific exchanges; fisheries; and border trade.

Additional indications of growing cordiality included the signing of border patrol crossing agreements in July 1975; evidently these were updated versions of agreements first signed in July 1956. To be enforced by the naval commands of both countries, these accords were designed to ensure that the land areas, waters, and airspace of the two countries would not be utilized "as staging areas for illegal activities or as places of refuge" for outlaws (see ch. 17). Moreover in September 1975 the two countries initialed a draft extradition treaty, said to be the first such pact that the Philippines had entered into with any foreign state.

Relations with Malaysia were alternately warm and cool, depending on the depth of discord over the long-standing Philippine claim to Sabah. The dispute surfaced officially in the 1962–63 period, but until then the two countries had cordial ties. The Philippines had promptly extended diplomatic recognition to Malaya when it gained independence in 1957. The two countries sought mutual cooperation through ASA, and in 1962 in recognition of the close historical ties between the peoples of the two countries President Macapagal even proposed the formation of a Malayan-Philippine confederation to include Singapore and the British-held territories of Sabah (North Borneo), Sarawak, and Brunei. In the following year the two countries joined with Indonesia in agreeing to the creation of MAPHILINDO.

The Philippines' territorial claim is based on the argument that the sultan of Sulu "leased," not "ceded" as Malaysia contended, parts of Sabah to the British North Borneo Company in 1878. The issue became public in 1957 when a Muslim delegation from Mindanao appealed to

President Ramón Magsaysay for the recovery of that part of Sabah that had originally been ruled by the Sultanate of Sulu. In April 1962 the Philippine government took an official stand on this question and in January 1963 formally notified the government of the United Kingdom of its claim to "a certain portion of the island of Borneo and adjacent islands." The British countered that the status of North Borneo was not in dispute and in any case let it be known that the territory in question would become part of Malaysia.

Diplomatic relations were severed in September 1963 almost immediately after the inauguration of the Federation of Malaysia. They were restored in June 1966 but without solving the territorial issue. The Philippine claim, dormant for several years, was revived in 1968 and was the subject of acrimonious negotiations held at the neutral site of Bangkok in June and July 1968. The Philippines demanded that the issue be referred to the International Court of Justice in The Hague; Malaysia angrily refused. Diplomatic relations were not ruptured but for all practical purposes were suspended, as each government withdrew its ambassador from the other's capital.

The situation was exacerbated in September 1968 when President Marcos signed into law a bill redefining the national boundaries; the new territorial map included most of Sabah. Malaysia immediately not only suspended diplomatic relations but also abrogated the antismuggling agreement the two countries had signed earlier in the year. In October 1968 the Philippines reiterated its demand that the dispute be taken to the world court and in the following month, because of violent mass reactions in Kuala Lumpur, withdrew its entire diplomatic staff from Malaysia.

Coolness in bilateral relations did not affect Philippine and Malaysian participation in ASEAN meetings. In fact the decision to resume full diplomatic relations was announced at the opening session of the ASEAN conference held at Cameron Highlands, Malaysia, in December 1969. The territorial question cropped up again, however, in the fall of 1970 when the Philippines renewed its appeal to Malaysia to settle the issue through the world court. In the mid-1970s it appeared that the two countries did not wish to see their relations affected by the dispute and that they wanted to focus more attention on seeking common ground for mutual cooperation. In August 1975 Secretary of Foreign Affairs Romulo announced that Malaysia and the Philippines agreed to "put in the background" his government's claim to Sabah for the sake of regional cooperation. He acknowledged that this issue had been detrimental to ASEAN cooperation. At the same time the Philippine government expressed continued concern that Sabah's chief minister, Tun Mustapha, was aiding Muslim rebels in southern Mindanao. According to unconfirmed reports emanating from Manila, Tun Mustapha's ambition was to create a separate state consisting of Mindanao, Palawan, Sulu, Tawitawi, and Basilan in the Philippines and the Malaysian state of

Sabah. These reports also speculated that Sabah was in fact serving as a training ground and entry point of smuggled arms for Filipino rebels in Mindanao (see ch. 17).

Relations with Thailand were as cordial in the mid-1970s as they had been since the establishment of diplomatic ties in 1949. The Philippines' concern about the expansion of communism in Southeast Asia had been shared by Thailand for many years. As a result in the 1950s both countries had sent combat ground troops to Korea in support of the UN-sanctioned military action, both joined SEATO in 1954 and ASPAC in 1966, and both were involved in the Vietnam conflict.

The two countries also shared a strong interest in regional cooperation. They were founding members of ASA in 1961 and, when diplomatic relations were broken between the Philippines and Malaysia in 1963, Thailand offered to represent the interest of the disputants in each other's capital. The Thai government played a similar role as an intermediary and peacemaker in 1968, when the Philippines, Thailand, and Malaysia were members of ASEAN.

In the 1970s both the Philippine and Thai governments increasingly demonstrated their flexibility in adapting themselves to the shifting currents of international politics in general and the thaw in Sino-American relations in particular. This was especially the case in their response to the collapse of anticommunist governments in Phnom Penh and Saigon in April 1975.

In July 1975 Thai Prime Minister Khukrit Pramot paid a four-day visit to Manila to discuss a wide range of issues facing the two countries. He and President Marcos reaffirmed the need to promote and expand their relations with "other countries without regard to ideology" and the view that "foreign military bases in the region were temporary in character." The Philippine and Thai leaders took the occasion also to reaffirm the need for the United States to remain a Pacific power for the time being. It was also reported that the two leaders agreed in principle to phase out SEATO in accordance with developing circumstances.

The Philippines also maintained cordial ties with Singapore, a fellow member of ASEAN, and Australia and New Zealand, both of which showed much interest in the concept of a neutralized Southeast Asia. Relations with Burma were correct; the Philippines continued to express the hope that Burma would become a member of ASEAN. Japan, South Korea, India, Pakistan, Bangladesh, and Sri Lanka had diplomatic and trade relations with the Philippines, but in the mid-1970s, despite President Marcos' announced intention of strengthening regional cooperation, relations with these Asian states—with the notable exception of Japan—were generally viewed in Manila as a matter of less than critical importance.

In the mid-1970s the Philippine government pursued a pragmatic policy of peaceful coexistence with communist-led neighbors in Southeast Asia—the Democratic Republic of Vietnam (North Vietnam), the

Provisional Revolutionary Government of South Vietnam (South Vietnam), Cambodia, and Laos. In mid-April 1975 the government officially announced the urgent need for establishing a "direct communications line to Hanoi" in view of the rapidly changing situation in Indochina. On April 18, the day after the fall of President Lon Nol's anticommunist regime in Phnom Penh, the Philippines and other ASEAN members jointly extended diplomatic recognition to the new communist-led government in the Cambodian capital. In late July 1975 a two-man Philippine government mission that had been looking into the evacuation of Filipinos from South Vietnam journeyed to Hanoi, and on August 7 it was announced in Hanoi—but not in Manila—that the two countries had signed a communiqué on the establishment of diplomatic relations.

At the end of 1975 the Philippine government remained officially silent on the Hanoi announcement. It was unclear whether this meant Manila's repudiation of the Hanoi communiqué, signed by the Philippine envoy Augustine P. Manguila. In any case shortly after his return from Hanoi Manguila "resigned" for reasons of health, according to an official announcement in Manila. Before his resignation the envoy had been quoted as having "personal knowledge" that North Vietnam was not selling arms to Filipino Muslim rebels and apparently had no intention of doing so. For its part the Philippines was said to have assured North Vietnam, according to Radio Hanoi, that it would not allow the United States to use Philippine territory against the Indochinese people. While in Hanoi, Manguila also discussed the possibility of establishing diplomatic relations with South Vietnam. North Vietnam reportedly assured him that it would inform Manila as soon as Saigon was ready to negotiate on this issue.

In any case the Philippine intention of bringing the Indochinese states into a regional cooperative forum, preferably ASEAN, was clearly indicated during 1975. In June 1975 an editorial in the progovernment daily *Times Journal* stated: "The enlargement of the ASEAN to include all communist states in the region will not only strengthen the organization but also hasten the formation of the dream of the zone of peace and neutrality." Secretary of Foreign Affairs Romulo said in August: "We are in one region belonging to one group and one racial stock. There is no reason why we cannot cooperate with each other. . . . We can be a formidable bloc."

RELATIONS WITH COMMUNIST COUNTRIES

As of late 1975 the Philippines had diplomatic relations with nearly all socialist states—except the Soviet Union, the Democratic People's Republic of Korea (North Korea), Albania, North Vietnam, and South Vietnam. Active discussions were under way during 1975 with both the Soviet Union and North Vietnam on the possibility of opening relations, but evidently there were still issues that remained unresolved.

Diplomatic relations with the socialist states were envisioned as early as 1968 but were not realized until March 1972, when the Philippines established formal ties with Romania and Yugoslavia. Later in that year ties were established with other socialist countries of Eastern Europe. Relations with Cuba were restored in September 1975. In late 1975 Manila was also studying the possibility of establishing trade relations with North Korea in response to the latter's offer to supply rice, corn, flour, steel products, pig iron, light machine tools, and nitrate fertilizers.

In the Philippine search for a new direction in foreign policy, by far the most noteworthy development was the establishment in June 1975 of diplomatic contact with the PRC. This was all the more significant in that for a quarter of a century the PRC had been pictured in Manila as "an illegitimate, evil and expansionist regime that would subvert—directly or indirectly—the existing institutions and government in the Philippines," as a leading Filipino statesman had put it in 1972. The foundation upon which rested the long-standing fear of the PRC began to crumble in early 1971 when the PRC and the United States—until then enemies—initiated steps toward mutual reconciliation and détente. Jolted from their customary assumptions about the cold war, Filipinos soon established unofficial trade contacts with Peking during 1971. They also quickly realized the impracticality of their old China policy, especially after the PRC was finally seated in the UN in October 1971. The rapidly rising international stature of the PRC, coupled with President Nixon's visit to Peking in February, 1972, dictated a new, realistic China policy; the Filipinos found it difficult to continue to accept the old notion that the world was divided into such dichotomies as "free" and "communist" or "friendly" and "hostile."

In March 1972, less than two weeks after PRC Premier Chou En-lai and President Nixon signed a joint communiqué in Shanghai, Philippine Senator Salvador Laurel flew to Peking to explore the possibility of the two countries' establishing diplomatic relations. This was a reversal of the Philippine policy of no relations with the PRC that had been reiterated in September 1970, at which time, however, the government expressed its readiness to enter into diplomatic relations with the Soviet Union and other socialist states in Eastern Europe.

The countries moved a step closer toward diplomatic rapprochement in September 1974 when Imelda Romualdez Marcos paid a visit to Peking and met with both Mao Tse-tung and Chou; at that time the two countries signed a trade document under which the PRC agreed to supply a total of 1 million tons of crude oil to the Philippines in 1974 and 1975 (see ch. 15). Formal relations were finally established on June 9, 1975, at the end of President Marcos' visit to Peking—the first visit to the PRC by an ASEAN head of state. President Marcos recognized the PRC as the sole legal government of China and on the same day announced the termination of all existing official ties with Nationalist China, with which the Philippines had had diplomatic relations since 1946. He also signed a new trade agreement with the PRC, in which each granted the other most-favored-nation treatment (see ch. 15).

Secretary of Foreign Affairs Romulo described the normalization as "the crystallization of an independent foreign policy" and an essential part of the Philippine effort to "reorient ourselves toward Asia." The new relationship with Peking was said to be valuable in that it widened the range of Philippine political and economic options; it was also meaningful, according to Romulo, partly because the Philippines had much to learn from Peking's successful efforts to bring about "unity and discipline" and partly because the Chinese Communists shared with the Filipinos the same problem of economic development. The government stressed, however, that the Philippines would not change its own social system along the Communist Chinese model nor abandon or neglect old friends. Shortly after President Marcos' return from Peking, it was also announced in Manila that the Communist Chinese leaders had assured him that the PRC would not intervene in the internal affairs of the Philippines and that the Philippine government should be "free to deal with any insurgency, subversion or rebellion in accordance with the security and well-being" of the Filipinos. The Communist Chinese leaders were also said to have expressed full support of the ASEAN policy of creating "a zone of peace, freedom, and neutrality" in Southeast Asia.

Relations with Nationalist China were not completely severed, however. The Philippines continued to carry on trade with Nationalist China through trade offices that both sides agreed to set up in Taipei and Manila. As for the sometime controversial issue of who should control Chinese schools in the Philippines, the government in Manila announced on June 4, 1975, that these institutions would be operated as Filipino schools beginning in 1976.

Originally the intention of the Philippine government was to normalize relations with the Soviet Union first and not with the PRC. But by early 1972 this policy had obviously changed. On March 15, 1972, Manila sent Mrs. Marcos to the Soviet capital—on the same day that Senator Laurel visited Peking—to sound out the possibility of opening diplomatic relations. This so-called equidistance policy was reaffirmed throughout 1974.

In the mid-1970s there were many unofficial contacts between the Philippines and the Soviet Union. Trade was carried on indirectly, through third countries, such as Japan. Negotiations were under way to end this inconvenience. In January 1975 the two countries signed an agreement on expanding scientific and cultural exchange.

According to Philippine government statements, diplomatic ties with the Soviet Union were to have been established sometime in the latter half of 1975. In mid-June, for example, Secretary of Foreign Affairs Romulo described as "impending" the opening of such a relationship. The relationship was not opened, however, and it was speculated in Manila that the delay was caused by Soviet displeasure over the Philippine decision to normalize relations with the PRC first. In September, in denying reports that there was an unanticipated complication, Romulo stated that President Marcos' projected trip to Moscow had been postponed because of "the hard Russian winter." By the end of 1975 the Philippines still had no formal ties with Soviet Union.

RELATIONS WITH COUNTRIES IN OTHER REGIONS

Diplomatic, trade, and cultural relations were maintained with a number of countries outside Asia, mostly in Western Europe and a few in Latin America, the Middle East, and Africa. In the mid-1970s there was a concerted effort on Manila's part to broaden its contacts with the previously neglected third world countries. At a conference of nonaligned nations held in Lima, Peru, in August 1975 the Philippines sought membership as a third world nation; the application was rejected.

The Philippines' pragmatic foreign policy posture was plainly evident in the reversal of its pro-Israeli policy after the Arab-Israeli war of 1973. Until then it had generally supported the Israeli cause against the Arab bloc but, in the fact of the Arab oil embargo in late 1973, Marcos announced a shift in policy. This shift was justified on two grounds: the need for a new, development-oriented foreign policy and the need to identify the Philippines unequivocally with a large number of Islamic countries and, by implication, with the third world.

In the Philippine attempt to penetrate the third world, much emphasis was placed on the World Islamic Conference, a group of forty-two countries having a common religious and cultural heritage. Through the good offices of Saudi Arabia, this conference arranged peace talks between the Philippine government and the Muslim rebels in southern Mindanao. For this purpose the conference appointed an ad hoc commit-tee consisting of Libya, Senegal, Saudi Arabia, and Somalia, and the first peace talks were held in Jiddah, Saudi Arabia, in January 1975—but with few results; a second series of talks took place at the southern Philippine port city of Zamboanga in July 1975—again with few results (see ch. 10).

In January 1975 the Philippines established diplomatic ties with Algeria in an apparent effort to strengthen relations with the third world through that country. For years Manila's principal listening post in the Arab world has been the Philippine mission in Cairo; the city has long been regarded by Filipino Muslims as the center of Arab nationalism and a major source of religious and cultural inspiration.

INTERNATIONAL AND REGIONAL COOPERATION

As a charter member of the UN the Philippines took an active interest in its functioning from the beginning. In 1949 Romulo became the first Asian leader to be elected to the presidency of the UN General Assembly. The Philippine delegates to the world organization and its specialized agencies consistently supported all resolutions on decolonization, disarmament, the peaceful uses of atomic energy, and the promotion of fundamental human rights and freedoms throughout the world. They also played a leading role in advocating international freedom of the press and information. Manila played host to numerous conferences related to the world organization. In the mid-1970s the Philippines held membership in nearly all of the intergovernmental organizations related to the UN.

As of late 1975, however, it was evident that the country's emphasis had shifted from the UN to regional cooperation. Apparently the Filipino leaders concluded that they could secure more tangible results from bilateral and multilateral exchanges with their immediate neighbors than within the "rhetoric-filled" halls of international organizations. When President Marcos laid down his six new foreign policy guidelines in May 1975, the UN was not explicitly mentioned; in the past he and his predecessors had invariably included it as a principal forum for the country's foreign relations.

Basic to Manila's scheme of regional collaboration were SEATO for collective defense against communist aggression and ASEAN for broad-gauged multilateral cooperation in nonmilitary fields. The beginning of Sino-American reconciliation in 1971, over which the Philippines and its neighbors had no control, was to have far-reaching repercussions on these regional organizations. Philippine reaction to the Sino-American quest for détente was expressed in the determination to refashion a more flexible approach and a more agile response to a changing foreign policy environment. This entailed a sweeping reassessment of the orthodoxies and rigidities of the cold war-oriented foreign policy as exemplified in Philippine participation in SEATO and to a lesser degree in ASPAC.

Specifically the initial response was in the form of a renewed emphasis on ASEAN as a forum for mutual regional assistance. At the ASEAN foreign ministers conference in November 1971, the Philippines joined other member states in signing the Kuala Lumpur Declaration, which set aside Southeast Asia as "a zone of peace, freedom, and neutrality" and appealed to the United States, the Soviet Union, and the PRC to "guarantee", ASEAN neutrality.

The sentiment in Manila, as in other ASEAN capitals, that SEATO was anachronistic was brought home dramatically after the noncommunist regimes in Cambodia and South Vietnam capitulated in early 1975. In May 1975 the semiofficial daily *Times Journal* asserted that SEATO, which it dubbed "a provocative nuisance," should be allowed "to die . . . with whatever little dignity it may still retain." The government-controlled mass media began to picture President Marcos as being "among the first doves in the SEATO." In August 1975 the president and his Thai counterpart announced their agreement on the phasing out of SEATO; this was confirmed the following month at the SEATO ministerial conference held in New York. The Thai government, however, expressed the reservation on both occasions that, although the organization could be gradually dissolved, the Manila Pact of 1954 should be preserved. Thailand, the only SEATO member that did not have a bilateral or multilateral defense arrangement with the United States, argued that it would not do any harm to retain the treaty.

In the mid-1970s the Philippines had much empathy toward ASEAN but was realistic about the difficulty of bringing about a truly cooperative regional scheme. In the spring of 1971 ASEAN leaders met in Manila to explore such possibilities as a free-trade zone, an Asian payments union, a regional investment bank, and eventually an Asian common market.

Meeting in Manila in August 1974, the ASEAN ministers also discussed a number of feasible projects and agreed to include such industries as iron and steel, farm machinery production, telecommunications equipment, petrochemicals, and newsprint production. The need for regional self-reliance and the 1971 agreement on Southeast Asian neutrality assumed critical importance in the spring of 1975 because of the Indochinese development. In mid-April 1975 President Marcos proposed an ASEAN summit to discuss the implications of Indochinese events for the region; three months later he called on the ASEAN members to begin immediately a regional economic cooperative scheme, such as an Asian common market. Both proposals failed to evoke positive response. Not unexpectedly Marcos stated that a more vigorous push toward mutual cooperation would be required "if the ASEAN were to realize its full potential." He sounded particularly hopeful when he suggested that an "industrial complementation plan" might provide strong inducement toward expanded cooperation.

SECTION III. ECONOMIC

CHAPTER 12

CHARACTER AND STRUCTURE OF THE ECONOMY

In the mid-1970s economic activity in the Philippines was based on private enterprise. The government's role consisted essentially of the traditional functions of defense, administration, and public works, but the government has at times undertaken various industrial enterprises and from about 1974 began to handle trade in certain major commodities. In addition the government had taken steps to promote economic policies it considered essential for speeding up the rate of economic development. Policy initiatives promoted by the government and responded to by the private sector have included a prolonged import-substitution phase of industrialization from 1950 to 1970 and, since 1970, a redirection of the industrial sector toward exports and more efficient reform after 1972 was strengthening the government's development planning and rationalizing the national economy. The economic goals in 1975 as stated in the Four Year Development Plan (1974–77) included increased economic growth and employment; more equitable distribution of income and wealth; and regional development and industrialization.

The economy remained rooted in agriculture, for both export and consumption. The growth pattern of the net domestic product (NDP—see Glossary) for various periods between 1946 and the mid-1970s, however, showed an increase in the relative importance of the manufacturing sector. The share of agriculture, fishing, and forestry in NDP during the postwar period followed a path inverse to that of manufacturing, falling from 38 percent in 1948 to about 30 percent in 1974. As is typical of developing countries in the 1970s, the share of labor employed in agriculture was much larger than the share of agriculture in NDP. In 1948 the labor force share in agriculture was 71.5 percent, whereas in the mid-1970s it was about 56 percent. Manufacturing absorbed about 6 percent of the labor force in 1948 and about 11 percent in the early 1970s.

The overall economic growth rate in the Philippines during the first half of the 1970s, as in the 1960s, averaged about 6 percent per year in real terms, except for 1973 when the growth rate achieved 10 percent. The important contributors to economic growth have been the export agricultural, industrial, and services sectors. Domestic agriculture, primarily rice and corn production, stagnated during most of the 1960s but expanded in the late 1960s after adopting high-yield seeds and related agricultural technology. Rice production declined from 1970 to 1972 because of adverse weather but recovered in 1973 and 1974 under the stimulus of expanded government food production programs. Gross national product (GNP—see Glossary) per capita was the equivalent of about US$250 in 1974 compared to the equivalent of US$155 in 1960.

Economic growth in the post-World War II years was not matched, however, by improvements in employment and income distribution. The unemployment rate was between 7 and 8 percent during the 1960s. In 1973 an International Labor Organization mission estimated that about 30 percent of the labor force was either unemployed or underemployed and that the labor force was growing at an annual rate of about 3 percent.

After 1960 the effort to mobilize resources for growth was reflected by the increase in the investment rate from about 17 percent in 1960 to a 1974 level of about 20 percent of GNP. Although information on the sectoral allocation of investment was not available, it appeared that infrastructural and agricultural investment was relatively neglected during most of the 1960s and early 1970s. Public investment during the 1960s constituted only 10 percent of total investment, and its ratio of GNP rarely rose above 3 percent; capital expenditures accounted for less than 15 percent of total budgetary expenditures. The low levels of infrastructure investments were attributed to the traditional low tax effort and collection capabilities—about 10 percent of GNP—and to serious gaps in the public sector's capability to plan and manage development programs and projects. Reforms instituted after martial law was declared indicated that these conditions were being rectified: in the early 1970s the ratio of tax revenue to GNP increased to about 12 percent; the share of capital expenditures in total budgetary expenditure rose to 40 percent by 1974; and in 1974 the government accounted for about 12 percent of total investment.

Foreign capital inflows—both private commercial and official development assistance—were small during the 1960s but expanded greatly in the 1970s. After martial law was declared in 1972, private direct investment responded vigorously to various investment incentives offered by the government.

Balance-of-payments difficulties have been a chronic problem of the economy owing to the slow growth of exports and the heavy dependence of domestic industry on imports. In the late 1960s a severe external debt service problem emerged, coupled with excessive spending associated with the 1969 presidential election campaign and on expansion in liquidity. The Philippines entered into a standby agreement with the International Monetary Fund, and the peso underwent a major devaluation in 1970; it was allowed to float freely downward again in 1974 and 1975 to about ₱7.50 per US$1. After 1970 the balance-of-payments position improved, and the external debt burden was reduced to manageable levels through careful management and export growth. The Philippine economy benefited greatly from high export prices of primary commodities, especially minerals and sugar, up until early 1974. Since mid-1974, however, prices received for ex~~rts have dropped while the prices of oil and other imports have rise   a result the trade surplus that was realized in 1973 was again con\   d into a deficit in 1974 and 1975.

International trading patterns and relations have changed slowly over the years since World War II. Traditionally dependent solely upon primary product export trade mainly with the United States, the economy in the 1970s witnessed the increased exports of manufactures and diversification of foreign markets. Philippine foreign economic relations were being revised to reflect the expiration of the Revised United States-Philippine Trade Agreement of 1955 (Laurel-Langley Agreement), the continued growth of economic ties with Japan, the opening of trade with various communist countries, and the rising importance of the Middle Eastern oil-producing countries.

STRUCTURE AND GROWTH OF THE ECONOMY

The Colonial Heritage

When the Americans assumed control of the Philippines in 1898, the island nation was ill prepared for modern economic growth. Spain, which had dominated the islands for more than 300 years, was without an industrial revolution or tradition of its own and was in no position to export these to the Philippines. The cash-crop economy established during the late stages of Spanish rule was only slightly modified although greatly expanded during the American period. The economy inherited by the newly independent Republic of the Philippines in 1946 was a legacy of the classic colonial stereotype in which foreign political control, superimposed upon an agrarian base, had enforced a mode of operation based on agricultural exports.

The institution of free trade with the United States favored development of agriculture and such extractive industries as logging and mining (see ch. 15). The kinds of industries that did develop consisted mainly of processing the products of mining, agriculture, and logging for export: sugar milling; abaca stripping; producing coconut oil and desiccated coconut; manufacturing cigars; processing gold and other minerals; and producing lumber. Foreign investment, primarily American, dominated these export industries. Little incentive existed to develop manufacturing for the local market in competititon with the American products entering the country tax free.

The colonial economy may be visualized as a resource flow in which such primary product exports as sugar and abaca moved from a commercial agriculture sector in the colony to the mother country. Agricultural exports provided the foreign exchange for importing manufactured goods to service a domestic market with consumer goods and commercial services. Colonial development resulted in a dualism in which there was a distinction within the domestic economy between the nonagricultural and the agricultural sectors. The agricultural sector was further subdivided into a commercial sector producing for export and a traditional sector that was large, uncommercialized, and relatively backward.

The economic goal of colonialism was the realization of profits for the mother country through production and export of primary products. Colonial profits were employed to expand export production through reinvestment within the Philippines, or they were transferred abroad. The colonial period alternated between active and passive growth phases, dependent to a great degree on the state of foreign demand for primary product exports. In periods of rising demand export profits were reinvested, leading to imports of capital goods. During periods of falling world demand export profits were repatriated to the mother country, tantamount to capital export and causing stagnation of the domestic economy.

The colonial heritage left behind conditions that profoundly affected the course of Philippine development. Structurally the economy was compartmentalized into two mutually insulated parts: a modern, export-oriented enclave situated in Manila and a large traditional agricultural sector. Under colonialism the nonagricultural sector was characterized chiefly by provision of commercial services related to exports. Investment was concentrated in these export services, and the pace of investment was controlled by foreign demand. The domestic industrial sector developed no internal growth momentum of its own. Traditional agriculture, isolated from the commercial export sector, tended to stagnate and remained characterized by low labor productivity, primitive technology, an unfavorable land-labor ratio, and noncommercial attitudes.

Although the post-World War II Philippine government has been firmly committed to a private enterprise economy, it has experimented with bureaucratic entrepreneurship. Within the first two decades of the twentieth century a number of Philippine government-controlled corporations were established whose purpose was to aid economic development and provide essential social services; only a few of these corporations engaged in manufacturing. After the inauguration of the commonwealth period in 1935 and the prospect of Philippine independence and the loss of tax-free entry to the American market for Philippine agricultural products, plans were drawn up for a vigorous industrialization program in which government corporations were to play an important role. The principle of public enterprise was codified into law by an article of the 1935 Constitution that provided that the "State may . . . establish and operate industries and means of transportation and communications."

In 1936 the policy of direct government participation in economic activity initially resulted in converting the National Development Company (NDC), originally organized in 1919 as a semipublic holding company to operate agricultural estates, into a government-owned corporation. The NDC subsequently established various corporations involved in milling rice and corn, producing footwear, refining sugar, and producing various foodstuffs. These preindependence government-sponsored plans for development and efforts to encourage an indigenous industrial group were interrupted by World War II.

The government continued to experiment with public corporations after World War II as an instrument for transforming the economy. By the early 1950s the government was operating railroads, hotels, electric power, gas, and water works as well as producing cement, coal, fertilizer, steel, textiles and yarns, and operating a shipyard and engineering shops. Through the NDC the government was engaged in the production of nails, lumber, footwear, sugar, textiles and yarns, food preserving, and packaging and warehousing. A central bank, which was established in 1949, was granted authority to create money and credit to support economic development by both public and private sectors.

The nations' faith in bureaucratic entrepreneurship waned in the early 1950s as evidence of corruption, nepotism, and mismanagement within government-run enterprises became apparent. After Ramón Magsaysay's inauguration in 1954 the government initiated action to sell or lease to private management activities in which private enterprise was interested. With the termination of its direct involvement in the productive sectors, the government confined its operations to guiding and stimulating the direction of the private sector.

The 1946–70 Period

Rapid industrialization did not occur in the aftermath of World War II or after political independence in 1946; rather, a situation that approximated the prewar economic pattern existed. The economic framework for the rehabilitation of the economy was initially established by the Philippine Trade Act of 1946 (Bell Act) (see ch. 15). This act continued mutual free trade between the United States and the Philippines until 1954, from which time the two economies would gradually disengage over a twenty-year period. The postponement of disengagement continued to confine the Philippines to the colonial pattern of raw materials specialization and export orientation. This continuity was evident in that between 1946 and 1951 approximately three-fourths of all Philippine exports went to the United States and two-thirds of all Philippine imports originated in the United States. The prewar commodity structure persisted: exports were concentrated in processed sugar, copra, abaca, and other raw materials. Imports consisted chiefly of finished textiles, petroleum products, machinery, automobiles, trucks, and processed food products. Although investment was concentrated in reconstructing war-damaged facilities, replenishing trading inventories, real estate construction, and opportunities in export agriculture, all competed for available private capital. No real change in the island's colonial economic structure appeared likely.

Large foreign exchange reserves and disbursement of United States grants and aid made possible the prompt reconstruction of prewar productive capacity. Despite this achievement a formidable balance-of-payments crisis appeared in 1949 and 1950. A pent-up Philippine desire for imports was a prominent feature of the immediate postwar economy, and the eagerness of businessmen to meet this demand far outweighed their interest in balanced economic development. The inability of the traditional economic structure—even when fully rehabilitated—to provide through exports the foreign exchange requirements necessary for soaring imports was clear.

The immediate postwar performance of the economy confirmed the need for drastic policy changes to promote economic development, particularly in the industrial sectors of the economy. This implied a transformation of the government away from a minimal colonial-style administration, which could not speed economic development. The dual colonial economic structure could not support an economically viable, independent country in which the benefits of economic development would accrue to all.

National economic planning commenced in the early 1950s as the government recognized that import and exchange controls could be powerful instruments for restructuring the economy. Such controls were used to direct investment and income distribution in accordance with planned objectives. Between 1950 and 1955 economic planning goals called for industrial development, and plan implementation had some impact on growth and structural change. GNP increased between 1950 and 1955 at an annual rate of almost 11 percent. The manufacturing sector of the economy doubled its contribution to total output as domestic manufacturing grew in response to the new market opportunities created by banning or restricting imports of finished goods. The proportion of total income generated by manufacturing increased from 11 percent in 1949 to 17.5 percent by 1959.

The exchange and import controls applied in the 1950s led to the development of a manufacturing sector directed mainly to substituting domestic products for imports. The import-substitution strategy held the promise of lowering imports of manufactured goods, which it achieved to some extent. Exchange controls protected an emerging Filipino entrepreneurial community, which for the first time was able to challenge American industries. But exchange controls on the overvalued peso also encouraged the establishment of a manufacturing sector whose products were not competitive in world markets. The policy, moreover, did not alleviate the constant battle to raise exports and lower imports to reduce recurring balance-of-trade deficits; heavy imports continued in the form of raw materials, equipment, semifinished products, and capital goods to meet the needs of the domestic manufacturing sector, but the exports needed to pay for these goods did not materialize.

Since the control system severely limited imports of consumer goods while permitting the liberal import of producer goods, manufacturing tended to concentrate on the finishing stages, most of the industries being involved in the assembly or processing of imported goods and materials. Thus while the share of consumer goods in imports fell from 28 percent in 1950 to 17 percent in 1957, total imports as a proportion of GNP remained constant. Moreover, given the nature of the policy measures—including overvalued exchange rates and low interest rates—industrial development tended to be overly import and capital intensive in a labor-surplus economy.

The failure of import-substitution manufacturing to reduce the country's dependence on imports continued to place the burden of providing foreign exchange on the primary sector, which under the policies of the 1950s was less and less able to provide both sufficient exports and domestic food supplies to keep pace with the growth in GNP. The result was continuing balance-of-payments difficulties and a further tightening of import controls after 1957. These, plus the fact that many of the easy import-substitution opportunities had been exploited by the late 1950s, brought a sharp retardation in industrial growth.

The Diosdado Macapagal administration (1961 to 1965) abandoned import and exchange controls in 1962 in favor of a free market in foreign exchange. Although economists agreed that this might have provided a means of redirecting the manufacturing sector away from its extreme import-substitution bias and toward exports, the results were disappointing. Agricultural growth was not rapid enough both to earn the needed foreign exchange to further industrial growth and to feed a population that grew at over 3 percent a year between 1950 and 1970. The devaluation in fact shifted land to food export crops. In addition decontrols did not result in substantial trade liberalization since highly protective tariffs surfaced as the dominant instrument for limiting imports. Accordingly import substitution continued; the industrial sector remained dependent on the primary sector to provide foreign exchange; and devaluation had only a minor impact on the development of new export industries.

The Philippine economy grew at an average annual rate of about 6 percent during the 1960s, and real GNP per capita reached US$200 by 1970 compared with US$155 in 1960. The growth in output in the 1960s included an industrial expansion of about 5 percent a year, a growth in agricultural exports, and a large increase in the services sector. On an aggregate level this was considered satisfactory performance—relative to other developing countries—but was disappointing given the potential of the Philippines, its rich natural resources, and its dynamic private sector. A major problem during this period was the failure of government policies to give sufficient social and economic direction to the country and to rectify structural deficiencies. Infrastructure—roads, bridges, water-control facilities, and the like—was neglected; public investment was low, as was agricultural investment. A weak export performance combined with a failure to reduce the import dependence of domestic industry resulted in a steady deterioration in the balance-of-payments position. The economy was unable to create sufficient employment to absorb a rapidly expanding labor force; as a result overt unemployment stood at about an estimated 8 percent by 1970. The benefits of this growth remained unevenly distributed. Between the late 1950s and the beginning of the 1970s the top 10 percent of the population continued to receive well over 30 percent of total family income while the income position of the lowest 20 percent of the population actually deteriorated (see table 7).

The relative importance of the major sectors of the economy was fairly stable through the 1960s, and by 1969 sector contributions to NDP included agriculture, 36 percent; mining, 2 percent; manufacturing, 17 percent; construction, 3 percent; transportation, 4 percent; commerce, 14 percent; and services, 24 percent. The 1960s witnessed a substantial change in the distribution of the labor force. Employment in agriculture increased by only 1.2 percent a year during that decade, but agriculture absorbed 23 percent of the increase in the labor force. The share of the labor force employed in this sector fell from about 61 percent at the start of the decade to 54 percent by 1969. Because of the heavy emphasis on import capital-intensive technologies, industry absorbed only 10 percent of the increase in the labor force, and its share of employment remained at around 12 percent throughout the decade. The share of the remaining sectors in employment rose from 27 percent in 1960 to 34 percent in 1970. The main shift of labor was to service industries, reflecting in part the substantial movements of population from rural to urban areas—

Table 7. Philippines, Distribution of Total Family Income, Selected Years, 1956–71

Families	Percent of Total Family Income			
	1956	1961	1965	1971
Lowest 20 percent	4.5	4.2	3.5	3.6
Second 20 percent..................	8.1	7.9	8.1	8.1
Third 20 percent	12.4	12.2	12.8	13.3
Fourth 20 percent..................	19.8	19.3	20.2	21.0
Highest 20 percent	55.2	56.4	55.4	54.0
(Top 10 percent)*	(39.4)	(41.0)	(40.0)	(37.1)
TOTAL	100.0	100.0	100.0	100.0

*Top 10-percent figures are included within highest 20 percent.

Source: Based on information from U. S. Department of State, Agency for International Development, *Development Assistance Program for the Philippines*, Manila, 1974.

particularly to Manila—where migrants have been largely absorbed into various service occupations at low-level earnings.

In contrast to an adequate overall savings performance, public savings were less than 1 percent of GNP throughout the decade of the 1960s, a consequence largely of the slow growth of tax revenues; the ratio of tax revenues to GNP remained little changed at about 10 percent throughout the decade. About 85 percent of total government budgetary expenditures during the 1960s was for current outlays; education alone took 25 percent of the total. Capital expenditures accounted for less than 15 percent of total budgetary outlays. Limited capital expenditures and low levels of maintenance resulted in an increasingly inadequate level of infrastructure that by the end of the decade had become a serious bottleneck to expanding output.

Throughout the 1960s agriculture and related processing industries together with the minerals sector provided most of the foreign exchange needed for the heavily import-dependent industrialization process. During the decade merchandise exports increased at an average rate of only 4.8 percent while merchandise imports grew at an average rate of 6.8 percent a year. A large proportion of the private industrial investments undertaken in the late 1960s was financed by heavy borrowing of foreign commercial loans that had relatively short maturities. As a result the total external debt increased from US$600 million in the mid-1960s to US$1.9 billion by the end of 1969, almost 60 percent in maturities of less than five years. With a sharply mounting debt service obligation and only slow growth in export receipts, a foreign exchange crisis that threatened to disrupt the economy and constrain further growth emerged in 1969. This situation was exacerbated by the inflationary policies of the government at the time of the 1969 elections, and there followed in early 1970 a major devaluation of about 40 percent, a rescheduling of some short- and medium-term external debt, tighter controls over borrowing abroad, and implementation of a postdevaluation stabilization program.

The 1970–75 Period

Beginning in 1970 the government initiated numerous economic and social reforms designed to provide the institutional and policy environment for the attainment of economic and social goals. Between 1970 and the declaration of martial law in September 1972, several significant reforms were undertaken. In early 1970 a foreign exchange reform that devalued the peso and adopted a floating rate was implemented. Technocrats were recruited into high-level posts in the government, and the quality of development management was greatly improved. Studies and plans were undertaken laying the groundwork for the rapid implementation of additional reforms initiated under martial law.

Although between 1970 and 1972 authorities pursued policies of financial and fiscal restraint, the performance of the economy was disappointing: real GNP increased at a rate below 6 percent, and real gross national income per capita leveled off at about the equivalent of US$200. The economic slowdown was the result of a number of factors, including a series of natural disasters between 1970 and 1972—which seriously retarded agricultural growth—and a general falling off of export prices. At the same time import prices increased substantially, and the economy experienced a renewed period of rapid inflation at an annual rate of 20 percent owing to the combined effects of devaluation, inflated import prices, and shortfalls in domestic food production. Despite the slow growth rate between 1970 and 1972, public revenues improved slightly over the 1960s level. The revenues rose from about 10 percent of GNP in 1969 to about 11 percent in 1972, mainly as the result of an export tax introduced in 1970 after the devaluation.

The Philippines entered the 1970s facing serious economic challenges. The disappointing economic performance of the 1960s was accompanied by political disenchantment, focusing on issues that included agrarian reform and the extreme inequality in the distribution of wealth and income. Major economic reforms instituted since 1972 to combat the economic ills of the society have included an agrarian reform program; reorganization of government; tax and tariff reforms to improve the tax system as a means of income redistribution and to enhance the investment climate; banking and financial reforms to help mobilize resources for development and to establish a more stable and better regulated financial structure; liberalization of regulations on foreign investment; reorientation of industrial policies toward export expansion, industrial dispersal, and labor intensification production techniques; and the reinforcement of the family planning program (see ch. 2; ch. 9; ch. 13).

A major focus of the measures taken initially after martial law was the strenghtening of the government's development planning capabilities. The past disjointedness of planning activities was remedied by the creation of a single planning agency in 1972, the National Economic Development Authority (NEDA). NEDA was designated to link policymaking and planning to program and project implementation. It was chaired by the president and was composed of cabinet-level officials involved in formulating and executing sectoral development activities. It was expected, however, that substantial amounts of capital would be needed for the Philippines to achieve its growth targets. Since the 1973 economic performance enhanced the country's credit standing, medium- and long-term funds have been provided from individual countries, such as Japan and the United States, and such international lenders as the Asian Development Bank (ADB) and the International Bank for Reconstruction and Development (IBRD—commonly known as the World Bank). Domestic sources of investment remained inadequate for the tasks of structural reform and economic growth. The personal consumption component of GNP, though declining, still accounted for about 68 percent of GNP in 1975. During the first half of the 1970s the government component fluctuated between 7 and 9 percent. Though savings were rising—meaning that more domestic funds would be available for investment—it was expected that it would be many years before the Philippines approached the point when sufficient resources for its investment needs would be generated from local sources.

There were no dramatic shifts in sectoral contributions to NDP (see table 8). Agriculture, in addition to contributing close to one-third of NDP in 1974, provided about two-thirds of Philippine export earnings. Its role in earning foreign exchange and providing employment generated considerable feeling that growth in this sector was a key to overall growth and any serious production losses would inhibit total economic growth. Despite continued efforts to stimulate the agricultural sector, growth was disappointing. Institutional and social factors were partly to blame, including the unequal distribution of land and the prevalence of tenant farmers. Moreover the uncertain nature of the world market for Philippine products tended further to discourage private investment in agriculture in 1974, but this was changing in 1975 as physical plants expanded in both sugar and coconut oil mills.

Mining, with a 1974 contribution to NDP of about 2 percent, accounted for about 23 percent of export earnings. Of total mineral exports, copper concentrates accounted for about 65 percent of earnings. After a spectacular 1973 earnings performance, largely because of temporarily soaring world prices, the sector suffered a considerable decline in 1974 in both volume and earnings. Authorities felt, however, that despite the slowdown the prospects for the mining sector appeared good because of

Table 8. *Philippines, Sectoral Origin of Net Domestic Product, Selected Years, 1969–73*
(in millions of pesos at 1967 prices)[1]

Sector	1969		1970		1972		1973	
	Amount	Percent	Amount	Percent	Amount	Percent	Amount	Percent
Agriculture, fishery, and forestry	8,822	34.2	8,962	33.5	8,948	30.8	9,559	30.5
Mining	468	1.8	558	2.1	686	2.4	732	2.3
Manufacturing	4,811	18.6	5,144	19.2	5,828	20.1	6,527	20.8
Construction	820	3.2	689	2.6	1,014	3.5	1,245	4.0
Transportation and communications	999	3.9	1,035	3.9	1,217	4.2	1,306	4.2
Commerce	3,935	15.3	4,149	15.5	4,594	15.8	4,903	15.6
Services	5,955	23.1	6,196	23.2	6,735	23.2	7,101	22.6
Total Net Domestic Product at Factor Cost ...	25,810	100.0[2]	26,733	100.0	29,022	100.0	31,373	100.0

[1] For value of the peso—see Glossary.
[2] Figures do not add to 100.0 because of rounding.

Source: Based on information from Business International Asia-Pacific, *The Philippines: Operating for Profit in the New Society*, Hong Kong, 1974.

the existence of untapped resources and substantial new investment in projects to process local minerals.

The contribution of manufacturing to NDP in 1974 increased to about 21 percent compared to about 18 percent in 1969; the food industry was the largest sector, followed by chemicals, textiles, and beverages. The industrial sector was characterized by a small number of large, highly capitalized firms and a great number of small firms, in which about 70 percent of the industrial labor force was employed. Manufacturing was heavily concentrated in the Manila area, where about 47 percent of the enterprises employing twenty or more workers were located.

The commerce sector contribution to NDP has remained fairly constant at about 15 to 16 percent since 1969. It was the fourth largest sector of the economy, banking having the fastest growth. The largest contribution to the services sector represented government services. Growth in transportation, communications, and utilities was moderate but was expected to increase as the government's plans for infrastructure development got under way.

MECHANISMS OF CONTROL

Fiscal Policy

Like many former colonies the Philippines inherited a legacy of minimal government. Colonial fiscal policy ensured only that the colony would pay its own way; colonial administrations provided for a modest level of social services, and public investment was concentrated on extending transportation facilities. After 1946 the government's role expanded to provide for higher levels of social capital services, and the public sector underwent growth relative to the private sector.

Despite the postindependence expansion of the public sector, tax revenues and expenditures remained low compared to the needs of a rapidly growing population. In the mid-1950s total expenditures were equal to about 9 percent of national income and tax revenues to only 6 percent; through the 1960s these proportions increased to about 14 percent and about 9 to 10 percent respectively. Moreover, although overall national government expenditures increased more than three times in absolute amount during the 1960s, the ratio of government capital expenditures to national income remained unchanged at about 2 percent.

Between 1972 and 1974 the fiscal performance of the government showed improvement. The ratio of government tax revenues to GNP increased to 12 percent in fiscal year (FY) 1974. The growth was mainly due to long-needed tax reforms and improvements in tax administration. During FY 1973 the government was able both to restrain the growth of current expenditures and to increase capital expenditures by about 40 percent. Outlays for FY 1974 reflected an increased emphasis on agriculture, maintenance of infrastructure, and defense.

The improvements in the tax system after 1972 can be best appreciated in the context of the Philippines' prior performance and the record of other developing countries. The inadequacies of the Philippine tax system had included low levels of direct taxes and a heavy reliance on regressive taxes; low rates of import tariffs and generous exemptions; low levels of taxes on commodities; and deficiencies in tax collection and administration. In 1971 the ratio of government taxes to GNP had been well below the average of other developing countries; by 1974 this gap was being closed.

After the imposition of martial law over 100 presidential decrees related to tax provisions were issued with a view to increasing tax revenues and improving administration, providing incentives for tax payments and productive investment, and redistributing income in a more equitable manner. The major revenue-earning reforms included a revised tariff and customs code, revised duties on exports, higher property taxes, and higher excise taxes. In addition the government granted amnesties to nonfilers on previously untaxed income, provided a portion of the taxes due was paid. The administrative reforms included reorganization of tax collecting institutions and dismissal of a substantial number of persons in the internal revenue and customs bureaus in an effort to reduce corruption. In general, however, the tax structure continued to be largely regressive, emphasizing various sales and service taxes.

Monetary Policy and Banking

In 1975 the financial system was governed by the Monetary Board and the Central Bank of the Philippines. The Central Bank, founded in 1949, had wide powers to establish monetary policy, administer the building and credit system, and act as fiscal agent of the government. It dealt in government securities, varying the reserve and other ratios of the commercial banks, adjusting rediscount rates, and setting maximum interest rates of other financial institutions. It also managed the country's external debt, monitored foreign exchange transactions, and issued regulations affecting exports, imports, and invisible transactions. The Central Bank's powers and functions were directed by a monetary board headed by the governor of the Central Bank. Other members included the secretary of finance, the director general of members included the secretary of finance, the director general of NEDA, and the chairman of the Board of Investment.

In 1974 the banking system had total assets of about ₱35 billion (for value of the peso—see Glossary). More than 90 percent of bank assets were held by commercial banks, the remainder by various rural banks and private development banks. The banks consisted of thirty-six commercial banks, eleven savings banks, thirty-six savings and loan associations, several hundred rural banks, and about thirty development banks. Two government-owned banks dominated their respective fields.

The Philippine National Bank (PNB), the largest commercial bank, controlled about 24 percent of the total assets of the commercial banking system. The Development Bank of the Philippines (DBP) dominated its field with about 86 percent of total assets in the sector.

Banking reforms enacted after 1972 included the requirement that commercial banks maintain a minimum capitalization of ₱100 million, and a presidential decree allowed foreign equity participation in commercial banks up to 40 percent of total capital. As of 1974 several United States, Canadian, and Japanese banks had availed themselves of this opportunity, and by mid-1974 it was estimated that the equivalent of about US$300 million would be invested in the Philippine banking system.

The commercial banks were the major source of credit to the private sector in the mid-1970s. There was growth in credit in 1974 of 38 percent over the 1973 level. This growth was attributed to an increased demand that arose from the higher level of prices, especially of imported goods. The financial institutions that extended credit to the agricultural sector included the PNB and other commercial banks, rural banks, the DBP, the Agricultural Credit Administration, and the Land Bank. A potentially important means of directing credit to rural areas was the requirement that 25 percent of the lendable funds of the various lending institutions be made for agricultural purposes. Other priority areas where the authorities wanted credit directed included export-oriented industries, medium- and small-scale enterprises, and labor-intensive industries. As of mid-1975, however, the steps taken to direct credit to these areas had not had a major impact.

Planning and Development

National economic planning commenced in 1936 with the formation of the National Economic Council (NEC). It was not until the 1950s, however, when import and exchange controls were used as instruments for restructuring the Philippine economy, that the nation had anything more than paper plans. Despite the industrialization policies of the 1950s, plans for other sectors of the economy—such as agriculture and infrastructure—suffered because the NEC was plagued with problems of project implementation, ambitious plans beyond the limits of government resources, and an inability to attract or maintain a well-qualified staff. The Program Implementation Agency (PIA) of 1962 and the succeeding Presidential Economic Staff (PES) of 1966 represented attempts to buttress planning by placing the technical economic staffs under the Office of the President. Congress asserted its role in economic planning with the formation of the Congressional Economic Planning Office (CEPO) in 1969, which revived the concept of a national economic development authority, first proposed in the mid-1950s. NEDA, which came into existence in 1972, has replaced the NEC, the PES, and other agencies having planning and execution functions. Its major functions have been to plan and implement a four-year development plan.

264

The Philippine government began annually reviewing development plans in 1972; the plan revised every year to account for changing developments. The plan for the 1973–76 fiscal years, prepared in 1972, was never published because of the economic uncertainties caused by severe floods and the altered political situation created by martial law. The four-year development plan inaugurated in FY 1974 incorporated major revisions to take into account the social and economic reforms instituted after the proclamation of martial law in 1972.

The Four Year Development Plan (1974–77) has as its goals increased economic growth and employment; a more equitable distribution of income and wealth; regional development and industrialization; promotion of social development; and maintenance of price and balance-of-payments stability. The NDP was targeted to expand by 6.5 percent each year from 1974 to 1977, and GNP was expected to increase by 7 percent per year (see table 9). To achieve these targets it was estimated that gross total investment would have to expand at a 10-percent annual rate. The plan's sectoral target growth rates for the four-year period were agriculture, 5 percent; mining, 18 percent; manufacturing, 10 percent; construction, 10 percent; transportation, 4.9 percent; commerce, 4.7 percent; and services, 4.5 percent. The employment target was ambitious, and unemployment was expected to be reduced to 3 percent by FY 1977.

The prospects for meeting these goals depended on the ability of the economy to mobilize the necessary resources, requiring substantially greater amounts of both private and public investment than had been achieved. About 82 percent of investment requirements for FY 1975 were expected to come from the private sector. Financing was to be derived mostly from domestic savings; about one-third was expected from direct foreign investment, credit, and loans. It was anticipated in 1975 that the implementation of the various government programs at planned levels would necessitate a continuing increase in total public expenditures. Budgetary expenditures—current and capital—for FY 1975 were programmed at about ₱17.7 billion, a 27-percent increase over the 1974 level; about 53 percent of these expenditures were earmarked for economic development, 19 percent for social development, and about 12 percent for national defense.

The Philippine government planned to expand its capital expenditures as a ratio of the country's total investment over the duration of the plan. Its share of total investment was to be increased from a level of about 12 percent in FY 1972 to 18 percent by FY 1977. The rise in public capital expenditures was to be financed by increased tax revenues and official foreign assistance.

The plan's basic strategy for achieving the economic and social goals involved balanced growth and complementary development of the various sectors of the economy. The strategy of balanced growth represented a departure from the strategy pursued in the 1950s and 1960s, which strongly emphasized import substitution in the industrial

Table 9. Philippines, Sectoral Targets of the Four Year Development Plan (1974–77)
(in millions of pesos at 1967 prices)[1]

	Targets				Average Annual Growth Rate 1974–77[2]
	1974	1975	1976	1977	
Agriculture............	8,649	10,132	10,649	11,182	
Growth rate	4.8	5.0	5.1	5.0	5.0
Percent of NDP[3] ...	30.2	29.8	29.4	28.9	
Mining	897	1,059	1,250	1,475	
Growth rate	18.0	18.0	18.0	18.0	18.0
Percent of NDP[3] ...	2.8	3.1	3.4	3.8	
Manufacturing	6,730	7,403	8,143	8,957	
Growth rate	9.0	10.0	10.0	10.0	10.0
Percent of NDP[3] ...	21.1	21.8	22.5	23.2	
Construction	1,243	1,367	1,504	1,654	
Growth rate	10.0	10.0	10.0	10.0	10.0
Percent of NDP[3] ...	3.9	4.0	4.1	4.3	
Transportation	1,204	1,264	1,328	1,396	
Growth rate	4.5	5.0	5.1	5.1	4.9
Percent of NDP[3] ...	3.8	3.7	3.7	3.6	
Commerce	4,907	5,142	5,390	5,649	
Growth rate	4.5	4.8	4.8	4.8	4.7
Percent of NDP[3] ...	15.4	15.2	14.9	14.6	
Services	7,283	7,611	7,990	8,351	
Growth rate	4.5	4.6	4.5	4.5	4.5
Percent of NDP[3] ...	22.8	22.4	22.0	21.6	
Net Domestic Product	30,913	33,978	36,254	38,664	6.5
Growth Rate ..	6.1	6.5	6.7	6.6	6.5
Gross National Product	39,700	42,479	45,452	48,861	7.0
Growth Rate ..	6.5	7.0	7.0	7.5	7.0

[1] For value of the peso—see Glossary.
[2] Fiscal years.
[3] Net domestic product.

Source: Based on information from *Asia Research Bulletin,* 4, No. 6, Singapore, November 30, 1974, p. 26.

sector and neglected the development of the agricultural and rural sectors. The major aspects of balanced growth as stated in the plan included greater emphasis on increasing agricultural output and the production of wage goods needed by low-income groups, greater stress on agricultural and infrastructural investment as well as provision of social services, and greater attention to the distribution of growth benefits.

Within the framework of this development strategy, the government concentrated its efforts on strengthening and expanding selected programs. Land reform and food production programs, supported by the development of cooperatives and rural agriculture, were to be the major means for achieving agricultural and rural development (see ch. 13). Priority infrastructure projects included those directly supportive of increased food production, such as irrigation and feeder roads. The major thrust of the government's industrial development efforts was the promotion of exports, labor-intensive methods of production, and geographically dispersed small and medium-sized industries. In response to the energy crisis the government attached high priority to nonpetroleum energy development projects, including hydroelectric, geothermal, and nuclear power plants. Major programs for social development included programs for population and family planning, health and nutrition, and educational and manpower development geared to the skill requirements of agriculture and industry.

As early as 1974 the government confronted problems of project implementation that saw current expenditures increase at the expense of capital expenditures. The ability to implement large infrastructure projects was hampered by shortage of construction materials, fuel oil, and other raw materials and by the adverse effects of inflation. Many public sector projects had been subcontracted to the private sector at fixed contract prices without cost escalation clauses; with the rapid rise of prices in 1974 contractors refused to continue work on projects unless contracts were renegotiated to take into account cost overruns. The slow pace of project implementation in 1974 was also reflected in the lag of actual cash disbursements behind obligated capital expenditures. In May 1974 President Ferdinand E. Marcos decreed a more liberal adjustment of contract prices so that capital disbursements reflected not only current obligations but also obligations from previous years.

The FY 1975 budget was highlighted by large estimated increases in both cash income and capital expenditures. Revenues from traditional tax sources were expected to be augmented by the proceeds from a new levy imposed on all primary sales of coconut products. Current expenditures in the 1975 budget were projected to increase by 50 percent over the previous year while capital expenditures were estimated to increase by 138 percent. On a cash basis the 1975 budget was projected to show a deficit to be financed substantially through foreign borrowings and reliance on the domestic issue of long-term public bonds.

PROBLEMS AND PROSPECTS

The Philippines entered the second half of the 1970s facing very serious economic and social problems. Since World War II the large rural sector has remained essentially traditional in outlook, technology, and organization at the same time that rapid, urban industrial growth based on a policy of import substitution has taken place. These factors led to a deterioration in the ability of the rural sector to finance further industrial growth as well as feed the country. Despite the improvements that have taken place in agriculture—especially the introduction of high-yield seed varieties and fertilizers and improved technology—the rural sector has been less able to provide sufficient opportunities for employment, and the industrial sector has been threatened by saturated domestic markets.

The problems confronting the Philippines in mid-1975—unemployment, income inequality, inflation, and balance-of-payments difficulties—have been identified as the consequence of the urban industrial development strategy pursued since 1946. The effort to break with the colonial pattern of trade and investment has only been successful because domestic industrial capacity was built up by replacing imported consumer and industrial goods with domestic production. The entire process was dependent on the agriculture sector's ability to fuel industrial growth by the export of traditional products. Thus the traditional sector, formerly used to create colonial profits, found itself in a situation after World War II of funding limited industrial growth while attempting to feed a population increasing by over 3 percent annually.

The industrial growth of the 1950s slackened greatly in the 1960s as the more difficult backward linkage varieties of import substitution were resorted to and as the domestic markets became saturated (see ch. 14). The growth that did take place was purchased at very high cost. These problems were the direct result of the deliberate continuation of policies that fostered inefficient industries and neglected viable development opportunities in the rural sector.

In November 1975 President Marcos announced in Manila that "the principal threat to the stability of the government is economic." By the mid-1970s, however, despite almost four years of martial law and the New Society, a gap between the promises of the Four Year Development Plan and actual performance was evident. Land reform, described by the government as the most important New Society program, had barely made a beginning by the end of 1975 (see ch. 13). Although President Marcos has done more for land reform than previous presidents, as of 1975 only about 10 percent of the people it was aimed at have benefited.

At least through 1976 the economy would have to contend with inflation and a worsening balance-of-payments situation as import costs continued to increase relative to export commodity prices. Between mid-1973 and mid-1975 consumer prices rose more than 40 percent annually. Inflation was initially generated by demand factors associated with the increased liquidity from the export boom of 1973. In 1974 cost factors became apparent that were associated with the higher rates of world inflation, domestic food shortages, and increased petroleum costs. The government was only partly successful in containing inflation through monetary and fiscal policies aimed at absorbing excessive liquidity and putting price ceilings on various foodstuffs. Inflation has hit wage earners particularly hard, since salaries and interest rates have not increased at an equivalent rate.

Through the remainder of the 1970s the Philippine economy will continue to confront problems of reducing unemployment and underemployment and trying to improve the highly skewed income distribution that found 54 percent of family income concentrated in 20 percent of the households in 1971. Programs to alleviate these conditions centered on departure from the capital-intensive industries of the 1950s and 1960s to a development program that would place emphasis on the more labor-intensive small- and medium-sized industries. International agencies have suggested that large investments in capital-intensive industries, which require large amounts of foreign exchange and imports and do not make a clear contribution to employment, should be postponed. Data available in the mid-1970s indicated, however, that a significant proportion of investment and credit extension—often to foreign concerns—was still being made in large, capital-intensive plants, tending to perpetuate the earlier industrial pattern.

Balance-of-payments difficulties and external debt servicing continued as persistent constraints on the pace of development. High prices for the Philippines' chief exports in 1973, including coconut products, sugar, copper, and wood products, were largely responsible for a trade surplus. In mid-1974, however, a large trade deficit emerged, chiefly because prices for traditional exports dropped and manufactured exports were unable to account for more than 10 percent of total exports. Import prices continued to rise rapidly. The government announced in the fall of 1975 that, since 95 percent of the country's imports consisted of essential items, import restrictions were not available as a policy alternative. At the end of 1975 the balance-of-trade deficit for the year was placed at the equivalent of US$1 billion, roughly US$350 million more than had been predicted. Thus a fundamental economic problem continued into the mid-1970s—the traditional reliance on agricultural products as the main foreign exchange earners and the vulnerability to world market conditions over which the government had little if any control. Whereas the favorable trade picture of 1973 allowed for a considerable reduction in the foreign debt estimated to be the equivalent of US$1.8 billion, the deterioration in the external terms of trade, which commenced in 1974 and was projected to continue through 1976, required a shift of foreign exchange from developmental projects to debt service and raised questions about continued Philippine ability to finance the investment needed to maintain current growth rates.

It was widely agreed in 1975 that government expenditure for infrastructure development would have to expand rapidly for the remainder of the 1970s in order to meet development requirements and create employment. Despite scheduled increases in these areas, substantial budget deficits totaling the equivalent of US$587 million were foreseen for FY 1976. Accordingly President Marcos ordered forced savings by all government offices by imposing a 5-percent cut on all programmed expenditures and a complete suspension of fund releases for building construction. Compounding the budget difficulties were the problems of maintaining GNP growth momentum. Development plans called for GNP growth at an average rate of 7 percent, and independent analysts concluded that the economy would have to expand at just that rate if it were to feed the population adequately, provide minimal increases in public services, and absorb a rapidly expanding labor force. In fact GNP growth for 1974 and 1975 reached only 5.8 and 5.9 percent respectively.

Labor force growth, in conjunction with continued high rates of population growth, signaled an additional constraint on the Philippines' ability to meet its development objectives. It was estimated that by 1980 the population would number 50 million. If the level of rural-urban migration of 5 percent annually persisted, the urban population would increase by another 5 to 6 million during the 1970s, making if difficult to reverse the trend of urban deterioration, particularly evident in Manila. Another dimension of the population problem was heavy pressure on the labor market. Available data indicated that there would be about 4 million people entering the labor market in the 1970s, implying than at least 3.5 million new jobs would have to be created during the decade—considerably more if the widespread problem of underemployment was to be remedied.

These problems, although of long standing, were exaggerated by the concurrent impact of the mid-1970s worldwide recession. Various international agencies felt that the government would be able to reverse the inequities and poorly balanced growth record of the past. They cited the natural resources of the country, especially its vast mineral deposits, and the human resources, represented by one of the highest literacy rates in Asia, as positive elements supporting long-term development projects. In addition the government had adopted economic reforms that if properly implemented would contribute to an environment for sustained economic development.

CHAPTER 13

AGRICULTURE

The agricultural sector has traditionally been the economic foundation of the economy. This remained true in the mid-1970s, when agriculture, forestry, and fisheries provided one-third of the net domestic product (NDP—see Glossary), over one-half of employment, and seven-tenths of export earnings. Agriculture was thus the most important economic sector both as the principal source of income and employment and as the principal source of foreign exchange earnings, which in turn supported industrialization (see ch. 14).

Indeed the agricultural sector has generally been looked to as a source of surplus earnings to be used for investment elsewhere in the economy rather than for reinvestment in agriculture. Until the late 1960s little was done to realize or develop the full potential of agricultural resources, and agriculture remained highly labor intensive and at low levels of productivity. Commercial crops grown for the export market took up a considerable proportion of available resources and investment, with the result that food crops were unable to meet growing consumption demands and had to be supplemented with major imports of rice, corn (maize), and wheat. Since the late 1960s attempts have been made to ameliorate the problem; high-yield varieties of seed, improvements in irrigation, subsidies for fertilizer, and technical extension services were all being pursued in the mid-1970s in the hopes of increasing crop yields and achieving food self-sufficiency. Agrarian reform and the improvement of rural credit institutions had been undertaken, if slowly, in an attempt to counter the uneven distribution of rural incomes that bore most heavily on the small-holding owners and tenant farmers who make up the majority of the rural population.

It was uncertain in the mid-1970s whether these measures could succeed in solving the most fundamental problem confronted by the primary sector, the problem of a growing population in the face of the virtually complete exhaustion of easily accessible arable land. Land reform programs, started and postponed or left unimplemented time and time again during the twentieth century, might achieve some redistribution of rural income but could no longer address the problem of a finite amount of land forced to support what seemed to be an indefinitely expanding population, more and more of whom were slowly being reduced to the status of landless laborers.

LAND USE AND RESOURCES

The Philippines is well endowed with a potential resource base for agriculture, forestry, and fisheries. For a variety of reasons these resources have not been tapped to the full extent of their potential. Climatic conditions are generally favorable to agriculture, although the lack of irrigation, drainage, and flood control systems leave most crops vulnerable to the vagaries of drought or flooding.

Of the roughly 30 million hectares (one hectare equals 2.47 acres) of land in the Philippines, 9.2 million were under crop cultivation in the mid-1970s—about 31 percent. This represented an increase of almost one-third since the mid-1950s, but it must be noted that, when the area under cultivation passed the 8-million-hectare mark in the mid-1960s, the limits of land area with sufficiently level gradients and proper soil and water conditions had been reached. Since then most expansion has taken place on land with steep gradients susceptible to erosion and on land of marginal fertility. Land use for cultivation was dominated by rice, corn, and coconut, and significant areas were devoted to fruits (especially bananas) and sugarcane.

Forestry resources are considerable, although somewhat endangered by overcutting. Over 14 million hectares were covered by potentially productive forests—in the mid-1970s almost half of the total land area in the Philippines. Fishing resources are also impressive, the territorial waters encompassing over 600,000 square miles; most suitable fishing grounds are found in shallow waters close to shore—about 71,400 square miles. There are an additional 3,100 square miles of fresh water for fishing and a small fishpond industry.

There remain sizable marginal lands, mostly government owned, that could be exploited or cultivated; much was already occupied by squatters or so far removed from population centers and market access that it was difficult to induce resettlement. Significant resettlements have taken place in Mindanao, but these have resulted in bloody conflict between Christian settlers and Muslim inhabitants (see ch. 4). By the mid-1970s the pressure of population on the land was increasing, and room for expansion had virtually vanished.

Climate, Terrain, and Soils

Extending little more than 20° north of the equator, the Philippine archipelago has a tropical climate, a year-round growing season and a high but variable rainfall. Even though the distance from the northernmost to the southernmost parts of the country is considerable, the temperature range is slight, both from one part of the country to another and from one season to another. The greatest range in temperature is found in northern Luzon between the January mean of 73.4°F and the July mean of 84.2°F; temperatures in Mindanao scarcely vary. Virtually all parts of the country register more than fifty-nine inches of rain annually. The distribution of rainfall during the year follows a regular pattern depending on which side of the generally north-south mountain ranges the land lies. In winter and spring the western side of Luzon and of other islands is relatively dry; on the eastern side of the ranges the pattern is reversed, although it is never as dry as on the western side. Each year an average of twenty typhoons descend on the islands between July and October; they have frequently caused major crop losses. Flooding from typhoons in 1972 was responsible for enormous crop losses and resulted in significant food shortages.

The most fertile soils in the country are found in the plains and valleys where alluvial deposits are regularly augmented by rivers and streams. The lowland soils, sometimes enriched by volcanic materials, are considered to be of high potential quality; however, much of this cropland has been under cultivation for generations, and a number of problems have developed. Paddy lands in particular have lost some of their fertility because constant flooding and poor drainage have caused the soil to become waterlogged, allowing valuable nutrients to leach out of the soil. Lack of proper drainage systems has also contributed to erosion, a serious problem in many parts of the country. Cebu in particular has been prone to soil erosion; more than half the arable land has lost 75 percent or more of its topsoil. On Luzon the northwestern coastal plains and those south of Manila have been seriously eroded, as have parts of the islands of Bohol and Masbate.

A primary cause of erosion has been the double-and triple-cropping of corn on steep hillsides. Another contributing factor has been a failure to follow the practice of contour plowing. Moreover centuries of planting corn on the same land without rotating crops has, even in relatively level areas, exhausted the soil, broken down its structure, and left it open to erosion by water and wind.

The climate, terrain, and soils of available arable land have been important factors affecting crop distribution. The plains of the coastal lowlands have been predominantly turned to the cultivation of paddy rice. Hillsides and soil with a coarse or granular texture have been devoted to cultivation of corn, sugarcane, and tobacco. Tree crops are usually found in the areas that have even rainfall and are protected from high winds, although coconut trees are ubiquitous. Where market channels are available, flat terrain is devoted to vegetable production; rolling and hilly terrain, to root crops.

Cropland Distribution

As the Philippines over the years has looked increasingly to the agricultural sector as a source of foreign exchange, the area devoted to commercial crops has grown at the expense of food crops (see table 10). Although the total area of harvested cropland has increased, the area devoted to rice and corn, the two largest crops, has remained relatively constant since the mid-1960s while the area devoted to the cultivation of sugarcane, coconuts, and commercial crops as a whole has increased, not

Table 10. Philippines, Cropland Distribution, Selected Years, 1955–73

Crop	Area Harvested (in thousands of hectares)[1]					Percent of Total Area				
	1955	1960	1965	1970	1973	1955	1960	1965	1970	1973
Palay (unmilled rice)	2,656	3,306	3,200	3,113	3,112	41.3	43.5	38.8	34.8	33.8
Corn	1,388	1,846	1,923	2,420	2,325	21.6	24.3	23.3	27.0	25.2
Citrus fruit	20	23	29	21	19	0.3	0.3	0.3	0.2	0.2
Other fruits and nuts	332	320	372	380	389	5.2	4.2	4.5	4.2	4.2
Root crops	273	289	274	252	266	4.2	3.8	3.3	2.8	2.9
Vegetables	98	81	54	63	68	1.5	1.1	0.6	0.7	0.7
Beans and peas	68	78	56	50	47	1.1	1.0	0.7	0.6	0.5
Coffee	19	31	44	54	61	0.3	0.4	0.5	0.6	0.7
Cacao	7	7	10	8	7	0.1	0.1	0.1	0.1	0.1
Peanuts	28	24	24	32	33	0.4	0.3	0.3	0.4	0.4
Other food crops	2	4	11	12	17	..[2]	..[2]	0.1	0.1	0.2
Total All Food Crops[3]	4,891	6,008	5,996	6,406	6,345	76.0	79.1	72.6	71.6	68.9
Coconuts	990	1,059	1,605	1,884	2,133	15.4	13.9	19.4	21.1	23.2
Sugarcane	268	242	351	366	455	4.2	3.2	4.2	4.1	4.9
Abaca	217	175	199	173	163	3.4	2.3	2.4	1.9	1.8
Tobacco	53	96	76	87	84	0.8	1.3	0.9	1.0	0.9
Rubber	5	5	17	22	26	..[2]	0.1	0.2	0.2	0.3
Other commercial crops	12	10	9	9	6	0.2	0.1	0.1	0.1	0.1
Total All Commercial Crops[3]	1,544	1,588	2,257	2,540	2,868	24.0	20.9	27.3	28.4	31.1
Total All Crops[3]	6,434	7,596	8,252	8,946	9,213	100.0	100.0	100.0	100.0	100.0

[1] One hectare equals 2.47 acres.
[2] Negligible.
[3] Figures may not add to totals because of rounding.

only in absolute size but also as a proportion of total cropland. Thus crops grown for export have been expected to generate greater revenue than food crops for domestic consumption, the expectation being that higher yields and greater cropping intensity of food crops would meet growing consumer needs without large food imports. Rice, corn, and coconut are the three major crops, taking up about 34, 25, and 23 percent of all cropland respectively in 1973. Fruits, nuts, and sugarcane accounted for over 9 percent of harvested land. Other important crops, in order of size, include root crops, abaca, tobacco, coffee, vegetables, rubber, and cacao. The remainder was taken up by ramie, maguey, kapok, cotton, and others.

The bulk of rice production takes place in central Luzon, which in 1970 produced 27 percent of the nation's supply (see fig. 9). The "rice bowl" of central Luzon, made up in part of the provinces of Pangasinan, Tarlac, Nueva Ecija, and Bulacan, was responsible for most of this production. The Cagayan Valley on the northeastern coast of Luzon was also a large producer of surplus rice, as were the Bicol Peninsula, the western Visayan Islands, and southern and western Mindanao. The principal deficit regions were the areas south and east of Manila, northern and eastern Mindanao, and the eastern Visayan Islands. Over half the corn is produced in the Visayan Islands and southern and western Mindanao. Coconuts are concentrated in Mindanao and the eastern Visayan Islands, and sugarcane plantations are heavily concentrated in the western Visayan Islands. Almost half of the nation's banana production comes from the Visayan Islands. Most tobacco is grown in northern Luzon.

Resource Development

Agronomists agree that the productive potential of Philippine agriculture has remained largely untapped. Poor soil management practices, poor crop management, little mechanization and rural electrification, low fertilizer application, and lack of adequate drainage and irrigation facilities have all contributed to low yields and low labor productivity in the agricultural sector. Lack of irrigation and drainage facilities has tended to exacerbate problems of soil management and has made for less cropping intensity than could otherwise be practiced. Price and marketing structures as well as shortages of credit have also inhibited growth in production. In the early 1970s less than 30 percent of rice paddy land was under controlled irrigation. A few large sugarcane plantations were irrigated, but even in areas with a pronounced dry season most crops were entirely rain fed. Reliable sources estimated that fewer than 900,000 hectares were under irrigation, almost all of which were served by gravity-fed systems. Moreover many existing irrigation facilities have deteriorated. Roughly half of the irrigation systems were operated by the National Irrigation Administration, a government agency. Improvement of irrigation facilities could increase cropping intensity significantly; lack of proper irrigating facilities impeded maximum use of fertilizers. In the mid-1970s virtually none of the existing irrigation systems included drainage facilities. Crop losses resulting from the ensuing flooding and waterlogging of soils have been enormous at times.

Agriculture in the mid-1970s was extremely labor intensive and appeared likely to remain so. Indeed growing population pressure seemed likely to make the sector even more labor intensive in the future as the land becomes a source of employment for increasing numbers of people, many of them landless agricultural day laborers. The level of mechanization in the sector, aside from the larger holdings and commercial plantations, was very low. Imports of agricultural machinery in 1974 were valued at roughly US$1.2 million, mostly for tractors. Most farmers depend on draft animals for motive power. It was estimated that less than 5 percent of the rural population was reached by electric power in the mid-1970s.

The most important changes in resource development have come in the form of increased use of fertilizer, the introduction of high-yield seed varieties, the greater availability of extension services, and improvements in rural infrastructure. Impressive gains were made in the second half of the 1960s, rice production increasing by roughly 6 percent each year (see Production, this ch.). The gains were somewhat neutralized in the early 1970s by three years of bad weather, severe flooding, and drought but had resumed growth levels by the mid-1970s. Even so, average yields of approximately 1.7 tons of palay (unmilled rice) per hectare in the mid-1970s were among the lowest in Asia.

Production and yield increases have been attributed almost entirely to the introduction of high-yield varieties of rice—popularly known as "miracle rice"—although some expansion of cultivated area played a role. The Philippines has been a leader in the development of high-yield variety technology, not only through the International Rice Research Institute (IRRI) in Los Baños but through the country's Bureau of Plant Industries (BPI) and College of Agriculture. High-yield varieties were first introduced on a large scale in 1967. By the early 1970s they were being cultivated in roughly half the lowland paddies. At first IRRI 8 was the most widespread, but it was later found unsatisfactory because it had a chalky taste and was particularly susceptible to a viral disease known as tungro. It has largely been replaced by IRRI 20 and 24 and to a lesser extent by BPI 76 and College of Agriculture varieties, although parts of the country isolated from extension services still use traditional varieties and IRRI 8.

Extension of high-yield varieties to corn and sugarcane production has been far slower. Susceptibility to downy mildew disease has been the major impediment to the adoption of high-yield varieties of corn, which covered less than 15 percent of corn areas in the mid-1970s. Sugarcane yields have dropped considerably, although between the mid-1960s and mid-1970s production increased through expansion of the area under cultivation. Reduction of yields is attributed to insects and disease,

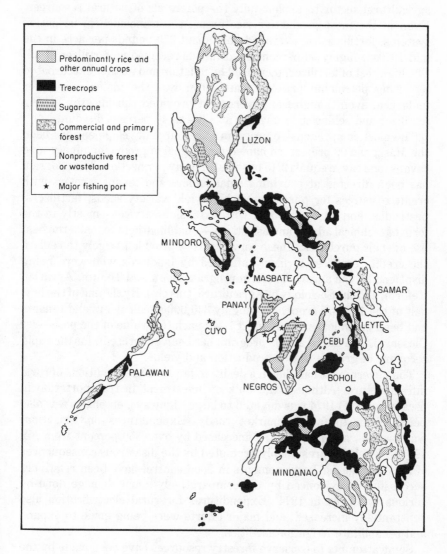

Figure 9. Philippines, Land Use, 1972

The legend of the map reads:

- Predominantly rice and other annual crops
- Treecrops
- Sugarcane
- Commercial and primary forest
- Nonproductive forest or wasteland
- ★ Major fishing port

Labels on the map: LUZON, MINDORO, MASBATE, SAMAR, PANAY, LEYTE, CUYO, CEBU, PALAWAN, BOHOL, NEGROS, MINDANAO delays in processing, and expansion into marginally fertile lands.

Underuse of fertilizer has been a principal reason for the inability of the agricultural sector to exploit fully the potentials of natural resources. Even in the most productive rice areas, those included in irrigation systems, fertilizer use averaged only about 270 pounds per acre in the mid-1970s; roughly 90 percent of cornlands received no fertilizer at all. The high cost of fertilizer, increased by inflation and further exacerbated by rising petroleum prices in late 1973, was the major reason for underuse, even though the government provided subsidies by buying fertilizer and selling it to farmers at a 30- to 40-percent discount.

The most comprehensive program of resource development has been the Masagana 99 project, so named for its goal of producing ninety-nine cavans (one cavan equals 2.13 bushels) of palay per hectare. The program has been directed at providing smallholders and tenant farmers with credit resources for purchases of high-yield variety seeds, fertilizers, pesticides, and herbicides and with extension services—mostly in the form of technical advice and assistance—enabling them to make the best use of their purchases. These services were provided largely to replace the credit resources formerly afforded by landlords who were being displaced by the agrarian reform program (see Land Tenure, Agrarian Reform, and the Sociology of Agriculture, this ch.). By the end of the first half of the 1974–75 crop year roughly 340,000 smallholders and tenants had been given loans averaging ₱1,327 each (for value of the peso—see Glossary). The Masagana 99 program has been given credit for the rapid recovery of growth in rice production and yields.

The government has shown a desire to improve the conditions of rural infrastructure. Although the bulk of investment in transportation in fiscal year (FY) 1974 was devoted to large highways, emphasis was also being given to farm-to-market roads. Expenditures on irrigation, waterworks, and flood control increased by over 350 percent from FY 1971 to FY 1974, presumably prompted by the disastrous consequences of the 1972 floods. Improvements in flood control have been relatively successful, as evidenced by the comparatively minor damage done by serious typhoons in 1974. Expenditures for rural electrification also substantially increased, and major efforts were being made to expand and rehabilitate irrigation facilities.

Some attempts to conserve forestry resources have been made by the government. All forest reserves have been declared public forests, and logging is licensed, presumably in an attempt to control overcutting. It was apparent, however, that permits were frequently abused, that public forests were often logged illegally, and that squatters and slash-and-burn agriculturists had further denuded forests to bring land under cultivation. Remedial action on the part of the government included suspensions of licenses, closer supervision, and reforestation projects. In an attempt to expand the area for crop cultivation, the government has declared over 3 million hectares of forestland "alienable and disposable" for agricultural purposes—usually large blocks of relatively level terrain—and has granted farmers patents to logged lands.

Fishery resources are generally divided into two categories, municipal and commercial. Fishing by large vessels in waters within three miles of the shoreline is licensed by local municipalities; the government licenses fishing beyond these waters. There has been considerable poaching by commercially licensed vessels in municipal waters. A far greater proportion of the potential catch is made in municipally controlled waters.

PRODUCTION

Rebounding from severe setbacks because of poor weather in the first three years of the 1970s and benefiting from resource development projects and higher prices offered, agricultural production has increased dramatically. Crop production in calendar year 1974 increased by almost 7 percent, livestock and poultry by 6.7 percent, and fishing by almost 12 percent over 1973. Forestry production, however, fell considerably (by roughly 35 percent), mostly as a result of declining import demand in the United States and Japan. Most percentage increases in 1973 and 1974 represented a recovery from the earlier setbacks rather than actual growth.

Crop Production

Growth in crop production is attributed to increased yields and to some increase in area harvested (see table 11). In the 1973–74 crop year the total supply of cereal grains was roughly 7.4 million tons, 6 percent more than the previous year's supply. The supply was expected to reach 7.8 million tons at the end of the 1974–75 crop year. Although in the 1973–74 period rice production increased by 23 percent over the previous year and reached a level of 5.5 million tons of palay, the increase was only slightly better than production four years earlier. Much of the large percentage increase was credited to the recovery of damaged land and expansion of cultivation in northeastern Luzon and Mindanao. The 1974–75 rice crop was expected to produce 5.9 million tons of palay, a 6-percent increase over the previous year. Nevertheless production increases have characteristically lagged behind demand, and it was expected that rice imports would once again be necessary in 1975.

Corn production also increased in the 1973–74 crop year, recovering from the extremely bad crop of the 1972–73 period. Corn production for the 1974–75 period was forecast at 2.35 million tons, the area harvested growing to 2.83 million hectares. Coconut production was expected to increase to 1.85 million tons of copra in the 1974–75 crop year. This would represent a substantial increase over the previous year, when yields

Table 11. Philippines, Production of Selected Crops, Selected Years, 1955–73
(in thousands of metric tons)

Crop	1955	1960	1965	1970	1973
Palay (unmilled rice)	3,202	3,739	3,992	5,233	4,415
Corn.............................	770	1,165	1,313	2,008	1,831
Citrus fruit.......................	32	43	71	71	64
Other fruits and nuts	596	675	1,214	1,569	1,803
Root crops	1,200	1,412	1,537	1,316	1,221
Vegetables	184	186	216	306	322
Beans and peas	40	42	26	23	26
Coffee	7	26	44	49	51
Cacao............................	2	3	4	4	4
Peanuts (unshelled)	18	15	13	17	18
Copra............................	1,103	1,075	1,471	1,656	1,698
Desiccated coconut	40	42	63	70	99
Sugar (centrifugal and muscovado)*.....................	1,304	1,439	1,621	1,987	2,305
Molasses	242	369	414	608	886
Abaca	105	95	134	122	119
Tobacco	30	64	46	61	65
Rubber	2	3	6	19	23

*Muscovado is partially refined sugar; centrifugal is more completely refined.

were low because immature nuts were harvested to take advantage of high prices early in the year and because recovery from a severe drought the year before had not been complete.

Sugar production for the 1974–75 period was predicted at 2.6 to 2.7 million short tons of refined sugar. Sugarcane production increased from 52.2 tons per hectare in the 1972–73 period to 56.8 tons the following year, but yield in sugar produced dropped from 219 pounds per ton of cane to 208 pounds, largely as a result of bad weather and reduced fertilizer applications. Production forecasts for other commodities in 1975 included 42,000 tons of tabacco and 2.5 million tons of fruits and vegetables. Significant imports would be required for rice, corn, wheat, cotton, and tobacco.

Livestock and Poultry Production

Livestock and poultry constitute roughly 20 percent of gross value of agricultural production. Production in 1975 was predicted at 450,000 tons of beef, pork, and carabao (water buffalo), roughly half of which was to be provided by swine. About 28,500 tons of milk were expected to be produced, far short of consumer requirements. The government has encouraged livestock and poultry production, seeking self-sufficiency in meat; experts feel this is likely to be achieved for swine but are less than optimistic about beef.

Pigs, chickens, and carabao are found on nearly every farm. Ducks, goats, pigeons, turkeys, and geese are also frequently raised. Horses and sheep are of minor importance. Dairy farming is confined to the Manila area and to a few other large cities. Beef is raised primarily on Mindanao, central Luzon, and Masbate. Beef numbered over 2 million head in the mid-1970s, carabao over 5 million, pigs over 9 million, and goats roughly 1 million.

Forestry Production

Forestry production is a major earner of foreign exchange, and forest products are basic to the domestic economy, supplying building materials and raw materials for a variety of industries (see ch. 14). A great volume of forestry products, particularly lumber, logs, and plywood, is exported to the United States and Japan; roughly 80 percent of the logs produced are exported, and forestry products characteristically rank among the country's top four categories in export value. Nevertheless paper and pulp production lagged behind demand, and imports of both were necessary in the mid-1970s.

Two varieties of pine and several kinds of hardwood are produced; Philippine mahogany is a major export. Logs and lumber were the principal components of the subsector; other components included poles and pilings, railroad ties, mine timbers, rattan, bamboo, firewood, charcoal, and gums and resins. Log production increased rapidly in the 1960s but appeared to have leveled off after 1968; production in the mid-1970s approached 4 million board feet.

Fishery Production

The traditional Filipino diet is one of rice and fish, and fish products provide the bulk of protein consumed (see ch. 6). Even though fishery production doubled in the 1960s and continued to increase in the 1970s, although more slowly, it was far outstripped by rising consumer needs, and large imports were required. Gross production was 989,000 tons in 1970.

Subsistence and commercial fishing provided about 90 percent of the total catch, the remainder being made up by fishpond production. Subsistence fishing carried out in small, usually unpowered craft operating in municipally controlled waters, provided most of the production and employed about 500,000 fishermen. Commercial fishing relied on larger vessels, most of them more than ten years old, and employed more than 30,000 workers. Most of the commercial catch is landed in the Manila area. There is evidence that municipal waters have reached their potential yields, and catches in some commercial grounds have begun to decline.

MARKETING AND CREDIT

The planting, tending, harvesting, and selling of agricultural products is undertaken in a generally private and noninstitutional fashion. The greatest contact between the government and the farmer takes place in the marketing of crops and the securing of credit, but even in these areas most activity takes place in a noninstitutional framework. Only after 1972 and the start of an intensified agrarian reform program did government policies begin to have a serious impact on the day-to-day activities of agriculture.

Marketing

Marketing patterns are characterized by considerable complexity and a large number of middlemen. Produce changes hands many times on its way from the fields to the consumer's table. Milling operations for rice, for example, may take place some distance from the farm, and the task of moving palay to the mill is accomplished by a variety of means in both interisland and intraisland transportation systems (see ch. 15). At almost every stage a different middleman takes charge and makes a profit. Much of this accumulation and transmission was formerly undertaken by ethnic Chinese and Chinese mestizos and, although this was almost certainly no longer the case in the mid-1970s, the stereotype of the unscrupulous Chinese trader has lingered in the popular mind (see ch. 4).

A significant, most likely the major, proportion of food crops never reaches market channels. A large portion is consumed by the farming family, and a considerable amount is used to pay laborers assisting in harvesting or threshing and to repay small debts. Once food enters market channels, losses from inadequate storage and transport or theft further reduce the amount that ultimately reaches the consumer; it was estimated that roughly 7 percent of the rice that reaches market channels is lost in this way.

Marketing for corn tends to be simpler and more efficient than for rice inasmuch as the general pattern of double- and triple-cropping spreads corn production more evenly throughout the year. Like those for rice, however, market channels for corn are in private hands, and a number of middlemen participate. Marketing channels for coconuts are also characterized by numerous intermediaries, largely because the crop is so widely dispersed. Sugarcane is generally bought on consignment by mills, which share a portion of the proceeds with the grower.

Government involvement takes four forms: indirect subsidies, price controls, direct purchases from farms, and import-export monopolies. Rice, corn, and banana production is indirectly subsidized by below-cost sales of fertilizer through the Fertilizer Industry Authority.

Government control of rice marketing is principally designed to prevent shortages and their accompanying price rises. The Department of Agriculture, National Grains Authority, National Economic Development Authority, and the secretary of finance share responsibility for the determination of rice import needs in a given year. Low-quality, mainly imported rice is purchased by the government and is sold to the consumer at a discount—about 40 percent in 1975. Producers are guaranteed a purchase price floor, and the farmer's profit is further assured by fertilizer subsidies. Not surprisingly a thriving black market existed for higher quality rice. Private mills paid slightly more than the National Grains Authority for this rice, knowing that retailers could (illegally) sell better quality rice well above the price ceiling set by the government. Corn also falls under price controls. Minimum purchase prices in 1975 were ₱0.80 per kilogram (one kilogram equals 2.2 pounds), and the retail price ceiling was set at ₱1.45 per kilogram.

In June 1974 the Philippine National Bank assumed control of sugar marketing. The proportion of a year's crop to be exported was determined by the Sugar Quota Administration; the 1974–75 crop, for example, was divided thirty-five to sixty-five in favor of exports. A farmer was paid ₱49.80 per picul (one picul equals 139.4 pounds) for sugar destined for domestic consumption. This was far below production costs but was made up for by a purchase price of ₱180 for the 65 percent of the crop exported. Milling took place at fewer than forty mills (*centrals*) in the mid-1970s. Retail prices for coconut oil were set at ₱1.65 per pint, discounts being given for larger quantities. A complicated subsidy system of rebates, designed in part to ensure adequate domestic supplies at reasonable prices, governed oil milling. After November 1974 wheat imports and sales were also handled by the government.

Credit

Filipino farmers have traditionally relied on their own resources or on informal borrowing to finance farm investment. For tenant farmers in particular the landlord was a frequent source of easily available, if often usurious, loans. As traditional patterns of landlord-tenant relationships have broken down and as investment costs for fertilizer and seed stocks have increased, however, a greater need for institutional credit for farmers has emerged. The Masagana 99 program was designed to serve that need, as were the forced savings programs of the *barrio* (smallest administrative division) cooperative components that are part of the agrarian reform program (see Land Use and Resources; Land Tenure, Agrarian Reform, and the Sociology of Agriculture, this ch.). Nevertheless in the early 1970s it was estimated that only one farmer in four borrowed during a given crop year and that half the borrowers relied on landlords, friends, relatives, or small moneylenders rather than on institutional credit.

Rural banks are the major source of institutional credit for small farm owners. They numbered roughly 1,000 in the mid-1970s. Although partially funded by the government, rural banks are locally owned and operated for profit. Most poorer farmers and tenants have been excluded from using the rural banks as a source of credit because the banks require heavy collateral to secure the loans, something that those most in need of credit can rarely provide. Denied easy access to institutional credit, poor farmers and tenants are forced into the more expensive financing of noninstitutional arrangements. The unavailability of reasonably priced institutional credit was a contributing factor in the rapid growth of tenancy in the second quarter of the twentieth century (see Land Tenure, Agrarian Reform, and the Sociology of Agriculture, this ch.).

Under provisions of the agrarian reform program, beneficiaries of agrarian reform are entitled to post up to 60 percent of the value of lands transferred to them as collateral for loans even though the land is still not completely amortized. In mid-1975 there was insufficient information available to determine the extent to which this was being done. Cooperative components at the *barrio* level were also envisioned as a source of credit and debt insurance for poor farmers, but the forced savings programs appeared to be too expensive for most poor peasants or were simply mistrusted, and many were either thus dissuaded from joining or failed to participate fully.

LAND TENURE, AGRARIAN REFORM, AND THE SOCIOLOGY OF AGRICULTURE

Land tenure patterns are the product not only of economic and political influences but of a number of important historical, social, and cultural influences as well. To most Filipinos the ownership of land has in both traditional and modern times been the single most important—if not the only—means of establishing wealth, security, and social status. For the peasant in particular the right to till a given plot of land as a tenant, if not as an owner, has been equated with survival itself. Throughout the history of the Philippines, militant political movements, including the Hukbalahap (see Glossary) movement in the 1940s and 1950s and the New People's Army in the 1970s, have drawn heavily on peasant dissatisfaction with land tenure inequities for support. Scholars are in almost unanimous agreement that agrarian reform programs have always come about as a response to actual or potential peasant unrest.

Before the arrival of the Spanish late in the sixteenth century, agricultural communities were composed of small groups of related families who owned the land communally. Although the local chief supervised activity and along with lesser members of the local elite could call upon the labor services of commoners and slaves, there was no real sense of private ownership of land (see ch. 3). All members of the community shared in the harvest, and the maintenance of families who had fallen on hard times was a community responsibility.

Under Spanish rule a series of changes gradually took place. In the seventeenth century many of the local chiefs began to assume formal private ownership of community lands, a legal concept introduced by the Spanish. Large grants of land were also made by the Spanish authorities to the descendants of local chiefs and nobles and to the descendants of Spaniards who had formerly been given feudal tribute and labor rights over the peasantry under the short-lived *encomienda* (tribute rights to a certain area) system (see ch. 3). By the eighteenth and nineteenth centuries large estates had been established, including those of the

Catholic religious orders. Merchants, often Chinese mestizos who had grown rich on the expanding trade of the Philippines in the nineteenth century, also had come to accumulate large landholdings ranging from fifty to several hundred hectares.

Increased Tenancy and the Erosion of Landlord-Tenant Relations

Those peasants who farmed the estates of the large landowners (who were known as *caciques*) and of the religious orders became tenants, sometimes as lessees but most often as sharecroppers. A well-established system of patron-client relations came to exist between the landowner and his tenants. In exchange for a share of his crop (usually one-half), labor on demand, and social deference, the tenant could legitimately expect a supply of seed rice, the use of draft animals, loans of rice at no interest during periods of scarcity, loans of cash—often at usurious interests—and gifts and personal attention at times of birth, baptism, marriage, sickness, and death. Other ties, noneconomic in nature, also bound the landowner and tenant together. The landlord depended on the political loyalty of his tenants at election time and in return served as a powerful intermediary on their behalf in dealing with state authority and as an adjudicator and mediator in local disputes.

Several factors operated to maintain a balance in the patron-client relationship and to prevent the system from becoming overly exploitative. There was sufficient unclaimed land that could be settled by peasants willing to forsake the security of the patron-client relationship and for the gradually expanding population. The rapidly growing sugarcane industry also provided a small outlet for excess population in the form of untenured employment, although most sugarcane plantations also used a form of share tenancy that involved a division of monetary proceeds rather than harvested crops. Room for expansion to some extent prevented the development of competition among peasants for the favors of the landowner and impelled the landlord to live up to his obligations. Moreover the tenant was often related to his landlord by blood or marriage, and the dictates of social values encouraged the landlord to take a paternalistic approach in dealing with his tenant-relative.

Some of the land for settlement or conversion to peasant ownership became available through the first attempt at agrarian reform in the Philippines. In 1907 American authorities began purchasing most of the large landholdings owned by the Roman Catholic Church and distributed them to some tenants. The number of tenants involved was relatively small, however, and much of the land ultimately fell into tenancy as tenants who had received ownership themselves became landlords to other tenants or *caciques*, and merchants acquired the land and returned it to tenancy. Other United States colonial policies in agrarian reform were modeled after the American experience with homesteading and were designed to give title to those small-holding squatters on public lands and to control and encourage settlement of virgin lands. The policies did little to achieve their goals, however, as the legal procedures and costs were usually beyond the ability or means of the peasant; and Filipino administrators, who were almost always landowners, were sympathetic to landlord interests. Nevertheless land tenure patterns at the beginning of the twentieth century were characterized by roughly 80 percent owner-operated farms, the remainder being operated by tenants. The highest proportion of tenants was found in the rice bowl of central Luzon.

Throughout the first three-quarters of the twentieth century land tenure patterns and agrarian relations have tended toward change in two directions. The first has been a rapidly accelerating rate of tenancy. By 1939 the proportion of farmers who were share tenants had reached 34 percent, and an additional 16 percent were only part owners of the land they tilled. In the ensuing twenty years the proportion of tenant farmers grew to 40 percent, and in the early 1970s it was estimated that 45 to 50 percent of Filipino farmers were tenants. By far the greatest concentration of tenancy was found on land devoted to the subsistence cultivation of the two principal food crops, rice and corn. As early as 1960 tenancy had reached a level of 70 to 85 percent in the central Luzon rice bowl.

The second general trend has been toward a breakdown of traditional patron-client relations. Although there have been exceptions, the traditional relationship of exchange has frequently become a one-sided affair in which tenants have found their burdens increased while their expected return from the landlord has diminished if not vanished. More and more the landlord-tenant relationship has become a purely economic one; the sons of landlords who had observed the obligations of their position have moved into the cities, leaving the management of the estate in the hands of paid overseers (*katiwalas*). One estimate placed the proportion of absentee landlordism at 90 percent in the early 1970s. Visayan and Bikolano patron-client relations have retained much of their traditional character, however, and peasant dissatisfaction and unrest in these areas have generally been much lower, although considerable discontent has been reported in the Visayan Islands sugar industry among laborers who have been displaced by mechanization.

The increase in tenancy and the decline of the traditional patron-client character of landlord-tenant relationships is attributable to a variety of factors. A principal factor was the monetization of the rural economy. At the same time that cash became the principal means of economic exchange, prices rose and the supply of available cash in the rural economy contracted. Smallholders were increasingly forced to borrow from moneylenders at usurious rates and often had to sell all or part of their land—much of which was bought in the 1920s and 1930s in relatively small parcels (less than twenty-four hectares) by the class of merchants, teachers, professionals, and petty officials. Many smallholders thus lost ownership but remained on the land as tenants. Tenants, borrowing from their landlords, also found themselves deeper and deeper in debt and were thus bound closer to their landlords in a way that began to upset the delicate balance of the patron-client relationship.

The position of the tenant was further weakened by the rapidly increasing pressure of population on the resources of the land. As Philippine agriculture became commercialized, more and more land was turned to the cultivation of cash crops that often used low-paid labor rather than tenancy. At the same time the population increased relentlessly, tripling during the five decades of American rule and doubling again between 1948 and 1970, growing by over one-third in the 1960s alone. Moreover some ethnic groups had a cultural bias that made them less willing than others to leave their homes. Tagalogs in particular were firmly attached to the land on which they lived, whether as owners or tenants, and, unlike the home regions of the Ilokanos, central Luzon began to experience intense population pressure at an early date (see ch. 4).

Landowners, aware of their advantage and increasingly becoming involved in commercial enterprises, gradually lost personal involvement in their landholdings and their tenants and, no longer living on the land, came to look upon both as a source of capital for investment rather than as a social commitment. Bit by bit they demanded greater shares and greater provision of agricultural resources from their tenants and provided less and less of the social insurance that had formerly been their implicit responsibility.

The land tenure patterns that existed at the beginning of the 1970s were a product of all these historical, economic, political, social, and cultural influences. By the 1950s resettlement and migration to more sparsely populated parts of the archipelago had exhausted most of the land that could be economically converted to agricultural use; even in Mindanao, which had once been looked to as a bountiful source of virgin land, population pressure in the 1960s and 1970s triggered serious conflicts between resident Muslims and Christian settlers (see ch. 2; ch. 4). Population density grew from 166 persons per square mile in 1948 to 317 per square mile in 1970. In central Luzon the density in the 1970s was over 558 persons per square mile. The roughly 1 million tenant families on ricelands and cornlands farmed only 1.8 million hectares, providing the average tenant a holding of less than 4.5 acres in size. Landlords frequently took one-half to two-thirds of the harvest, reducing the tenant to a bare subsistence level.

Tenant rice and corn farms were generally not part of large estates; 80 percent were part of landlord holdings of less than seven hectares, usually owned by the petty bureaucrats, teachers, and others who had acquired land in the 1920s and 1930s. High proportions of share tenancy were also found in sugarcane cultivation, where holdings tended to be considerably larger; tenancy made up a lesser proportion of other farms. Most owner-cultivators were in an only slightly better position than tenants; the average farm size for owner-cultivators in 1960 was 4.27 hectares, but it must me noted that significant land fragmentation has taken place since then and that 40 percent of all farms in 1960 were less than two hectares in size.

Not unexpectedly rural incomes were extremely low and their distribution extremely uneven. The mean income of rural families in 1971 was ₱2,818—less than one-half of the urban mean. Almost one-fourth of rural incomes were received by only 5 percent of the families; 40 percent of the families received less than 12 percent of rural incomes, and one-half of them received less than 4 percent. The meagerness of rural income can partly be explained by widespread underemployment and unemployment. Landholdings themselves very frequently provided an insufficient source of income to farmers, who were typically active less than six months of the year on their farms. Many have attempted to supplement their incomes by working as paid laborers on sugar plantations and elsewhere at harvesttime. The competition for paid labor has kept wages extremely low. Personal income for the estimated 14 percent of the agricultural labor force that comprised landless workers in 1971 was about ₱1,200, and almost one-third of the rural population depended on some kind of wage labor for income.

Agrarian Reform

The history of agrarian reform in the Philippines presents a complex mosaic of laws, amendments, decrees, letters of instruction, and circular memoranda creating, directing, and governing a variety of departments, agencies, funds, banks, authorities, and administrations (see table 12). Before the declaration of martial law in September 1972, reform measures usually took an ad hoc "Band-Aid" approach to the problems of land tenure and tenant misery. Reform measures were passed but were generally applied only in areas where serious peasant unrest had erupted or threatened to do so. This was true of land reform measures enacted in 1933 and 1954, though it was somewhat less true of the 1963 act. Implementation of the more comprehensive agrarian reform measures adopted under martial law had, as of mid-1975, also been rather selective, proceeding more rapidly in areas of insurgency than elsewhere

The most meaningful gauge of the failure of agrarian reform before 1972 was found in the rapid increase of tenancy, especially share tenancy, throughout the period. Land reform programs have failed for a variety of specific reasons; most often, however, these reasons have had their root in the continuing hold by landlords on political power in the Philippines, not only at the higher levels of government but at the local level as well. Judges, teachers, sheriffs, provincial and *barrio* officials, bureaucrats— in short all these occupying positions of influence, respect, and power at the local level—have usually been landlords or the children of landlords. The 1933 Rice Share Tenancy Act failed because it left the proclamation of areas under reform to municipal authorities who had no desire to see their

Table 12. Philippines, Chronology of Important Agrarian Reform Measures, 1904–75

Year	Measure	Remarks
1904	Philippine (Commission) Act 1120	Purchase of Roman Catholic Church lands; resale to tenants; put into effect 1907; negligible results.
1933	Rice Share Tenancy Act	Regulate share tenancy relations; not proclaimed until 1946; little effect.
1934	Commonwealth Act 4113	Regulate tenancy relations on sugarcane plantations; not enforced.
1950	executive order	Create Land Settlement and Rehabilitation Administration to deal with settlement of public lands.
1954	Republic Act 1160	Replace with National Resettlement and Rehabilitation Administration.
	Republic Act 1199 (Agricultural Tenancy Act)	Limit landlord's share to 30 percent; secure tenant tenure; never enforced.
1955	Republic Act 1267	Establish courts of agrarian reform.
	Republic Act 1400 (Land Reform Act)	Distribute public lands and expropriate private lands where conflicts exist, for instance in areas of Hukbalahap activity; never enforced; expropriation limited to very large landholdings.
1963	Republic Act 3844 (Agrarian Land Reform Code)	Outlaw share tenancy and convert to leasehold; most cash crops excepted; tenants given right of first refusal. Landlord allowed to retain seventy-five hectares* under RA 3844, reduced to twenty-four hectares by RA 6389; rents fixed at 25 percent of average harvest; tenants protected from eviction; underfinanced; little effect.
1971	Republic Act 6389 (Code of Agrarian Reforms)	Revise RA 3844; create Department of Agrarian Reform.
1972	Presidential Decree 2	Reconfirm RA 3844 as amended.
	Presidential Decree 27	Rice and corn tenants "deemed owners"; fifteen amortization payments on the basis of 2.5 times average harvest as total price plus 6-percent interest; tenants to become cooperative members; landlords permitted to retain seven hectares for "personal cultivation" but hired labor permitted.
	Presidential Decree 85	Establish Land Reform Fund.
	Presidential Decrees 251, 338, 444, and 462.	Strengthen Land Bank.
1973	Presidential Decree 175	
	Presidential Decree 316	Prohibit eviction of tenants.
	announcement	Implementation of PD 27 extended to landholdings of more than twenty-four hectares.

Table 12—Continued.

Year	Measure	Remarks
1974 . . . . . .announcement		Implementation of PD 27 extended to landholdings of more than seven hectares.
	Presidential Decree 583	Reinforce PD 316.
1975 . . . . . .announcement		PD 27 not to extend below seven hectares; RA 3844 and RA 6389 to be applied to tenants.

*One hectare equals 2.47 acres.

own landholdings reformed. The Land Reform Act of 1955 was never fully implemented; only forty-one estates were purchased and redistributed under the provisions of the act. Land reform legislation enacted in 1963 was watered down by congressional amendment from the outset; funds were never fully appropriated and when appropriated were not spent. Administrative duplication and division of responsibility hampered the efficiency of implementation; the 1963 act was amended in 1971 by Republic Act (RA) 6389 to place general administration under the unified Department of Agrarian Reform, to establish the Land Bank for financing, and to extend coverage. Even so, funding was generally deemed inadequate, and many landowners employed a variety of subterfuges to escape compliance.

Between 1963 and 1972 agrarian reform programs were primarily focused on the conversion of share tenants to controlled leaseholders. A second stage, the conversion of leaseholders to amortizing owners, was contemplated but never actively pursued. The 1971 revision of RA 3844 declared that all tenants growing rice and corn were covered by provisions of the code. The number of share tenants actually converted to leasehold, however, has been difficult to determine. One reliable source placed the number at 53,420 in February 1972—a mere 9 percent of the total covered. Conversions to leasehold were concentrated in the province of Nueva Ecija, a prime area of peasant dissatisfaction, where 67 percent of all conversions took place. The effectiveness of conversions to leasehold is further brought into question by the fact that two-thirds to four-fifths of the conversions were by oral contract only, and there is considerable evidence that in many of these instances the rents paid continued to follow former sharecropping arrangements. In a few cases share tenancy was effectively retained by converted farmers who had maintained traditional patron-client relations with their landlords and felt unable to discharge their moral obligation to them in any other way. Such arrangements were illegal under the code inasmuch as rents were fixed at a maximum of one-fourth of an average year's harvest. The second phase of the program, the conversion of leaseholders to amortizing owners, was accomplished for roughly 30,000 farmers according to a

Department of Agrarian Reform official—a figure fully ten times greater than the one cited by Land Bank sources.

Even as amended, progress under RA 3844 was extremely slow, and the need for greater executive power in order to revitalize agrarian reform was one of several reasons given by President Ferdinand E. Marcos for declaring martial law in 1972. Indeed Marcos at least rhetorically has staked the legitimacy of his rule by decree on the success of land reform: "The land reform program is the only gauge for the success or failure of the New Society. If land reform fails, there is no New Society." Critics of martial law, however, have suggested that Marcos' motives in land reform have been to avert agrarian unrest, win over the rural population to his regime, assure foreign investors of the social and political stability of the country, and emasculate his political opposition, which has been made up in part by members of the landholding elite. It should be noted, however, that many if not most observers have not questioned the sincerity of Marcos and the top-level agrarian reform officials, although a great number of these doubt the extent to which the administration has been willing to take political risks in implementing the program.

Immediately after the declaration of martial law, Marcos proclaimed Presidential Decree (PD) 2, which in effect confirmed RA 6389 as the guiding law in agrarian affairs. The whole of the Philippines was thus declared a land reform area, but lands devoted principally to the cultivation of most commercial crops were exempted, including tree crops and crops exported under quotas, such as sugarcane. The net effect, then, was to limit agrarian reform to tenanted rice and corn lands. Even though the sugar quota was no longer in effect in mid-1975, sugarcane lands had not been brought under reform.

On October 21, 1972, President Marcos promulgated PD 27. The announced goal of this decree was to effect the immediate transfer to amortizing ownership for rice and corn tenants on "family-size" farms of five hectares of unirrigated land or three hectares of irrigated land. The scarcity of land made the family-size farm of PD 27 more a dream than a reality; at most tenants have been "deemed owners" of the land they till. Landlords would be permitted (as under RA 6389) to retain seven hectares for "personal cultivation," but personal cultivation has since been interpreted to include the use of hired labor. Although deemed owner of the land, the tenant does not receive title until he has paid for the farm in fifteen equal amortization payments plus 6-percent interest on the unpaid balance. The title received cannot be sold or fragmented but only transferred to a single inheritor or to the government. The landlord is to be compensated by one of several means, most frequently through a 10-percent cash payment and the remainder in twenty-five-year Land Bank bonds earning 6-percent annual interest. The value of the land thus bought and sold is to be set at 2.5 times the average yearly harvest of the previous three "normal" crop years.

Implementation of PD 27 first required the determination of precisely who were tenants and precisely what lands they tilled. After such a determination land transfer certificates were to be printed and issued to the tenant upon his becoming a dues-paying member of a Samahong Nayon, one of the elements of agricultural cooperatives at the *barrio* level. In the meantime conversion of tenants to leasehold was to continue under provisions of RA 6389. The total of potential beneficiaries initially envisioned under PD 27 was 956,000 tenants on 1.5 million hectares of land, but some confusion has arisen over the provision for retention of seven hectares by the landlord. A September 1975 ruling by the Department of Agrarian Reform provided that owners of tenanted riceland and cornland were eligible to retain seven hectares if they owned no other agricultural lands totaling seven hectares or any other land devoted to residential, commercial, or industrial use serving as a source of income. Nevertheless in May 1975 PD 27 was also amended to provide for leasehold conversion for tenants on retained land rather than "personal cultivation" only, as originally announced. According to estimates in September 1975 this would reduce potential beneficiaries to roughly 450,000 tenants, less than half the original total.

Progress under PD 27 between 1972 and 1975 was extremely slow. Roughly 203,000 certificates of land transfer had been printed by August 1975 covering plots averaging somewhat smaller than 1.8 hectares. The number of certificates actually issued, however, had been much fewer. One estimate placed the number in early 1975 at about 75,000. Moreover, as implementation of the decree successively extended from landholdings of over twenty-four hectares in late 1973 to landholdings of over seven hectares in late 1974, the pace of reform slowed rapidly. More than 50,000 certificates were printed in September 1973; by August 1975 monthly printings had slowed to 2,500. At the rate of printing that prevailed in the first two-thirds of 1975, the total number of certificates planned would not be printed—much less issued—until 1989, well beyond the December 1976 target date set by the Department of Agrarian Reform. Compensation of landlords by the Land Bank, the last step in transfer and the beginning of amortization payments by tenants, had progressed to an even lesser extent. By August 1975 fewer than 400 landlords had been compensated for lands occupied by roughly 11,500 tenants.

The slow progress under PD 27 has been attributed to a variety of impediments; some were administrative, and others stemmed from landlord resistance. The extension of implementation to landholdings between seven and twenty-four hectares greatly exacerbated both kinds of problems. The number of individual landholdings, landlords, and tenants to be administered increased dramatically after 1974, and agrarian reform in the mid-1970s consistently found its most virulent opposition in the smaller landlords who, unlike large-holding owners, depend on their holdings for a far greater proportion of their incomes.

In September 1975 Conrado F. Estrella, secretary of the Department of Agrarian Reform, pinpointed the most important administrative problems as slowness of action by the Courts of Agrarian Reform, slow formation of Samahong Nayons, and understaffing of survey teams, legal personnel, and other administrators. At that time the department proposed the abolition of the Courts of Agrarian Reform, to be replaced by district offices of an agrarian relations commission under department supervision. One department official described the courts as "the last bastion of the landlords in actively opposing the agrarian drive." The problem was further aggravated by the loss of many department lawyers who had become dissatisfied with low wages and overwork; the legal staff in late 1975 was at half strength. According to officials the problem had reached "critical proportions" and threatened to become a major obstacle in implementing land transfers.

Samahong Nayons have developed slowly, and considerable question has been raised as to their potential ability effectively to represent tenants and to fulfill their intended role—ultimately to replace the functions of social insurance and source of credit traditionally performed by the landlord. Receipt of a land transfer certificate was made contingent upon membership in a Samahong Nayon. In order to join, a farmer had to pay a ₱10 membership fee and agree to contribute 5 percent of his loans from the Land Bank to a cooperative investment fund as well as one cavan of unmilled rice for each hectare he tills annually to an amortization guarantee fund. The expense of membership has been too high for some of the poorer tenants, and instances have been reported of farmers who have returned their certificates because of the high cost of membership. Other tenants have presumably been discouraged from joining for this reason as well. Less than half of the farmers who had joined were reported to have made the necessary contributions.

Roughly half of the *barrios* in the Philippines had formed Samahong Nayons by mid-1975; half of the farmers in those *barrios* had joined them; and only 40 percent of the membership were actually tenants. Samahong Nayons have come under considerable criticism for opening membership to landowners and nonfarmers, thus permitting other interests to dominate those of tenants. Large landowners are prohibited from holding positions of power, but smaller landlords are not, and firsthand reports indicate that some Samahong Nayons have quickly been demoralized by what one peasant organization head called "old foxes dressed in new sheep's clothing." Department of Agrarian Reform officials have reported that peasants have been most easily organized in areas of former Hukbalahap activity, where a basis of organization has presumably remained.

But the most significant obstacles to agrarian reform have been those created by the landlords. The history of the Philippines has left a legacy of landowner control over almost every level of social, political, legal, and economic organization. In the past landlords were easily able to thwart agrarian reforms through complicated processes of litigation that the peasant could neither understand nor afford, in a legal system dominated by other landowners. This was still largely the case in mid-1975, as evidenced by Department of Agrarian Reform complaints against the Courts of Agrarian Reform. Landlords are reported to have resorted frequently to illegal and extralegal means of opposing PD 27 as well. Almost immediately after the promulgation of the decree landlords began to evict tenants—sometimes by physical force—in order to turn the land to "personal cultivation" and thus evade reform. Through later decrees President Marcos ordered a stop to such evictions and the maintenance of the status quo; enforcement of these decrees has only rarely been reported, however, and the extent to which this practice has ceased was difficult to determine. A more common subterfuge was the simple refusal of landlords to recognize their tenants' tenure. Because tenancy arrangements are almost always concluded orally, the burden of proof in such cases was shifted to the tenant. As one official noted in mid-1975, "As of now, it appears that landowners can stop the government from carrying out land reform by merely refusing to recognize farmers as their tenants."

Another means of evading PD 27 has been the conversion of ricelands and cornlands to other crops or to nonagricultural uses. Landowners can obtain permits for land conversion provided they pay tenants compensation equal to five times an average year's harvest. It was impossible to determine the extent of legal or illegal conversions, but evidence suggests that the practice has not been uncommon. The process of valuing the land for sale to the tenant has also been used as a delaying tactic by landlords. After martial law land value was determined by a *barrio* committee with a composition weighted slightly in favor of tenants. There were 1,900 of these committees in mid-1975. By simply refusing to attend committee meetings, however, landlords were able to undermine their effectiveness. The effectiveness of the *barrio* committees was further undermined by a February 1974 decision to bring landlords and tenants together in face-to-face negotiations under the auspices of the Department of Agrarian Reform. These negotiations were to determine a cash price that was later to be converted into an average year harvest figure so as to conform with the decree's valuation system. Landlords were more willing to participate in these negotiations, finding their superior knowledge and bargaining abilities a significant advantage. The price of land thus negotiated has been reported to be extremely high—an average of ₱6,400 per hectare—and constituted a very large proportion of the average tenant's income even when spread over fifteen amortization payments.

Philippine agrarian reform in the mid-1970s was thus beset with a number of ambiguities and contradictions. The conditions it has sought to ameliorate are rooted in problems that may be beyond the scope of reform measures. One root problem has been the breakdown of traditional landlord-tenant relations and an unbalancing of power and advantage in favor of the landlord. In areas where traditional arrangements have remained intact, tenants have repeatedly returned their land transfer certificates, preferring the security of old ways. Moreover perhaps one-third of the tenants are related to their landlords, creating a serious conflict between social values and agrarian reform (see ch. 5). Elsewhere the task of breaking the landlord's grip on the lives of his tenants has proved too difficult. Landlords with superior access to civil, constabulary, and military authorities—most often landlords themselves—have maintained their pervasive influence; according to one peasant organizer "two or three landlords [on a Samahong Nayon or *barrio* committee] are enough either to misinterpret directives, or confuse the issue, or otherwise cow the tenants into submission."

If fully implemented, the agrarian reform program would presumably result in the redistribution of rural income, but the program completely omits reference to the numerous tenant farmers on croplands other than rice or corn. Moreover an estimated 80 percent of landlords own less than seven hectares, and their tenants would merely be converted to leaseholders. Many of those tenants who have acquired amortizing ownership of the land they till have found that property taxes and the rapidly increasing expenditures for fertilizer and other capital investments—which accompanied the greater requirements of the high-yield seed varieties that were being introduced at the time—have largely absorbed much if not all of the surplus that the landlord formerly took.

It is possible that the creation of a viable Samahong Nayon movement could successfully replace the role formerly filled by responsible land-lords and protect the new owners from the effects of inflating costs. But the far more fundamental problem of growing population densities and the exhaustion of land for expansion poses a threat to rural livelihood that may not be overcome by a mere redistribution of landownership. It would appear that the process of what anthropologist Clifford Geertz calls "agricultural involution" was already under way in many parts of the Philippines in the mid-1970s. In Geertz' model, agriculture becomes increasingly labor intensive, with a labor force composed largely of landless workers accommodated by elaborate mechanisms for sharing a supply of work and produce that is growing much more slowly than the population. The number of landless rural families in the Philippines appears to be on the rise. Duncan A. Harkin, at a 1975 conference on land reform in the Philippines, concluded his paper with the observation:

The land reform preserves the labor absorptive incentives of the family sized farm and thereby buys some time for the more fundamental balancing of population to resource capacity. Also the reform, by redistributing wealth, will probably increase employment in wage goods industries, again gaining some time for the solution of the more basic problem. However, until the ratio of population dependent upon land stabilizes, this generation's land reform beneficiaries can be expected to become the next generation's landlords. The form of the relationship may be different, but so long as there are persons without access to resources and without alternative employment opportunities, it appears almost inevitable that they will be reduced by competition against each other to a near subsistence level of living. Already many tenants are not actually cultivators, but because they have use rights in land, they function as intermediaries between the nominal owner (landlord) and the actual tillers who are increasingly day wage laborers.

CHAPTER 14

INDUSTRY

Although still a relatively small sector of the economy, industry, including manufacturing, mining, and construction, accounted in 1973 for 27 percent of net domestic product (NDP—see Glossary), absorbed over one-third of total fixed investment, and provided employment for about 15 percent of the total labor force. Government policies in the mid-1970s were aimed at the creation of a climate conducive to industrial growth and the provision of necessary social overhead capital and services for the accelerated growth and development of the industrial sector.

In 1972 the growth rate of the gross national product (GNP—see Glossary) fell to 4.1 percent, but the average growth rate during the preceding five years had been 5.9 percent, and 1973 saw a recovery; statistics indicated that the real growth rate for that year was 10 percent. Although it was too early to judge the magnitude of the effect on the Philippines of recession in the industrial countries of the world and the increasing rise in oil prices, the economy was expected to achieve a real annual growth rate of from 6 to 8 percent between 1975 and 1980, manufacturing output growing at a rate of around 7 percent per year and manufactured exports increasing annually by about 20 percent. Prospects for continued industrial growth thus appeared promising. The economic reforms of the early 1970s laid a potential base for a comprehensive developmental effort in which small-, medium-, and large-scale industries were expected to play an important role in expanding and diversifying production and exports.

The government's industrial strategy beginning in the late 1960s placed special emphasis on the processing of local raw materials, the growth of manufactured exports, the generation of employment, and the regional dispersion and development of small- and medium-scale industries. The government provided, mainly through the Board of Investments (BOI), various tax and other financial incentives to projects emphasizing labor-intensive techniques of production or having a strong export potential. Priority plans provided additional inducements to export-oriented industries and gave increased emphasis to the promotion of exports and manufactured goods processed from local raw materials.

Manufacturing, which accounts for over two-thirds of all industrial output, continued to be predominantly privately owned and was generally concentrated in large-scale, vertically integrated, capital-intensive units. The structure of the manufacturing sector reflected the dual nature of the economy—large-scale modern operations on the one hand and a multitude of small, minimally productive firms on the other—and the limited labor-absorptive capacities of modern plants established after World War II. Thus in 1971 a comparatively small number of firms that employed only 17 percent of the manufacturing labor force accounted for some 70 percent of the value added in manufacturing—a standard indicator of the relative importance of an industry that measures the difference between the value of goods produced and the cost of materials and supplies that are used in producing them. A great number of small and medium-sized firms that employed about 76 percent of the manufacturing labor force accounted for only 10 percent of the value added. The scanty data available suggested that of these small and medium-sized firms the so-called unorganized sector—firms having from one to five workers—accounted for more than 70 percent of all employment in manufacturing.

Food and beverages constituted the largest manufacturing sector. Chemicals and petrochemical were second and textiles third. Over 65 percent of manufacturing enterprises were concentrated in the Manila area and the southen Luzon region. Increasing industrialization has also been taking place in northern Mindanao and the Visayan Islands of the central Philippines.

For most of the period after World War II industrial production was geared mainly to meeting the needs of the domestic market. Reliance on the industrial sector as a major vehicle for enhancing export earnings has been a relatively new development, signaled by the Export Incentives Act of 1970 and by other policy measures, such as the floating of the peso—resulting in a substantial devaluation that made Philippine exports more competitive in international markets.

The construction industry enjoyed the highest growth rate among major sectors of the economy in the early 1970s. After a falling off of activity in 1970, the sector recovered fully in 1971 with a 17.2-percent growth rate and experienced even higher growth rates in 1972 and 1973. Much of this increase has been the result of expanded government construction aimed at improving the infrastructure. Roads, airports, waterworks, schools, and similar public works have received first priority. Government construction activity has also been directed at overcoming the serious shortage of housing facilities for low-income families.

The country contains vast natural resources. Mining is thought to have barely scratched the surface of the mineral wealth available, although it earned the equivalent of approximately US$300 million annually in 1975. Copper and gold are the most important minerals, followed by nickel, chromium, and various nonmetallic minerals.

Tourism has developed into an important industry, elevated administratively to cabinet level in recognition of the rising influx of foreign visitors, who numbered some 250,000 in 1973 as against 160,000 the previous year. Projections of a 13-percent annual increase in the flow envisioned close to 400,000 arrivals by 1977, spurring such related activities as hotel construction and investment in retail establishments catering to the tourist trade.

In the mid-1970s industrial development was guided by the Four Year Development Plan (1974–77), which is the successor of the Four Year Development Plan (1972–75). The 1974–77 plan was revised to take into account recent developments in the economy stemming from martial law. Although the global economic recession brought about by the energy crisis has caused some doubt about achieving the plan's economic goals, basic guidelines remain the same, and the government announced its intention of pursuing the same objectives as set in the plan. Industry's goals have been defined in the plan as promotion of intermediate and capital goods industries and industrial dispersal to different regions (see ch. 12).

From 1953 to 1972 labor-management relations in industry were governed by a system of collective bargaining. This system resulted in an increase in the number and strength of trade unions; at the time of the proclamation of martial law in 1972, it was estimated that there were more than 6,000 unions in the country. The labor movement, however, was fragmented and weakened by internal rivalries; the great number of small manufacturing firms also handicapped effective labor organization. The collective-bargaining system was replaced in October 1972 by a presidential decree that prohibited strikes and lockouts. All matters involving employer-employee relations were referred for decision to the National Labor Relations Commission composed of officials from the Department of Labor. Before 1972 elaborate legislation governed—in addition to labor relations—such aspects of working conditions as hours of work, minimum wages, workmen's compensation, employment of women and children, medical care, leave, and termination of employment. The provisions, however, were very unevenly implemented and enforced. They were greatly amended and consolidated in an abbreviated labor code that became effective in late 1974. In some areas the abbreviated code lacked implementing mechanisms, and it tended to strengthen the role of central authorities in labor relations.

TRENDS AND PROBLEMS IN THE INDUSTRIAL SECTOR

Manufacturing Trends Through the 1960s

Because the economic goal of colonialism was the realization of profits for the mother country through production and export of primary products, industrial development during the colonial period was not impressive. The foundation of a dualistic economy was laid during the colonial era: the rural and industrial sectors were linked to each other and the outside world through trade. Primary raw materials consisting of agricultural commodities, abaca, sugar, tobacco, and coconut were exported in exchange for such manufactures as textiles, clothing, machinery, capital equipment, and various foodstuffs. The pattern that emerged from this mode of economic exchange was one in which the rural agricultural sector provided the product exports to pay for imports of manufactured goods. In general Filipinos dominated the agricultural resource activities engaged in export production, and Western interests—primarily American—were involved in exporting, importing, and wholesaling. In addition the Western interests provided the entrepreneurial skills and capital for the development of mining and forest resources and for the processing of agricultural crops for export.

The dominant factors inhibiting growth of this agricultural export economy were the fluctuations in foreign demand for primary products. In periods of rising demand, export profits were reinvested locally in order to expand capacity. As world demand fell, export profits were repatriated, resulting in capital export and domestic stagnation. Thus the dominance of the export sector, the importance of foreign investment in this sector, and the dualistic nature of the economy inhibited industrial development, especially manufacturing.

The desire to stimulate greater Filipino involvement in the transition toward a modern industrial economy emerged in 1935 with the inception of the commonwealth period. From 1935 to 1941 the Philippine government established public corporations and experimented with bureaucratic entrepreneurship that was expected to precede the eventual takeover of these activities by private enterprise. The commonwealth period, however, produced few changes in the colonial pattern. On the eve of World War II control of industry was about 40 percent Filipino, 30 percent American, and 25 percent Chinese. American participation lay largely in the agricultural processing industries, mining, public utilities, and power development. Filipino investment primarily reflected government participation; of the few private Filipino concerns, most were small or poorly capitalized.

Although the impetus for post-World War II development of the industrial sector can be traced to legislation adopted as early as 1946, the 1946–49 period primarily witnessed the effort to rehabilitate the economy after the severe damage caused by the war and to achieve prewar levels of production. The immediate postwar rehabilitation was financed primarily with funds provided by the United States. Within the three years following 1945 reconstruction was completed and prewar levels of output restored. The use to which these funds were put and the inability of the government to take firm economic steps, however, led to certain economic crises that in turn strongly affected postwar industrialization strategies. As a result of the failure to channel funds into primary investment, together with overvaluation of the peso and termination of reconstruction aid, the late 1940s saw exports lag and imports of all kinds soar. Although production recovered, the trade deficit expanded. From

1948 to 1949 foreign reserves dropped precipitously from US$420 million to US$260 million.

In response to the large balance-of-payments deficit and the foreign exchange crisis, the government imposed restrictions in 1950. This decision acted as the principal stimulus from which an import-substitution industrialization strategy evolved, an approach that the Philippines shared with most other developing countries of the period and that was accompanied by the usual policies of exchange and import controls, low interest rates and credit rationing, and often direct controls on industries.

The import-substitution strategy focused on the development of industries producing consumer goods and other light products that had formerly been imported. Very little attention was given to production for export. In fact export manufacturers were handicapped by government policies; in this the Philippines differed from such countries as the Republic of China (Nationalist China) and the Republic of Korea (South Korea). The strategy thus resulted in an inward-looking concentration on a protected—but limited—domestic market. Even after the limitations of this strategy had become apparent in the late 1950s, the industrial system that had been created proved very resistant to change. The system incorporated the strong interests of the elite and of foreign investors, who continued to benefit from government policies relating to trade protection, tax incentives, investment financing, and foreign exchange rates.

Initial legislative support for the provision of incentives to import-substitution industries, especially in consumer goods, was found in the 1946 Republic Act 35, which excepted certain industries deemed "new and necessary" from the payment of industrial revenue taxes. In 1949 several efforts were made to invigorate these provisions, and in 1951 the act was replaced by Republic Act 901, which extended exemptions from internal taxes to all taxes, including customs duties. A rider to the new act liberalized the requirements for classification as "necessary" industry and provided significant loopholes for industries that were capital intensive and heavily dependent on imported equipment and materials. The provisions of the act were effective until December 1958, when the porportion of the taxes to be exempted would begin to diminish, reaching zero by 1962.

Together with the import and exchange controls, the new law gave a powerful impetus to import-substitution industries. For several years after 1950 the industrial sector expanded rapidly, and the strategy appeared effective. Between 1950 and 1957 manufacturing grew by 11 percent a year. Since the controls established allowed the liberal importation of producer goods (as distinct from consumer goods), manufacturing tended to concentrate on the finishing stages of production; thus while the proportion of imported consumer goods dropped from

28 percent in 1950 to 17 percent in 1957, total imports as a proportion of GNP remained fairly constant. In effect the industrial sector was induced to become an assembler of imported components.

Economists have identified two constraints that act negatively on growth induced by an import-substitution strategy, and the Philippines fell victim to both. The first is the shortage of foreign exchange, which in the Philippines had become an acute problem by the late 1950s. The second is the limited size of the domestic market for consumer goods. As the domestic market becomes saturated, sustaining the earlier pace of industrial growth is impossible unless alternative outlets are found, mainly through breaking into the international market. The protection used to develop import substitutes, however, also fostered inefficient production that was unable to compete internationally. Throughout the 1960s manufacturing grew at a rate of only 5 percent a year, although there was some entry into new product lines.

Manufacturing development in the 1950s, therefore, did not reduce the country's dependence on imports; the principal burden of earning foreign exchange continued to be placed on the agricultural sector, and industrial growth began to lag. There were, in addition, other undesirable consequences. The policy of stimulating industry by tax exemptions was tantamount to indirect government subsidies, and the investor came to obtain much of his return not by adding to output but by keeping what would otherwise have been government tax revenue. The policies used, moreover, favored capital-intensive development, and employment in industry increased only slowly during the 1950s.

The Philippines was again faced by balance-of-payments problems in the late 1950s. Having exhausted the usefulness of trade and exchange controls as a means of solving these problems, the government opted for decontrol and devaluation in a series of steps completed by 1962. Although these moves might have provided the basis for a restructuring of industry, their effect was minimized in several ways. For example, decontrol did not result in a truly substantial trade liberalization that would have injected a sorely needed element of competition into Philippine industry. Moreover, as the expiration date for Republic Act 901 approached, industrialists exerted strong pressure on the government to enact a new incentive law, and in 1962 the Basic Industries Act was adopted. The new act recognized the errors of the extensive tax exemptions of the earlier law and provided exemptions on importation of machinery only for certain basic industries. For this purpose a list of eighteen industries defined as basic were cited in the law. The list, however, was broad enough to include many of the "new and necessary" industries already in existence.

Subsequently, in 1964, the government enacted legislation to reduce the scope of the definition of basic industries; yet again the main beneficiaries were firms already in operation. Through 1966 about 40 percent of the firms that received incentives had received exemptions under earlier laws. Over 64 percent received their exemptions for expansion of existing capacity as distinct from new projects and, out of a total of the equivalent of US$143 million of basic industry imports from 1964 to 1966, only 5 percent was imported by new firms.

The government's financing and incentive policies had the effect of making capital goods and imported materials relatively cheap compared to domestic resources; industries were built requiring more capital equipment and less labor and domestic materials. Toward the end of the 1960s several industries experienced problems of excess capacity but were able to withstand these difficulties because of low investment costs. Government funds were preferentially channeled to industries at low interest rates and on easy terms. Default on loans from the Development Bank of the Philippines (DBP), the most important source of long-term finance for industry, was sometimes avoided by debt rescheduling and relending to distressed firms. Although the DBP lent to a wide range of manufacturing industries in the 1960s, it concentrated on a handful of privileged enterprises. The paper, steel, sugar, textile, cement, radio, and television industries and certain branches of the metal products industry received 60 percent of DBP loans in the 1960s while accounting for less than one-fourth of total manufacturing output.

Through the 1960s, therefore, the industrial sector, in particular manufacturing, displayed several features that were increasingly regarded as contributing to the fundamental economic problems confronting the country. Emphasis on import-substitution strategies and associated policies proved to be self-limiting and failed to relieve the country of periodic balance-of-payments crisis. In a labor-surplus economy, reliance on capital-intensive technologies was basically wasteful. The development of capital-intensive industry and its concentration in and around Manila limited access by the labor force to the entire process of industrialization and economic modernization. Despite various partial reforms, these patterns were remarkably persistent. It was not until a severe balance-of-payments crisis occurred in the late 1960s, as an earlier one had in 1949, that the government began seriously to redirect its industrialization policy.

General Characteristics of Industrial Structure

Philippine economic development has depended upon a sympathetic relationship between government policy and private economic activity. The industrial promotion policies and the development of import-substitution industries in the 1950s were in part an illustration of this relationship. As industry lagged after the initial gains of the 1950–57 period, new policy measures were required to strengthen the basis of industrialization and spread its benefits more equitably throughout the society; such measures would include, for example, backward integration through small and medium-sized labor-intensive industries, dispersal of industry out of the Manila enclave, expansion of employment, and the stimulation of industrial exports. These measures were not taken in the 1950–70 period, largely because of the nature of the government's protection and incentive policies and the entrepreneurial response—both domestic and foreign—to them.

The economy, aside from earlier government-owned and bureaucratically managed enterprises of the commonwealth period, which included cement, fertilizer, and textile plants, has been based on private enterprise. The principal source of domestic entrepreneurs was the traditional elite. Their power was rooted in colonial history, and their economic base grew out of a dominant position in exports of primary products. The postwar period saw this group become the major source of private entrepreneurs and assume positions of political and government leadership.

The structure of the manufacturing industry reflected a bias toward large-scale capital-intensive firms, enhanced by the policies adopted by the government in the 1950s and 1960s. The import control policies of the 1950s and the sudden opening of a protected domestic market, aided by laws that gave the most liberal benefits to highly capitalized enterprises, provided immediately profitable opportunities for large investments of capital. Members of the elite group moved quickly from commerce and primary exports into manufacturing. Small and medium-sized firms failed to develop as a viable market force since they found it difficult to qualify as "new and necessary" and were subject to import controls that favored high capitalization. The capital-intensive nature of manufacturing in a labor-surplus economy was reflected in employment and output patterns; between 1969 and 1971 firms having 100 or more workers employed only 17.0 percent of those employed while contributing 70.1 percent to value added in manufacturing (see table 13).

In industry as a whole as well as in individual subsectors a few large firms were predominant in output, sales, equity, and profits. Concentration was pronounced in beverages, tobacco, cosmetics, paper and paper products, and household appliances as well as in mining but somewhat less so in textile and food-processing industries. Consolidation of ownership in the elite and the subsequent predominance of already established firms were particularly noticeable in the period after 1950 (see ch. 12). Opportunities for small-scale entrepreneurs diminished.

Because Filipino manufacturing entrepreneurs have come from the traditional elite, relations between national politicians and the top economic group often operated to make entry into the entrepreneurial class difficult. The big exporters, importers, and manufacturers received protective legislation, liberal loans from government banks, and appointment to public offices and corporations. The close association between economic and political power was also evident in the number of public officials or relatives of officials on corporate boards. A study of the economic elite's political relationships has shown that 88 percent of the

Table 13. Philippines, Shares in Employment and Value Added in Manufacturing
by Size of Firm, 1969–71

Firm Size (number of workers)	Number of Firms (1970)	Share of Total Employment	Share of Total Value Added[1]
		(in percent)	
1–5................	58,500[2]	71.2 }	10.1
6–19..............	8,340	5.0 }	
20–99............	1,900	4.8	9.5
100–199.......... }	260	2.0	10.3
200+ .... }		17.0	70.1
TOTAL	69,000	100.0	100.0

[1] Value added is the difference between the value of goods and the cost of materials or supplies that are used in producing them. It is a gauge of the relative importance of an industry because it measures that industry's contribution to the economy rather than its gross sales.
[2] Estimate based on available data.

Source: Based on information from International Labour Organization, *Sharing in Development: A Programme of Employment, Equity, and Growth for the Philippines*, Geneva, 1974, p. 142.

thirty-three private commercial banks existing in 1963 had public officials or their close relatives on the boards of directors.

The protected Philippine market also reinforced the already important role of foreign investors. Foreign manufacturers, threatened with the loss of their market in the Philippines as a result of import controls, were attracted to establish industries there in the 1950s and early 1960s. Government policy encouraged joint ventures by foreign and domestic investors in import-substitution enterprises. Oil refining, pharmaceuticals, and metallic and nonmetallic manufacturing, as well as wholesale trade and commerce, were dominated largely by American investment. Between 1950 and 1963 American investment in commerce and manufacturing rose from US$53 to US$340 million. The growth within these two sectors exceeded the total growth in American direct investment in the Philippines and reflected the system's powerful incentives to invest in manufacturing for the domestic market and in final processing and distributing facilities.

Manufacturing was heavily concentrated in the Manila area and adjoining provinces. In large part this reflected economic and market considerations, such as the heavy reliance on equipment, semiprocessed products, and certain raw materials imported through Manila, the country's main port. In part it reflected the social preferences of elite businessmen and the advisability of locating close to the heart of political and financial power. Data indicated that 45 percent of all industrial workers in the organized industrial sector (comprising those firms employing five or more workers) were employed in the greater Manila area in 1969. More detailed information for establishments employing twenty or more workers indicated that 156,000 of a total of 332,000 industrial workers were employed in greater Manila, 100,000 in other parts of Luzon, and only 76,000 in the rest of the country, chiefly in Negros, Cebu, and three industrial centers in Mindanao.

Policy and Institutional Reforms

By the end of the 1960s it was apparent that the industrialization policies of the 1950s and 1960s had resulted in growth that was both disappointing and costly. Largely because of the relative failure of the earlier policies, the government enacted the Investment Incentives Act in 1967 to provide a policy and institutional environment for the achievement of economic and social goals. Through this legislation the government hoped to exert a greater influence over private investment decisions.

The Investment Incentives Act provided substantial incentives relating to the import or domestic purchase of capital goods and to depreciation and taxable income—especially if the latter was reinvested—for firms in preferred areas in manufacturing, mining, and agricultural industries. As amended by presidential decree in 1973, labor intensity was added as an additional criterion for the granting of incentives. The government hoped that these incentives would provide, through the Board of Investments (BOI) created to administer the act, a degree of control over the creation of new capacity in desired areas that would avoid the problems of inadequate scale and excess capacity characteristic of the 1960s.

An outgrowth of the Investment Incentives Act was the Export Incentives Act of August 1970. Like the investment act, the Export Incentives Act is administered by the BOI. The BOI has annually issued an export priorities plan indicating product areas that qualify for export incentives according to criteria of competitiveness, foreign exchange contribution, and profitability to the economy. The industrial strategy of the government placed such strong emphasis on the growth of manufactured exports that projects having export potential were allowed exemption from the labor-intensity criteria of 1973.

The deteriorating balance-of-payments situation of the late 1960s also led to reforms in the area of exchange rates and financing. Devaluation of the peso in 1970 raised the price of imports and made exports more attractive; subsequently the peso was allowed to float freely, and toward the end of 1974 and in July 1975 it depreciated further against the United States dollar. The more realistic exchange rate made Philippine manufactured exports more price competitive. Although those industrial firms heavily dependent upon imported materials were hard hit by the original devaluation, the resulting problems appeared to have been ironed out.

Since its inception the BOI has sought to promote, through its investment priorities, several additional aims: more favorable ratio of capital to employment, balanced regional development, growth of small-scale industries, and more efficient use of foreign capital resources. In pursuit of its objectives it established policies for linking employment and export criteria to new investment proposals. Especially in such problem industries as steel and cement, it has helped formulate policy that is both profitable and economically more efficient. In such industries as synthetic fibers, plastic resins, and automobile components, the BOI has moved to limit the number of enterprises to avoid problems of excess capacity.

Initial BOI involvement in the area of small- and medium-scale industry emphasized finding markets and removing institutional rather than financial barriers. Subsequently, however, there has been increasing realization of the economic, and particularly the employment potential of small- and medium-scale industry. Since 1973 the Philippine government's interest in expanding small- and medium-scale industries has been highlighted by the participation of the International Bank for Reconstruction and Development (IBRD, commonly known as the World Bank). Through the medium of a US$30 million loan, two priority needs of small and medium enterprises were to be addressed: increased access to sources of credit and technical assistance aimed at solving problems of production, marketing, and accounting. Although there is no one uniform definition of the terms *small* and *medium scale*, the World Bank has included all units employing up to ninety-nine people, thus including the so-called unorganized manufacturing sector composed of very small firms.

In the period after the enactment of the Investment Incentives Act, the government moved to more active forms of industrial promotion by playing a greater planning role in industry. The BOI, through its annual investment priorities plan, lists those activities that qualify for incentives. The plan also presents a broad range of data on market site, production requirements, and levels of protection needed. Qualifying activities are divided into preferred nonpioneer and preferred pioneer categories. A preferred area is defined according to several economic criteria, the most important of which is measured capacity—a market with room for enough extra capacity to justify at least one "recommended economic size plant." A pioneer industry operating in new product and process areas receives tax incentives on a sliding scale and some tariff protection. Only in a pioneer industry may the equity share of foreign investors go up to 100 percent. Preferred areas are allowed no more than 40-percent foreign equity participation unless Filipino investment has not been made after three years of preferred area designation.

The major reforms affecting industry enacted after martial law in 1972 were the creation of the National Economic Development Authority (NEDA) and the creation of the Department of Industry. The BOI, although originally designed as the principal regulatory agency that would guide industrial investment, had by default become increasingly involved in policymaking. In order to relieve it of an enormous work overload NEDA was created in 1973 and made the principal policymaking institution responsible for the preparation of the four-year development plan (see ch. 12).

In June 1974 the Department of Industry was created by presidential decree and made "the primary policy, planning, programming, coordinating, implementing and administrative entity of the executive branch of government in the development, expansion and diversification of industry." The department had three subdivisions: the Commission on Small and Medium Industries, the Bureau of Industrial Coordination, and the Bureau of Industrial Information and Programs. The two bureaus were concerned with policy and programs relating to medium- and large-scale industries, defined as firms with total assets over ₱1 million (for value of the peso—see Glossary) or 100 or more employees. The commission was made responsible for coordinating all small- and medium-scale industry assistance programs and for providing direct technical assistance to such firms, particularly those located outside of Manila; these assistance programs, however, defined small scale as firms having twenty to ninety-nine employees, thus slighting the unorganized sector in which employment tended to be concentrated.

MANUFACTURING

Manufacturing industries occupy a significant place in the economy. Production has steadily expanded and diversified since World War II. Growth, however, has been relatively slow since the early 1960s. Manufacturing accounted for about 21 percent of NDP in 1963, declined gradually to about 18 percent by 1969, and recovered to about 21 percent in 1972. There was an upsurge in manufacturing production in 1973. The largest increases were in food products, up 24 percent; basic metals, up 149 percent; and wood products, up 27 percent. Substantial increases were recorded in the production of nontraditional manufacturers for the export market, such as garments, textile fabrics, cement, electronic parts, and wood products. Preliminary estimates made in January 1975 showed that in 1974 manufacturing accounted for 21.6 percent of NDP at constant 1967 prices, or 26 percent at current prices.

Production is primarily centered on processing and assembly operations comprising food, beverages, tobacco, and rubber products; textiles, clothing, and footwear; pharmaceuticals; paints; plywood and veneer; paper and paper products; small appliances; and automobiles. Among heavier industries there is some production of cement, glass, industrial chemicals, fertilizer, iron and steel, and refined petroleum products.

A considerable number of manufacturing enterprises suffer from a weak capital base, shortage of credit and foreign exchange, and inadequate power and transportation facilities. Government programs to strengthen industrial development have included protective import duties and taxes, refinancing of distressed industries, and investment and export incentive legislation under which tax and credit incentives are granted to selected industries and firms. In addition the government has played a major role in expansion of such infrastructure elements as telecommunications, roads, and electric power and has contributed to private industrial growth through such long-term financing institutions as the DBP.

Manufacturing, which accounts for over two-thirds of all industrial activity, is predominantly privately owned; and large-scale, vertically integrated, capital-intensive units accounted for the major share of production. Until 1969 manufactured exports (excluding traditional manufactures related to sugarcane, coconut, pineapple, abaca, and tobacco) accounted for only 6 to 7 percent of total exports. Since then, largely in response to the peso devaluation, exports of various manufactures have risen; and in 1972 they accounted for about 13 percent of total exports. Conscious of the scope available for growth and employment in industries directed to foreign markets, the government has taken measures to encourage export industries.

One of the main government projects to stimulate export production was the creation of the Export Processing Zone Authority. This agency was charged with the responsibility for constructing and operating the Free Trade Zone at Mariveles on Bataan, which allows enterprises to bring in needed capital or raw materials for processing, manufacturing, or assembling for export, free from customs duties and internal revenue taxes. Development work on this site was completed by 1975, but transport links with Manila harbor and facilities for labor, banking, and communications still required work. In November 1974 there were about a dozen export-oriented companies operating at Bataan and at least the same number constructing premises. There were expected to be over 100 export producers in the zone by 1978, exporting industrial goods exceeding US$300 million in value. The biggest plant nearing completion in late 1975 was Ford Motor Company's US$35 million motor vehicle stamping plant—the biggest foreign investment made since the imposition of martial law.

Through the 1960s and into the early 1970s manufacturing contributed disappointingly little toward alleviating the persistent problems of unemployment and underemployment. Between 1960 and 1970 employment in manufacturing grew at an annual rate of about 2.5 percent; in 1972 it fell by 0.3 percent and in 1973 by 3.3 percent. The share of manufacturing in total employment actually dropped from 12.1 percent in 1960 to 10.7 percent in 1973. The distribution of manufacturing employment in the Philippines is unusually dualistic in its concentration in the unorganized cottage industry sector on the one hand and in a few very large firms on the other. Although data on employment are not completely reliable, it appeared that 1.4 million people were employed in the manufacturing sector in 1970. The organized sector (establishments having five or more employees) accounted for about 29 percent. The balance were employed in units of five or fewer employees. In an effort to reduce these economic and employment disparities, the government was endeavoring to promote small and medium-sized enterprises.

The government also sought a wider geographical distribution of organized manufacturing employment and appeared to recognize the complementary role of large and small industries in the process. It encouraged expansion of some large industries in areas where little or no industry had developed and prohibited such growth in the greater Manila area. The textile industry was an example of this trend, for it is known to provide substantial employment per unit of capital invested. It was felt, however, that some large industries had substantial infrastructural and other support needs that could be provided more economically in areas of industrial concentration. It was therefore considered impractical to insist on dispersal of individual units unless those units were large enough or dependent on local availability of raw materials to an extent that justified the creation of necessary supporting facilities at a new location.

Various small-scale industries are quite suitable for development of a geographically dispersed pattern because of their link with domestic raw materials and rural markets. In the past the government did not take adequate steps to develop small industries as a means of regional development. In 1974, with financial assistance from the World Bank, the BOI embarked upon an experimental regional development plan based on small industry promotion for several provinces in the northern Mindanao area. The experiment was to focus on the scope for agriculture-based and labor-intensive small industries, such as feed mills, lumber products, tanneries, handicrafts, and power tillers, using local cooperatives and small entrepreneurs as promoters. The BOI was to provide technical assistance and arrange for financial assistance from the DBP.

Food processing, beverages, and tobacco have consistently been the most valuable categories of consumer-oriented manufacturing. Food-processing plants are widely dispersed throughout the islands. Fish, meat, and fruits are canned locally for domestic consumption. Pineapple canning, which is the only large-scale food-processing industry with the exception of sugar, produces for export as well as for the domestic market. The sugar-processing industry is important both as an employer of labor and as an important earner of foreign exchange (see ch. 13). One firm, the long-established San Miguel Corporation, dominated the beverage industry. It produced all the beer consumed in the country and also manufactured soft drinks, such as Coca-Cola, under licensing agreements. In 1974 it was reported that twenty-six tobacco firms manufactured cigars and cigarettes for domestic use and export. One factory in Manila, Telangtan Bros. and Sons, dominated the market and produced such United States brands as Marlboro and Philip Morris.

The pulp and paper industry began in 1941 with the construction of the world's first bagasse pulp mill. Since then the industry has expanded to include six integrated pulp and paper mills with an annual capacity of 194,000 tons. Paper and paperboard consumption has grown at a higher rate than in other countries with comparable per capita national income. The Philippines lacks long-fiber pulpwood but has large short-fiber pulpwood and bagasse resources that could be utilized both to satisfy growing domestic demand and to provide export earnings.

The textile industry, once described as overcrowded as a result of a policy structure that discouraged textile exports and saturated the domestic market, was again granted investment incentives by the BOI in the early 1970s for new textile mills to be located outside the greater Manila area and for export expansion. The garment industry made a substantial contribution to both exports and employment. In 1973 there were approximately 54,000 workers in organized units and about 160,000 outworkers. Wearing apparel and undergarments have become far more important than the traditional embroidered goods for both domestic and export markets. The industry, through its links with foreign principals in the area of raw materials, product specifications, and marketing channels, had prospects for substantial expansion. Although in the 1950s and 1960s the garment industry did not provide much stimulus to the domestic textile industry, this situation had changed by 1975 as textile mills became increasingly interested in forward integration into the garment industry.

The footwear industry includes both large and small factories. The industry is labor intensive and has been an active exporter for years. In common with other small-scale industries it required government and institutional help to obtain financial credit for expansion. The expansion of this industry in line with government policy could have significant implications for regionally dispersed industrialization and employment generation.

Foreign investment in manufacturing has consisted largely of United States investment, which was allowed easy access to the Philippines under various bilateral agreements. This investment was largely aimed at establishing import-substitution industries. As these opportunities declined, so did foreign investment. In the early 1970s, however, foreign participation in manufacturing was still important, and foreign-controlled corporations accounted for around one-fifth of manufacturing NDP.

The government's strategies in the early 1970s placed high priority on the development of small and medium industries and on regional dispersal. Data indicated that these efforts had still been only marginally successful by 1975. The manufacturing sector was still concentrated in a few big firms (see fig. 10). In 1973 the 100 largest companies accounted for 68 percent of total sales and 60 percent of net profits. The share was

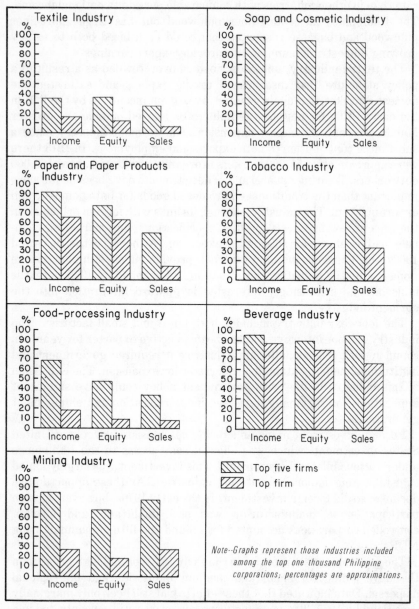

Figure 10. *Philippines, Corporate Domination in Selected Industries by Percentage of Industry Total, 1972*

Source: Based on information from *"Business Asia* Analyzes Concentration in 12 Philippine Industries," *Business Asia*, V, No. 9, Hong Kong, March 1, 1974, pp. 68–69.

reduced, however, to 56 percent of sales and 52 percent of net profits in 1974. Whether income concentration continued to decline would serve as a major indicator of the success of stated government goals.

MINING

The Philippines has rich deposits of such minerals as gold, iron, coal copper, manganese, and chromite (see fig 11). The actual mineral base is still only imperfectly known, however; only slightly more than 10 percent of the nation's area had been systematically surveyed for minerals by the early 1970s. As geologic structures and composition become better known, there is strong indication that the number of proven mineral reserves will be increased tremendously.

Base metals, especially copper, accounted for the bulk of aggregate mineral output in 1974. The Philippines is the largest copper producer in Asia and also ranks among the top producers of refractory chromite in the world. At the end of 1971 the Philippines had an estimated copper ore reserve of 1.7 billion tons. Other ranking mineral exports included iron, chromite, nickel, manganese, and gold. The rest of the country's metallic exports, such as platinum, palladium, lead, molybdenum, and cadmium, are by-products in the metallurgical processing of other ores and concentrates and follow a production trend similar to that of the primary metals to which they are related.

Nonmetallic minerals consist primarily of construction materials—cement, adobe, sand, gravel, earth, marble, perlite, and lime. The value of the output of cement, produced by seventeen firms, increased by 52 percent in 1973 over 1972. This increase accounted for a substantial share of the total increase in the gross value of mineral production and was explained largely by the expanded national demand brought about by the increasing tempo of infrastructure and other construction projects initiated in the period.

Oil exploration, a sporadic activity in the Philippines since 1896, received a boost in late 1972 when President Ferdinand E. Marcos decreed highly liberalized terms for foreign participation. Since then service contracts have been signed with the government's Petroleum Board by consortia involving local concessionaires and international companies. Some US$70 million has been committed for periods of from five to seven years, and fresh drilling efforts were initiated, chiefly in the southern Sulu and Palawan waters where interest has been heightened by recent strikes in nearby Malaysia. Foreign companies that joined in the oil exploration included Chevron-Texaco, Phillips, Champlin Philippines, Mosbacher, and Sun Oil of the United States; Husky Oil of Canada; Superior-Endeavor of Australia; and the Chinese Petroleum Corporation of Nationalist China.

The mining sector accounted for 2.4 percent of NDP in 1973. From 1963 to 1973 the mining sector grew by 11.3 percent annually while NDP grew by 4.8 percent. A decline in mining's growth rate, however, took place in

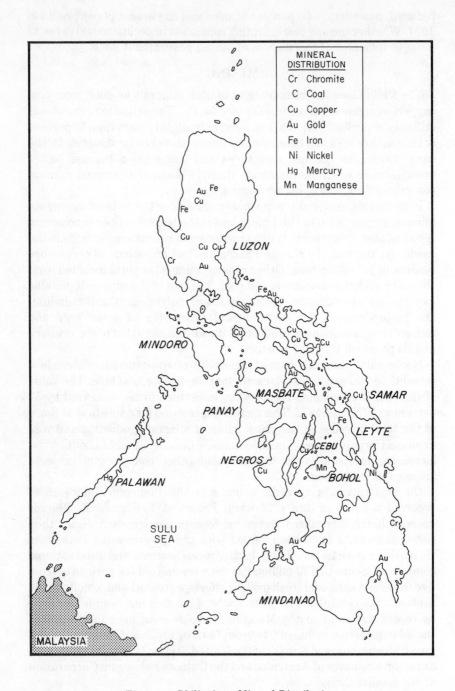

MINERAL
DISTRIBUTION
Cr Chromite
C   Coal
Cu Copper
Au Gold
Fe Iron
Ni Nickel
Hg Mercury
Mn Manganese

Figure 11. Philippines, Mineral Distribution

1974. Copper output rose by 4.9 percent in the first quarter of 1974, primarily in response to the high copper prices prevailing in the early part of the year. Copper production has tapered off since mid-1974, however, largely as a result of import reductions by Japan, a fall in copper prices from a high of US$1.40 per pound in early 1974 to about US$0.58 by the summer of 1975, and a major company's technical problem of an excessively high arsenic content in its copper concentrate. Iron ore and chromite production declined in 1974 while coal and gold witnessed the onset of depletion of high-yielding mines. Stone quarrying and clay and land pit output rose by 22 percent in the first half of 1974 because of the increased demand for local raw materials for the construction sector in early 1974.

Despite the decline in overall production growth in 1974, mining continued to be the most profitable sector of Philippine industry in 1974. Although the Philippines' ten biggest corporations—on the basis of gross sales—included only one mining company, six of the ten corporate leaders in net profits earned were engaged in copper- and gold-mining operations. Marcopper Mining Corporation was the best earner among mining corporations. Other big earners were Philex Mining Corporation; Benguet Consolidated, a gold producer; and Atlas Consolidated, the eighth largest corporation in the Philippines in 1974.

Mining was second only to sugar as a foreign exchange earner in 1974, but the industry's contribution to GNP remained below 4 percent. Because of the high prices for mineral products prevailing during most of the year, Philippine mineral production increased in value by 31 percent over 1973. The value of metals output increased by only 24.3 percent, and that of nonmetals, such as cement, coal, and gypsum, rose by an average of 62.2 percent.

Although only a minor percentage of total nonmetal output, coal production increased to 50,746 tons in 1974 from 39,004 tons in 1973, and the value increased by 33.1 percent over that of the previous year. This reflected, in part, the new boost that the rising cost of energy has given the search for other forms of power in the Philippines.

Production of all precious metals, including gold, decreased in quantity. But the overall value rose by 55.3 percent from 1973 to 1974. Gold production, at 16,682 kilograms (one kilogram equals 2.2 pounds) in 1974, dropped by 6.3 percent from the preceding year, but the value rose by 53.9 percent.

Despite the slowdown in the growth rate of the mining sector in 1974, future prospects for the sector appeared good because of the existence of untapped mineral resources and substantial investment in projects to process local minerals. As of January 1975 sixteen new copper mines were either under development or in the prospecting stage. At the same time the Philippines sought to reduce its dependence on the Japanese market for ores and concentrate, and there were plans to establish two smelter-refining projects. Not only will local processing increase the value added of exports—by about 20 percent—but it will enable the Philippines to diversify its export markets.

One of the largest expansion projects being pushed was that of Atlas Consolidated, which operated the biggest open-pit copper mines in Southeast Asia. A new property, the Carmen mine, which adjoins the mines in operation on the island of Cebu, was being developed and, when in full operation, will increase Atlas' existing 70,000-ton daily capacity to over 100,000 tons.

A major new mining industry was nickel mining and processing. The Marinduque Mining and Industrial Corporation nickel project became operational in 1975. The complex is located on Nonoc Island off northeastern Mindanao. The plant will have a capacity of 75 million pounds of nickel metal and alloy. When in full operation the project is expected to earn an additional US$100 million annually.

According to regulations promulgated after the establishment of the commonwealth, resources in the ground are the property of the state, and exploration and exploitation may be carried on only with the sanction of the government. Exploitation of natural resources was reserved to citizens of the Philippines or to corporations or associations at least 60 percent owned by citizens. Special exceptions were granted in 1946 to United States citizens, conferring rights of exploitation of natural resources and all other kinds of economic activity equal to those of Filipinos. In 1974, however, the pattern of American rights changed (see ch. 15).

The government moved, through the Mineral Resources Development Decree of 1974, to strengthen the law relating to mining. Lease and exploration requirements were made more rigorous by establishing eighty-one hectares (one hectare equals 2.47 acres) as the minimum claim area, thus reducing the proliferation of small claims. The decree also provides for the Bureau of Mines to carry out exploration for leaseholders and to enter into contracts with foreign contractors, whose share is not to exceed 40 percent.

Government measures have also reduced some of the speculative potential in mining entrepreneurship. The mining depletion allowance, which formerly amounted to 50 percent of gross revenue, was completely eliminated, although it may be replaced by a less generous 120-percent write-off of development costs. At the same time the government has made greater use of export taxes and premiums to skim off profits when prices are high. This practice was suspended with the fall in mineral prices in 1974 but will almost certainly resume when prices recover.

Private ownership predominates in the mining industry. The individual companies tend to be large, and data for 1971 indicated that 50 percent of all employment generated was in firms having more than 500 workers. In addition the industry tends to be dominated by a few large firms. In 1974 the top five corporations, out of a total of nineteen, accounted for close to 80 percent of all sales and over 80 percent of profits in the mining sector.

COTTAGE INDUSTRIES

Cottage industries are the most dispersed of all Philippine manufacturing enterprises. They are less dependent on power and tend to process locally available materials. Two forms of cottage manufacturing activity have developed, namely, household industries manufacturing traditional products and handicrafts for the domestic market and for export and small workshops providing services and minor product fabrication for rural areas. Apart from the limited use of capital equipment and the probable underestimation of value added in national accounts, an explanation for the generally low productivity of workers in this sector is the part-time nature of many of the activities pursued. To a large extent the motivation for small-scale, rurally based enterprise was to add to meager household incomes in a rural economy that was being transformed from barter to cash.

Approximately three-fourths of the smallest establishments are in food industries and wearing apparel. There are a large number of textiles, metal products, electrical machinery, and transport equipment, providing services as well as fabricating small parts and components. Efforts to improve the handicraft industries have led to regional specialization in such crafts as woodcarving, embroidery work, abaca products, *tikiw* fiber for baskets and bags, pina items, and brasswork.

There is no one uniform definition to differentiate cottage industries and small-scale industries. Initially the government identified cottage industries as its policy target for the expansion of industry out of Manila, and in 1962 it created the National Cottage Industries Development Authority (NACIDA). NACIDA defines a cottage industry as a small-scale economic activity carried on for profit mainly in the home and principally by family members. In addition a cottage industry unit should not have a capital investment in excess of ₱15,000. Under the law certain incentives are provided to cottage industries, including exemption from business taxes and from the minimum wage law.

Data on cottage industries are scanty. The law that created NACIDA provided for registration of cottage industries with that authority as a requirement for making them eligible for tax exemptions and incentives, but registration was not compulsory. In 1974 there were 50,000 units registered with NACIDA; unofficial estimates placed the number of active units at about 35,000. Perhaps an equal number were not registered.

Cottage industries' export earnings, as reported by NACIDA, doubled in 1973, making them the sixth-ranking export group. Ninety countries bought cottage industry products from the Philippines: the United States, Japan, and the Federal Republic of Germany (West Germany) were the three largest buyers. Woodcrafts were the major export group, followed by needlecrafts, shellcraft, embroidery, mat weaving, and bamboo and rattan items. Through its Buy-Filipino campaigns and product acceptance on the world market, this sector has good potential for expansion.

The government has actively supported handicraft activities. In order to satisfy demand, adjust to style changes, and maintain quality standards, the Design Center Philippines was created by Presidential Decree 279 in August 1973. The center's mission was to create, develop, promote, and improve product design of handicraft industries. The center also maintained a design research and product development program.

NACIDA reported that in 1972 cottage industries provided employment for more than 800,000 workers. Impartial observers, however, placed the number much higher since NACIDA only accounted for registered firms. Cottage industries, being labor intensive, undemanding of major capital investment, and rurally located, are in general congruence with the Four Year Development Plan (1974–77), which calls for promotion of export-oriented activities and dispersal of industries to the countryside. In addition to those cottage industries producing handicrafts and exotic curios, rural industries engaged in producing a variety of other items with a mass market potential were regarded as having an important role in improving rural income distribution and reducing pressures for migration to urban areas.

CONSTRUCTION

In 1974 construction accounted for approximately 2.6 percent of NDP. The growth rate of value added in construction was higher than that of NDP during the first half of the 1960s, slowed to a standstill in the latter part of the decade, and picked up again in 1971, 1972, and 1973, mainly because of the substantial growth in government construction.

Construction is a sector having a high potential for absorbing labor productively, especially unskilled labor. The growth of its labor force has been greater than that of the total labor force. The technology of the sector, however, has been biased toward capital and import intensity. In the 1960s the capital-to-output ratio was high: investment by the construction sector in durable equipment grew at an annual rate of 25 percent, but the growth of output amounted to only 9 percent, reflecting the increasing capital intensity.

Available evidence indicates that construction activity, like manufacturing, was concentrated in urban areas. Similarly between 1965 and 1972 almost half (47.5 percent) of government expenditure on infrastructure took place in only two regions: Rizal Province (which includes Manila) and central Luzon (the provinces of Pampanga and Nueva Ecija).

The heavy concentration of construction in urban areas and central Luzon meant that a more equal regional distribution of construction was limited. Even within the urban areas there was comparatively little construction of low-cost housing. There was some evidence that the government's credit institution in the housing field favored government employees having high salaries while very little public effort went into low-cost housing or improving the condition of squatter settlements.

The government appeared to recognize that the level of public infrastructure expenditure has been inadequate in the past, and the 1974–77 development plan stated: "Public construction will remain the biggest force propelling total construction activity to higher levels. Efforts at infrastructure development remain a top priority of the Development Plan." For the period of the Plan, investment in construction was to be allocated to: transportation (highways, railroads, airports, air navigation, and ports), 43.2 percent; water resources (irrigation, water supply, flood control, and drainage), 28.4 percent; power and rural electrification, 18.0 percent; buildings and schools, 5.8 percent; telecommunications, 4.0 percent; and preinvestment studies, 0.6 percent. About 40 percent of the program was to be funded by foreign assistance.

POWER

The power sector experienced rapid growth in the 1960s. Despite the expansion, electricity reached only about 20 percent of the population, mostly in big cities and towns, by the end of the decade; this proportion climbed to 30 percent in 1973. Installed capacity increased by 15 percent during the 1966–70 period. In order to meet a continuing growth in demand for energy, it was expected that capacity would have to increase by at least 19 percent per year through 1977. Because of the projected growth in demand and the larger share of future power to be provided by the government-owned National Power Corporation (NPC), investment in power would have to increase substantially.

The country is not rich in known energy resources. Hydroelectric sources, which accounted for about one-third of installed power capacity in the mid-1970s, are limited. Geothermal sources have not been exploited, but they could provide a significant energy base in future years. Thermal and hydroelectric energy provided 92 percent of the total electrical energy generated in the Philippines in 1974. A greater reliance on thermal power, however, could add balance-of-payments problems because of the increased demand for imported oil. The effect of oil prices was already apparent in 1974, when total sales of electricity declined by 1.9 percent from a volume of 5,567 million kilowatt-hours in 1973 to 5,459 million kilowatt-hours. Sales were lower to all sectors except the industry sector, which increased consumption by 2.5 percent in 1974 over 1973.

The sector has been dominated by two utilities—the Manila Electric Company (MERALCO) and the NPC, which together accounted for about 90 percent of total power generation. There were also some 460 small private or municipal utilities that distributed power received from

NPC and MERALCO or produced by their own generating stations. Of the 30 percent of the population enjoying the benefits of electricity in 1973, some 61 percent resided in Manila or other urban centers. The government hoped to establish electric cooperatives and provide electricity to all provinces by 1977. Its aim was to bring low-cost electricity to the rural areas by using both geothermal and nuclear power.

In 1973 about 77 percent of the total installed capacity of all electric plants in the Philippines belonged to the private sector. This proportion was expected to fall as a result of a presidential decree in November 1972 that stated: "It is the ultimate objective of the state for the NPC to own and operate as a single integrated system all generating facilities supplying electric power to the entire area embraced by any grid set up by the NPC."

Since imported petroleum provides more than 90 percent of the Philippines' total energy requirements, the higher petroleum prices that commenced in 1973 had an impact upon domestic power prices. MERALCO rate increases have been rather large, reflecting its almost total dependence on fuel oil for power generation. NPC's rate increases have not been as substantial because most of its generating capacity is in hydroelectric power plants.

In 1973 of a total of 1,002 electric plants in the country, 954 were driven by internal combustion engine, thirty by thermal power, and eighteen by hydroelectricity. Although thermal plants constituted only 3 percent of the total, they generated 60 percent of the total installed capacity. The government's power development program was aimed at reducing the dependence on oil for power generation.

CHAPTER 15

FOREIGN ECONOMIC RELATIONS, TRADE, AND TRANSPORTATION

Foreign economic relations in 1975 were in a stage of transition characterized by a loosening of the ties of dependence upon the United States as a market for exports and the continued growth of Japan as a major supplier of imports. Dependence on the United States was established before World War II and was continued after the war by the provision of an eight-year period of mutual free trade as set forth in the Philippine Trade Act of 1946 (Bell Act). The special Philippine-American economic relationship was maintained under the Revised United States-Philippine Trade Agreement of 1955 (Laurel-Langley Agreement), which expired on July 4, 1974. The United States, traditionally the Philippines' major trading partner, has in recent years seen Japan assume that position. Trade has also increased with other countries of Asia, the Middle East, and Western Europe. Since 1974 Philippine trade with communist countries has increased greatly.

Exports have maintained the same basic pattern of dependence upon a few primary commodities that was established before World War II. The composition of imports, however, has changed. The emphasis on producer goods rather than consumer goods reflected the growing industrialization oriented toward the production of domestically produced consumer goods (see ch. 14).

Domestic trade was dualistic in character, consisting of modern trade outlets using sophisticated distribution methods in urban areas and trade by traditional means in rural areas. The government embarked in the early 1970s on a program to modernize and improve the country's transportation network, rehabilitation of the country's highways receiving particular attention.

PATTERNS IN FOREIGN ECONOMIC RELATIONS

The development of Philippine foreign economic relations combined elements that related both to its geographical location on the fringes of the Asian continent and to its changing political history. Trading relations with the outside world developed well before the initiation of the Spanish period in the early sixteenth century. The geographic location and character of the islands with their many ports made them a logical point of exchange for goods carried by traders of many nationalities, including Chinese, Indonesians, Annamese, and Indians. A barter trade developed between foreign traders and inhabitants of the various islands; local items, including gold, abaca, and coconuts, were exchanged for such products as bronze and iron, porcelains, metal fabrications, and jewelry. Trade tended to be localized, and no overall pattern developed throughout the archipelago, nor did any one island or port dominate this commerce.

Commerce expanded after the arrival of the Spanish in the early sixteenth century, and for a period the islands became the center of the galleon trade involving the reshipment of goods from China to Mexico and Spain via Manila. Products of Philippine origin constituted only a very small volume of exports, so few of the benefits of commerce accrued to Filipinos. Except for the brief British occupation of Manila from 1762 to 1764 the Philippines was officially closed by the Spanish to foreign commerce, although the old barter practices were continued in the areas outside of Spanish control. Significant expansion of foreign trade began when the port of Manila was opened to general foreign commerce in 1834. Its primacy as a port was founded upon the concentration of Spanish shipping there, the existing pattern of internal trade, and the relatively better facilities at Manila, as the seat of Spanish authority, than at other ports.

At the beginning of the nineteenth century China assumed a leading position in Philippine import trade, primarily as a legacy of the earlier galleon trade. The modern transformation of foreign commerce, however, resulted from the activities of British and American shippers engaged in trade with Philippine producers. By the late nineteenth century foreign commerce had assumed a characteristic pattern—raw materials comprising agricultural and forest products provided the exports in exchange for such imports as manufactured consumer and producer goods and various foodstuffs.

By 1898, when sovereignty of the Philippines passed from the Spanish to the Americans, the United States was the dominant market for Philippine products, absorbing from 30 to 40 percent of export production. Nevertheless between 1870 and 1898 the Philippines imported from the United States only between 2 and 6 percent of import requirements. Commencing with the United States acquisition of the islands and extending beyond the granting of independence in 1946, American commercial policy dictated the structure and growth of Philippine foreign economic relations through variants of mutual free trade.

During the Spanish regime preferential treatment was granted to Spanish goods and shipping. Beginning with the United States administration in 1901, steps initiating closer trading relations between the Philippines and the United States were undertaken by providing for reduced duties on import goods that Spain did not produce. This step, which had the effect of increasing Philippine dependence on American products, was accompanied by moves giving advantages to Philippine exports in the American market. Furthermore the United States

Supreme Court, as a result of the "Insular Cases," established the constitutional status of the Philippines as a nonforeign country for the purposes of trade and granted the United States Congress authority to formulate commercial policy governing such trade.

After the passage of the Philippine Trade Act of 1909 commercial relations entered a phase of reciprocal free trade whereby quota limitations were removed and duties on products entering the United States from the Philippines were eliminated. During this period, which continued until 1934, the character of the Philippines as an export-oriented economy was established. The demand for Philippine commodities during World War I, coupled with the high demand for sugar and coconut products in the following decade, greatly increased the value of exports. At the same time the free entry of manufactured goods from the United States discouraged industrialization.

With the establishment of the commonwealth in 1935, a new commercial policy was initiated, preparing for the termination of the preferential relations that had rendered Philippine foreign trade excessively dependent upon the United States for export markets and for manufactured consumer goods. The economic provisions contained within the Philippine Independence Act of 1934 (Tydings-McDuffie Act) stipulated an orderly transition to Philippine economic sovereignty in which the preferred position of each country within the market of the other would be reduced. Mutual free trade was to be continued until 1940 except in the cases of sugar, coconut oil, and cordage, upon which quotas were imposed. No restrictions were placed on United States exports to the Philippines. During the 1941–46 period Philippine exports were to be subject to a gradually increasing export tax, and full tariffs were to be paid after 1946, the scheduled independence date. The war with Japan interrupted this planned transition.

By 1940 the United States share of total Philippine trade had reached 81 percent. The orderly dismantling of the "special economic relationship" as provided by the Tydings-McDuffie Act was interrupted by World War II. Subsequently, although independence was granted on schedule, the United States Congress passed two linked pieces of legislation—the Philippine Trade Act of 1946 and the Philippine Rehabilitation Act of 1946—that impinged directly on Philippine economic sovereignty.

The Philippine Trade Act of 1946

The policy governing commerce between the new republic and the United States was defined in an executive agreement signed by the two governments in 1946. The Philippine Trade Act provided for an eight-year transitional period of tariff-free mutual trade to be followed by a twenty-year period in which each country would collect increasing proportions of usual tariff rates until full duties would be imposed on mutual trade beginning in 1974. In addition absolute quotas were continued on selected Philippine exports to the United States; the economically significant quotas—to be maintained at levels established in the Tydings-McDuffie Act—were on sugar, coconut oil, and cordage.

In addition to providing for a gradual elimination of the preferred trade position, the trade act included a number of infringements on Philippine sovereignty: a commitment not to levy export taxes—deemed necessary so as to ensure the profitability of export activities attractive to foreigners; a parity clause amendment to the Philippine constitution establishing equality of opportunity for United States citizens in the area of natural resource exploitation and the operation of public utilities; and a restriction on monetary autonomy through a Philippine commitment not to change the par value of the peso (for value of the peso—see Glossary) without agreement of the president of the United States. Although the Philippine agreement not to levy export taxes was reciprocated by the United States, the absence of exchange rate autonomy, establishment of United States citizens' parity rights, and the quota limitations on duty-free Philippine exports to the United States were not matched by comparable United States commitments.

The trade act was coupled with another piece of legislation, the Philippine Rehabilitation Act, which provided United States compensation for war damage suffered by the Philippines. This act had its origins in a 1943 amendment to the Tydings-McDuffie Act providing for the establishment of a joint commission to formulate measures for postwar rehabilitation as well as future trade relations. The rehabilitation act furnished war damage payments of US$620 million and extensive technical assistance by United States government agencies in restoring the economy to its prewar levels. The two acts were complementary since acceptance of the trade act—and the necessary constitutional amendment to allow the United States parity rights—was made the price for war damage payments. In view of the prevailing economic circumstances the Philippine leadership, although resentful of the infringement and after considerable controversy, had no alternative but to accept.

The eight-year free trade provision of the trade act, designed to provide the opportunity to rehabilitate a war-torn economy, achieved results that were not completely satisfactory. Given the free trade provision and an overvalued peso, imports soared, especially for nonessential items, and led to a severe drain on the country's foreign reserves. The level of imports over the eight-year span of free trade—about 20 percent of national expenditures—indicated the inadequacy of the country's production structure. This state of affairs highlighted the shortcomings of Philippine industrial efforts, especially in the manufacturing sector (see ch. 14).

The first eight years of the trade act witnessed significant changes in the commodity composition of Philippine imports. The pattern of exports, however, which had been characterized by excessive dependence on a few primary products, underwent little qualitative change. Major Philippine exports during this period paralleled the unbalanced prewar patterns, the primary agricultural sector being dominant. Coconut products, especially copra, accounted for an average of 51 percent of the total value of exports. Sugar in its various forms was the next most important export commodity, representing 19 percent of total export value. Other important exports during this period were abaca, cordage, and mineral ores.

Philippine imports during the first postwar decade reflected the adoption of an import-substituting industrialization policy (see ch. 14). The imposition of import controls in 1949 produced shifts in the commodity composition of imports. Imports of producer goods were stimulated while luxury imports were discouraged by government policy. Accordingly machinery and transport equipment, mineral fuels, and lubricants gained at the expense of textile yarns, fabrics, manufactures, footwear, and clothing. Food imports remained substantial through 1954, accounting for approximately one-fifth of total imports.

The mutual free trade policy and the prior colonial relationship tended to concentrate Philippine trade with the United States. Between 1946 and 1954 an average of 65 percent (by value) of total exports went to, and 75 percent (by value) of imports came from, the United States. Within Asia Japan was the only significant export market, and within Western Europe the United Kingdom, the Netherlands, and Belgium accounted for more than 50 percent of export value. The geographic composition of the import trade saw Indonesia join Japan as an important Asian supplier, the United Kingdom and Canada being other important suppliers.

The Laurel-Langley Agreement

In 1955 the Philippines and the United States signaled an end to the eight-year free trade period provided for in the 1946 trade act by signing the Revised United States-Philippine Trade Agreement of 1955. This agreement, usually called the Laurel-Langley Agreement after the chairmen of the Philippine and United States negotiating panels, was a compromise in which progress toward the American goal of normal third-country relations remained intact while concessions were granted to the Philippines.

Under the new agreement the Philippine government was granted control of its currency and was able to fix the exchange rate between the peso and the dollar. In like manner the parity rights that were conferred upon citizens of the United States under the earlier agreement were made reciprocal in the United States for citizens of the Philippines. The Laurel-Langley Agreement also modified many of the then existing provisions concerning quotas, export taxes, and the Philippine foreign exchange tax. Tariff rates on goods were revised to favor the Philippines. Duties were to be applied gradually over the period, maturing at expiration of the agreement in 1974, the preferences diminishing more rapidly for American than for Philippine products.

The concessions granted to the Philippines under the new agreement restored rights denied them under the 1946 agreement. In return the United States gained a provision that provided that "new limitations imposed by either party upon the extent to which aliens are accorded national treatment with respect to carrying on business activities with its territories, shall not be applied as against enterprises owned or controlled by citizens of the other party which are engaged in such activities therein at the time such new limitations are adopted." This provision, in which "national treatment" is explicitly extended to the citizens and enterprises of each country, provided American-owned business with protection against Philippine legislation restricting the economic activities of foreigners.

The Laurel-Langley Agreement resulted in a dramatic change in the commercial relations between the United States and the Philippines. Acceleration in the collection of Philippine duties on imports from the United States rapidly reduced the concentration of Philippine trade with the United States. By 1958, for example, the ratio for both imports and exports had declined to 50 percent. For the same three-year period total trade with Asia, especially Japan, increased, as did total trade with Western Europe.

As the era of special economic relations with the United States drew to a close, Philippine anxiety over the loss of American trade concessions was unmistakable. Under a Laurel-Langley Agreement provision that called for intergovernmental discussions in anticipation of the termination of the agreement, the Joint Preparatory Committee met in 1967 to discuss the concepts that would underlie a new instrument to replace the agreement. A divergence of interests was evident in that the Philippines favored a continuance of a preferential trade relationship beyond 1974, whereas the Americans were not interested in continuing the old system and favored moving toward the usual third-country basis.

A major Philippine concern over termination of the agreement was the status of the sugar quota. Of the various categories of major exports during the operative life of the Philippine Trade Act and the Laurel-Langley Agreement, sugar had proved to be wedded to the American market. From 1952 to 1974 Philippine exports of sugar usually matched the Philippine quota in the American market, and 98 percent of Philippine sugar exports went to the United States. The Philippine sugar industry developed solely on the basis of the United States quota. Foreign exchange generated by sugar exports to the United States was thought to be irreplaceable because from 1951 to 1969 the United States market price for sugar averaged US$53 per short ton greater than the average world market price. Philippine sugar production, which was relatively high cost and inefficient, had been entirely oriented toward the protected American market and was not considered competitive on the world market.

Parity rights, another backbone of Philippine-American economic relations, were to terminate at the expiration of the Laurel-Langley Agreement by mutual agreement as announced in a joint communiqué by presidents Lyndon B. Johnson and Ferdinand E. Marcos in December 1966. The agreement to abolish these rights did not make explicit the form that termination would take. The most important issue concerned the future of United States holdings acquired before or under parity.

The Philippine attitude toward termination of the Laurel-Langley Agreement was not characterized by a unanimity of viewpoint; in the late 1960s and early 1970s Filipino views varied in their degree of nationalism. In early 1972 a Supreme Court decision maintained that the expiration of both the Laurel-Langley Agreement and the parity amendment to the Philippine Constitution would automatically eliminate American rights, not only to acquire land but to retain land acquired since 1946. The discussion of land retention—for example, in the Constitutional Convention during the 1971–72 period—was characterized by a wide range of sentiments: from considerations of fairness to the American property holders upon termination of parity rights, through just compensation for divested land or an extended period for land divestment, to strongly nationalistic calls for immediate American divestment in 1974.

All uncertainty ended after martial law was declared. Although the government continued to insist that American firms comply with the constitutional restrictions on foreign landownership the government facilitated their doing so in ways that would permit them to continue operations. In some cases this meant the sale by an American firm of 60 percent of its corporate ownership to Philippine citizens. More frequently it meant transferring the land to Filipinos or Philippine organizations and leasing it back on a long-term basis, while retaining title to the facilities on the land. Long-term residents and former Filipino citizens were permitted to retain residential land not exceeding one-half hectare (one hectare equals 2.47 acres). In addition President Marcos granted a grace period for American firms to divest themselves of landholdings.

Philippine willingness to prolong parity rights was thought to stem partly from the cost of United States disinvestment and partly from fear that abrupt termination of parity rights might create an unfavorable investment climate in the future. By 1974 United States holdings were variously estimated to range from US$1 to US$2 billion. Of this, disinvestment could involve sums of between US$180 and US$900 million, having actually reached US$119 million by the early 1970s. Regarding new investment, the government was anxious to attract private foreign investment since foreign capital played an important part in its economic development strategy (see ch. 12). In addition inflows of foreign capital were heralded as bearing testimony to the order and stability of the post-martial-law society.

Several American companies have voiced objections to the government's decision that landownership, although legally acquired under the Laurel-Langley Agreement, could not continue after its expiration. They pointed out that ownership of land, if legally acquired under the laws of the land, became a vested right that could not be taken away after the laws changed. The Philippine government rejected this view in favor of its own interpretations. President Marcos issued two decrees in 1974, however, that made it possible for companies to use donation schemes for the transfer of land to Philippine entities. Many companies appeared to take advantage of this option, subsequently leasing back the property.

In 1975 there was speculation that the Philippines had softened its stance on parity in an effort to gain maximum concessions from the United States in negotiations over a new trade agreement. As of 1974 the Philippines had asked for reduction in tariffs for such commodities as coconut oil and Philippine mahogany plywood, on which the duties were higher than on competitive products. The United States, however, was not prepared to go beyond a system of generalized preferences as stipulated in the Trade Reform Act of 1973. The sugar quota ceased to be a significant negotiating item when the United States House of Representatives stopped all domestic and import quotas in 1974.

The initial economic impact of the expiration of the Laurel-Langley Agreement was not as great as feared. Several major export commodities, including copra, abaca, logs, chromite ore, copper ores and concentrates, and gold were on United States duty-free lists and thus not affected by the termination of preferential trade tariffs; for several years before 1974 these commodities accounted for almost 60 percent of the total value of Philippine exports. Because they were not subject to United States duties, they enjoyed no distinct advantage in the American market. Moreover primary exports in general benefited until mid-1974 from a rise in world prices and contributed to an increase in foreign exchange reserves, although the increase in oil prices after 1973 cut into these reserves. Sugar exports had been the main worry at the expiration of the agreement but, when the United States quota was lifted, the world market price was higher than the American market price, and the sugar industry was temporarily cushioned against the full impact of the loss.

The United States Department of Commerce announced in the summer of 1975 that negotiations for a replacement of the Laurel-Langley Agreement, which had been initiated in 1974, would resume in the autumn of 1975; they were, however, rescheduled to resume sometime in 1976. The expiration of the Laurel-Langley Agreement had no perceptible effect on the commercial and economic relations between the two countries since the United States continued to be the principal market for Philippine exports, absorbing 42 percent of the total export value in 1974, and since American equity investments rose in 1974 by 10 percent over the 1973 level.

New Foreign Economic Policy Moves

The response of the Philippine government to these changes in Philippine-American economic relations was to diversify foreign economic policy. A series of policy steps, especially after the declaration of martial law in 1972, were initiated, according to a high government official, in order to "insulate the country from the narrow confines of any special relations with a particular country." Among the steps taken were a vigorous investment policy to encourage the participation of all foreign nationals; application in 1973 for accession to the General Agreement on Tariffs and Trade (GATT), which makes available most-favored-nation status to all member nations; and, perhaps more important, a vigorous effort in trade promotion that saw the expansion of trade with new partners, including the communist countries.

Expanded economic ties with Japan were made official in 1974 by the ratification of the Treaty of Friendship, Commerce, and Navigation by presidential decree; the treaty had been awaiting approval from the Philippine Senate since 1961. The absence of a formal treaty had not prevented a steadily increasing trade between the two countries, however. The decade from 1957 to 1967 saw Philippine exports to Japan grow from 17 to 31 percent of total exports and imports increase from 10 to 27 percent of total imports. By June 1975 trade statistics indicated that Japan had replaced the United States as the Philippines top trading partner.

Trade with the communist nations of Europe, the Soviet Union, and the People's Republic of China (PRC) was also increased, representing a departure from earlier policy. The initiation of a more flexible trade policy toward these countries had political benefits, by recognizing the new pattern of great power competition, and economic benefits, through balancing the country's economic ties (see ch. 11). A Soviet mission arrived in Manila in 1973 to discuss oil exploration and a trade treaty; and in June 1975 a trade agreement was signed between the Philippines and the PRC.

The government introduced measures during 1973 to increase the attractiveness of foreign investment in the Philippines. These measures have included a more liberal policy in regard to the repatriation of capital and permitting foreign-owned enterprises whose activities were geared toward the export market to qualify for incentives under the Export Incentives Act of 1970 (see ch. 14). The success of this policy was attested to by the increasing diversification of foreign investment applications. The breakdown of the value of applications received during 1974 was United States, 21 percent; Europe, 20 percent; Australia and Canada, 18 percent; Japan, 14 percent; and other countries, 27 percent. At the end of 1970, in contrast, 80 percent of the foreign investment applications had come from the United States.

TRENDS IN FOREIGN TRADE

The Philippines has traditionally had a trade deficit (see fig. 12). Except for 1973, when world prices for Philippine products were quite high, the value of imports exceeded the value of exports. There was little

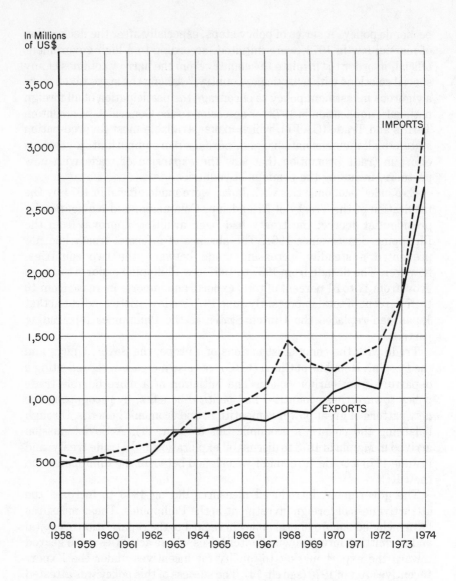

In Millions of US$

Figure 12. Philippines, Exports and Imports, 1958-74

change in the composition of foreign trade between World War II and the mid-1970s. The country remained almost completely dependent upon primary products as the source of its exports. Although exports of manufactured goods began to rise after 1970, they were still only 12 percent of total merchandise exports in 1973. In view of the recession in the economies of key trading partners and the competition posed by the country's nearby Asian neighbors, the short-run prospects for a major substitution of manufactured goods for exports of primary products was judged to be dim by economic analysts in the mid-1970s.

Imports have shifted from an emphasis on consumer goods before 1949 to an increase in producer goods since then. Imports have tended to be higher than exports, accounting for periodic balance-of-payments problems. The trade account, which turned from its traditional deficit in 1973, reverted sharply to a deficit in 1974 in the face of a doubling of imports, caused mainly by a nearly threefold increase in the import bill and an increase in non-oil imports. The trade deficit in 1974 amounted to the equivalent of approximately US$770 million. Invisible earnings made up for part of the deficit, and extensive foreign private credits were obtained, enabling the Philippines to achieve an overall surplus for the year and to maintain a high reserve level. The Philippines also took advantage of a special oil facility allocated to the country by the International Monetary Fund (IMF) as well as substantial foreign loans provided by the International Bank for Reconstruction and Development (IBRD, commonly known as the World Bank) and other international lending institutions, including the Asian Development Bank (ADB).

The direction of Philippine trade has altered considerably. The period from 1955 to the mid-1970s witnessed a decline in dependence upon the United States both as a supplier of goods and as a market. By 1974 the Philippines had two major trading partners—Japan and the United States—between whom about two-thirds of the country's total trade was divided. By 1973 Japan had taken over as the leading trading partner, although in 1974 the United States regained the top spot. Midyear statistics for 1975 indicated that Japan would again be the Philippines' major trading partner. Beyond these two nations trade was carried out with nations of Western Europe, particularly those of northwestern Europe, and with various nations of the Middle East upon whom the Philippines was largely dependent for oil.

Composition of Trade

Exports

In 1974 the total value of exports was the equivalent of US$2.7 billion, an increase of about 42 percent over US$1.9 billion in 1973. The 1975 figures were less favorable, however; preliminary estimates placed the value of exports at the equivalent of US$2.3 billion. Although primary exports jumped in value from 1972 to 1974, almost all of this increase was because of increased prices for the major export groups—coconuts, sugar, copper, and forest products. In fact there were sharp declines in the export volumes of coconut and forest products. These declines were attributed to the continued effects of the 1972-73 drought and poor coconut yields since 1973 because of widespread harvesting of immature nuts to take advantage of high prices. The drop in export volume of logs was attributed to a slowdown in construction activity in Japan and the United States. Sugar production increased by 7 percent in 1974 over the 1973 levels while earnings more than doubled, jumping from an equivalent of US$274.7 million in 1973 to US$737.4 million in 1974. By early 1975, however, sugar too felt the effects of price fluctuations as world prices plummeted from US$0.89 per pound before 1974 to about US$0.12 per pound by June 1975. Prices of the other major exports had declined earlier and remained low throughout 1975 while prices of petroleum and other imports continued to rise.

The commodities exported were largely raw materials and slightly processed agricultural and mineral products, many of which were already important before the beginning of the twentieth century. The composition of exports has remained relatively unchanged since 1949, although there were changes in the value and ranking of commodities. In 1974 the ten principal exports were, in descending order of value, sugar, copper concentrates, coconut oil, logs and lumber, copra, gold, dessicated coconut, bananas, abaca, and canned pineapple (see table 14). This group accounted for almost 79 percent of the total value of exports that year. Among other less important products that nevertheless contributed to total export value were cement, petroleum pitch and residue, and plywood.

The Philippine government has expressed concern about the narrow range of primary products earning the foreign exchange required to import commodities needed for industrialization of the country. Long-range plans for the improvement of foreign trade have taken into consideration the desirability of developing exportable industrial commodities as a counterbalance to price fluctuations in the world market that affect primary product exports. Such a development would also be a hedge against loss of exports of primary products occasioned by natural disasters. Although there was progress in 1973—nontraditional industrial exports accounting for 12 percent of total merchandise exports—1974 saw a falling off to 9 percent. Projections through 1976 predict industrial exports leveling off at about 10 percent of total exports. Nontraditional exports that have contributed most to export earnings included textile products, clothing, footwear, engineering industry products, and handicrafts.

High prices for the Philippines' chief exports, including coconut products, sugar, copper, and wood products, were largely responsible for an increase in merchandise receipts of almost 70 percent in 1973. In mid-1974, however, a large trade deficit appeared, largely because the growth in export prices moderated while import prices rose rapidly. This abrupt deterioration in the external terms of trade and the recession in the economies of key trading partners, together with uncertainty about how quickly they would recover, threatened some of the Philippines' economic gains made in the early 1970s. Problems faced by major export products deepened the government's concern that an export-oriented

Commodity	1952	1972	1974
Sugar...........................	90	208.6	737.4
Copper concentrates	4	190.9	393.2
Coconut oil	15	84.3	380.7
Logs and lumber..................	19	174.4	246.4
Copra...........................	91	110.5	139.8
Gold	...	26.9	74.3
Desiccated coconut	10	17.6	60.3
Bananas	...	24.3	45.5
Abaca, unmanufactured............	41	...	37.5
Pineapple, canned.................	11	...	30.6
Total Ten Principal Exports...	281	837.5	2,145.7
Total Exports	335	1,145.0	2,725.0

... means not among ten principal exports for that year.
* Free on board.

economy dependent upon primary products might be too vulnerable to outside market factors such as inflation and recession, which are beyond the reach of policymaking by the exporting country. Worldwide price fluctuations and the possibility of peso devaluation led to speculation in mid-1975 that the Philippines would consider readopting a variant of the import substitution strategy that had been pursued in the 1950s (see ch. 14).

Imports

Total imports were valued at the equivalent of US$3.4 billion in 1974 and were estimated to be about the same for 1975. Despite fluctuations in the value of imports from year to year, the trend has been upward, and the period from 1952 to 1974 saw the value of imports increase eightfold. The composition of the principal imports did not change from 1952 to 1974, although values and commodity ranking changed significantly (see table 15). The value increase in imports up to 1973 was largely due to price factors. Overall import volume rose by less than 1 percent a year during the 1970–72 period. In 1974 price increases were also responsible for the sharp rise in import payments, but import volume also rose significantly. Compared to 1973 imports rose by approximately 108 percent in value during 1974; excluding oil imports the increase was 96 percent. Import volume rose by about 16 percent in 1974 over 1973. Because the volume of oil imports was practically unchanged from the 1973 level, the overall volume increase in imports was in other commodities.

In contrast to the concentration of exports in agricultural products, Philippine imports were composed of a wide range of foodstuffs, fuels, raw materials, and production-oriented manufactured goods. Imports of

Table 15. Philippines, Ten Principal Imports, 1952, 1972, and 1974
(FOB* value in millions of United States dollars)

Commodity	1952	1972	1974
Machinery (other than electric)	32	239.9	418.1
Mineral fuels and lubricants	42	148.8	648.9
Base metals...................................	21	112.4	291.9
Cereals and cereal preparations	35	84.3	154.7
Electric machinery, apparatus, and appliances ...	11	54.0	104.9
Explosives and miscellaneous chemicals	3	54.3	113.1
Chemical elements and compounds	...	48.2	211.7
Transport equipment	21	123.7	263.6
Textile fibers not manufactured into yarns	2	45.8	88.7
Dairy products	18	45.6	74.3
Total Ten Principal Imports	185	957.0	2,369.9
Total Imports	431	1,596.6	3,400.0

... means not among ten principal imports for that year.
* Free on board.

producer goods used in the pursuit of industrialization were stimulated by government policy. Until 1955 the Philippines could not rely on tariffs to protect domestic production because of the duty-free privileges accorded to Americans under the 1946 trade agreement. Beginning in 1950 local industries were afforded protection, however, through exchange and import controls, which were imposed initially as exchange conservation measures and then as stimulants to the domestic production of manufactures. These directly protective measures were replaced by tariffs in 1962 after the elimination of import controls and a devaluation of the peso. In the meantime the development of domestic manufacturing reduced imports of consumer goods and such manufactures as textiles, tobacco, and rubber products and led to increases in imports of industrial raw materials. Although more than one-third of Philippine imports in 1949 were consumer goods, by 1974 the share had dropped to about 8 percent.

Direction of Trade

The expansion of the country's trade has brought with it considerable change in the pattern of both export markets and import suppliers (see table 16). Major changes have occurred in the roles of the United States, Japan, and various nations of the Middle East. During 1974 the Philippines enjoyed a favorable balance of trade with fifty-nine trading partners, led by the United States, Japan, the Netherlands, Hong Kong, the Republic of Korea (South Korea), the Soviet Union, and Indonesia (see fig. 13). The Philippines suffered unfavorable balances with seventy-one countries, however, led by such oil-exporting countries as Saudi Arabia, Kuwait, Iran, and Qatar. The country also had deficits with non-oil-exporting countries, such as Canada, the United Kingdom, and the Federal Republic of Germany (West Germany).

Table 16. *Philippines, Direction of Foreign Trade, Selected Years, 1958–74*
(in millions of United States dollars)

Country	Exports				Imports			
	1958	1965	1972	1974	1958	1965	1972	1974
United States	275	349	434	1,133	289	312	352	829
Japan	97	217	358	932	81	213	424	924
United Kingdom	6	9	25	56	19	37	52	138
Canada	2	2	7	13	12	26	29	50
Western Europe	88	144	142	280	56	108	159	330
Saudi Arabia	...	...	...	7	4	17	68	370
Other Middle Eastern countries	1	...	...	21	...	31	126	264
Other Asian countries	10	29	69	122	62	108	92	204
Communist countries	2	...	4	32	...	...	2	34
Other countries	11	17	30	77	24	43	62	301
TOTAL	492	767	1,069	2,673	547	895	1,366	3,444

... means less than US$500,000.

The Philippines' major trading partners have been the United States and Japan. Combined trade with these two countries reached 62 percent of total trade in 1974. On the one hand the United States remained a primary market for Philippine goods, accounting for 42 percent of total export revenue. Japan accounted for 35 percent. On the other hand 27 percent of total Philippine imports came from Japan in 1974, and 24 percent were supplied by the United States. The increase in oil prices was instrumental in making Saudi Arabia the country's third largest trading partner, having a 6-percent share of the total trade in 1974.

In 1974 the United States purchased the equivalent of about US$1 billion in Philippine commodities. More than half of this total represented shipments of sugar, amounting to approximately US$574 million. Additional products for which the United States market had traditionally been of special importance included coconut oil, desiccated coconut, plywood, copper concentrates, and copra. Philippine imports from the United States amounted to the equivalent of US$829 million in 1974. The major imports from the United States were mining, construction, and other industrial machinery; wheat; cotton; and electric machinery, apparatus, and appliances.

Sales of Philippine commodities to Japan were equivalent to US$932 million in 1974. Japan was a principal market for copper concentrates, logs and lumber, bananas, molasses, and copra, which together accounted for approximately 80 percent of the total Philippine export value to Japan for that year. The Philippines imported from Japan iron and steel, mining equipment, transport equipment, machinery, and chemicals. Japan during the 1960s had gradually supplanted the United States as the supplier of many manufactured goods. Statistics for the first six months of 1975 indicated that Japan had regained the position as the

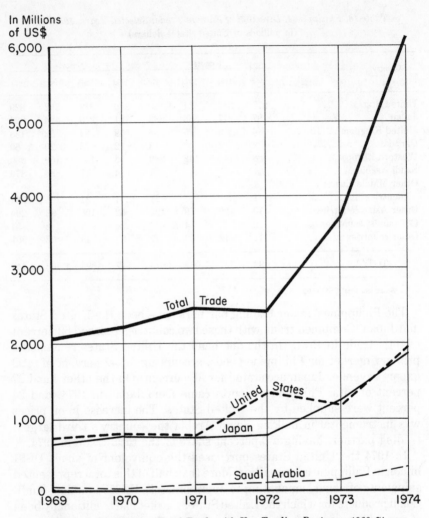

Figure 13. Philippines, Total Trade with Key Trading Partners, 1969–74

Source: Based on information from International Monetary Fund, *Direction of Trade Annual, 1970–74*, Washington, 1974, p. 245; and International Monetary Fund, *Direction of Trade Annual, 1966–70*, Washington, 1970, p. 288.

Philippines' top trading partner, a position it also held in 1973. The Japanese ascendancy to the top position was brought about by increased imports of processed sugar, which offset cutbacks in Japanese imports of copper, logs, and lumber and complemented the sharp decline in exports of sugar to the United States, which followed expiration of the United States sugar quota system at the end of 1974.

Several factors, including the complementary nature of the production systems of the two countries, whereby the Philippines provided raw materials for Japanese industry in return for manufactured and semi-finished commodities, contributed to the growing closeness of trading relations between the countries. Trade was also encouraged by geographic position and by the terms of the Japanese reparations agreements with the Philippines (see ch. 11).

In 1973 and 1974 imported petroleum provided more than 95 percent of the Philippines' total energy requirements. The bulk of these imports came from the countries of the Middle East, principally Saudi Arabia and Kuwait in 1974. In 1973 the country imported the equivalent of 71 million barrels of petroleum crude and petroleum products at a cost of approximately the equivalent of US$152 million. By 1974 an equal amount of imports cost the Philippines the equivalent of US$634 million. Although Philippine exports to the Middle East amounted to only the equivalent of US$19 million in 1974, this represented more than a 500-percent increase over the 1973 level. The Philippine government was hoping that the Middle East would prove to be a new and growing market for such products as food, industrial equipment, and consumer goods.

In 1974 Philippine exports to the countries of the European Economic Community (EEC—also known as the Common Market) were about 12 percent of total exports, and imports from these countries were almost 13 percent of total imports. The principal Common Market buyers of Philippine commodities were the Netherlands and West Germany, both of whom absorbed large quantities of Philippine coconut products, whereas imports were mostly from West Germany and the United Kingdom in the form of nonelectrical machinery, transport equipment, and electrical machinery and appliances.

Exports to Asian countries (excluding Japan) were about 6 percent of total exports in 1974, and these countries supplied about 12 percent of all imports in that year. The major trading partners were Australia, Indonesia, Malaysia, and the Republic of China (Nationalist China).

The Philippines carried on trade with nine communist countries in 1974. Total trade—both exports and imports—amounted to the equivalent of US$66 million. Philippine exports to these countries consisted mostly of copra, coconut oil, dessicated coconut, cement, and plywood. Imports comprised cereals, base metals, foodstuffs, and machinery.

In June 1975 the Philippines and the PRC signed a trade agreement. The agreement called for the promotion and expansion of trade and economic relations between the two nations, as well as the establishment of most-favored-nation treatment in regard to customs duties and other taxes applicable to bilateral trade. Among the products accorded preferential treatment by the Philippines were petroleum, chemicals, machinery, and various foodstuffs. The Philippines primarily would export sugar, coconut products, and mineral ores. Late 1975 witnessed a pledge from the PRC to increase its supply of oil to the Philippines at a preferential price. Under this agreement oil would be supplied to the Philippines at costs lower than the Organization of Petroleum Exporting Countries (OPEC) price. In addition the PRC agreed to purchase various Philippine primary products at prices higher than on the world market.

DOMESTIC TRADE

Domestic trade in the Philippines has evolved in a manner related both to the insular character of the country and to historical sequences of development. Water transport has been more significant than land transport, and the commercial significance of ports has been much greater than the centers of inland transport. The Spanish developed Manila as their political and economic base, and in 1975 the Manila metropolitan region still remained dominant as the economic center of the country.

Modern domestic trading grew out of a barter background that still exists in rural *barrios* and on small islands distant from market centers. Well into the twentieth century commercial trading operations were dominated by the Chinese. Since World War II, however, there has been an increasing development of Filipino entrepreneurship in both foreign commerce and domestic trade. The most notable trend in public policy toward domestic trade has been the rise of economic nationalism, which, although not limited to domestic trade, has nevertheless brought about substantial changes in the pattern of its composition. Economic nationalism in the Philippines has been expressed in the principle of reserving to Filipinos, or encouraging their greater participation in, various sectors of the economy through either legislation or administrative action or both. Most significant in this regard has been the legislative action banning aliens from trading and milling rice and corn (maize) in the Philippines and the legislation known as the Retail Trade Nationalization Law, which was promulgated in 1954 and became effective in June 1964. This law reserved retail trade to Philippine citizens or to Philippine firms wholly owned by Philippine citizens.

Despite the 1954 law the distinction between wholesale and retail trade in the Philippines remained unclear until the meaning was clarified through presidential decree in June 1975. Whereas the concept of "wholly owned" has been given a consistently literal interpretation, the definition of retail trade has been interpreted differently by various Philippine administrations and lower courts. At times retail trade was interpreted to include, among other things, large-volume sales for industrial or commercial consumption or transformation as well as any sale to an end user. In June 1975 President Marcos clarified the meaning of retail trade because he believed that bulk sales to industrial consumers should not be considered retail sales. The decree, which amended the Retail Trade Nationalization Law of 1954, stated that sales by manufacturers to industrial and commercial consumers who use the products to render services or to produce goods for the general public shall not be considered retail trade under the old law. The inflation of 1973 and 1974 also brought a substantially increased governmental role in the domestic economy, with imposition of ceiling prices on key consumer commodities and government monopolization of foreign trade in sugar and imported grains, as well as a more active role than formerly in marketing.

Foreign investment in the Philippines was encouraged, subject to limitations in certain areas as to the scope of activity and participation. Only Philippine citizens or corporations at least 60-percent Filipino owned could own land, develop natural resources, or operate public utilities. Other businesses that required varying amounts of Filipino equity included finance companies, commercial and private development banks, and rural banks.

Domestic trade remained family oriented in 1975. Most enterprises were small and individually owned, although some were partnerships. Corporate forms of organization were used only in larger economic entities. When incorporation was used, ownership, financing, and management were still mostly family oriented.

Despite periodic programs for decentralizing commercial and industrial activities, in the mid-1970s the Manila metropolitan area was the center of domestic trading operations, commercial organizations, and financial structuring and was the primary market. It also served as an interregional center for all the northern provinces of Luzon and as a major center for the large immediate hinterland. Approximately 85 percent of Philippine foreign trade passed through the port of Manila; 70 percent of imports entered this port to be distributed to the other principal cities via trucks and interisland shipping. In 1974 about 90 percent of all Philippine industries were located in the greater Manila area.

Cebu, the second largest city in the Philippines, was the second-ranking trade center of the Philippines. It had an advantage over Manila in domestic trade carried on by water since its hinterland was accessible by boat. Although Cebu was a major port for abaca, sugar, and copra, it operated chiefly as an interregional center for gathering and distributing such products as corn, rice, livestock, fish, fruits, and vegetables. Its hinterland includes the eastern Visayan Islands and the northern half of Mindanao.

Iloilo shared with Cebu the servicing of the central area of the country. Formerly a key port in foreign commerce and for the export of sugar products, by 1974 it served chiefly as an interregional center in domestic trade, distributing rice, corn, and various manufactured goods.

Davao was the fourth-ranking center of the interisland trade and enjoyed a dominant position in the trade of southern Mindanao. Davao's position dated from 1935, but since the 1960s it has played an increasingly large role in interisland trade. The city served primarily as the gathering point for regional surpluses of corn moving to Cebu, Negros, and Manila. Zamboanga, an old established port, was the last major interregional center, handling rice, copra, and fish and smaller volumes of timber, abaca, and fruit. Transportation to the hinterland from Zamboanga was almost entirely by water since the roads in that part of Mindanao were poor.

Nationwide marketing, as contrasted with selling in Manila, still was limited by an inadequate distribution system for most products. Also for many products limited demand outside the urban areas often did not warrant establishment of a nationwide distribution system. Buyers from throughout the islands visited Manila periodically. In many instances a sales agent in Manila having branches and travelers or representatives regularly covering the interregional centers could provide adequate coverage of the country. The product or product line itself helped decide what kind of representation was called for.

In the 1970s a high percentage of import orders was handled by large trading companies. These firms, most of which were situated in Manila, represented as many as 600 foreign suppliers. The trading houses emphasized customer relations rather than specific product selling in order to assure a steady flow of orders. Some firms specialized in commodity lines, and others handled a wide variety of commodities and were divided into specialty departments. Import trading firms were organized in all major port cities, but Manila dominated in volume of trade.

In addition to the large trading houses there were a number of smaller firms that represented the traditional trading economy. They generally handled a more limited range of products and had more limited promotional activites. These firms have proved effective in providing for the small, quality market—department stores and the established larger wholesale and retail outlets in the urban areas—and the traditional market of petty traders and *sari-sari* stores (small rural general stores).

Urban retail needs were served by outlets that ranged from the department store to the traditional peddler. Department stores in downtown Manila and its suburban shopping centers, organized like their Western counterparts, provided quality merchandise for higher income groups. Other major cities were also served by similar stores. Major urban areas also had a wide variety of specialty shops, and stores handling similar kinds of products tended to cluster in the same area.

Sari-sari shops and muncipal markets were used by the less wealthy. The general stores, many of which were managed by women and established in one room of a residence, carried a limited stock of canned goods and small articles for everyday use. Municipal markets comprised privately owned stalls set up under a roof or awning. These stalls usually sold such items as hardware, utensils, clothing, and textiles. Others sold vegetables and various other foodstuffs. In Manila large municipal markets constituted an important link in the retail chain, which was further augmented by street vendors and peddlers. In rural areas retail facilities were much less abundant and were essentially restricted to general stores, nearby markets, and peddlers.

The introduction of high-yielding varieties of rice in the mid-1960s and the subsequent rise in production brought about serious deficiencies in the marketing system of rice. Traditional milling and handling techniques had proved increasingly inadequate to handle the commercial flow of paddy in major producing areas. Because of transportation bottlenecks, the processing and marketing of rice was widely dispersed, involving the services of intermediaries and buying agents, rice traders, and other wholesalers who benefited from the farmers' immobility and lack of knowledge of prices by buying at relatively low prices and selling at substantial profits. In some cases paddy changed hands two or more times before arriving at the mill.

Retailing of rice was handled mainly by small shops and by vendors in public markets. Usually the unit of sale was not standardized. Brand names were unimportant, but the various varieties were classified into "ordinary," "fancy," or "special" categories, their prices varying accordingly.

TRANSPORTATION

Until the late 1960s development of transportation was oriented toward island and overseas trading. The main characteristic of the Philippine transportation network and the source of many of its problems is the fact that it serves a population scattered over hundreds of islands. The major transport modes of the islands consisted of road transport, interisland and coastal shipping, railroads, and domestic aviation (see fig. 14).

Road transport was the dominant mode within the two major islands of Luzon and Mindanao and accounted for approximately 60 percent of total freight movement and over 80 percent of passenger traffic in 1973. Interisland and coastal shipping was the second largest transport mode, serving a widespread population and having accounted for about 40 percent of freight traffic and under 8 percent of passenger movement. The railroad was of marginal importance and carried a small fraction of total traffic. Domestic aviation, although of small importance and mainly serving passenger traffic, was developing rapidly.

Investment within the transportation sector has been relatively important, having accounted for over 50 percent of public capital formation in the 1968–72 period. Transportation expenditure as a percentage of total public infrastructure expenditure during the 1974–77 period was targeted at 43 percent. These expenditures have been insufficient to cope with transportation demands and to eliminate infrastructure bottlenecks, however. The transportation network had deteriorated considerably by the 1970s, as maintenance suffered from inadequate funding and poor administration. Also, excessive political interference and expediency had hampered rational planning and efficient project execution.

Highways

The highway network of about 10,000 miles of paved roads, 24,000 miles of gravel roads, and about 13,000 miles of unimproved roads was concentrated on Luzon and Mindanao; the balance was mostly concen-

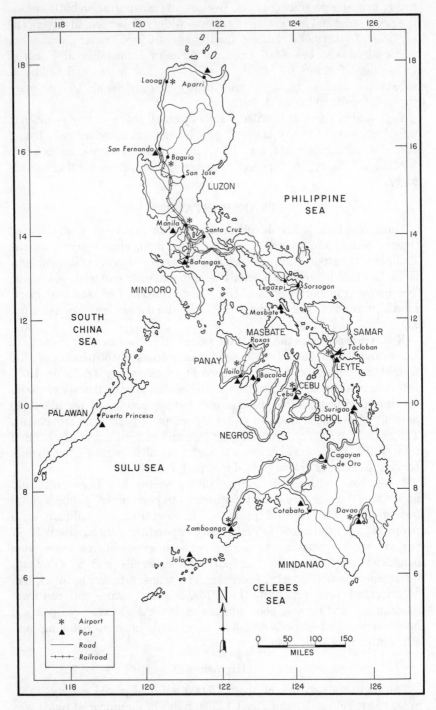

Figure 14. Philippines, National Highways, Railroads, Principal Ports, and Airports

trated on Cebu, Negros, and Panay—the main islands of the Visayan Islands. The principal road artery of the country was the Pan-Philippine Highway, which extended for over 1,250 miles from Aparri in northern Luzon through Samar and Leyte to Davao in southern Mindanao. It had two major interisland crossings that were served by regular ferries.

Highways were divided into five classes: expressway, primary, secondary, municipal, and feeder. The Bureau of Public Highways was responsible for the planning, construction, improvement, and maintenance of the national road network. This consisted of the expressways, primary roads, and about one-third of the secondary roads. The rest of the road system was largely in the hands of provincial and city administrations.

Most of the national primary and secondary roads were in a deteriorated condition because of inadequate maintenance over the years. The condition of the gravel and earth roads was poor, only a small proportion of them being serviceable throughout the year. There was a lack of adequate, low-cost feeder roads that could provide better farm-to-market movements. Most of the existing secondary and feeder roads were isolated and poorly connected to main highways. Government efforts to improve this situation included allocating a large share of infrastructure investment to highway improvement. The government launched an ambitious highway program for the 1973–77 period using both domestic and foreign capital.

Railroads

Railroads have not achieved a dominant position in transportation because of the fragmentation of land areas and the high investment necessary to build, maintain, and expand operations. After the destruction from World War II existing railroad facilities were rehabilitated, but their importance was overshadowed by the growth of motor highways and motor transportation. In 1975 railroads carrying freight and passengers were confined to the islands of Luzon and Panay. Industrial railroads operated by sugar mills (*centrals*) and logging companies also added to the facilities for moving goods.

There were two government-owned railroads, the Philippine National Railways (PNR) and the Philippine Railroad Company. The latter was located on the island of Panay and consisted of about seventy-three miles of antiquated track. The network of the PNR totaled 643 miles of main line and about 625 miles of branch lines and siding. It was located on Luzon and ran from San Fernando in La Union Province on the northwestern coast of Luzon to Legazpi on the southeast.

The government has adopted a railroad rehabilitation plan for the 1973–77 period, during which time it plans to acquire new rolling stock and to improve dilapidated roadbed, track, and crossties. Besides this rehabilitation the government was expected to initiate new projects, including an extension line to the Cagayan Valley in the north of Luzon and another in the south, the Sorsogon extension.

Ports and Shipping

The insular nature of the Philippines and the extent of the country's foreign trade have made ports and shipping especially important to the economy. Port facilities in the mid-1970s included eighty ports operated by the national government and another 390 ports under the direction of municipalities. There were also numerous wharves and piers owned and operated by commercial firms, among them sugar mills, flour millers, pineapple growers, and copra mills. Petroleum importers also had their own piers equipped with special pipelines for unloading tankers.

Manila was the country's most important harbor for the handling of foreign trade. In the mid-1970s about 70 percent of the national imports and 5 percent of exports passed through this port. A distinguishing feature of the Philippines was that the bulk of exports and imports was handled through private port facilities and piers. Port statistics, therefore, were misleading because the data did not indicate whether exports were shipped from public or private piers. Ports handling substantial volumes of domestic traffic included Iloilo, Manila, Batangas, and Zamboanga.

Administration and control of the national ports have been in the hands of the Bureau of Customs, and physical planning, construction, and maintenance were the responsibility of the Bureau of Public Works. In the 1970s the government created a national port authority to take over from the Bureau of Customs the responsibility of administering and operating the ports.

The Philippine merchant fleet totaled approximately 1.6 million gross registered tons in 1971 and included 130 oceangoing vessels and 156 interisland vessels. The fleet tended to be old, close to 50 percent of the interisland and oceangoing fleet having been in operation nineteen or more years.

Philippine vessels maintained regular service to Asia, North America, and Europe. A considerable number of foreign shipping firms also had regular routes to the Philippines. Within the country's territorial waters coastal vessels furnished adequate interisland passenger and freight service to all but a few of the smaller outlying islands.

Airlines

Manila's airport served as the country's primary international airport. It was served by fifteen major international airlines, as well as Philippine Air Lines (PAL), which operated both internationally and domestically. A secondary international airport was located at Mactan, Cebu. An extensive network of domestic airports was served by PAL, which in 1974 absorbed two local carriers—Air Manila and Filipinas Orient Airways. Domestic passenger service has been increasing by about 17 percent per year. Air freight was insignificant domestically but has shown growth on international routes. In 1972 there were seventy-six national airports plus a number of private ones.

Airport infrastructure was in most cases inadequate. Terminal facilities were almost nonexistent and runways poorly surfaced. A study conducted in 1967 reported that only thirteen of the seventy-six national airports had adequate surfacing. The most pressing problem was the improvement of the international airport of Manila. The financing of the project was to be undertaken with the assistance of the ADB. In addition plans for an alternative international airport at Bulacan—fifteen air miles from Manila—were under way.

Communications

Communication facilities were operated by government and private facilities. Private telephone companies, of which the Philippine Long Distance Telephone Company was the largest, had more than 171,000 lines operating from forty-eight telephone exchanges, and the government Bureau of Telecommunications had another 28,000 lines and twenty-seven exchanges. A public telegraph service interconnected by radio, radiotelephone, and telephone stations and consisting of 1,318 telegraph stations in municipalities throughout the country was also operated by the Bureau of Telecommunications. Overseas communication was provided through a trans-Pacific cable system and a permanent satellite earth station.

SECTION IV. NATIONAL SECURITY

CHAPTER 16

THE ARMED FORCES

Philippine defense policies and institutions were undergoing unprecedented changes in the mid-1970s as a consequence of altered power relationships in the Pacific region and a new upsurge of domestic disturbance. In response to new perceptions of national defense, the armed forces establishment was experiencing substantial expansion and was moving toward a more central position in national life. Also, a serious armed insurgency in Mindanao and the Sulu Archipelago have since 1973 kept the military services embroiled there in a large-scale and costly internal security operation (see ch. 17).

The Armed Forces of the Philippines (AFP) embraced the three military services, army, navy, and air force, along with the constabulary under a unified command in the Department of National Defense. As of late 1975, under interim authority pending the coming into force of certain provisions of the 1973 Constitution, President Ferdinand E. Marcos remained commander in chief of the armed forces (see ch. 9).

An established principle of national defense policy since the founding of the republic was to limit the size of the standing military force while maintaining a large body of reserves. Defense policy has also stressed basic weaponry in preference to sophisticated equipment in keeping with the capacity of the national economy. National defense policy assumed that the armed forces were not, and over the foreseeable future would not be, capable of preventing an invasion of Philippine territory.

Although the constabulary remained the largest of the four services by a small margin, the army was the largest of the military services. In 1975 force levels of the regular army, air force, and navy were together estimated at 67,000 enlisted personnel and officers including some, women; inclusion of the constabulary, which functioned more as a military than as a national police force, would increase this level to over 100,000 (see ch. 17). Force levels had more than doubled between 1972 and 1975. Various categories of reserves and conscripted trainees on extended duty added up to several times this number under stepped-up training programs put into effect beginning in 1972.

Civic action programs, which had proved successful on a limited basis against the Hukbalahap (Huk—see Glossary) insurgency in the 1950s, were greatly expanded by the Marcos government in the 1970s and given an important place in the military mission. Under the Home Defense Program the human and material resources mobilized in the course of raising an expanded citizens army were to be directed to national social and economic betterment through an interrelationship between military training and civic action. Historically the military establishment has made only modest demands on national resources. One aim of the Home Defense Program was to expand the national defense capability through a minimum of additional economic and fiscal burden on the underdeveloped Philippine economy.

President Marcos' imposition of martial law in September 1972 set the stage for an enlarged role for the armed forces in national affairs. Although martial law did not mean rule by the military but rather use of the military by the president in his role as commander in chief—what President Marcos termed a "constitutional authoritarian regime"—the institutional arrangements brought direct military intervention into the management of the economy and the administration of criminal justice. Since there was no official prospect held out for an early end to the martial law regime, in the support of which the armed forces appeared to be the president's main power base, the potential was clearly present for enlargement of the historically uninfluential military elite and for growth in the influence of this elite over the course of political change in the Philippines.

Although martial law had had a salutary effect in relation to the communist-led insurgency in Luzon, it had exacerbated the problem in Mindanao to the point of open rebellion. Fighting there between government forces and Muslim insurgent forces escalated to full-scale though sporadic warfare, such as that which devastated the city of Jolo in early 1974. There was clear evidence of outside support for the Mindanao insurgent forces, almost certainly from Sabah in northern Borneo and possibly from as far as Libya, which had proclaimed its support for Muslim rebels everywhere. Official Philippine statements, however, tended to treat the question of foreign intervention gingerly.

Changing power relationships in Southeast Asia, including the establishment of relations between the United States and the People's Republic of China (PRC) and the collapse of the Republic of Vietnam (South Vietnam) in 1975, led the Philippine government to emphasize a strategy of national mobilization. The government continued to view its defense relationship with the United States as indispensable to its own strategic defense for the foreseeable future. This relationship, however, was undergoing a continuing process of adjustment and accommodation, particularly with regard to the status of United States military bases and forces in the Philippines.

No issues likely to disturb the peace were evident between the Philippines and any of its neighbors, although relations with the two Vietnamese governments remained to be settled. Unresolved territorial claims and other problems that arose over the Malaysian state of Sabah in northern Borneo remained an irritant in Philippine-Malaysian relations, but both sides appeared committed to keeping the issue from becoming a threat to security in the area.

ORIGIN AND DEVELOPMENT

No Philippine armed force other than police existed in the Philippines before the establishment of the Commonwealth of the Philippines on November 15, 1935. One of the first acts of the commonwealth government of President Manuel L. Quezon was to provide for a national army. Commonwealth Act 1, the National Defense Act of 1935 provided the legal base under which the president established the Army of the Philippines, comprising all eventual land, sea, air, and national police forces. A manpower ceiling of 10,000 was set for the new army. A reserve force with a projected strength of 400,000 by 1946 was to be built up through national conscription. The army was to be directly subordinate to the president of the commonwealth; operational control was vested in the chief of staff, who would have headquarters in Manila.

The existing national police force, the Philippine Constabulary, was abolished and used as the nucleus of the new army. Command was given to a retired constabulary officer who was recalled to duty as acting chief of staff in the rank of brigadier general. The constabulary's air force became the air arm of the new army; a small maritime element, the Off-Shore Patrol, was added in 1939. General Douglas MacArthur, retired from the United States Army and having long experience in the Philippines, was engaged by President Quezon as military adviser to organize and train the army. The army's mission, defined by MacArthur as that of a holding force against external attack pending the arrival of American reinforcements, remained essentially unchanged until the early 1970s.

In anticipation of a Japanese military threat to the Philippines, President Franklin D. Roosevelt in July 1941 ordered the induction of the Philippine forces into the United States Army, Far East. Philippine units retained their identity in the United States forces. At the time of the Japanese attack on Clark Air Base near Manila on December 8, 1941, trained Philippine army reserves totaled about 132,000.

Philippine forces fought in the battles of Bataan and Corregidor. After the capitulation to the Japanese in May 1942 many officers and men of the Philippine forces went into the resistance. Some formed or joined guerrilla units that harassed Japanese forces during the occupation period and provided intelligence to the American forces of the Southwest Pacific Area Command. Many later fought again with the United States forces when the latter reentered the Philippines at Leyte in October 1944. After the end of the war in 1945 the Philippine elements were released from United States control and reconstituted as a national force.

Coincident with a reorganization of the government in October 1947, President Manuel A. Roxas redesignated the military forces the Armed Forces of the Philippines. This was essentially an army command under which air force, maritime, and police internal security elements (then known as the Military Police Command, later to become the reconstituted Philippine Constabulary) were constituted as subordinate commands and had their own staffs. A more fundamental reorganization of the military establishment was carried out beginning in early 1951, brought about in part by the need for more effective action to counter the growing Huk insurrection. Executive Order 389 of December 1950 established four separate services, army, air force, navy, and national police, under a joint headquarters. The army continued to dominate the command structure through its staffing of the key positions in the headquarters until about 1960, when the headquarters was changed into a truly joint command post.

Two developments that were to have a strong formative influence on the armed forces were the appointment of Ramón Magsaysay, later president of the Philippines, as secretary of defense in 1950 and the Military Assistance Agreement of 1947, which established the basis for United States military assistance to the Philippines.

Drawing upon both his experience and his associates in the guerrilla campaign against the Japanese occupation, Magsaysay brought young officers and fresh concepts to the molding of a new style of army capable of dealing with the problem of the Huk insurrection. Magsaysay's force-and-persuasion approach to the Huk campaign included on the "force" side recasting the combat forces into more flexible and effective battalion combat teams of about 1,200 men. The "persuasion" half of the formula stressed building national confidence in the army as a public protector. In the process some traditional military ways were changed. Soldiers were instructed to pay for the rice and chickens they acquired from villagers; social conscience was to go hand in hand with combat effectiveness. The combination worked. In expanded form it was being tried again in the 1970s.

The initial 1947 military assistance agreement with the United States provided for equipment, training, and logistical support for the development of the Philippine armed forces. This agreement continued the military relationship that had existed since the Spanish-American War. The effect on the shaping of the AFP would be hard to exaggerate. For the United States the relationship has been no less critical to its strategic actions and policies in the Pacific and Southeast Asia, as evidenced in both the Korean and the Vietnam conflicts.

Since World War II Philippine contingents have been dispatched abroad on three occasions. Philippine expeditionary forces served in Korea under the United Nations Command between 1950 and 1955. Also under United Nations auspices the Philippines sent seventy-seven air force officers and men to the Republic of the Congo (present-day Zaire) in February 1963. From the mid-1960s until the early 1970s the Philippine Civic Action Group (PHILCAG), composed mainly of engineer, security, medical, and rural community development teams, was active in South Vietnam.

PHILIPPINE SECURITY IN THE POST-VIETNAM CONTEXT

In the mid-1970s Philippine national defense policy was in the process of its first fundamental realignment since independence. This was undertaken in response to changes that had been mounting for a decade in the international environment of Southeast Asia. Underlying shifts included the fragmentation of the bipolar world of the cold war era, the partial disengagement of Western power as signified by the 1969 Nixon Doctrine, the British withdrawal from Singapore and Malaysia, and the United States withdrawal from South Vietnam. Accompanying these shifts and largely induced by them was a new consideration on the part of Southeast Asian nations, including the Philippines, of neutralism, self-reliance, and ideological accommodation as lines of national defense.

The fall of Saigon in the spring of 1975 had a traumatic effect on Philippine defense thinking. More than any other event it was responsible for inducing a fresh look at the assumptions and purposes of national defense. Defense policy under the republic had changed little from preindependence times: defense was designed to protect the country against external communist aggression, the controlling assumption being that this was best assured through mutual defense arrangements and alignment with a powerful patron. The cornerstone of this defense policy was the Southeast Asia Treaty Organization (SEATO) and a bilateral defense relationship with the United States.

The case was stated by President Marcos to military academy graduates in 1966: "The Philippines must depend upon collective security for its defense and safety. Collective security is its only means of survival. . . . I cannot foresee in the next several decades any alteration of this imperative."

By 1972 President Marcos and his defense chiefs no longer held this view. The potential threat to national security for the foreseeable future was perceived to stem from domestic subversion, not external aggression. Greater reliance had to be placed on the country's own resources, material and moral. Salvation through the intervention of an outside power as in World War II no longer seemed workable for the Philippines in the post-Vietnam world. In 1975 the Philippines was in the process of bringing its military arrangements into line with the new reality.

Other than its bilateral treaty with the United States, the Philippines' only defense commitment since independence has been as a member of SEATO, a joint defense planning and coordinating body that grew out of the 1954 Southeast Asia Collective Defense Treaty. Besides the Philippines and the United States, original signatories of the treaty were Australia, Great Britain, France, New Zealand, Pakistan, and Thailand. Pakistan quit the treaty in 1973, and France ceased participating the following year.

In June 1972 President Marcos informed the SEATO Council meeting in Australia of the Philippine view that SEATO had outlived its usefulness in its present form and that it should be redirected "to take full account of the new realities of the international situation." In September

1975, largely on Philippine initiative, the SEATO Council agreed to phase out the organization within two years.

Although not conceived as a defense alliance, the Association of Southeast Asian Nations (ASEAN), formed in 1967 by the Philippines, Indonesia, Malaysia, Singapore, and Thailand, has tended to edge into logistical and military concerns in connection with its widening technical consultations and other activities. Some observers saw the possibility that ASEAN would gradually take on a regional security interest, filling some of the requirements left by the demise of SEATO.

A more fundamental and difficult realignment for the Philippines involved its military relationship with the United States. The formal basis of this relationship was the Mutual Defense Treaty of August 1951 and related military assistance and base agreements.

At the crux of the relationship were the United States naval base at Subic Bay, which included the Seventh Fleet fitting station, and Clark Air Base, the largest United States overseas installation. Some 17,500 American military and civilian personnel were stationed at these bases in 1975. Many times that number of Filipinos were directly employed in connection with them—roughly 18,000 at Subic Bay alone.

The Philippines shared with the United States a strategic interest in not overly restricting the operational use of the bases by American aircraft and ships covering the approaches to the Philippines. The basis of the Philippine interest was defined simply by President Marcos: the task of securing the sea and air links over which the nation's commerce moved, which were also the corridors of any hostile approach, would remain beyond Philippine resources for the foreseeable future.

There was, however, a long history of Filipino irritation and political agitation over the housekeeping arrangements that governed the American presence. Philippine grievances centered on both perceived affronts to national pride because of United States control of the bases and the sensitive matter of criminal jurisdiction. The latter was regulated under various agreements and amendments to the original base agreement of 1947, which taken together constituted a status-of-forces agreement between the two countries. At the end of 1975 the United States and the Philippines were gradually working toward a new accommodation that, while preserving the strategic utility of the bases, would accord with the new thrust of Philippine policy and end any vestiges of what Philippine spokesmen described as extraterritorial privileges in the base agreement.

Strategic and political readjustments notwithstanding, the symbiotic military relationship between the Philippines and the United States was regarded as likely to continue without substantial change through at least the rest of the 1970s, if not well beyond. The Philippine armed forces were modeled in all important respects after those of the United States. All but an insignificant portion of weaponry and matériel was of American origin, and much depended on American parts and replacements. From independence in 1946 until 1975 United States direct military assistance to the Philippines, mostly grant aid, totaled an estimated US$750 million. No change in the existing overall level of aid was contemplated as of late 1975. Proposed fiscal year (FY) 1976 security assistance was US$37.6 million, of which just over half was grant aid. American base-related expenditures themselves had a far from negligible impact on the Philippine economy.

THE ARMED FORCES AND THE NATION

Neither the 1935 Constitution nor the 1973 Constitution contains specific provisions relating to the nature or composition of the armed forces. Article II of the new charter states that "the defense of the State is a prime duty of the Government and the people, and . . . all citizens may be required by law to render personal military or civil service." The National Defense Act of 1935 has remained the basic enabling law providing for the armed forces establishment.

In keeping with the change from a presidential to a parliamentary form of government, which was called for in the new constitution, the authority of commander in chief of the armed forces (including the national police) was vested in the prime minister, who was given constitutional power under certain circumstances to call out the armed forces, to suspend the writ of habeas corpus, and to place part or all of the country under martial law. Pending the coming into effect of the provisions relating to the change to parliamentary government, President Marcos remained commander in chief of the armed forces under transitory provisions of the 1973 Constitution. (see ch. 9).

In his role of commander in chief the president had the advisory assistance of the National Security Council and the National Intelligence Coordinating Agency. The National Security Council is a body of top civil and military officials created in 1958 to plan national strategy and determine policies for the attainment of national goals, including defense. The National Intelligence Coordinating Agency gathers and evaluates intelligence related to national defense.

Martial influence in Philippine national life has historically been small, and military interference in the political process has not been significant, at least before the transforming events of the early 1970s. The nation traditionally has been suspicious of and has eschewed large professional military forces. It has continued to favor the citizen army concept of a large conscript reserve force composed of men who have completed a period of formal military training. The principle of civilian supremacy was rooted in law and practice. Apart from those limited areas of the country where counterinsurgency operations have concentrated the presence of military and police forces, the visibility of the army's relatively few, widely scattered units has usually not been great.

Lack of a powerful national constituency was evident in a record of congressional penury in military appropriations and a tendency on the part of some to see militarization behind the armed forces' civil affairs programs. President Marcos stated the military case in his *Notes on the New Society of the Philippines*:

> [It was always] a source of scandal for me that the . . . Congress exposed the military to ridicule whenever the latter testified about the state of rebellion in the country. . . . [Military] leaders and officers had to face the annual comic ceremony before the Congress. . . . The effectiveness of the armed forces was affected by the seeming lack of support given them by the civil authorities. . . . The armed forces were protecting the government of a society which seemed indifferent to its own salvation.

It was questionable, however, how accurate this traditional portrait was in the Philippines of the mid-1970s. The military services were undergoing substantial enlargement; their historic role of defender against external aggression was now subordinate to the roles of defender of domestic order and guiding force for national development. It remained to be seen whether the new interventionist role in which the military establishment had been cast under the martial law regime would permanently end the military's traditionally low profile in national life.

The Armed Forces and Martial Law

In proclaiming martial law in September 1972 President Marcos made it clear that the military was not instrumental in this decision and that the direction of government would remain in civilian hands. The armed forces establishment, however, was given a leading institutional role in enforcing the martial law regime. Military forces and installations probably operated with the police in the initial roundup of thousands of people proscribed by the government as "dissidents, activists, subversives, and corrupt elements." A system of military tribunals was established that had nationwide jurisdiction over a broad range of offenses previously within the purview of the civil courts.

Enforcement of controls over the national media was placed in the hands of the army's Office for Civil Relations, under the direction of a committee of which the secretary of national defense was cochairman. Although direct media control was later abolished, an important element of indirect military control remained in late 1975 through the requirement that work permits needed by all media employees depended upon a security clearance from the military.

Sensitive areas of the national economy were placed under military control. These included in some measure critical public utilities, communications, transportation services, and industries that the government had marked for possible restructuring. Other measures included the takeover of the country's three steel companies in December 1972 and the president's directive of April 1975 to the defense secretary to oversee the trading and exporting of Philippine sugar (later placed under the control of the Philippine National Bank). Three years after the imposition of martial law there was no indication from President Marcos as to how long martial law, or the military's role in administering it, would last.

The Home Defense Program

A leading part in President Marcos' New Society program initiated under martial law was assigned to the armed forces' Home Defense Program. This was a military-directed socioeconomic and civic action program that married the concept of a trained reserve citizen army to the purposes of national development. The Home Defense Program existed in its essential elements before martial law; under the New Society program it took on a larger and more central role. This new role did not alter the underlying rationale of the Home Defense Program, which was to enhance military preparedness by building an effective, trained military reserve force. Henceforth, however, the public emphasis was to be on moral rearming and national development.

Since 1972 particular application of this civic action approach was evident in the government's policy toward the Muslim Filipino insurgency in Mindanao and the Sulu Archipelago, the policy of force and persuasion. Military means were needed to restore law and order, but only reforming the ills that fed the rebellion and winning over the people could eliminate the problem.

Neither the carrot-and-stick approach to insurrection nor the use of military units for civil affairs missions was novel. Magsaysay had successfully applied both concepts against the Huk movement in the early 1950s. Whereas the Magsaysay approach had been limited essentially to the Huks, however, the Home Defense Program was conceived as being applicable on a national scale.

Three fields of civic action were defined in the armed forces' Home Defense Program of the mid-1970s: community relations, civic assistance, and agromilitary activities. A fourth field, reserve affairs and manpower development, remained both the core activity and the chosen instrument for promoting the others (see Mission and Organization of the Military Forces, this ch.). The three military services along with the constabulary all had parts in carrying out both the military and the socioeconomic aspects of the program in cooperation with various ministries and local institutions of the civil government.

Military involvement in civic action had its beginning in a 1958 appropriation act that authorized the armed forces to employ their personnel in activities related to public works construction, food production, land resettlement, and rural development. This mission was greatly expanded by a governmental decision in 1966 to apply military resources to national and local development programs. Civic action has since become probably the most visible of the Home Defense Program activities. Under its aegis military units were involved in development work, such as the construction of roads and the erection of prefabricated schoolhouses, disaster control and emergency relief and evacuation, assistance in the maintenance and security of public utilities, and law enforcement and other support to local authorities. According to official figures, armed forces medical and dental teams treated some 500,000 Filipinos, most in rural areas, who had no access to civilian doctors, nurses, and dentists.

The community relations aspect of the Home Defense Program was concerned mainly with the information and public relations side of military-civil relations. An inner-directed program has aimed at reeducating the military man, enlisted as well as officer, to awareness of the importance of military ties with the community and how this relates to military conduct. An outer-directed public information program was intended to foster public confidence in the armed forces as a contributor to nation building.

Agricultural activities were among the earliest forms of civic action, a response to the agrarian nature of the Huk movement. So-called Socioeconomic Military Program farms and "green revolution" projects aided the national food production campaign by putting idle military lands to work in agricultural and livestock production while providing training in agricultural skills. The program was a vehicle for assisting other government agencies in land resettlement projects and the distribution of public lands to landless farmworkers.

Direction and execution of the Home Defense Program lay with the assistant secretary of national defense for home defense and the assistant chief of staff for home defense in each major service headquarters. The Home Defense Center (army-run) or Community Relations Unit (run by the constabulary, air force, or navy) served as the coordinating center and point of direction within a district or province for joint civil-military activities under the Home Defense Program. Plans called for at least one such center or unit in each province. As of late 1972 thirty-eight were in existence, twenty-two of which fell into the category of Home Defense Center.

The Military Establishment and the National Economy

In comparison with other developing countries in Asia and worldwide, the Philippines maintained a relatively low level of military expenditures, at least until 1972. Such expenditures (not including those for the constabulary) averaged less than 2 percent and generally closer to 1.5 percent of the gross national product (GNP—see Glossary) during the decade through 1973.

The substantial expansion of the armed forces, including the police, under way after 1972 has exerted a pronounced upward pressure on the military budget. In the absence of clearly defined official budget figures, it was not clear how much of the increased armed forces budget, if any, was attributable to expanded socioeconomic activities. Stated government policy was to continue to tailor the military establishment to the capacity of a developing economy. Nevertheless substantial increases in standing-force levels, announced plans for additional military-related capital expenditures over a five-year period beginning in 1972, and increases in certain categories of military pay and allowances since 1972 suggest that a larger proportion of the national budget will be devoted to direct military purposes during the late 1970s.

In the second half of the 1970s a stronger indirect impact on the economy also appeared likely from the effects of the Home Defense Program and of the shift in defense policy to a stance of greater self-reliance. This policy as it was enunciated in 1972 and thereafter called for an "army of development" that, operating through the institutional form of the Home Defense Program, anticipated a greater linking of national defense assets and resources to national development.

No statistical estimates were available of the economic contribution of the armed forces through its civic action activities in the past. It is likely, however, that the Home Defense Program, if developed as planned in the 1970s, would contribute materially to national economic development. Whether it would have the intended seed effect on the growth of local civilian initiative was not clear. One field in which the military services have been in a unique position to assist national development has been the construction of infrastructure projects in remote areas. In areas where qualified civilian contractors could not or would not operate, the military services have provided the skills and technology for building roads, power facilities, and communications. A major force in such projects were the 51st and 52nd Engineer Brigades, both of which originated in the late 1960s. The greatly expanded and extended reserve training program was also expected to contribute to manpower development in the civil economy by providing a steady spillover of reservists returning from conscription with new vocational skills ranging from radio and automotive repair to animal husbandry.

The nation's industrial economy would probably experience some stimulus from the government's five-year program, announced in 1972, to foster certain military-related industries and manufactures as part of its policy of greater self-reliance in the area of national defense and security. This program for a "military-industrial complex" included the establishment of an arms industry producing small arms and ammunition and such military hardware as rockets and employing indigenous resources entirely. It remained to be seen whether the temporary role being played by the armed forces in carrying out certain of the industrial and economic controls imposed under martial law would harden into a permanent feature of military influence in economic life.

MISSION AND ORGANIZATION OF THE MILITARY FORCES

National defense policy underwent a fundamental reassessment in the early 1970s, the result of which was a sharp break with the past. Since before World War II the national defense had been tailored to a holding strategy of which General MacArthur was the leading architect: mobilized reserves would bolster a small standing force in resisting conventional attack on the national territory until decisive outside assistance (from the United States) could be brought to bear. Defense strategy beginning in the 1970s, however, called for a people's army capable of coping with externally supported subversion. Both Maoist and Israeli models were referred to as applicable to the Philippines.

The contemporary threat, President Marcos said, was from "a massive type of infiltration which will probably seek to support with arms, equipment, funds and supplies from outside, whether covertly or openly, an indigenous rebel force within the Philippines that seeks to overthrow the established government." The lesson of Vietnam was that "the armed forces collapsed not so much because of enemy pressure from the outside, but more because of disintegration from within brought about by the lack of will to fight on the part of the armed forces and on the part of the civilian population."

A defense that relied primarily on outside assistance was both inappropriate to this kind of threat and no longer credible in post-Vietnam Asia. The postulates of a defense posture suited to the new circumstances were that it be "unilaterally self-reliant, viable, and economically feasible" for an underdeveloped country.

The essential ingredient of a people's army strategy was a citizenry that was capable of being aroused and that was equipped with the training and the organization necessary to sustain protracted territorial warfare. This was the seminal purpose of the Home Defense Program. "If the people are again called to fight and defend the country," in the president's words, it must be in a position "where every able-bodied citizen, armed or unarmed, shall form part of the country's total effort, [fighting] the entire spectrum of warfare, conventional to unconventional."

Operations against the Mulsim insurgency in Mindanao provided a practical application of the national defense strategy on a limited scale. Government claims of growing success with its force-and-persuasion policies in the form of increasing insurgent defections were difficult to assess as of late 1975. It was estimated that the organized Muslim forces, known as the Bangsa Moro Army, were tying down some 35,000 to 50,000 government armed forces, both regular and irregular, in the Mindanao area in 1975. Included were most of the standing Philippine army and one or more special battalions of conscripted trainees (see ch. 17).

Under the designation Armed Forces of the Philippines (AFP) were included the Philippine Army, largest of the military services, the Philippine Navy and the Philippine Air Force—each about half the size of the army—and the army-sized Philippine Constabulary, a centralized police force, with a substantial paramilitary capability. The army, navy, and air force form the military forces proper.

Operational control over the four branches of the armed forces lay with chief of staff under the administrative direction of the secretary of national defense, who was a civilian member of the cabinet. Under the 1973 Constitution the secretary of national defense was to be responsible to the prime minister as commander in chief; in late 1975 President Marcos retained the position of commander in chief under interim provisions.

The chief of staff, who was the senior armed forces officer, exercised command through the General Headquarters, AFP, located in the Department of National Defense in Manila. Immediately subordinate to him were a vice chief of staff, who was the commander of the Philippine Constabulary, and a deputy chief of staff, who was his chief administrative officer. The chief of staff presided over the General Military Council, an advisory body to the commander in chief on defense matters. Other members of the council included the chiefs of the services and certain other designated general officers.

Of the three combined tactical commands directly subordinate to armed forces headquarters, two operated in the southwest of the country, the areas of the Muslim insurgency. These were the Central Mindanao Command, headed by an army commander, and the Southwest Command; the Sulu Sea Frontier Command, headed by a rear admiral, came under the Southwest Command. The third command, the Northeast Command, was located in northern Luzon.

Numerous organizational changes in the armed forces since 1970 both at the headquarters and at subordinate levels were designed to give greater emphasis to the home defense and civic action functions of the military services and the constabulary. As of late 1974 many elements within the general headquarters of the armed forces were related to these functions and had counterparts in subordinate units or organizations throughout the country.

The Food Production Corps was in charge of the program converting former idle military lands into productive farms. The Office of Manpower and Reserve Affairs was in charge of the training program under which selected twenty-year-old youths were conscripted for a period of compulsory military training. The Directorate for the Reserve Officers Training Corps and the Office of Citizen Army Training and Youth Affairs managed the military training programs in the high schools and in the institutions of higher learning. The Office for Civil Relations, as described in an official publication, had the public relations mission "to project the army as protector of the people and their part in national progress." Directly under the Department of National Defense was the Office of Civil Defense, whose peacetime function was disaster relief.

A five-year armed forces development program initiated in 1972 called for a substantial rise in strength levels of the country's armed forces, including the constabulary. Authorized strength of 60,000 in 1972, which was substantially higher than force levels at the beginning of the 1970s, was increased to a new authorized level of 80,000 by the end of 1975. Actual force levels increased from an estimated 54,000 in 1972 to 102,000 in 1975, including the constabulary. Even larger increases were put into effect for the various military and paramilitary reserve forces. President Marcos spoke in May 1974 of more than doubling the nation's total armed forces-related personnel, active and reserve, from 100,000 at the time of the imposition of martial law to 250,000 by mid-1975. He termed this an "army for development." He justified it to the nation as being dictated by the shift from a policy of defense based on military alliances to one based on self-reliance. The escalation of fighting in the Muslim areas of the south after 1972 was probably an added consideration.

The government unveiled in 1972 a long-range priority program, second only to national development, to "upgrade and broaden the domestic component of the country's defense." Increased arms and equipment were to include unspecified advanced land warfare weaponry, a naval and air weapons system, improved communications electronics, combat and service support systems, and other military matériel. Accelerated deliveries under the United States Military Assistance Program were expected to provide a portion of this equipment.

The Philippine Army

The structure of the ground forces includes both operational and territorial commands under a conventional headquarters and staff organization located at Fort Bonifacio near Manila. The oldest (established January 1936) and largest of the three military services, the army in 1975 was commanded by a major general. The highest military rank, that of general, was held by an army officer who also held the post of chief of staff of the armed forces.

Regular army strength in 1975 was an estimated 39,000 enlisted and officer personnel. This represented a sizable increase over the three-year period since the imposition of martial law and roughly a doubling of the army's strength since the beginning of the 1970s. It was not clear whether this figure included conscripts on eighteen-month training duty.

The major tactical units included three infantry divisions, one of which, the 1st Infantry Division, was a central reserve force; two independent infantry brigades; an artillery group; a Hawk ground-to-air missile unit; the 51st and 52nd engineer brigades, composed of some thirteen battalions; and an unconventional warfare unit with an airborne capability. One unofficial estimate in early 1975 placed the total of operational units at thirty-seven battalions, compared to an estimated seven effective battalions before martial law. Many of these battalions reportedly were under strength, a result in part of a tendency to create new battalions to replace units depleted in the Mindanao operations. Under a 1975 change the standard army infantry (as well as marine and constabulary) battalion was increased from three to four companies.

An important specialized unit was the Home Defense Forces Group, formerly the AFP Special Forces, a body of some 200 men in 1975 trained in unconventional warfare. It was formed in the 1960s under American tutelage as a Philippine counterpart of the Special Forces (Green Berets) of the United States Army in South Vietnam and served with the Philippine contingent there. Partly to dissociate the force from the Vietnam combat context and partly to emphasize the civic affairs mission, the unit designation was changed from Special Forces Units to Home Defense Forces Group. In addition to its operational mission the unit also served as a training cadre for specialist personnel in other army and constabulary units.

Under a 1970 administrative reorganization the former four military areas into which the country had been divided were redesignated territorial commands. These were believed to be administrative headquarters rather than tactical commands, whose peacetime responsibilities lay mainly in the areas of reserve training and civic action.

Major ground forces arms included a number of half-tracks and late-model M-113 armored personnel carriers and light and medium artillery. The army also had about twenty light aircraft and 200 ground-to-air Sidewinder missiles. The standard infantry arm of the regular forces was the American M-16 rifle. Virtually all arms and equipment were of American design and manufacture.

The Philippine Air Force

The air force had its beginnings in 1935 as the air arm of the constabulary. After the activation of the Philippine Army at the end of that year it was transferred to the new force. Under the 1947 reorganization, which established the AFP, the air arm was redesignated the Philippine Air Force as an autonomous element of the army-dominated armed forces. Executive Order 389 of December 1950 established the air force along with each of the other three services as an independent service.

Air force strength of about 14,000 in 1975 constituted an increase of about two-thirds over force levels for the 1970–71 period. The commander of the air force in 1975 held the rank of major general. The fifteen operational squadrons of the force were organized into two air divisions that included a fighter wing, a strike wing, two airlift wings, and two aircraft control and warning wings. Combat elements included three F-86 fighter squadrons, one of which was an all-weather interceptor squadron, and a fighter-bomber squadron equipped with F-5 aircraft. In the airlift wings were five troop carrier squadrons, two aviation engineer squadrons, and liaison air-sea rescue, special mission, and counterinsurgency squadrons.

Combat aircraft included some forty F-86s, of which eighteen were of the F-86D all-weather interceptor type, and about twenty-two fighter bombers, mostly of the F-5A type. The sizable inventory of more than 200 support aircraft included about forty transport aircraft ranging from two C-130s due for delivery in late 1975 or 1976 to the small Japanese-made YS-11. It also included more than 140 training and utility craft and an estimated thirty or forty helicopters of various types. All of the combat and most of the other aircraft were of United States origin. Some support craft, such as the YS-11 and the T-34, were received from Japan in the late 1950s as part of war reparations. The counterinsurgency squadron was equipped with sixteen armed versions of the Italian-made SIAI-Marchetti SF-260.

The primary missions of the air force were to provide airlift services for the ground forces, both constabulary and army, and close-in tactical air support for ground combat operations. A regional air command was reportedly established in Mindanao in late 1972 to provide a ready deployment of aircraft for tactical support of other forces engaged in operations in that area. In May 1972 the Philippine Air Force assumed control from the United States Air Force of the air defense system for the Philippines. Major air bases in addition to Clark Air Base used by the United States air forces in the Philippines included Basa Air Base at Florida Blanca; Fernando Air Base, Lipa, Batangas; Sangley Point Air Base, Cavite; Mactan Air Base, Cebu; Edwin Andrew Air Base, Zamboanga; and Nichols Air Base, Manila.

All flight training was conducted in-country and was centered at the Air Force Flying School at Fernando Air Base. Seventy-four officers were graduated in the 1974–75 class.

The Philippine Navy

Newest of the services, the navy traces its ancestry to the Off-Shore Patrol, which was formed as part of the army in February 1939. Redesignated the autonomous Philippine Naval Patrol in 1947, it became the Philippine Navy after the armed forces reorganization of January 1951. Command rank was raised from commodore to rear admiral in late 1974.

Like the other services the navy experienced much growth during the first half of the 1970s. Force levels of over 14,000 men and officers in 1975 included a nucleus of marine and coast guard units and the small Naval Air unit of helicopters. Headquarters of the navy is in proximity to its main base at Cavite, near Manila on Manila Bay. The shore establishment included four major activities: the Naval Shipyard, the Naval Supply Center, the Naval Training Command, and the Naval Stations Systems Command. The naval base complex at Subic Bay facing the South China Sea west of Manila was probably without peer as a deepwater facility in the South Pacific. It continued to be used mainly by United States naval forces in the 1970s. Subic Bay owed much of its high state of development to the important part that it played in the United States operations during both the Korean and the Vietnam conflicts.

The navy's principal mission was related to protecting and policing the nation's more than 7,000 islands, which have a combined coastline double that of the United States and are distributed over some 700,000 square miles of claimed territorial waters. The navy also had an important support mission for the other armed services and agencies of the government. Its operational tasks included naval reconnaissance and antisubmarine warfare, amphibious warfare, harbor defense, antipoaching and antismuggling operations, enforcement of maritime regulations, and logistic and transport services. In mid-1970s it was engaged, in cooperation with the other services, in operations against the Muslim insurgents in the Sulu Archipelago region.

Major subordinate commands under naval headquarters were the Naval Operating Force, the navy's combat arm; the Philippine Coast Guard; and the Philippine Marine Brigade. Operational groups included the Underwater Operations Unit, the Naval Construction Force (Seabees), the Mine Force, the Anti-Submarine Force, the Naval Air Unit, and the Ready Force under the direct control of naval headquarters.

The coast guard, established in October 1967, was the navy's law enforcement arm. Its responsibilities also included such maritime affairs as testing and licensing seamen and vessels, aids to navigation, and protecting life and property at sea. The marines had grown from a company-sized force of 230 when organized in November 1950 to a major unit in 1975 of some three infantry battalions, a headquarters service group, and a combat support group. Its nucleus of landing ships, tank (LSTs), and landing ships, mechanized (LSMs), were believed capable of mounting and supplying a full brigade-sized landing operation. Authorized rank of the marine commander reportedly had been raised to commodore in late 1974 or early 1975.

Consistent with the navy's mission, about two-thirds of the fleet strength of some sixty-one line vessels in 1975 consisted of patrol boats and larger patrol vessels. None of these was known to have a missile capability as of late 1974. Particularly suited for antismuggling work were four hydrofoil patrol boats, two of Italian and two of Japanese origin. Other vessels of fleet strength were a destroyer escort and a frigate, believed used as command ships, eleven infantry and tank landing craft, minesweepers, and about eighteen auxiliary vessels ranging from oilers to lighthouse tenders. Another fifteen or sixteen vessels, virtually all forty-foot utility boats acquired from the United States Coast Guard, were assigned to the navy's coast guard. Much equipment was believed to be in need of upgrading and modernization.

According to the authoritative *Jane's Fighting Ships, 1975–76* the navy was expected to add ships of destroyer size to the fleet during the 1970s. There were no known plans to acquire submarines. With few exceptions fleet vessels were of United States origin. Some smaller vessels of American design were constructed in the Philippines. Virtually all of the patrol craft and some other line vessels were no more than twenty years old in 1975; most of the others and the auxiliary vessels were of World War II vintage.

The Reserve Forces

National defense policy, particularly since martial law, has assigned a leading role to a citizen army of trained and motivated reservists. Most of the elements of the reserve program had existed for a number of years, in some cases since before World War II, but new policies in the mid-1970s gave these programs a priority and a commitment they had lacked earlier.

Several purposes were to be served by the expanded and improved reserve program called for by President Marcos. One, insisted upon by the Congress in approving the Marcos administrations' request for increases in the standing armed forces, was the preservation of the citizen army principle. This principle was embodied in the National Defense Act of 1935. It called for a defense based not on large conscript forces but on a limited professional cadre force supported by a mass base of citizen reservists. A second purpose was to meet the demands imposed by a policy of increased self-reliance in national defense. A third was to harness military training to national development.

Although no breakdown of the numbers and categories of reserve forces was available in 1975, the total number of active reservists may have been on the order of 200,000. Additions to the reserve forces came from a variety of sources and programs. The core of the enlisted reserve program was the Trainee Program, under which a limited number of twenty-year-old males (about 10,000 annually as of 1975) were conscripted for a period of active military training. The training period was eighteen months in all services in 1975, an extension of the term in effect before 1972. A small number of reservists were veterans of the career military services, who were automatically placed on the reserve until a certain age.

A basic military training and indoctrination course was compulsory for all high school students. Boys belonged to the Citizen Army Training and girls to the Women's Auxiliary Service. Physically fit male college students were required to join the Reserve Officers Training Corps (ROTC) of one of the services. A counterpart organization for women students, the Women's Auxiliary Training Corps (WATC), was voluntary. Enrollment in both was an estimated 175,000 in 1973. The ROTC program was the major source of officer personnel for the components of the respective services and of leadership cadres for other defense mobilization programs.

More specialized reserve programs included the "36–70 project," under which certain key technical and executive personnel received reserve commissions and annual active duty assignments in their specialties. The Integrated Civilian Home Defense Forces program under the constabul-

364

ary was a form of civilian police that, particularly in the metropolitan areas, provided a reserve organization for personnel in government or private industry who held police and security guard positions. the "weekend warrior" program, such as in the air force, brought reservists on active duty for a number of weekends each year.

A key element of the government's long-range plan for building up the reserves was the Home Defense Program. An authoritative statement described it as "aimed primarily at a more progressive development of the Reserve Force of the AFP and its auxiliaries such as the ROTC. Secondarily the program seeks to provide active and effective AFP participation in national development." Emphasis was placed on integrating reserve training and reserve manpower resources into the armed forces' Home Defense Program activities at all levels. ROTC and other forms of reserve training were broadened to include theoretical and practical work in the civil affairs field. The talents of reservists who had professional and technical skills would be used for community or public relations purposes.

Plans called for the eventual creation of local civil defense units, called *barrio* self-defense units, in each of some 40,000 *barrios* of the country. Each unit was a basic village militia typically under the direction of a noncommissioned officer from the regular forces stationed in the vicinity. As of 1975 only a small number of such units were in existence, in insurgency-affected areas of Mindanao and northern and central Luzon.

PERSONNEL AND LOGISTICS

Enlisted Procurement and Training

Manpower needs of the regular armed forces have consistently been met through voluntary enlistment. The large number of applicants seeking enlistment has generally enabled the services to be selective. Initial enlistment in all services was possible to the age of thirty with three-year reenlistments. Retirement was at sixty or voluntarily after twenty years of service. Potential military manpower was large: in 1975 an estimated 60 percent of the total population of over 42 million was under the age of twenty-five.

Augmenting the standing forces were those performing military training under conscription. All Filipino males were required to register for conscription in the province of their residence on reaching the age of twenty. Although men remained subject to call-up until the age of forty-nine, the practice has been to confine the selection to youths just turned twenty. About four classes a year were inducted. Even the considerably enlarged contingent of inductees in the mid-1970s, as compared to the annual number of 6,000 or so usual before about 1973, represented a tiny proportion—less than 2 percent—of the age cohort.

In accordance with a major change in mobilization policy that took effect in 1973, certain inducted men receive their training in special battalions called Kamagong (after a native hardwood tree known for its strength and beauty). These were in effect rotational training units that included a cadre of regular officers and noncommissioned personnel. In time of mobilization Kamagong units would be called up first. The high degree of physical and military readiness of freshly trained young Kamagong men meant that they were quickly available for operational use, in contrast to the regular reservists. The mobilization of young, mainly unmarried men also entailed less social hardship and economic disruption.

A presidential decree of May 1973 empowered the armed forces to induct Kamagong trainees for emergency service periods of up to two years. It also provided preferential consideration after such service in application for government employment or for enlistment in the regular forces. Kamagong units reportedly have been used with regular forces in military operations against the Muslim insurgents.

Noncommissioned officers for the regular services are obtained from the ranks of enlisted men who have demonstrated professional aptitude and leadership. Those selected usually have had more than three years' service and have undergone special training in a service school.

In the reserve, noncommissioned officers are procured only after they have completed formal training in the ROTC. Men who complete the two-year basic ROTC course qualify for appointment, as do those who take the two-year additional advanced course but do not qualify for commission as an officer.

Advanced specialized training for both officers and enlisted men of all services is accomplished at formal service schools. Army and constabulary personnel attend schools of the Army School Center at Fort McKinley, naval personnel at the Naval School Center in Cavite, and air force personnel at schools of the 100th Training Wing at Lipa Air Base, Laguna.

The army operates separate schools for the various arms and branches, all of which offer appropriate basic and advanced courses as well as specialized technical courses. The School for Combat Arms offers four- to five-month courses in artillery, armor, and infantry; the School for Technical Services offers courses for signal, engineer, ordnance, quartermaster, and chemical service personnel; the School for Administration and Finance offers courses ranging from nine to twenty weeks in length in finance and administration.

Officer Procurement and Training

Career officers of the three military services and the constabulary have been drawn in the main from graduates of the Philippine Military Academy at Fort Del Pilar, Baguio. About half the regular officer corps in 1973 were academy graduates, the rest being integrated reserve officers. The academy accepts cadets between the ages of seventeen and twenty-three who are selected, after examination, from their congressional districts (by congressional nomination before suspension of the Congress in January 1973) and appointed by the president. After a four-year course patterned on that of the United States Military Academy at West Point, graduates receive bachelor of science degrees and are commissioned second lieutenant or ensign. Service assignment is made at graduation on the basis of the annual quotas set for each service by armed forces headquarters. Within quota limits cadets are given their preference, being asked in order of class standing. Those who elect the navy or air force usually attend orientation courses of those services before being assigned to their units.

Of the ninety-one cadets scheduled for graduation in 1975, thirty-two (35 percent) were apportioned to the army, twenty-eight (31 percent) to the navy, sixteen (18 percent) to the air force, and the remaining fifteen (16 percent) to the highly preferred constabulary. This constituted a significant shift in the navy and constabulary quotas from past years; of the 1,545 academy graduates in the period from the end of World War II to 1974, about 20 percent had gone to the navy and 27 percent to the constabulary. It was not clear to what extent the 1975 increase in the navy quota reflected a temporary demand arising from rapid naval expansion.

Most reserve officers and some regular officers receive their commissions through either the ROTC at selected universities or the course at the School of Reserve Commissions. The ROTC program is divided into an initial two-year basic course and an advanced course covering an additional two years. The four-year course has been a prerequisite for the final probationary training, leading to commissioning as a reserve second lieutenant or, for a small number, regular commissions. Two-year-course graduates qualify as candidates for reserve noncommissioned status. Commissions for women can be had through the WATC, whose members are termed cadettes. Women are commissioned in the Women's Auxiliary Corps, of which each service has a counterpart. There was still a good deal of ambivalence both in and outside the service over the idea of military careers for women, enlisted or commissioned. A service publication noted the persistent discrimination in assignment and promotion of women officers: the highest rank was major. Women also serve as commissioned officers in the nurse corps.

The armed forces' School of Reserve Commissions was an officer candidate school open to enlisted men in the regular forces. Formerly an army school, it was placed under the Home Defense Training Center of the Armed Forces in 1974 and open to personnel of all services. Admission was highly selective on the basis mainly of competitive examination. Applicants had to be noncommissioned officers between the ages of twenty-four and thirty-five, have at least three years of continuous military service, and have completed some college-level academic work. The twelve-month course included a final four-month period of on-the-job training as probationary second lieutenants. There was provision for direct commissioning of persons having certain technical and professional qualifications and for direct battlefield commissioning of noncommissioned officers for outstanding service in wartime.

In-service professional training for officers consisted of three levels of institutions. These were the service schools, such as the Air Force Officer School, for preparing company-grade officers for command and staff responsibility; the AFP Command and General Staff College for field-grade officers; and the top-level National Defense College of the Philippines.

Created in 1963, the National Defense College provides a broad, last-step professional education for senior officers destined for high command and policymaking responsibilities. Originally open only to military and government officers (later including women), the college broadened its scope in 1972 to include key civilian executives from industry, national organizations, and education. Persons from outside the government outnumbered both military and civil government students in the thirty-nine-member class of 1975. The eleven-month course led to a master's degree in national security administration.

The senior institution of tactical military education is the AFP Command and General Staff College, now virtually obligatory for appointment to battalion-level command. The institution is a combined service school created in 1969 out of the separate service command schools. It was closely patterned after the United States counterpart at Fort Leavenworth, Kansas. Enrollment as of 1974 was limited to sixty each year, selected from among field-grade officers on the basis of competitive examination and other requirements. The ten-month curriculum was broadened in the early 1970s to include geopolitical and sociopolitical studies as well as such subjects as insurgency and internal stability. Plans were under way in 1974 to open the school to inactive reserve officers. Weekend classes would be available to those in the greater Manila area and correspondence study to students elsewhere.

Conditions of Service

Armed forces grades and ranks were identical with their counterparts in the United States forces with minor exceptions. The army, air force, and constabulary used the same rank terminology and insignia. The lowest navy flag rank was commodore rather than admiral as in American terminology. No rank of warrant officer existed in any of the services. By 1975 uniform khaki dress had been adopted for all services, and the color of rank insignia rather than uniform differentiated the service of officers. Details of rank insignia had undergone modification between 1972 and 1975.

Pay and other emoluments in the armed forces have traditionally been attractive in relation to the civilian economy and the standard of living of the average Filipino. Substantial increases in the kinds and levels of military compensation, particularly for officers, were announced in 1972 and 1975 as a concomitant of the government's policy of priority development of the national defense establishment (see table 17). This has included not only increases in base pay scales but also improved allowances, housing, combat pay, and retirement benefits and enhanced promotional opportunities for senior officers.

Service emoluments included a commissary service established in 1973 and the Government Service Insurance System, which was extended after 1972 to include armed forces personnel. There was, however, a continuing severe shortage of doctors and trained medical personnel. English was the language of official communication as well as the lingua franca of the multilingual troop units. Pilipino was coming into use in certain ceremonial and other situations.

A campaign to tighten standards of discipline and integrity within the armed forces resulted in the dismissal or punishment of some 1,800 officers and enlisted men in the first three years of the campaign, to August 1975, according to the secretary of national defense. Discipline remained a serious problem, according to official indications. In the autumn of 1975 there were reports that the president intended to purge a number of officers from the top echelons of the military, which many regarded as tainted by corruption. Subsequently the secretary of national defense indicated that the military would purge its own ranks; at year's end no significant retirements had been announced. Among other

Table 17. Philippines, Military Ranks and Pay Scales, 1975

Rank		Monthly Base Pay (in pesos)[1]	
Army and Air Force	Navy	December 1975	January 1976
General or Chief of Staff	(Chief of Staff)[2]	2,200	4,000
Lieutenant General	...[2]	1,925	3,500
Major General	Rear Admiral	1,650	3,000
Brigadier General	Commodore	1,430	2,500
Colonel	Captain	1,210	2,000
Lieutenant Colonel	Commander	990	1,700
Major	Lieutenant Commander	770	1,400
Captain	Lieutenant Senior Grade	605	1,100
First Lieutenant	Lieutenant Junior Grade	495	900
Second Lieutenant	Ensign	407	700
Master Sergeant	Chief Petty Officer	286	410
Technical Sergeant	Petty Officer First Class	264	360
Staff Sergeant	Petty Officer Second Class	242	325
Sergeant	Petty Officer Third Class	225	300
Corporal	Seaman First Class	214	275
Private First Class	Seaman Second Class	203	255
Private	Apprentice Seaman	198	240

[1] For value of the peso—see Glossary.
[2] No equivalent to United States naval rank.

measures to cleanse the military ranks of corrupt practices, President Marcos in early 1975 ordered certain military and other officials to declare their financial assets.

At least nineteen awards and decorations exist for which military personnel are eligible. Of the awards for gallantry, the highest is the Medal for Valor, corresponding to the Medal of Honor of the United States. It is awarded for conspicuous gallantry and intrepidity above and beyond the call of duty in action against an enemy.

Regular military courts were patterned after the courts-martial of the United States forces. The system contained three levels of courts in ascending order according to the gravity of the offenses assigned to them: summary courts-martial, special courts-martial, and general courts-martial. Review of court-martial sentences was conducted within military command channels. Final appeal of a sentence lay with the president as commander in chief.

Logistics

National defense policy after 1972 placed priority on reducing over the long term the heavy dependence of the armed forces on outside—mainly United States—sources of arms and matériel. Oil exploration in Philippine territory has raised official hopes of an eventual domestic source of petroleum that would reduce somewhat the nation's vulnerability in this respect.

Two main elements of this policy, as stated in the self-reliant defense posture program, were to provide for as large a portion as possible of defense needs from the country's own resources and production and to encourage the development of a civilian defense industry through military and governmental assistance and partnership. Preference would be given in the procurement of arms and matériel to indigenous industry and raw materials. When feasible, sophisticated equipment would be avoided in favor of simpler models more in keeping with the production and maintenance capabilities of a developing economy.

Under way in 1975 was the construction of a plant for the manufacture of M-16 rifles. Plans also called for the domestic production of assault rifles as part of a larger basic-weapons production program. As of late 1974 a facility was in operation for the assembly of helicopters of European manufacture for the navy's air unit. The navy's self-reliance program also included a shipbuilding program under the Maritime Industrial Authority. The accent was on production of small craft and patrol vessels, including ships up to 120 feet. A program for the manufacture of automotive parts and components was planned so as to create manufacturing facilities that would be quickly adaptable to military transport purposes as well as to the manufacture of arms and ammunition. It was also announced, after the firing of a prototype rocket in early 1972, that the government planned at an unspecified time to enter into the production of a tactical rocket.

Instrumental in the self-reliance program was the AFP Research and Development Center. The center's tasks included scientific inquiry into native resources and materials of military significance, weaponry development, keeping abreast of military-related research and development, and statistical and planning work related to national mobilization.

Poor surface mobility, lack of terrain knowledge, and logistics unsuited to local conditions have been noted as shortcomings that have hindered government forces in conducting unconventional warfare operations against insurgent groups, particularly in Mindanao. In economic planning a strong emphasis on roadbuilding has probably contributed to some improvement in these operations.

Among developments leading to improved logistical services was the establishment in 1970 of an integrated AFP Logistics Center and six regional military supply points. This was the major armed forces facility for the procurement, storage, and distribution of matériel. The center was assuming a growing role in fabrication, experimentation, and design of military-related matériel. It operated the commissary and exchange system. Computerization was coming into increasing use in personnel and logistics management, using the resources of the National Computer Center. A unified budget process was inaugurated beginning with FY 1975 under the annually updated five-year AFP Strategic Objective Plan. Great strides have been made since the mid-1960s in providing the military forces with a modern communication system. In 1975 virtually all tactical units, according to the government, were linked with armed forces headquarters by microwave communications.

Some logistic services that previously had been performed by United States elements, such as air traffic coordination at Clark Air Base and a water terminal at Manila, were taken over by Philippine forces in June 1974 after discontinuance of the United States Army Support Element in the Philippines.

CHAPTER 17

PUBLIC ORDER AND INTERNAL SECURITY

By the end of 1975 the Philippines had entered a fourth year under a state of martial law, proclaimed on September 23, 1972, by the president on the basis of his power to call out the armed forces "to prevent or suppress lawless violence, invasion, insurrection, or rebellion" (see ch. 9). All of these conditions except invasion were major preoccupations of the leadership during the first half of the 1970s. Armed challenges to the authority of the government were posed by the Maoist Communists centered on the main island of Luzon and by dissident Muslims engaged in both political and communal warfare in the south in Mindanao and the Sulu Archipelago.

Dissident movements have emerged periodically throughout modern Philippine history. A wellspring of such movements has been the central Luzon agricultural region where a densely settled peasantry—cast adrift from its earlier security and community values and increasingly impoverished—has responded alternately to quasi-religious exhortation and radical political organization. Geographically adjacent to this region and also burdened by problems of rapid urban growth, metropolitan Manila has been especially vulnerable to these twin threats to public order. Most such movements, like that of the Hukbalahap (see Glossary) of the 1950s, faded into banditry or oblivion. Although government efforts to suppress the Maoist New People's Army (NPA) and the Muslim separatists remained inconclusive as of the end of 1975, neither appeared to constitute a critical threat to the established order in the nation as a whole. They did constitute, however, a serious disturbance of domestic tranquillity and a drain on national resources.

The root cause of much of the national malaise was social as well as political and included deep-seated grievances over land tenure arrangements and corruption. Under the mantle of martial law the central government applied the coercive power of the police and the army to the pressing problem of restoring order while espousing measures designed to tackle the long-term task of reform.

A serious increase in lawlessness and violence in the early 1970s provided further cause for the imposition of martial law. Before martial law, statements of the president and other national leaders painted a picture of nearly anarchic conditions in the Manila metropolitan area and elsewhere. Some, observing soaring crime rates and other evidence of social deterioration, sweepingly proclaimed the Philippines a "failing democracy."

A disproportionate share of crime and violence, however, occurred in the city of Manila and its metropolitan environs. The Tondo slum district of Manila epitomized the worst social consequences of sustained and rapid urbanization in an Asian primate city. Such measures as the confiscation of private weapons and the disbanding of private armies contributed to a sharp decline in many forms of crime and violence, at least during the early period after the imposition of martial law.

Reform of the criminal justice system to achieve speedier justice made some headway under the martial law regime. This has been accompanied by the at least temporary sacrifice of some established constitutional safeguards and civil rights. Losses included the denial of recourse to habeas corpus in the case of political detainees and the institution of military tribunals that have civil jurisdiction. Martial law rule—what President Ferdinand E. Marcos termed a "constitutional authoritarian regime"—if prolonged could tend to erode the relative independence formerly enjoyed by the judiciary.

The agency primarily charged with the maintenance of law, domestic order, and security was the new Integrated National Police (INP). The core force of the police was the 27,000-man Philippine Constabulary, one of the four armed services under the ultimate direction of the president as commander in chief. The supporting role of the army in matters of internal security has drawn it, along with the other military services, into large-scale operations with the constabulary in the areas of the Muslim insurgency.

DOMESTIC ORDER AND MARTIAL LAW

A prelude to the martial law Proclamation 1081 of September 1972 was the erosion of domestic tranquillity and national stability after the bitter election year of 1969. Political violence and criminal activity—the two often merging—had long been endemic to the Manila metropolitan area but in the early 1970s reached intense levels. Even allowing for hyperbole, the national condition as described by President Marcos in his speech to the nation accompanying Proclamation 1081 was stark:

> There is no doubt in everybody's mind that a state of rebellion exists in the Philippines. . . . It has paralyzed the functions of the national and local governments. The productive sectors of the economy have ground to a halt. Many schools have closed down. Many of our businessmen, traders, industrialists, producers, and manufacturers have stopped their operations. In the Greater Manila area alone, tension and anxiety have reached a point where the citizens are compelled to stay at home. Lawlessness and criminality like kidnapping, smuggling, extortion, blackmail, armed robbery, illegal traffic in drugs, gunrunning, hoarding, and manipulation of prices, corruption in government, and tax evasion perpetrated by syndicate criminals have increasingly escalated beyond the capability of local police and civilian authorities.

The government claimed dramatic declines in crime rates in the initial months of martial law. These claims were attested to both by observers and by the relief often expressed by individual citizens. Two potent sources of violence and disorder—illegal handguns and the private armies of politicians, wealthy families, and criminal syndicates—were greatly weakened if not eliminated as the result of the government's sweeping use of its new police powers. Some 12,000 people were detained in the first year of martial law. The relatively quiet fashion in which the martial law regime was imposed appeared to contribute to the sense of public relief. To many it was the lesser of evils—a price to be paid for a return to security and stability.

In the area of internal security initial martial law measures had a mixed effect. Acts of overt confrontation and political violence stemming from the communist insurrection and subversion centered on Luzon appeared to have subsided. But long-smoldering Muslim dissidence in Mindanao was fanned into open separatism and communal warfare by measures taken under martial law.

Part of the price paid for the law-and-order benefits of martial law was diminished civil liberties and freedoms for the Philippine citizen. Political dissent was sharply curtailed as was freedom of the press and broadcasting media. Constitutional safeguards against arbitrary arrest and detention were circumscribed; due process was for some no longer a safeguard against authority. Under its new powers the state imposed a nationwide curfew from midnight to 4:00 A.M.; controlled all communications; prohibited demonstrations, strikes, and many kinds of political activities; removed certain students and teachers from their schools; temporarily seized all private aircraft and watercraft of Philippine registry; and forbade Filipinos to leave the country without permission (see ch. 7).

At the end of 1975, three years after the institution of martial law, Marcos held out no prospect of its early end, although some measures, such as direct control of the media, had been softened. One consequence was a backlash against martial law itself, including charges by critics that the president's purpose had less to do with the advancement of the national welfare than with the retention of political power.

Dissent and Insurrection

Major centers of dissidence or subversion to the regime as viewed by the authorities administering the martial law sanctions against them were the Maoist NPA, the Muslim separatists, certain student groups and other elements of the intelligentsia, and elements of the Roman Catholic Church and other religious organizations. Church-state relations in particular came under increasing strain after the imposition of martial law. There was no indication that the Roman Catholic Church or other religious groups posed a temporal challenge to the state. Nevertheless the fact that some 83 percent of the Philippine population counted themselves Roman Catholics made the church an alternate focus of loyalty and a powerful influence in molding national opinion, particularly in the absence of alternative outlets, such as those formerly provided by the political parties and a free if irresponsible press (see ch. 7; ch. 8).

Increasingly after the first year of martial law church leaders publicly criticized the suppression of civil liberties under the government's policy. In early 1974 the Roman Catholic bishops of the country formally called on Marcos to lift martial law. Later that year a church-sponsored mass protest against the Marcos regime was held at the Manila cathedral. Initial opposition was expressed by the younger activist element of the hierarchy and the religious orders but, as martial law was prolonged, some orders and more conservative church leaders also inclined toward outspoken criticism. Some Protestant leaders also joined the call for an end to martial law.

The government viewed several of the more activist religious elements as subversive. Arrests of Catholic priests and nuns and raids on church-affiliated establishments by martial law authorities were major sources of church-state tension. The 1974 protest at Manila cathedral was triggered by the detention of a number of persons after a police raid on the Sacred Heart Novitiate in Quezon City. At about the same time in mid-1974 authorities arrested a number of leaders of the National Council of Churches in a series of night raids. In late 1975 criminal charges reportedly were filed against a Catholic priest among others for alleged conspiracy to commit rebellion by publicly circulating and possessing subversive material.

Confrontation between government and campus was one of the contributors of the violence that increasingly scarred national life between 1969 and 1972. If not a direct threat to national authority, the some 500,000 college students in and around Manila had a potential for disruption that the government viewed with at least strong suspicion. The University of the Philippines in Manila, which radical students tried to seize in a violent incident in 1971, was the source of support for the NPA and other antistate groups through such front organizations as the Patriotic Youth (Kabataang Makabayan—KM) and the fanatical Youth Democratic Association (Samahang Demokratiko ng Kabataang). Among the evidences of gathering rebellion cited in Proclamation 1081 was "the disappearance and dropping out of school of some 3,000 high school and college students . . . who are reported to have joined with the insurgents for training in the handling of firearms and explosives."

Radical students reportedly constituted a large portion of the thousands of people arrested and held in detention by the martial law authorities in the police operations that characterized the first flush of enforcement of the law. Such measures, as well as infiltration of universities by government security agents, appeared to have effectively contained campus activism after 1972. One result, however, was to drive the hard-core element of student militants into the NPA or to other forms of armed opposition.

In Proclamation 1081 and in his speech to the nation on September 23, 1972, President Marcos gave as a major reason for the imposition of martial law the existence of a "state of rebellion." He singled out in this respect the Maoist NPA. Although many questioned whether the NPA and other groups constituted a clear and present danger to the established political order, it was evident that by 1972 NPA guerrilla activity had become a major security problem for the central government. It remained so three years later, although on a somewhat diminished scale.

The NPA was the military arm of the Maoist-oriented faction of the Communist Party of the Philippines (Partido Komunista ng Pilipinas— PKP). This faction distinguished itself when necessary from the pro-Soviet faction of the PKP by adding the words "Marxist-Leninist" or "Mao Tse-tung's Thought" after its name and was referred to as the PKP-ML or CPP-ML. Both the NPA and the PKP-ML were established in 1969. The PKP-ML was the most militant of several communist factions in the Philippines and espoused a Maoist strategy of revolutior. based on guerrilla warfare. Although all communist organizations were illegal under the Antisubversion Act of 1957, the pro-Moscow PKP had turned after 1972 to a tactic of "legal struggle" and accommodation with the Marcos government. Remnants of the Huk movement of the post-World War II period represented little more than local organized crime and banditry by the late 1960s. It was the PKP-ML and its youth front, the KM, that were the principal objects of the government's concern.

Early in the 1970s the NPA established its base of operations in the rural sanctuary of Isabela Province in northeast Luzon. A secondary foothold was in the Bicol Peninsula in southeast Luzon. Both were remote areas where central government control was weak. The NPA also organized an undergound urban guerrilla movement in part using radical students. By late 1972, according to President Marcos, the NPA controlled thirty-three of the thirty-seven municipalities in Isabela Province and had 207 barrio organizing committees in twenty-five towns. Tax collection was one of the functions of the committees.

Government tactics against the NPA under martial law have been a combination of carrot and stick. Aggressive patrolling along with periodic "encirclement and suppression" actions were proving effective, according to the government, in keeping NPA militancy under control. A presidential amnesty program, part of an alternative psychological warfare approach, was aimed at encouraging defections from NPA and party ranks. The government claimed some success in this "carrot" approach as well.

Perhaps in response to the effectiveness of the police counteraction, the NPA after 1972 tended to avoid contact with security forces and to downplay military action while concentrating on political subversion and building its power base. Links between the NPA and the Muslim dissidents in the islands to the south were judged by most observers to be tenuous, despite official formulations suggesting some form of operational connection. Few denied, however, that the Filipino Maoists, notably the NPA, had the support of the People's Republic of China (PRC). The Philippine diplomatic policy of rapprochement with Peking and the official endorsement of some Maoist models for emulation have further complicated the task of suppressing domestic Maoists.

Official and unofficial estimates of Maoist strength have varied widely partly because of the loose definition of and lack of criteria for what constitutes support. The proclamation of martial law put the figures as of July 31, 1972, at 7,900, of which 1,028 were termed regulars, 1,800 combat support, and the remainder service support. Another credible estimate was somewhat lower: as of early 1975 about 1,000 operational NPA adherents, about 2,000 PKP-ML cadre personnel, and between 2,000 and 3,000 sympathizers and supporters in front organizations. NPA militant activity by that time was confined mainly to sporadic acts in east-central Luzon. Scattered pockets of militancy also persisted in the Visayan Islands, Mindanao, and the Sulu Archipelago. Unlike the Muslim insurgents in the south the NPA had not proved capable of denying territory to the government's security forces. Nevertheless in 1975 the NPA continued to be a potentially effective and well-supplied revolutionary force within its limited area of operation. Official sensitivity to the NPA was heightened by the fact that NPA activity was concentrated in an area that was close to Manila and included the outskirts of the city itself.

The Muslim Rebellion

In 1975 a more vexing security problem than that of the NPA was that of the militant Muslim separatist movement in Mindanao and the Sulu Archipelago. Most of the Philippine Muslim minority, roughly 5 percent of the population, were concentrated in this southernmost area of the country. Ambivalent loyalty toward a national or political Philippine entity and rejection of the authority of a distant and culturally alien government in Manila have been constant features of Philippine Muslim history, active Muslim resistance dating back to the early Spanish colonial period. In the 1970s this historic alienation was exacerbated by land tenure problems, official neglect, private exploitation, and fears of being overrun by the Christian influx from the north, which had made the Muslims a minority in some of their ancestral lands by the 1970s (see ch. 4).

The insurgency of the 1970s began with the formation in August 1968 of the Mindanao Independence Movement (MIM) sparked by an embittered Muslim political leader, Datu Utdong Matalam. The movement became a part of the upsurge of militancy and national violence that affected the

Philippines from 1969 until the imposition of martial law. The MIM was named in Proclamation 1081 as one of "certain lawless organizations" whose acts had brought parts of Mindanao and the Sulu Archipelago to "a state of actual war."

In contrast to the damping effect of martial law on NPA militancy, the effect of martial law in the south was to drive a portion of the Muslim community into open revolt. Muslim rebels might have planned an offensive even before the declaration of martial law, as official sources claimed. Nevertheless certain government acts such as the attempt to include the Muslims in the nationwide police campaign to confiscate illegal arms, contributed directly to the Muslims' resorting to warfare. From the initial outbreak in Marawi City in Lanao del Sur Province of western Mindanao in October 1972, fighting extended rapidly into Lanao del Norte Province and the major islands of Basilan, Jolo, and Tawitawi in the Sulu Archipelago. Fighting reached a peak in early 1974, which saw the devastation of the city of Jolo. By 1975 endemic if sporadic warfare in the south had displaced an estimated 1.5 million Muslims and Christians and had cost the lives of at least several thousand government and rebel soldiers (neither side publicized its casualties). Brutalities were practiced on both sides.

The fighting caused serious economic loss in the area and affected the government's overall development program. The maintenance of a greatly expanded military and police force in the area was also a heavy fiscal drain. Total government forces engaged against the Muslims were estimated as of 1975 at about 35,000, to which were added some 15,000 local militia and *barrio* defense forces.

The Muslims of the MIM were not a single group, nor did they have a unified command or share a common outlook and set of goals. Ethnically they included three distinct groups: the traditionalist Maranao of Lanao del Sur; the Tausug, found mainly in the Sulu Archipelago and known for their fighting nature; and the Maguindanao in Maguindanao Province and the hinterlands of the city of Cotabato. All were involved in the fighting in some fashion. It was, however, the Moro National Liberation Front (MNLF), composed of all elements of the Muslim community, that emerged after 1972 as the driving force behind the insurgency. By 1975 the MNLF was believed to possess a sophisticated organizational structure and a regular military force known as the Bangsa Moro Army, which constituted the main fighting arm of the Muslim rebellion.

Estimates of MNLF strength in late 1975 ranged from 8,000 to about double that number of armed regulars and 20,000 to 30,000 active supporters. The mass base of sympathizers might have been as high as 400,000 according to a government figure. Centers of concentration of the MNLF were in southwestern Mindanao and the provinces of Lanao del Norte and Lanao del Sur in western Mindanao bordering on the Moro Gulf; in Zamboanga Province; and in Jolo, Basilan, and Tawitawi. Despite official statements tending to link the Muslim insurgents with the NPA, all evidence was that the Muslims had shunned any operational links with the Communists, whom they regard as ideologically alien.

After the heavy fighting of early 1974 government policy tended in the direction of a political settlement. This policy would grant the Muslims some measure of autonomy. It would also include legal and cultural recognition of the Muslim community's particular needs in a country where national institutions had been built upon a Western and Christian cultural base alien to the Muslim tradition. Although downplaying the religious aspect of Muslim dissidence, President Marcos freely conceded that the economic and other grievances of the Muslims were contributing causes of the rebellion. Prominent among these grievances were official corruption and the "grasping attitude of big Christian landowners, ranchers, loggers and others." Nevertheless government operations tended to reinforce the communal aspect of the fighting in that the government forces sent to suppress the Muslims were composed largely of Christians from the north who had little sympathy for or understanding of the Muslims. Furthermore government forces armed the local Christians for action against their Muslim neighbors.

Government sensitivity to the Muslim problem was compounded by concern over the strategic vulnerability of the "soft underbelly" of the Philippines in the Mindanao and Sulu land-sea frontier region. This formed part of an extensive island area where the Philippines, Malaysia, and Indonesia meet and where competing territorial claims remained unresolved. The Muslim state of Sabah, which is a Malaysian portion of the island of Borneo, helped sustain the pan-Islamic sentiment of Muslims in the Philippines as well as aiding them in more material ways. Neither the Malaysian government nor the Philippine government was able to exert its full authority in these distant and hard-to-govern territories under their respective sovereignties. Smuggling, piracy, and banditry have long been practiced in these regions of permeable frontiers in and around the Sulu Sea to the despair of governments and inhabitants alike. The breakdown of law and order did not make Manila's task any easier (see ch. 11).

The Marcos regime also had to contend with the reaction of Muslim countries elsewhere, particularly its Middle East oil suppliers, to its handling of the domestic Muslim minority. Colonel Muammar al Qudhaafi, the Libyan leader, openly proclaimed in early 1974 that he was providing support to the Philippine Muslim rebels in line with his policy of supporting Muslim dissidents everywhere. Although the statements were not necessarily related, President Marcos claimed in late 1975 that from 1972 to that time an estimated 30,000 assault rifles had entered the Philippines "from foreign sources."

As of late 1975 the government claimed considerable success for its "policy of attraction" by which Muslim dissidents were encouraged to rejoin the government under an amnesty that offered such inducements as monetary loans and commissions in the government armed forces. Using the good offices of the World Islamic Conference, talks had been opened with Muslim leaders in Jiddah, Saudi Arabia, in 1974 and in Zamboanga in mid-1975. Programs aimed at land reform, developmental assistance, and improved rice supply were being promoted. President Marcos stated the government's willingness "to give them the utmost autonomy." Hard-core rebel resistance, however, appeared relatively unaffected. At the end of three years of martial law substantial government forces remained tied down in the south. Official claims of having stabilized the situation and of having contained the rebel forces in a few isolated areas were disputed by reports from sources outside the government that the dissidents continued to control much of the countryside. Neither military victory nor political settlement appeared imminent in late 1975.

Crime and Violence

Regarding his decision to impose martial law Marcos wrote in 1973:

> My first concern was not only to secure the Republic against any uprising . . . but also to secure the entire citizenry from the criminal elements, the private armies bred by local politics, and the outlaw bands in the countryside. . . . It was imperative that we dismantle not only the apparatus of the insurgency movement, but also the whole system of violence and criminality that had virtually imprisoned our society in fear and anarchy.

He suggested that the problem of civil disorder was rooted in the inequities of Philippine society.

Several other characteristics of Philippine society have been regarded as related to the problems of violence and criminality. Few, however, have been systematically examined. Among these characteristics are a family-centered morality that, for example, overlooks theft when the victim is outside the immediate circle of family and friends; local factional rivalries and interfamily feuds that often erupt into physical assault or murder; the armed violence that almost invariably surrounds elections; and the rapid pace of urbanization, principally in the Manila area. Compounding these have been the public's unwillingness to cooperate with police in criminal matters and doubt about the impartiality of local police and criminal justice authorities.

Promising what would have to be a long-term effort at reform, the martial law authorites mounted an immediate attack on two sources of violence: the private armies and the private possession of arms. Threatened or actual violence had been closely related to the existence of these private armies as well as to ties between some political figures and criminal syndicates employing such armed groups. The authorities disbanded 145 of these groups during the first nine months of martial law and arrested several prominent political figures who had apparent criminal associations.

The outlawing of the unlicensed possession of firearms and certain other weapons, under maximum penalty of death, led to a particularly violent reaction on the part of the Muslims. As a result the authorities abandoned the effort to enforce the new decree in Muslim areas. For the most part, however, the government claimed great success: 130,000 firearms were surrendered during the initial one-month grace period; and more than 500,000 firearms in addition to quantities of bladed weapons, explosives, and at least one armored car were surrendered during the first nine months.

The Manila metropolitan area's very high crime rate has long made the city a special case. Much of the apparent crisis of soaring crime rates in the 1960s and early 1970s was actually a metropolitan rather than a nationwide problem, according to certain authorities. Greater Manila accounted for 87 percent of all reported crime nationwide in 1974.

As have other so-called primate cities in developing countries, the Manila metropolis has attracted and continues to attract the best and the worst from the rest of the country. The metropolitan area population, placed at 1.1 million in 1960 and 3 million in 1968, was projected by a University of the Philippines study to rise to 5.9 million in 1980 and 11.7 million by the end of the century. Industrialization and economic development have not kept pace. Resulting unemployment coupled with inadequate housing and services have forced a large part of the newcomers into some of the world's worst slum and squatter settlements. The notorious Tondo slum district alone, having about one-sixth of the metropolitan population, accounted for more than one-third of the reported crime victims in the mid-1960s. A 1969 study concluded that the Manila-area rate of murder and other homicides, abnormally high even by international standards, was rooted in the social effects of high growth and population density and was not greatly diminished by an increase in police.

Initially martial law measures appeared to have caused a sharp drop in national crime rates, particularly with respect to homicide and other crimes against persons and to syndicated crime (see table 18). Indications were that by the mid-1970s the rates were working back toward pre-martial law levels. The public's perception of improved order nationwide might have persisted because of greatly reduced crime reportage in the press, which had formerly provided detailed coverage. Juvenile crime, aggravated by the youthfulness of the urban population and by the large numbers of school-aged youths not in school or unemployed, reportedly accounted for much theft, robbery, and physical assault. Drug abuse was a serious problem affecting youth.

Drug trafficking and the smuggling of drugs and taxable commodities were organized criminal activities of particular concern to the government. A number of special interagency organs were involved in major enforcement efforts in these areas. The poor, although improving, crime reporting system and the fact that as many as half of all crimes were not reported by victims have stood in the way of any accurate statistical picture of the kinds and incidence of crime.

Table 18. Philippines, Incidence of Major Crimes Before and During Martial Law

Crime	Number		Rate per 100,000 Population	
	Before Martial Law[1]	During Martial Law[2]	FY 1972[3]	FY 1973[3]
Murder	6,510	2,424	10.5	5.0
Other homicide	8,669	3,530	13.4	6.8
Robbery	23,061	17,491	34.8	22.8
Assault	25,134	20,143	34.0	29.6
Rape	1,347	1,435	1.7	1.8
Theft	22,029	20,924	34.2	28.4

[1] January 22, 1971, to September 21, 1972.
[2] September 22, 1972, to May 21, 1974.
[3] Fiscal year is July 1 through June 30.

Source: Based on information from *Fookien Times Yearbook, 1974,* Manila, 1974, p. 63; and U.S. Department of State, Agency for International Development, Office of Public Safety, *Termination Phase-out Study: Public Safety Project, Philippines,* Washington, May 1974, p. 74.

THE ORGANS OF NATIONAL SECURITY

The enforcement of laws and regulations, the maintenance of public order and safety, and the suppression of crime are fundamental responsibilities centralized in the president as chief executive. Under both the 1935 and 1973 constitutions he may employ one or more of the armed forces to put down rebellion, insurrection, or invasion. If national security is threatened, he may declare martial law throughout the land or in any specific portion of it. When the situation seems to warrant it, he may suspend the right of habeas corpus. After his proclamation of martial law in September 1972, Marcos exercised sweeping discretionary powers to arrest and detain persons and to remand them to trial in special military courts.

Among security measures instituted after martial law was a national registration number and identifying card. Mandated by Presidential Decree 278 of August 1973, this required that all citizens and resident aliens be assigned a registration number and identifying card. Personal data acquired through the registration system have been computerized and made available to police and security authorities as an added surveillance tool in criminal investigation and the control of subversive activities.

The principal security agencies were the National Intelligence Coordinating Agency, the National Police Commission, the National Bureau of Investigation, the Integrated National Police, and the Philippine Constabulary. Other operating agencies were reportedly active whose organizational affiliations were not known. These and other parts of the security apparatus expanded substantially under the martial law regime and stepped up their operations against elements within the Catholic and Protestant churches and the campuses. A newly established agency, the Civil Intelligence and Security Agency, was said to have concerned itself with teachers, students, and nonacademic personnel in schools and universities.

National Intelligence Coordinating Agency

The National Intelligence Coordinating Agency, under the Office of the President, prepared foreign and domestic intelligence estimates for the president. Originally a staff organization, it was subsequently given some operational responsibility in the control of smuggling.

National Police Commission

The National Police Commission was established pursuant to the Police Act of 1966 for the purpose of improving the administration and operation of local police forces and establishing professional standards for all police. Its five authorized commissioners included in 1974 the secretary of national defense as chairman, the president's military affairs advisor, and the commander of the Philippine Constabulary. It was transferred from the Office of the President to the Department of National Defense in August 1975.

National Bureau of Investigation

The National Bureau of Investigation is a subordinate agency of the Department of Justice patterned after the Federal Bureau of Investigation in the United States. The organization began as an investigative division in 1936 but was expanded and raised to full bureau status in 1947. In 1960 the bureau was considerably expanded and reorganized. The original intent in creating the bureau was to relieve the equivalent of the constabulary of the tasks of ordinary crime detection and investigation, freeing it to concentrate on peace and order. Since the 1960 reorganization the bureau has been both an investigative organ and a research and service agency. Its investigative scope included all forms of graft and corruption; it had powers of arrest in certain kinds of cases. Its research and service functions included providing advanced police training and such technical services as maintenance of crime laboratories, which were at the disposal of police throughout the nation.

The bureau is organized into a headquarters under a director appointed by the president, an administrative element, and investigation and technical services. It operates through ten regional offices located at Manila, Batangas, Naga, Dagupan, Ilagan, Vigan, Iloilo, Cebu Island, Zamboanga, and Cagayan de Oro. Most have one or more suboffices.

Bureau personnel include agents, laboratory technicians, fingerprint experts, communications specialists, and administrative personnel. Recruitment is on the basis of rigid physical and mental examination. Agents selected for assignment to investigative divisions must also possess a degree in law or accounting. Bureau personnel generally have been regarded as among the best and most efficient law enforcement agents in the nation.

Integrated National Police

A major restructuring of police institutions was begun with the establishment on August 8, 1975, of the Integrated National Police (INP). This marked the completion of a program initiated in March 1974 for combining local police forces into a national force under Philippine Constabulary command. The first phase of the program had involved the integration of forces in the Manila metropolitan area. Establishment of the INP represented the achievement of a major element of law enforcement reform under the martial law peace-and-order program. It carried out a constitutional mandate written into the 1973 Constitution (Section 12, Article XV) that "the state shall establish and maintain an integrated National Police Force whose organization, administration, and operation shall be provided by law."

Under the provisions of Presidential Decree 765, all municipal police, fire, and jail organizations were brought under the supervision and control of the chief of the Philippine Constabulary, who was named concurrently director general of the INP. The INP functioned directly under the Department of National Defense and was subject to the command and general supervision of the president as commander in chief of the armed forces. As newly constituted the INP consisted of sixty-four city forces and 1,447 municipal forces totaling about 37,000 men. The core of the INP was the Philippine Constabulary of an estimated 27,000 men.

The INP was assigned responsibility for public safety, protection of lives and property, enforcement of the laws, and maintenance of peace and order throughout the national territory. To carry out these responsibilities it was given powers "to prevent crimes, effect the arrest of criminal offenders and provide for their detention and rehabilitation, prevent and control fires, investigate the commission of all crimes and offenses, bring the offenders to justice, and take all necessary steps to ensure public safety." Integration of local police into the national force gave rise initially to some confusion regarding the relationship of local police with municipal mayors and provincial governors and complaints by the lattter that they had lost control over local police. Instructions issued in late 1975 sought to clarify the relationship.

Philippine Constabulary

Proclamation 1081 directed the armed forces under the secretary of national defense to "maintain law and order throughout the Philippines, to suppress all forms of lawless violence as well as any act of insurrection or rebellion, and to enforce obedience to all decrees, orders, and regulations promulgated" by the president or on his instruction. The actual task of administering the peace-and-order program under martial law devolved on the chief of the constabulary, who in 1975 was also head of the INP. The three military services augment the constabulary in matters of domestic security, a role that assumed major proportions after 1972 in the southern region of the Muslim insurgency. The navy, particularly its coast guard arm, also had a law enforcement role in antismuggling and general sea surveillance activities. It operated both in interisland areas and in the Manila Bay area.

As the nuclear organization of the integrated police the Philippine Constabulary would continue to play the central operational and managerial role in law enforcement and domestic security. The oldest and long the largest of the four armed forces, the constabulary traces its origins to 1901. It was the constabulary division of the Philippine army before being constituted as a national police force in 1936. Operating as a national gendarmerie having units dispersed throughout the country, the constabulary had concerned itself mainly with large-scale crime, wide-area operations, insurgency and subversion, and enforcing the peace and national law in remote areas where local forces are nonexistent or ineffective. Special constabulary units or task forces have been assigned to such crime prevention missions as the land and close offshore aspects of smuggling and piracy, drug traffic, kidnapping and ransom syndicates, "carnapping," and patrolling national and other highways.

Organization of the Philippine Constabulary was similar to that of the army; the constabulary corresponded to a light-infantry force. The commander since 1974 has been a major general. Tactical forces operated under a standard military-type headquarters; in 1975 they consisted of eight battalions of some 450 men each. The total of 134 companies included a K-9 (dog) company and a company of horse cavalry. Companies and battalions not in strategic reserve were assigned regionally to one of the five constabulary zones under which were seventy-one provincial commanders and 187 posts and stations manned by detachments of varying size. One of the five zone commands was that of the Philippine Constabulary Metropolitan Command (METROCOM), which through integration became the nucleus of the new Metropolitan Police Force for the greater Manila area.

The constabulary included a number of specialized units. The Antinarcotics Unit, formed in 1972, had functions that included rehabilitation as well as enforcement. The Constabulary Offshore Anticrime Battalion deployed its excellent speedboats and patrol craft as needed to support ths onshore operations of the regional constabulary commands and task forces. In the control of smuggling, arms movements, and insurgency the offshore battalion complemented the deep-water operations of the navy and its coast guard arm. The Presidential Security Command embraced the elite and distinctive Presidential Guards Battalion as well as special security units responsible for the police protection of the area around the presidential residence at Malacañang. The Highway Patrol Group of some 450 officers and men in 1974 operated throughout the country and had special responsibility for suppressing the traffic in stolen vehicles. After the imposition of martial law the new Command for the Administration of Detainees was made responsible for administering the system for detention and parole of political detainees. The constabulary as one of the armed forces was also involved in civic affairs projects under the Home Defense Program of the Department of National Defense.

One objective of police integration was to step up the program, begun by the creation of the National Police Commission in 1966, for standardizing local police forces and improving their training. Centralization of the local police under constabulary command was expected to contribute to the professionalization of the former, particularly through better training and through the removal of the local police from local political control and interference. A uniform national police manual setting standards of performance and administration was adopted as the result of a project begun in 1969 by the National Police Commission aided by the technical and financial assistance, through fiscal year (FY) 1975, of the Office of Public Safety of the United States Agency for International Development (AID). The gap was likely to remain wide between the personnel and conditions of service of the local police and those of the relatively elite Philippine Constabulary, whose officers, for one thing, were graduates of the Philippine Military Academy (see ch. 16). In December 1975, however, a decree was signed standardizing and upgrading police salaries; similarly the police gained access to commissary privileges enjoyed by the armed forces.

THE SYSTEM OF CRIMINAL JUSTICE

The modern Philippine legal and judicial system contains elements of both Roman law introduced during the long Spanish colonial experience and Anglo-Saxon law introduced during the American colonial administration. Procedural rules and the general judicial technique (but not the jury institution) of the American federal court system became the model for much of Philippine judicial practice. Contemporary American legal experience retains a strong formative influence over Philippine jurisprudence. Philippine tribunals are "steeped in the American judicial habits" in the words of a leading Philippine jurist.

The Spanish legal tradition retains its strongest hold in the field of civil law, particularly the law of property and the family. A distinct Muslim legal tradition has persisted among the minority Muslim communities of Mindanao and the Sulu Archipelago, where in many traditional areas it has retained its effectiveness as the preferred instrument of justice. Among the pacification proposals held out to the Muslim dissidents by President Marcos has been the legal recognition of elements of this tradition with particular respect to land and family matters.

Philippine jurisprudence also reflects an underlying cultural leaning toward an individual leader's arbitration rather than the law as the preferred ultimate recourse for the person seeking justice. At least before changes were adopted in 1973 to expedite the disposition of criminal cases, a common pattern of court litigation found disputants becoming involved after the opening of a case in a series of continuances and dilatory tactics that dragged on for months. Finally the frustrated litigants, often through a mediator, settled their differences out of court. In their minds there was no substitute for strong, personal negotiation.

The Administration of Criminal Justice

Major elements of the system of criminal justice in addition to the police are the courts, the prosecutors, the bar, and the penal institutions. Changes instituted under martial law have altered the criminal justice process in several important ways.

Civil trial courts competent to deal with criminal cases consist of the municipal and city courts (both formerly termed justice of the peace courts), the courts of first instance, and the circuit criminal courts in certain provincial areas. The first-echelon municipal and city courts had original jurisdiction over minor criminal offenses, more serious crimes being tried in the second-echelon courts, of which the courts of first instance had somewhat wider jurisdiction than the circuit courts. The former also had appellate jurisdiction. Special juvenile and domestic relations courts in Manila had limited jurisdiction in criminal cases involving persons under the age of sixteen.

Significant change was introduced into this court system after 1972 by the creation of two new kinds of court, the military court and the Sandiganbayan. The latter was a special court provided for in the 1973 Constitution. It had jurisdiction over civil and criminal cases involving corruption by public officials and employees. Military tribunals, of which a large number were created under army and constabulary administration, were assigned jurisdiction "exclusive of the civil courts" over a wide variety of criminal offenses designated as affecting the security of the state. In criminal matters the top-echelon Court of Appeals and the Supreme Court had appellate jurisdiction only.

The setting up of an autonomous system of military courts deprived the civil courts of jurisdiction in a substantial number of criminal offenses. Any case could be transferred to a military court on the authority of the president or the chief of staff of the armed forces. Military courts were either five-member commissions or lesser single-member provost courts. All were under the Judge Advocate General of the Armed Forces of the Philippines (AFP), who was also responsible for the prosecutorial function in the military courts. As of early 1974 somewhat over 6,000 cases had been referred to the twenty commissions and forty-eight provost courts then in existence. Military courts operated under their own rules of procedure but were required to accord the accused the same constitutional safeguards as in criminal trials in the civil courts.

One reason given for the creation of the new military tribunals was the progressive breakdown of justice in the civil courts, where the backlog of cases in some instances went back ten years. Delays and inefficiencies in the court system represented a long-standing problem. Reforms instituted in 1967 to cope with the problem included the creation of a number of additional courts, setting time limits on the disposal of cases, and simplifying preliminary investigation. Despite these efforts the problem of the denial of justice through delay has persisted.

Restoring public confidence in the system of justice was a stated goal of martial law. Steps taken to this end included substantial shortening of pretrial procedures, making trials less vulnerable to delaying tactics by the accused, and instituting administrative and personnel changes. A strict statute of limitations was set within which courts had to render judgment or dismiss the case. In 1975 it was still too early to assess the long-term effectiveness of these measures.

Constitutional guarantee of the rights of an accused included due process, presumption of innocence, prohibition against self-incrimination, and the right to a speedy public trial. The law protected the accused from ex post facto enactments, unreasonable search and seizure, double jeopardy, and cruel and unusual punishment. Although by 1975 these rights and the power of the courts to enforce them had not seriously been interfered with under martial law, some violence had been done at least temporarily to some aspects of the justice system.

Habeas corpus, perhaps the most fundamental of all legal protections for an accused, did not apply to deprivation of freedom under the preventive detention provisions of martial law. Thousands of persons were held for a year or more without trial during the early period of martial law. More subtle in their potential impact on the administration of justice were changes under transitory provisions of the 1973 Constitution that gave the president certain powers in dismissing and appointing civil justices. An additional threat hanging over the judiciary was the pro forma letter of resignation that President Marcos elicited from each judge of the courts of first instance and higher courts after the imposition of martial law; it needed only the president's acceptance to end a judge's tenure. Although not necessarily an indication of the use of this power, official sources indicated that as of late 1975 among the hundreds of officials dismissed for cause were at least fourteen judges of courts of first instance.

Some also saw in martial law a potential threat to the historic position of the Supreme Court as a generally respected champion of justice. There was some fear that the high national regard in which the Supreme Court was held might gradually be eroded as the court was increasingly called upon to enforce rules derived from presidential decree rather than from law legitimized by the legislative process (see ch. 9).

The Penal Code

Substantive criminal law is embodied in the Revised Penal Code of 1930 (effective January 1, 1932). The code is derived from the Spanish Penal Code of 1887 and acts of the Philippine legislature and its preindependence counterparts as limited by the Bill of Rights of the Constitution. In the manner of the Spanish legal tradition, common law is not a source of criminal law; there are no punishable acts or penalties other than those expressly stated in law. The penal code applies to Philippine nationals outside the national territory as to certain acts, such as those of public officers, and crimes against national security and the law of nations. The criminal statutes are to be construed strictly against the state and liberally in favor of the accused.

Criminal law from Spanish times to the present has rested on the classical or juristic school of criminal law, which treats crime as an objective act and stressed prevention and punishment of crime. This aspect of Philippine law has long been an object of reform effort. The official Code Commission created in 1947 to revise and codify existing substantive civil and criminal law recommended a new code of crimes based on the more modern positivist philosophy that "criminality depends mostly on social factors, environment, education, economic conditions, and the inborn or hereditary character of the criminal himself." This approach stresses reform over punishment. The Crime Law Reform Project of the University of Manila in the late 1960s drafted the Proposed Revised Penal Code. As of 1975 no definitive legislative action had been taken on these proposals.

Three principal parts of the penal code deal with basic principles affecting criminal liability, provisions on penalties, and definition of the fourteen classes of felonies. The code lists aggravating and mitigating circumstances. Among the latter are age (under eighteen or over seventy), "immediate vindication of a grave offense" against self or family, physical defect, and acting under "powerful impulse causing passion or obfuscation." Insanity or acting under irresistible force or uncontrollable fear are regarded by law as exempting circumstances. Penalties are classified as corporal (death), afflictive (six years to life imprisonment), correctional (one month to six years), and light (to thirty days). Other penalties include disqualification, fine, and public censure. Sentence of life imprisonment normally entitles the prisoner to pardon after thirty years. The code provides for parole and probation. Death is by electrocution or by firing squad; in the former case the prisoner may request that he be anesthetized before sentence is carried out.

Criminal Procedure

The sources of procedural criminal law are the Constitution, special laws, the Revised Penal Code of 1930, and the New Rules of Court of January 1964. The last governs the pleading, practice, and procedure in all courts as well as admission to the practice of law. Promulgated by the Supreme Court, which administers the entire court system, the rules have the force and effect of law.

Criminal actions can be initiated by the offended party, by an official concerned, or by a prosecutor (termed a *fiscal* at the provincial and municipal levels of government). Pretrial investigation consists of a preliminary examination (in the case of more serious offenses) to determine probable cause for arrest and preliminary investigation of the charge after arrest. Warrant for arrest is issued by a judge. Investigation can be conducted by a trial judge, a *fiscal*, or by a municipal mayor in extraordinary cases. A procedural change enacted in December 1972 further simplified procedure by limiting the investigation effectively to affidavit form. In mid-1975 the period for the preliminary investigation and filing of criminal cases was shortened from sixty to twenty-five days from the date of the first hearing. In principle persons are permitted bail except in certain corporal cases; in practice pretrial detention is common if not the general rule.

Prosecution is carried out under the control and direction of the state prosecutor or a *fiscal*. Under the New Rules of Court the accused in a criminal prosecution is presumed innocent. He must be informed of the nature and cause of the accusation, has the right to a speedy public trial, and may confront witnesses and compel the securing of witnesses in his own behalf. The right of the accused to be present and to defend himself in person was modified by a martial law decree in 1972 providing among other things for the indictment and trial in absentia by military courts of persons charged with subversion or rebellion.

Trial procedure consists of arraignment, where the accused pleads to the charge, the trial itself, and the judgment and sentencing by the court. At arraignment the accused is given the exact charge against him and the list of witnesses and is informed of his right to be represented by an attorney. No jury is employed; the judge determines all questions of law and fact; and employment of assessors to help the judge determine facts is provided for by law but is rarely used.

The trial proceeds with the prosecution's presenting evidence and witnesses, after which the defense presents its case. Both sides may cross-examine witnesses. Judgment may be appealed by either party. A case appealed to the court of first instance is tried anew as an original case. The death penalty is automatically appealed to the Supreme Court, where it must be upheld unanimously in order to carry. Parole instead of incarceration may be granted to first offenders.

Under the legal and constitutional principles of the due process and equal protection dating from the introduction of American jurisprudence in 1900, an indigent defendent in a criminal trial must be provided with counsel of appropriate experience appointed by the court. Such counsel was usually secured through the legal aid offices of the Integrated Bar of the Philippines, which was supported in this work by public funds and the dues of its members. The Citizens Legal Assistance Office created in late 1972 operated in several provinces as of 1975, providing free legal aid through the services of lawyers employed by the government. A number of private organizations also assisted in this field, particularly in the Manila area. By estimate of the bar, over 95 percent of Filipinos were financially unable to afford counsel. There was as yet no officially established legal aid services with a paid staff.

Allegations of torture and physical abuse of prisoners held under detention and interrogation by martial law authorities were raised frequently and were the subject of protest by Roman Catholic Church leaders and other prominent Filipinos. A 1973 report by Amnesty International noted that such allegations were more often directed at the Antinarcotics Unit and other elements of the constabulary than at the army and that physical abuse rarely was directed against prisoners of elite social backgrounds.

Penal Institutions

Institutions for the confinement of convicts and the detention of persons awaiting trial included a variety of national prisons and penal farms as well as provincial and local jails. A reorganization in October 1972 established a system of seven national regional prisons along with other changes directed toward segregation of hard-core from less serious offenders. The changes were also aimed at alleviating chronic overcrowding and promoting rehabilitation by confining prisoners nearer to family and friends. Specialized prisons for women and juveniles were located at Mandaluyong in Rizal Province. Each municipality had its own jail, often only a room or two in the police headquarters building. Provincial jails tended to be larger but often little better appointed than those in city or town. Most convicts in local and provincial jails were serving short terms. Persons awaiting trial constituted as much as 40 percent of the prison population in some areas. Jails and prisons were administered under police authority.

The new Bilibid Prison in Manila was the central national penitentiary for prisoners sentenced to death, life imprisonment, or long-term penalties and was the largest prison in the world. Despite its newness, in the mid-1970s it suffered from serious overcrowding and exhibited many of the conditions, from serious to appalling, that afflicted the nation's penal institutions elsewhere. A 1969 official inquiry found living conditions in most prisons "subhuman." The 9,000 Bilibid prisoners were found to fare no better.

Penal colonies have been established in Davao Province (Davao Penal Colony), Zamboanga (San Ramon Prison and Prison Farm), Mindoro Island (Sablayon Penal Colony and Farm), and Palawan Province (Iwahig Penal Colony). Prisoners are initially placed on probation for two months during which they undergo orientation, wear distinctive orange uniforms, work under guard, and are housed in segregated barracks that are locked at night. At the end of this period prisoners join the community of regular colonists, wear civilian clothes, and are free to move about without the presence of guards.

BIBLIOGRAPHY

Section I. Social

Abueva, Jose Veloso. "The Philippines: Political Tradition and Change," *Asian Survey*, X, No. 1, January 1970, 56–64.

"Adult Education in the Philippines," *Asian South Pacific Journal of Adult Education* [New Delhi], VI, Nos. 1–4 and Nos. 1–10, August 1971–May 1972.

"Adult Education in the Philippines," *Indian Journal of Adult Education* [New Delhi], 32, No. 12, December 1971, 13–16.

Agoncillo, Teodoro A., and Oscar M. Alfonso. *History of the Filipino People*. (Rev. ed.) Quezon City: Malaya Books, 1967.

Ahmed, Manzoor, and Philip H. Coombs (eds.). *Education for Rural Development: Case Studies for Planners*. New York: Praeger, May 1975.

Albarracin, Narciso. "Educational Reforms in the New Society." Pages 300–305 in Betty Go-Belmonte (ed.), *Fookien Times Yearbook, 1974*. Manila: Fookien Times Yearbook Publishing, 1974.

Aldaba-Lim, Estefania. "Social Welfare Today: A Development Instrument." Pages 332–335 in Betty Go-Belmonte (ed.), *Fookien Times Yearbook, 1974*. Manila: Fookien Times Yearbook Publishing, 1974.

Alip, Eufronio M. "Philippine Languages and Literature," *Journal of History*, 17, No. 1–2, 1972, 41–64.

Alonzo, Ruperto P. "Short-Term Employment Creation Projects in the Philippine Setting: Problems and Prospects." (Southeast Asia Development Advisory Group. Papers on Problems of Development in Southeast Asia, No. 73–10.) New York: SEADAG of the Asia Society, 1973 (mimeo.).

Anderson, Gerald H. (ed.) *Studies in Philippine Church History*. Ithaca: Cornell University Press, 1969.

Ando, Hirofumi. "A Study of the Iglesia Ni Cristo: A Politico-Religious Sect in the Philippines," *Pacific Affairs* [Vancouver], XLII, No. 3, Fall 1969, 334–345.

Ang, Milda. "A Study of Philippine Education and Its Developmental Role." Unpublished Ph.D. dissertation. Boston: Boston College, June 1971.

Apel, Willi. *Harvard Dictionary of Music*. Cambridge: Harvard University Press, 1955.

Asian Mass Communication Research and Information Centre. *Communication and Change in Rural Asia: A Select Bibliography*.

Singapore: 1973.

Aspillera, Paraluman S. *Basic Tagalog for Foreigners and Non-Tagalogs*. Rutland, Vermont: Charles E. Tuttle, 1969.

Asuncion-Landé, Nobleza. "Multilingualism, Politics, and 'Filipinism,' " *Asian Survey*, XI, No. 7, July 1971, 677–692.

Ballweg, John A., and Donald W. MacCorquodale. "Family Planning Method Change and Dropouts in the Philippines," *Social Biology*, 21, No. 1, Spring 1974, 88–95.

Barker, Randolph, et al. "Employment and Technological Change in Philippine Agriculture," *International Labour Review* [Geneva], 106, Nos. 2–3, August–September 1972, 111–139.

Baretto, Felisa R. "Knowledge, Attitudes, and Practice of Family Planning in the Philippines, 1972," *Studies in Family Planning*, 5, No. 9, September 1974, 294–299.

Bastin, John, and Harry J. Benda. *A History of Modern Southeast Asia: Colonialism, Nationalism, and Decolonization*. Englewood Cliffs: Prentice-Hall, 1968.

Bautista, Romeo M. "Anatomy of Labour Absorption in Philippine Manufacturing, 1956–1966," *Economic Bulletin for Asia and the Far East* [Bangkok], XXIV, September –December 1973, 12–22.

————. "The Influence of Education on Manufacturing Productivity: The Philippines," *Developing Economies* [Tokyo], XII, No. 1, March 1974, 74–82.

Benda, Harry J. "Peasant Movements in Colonial Southeast Asia," *Asian Studies* [Manila], III, December 1965.

Benda, Harry J., and John A. Larkin. *The World of Southeast Asia: Selected Historical Readings*. New York: Harper and Row, 1967.

Benson, Louis Paul. "Changing Political Alliance Patterns in the Rural Philippines: A Case Study from Camarines Norte." Pages 130–152 in Benedict J. Kerkvliet (ed.), *Political Change in the Philippines: Studies of Local Politics Preceding Martial Law*. (Asian Studies at Hawaii, No. 14. Asian Studies Program, University of Hawaii.) Honolulu: University of Hawaii Press, 1974.

Brown, Brinton C. *The Mineral Industry of the Philippines: Preprint from the 1970 Bureau of Mines Mineral Yearbook*. Washington: GPO, n.d.

Bruton, William P. "New Movement in the Catholic Church: A Study of the Cursillo-Modernization: Its Impact in the Philippines." (Paper No. 7.) Quezon City: 1969.

Butwell, Richard. "The Philippines: Changing of the Guard," *Asian Survey*, VI, No. 1, January 1966, 43–48.

Cady, John F. *Southeast Asia: Its Historical Development*. New York: McGraw-Hill, 1964.

Carroll, John J. "Magic and Religion." Pages 40–74 in John J. Carroll, et al, *Philippine Institutions*. Manila: Solidaridad Publishing House, 1970.

————. "The Pope and the Philippines," *Philippines Free Press* [Manila], LX, No. 30, July 1967.

Carroll, John J., and John T. Keane. "Philippine Social Conditions and the Church," *Solidarity* [Manila], V, No. 10, October 1970, 25–41.

Carroll, John J., et al. *Philippine Institutions.* Manila: Solidaridad Publishing House, 1970

Castillo, Gelia T. "The Philippines: The Case for Non-Formal Education," *Spectrum* [Bangkok], 3, No. 1, October 1974, 66–75.

Catholic Almanac, 1975. Huntington, Indiana: Our Sunday Visitor, 1975.

Cespedes, C. H., and E. Gibbs. "New Middle Class in the Philippines: A Case Study in Culture Change," *Asian Survey,* XII, No. 10, October 1972, 879–886.

Coates, A. *Islands of the South.* London: Heinemann Educational Books, 1974.

Cockcroft, John. *The Philippines.* Melbourne: Angus and Robertson, 1969.

Communication and Change in Rural Asia: A Select Bibliography. Singapore: Asian Mass Communication Research and Information Centre, 1973.

Constantino, Ernesto. "Tagalog and Other Major Languages of the Philippines." Pages 112–154 in Thomas A. Sebeok (ed.), *Current Trends in Linguistics,* VIII, Pt. I. The Hague: Mouton, 1971.

Corpuz, Onofre D. *The Philippines.* (The Modern Nation in Historical Perspective Series.) Englewood Cliffs: Prentice-Hall, 1965.

Cruz, Patricia M. "Literary Situation Today from September 21, 1972." Pages 348 in Betty Go-Belmonte (ed.), *Fookien Times Yearbook, 1974.* Manila: Fookien Times Yearbook Publishing, 1974.

Cultural Policy in the Philippines. (Studies and Documents on Cultural Policies Series.) Paris: United Nations Economic, Scientific and Cultural Organization, 1973.

Cutshall, Alden. *The Philippines: Nation of Islands.* (Van Nostrand Searchlight Books.) Princeton: Van Nostrand, 1964.

Davis, William G. *Social Relations in a Philippine Market.* Berkeley: University of California Press, 1973.

Daza, Nora V. *Let's Cook with Nora.* Philippines: General Milk, 1965.

Deats, Richard L. *Nationalism and Christianity in the Philippines.* Dallas: Southern Methodist University Press, 1967.

Del Rey, Sister Maria. "Protestantism in the Philippines: Its Impact after 70 Years," Pt. I, *Christian Century,* 89, No. 37, October 18, 1972, 1047–1049.

————. "Protestantism in the Philippines: Its Impact after 70 Years," Pt. II, *Christian Century,* 89, No. 38, October 25, 1972, 1070–1073.

Demetrio, Francisco R. "Themes in Philippine Folk Tales," *Asian Studies* [Manila], 10, No. 1, April 1972, 6–17.

Desmond, G. M. "The Impact of National Development Policies on

Urbanization in South and Southeast Asia," *Ekistics* [Athens], 40, No. 238, September 1975, 167–173.

De Vega, Guillermo C. "A Look at Film Censorship." Pages 338–344 in Betty Go-Belmonte (ed.), *Fookien Times Yearbook, 1974*. Manila: Fookien Times Yearbook Publishing, 1974.

"A 'Developing Country' Shows How: The University of the Philippines Science Education Centre," *Australian Science Teachers Journal* [Melbourne], 17, No. 3, October 1971, 47–50.

Development Academy of the Philippines. Task Force on Human Settlements. "Manila and Its Outlying Areas: Emerging Concepts and Issues," *Ekistics* [Athens], 39, No. 233, April 1975, 255–257.

Dobby, E. H. G. *Employment Problems and Policies in the Philippines.* (Employment Research Papers.) Geneva: International Labour Office, 1969.

—————. *Southeast Asia.* London: University of London Press, 1967.

Doeppers, Daniel E. "The Development of Philippine Cities Before 1900," *Journal of Asian Studies*, XXXI, No. 4, August 1972, 769–792.

—————. " 'Ethnic Urbanism' in Philippine Cities," *Annals of the Association of American Geographers*, 64, No. 4, December 1974, 549–559.

"Don Bosco Lives in the Philippines," *American Vocational Journal*, XLVII, No. 9, December 1972, 54–55.

Douglas, Donald E. "An Historical Survey of the Land Tenure Situation in the Philippines," *Solidarity* [Manila], V, No. 7, July 1970, 65–79.

Douglas, J. D. (ed.) *The New International Dictionary of the Christian Church.* Grand Rapids: Sondervan Publishing House, 1974.

Douglas, Louis H. "Modernization in a Transitional Setting: A Philippines Case Study," *Civilisations* [Brussels], 18, No. 2, 1968, 204–231.

Duff, Robert Ward. *Neighborhood of Residence and Knowledge Attitudes and Practices with Regard to Conception Control in a Philippine City.* South Bend: University of Notre Dame, 1971.

East, W. Gordon, et al. *The Changing Map of Asia.* (5th ed.) London: Methuen, 1971.

East-West Center. East-West Population Institute. *Proceedings of the Conference on International Migration from the Philippines, 10–14 June 1974.* Honolulu: East-West Center Press, January 1975.

"Educational Development Decree," *Education in Asia: Notes*, 3, March 1973, 7–9.

Eggan, Fred. "Philippine Social Structure." Pages 1–48 in George M. Guthrie (ed.), *Six Perspectives on the Philippines*. Manila: Bookmark, 1968.

Eggan, Fred, and William Scott. "Ritual Life of the Igorots of Sagada: Courtship and Marriage," *Ethnology*, IV, No. 1, 1965.

—————. "Ritual Life of the Igorots of Sagada: From Birth to Adolescence," *Ethnology*, II, No. 1, 1963.

Eggan, Fred, et al. *The Philippines.* (Human Relations Area Files Subcontractor's Monographs, HRAF–16, Chicago–5.) New Haven:

HRAF Press, 1956.

Elwood, Douglas J. "Varieties of Christianity in the Philippines." Pages 366–386 in Gerald H. Anderson (ed.), *Studies in Philippine Church History*. Ithaca: Cornell University Press, 1969.

Espiritu, Socorro C., and C. I. Hunt. *Social Foundations of Community Development*. Manila: Garcia Publishing House, 1964.

Estrella, Conrado F. *The Democratic Answer to the Philippine Agrarian Problem*. Manila: Solidaridad Publishing House, 1969.

The Far East and Australasia, 1974: A Survey and Directory of Asia and the Pacific. London: Europa Publications, 1974.

Feldman, Kerry. "Squatter Migration Dynamics in Davao City, Philippines," *Urban Anthropology*, 4, No 2, Summer 1975, 123–144.

"Fertility, Social Class, and Outmigration: Some Philippine Data," *Rural Sociology*, XXXVIII, No. 3, February 1973, 312–324.

Filamor, Alberto E. "Realty Trends: 1974." Pages 196–199 in Betty Go-Belmonte (ed.), *Fookien Times Yearbook, 1974*. Manila: Fookien Times Yearbook Publishing, 1974.

Filipinas Foundation. *An Anatomy of Philippine Muslim Affairs*. Makati: 1971.

Flavier, Juan M. "The Philippine Rural Reconstruction Movement." In *Fookien Times Yearbook, 1967*. Manila: Fookien Times Yearbook Publishing, 1967.

———. "Population Planning Policy in the Philippines," *International Journal of Health Services*, 3, No. 4, 1973, 811–819.

Florentino, Albert S. (ed.) *Literature at the Crossroads: Three Symposia on the Filipino Novel, Poetry, Theater*. Manila: 1965.

Fookien Times Yearbook, 1971. Manila: Fookien Times Yearbook Publishing, 1971.

Friend, Theodore. *Between Two Empires*. New Haven: Yale University Press, 1965.

Fryer, Donald W. "Cities of Southeast Asia and Their Problems," *Focus*, XXII, No. 7, March 1972, 1–8.

Gatmaitan, Clemente S. "The State of the Nation's Health." Pages 312–313 in Betty Go-Blemonte (ed.), *Fookien Times Yearbook, 1974*. Manila: Fookien Times Yearbook Publishing, 1974.

Go, Purita. "RP Brain Drain," *Far Eastern Economic Review* [Hong Kong], LXXVIII, No. 42, October 14, 1972, 46–47.

Grecia, Bell H. "RP Is Getting Crowded," *Philippine Panorama* [Manila], V, No. 26, June 25, 1972, 10.

Grossholtz, Jean. "The Philippines: Midterm Doldrums for Marcos," *Asian Survey*, VIII, No. 1, January 1968, 52–57.

———. "The Philippines: New Adventures with Old Problems," *Asian Survey*, IX, No. 1, January 1969, 50–57.

Guillermo, Artemio Ramos. "A Readership Survey of 'Taliba,' a Philippine Newspaper." Unpublished Ph.D. dissertation, 1972. Syracuse: Syracuse University, 1973.

Gupta, M. L. "Outflow of High-Level Manpower from the Philippines with Special Reference to the Period 1965–1971," *International Labour Review* [Geneva], No. 107, February 1973, 167–191.

Guthrie, George M. "The Philippine Temperament." Pages 49–84 in George M. Guthrie (ed.), *Six Perspectives on the Philippines*. Manila: Bookmark, 1968.

Hall, D. G. E. *A History of South-East Asia*. (2 ed.) New York: St. Martin's Press, 1964.

Harman, Alvin J. *Fertility and Economic Behavior of Families in the Philippines*. (RM–6385–AID.) Santa Monica: Rand Corporation, 1970.

Hart, Donn V. "Culture and Curing in Filipino Peasant Society." In K. Ishwaran (ed.), *Contribution to Asian Studies*, V. Toronto: Canadian Association for South Asian Studies, 1974.

————. *The Philippine Plaza Complex: A Focal Point in Culture Change*. (Yale Southeast Asia Studies: Culture Report Studies.) New Haven: Yale University Press, 1955.

Hart, Donn V. (ed.) *Philippine Studies: Geography, Archaeology, Psychology and Literature: Present Knowledge and Research Trends*. (Special Report Series, No. 10.) Dekalb, Illinois: Center for Southeast Asian Studies, Northern Illinois University, 1973.

Hayden, Joseph Ralston. *The Philippines: A Study in National Development*. New York: Macmillan, 1942.

Hendershot, G. E. "Fertility, Social Class, and Outmigration: Some Philippine Data," *Rural Sociology*, 38, No. 3, Fall 1973, 312–324.

Hitchcock, D. I., Jr. *Provincial Press and National Development in Malaysia and the Philippines*. Singapore: Asian Mass Communication Research and Information Centre, 1973.

Hohenberg, John. *Between Two Worlds*. New York: Praeger, 1967.

Hollnsteiner, Mary Racelis. *The Dynamics of Power in a Philippine Municipality*. Quezon City: Community Development Research Council, University of the Philippines, 1963.

————. "Metamorphosis: From Tondo Squatter to Tondo Settler," *Ekistics* [Athens], 40, No. 238, September 1975, 211–215.

Huke, Robert E. "Settlement Patterns in Luzon," *Geographical Review*, 63, No. 1, July 1973, 399–401.

————. *Shadows on the Land: An Economic Geography of the Philippines*. Manila: Bookmark, 1963.

Human Relations Area Files. *Area Handbook on the Philippines*. New Haven: HRAF Press, 1955.

————. *The Philippines*, I, II, III, IV. New Haven: HRAF Press, 1956.

Ilustre, Macrina L. "The Medicare Programme of the Philippines," *Social Security Series for Asia and Oceania* [Geneva], No. 4, 1973, 5–7.

International Labour Organization. *Sharing in Development: A Programme of Employment, Equity, and Growth for the Philippines*. Geneva: 1974.

Jacobson, Helga E. "Some Aspects of the Structure and Organisation of a Provincial City, Cebu City, The Philippines," *Pacific Viewpoint* [Wellington, New Zealand], 10, No. 2, September 1969, 55–59.

———. "Urbanization and Family Ties: A Problem in the Analysis of Change," *Journal of Asian and African Studies* [Toronto], V, No. 4, October 1970, 302–307.

Joaquin, Nick. *Prose and Poems.* Manila: Alberto S. Florentino, 1963.

Jocano, F. Landa. "Conversion and the Patterning of Christian Experience in Malitbog, Central Panay, Philippines," *Philippine Sociological Review* [Manila], XIII, No. 2, April 1965.

Jocano, Felipe L., and Bangalese Alsaybar. "Cultural Context of Some Housing Needs among Filipinos," *Ekistics* [Athens], 39, No. 234, May 1975, 314–318.

Kann, Peter R. "The Philippines Without Democracy," *Foreign Affairs*, 52, No. 3, April 1974, 612–632.

Kaplan, Paul F., and Cynthia Hsien Huang. "Achievement Orientation of Small Industrial Entrepreneurs in the Philippines," *Human Organization*, 33, No. 2, Summer 1974, 173–182.

Kerkvliet, Benedict J. "Critique of the Rand Study on the Philippines," *Journal of Asian Studies*, XXXII, No. 3, May 1973, 489–500.

Kerkvliet, Benedict J. (ed.) *Political Change in the Philippines: Studies of Local Politics Preceding Martial Law.* (Asian Studies at Hawaii, No. 14. Asian Studies Program, University of Hawaii.) Honolulu: University of Hawaii Press, 1974.

Kim, Yun. "Net Internal Migration in the Philippines, 1960–1970," *Economic Research Journal* [Manila], 18, No. 4, March 1972, 206–224.

Kintanar, Agustin, et al. *Studies in Philippine-Economic-Demographic Relationships.* Quezon City: Economic Research Associates and the Institute of Economic Development and Research, School of Economics, University of the Philippines, 1974.

Koehler, John E. *The Philippine Family Planning Program: Some Suggestions for Dealing with Uncertainties.* (RM–6149–AID.) Santa Monica: Rand Corporation, February 1970.

Kolko, Gabriel. *The Politics of War.* New York: Random House, 1968.

Lachica, Eduardo. *The Huks: Philippines Agrarian Society in Revolt.* New York: Praeger, 1971.

Laing, John E. "Differentials in Contraceptive Use Effectiveness in the Philippines," *Studies in Family Planning*, 5, No. 9, September 1974, 302–313.

———. *Differentials in Philippine Contraceptive Continuation and Pregnancy Rates.* Manila: Population Institute, University of the Philippines, February 1973.

———. *Use Effectiveness of Family Planning in the Philippines, 1970–72.* Manila: Family Planning Evaluation Office, Population Institute, University of the Philippines, 1972.

Laquian, Aprodicio A. "Coping with Internal Migration in the Philippines: Problems and Solutions." Pages 235–252 in John F. Kanter and Lee McCaffrey (eds.), *Population and Development in Southeast Asia.* Lexington, Massachusetts: Lexington Books, 1975.

Lara, Ben. "Score Religion at Con-Con," *Manila Daily Bulletin* [Manila], May 4, 1972, 1, 5.

Larkin, John A. "The Causes of an Involuted Society: A Theoretical Approach to Rural Southeast Asian History," *Journal of Asian Studies,* XXX, No. 4, August 1971, 783–795.

―――. *The Pampangans: Colonial Society in a Philippine Province.* Berkeley: University of California Press, 1972.

Lathom, Vicki. "Report from Abroad: Building Day Care Centers in the Philippine Islands," *Children Today,* 1, No. 5, September-October 1972, 25–26.

Law and Population in the Philippines. (Law and Population Book Series, No. 9.) Medford: Law and Population Program, Fletcher School of Law and Diplomacy, Tufts University, 1974.

LeBar, Frank N. *Ethnic Groups of Insular Southeast Asia,* II: Philippines and Formosa. New Haven: Human Relations Area Files Press, 1975.

Lent,John A. *Asian Mass Communications: A Comprehensive Bibliography.* Philadelphia: School of Communications and Theater, Temple University, 1975.

―――. *Philippine Mass Communications: Before 1811, After 1966.* New York: Philippine Press Institute, n.d.

―――. "Philippine Media and Nation-Building: An Overview," *Gazette* [Deventer, Netherlands], XVI, No. 1, 1970, 2–12.

―――. "Philippine Newspapers from 1941–1947: The Occupation and Liberation Periods," *Journalism* [Lahore, Pakistan], IV, No. 1, 1971, 8–21.

―――. "Philippine Press Under Martial Law," *Index* [London], 3, No. 1, Spring 1974, 47–58.

Lesaca, Reynaldo M. "Pollution Control: The Philippines," *Development Digest,* XIII, No. 1, January 1975.

Lightfoot, Keith. *The Philippines.* (Nations of the Modern World Series.) New York: Praeger, 1973.

Littaua, Ferdinand Z. "Some Insights into the Student Movement in the Philippines," *Asia Quarterly* [Brussels], No. 3, 1972, 203–215.

"A Look at the Philippine Construction Industry." Pages 200–207 in Betty Go-Belmonte (ed.), *Fookien Times Yearbook, 1974.* Manila: Fookien Times Yearbook Publishing, 1974.

Lynch, Frank, and Alfonso de Guzman II (eds.). *Four Readings on Philippine Values.* (Institute of Philippine Culture Papers, No. 2.) Quezon City: Ateneo de Manila University Press, 1964.

Mabbett, Hugh, and Charles Coppel. *The Chinese in Indonesia, the Philippines and Malaysia.* (Minority Rights Group Reports, No. 10.) London: Minority Rights Group, 1972.

McCarthy, Florence E. *Third Cultural Networks of Philippine Physical Life and Social Scientists*. East Lansing: Michigan State University, 1972.

MacCorquodale, Donald W. "The Attitude of Philippine Family Planning Physicans Toward Sterilization," *Social Science and Medicine*, VIII, Nos. 11–12, December 1974, 591–594.

McKanghan, Howard. "Minor Languages of the Philippines." Pages 155–167 in Thomas A. Sebeok (ed.), *Current Trends in Linguistics*, VIII, Pt. I. The Hague: Mouton, 1971.

MacLeish, Kenneth. "Help for Philippine Tribes in Trouble," *National Geographic*, 140, No. 2, August 1971, 220–225.

Madigan, Francis C. *Birth and Death in Cagayan de Oro: Population Dynamics in a Medium-Sized Philippine City*. Quezon City: Ateneo de Manila University Press, 1972.

———. *Mapping for Recurrent Research: A Philippine POPLAB Report*. Chapel Hill: International Program of Laboratories for Population Statistics, Department of Biostatistics, School of Public Health, Carolina Population Center, University of North Carolina, 1973.

———. *The Mindanao Center for Population Studies: A Philippines POPLAB Report*. (Laboratories for Population Statistics, Scientific Report Series, No. 8.) Chapel Hill: University of North Carolina, 1973.

Mahar, Mangahas. *Income Inequality in the Philippines: A Decomposition Analysis*. (International Labour Organization, World Employment Programme Research, Population and Employment Working Papers, No. 12.) Geneva: ILO, February 1975.

Majul, Cesar Adik. *Muslims in the Philippines*. Quezon City: University of the Philippines Press, 1973.

Manglapus, Raul S. "Philippine Culture and Modernization." In R. H. Bellah (ed.), *Religion and Progress in Modern Asia*. New York: Free Press, 1965.

"Manila and Its Outlying Areas: Emerging Concepts and Issues," *Ekistics* [Athens], 39, No. 233, April 1975, 255–257.

Marcos, Ferdinand E. *The Democratic Revolution in the Philippines*. Englewood Cliffs: Prentice-Hall International, 1974.

———. *Notes on the New Society of the Philippines*. Manila: The Marcos Foundation, 1973.

Marcos, Pacifico E. "What Medicare Has Done So Far." Pages 314–317 in Betty Go-Belmonte (ed.), *Fookien Times Yearbook, 1974*. Manila: Fookien Times Yearbook Publishing, 1974.

Maring, Ester G. *Historical and Cultural Dictionary of the Philippines*. Metuchen, New Jersey: Scarecrow Press, 1973.

Medina, Florencio A. "Philippine Science is Proving Its Mettle." Pages 306–309 in Betty Go-Belmonte (ed.), *Fookien Times Yearbook, 1974*. Manila: Fookien Times Yearbook Publishing, 1974.

Meyer, Milton Walter. *A Diplomatic History of the Philippine Republic*.

Ann Arbor: University of Michigan Press, 1959.

Minerals Yearbook, 1969, IV: Area Reports, International. Washington: Bureau of Mines, U.S. Department of the Interior, 1971.

Morales, A. T. "Higher Education in the Philippines," *Bulletin of the UNESCO Regional Office for Education in Asia* [Bangkok], VII, September 1972, 114–124.

Moreas, Dom. *A Matter of People*. New York: Praeger, 1974.

Mucchi, Fabio, and Massimo Quinque. "Manila's Misery," *Far Eastern Economic Review* [Hong Kong], 88, No. 26, June 27, 1975, 21–23.

Nelson, Raymond. *The Philippines*. New York: Walker, 1968.

"New Labour Code Adopted," *Social and Labour Bulletin* [Geneva], No. 1, 1974, 3–5.

The 1975 Asian Press and Media Director. Manila: Press Foundation of Asia, 1974.

Nydegger, William F., and Corinne Nydegger. *Tarong: An Ilocos Barrio in the Philippines*. (Six Culture Series, VI.) New York: Wiley and Sons, 1966.

Ocampo, Galo B. "Cultural Patterns in Philippine Architecture," *Far Eastern University Journal* [Manila], 16, No. 3, March 1972, 288–292.

Onorato, Michael P. (ed.) *Philippine Bibliography, 1899–1946*. N. pl.: N. pub., 1968.

Orata, Pedro T. "Do-It-Yourself Schools in the Philippines, *"UNESCO Courier*, June 1972, 24–27.

Orosa, Rosalinda L. "Theater: An Obsessive Search for Identity." Pages 356–360 in Betty Go-Belmonte (ed.), *Fookien Times Yearbook, 1974*. Manila: Fookien Times Yearbook Publishing, 1974.

Overholt, William. "Martial Law Revolution and Democracy in the Philippines," *Southeast Asia: An Historical Quarterly*, II, No. 2, Spring 1973, 159–190.

Owen, Norman G. (ed.) *Compadre Colonialism: Studies on the Philippines Under American Rule*. (Michigan Papers on South and Southeast Asia, No. 3.) Ann Arbor: Center for South and Southeast Asian Studies, University of Michigan, 1971.

Pal, Agaton P., and Robert P. Polson. *Rural People's Responses to Change: Dumaguete Trade Area, Philippines*. Quezon City: New Day Publishers, 1973.

Pascual, Neri Diaz. "A Report on the Socio-Economic Present Status of the Cultural Minorities of the Philippines," *Unitas* [Manila], 40, No. 1, March 1967, 207–234.

Peck, Cornelius J. "Nationalism, Race, and Development in the Philippine Law of Citizenship," *Journal of Asian and African Studies*, II, Nos. 1 and 2, 1967.

Perfecto, Waldo S. "The Philippines: Control of Education and the Role of the Private Sector, *"Bulletin of the UNESCO Regional Office for Education in Asia* [Bangkok], No. 15, June 1974, 237–243.

Phelan, John L. *The Hispanization of the Philippines: Spanish Aims and Filipino Responses, 1565–1700*. Madison: University of Wisconsin Press, 1959.

Philippines. Department of Commerce and Industry. Bureau of the Census and Statistics. "Labor Force," *The BCS Survey of Households Bulletin* [Manila], Series No. 28, March 1971.

———. *1970 Census of Population and Housing*. 67 vols. Manila: N. pub., n.d.

———. *1970 Census of Population and Housing: Final Report*. Manila: 1972.

———. *1970 Census of Population and Housing: National Summary, Philippines: Advance Report*. Manila: 1972.

———. *Total Population of the Philippines and Each Province, City, Municipality and Municipal District, 1970*. Manila: Bureau of the Census and Statistics, October 1971.

Philippines. Department of Commerce and Industry. Bureau of the Census and Statistics. Central Research and Statistical Operations Training Staff. "The 'Brain Drain' Problem in the Philippines." Manila: 1967 (mimeo.).

Philippines. National Economic Council. *Four-Year Development Plan FY 1972–75*. Manila: National Media Production Center, 1971.

"Philippines: Policy Objectives of the Employment of Women," *International Labour Review* [Geneva], 106, No. 2, August–September 1972, 267–268.

Philippine Statistics: 1969 Yearbook. Manila: Bureau of the Census and Statistics, May 1971.

Pilar, Meliza del. "Divorce, Filipino Style," *Philippine Panorama* [Manila], V. No. 7, February 13, 1972, 8–9.

Poethig, Richard P. "Integrating Rural Migrants into Urban Life: Philippines," *Ekistics* [Athens], 34, No. 205, December 1972, 388–390.

Polsky, Anthony. "Politics in the Philippines: Theater of the Absurd," *Far Eastern Economic Review* [Hong Kong], LVIII, No. 6, November 9, 1967, 271.

Population Reference Bureau. *1970 World Population Data Sheet*. Washington: 1972.

Pride, Leo B. (ed.) *International Theater Directory: A World Directory of the Theater and Performing Arts*. New York: Simon and Schuster, 1973.

Ravenholt, Albert. *The Philippines: A Young Republic on the Move*. (Asia Library Series.) Princeton: Van Nostrand, 1962.

———. *Population Review, 1970: The Philippines*. (American Universities Field Staff. Fieldstaff Reports. Southeast Asia Series, XIX, No. 1.) New York: AUFS, 1971.

———. *So Many Makes for Malnutrition*. (American Universities Field Staff. Fieldstaff Reports. Southeast Asia Series, XXII, No. 5.) New York: AUFS, 1974.

Remotigue, Francisco E. F. "A Year of Social Work." In *Fookien Times*

Yearbook, 1966. Manila: Fookien Times Yearbook Publishing, 1966.

Reyes, Francisco G. *Science and Technology in Philippine Society*. Manila: University of Santo Tomas, 1973.

Reyes, Gracianus R. "Change and the Church," *Solidarity* [Manila], No. 10, October 1970, 42–47.

Reyes, Mario R. "Cottage Industries: Motive Power in Rural Areas." Pages 124–127 in Betty Go-Belmonte (ed.), *Fookien Times Yearbook, 1974*. Manila: Fookien Times Yearbook Publishing, 1974.

Rizal, José. *Noli Me Tangere* (The Social Cancer). (Trans., Leon M. Guerrero.) London: Longmans, Green, 1961.

———. *The Reign of Greed*. (2d ed.) (Trans., Charles Derbyshire, from the Spanish El Filibusterismo.") Manila: Philippine Education, 1912.

Robinson, Harry. *Monsoon Asia: A Geographical Survey*. New York: Praeger, 1967.

Roces, Alfredo R. "The Year of the Art Galleries." Pages 354–355 in Betty Go-Belmonte (ed.) *Fookien Times Yearbook, 1974*. Manila: Fookien Times Yearbook Publishing, 1974.

Rosenberg, David A. "The Development of Modern Mass Communications in the Philippines: A Case Study of Institutional Growth in a Developing Country." Unpublished Ph.D. dissertation, 1972. Ithaca: Cornell University, 1973.

Rosenberg, Richard W. "Social Security and Income Redistribution in Developing Countries: The Philippine Case," *Review of Social Economy*, 33, No. 1, April 1975, 43–61.

Saito, Shiro. *Philippine Ethnography: A Critically Annotated and Selected Bibliography*. New York: Paragon, 1972.

Salcedo, Juan, Jr. "The Progress of Science in the Philippines," *Solidarity* [Manila], VI, No. 4, April 1971, 20–25.

Sanders, Albert J. "An Appraisal of the Iglesia Ni Cristo." Pages 350–365 in Gerald H. Anderson (ed.), *Studies in Philippine Church History*. Ithaca: Cornell University Press, 1969.

Santiago, Sebastian B. "The Problems of Public Housing in the Philippines." Pages 208–211 in Betty Go-Belmonte (ed.), *Fookien Times Yearbook, 1974*. Manila: Fookien Times Yearbook Publishing, 1974.

Santillan, Felipe. "A New Era of Progress for Filipino Inventors and Inventions." Pages 310–312 in Betty Go-Belmonte (ed.), *Fookien Times Yearbook, 1974*. Manila: Fookien Times Yearbook Publishing, 1974.

Santos, Felix P., Rene R. Calado, and Fortunata C. Villamar. "Educational Administration in the Philippines," *Bulletin of the UNESCO Regional Office for Education in Asia* [Bangkok], No. 15, June 1974, 129–145.

Scott, James C. "The Erosion of Patron-Client Bonds and Social Change in Rural Southeast Asia," *Journal of Asian Studies*, XXXII, No. 1, November 1972, 5–37.

"Second Managers-Trade Union Leaders' Conference Sponsored by the

Family Planning Organization of the Philippines," *International Labour Review* [Geneva], 107, No. 1, January 1973, 87–89.

Sibayan, Bonifacio P. "The Philippines." Pages 1038–1062 in Thomas A. Sebeok (ed.), *Current Trends in Linguistics*, VIII, Pt. II. The Hague: Mouton, 1971.

Sibley, Willis E. "Social Organization, Economy, and Directed Cultural Change in Two Philippine Barrios," *Human Organization*, 28, No. 2, Summer 1969, 148–154.

Smith, Robert Aura (ed.). *Philippine Freedom: 1946–1958*. New York: Columbia University Press, 1956.

"Sociological Dimension of Population Growth in the Philippines," *Philippine Sociological Review* [Manila], 19, No. 3, July–October 1971, 149–276.

Solon, Florentino S. "Nutrition in the Philippines." Pages 318–324 in Betty Go-Belmonte (ed.), *Fookien Times Yearbook, 1974*. Manila: Fookien Times Yearbook Publishing, 1974.

Spencer, Robert F. (ed.) *Religion and Change in Contemporary Asia*. Minneapolis: University of Minnesota Press, 1971.

Stanley, Peter W. *A Nation in the Making: The Philippines and the United States, 1899–1921*. Cambridge: Harvard University Press, 1974.

Steinberg, David J. (ed.) *In Search of Southeast Asia: A Modern History*. New York: Praeger, 1971.

Stinner, William F., and Paul D. Mader. "Government Policy and Personal Family Planning Approval in Conflict Settings: The Case of Muslim Minority in the Southern Philippines," *Population Studies* London], 29, No. 1, March 1975, 53–59.

————. "Sons, Daughters, or Both? An Analysis of Family Sex Composition Preferences in the Philippines," *Demography*, 12, No. 1, February 1975, 67–79.

Stockwin, Harvey. "The Importance of Ethnic Origins," *Far Eastern Economic Review* [Hong Kong], 84, No. 18, May 6, 1974, 16–18.

Sturtevant, David R. *Agrarian Unrest in the Philippines: Guardia de Honor–Revitalization Within the Revolution and Rizalistas—Contemporary Revitalization Movements in the Philippines*. (Papers in International Studies, Southeast Asia Series, No. 8.) Athens: Center for International Studies, Ohio University, 1969.

————. "Sakdalism and Philippine Radicalism," *Journal of Asian Studies*, XXI, No. 2, February 1962, 199–213.

Szanton, David L. *Estancia in Transition: Economic Growth in a Rural Philippine Community*. (IPC Paper, No. 9.) Quezon City: Ateneo de Manila University Press, 1971.

Szanton, Maria Cristina. *A Right to Survive: Subsistence Marketing in a Lowland Philippine Town*. University Park: Pennsylvania State University Press, 1972.

Takahashi, Akira. *Land and Peasants in Central Luzon: Socioeconomic*

Structure of a Philippine Village. Honolulu: East-West Center Press, 1969.

Tan, Edita A., and Gwendolyn R. Tecson. *Patterns of Consumption in the Philippines with Particular Reference to Demographic Factors.* (International Labour Organization, World Employment Programme Research, Population and Employment Working Papers, No. 8.) Geneva: ILO, October 1974.

Tanco, Arturo R. "Philippine Demographic Realities, Agricultural Development, and Social Stability," *Asia*, No. 23, Autumn 1971, 99–112.

Tate, C. Neal. "Socioeconomic Development and Democratization in the Philippines," *Comparative Political Studies*, 7, No. 1, April 1974, 47–63.

Taylor, Alice (ed.). "Philippines," *Focus*, XXI, No. 7, March 1971, 1–12.

Taylor, Donald W., and Robert C. Gardner. "The Role of Stereotypes in Communication Between Ethnic Groups in the Philippines," *Social Forces*, 49, No. 2, December 1970, 271–283.

Taylor, George E. *The Philippines and the United States: Problems of Partnership.* New York: Praeger, 1964.

Tilman, Robert O. "Student Unrest in the Philippines: The View from the South," *Asian Survey*, X, No. 10, October 1970, 900–909.

Torrevillas-Suarez, Domini. "Philippine Protestant Churches Going It Alone," *Philippine Panorama* [Manila], V, No. 27, July 9, 1972, 8–10.

———. "Religious Instruction in School," *Philippine Panorama* [Manila], V, No. 22, May 28, 1972, 4–5.

Tuggy, A. Leonard, and Ralph Toliver. *Seeing the Church in the Philippines.* Manila: O.M.F. Publishers, 1972.

Tunnie, Martin, Jr. *Differential Response of Rural Communities to Modernization: A Study of a Philippine Trade Area.* Ithaca: Cornell University, 1971.

Umehara, Hiromitzu. *A Hacienda Barrio in Central Luzon: Case Study of a Philippine Village.* (I.D.C. Occasional Paper Series, No. 12.) Tokyo: Institute of Developing Countries, 1974.

United Nations. Department of Economic and Social Affairs. *Population and Vital Statistics Report.* (Statistical Papers, Series A, XXVII, No. 2.) New York: 1975.

———. *Population and Vital Statistics Report: Data Available as of 1 April 1972.* (Statistical Papers, Series A, XXIV, No. 2.) New York: 1972.

United Nations. Economic and Social Council. *World Survey of Education,* IV. New York: UNESCO Publications Center, 1966.

U.S. Congress. 94th, 1st Session. House of Representatives. Committee on International Relations. Subcommittee on International Organizations. *Human Rights in South Korea and the Philippines: Implications for U.S. Policy.* Washington: GPO, 1975.

U.S. Department of State. Agency for International Development.

Development Assistance Program for the Philippines. Manila: AID/ Philippines, 1974.

———. *FY 1973 Progress Report on Design Criteria and Methodology for Construction of Low-Rise Buildings to Better Resist Typhoons and Hurricanes*, by N. J. Raufaste and R. D. Marshal. (NBSIR 74-582.) Washington: 1973.

U.S. Department of State. Agency for International Development. Bureau for Population and Humanitarian Assistance. *Population Program Assistance.* Washington: GPO, May 1974.

U.S. Department of State. Agency for International Development. Bureau for Technical Assistance. Office of Population. *Population Program Assistance.* Washington: GPO, December 1971.

U.S. Department of State. Bureau of Intelligence and Research. The Geographer. *International Boundary Study: The Philippines, Straight Baselines.* (Series No. 33.) Washington: 1971.

———. *Philippines: Administrative Division.* Washington: May 12, 1975.

U.S. Department of State. Bureau of Public Affairs. Office of Media Services. *Background Notes: Philippines.* (Department of State Publication 7750.) Washington: GPO, September 1974.

U.S. Peace Corps—Philippines. "Philippine Literature in English," *Ang Boluntaryo* [Philippines], VIII, September 1, 1967.

Valencia, Teodoro F. "Philippine Press Two Years After Martial Law." Pages 336–337 in Betty Go-Belmonte (ed.), *Fookien Times Yearbook, 1974.* Manila: Fookien Times Yearbook Publishing, 1974.

Velasco, Rudolfo L. "The PMPPA Profile." Pages 345–355 in Betty Go-Belmonte (ed.), *Fookien Times Yearbook, 1974.* Manila: Fookien Times Yearbook Publishing, 1974.

Vizconde, A. C. "Adult Education in the Philippines," *Asian South Pacific Journal of Adult Education* [New Delhi], 6, No. 1–4, August 1971–May 1972, 1–10.

Wallace, Ben J. *Village Life in Insular Southeast Asia.* (Little, Brown Series in Anthropology.) Boston: Little, Brown, 1971.

Walsh, Tom. *Martial Law in the Philippines: A Research Guide and Working Bibliography.* (Southeast Asia Working Paper Series, No. 4.) Honolulu: Asian Studies Program, University of Hawaii, 1973.

Weightman, George H. "The Philippines-Chinese Image of the Filipino," *Pacific Affairs* [Vancouver], XL, Nos. 3 and 4, 1967–68.

Weintrau, Dov. *Development and Modernization in the Philippines: The Problem of Change in the Context of Political Stability and Social Continuity.* (Sage Research Papers in the Social Sciences, Serial No. 90–001.) Beverly Hills: Sage Publications, 1973.

Wernstedt, Frederick L., and J. E. Spencer. *The Philippine Island World: A Physical, Cultural, and Regional Geography.* Berkeley: University of California Press, 1967.

Wickberg, Edgar. *The Chinese in Philippine Life, 1850–1898.* New

Haven: Yale University Press, 1965.

———. "The Chinese Mestizo in Philippine History," *Journal of Southeast Asian History*, 5, No. 1, March 1964, 62–100.

Wideman, Bernard. "Health Care in Need of a Tonic," *Far Eastern Economic Review* [Hong Kong], 86, No. 47, November 29, 1974. 24–25.

Willoughby, Charles A. *The Guerrilla Resistance Movement in the Philippines: 1941–1945.* New York: Vantage Press, 1972.

Wolff, Leon. *Little Brown Brother.* Garden City: Doubleday, 1961.

World Communications 1975. New York: United Nations Educational, Scientific and Cultural Organization, 1975.

World Health Organization. *Fifth Report on the World Health Situation, 1969–1972.* (Official Records of WHO.) Geneva: 1975.

Wurfel, David. "The Philippines." Pages 679–777 in George McTurnan Kahin (ed.), *Governments and Politics of Southeast Asia.* (2d ed.) Ithaca: Cornell University Press, 1964.

———. "The Philippines: Intensified Dialogue," *Asian Survey*, VII, No. 1, January 1967, 46–52.

Yambot, Efren (ed.). *Philippine Almanac and Handbook of Facts.* Quezon City: Philippine Almanac Printers, 1973.

Yengoyan, Aram A. "Demographic and Economic Aspects of Poverty in the Rural Philippines," *Comparative Studies in Society and History* [London], 16, No. 1, January 1974, 58–72.

Ziegler, Oswald (ed.). *The World and South East Asia.* Sydney: Oswald Ziegler Enterprises, 1972.

(Various issues of the following periodicals were also used in the preparation of this section: *Bulletin Today* [Manila], January 1973–December 1975; *Christian Science Monitor* [Boston], June–December 1975; *Far Eastern Economic Review* [Hong Kong], January 1974–September 1975; *Foreign Broadcast Information Service: Daily Report, Asia and Pacific* [Washington], January 1973–July 31, 1975; *New York Times,* November 1975; *Pakayag* [Honolulu], December 1974; and *Washington Post,* January 1972–June 1975.)

Section II. Political

Abueva, Jose Veloso. "The Philippines: Political Tradition and Change," *Asian Survey*, X, No. 1, January 1970, 56–64.

Abueva, Jose Veloso, and Raul P. de Guzman (eds.), *Foundations and Dynamics of Filipino Government and Politics*. Manila: Bookmark, 1969.

Adkins, John H. "Philippines 1971: Events of a Year, Trends of the Future," *Asian Survey*, XII, No. 1, January 1972, 78–85.

―――. "Philippines 1972: We'll Wait and See," *Asian Survey*, XIII, No. 2, February 1973, 140–150.

Agoncillo, Teodoro A., and Oscar M. Alfonso. *History of the Filipino People*. (Rev. ed.) Quezon City: Malaya Books, 1967.

Alfonso, Caridad S. "Executive-Legislative Relations." Pages 343–346 in Jose Veloso Abueva and Raul P. de Guzman (eds.), *Foundations and Dynamics of Filipino Government and Politics*. Manila: Bookmark, 1969.

Aquino, Beningno S. "Youth in Revolt," *Far Eastern Economic Review* [Hong Kong], 76, No. 24, June 10, 1972, 22–24.

Aquino, Beningno S., Jr. "Reforms or Revolution: The Philippines in the Seventies," *Pacific Community* [Tokyo], 2, No. 1, October 1970, 189–201.

The Asian Policy of the Philippines, 1954–61. Vancouver: University of British Columbia Press, 1965.

Averch, Harvey A., Frank H. Denton, and John E. Koehler. *The Matrix of Policy in the Philippines*. Princeton: Princeton University Press, 1971.

Bathurst, Peter. "New Direction for the New Society," *Far Eastern Economic Review* [Hong Kong], 89, No. 24, June 13, 1975, 3–7.

Brackman, Arnold C. *Southeast Asia's Second Front: The Power Struggle in the Malay Archipelago*. New York: Praeger, 1966.

Corpuz, Onofre D. "Cultural Foundations." Pages 6–18 in Jose Veloso Abueva and Raul P. de Guzman (eds.), *Foundations and Dynamics of Filipino Government and Politics*. Manila: Bookmark, 1969.

―――. "Philippines Public Administration: Performance and Challenges," *Asia*, Autumn 1971, 23–35.

―――. *The Philippines*. (The Modern Nation in Historical Perspective Series.) Englewood Cliffs: Prentice-Hall, 1965.

―――. "Realities of Philippine Foreign Policy." Pages 50–66 in Frank H. Golay (ed.), *The United States and the Philippines*. (The American Assembly, Columbia University.) Englewood Cliffs: Prentice-Hall,

1966.

Cruz, Andres Cristobal. "Reformation of Philippines Bureaucracy: The Career Executive Service Development Program." Pages 294–299 in Betty Go-Belmonte (ed.), *Fookien Times Yearbook, 1974*. Manila: Fookien Times Yearbook Publishing, 1974.

Day, Beth. *The Philippines: Shattered Showcase of Democracy in Asia*. New York: M. Evans, 1974.

"Decree Changes Name of Barrios: New Barangays," *New Philippines* [Manila], XX, September 1974, 49–53.

De Guzman, Raul P. "Politics in the Philippines," *Asia*, No. 23, Autumn 1971, 36–44.

De Guzman, Raul P., and Arturo Pacho. "The Direction and Control of the Philippine Bureaucracy." Pages 409–413 in Jose Veloso Abueva and Raul P. de Guzman (eds.), *Foundations and Dynamics of Filipino Government and Politics*. Manila: Bookmark, 1969.

De la Costa, Horacio. *The Background of Nationalism*. Manila: Solidaridad Publishing House 1965.

Del Carmen, Rolando V. "Constitutionalism and the Supreme Court in a Changing Philippine Society," *Asian Survey*, XIII, No. 11, November 1973. 1050–1061.

———. "Philippines 1974: A Holding Pattern—Power Consolidation or Prelude to a Decline?" *Asian Survey*, XV, No. 2, February 1975, 139–147.

Fabella, Armand V. "Reorganization for Development." Pages 102, 104, 112–113 in Betty Go-Belmonte (ed.), *Fookien Times Yearbook, 1974*. Manila: Fookien Times Yearbook Publishing, 1974.

Far Eastern Economic Review Yearbook, 1967. Hong Kong: FEER, 1966.

Far Eastern Economic Review Yearbook, 1968. Hong Kong: FEER, 1967.

Far Eastern Economic Review Yearbook, 1969. Hong Kong: FEER, 1968.

Far Eastern Economic Review Yearbook, 1970. Hong Kong: FEER, 1969.

Far Eastern Economic Review Yearbook, 1971. Hong Kong: FEER, 1970.

Far Eastern Economic Review Yearbook, 1972. Hong Kong: FEER, 1971.

Far Eastern Economic Review Yearbook, 1973. Hong Kong: FEER, 1972.

Far Eastern Economic Review Yearbook, 1974. Hong Kong: FEER, 1973.

Far Eastern Economic Review Yearbook, 1975. Hong Kong: FEER, 1974.

Ferrer, Jaime N. "Electoral Reforms in the Constitution." Pages 44–47 in *Fookien Times Yearbook, 1971*. Manila: Fookien Times Yearbook

Publishing, 1971.

Fookien Times Yearbook, 1968. Manila: Fookien Times Yearbook Publishing, 1968.

Fookien Times Yearbook, 1969. Manila: Fookien Times Yearbook Publishing, 1969.

Fookien Times Yearbook, 1970. Manila: Fookien Times Yearbook Publishing, 1970.

Fookien Times Yearbook, 1971. Manila: Fookien Times Yearbook Publishing, 1971.

Fookien Times Yearbook, 1972. Manila: Fookien Times Yearbook Publishing, 1972.

Fookien Times Yearbook, 1973. Manila: Fookien Times Yearbook Publishing, 1973.

Fookien Times Yearbook, 1974. (Ed., Betty Go-Belmonte.) Manila: Fookien Times Yearbook Publishing, 1974.

George, T. J. S. "Marcos Says an Uprising Is Planned," *Far Eastern Economic Review* [Hong Kong], 76, No. 26, June 24, 1972, 11–12.

――――. "Mr. Marcos and a Reverse Revolution," *Far Eastern Economic Review* [Hong Kong], 77, No. 40, September 30, 1972, 10–13.

――――. "The Philippines under Martial Law: The Road Ahead," *Pacific Community* [Tokyo], 4, No. 4, July 1973, 525–534.

Golay, Frank H. "Economic Collaboration: The Role of American Investment." Pages 95–124 in Frank H. Golay (ed.), *The United States and the Philippines.* (The American Assembly, Columbia University.) Englewood Cliffs: Prentice-Hall, 1966.

――――. "The Nation of the Filipino Nationalism." Pages 511–517 in Jose Veloso Abueva and Raul P. de Guzman (eds.), *Foundations and Dynamics of Filipino Government and Politics.* Manila: Bookmark, 1969.

Golay, Frank H. (ed.) *The United States and the Philippines.* (The American Assembly, Columbia University.) Englewood Cliffs: Prentice-Hall, 1966.

Grossholtz, Jean. "The Philippines: New Adventures with Old Problems," *Asian Survey,* IX, No. 1, January 1969, 50–57.

――――. "Philippines 1973: Whither Marcos?" *Asian Survey,* XIV, No. 1, January 1974, 101–122.

――――. *Politics in the Philippines.* Boston: Little, Brown, 1964.

Human Relations Area Files. *The Philippines,* III. New Haven: HRAF Press, 1956.

Iglesias, Gabriel V., and Abelardo Tolentino, Jr. "The Structure and Functions of Congress." Pages 249–256 in Jose Veloso Abueva and Raul P. de Guzman (eds.), *Foundations and Dynamics of Filipino Government and Politics.* Manila: Bookmark, 1969.

Jocano, F. Landa. *Growing Up in a Philippine Barrio.* (Case Studies in Education and Culture.) New York: Holt, Rinehart and Winston, 1969.

Kann, Peter R. "The Philippine Without Democracy," *Foreign Affairs,*

52, No. 3, April 1974, 612–632.

Kerkvliet, Benedict J. (ed.) *Political Change in the Philippines: Studies of Local Politics Preceding Martial Law*. (Asian Studies at Hawaii, No. 14, Asian Studies Program, University of Hawaii.) Honolulu: University Press of Hawaii, 1974.

Kiunisala, E. R. "Illegal Spending and Partisanship in Elections." Pages 75–79 in Jose Veloso Abueva and Raul P. de Guzman (eds.), *Foundations and Dynamics of Filipino Government and Politics*. Manila: Bookmark, 1969.

Landé, Carl H. *Leaders, Factions, and Parties: The Structure of Philippine Politics*. (Monograph Series, Southeast Asia Studies, No. 6.) New Haven: Yale University, 1964.

Laurel, Salvador H. "The Philippines: Shaping a China Policy," *Pacific Community* [Tokyo], 3, No. 4, July 1972, 756–763.

Legarda, Benito, Jr., and Roberto Y. Garcia. "Economic Collaboration: The Trading Relationship." Pages 125–148 in Frank H. Golay (ed.), *The United States and the Philippines*. (The American Assembly, Columbia University.) Englewood Cliffs: Prentice-Hall, 1966.

Leifer, Michael. "The Nixon Doctrine and the Future of Indochina," *Pacific Community* [Tokyo], 2, No. 4, July 1971, 742–753.

Lichauco, Alejandro. *The Lichauco Paper: Imperialism in the Philippines*. New York: Monthly Review, 1973.

Locsin, Teodoro M. "The Philippines: Leadership and Poverty," *Pacific Community* [Tokyo], 3, No. 1, October 1971, 171–182.

———. "The Two-Party System and Democracy." Pages 200–203 in Jose Veloso Abueva and Raul P. de Guzman (eds.), *Foundations and Dynamics of Filipino Government and Politics*. Manila: Bookmark, 1969.

Majul, Cesar Adib. *The Political and Constitutional Ideas of the Philippine Revolution*. New York: Oriole Editions, 1974.

Makalintal, Querube C. "The Supreme Court under the New Constitution (Footnote to the Ratification Cases)." Pages 284–285 in Betty Go-Belmonte (ed.), *Fookien Times Yearbook, 1974*. Manila: Fookien Times Yearbook Publishing, 1974.

Manglapus, Raul S. *Philippines: The Silenced Democracy*. Maryknoll, New York: Orbis Books, 1975.

———. "The State of Filipino Democracy." Pages 538–546 in Jose Veloso Abueva and Raul P. de Guzman (eds.), *Foundations and Dynamics of Filipino Government and Politics*. Manila: Bookmark, 1969.

Marcos, Ferdinand E. *The Democratic Revolution in the Philippines*. Englewood Cliffs: Prentice-Hall International, 1974.

———. *Notes on the New Society of the Philippines*. Manila: The Marcos Foundation, 1973.

———. "Our Foreign Policy." Pages 486–494 in Jose Veloso Abueva and Raul P. de Guzman (eds.), *Foundations and Dynamics of Filipino Government and Politics*. Manila: Bookmark, 1969.

Mariano, Leonardo C. "Local Government Finance." Pages 453–465 in Jose Veloso Abueva and Raul P. de Guzman (eds.), *Foundations and Dynamics of Filipino Government and Politics.* Manila: Bookmark, 1969.

Meyer, Milton Walter. *A Diplomatic History of the Philippine Republic.* Ann Arbor: University of Michigan Press, 1959.

Milne, R. Stephen. "The Filipino Party System." Pages 181–187 in Jose Veloso Abueva and Raul P. de Guzman (eds.), *Foundations and Dynamics of Filipino Government and Politics.* Manila: Bookmark, 1969.

"The National Reformation: 2nd Year," *New Philippines* [Manila], XX, September 1974, 1–6.

Noble, Lela Garner. "The National Interest and the National Image: Philippine Policy in Asia," *Asian Survey,* XIII, No. 6, June 1973, 560–576.

Nowak, Thomas C., and Kay A. Snyder. "Clientelist Politics in the Philippines: Integration or Instability?" *American Political Science Review,* LXVIII, No. 3, September 1974, 1147–1170.

O'Campo, Romeo B. "The Formal Structure and Functions of Philippine Local Governments." Pages 437–446 in Jose Veloso Abueva and Raul P. de Guzman (eds.), *Foundations and Dynamics of Filipino Government and Politics.* Manila: Bookmark, 1969.

Paguio, Bernabe B. Pages 80–81 in Jose Veloso Abueva and Raul P. de Guzman (eds.), *Foundations and Dynamics of Filipino Government and Politics.* Manila: Bookmark, 1969.

Pangilnan, Roberto M. "The Civil Service System." Pages 383–390 in Jose Veloso Abueva and Raul P. de Guzman (eds.), *Foundations and Dynamics of Filipino Government and Politics.* Manila: Bookmark, 1969.

Pelaez, Emmanuel. "Philippine Foreign Policy: The Whole and Its Parts." Pages 480–486 in Jose Veloso Abueva and Raul P. de Guzman (eds.), *Foundations and Dynamics of Filipino Government and Politics.* Manila: Bookmark, 1969.

Philippines. National Economic Council. *Four-Year Development Plan FY 1972–75.* Manila: National Media Production Center, 1971.

Polsky, Anthony. "Politics in the Philippines: Theater of the Absurd," *Far Eastern Economic Review* [Hong Kong], LVIII, No. 6, November 9, 1967, 271.

Rama, Napoleon G. "The Supreme Court in Action." Pages 357–364 in Jose Veloso Abueva and Raul P. de Guzman (eds.), *Foundations and Dynamics of Filipino Government and Politics.* Manila: Bookmark, 1969.

Romulo, Carlos P. "Philippine Foreign Policy under the New Society." Pages 72 and 76–77 in Betty Go-Belmonte (ed.), *Fookien Times Yearbook, 1974.* Manila: Fookien Times Yearbook Publishing, 1974.

Rono, Jose A. "The Governing Role of the Barangays." Pages 290–293 in

Betty Go-Belmonte (ed.), *Fookien Times Yearbook, 1974.* Manila: Fookien Times Yearbook Publishing, 1974.

Ronquillo, Bernardino. "Philippines: Second Thoughts," *Far Eastern Economic Review* [Hong Kong], 89, No. 27, July 4, 1975, 26–27.

Rosenberg, David A. "Civil Liberties and the Mass Media under Martial Law in the Philippines," *Pacific Affairs* [Vancouver], XLVII, No. 4, Winter 1974–75, 472–484.

Roth, David F. "The Deterioration and Reconstruction of National Political Parameters: The Philippines During the 1970s," *Asian Survey*, XIII, No. 9, September 1973, 812–825.

Salonga, Jovito. "Myths and Realities in Philippine Foreign Policy." Pages 496–506 in Jose Veloso Abueva and Raul P. de Guzman (eds.), *Foundations and Dynamics of Filipino Government and Politics.* Manila: Bookmark, 1969.

Santos, Vincente Abad. "The Conduct of Justice under the New Society." Pages 280–283 and 293 in Betty Go-Belmonte (ed.), *Fookien Times Yearbook, 1974.* Manila: Fookien Times Yearbook Publishing, 1974.

Seah, Chee-Meow. "The Muslim Issue and Implications for ASEAN," *Pacific Community* [Tokyo], 6, No. 1, October 1974, 139–160.

Shafie, M. Ghazali bin. "The Neutralization of Southeast Asia," *Pacific Community* [Tokyo], 3, No. 1, October 1971, 110–117.

Sison, Jesus C. "The Power and Functions of the President." Pages 322–329 in Jose Veloso Abueva and Raul P. de Guzman (eds.), *Foundations and Dynamics of Filipino Government and Politics.* Manila: Bookmark, 1969.

Starner, Frances. "Philippines: Instant Revolution," *Far Eastern Economic Review* [Hong Kong], 75, No. 3, January 15, 1972, 18–20.

———. "The Philippines: Politics of the 'New Era'!" *Asian Survey*, III, No. 1, January 1963.

Sternberg, David T. "The Philippines: Contour and Perspective," *Foreign Affairs*, XL, No. 3, April 1966.

Stockwin, Harvey. "Marcos vs. Lopez: End of an Oligarchy?" *Far Eastern Economic Review* [Hong Kong], 81, No. 38, September 24, 1973, 47–48.

———. "Overhauling the New Society," *Far Eastern Economic Review* [Hong Kong], 90, No. 40, October 3, 1975, 13–15.

Suhrke, Astri. "US-Philippines: The End of A Special Relationship," *The World Today* [London], XXXI, No. 2, February 1975, 80–88.

Taylor, George E. "The Challenge of Mutual Security." Pages 67–94 in Frank H. Golay (ed.), *The United States and the Philippines.* (The American Assembly, Columbia University.) Englewood Cliffs: Prentice-Hall, 1966.

———. *The Philippines and the United States: Problems of Partnership.* New York: Praeger, 1964.

Thompson, W. Scott. "America Renegotiates with the Philippines," *Pacific Community* [Tokyo], 2, No. 4, July 1971, 819–830.

————. *Unequal Partners: Philippine and Thai Relations with the United States*. Lexington, Massachusetts: Lexington Books, 1975.

Tilman, Robert O. "The Philippines in 1970: A Difficult Decade Begins," *Asian Survey*, XI, No. 2, February 1971, 139–148.

Tōnan Ajia Chōsakai (comp.). *Tōnan Ajia Yōran, 1968* (South and Southeast Asia Factbook, 1968). Tokyo: 1968.

————. *Tōnan Ajia Yōran, 1969* (South and Southeast Asia Factbook, 1969). Tokyo: 1969.

————. *Tōnan Ajia Yōran, 1970* (South and Southeast Asia Factbook, 1970). Tokyo: 1970.

————. *Tōnan Ajia Yōran, 1971* (South and Southeast Asia Factbook, 1971). Tokyo: 1971.

————. *Tōnan Ajia Yōran, 1972* (South and Southeast Asia Factbook, 1972). Tokyo: 1972.

————. *Tōnan Ajia Yōran, 1973* (South and Southeast Asia Factbook, 1973). Tokyo: 1973.

————. *Tōnan Ajia Yōran, 1974* (South and Southeast Asia Factbook, 1974). Tokyo: 1974.

————. *Tōnan Ajia Yōran, 1975* (South and Southeast Asia Factbook, 1975). Tokyo: 1975.

U.S. Congress. 91st, 2d Session. Senate. Committee on Foreign Relations. Subcommittee on United States Security Agreements and Commitments Abroad. *United States Security Agreements and Commitments Abroad*, I. (Pts. 1–4, Hearings.) Washington: GPO, 1971.

Usher, Richard E. "Philippine-American Economic Relations," *Asia*, No. 23, Autumn 1971, 80–88.

Wernstedt, Frederick L., and J. E. Spencer. *The Philippine Island World: A Physical, Cultural, and Regional Geography*. Berkeley: University of California Press, 1967.

Wideman, Bernard. "Marcos' Sometimes Referendum," *Far Eastern Economic Review* [Hong Kong], 87, No. 4, January 24, 1975, 13.

————. "Philippines: Goodbye to the Maker of Dollars and Men," *Far Eastern Economic Review* [Hong Kong], 89, No. 30, July 25, 1975, 25.

————. "Philippines: The Ultimate Purge as Melchor Goes," *Far Eastern Economic Review* [Hong Kong], 90, No. 50, November 21, 1975, 18–19.

Wurfel, David. "Individuals and Groups in the Philippine Society." Pages 208–223 in Jose Veloso Abueva and Raul P. de Guzman (eds.), *Foundations and Dynamics of Filipino Government and Politics*. Manila: Bookmark: 1969.

————. "The Philippines." Pages 679–777 in George McTurnan Kahin (ed.), *Governments and Politics of Southeast Asia*. (2d ed.) Ithaca: Cornell University Press, 1964.

Zaide, Gregorio F. *Philippine Government: Development, Organization, and Functions*. (Rev. ed.) Manila: Modern Book, 1965.

————. *The Republic of the Philippines: History, Government, and Civilization*. Manila: Rex Book Store, 1963.

(Various issues of the following periodicals were also used in the preparation of this section: *Far Eastern Economic Review* [Hong Kong], January 1967–July 1975; *Christian Science Monitor* [Boston], June–December 1975; *Manila Bulletin* [Manila], January 8, 1972–August 7, 1972; *Manila Chronicle* [Manila], July 9, 1972–August 21, 1972; *Manila Times* [Manila] September 1–November 22, 1971; *New York Times*, January 1967–August 1975; and *Washington Post*, January 1967–August 1975.)

Section III. Economic

Abueva, Jose Veloso, and Raul P. de Guzman (eds.). *Foundations and Dynamics of Filipino Government and Politics*. Manila: Bookmark, 1969.

Alunan, J. A. "Cost Relationships in Beef Cattle Farms in the Philippines," *Philippine Agriculturist* [Manila], LIII, No. 2, July 1970, 126–131.

American-Philippine Yearbook, 1967. (Ed., American Chamber of Commerce.) Manila: Manila Times, 1967.

Ancheta, Constancio M. "Economic Planning in the Philippines: Programs and Problems," *The Philippine Economy Bulletin* [Manila], V, No. 4, March–April 1967, 22–36.

Asia Research Bulletin [Singapore], 4, No. 6, November 30, 1974, 26.

Asian Development Bank. *Asian Agricultural Survey*. Seattle: University of Washington Press, 1969.

————. *Southeast Asia's Economy in the 1970s*. New York: Praeger, 1971.

Baldwin, Robert G. *Foreign Trade Regimes and Economic Development: The Philippines*. (A Special Conference Series on Foreign Trade Regimes and Economic Development.) New York: National Bureau of Economic Research, 1975.

Barker, Randolph, et al. "Employment and Technological Change in Philippine Agriculture," *International Labour Review* [Geneva], 106, Nos. 2–3, August–September 1972, 111–139.

Bathurst, Peter. "New Direction for the New Society," *Far Eastern Economic Review* [Hong Kong], 89, No. 24, June 13, 1975, 3–7.

Beech, Keyes. "Corruption and Disillusionment in Marcos' New Society," *San Francisco Examiner*, October 14, 1975.

Bhalla, A. S. "Manpower and Economic Planning in the Philippines," *International Labour Review* [Geneva], XCIV, No. 6, December 1966.

Bird, Richard M., and Oliver Oldman (eds.). *Readings on Taxation in Developing Countries* (3d ed.) Baltimore: Johns Hopkins University Press, July 18, 1975.

Bowring, Philip. "Test of Strength in the Philippines," *Far Eastern Economic Review* [Hong Kong], 88, No. 14, April 4, 1975, 51–54.

————. "Where Has All the Money Gone?" *Far Eastern Economic Review* [Hong Kong], 88, No. 24, June 13, 1975, 8–10.

"*Business Asia* Analyzes Concentration in 12 Philippine Industries," *Business Asia* [Hong Kong], V, No. 9, March 1, 1974, 68–69.

Business International Asia-Pacific. *The Philippines: Operating for*

Profit in the New Society. Hong Kong: 1974.

Cameron, Virginia Shook (ed.). *Private Investments and International Transactions in Asian and South Pacific Countries.* (Conference on Private Investments and International Transactions in Asian and South Pacific Countries, held in Singapore, 1973.) New York: M. Bender, 1974.

Carroll, John J. "Filipino Entrepreneurship in Manufacturing." Pages 115–138 in Frank Lynch and Alfonso de Guzman II (eds.), *Four Readings on Philippine Values.* Quezon City: Atenco de Manila University Press, 1970.

————. *The Filipino Manufacturing Entrepreneur: Agent and Product of Change.* Ithaca: Cornell University Press, 1965.

Castillo, Gelia T. "Technological and Social Change: The Case of the Miracle Rice," *Solidarity* [Manila], IV, No. 3, December 1968, 37–47.

Castro, Amado. "Philippine Export Development." Pages 181–201 in Theodore Morgan and Nyle Spoelstra (eds.), *Economic Interdependence in Southeast Asia.* Madison: University of Wisconsin Press, 1969.

Corpuz, Onofre D. *The Philippines.* (The Modern Nation in Historical Perspective Series.) Englewood Cliffs: Prentice-Hall, 1965.

————. "Realities of Philippine Foreign Policy." Pages 50–66 in Frank H. Golay (ed.), *The United States and the Philippines.* (The American Assembly, Columbia University.) Englewood Cliffs: Prentice-Hall, 1966.

Cutshall, Alden. *The Philippines: Nation of Islands* (Van Nostrand Searchlight Books.) Princeton: Van Nostrand, 1964.

Darrah, L. B., and F. A. Tiongson. *Agricultural Marketing in the Philippines.* Los Baños: University of the Philippines, 1969.

Day, Beth. *The Philippines: Shattered Showcase of Democracy in Asia.* New York: M. Evans, 1974.

De Guia, Eric O. *Fertilizer Distribution in the Philippines.* Paris: Organization for Economic Cooperation and Development, 1970.

De Guzman, Raul P. "Achieving Self-Sufficiency in Rice: A Study of the Philippine Experience in Program Implementation," *Philippine Journal of Public Administration* [Manila], XIV, No. 2, April 1970, 136–168.

De Guzman, Sixto T., Jr., et al. *Credit and Security in the Philippines: The Legal Problems of Development Finance.* New York: Crane-Russak, 1973.

Deomanpo. N. R. "The Effects of Cropping Patterns on Farming Earning Capacity in Malvar, Batangas," *Philippine Agriculturist* [Manila], LIII, No. 1, June 1969, 17–27.

De Roos, Robert. "The Philippines, Freedom's Pacific Frontier," *National Geographic*, CXXX, No. 3, September 1966.

Dlouhy, David B. "Philippines-U.S. Pact to Expire, Trading Patterns Felt Altered," *Foreign Agriculture*, XII, No. 20, May 20, 1974, 9–11.

Douglas, Donald E. "An Historical Survey of the Land Tenure Situation in the Philippines," *Solidarity* [Manila], V, No. 7, July 1970, 65–79.

Dozier, Edward P. *Mountain Arbiters: The Changing Life of a Philippine Hill People.* Tucson: University of Arizona Press, 1966.

Emery, Robert F. "Philippine Inflation, Balance of Payments, and Economic Development," *Asia*, No. 23, Autumn 1971, 89–98.

Espiritu, Socorro C. "Folk Beliefs and Modernization in Agriculture," *Solidarity* [Manila], IV, No. 4, April 1969, 33–37.

Estrella, Conrado F. *Agrarian Reform in the New Society.* N.pl.: N. pub., 1974.

———. *The Democratic Answer to the Philippine Agrarian Problem.* Manila: Solidaridad Publishing House, 1969.

———. "Motivation for Agrarian Reform," *Solidarity* [Manila], V, No. 7, July 1970, 25–30.

Far Eastern Economic Review Yearbook, 1965. Hong Kong: FEER, 1964.

Far Eastern Economic Review Yearbook, 1966. Hong Kong: FEER, 1965.

Far Eastern Economic Review Yearbook, 1967. Hong Kong: FEER, 1966.

Far Eastern Economic Review Yearbook, 1968. Hong Kong: FEER, 1967.

Far Eastern Economic Review Yearbook, 1969. Hong Kong: FEER, 1968.

Far Eastern Economic Review Yearbook, 1970. Hong Kong: FEER, 1969.

Far Eastern Economic Review Yearbook, 1971. Hong Kong: FEER, 1970.

Far Eastern Economic Review Yearbook, 1972. Hong Kong: FEER, 1971.

Far Eastern Economic Review Yearbook, 1973. Hong Kong: FEER, 1972.

Far Eastern Economic Review Yearbook, 1974. Hong Kong: FEER, 1973.

Far Eastern Economic Review Yearbook, 1974. Hong Kong: FEER, 1973.

Far Eastern Economic Review Yearbook, 1975. Hong Kong: FEER, 1974.

Farquhar, J. D. *Demonstration and Training in Forest, Forest Range, and Watershed Management.* Manila: United Nations Development Program, 1967.

Fookien Times Yearbook, 1966. Manila: Fookien Times Yearbook Publishing, 1966.

Fookien Times Yearbook, 1967. Manila: Fookien Times Yearbook Publishing, 1967.

Fookien Times Yearbook, 1971. Manila: Fookien Times Yearbook

Publishing, 1971.

Fryer, Donald W. *Emerging Southeast Asia: A Study in Growth and Stagnation*. New York: McGraw-Hill, 1970.

George, T. J. S. "The Philippines under Martial Law: The Road Ahead," *Pacific Community* [Tokyo], 4, No. 4, July 1973, 525–534.

Golay, Frank H. "Economic Collaboration: The Role of American Investment." Pages 95–124 in Frank H. Golay (ed.), *The United States and the Philippines*. (The American Assembly, Columbia University.) Englewood Cliffs: Prentice-Hall, 1966.

———. "The Economic Consequences of the Bell Trade Agreement," *Pacific Affairs* [Vancouver], 28, March 1955, 53–70.

———. "Economic Nationalism in Southeast Asia." Pages 1–21 in Frank H. Golay, et al (eds.), *Underdevelopment and Economic Nationalism in Southeast Asia*. Ithaca: Cornell University Press, 1969.

———. "The Philippine Economy." Pages 199–279 in George M. Guthrie (ed.), *Six Perspectives on the Philippines*. Manila: Bookmark, 1968.

———. "The Philippines." In Frank H. Golay, et al (eds.), *Underdevelopment and Economic Nationalism in Southeast Asia*. Ithaca: Cornell University Press, 1969.

———. *The Philippines: Public Policy and National Economic Development*. Ithaca: Cornell University Press, 1961.

———. "The Revised United States-Philippine Trade Agreement of 1955." (Cornell Southeast Asia Program, Data Paper, No. 23.) Ithaca: November 1956 (mimeo.).

———. "Some Costs of Philippine Politics," *Asia*, No. 23, Autumn 1971, 45–60.

Golay, Frank H., and Marvin E. Goodstein. *Rice and People in 1990—Philippine Rice Needs to 1990: Output and Input Requirements*. Manila: Agency for International Development, U. S. Department of State, 1967.

Golay Frank H. (ed.) *The United States and the Philippines*. (The American Assembly, Columbia University.) Englewood Cliffs: Prentice-Hall, 1966.

Golay, Frank H., et al (eds.). *Underdevelopment and Economic Nationalism in Southeast Asia*. Ithaca: Cornell University Press, 1969.

Goodstein, Marvin E. *The Pace and Pattern of Philippine Economic Growth: 1938, 1948, and 1959*. Ithaca: Cornell University Press, 1963.

Grossholtz, Jean. *Land Reform and Rural Development in the Philippines: Political Imperatives and Political Impediments*. (Papers on Problems of Development in Southeast Asia, No. 27.) New York: Asia Society, 1967.

———. *Politics in the Philippines*. Boston: Little, Brown, 1964.

Guthrie, George M., and Richard E. Caller. "Dynamics of Barrio Changes." In *The Filipino Child and Philippine Society*. Manila: Philippine Normal College, n.d.

Harkin, Duncan A. "Strengths and Weaknesses of the Philippine Land Reform." (Paper presented at the Southeast Asia Development Advisory Group, Rural Development Seminar on Land Reform in the Philippines, Baguio, Philippines, April 24–26, 1975. SEADAG Paper, No. 75–5.) New York: SEADAG of the Asia Society (mimeo.).

Hartendorp, A. V. H. *History of Industry and Trade of the Philippines*. Manila: American Chamber of Commerce of the Philippines, 1958.

———. *History of the Industry and Trade of the Philippines: The Magsaysay Administration*. Manila: Philippine Education, 1961.

Haswell, M. R. "Economics of Agricultural Development in the Philippines," *Civilisations* [Brussels], XIX, No. 4, April 1969, 437–450.

Hicks, George L. *The Philippine Coconut Industry: Growth and Change, 1900–1965*. (Field Report No. 17.) New York: National Planning Association, 1967.

Hicks, George L., and Geoffrey McNicoll. *Trade and Growth in the Philippines*. Ithaca: Cornell University Press, 1971.

Hollnsteiner, Mary Racelis. *The Dynamics of Power in a Philippine Municipality*. Quezon City: Community Development Research Council, University of the Philippines, 1963.

Hooley, R. W., and Randolph Barker (eds.). *Growth of Output in the Philippines*. Los Baños: International Rice Research Institute, 1967.

Huke, Robert E. *Shadows on the Land: An Economic Geography of the Philippines*. Manila: Bookmark, 1963.

Human Relations Area Files. *The Philippines*, I, III, and IV. New Haven: HRAF Press, 1956.

Huq, Muhammad Shamsul. *Education and Development Strategy in South and Southeast Asia*. Honolulu: East-West Center Press, 1965.

"Implications of Demographic Factors on Rural Development," *Journal of Philippine Statistics* [Manila], XIX, No. 4, October–December 1968, 13–21.

International Bank for Reconstruction and Development. *Economic Growth of the Philippines*. N. pl.: January 19, 1962.

International Bank for Reconstruction and Development and International Development Association. *World Bank and IDA, Annual Report 1966–1967*. N. pl.: September 1967.

International Financial News Survey, XX, No. 12, March 29, 1968.

International Financial Statistics, XXI, No. 3, March 1968.

International Labour Organization. *Sharing in Development: A Programme of Employment, Equity, and Growth for the Philippines*. Geneva: 1974.

International Labour Organization. International Labour Office. *Report to the Government of the Philippines on the Development of Vocational Training for Industrial Occupations*. Geneva: 1967.

International Monetary Fund. *Direction of Trade Annual, 1958–1962*. Washington: International Bank for Reconstruction and Development, 1962.

————. *Direction of Trade Annual, 1966–70*. Washington: IBRD, 1970.

————. *Direction of Trade Annual, 1968–72*. Washington: IBRD, 1972.

————. *Direction of Trade Annual, 1969–73*. Washington: IBRD, 1973.

————. *Direction of Trade Annual, 1970–74*. Washington: IBRD, 1974.

————. *Direction of Trade, July 1975*. Washington: IBRD, 1975.

Joint International Business Ventures in the Philippines: A Group Study. (Country Studies, No. 3.) New York: Columbia University, 1958.

Kann, Peter R. "The Philippines Without Democracy," *Foreign Affairs*, 52, No. 3, April 1974, 612–632.

Kaut, Charles R. "Utang na Loob: A System of Contractual Obligation among Tagalogs," *Southwestern Journal of Anthropology*, XVIII, No. 3, 1961, 256–272.

Kerkvliet, Benedict J. "Land Reform in the Philippines since the Marcos Coup," *Pacific Affairs* [Vancouver], 47, No. 3, Fall 1974, 286–304.

Kerkvliet, Benedict J. (ed.) "Agrarian Conditions in Luzon Prior to Martial Law," *Bulletin of Concerned Asian Scholars*, September 1973.

Koone, Harold D., and Lewis E. Gleeck. "Land Reform in the Philippines." Pages 1–93 in *Spring Review of Land Reform*, June 1970, IV. (2d ed.) Washington: Agency for International Development, U. S. Department of State, 1970.

Krinks, Peter. "Old Wine in a New Bottle: Land Settlement and Agrarian Problems in the Philippines," *Journal of Southeast Asian Studies* [Singapore], V; No. 1, March 1974, 1–17.

Larkin, John A. "The Causes of an Involuted Society: A Theoretical Approach to Rural Southeast Asian History," *Journal of Asian Studies*, XXX, No. 4, August 1971, 783–795.

Laurel, Salvador H. "The Philippines: Shaping a China Policy," *Pacific Community* [Tokyo], 3, No. 4, July 1972, 756–763.

Lawas, Jose M. "Agricultural Diversification and Development: The Philippine Viewpoint." (Southeast Asia Development Advisory Group, Rural Development Panel Seminar, Manila, January 6–8, 1971. SEADAG Paper, No. 71–3.) New York: SEADAG of the Asia Society (mimeo.).

Legarda, Benito, Jr., and Roberto Y. Garcia. "Economic Collaboration: The Trading Relationship." Pages 125–148 in Frank H. Golay (ed.), *The United States and the Philippines*. (The American Assembly, Columbia University.) Englewood Cliffs: Prentice-Hall, 1966.

Leifer, Michael. "The Nixon Doctrine and the Future of Indochina," *Pacific Community* [Tokyo], 2, No. 4, July 1971, 742–753.

Lightfoot, Keith. *The Philippines*. (Nations of the Modern World Series.) New York: Praeger, 1973.

Lipsky, Seth. "Unravelling a Sensitive Land Deal," *Far Eastern Economic Review* [Hong Kong], 85, No. 26, July 1, 1974, 38.

McLennan, Marshall S. "Land and Tenancy in the Central Luzon Plain," *Philippine Studies* [Manila], No. 17, October 1969, 651–682.

Marcos, Ferdinand E. "Our Foreign Policy." Pages 486–494 in Jose Veloso Abueva and Raul P. de Guzman (eds.), *Foundations and Dynamics of Filipino Government and Politics.* Manila: Bookmark, 1969.

Mears, Leon A. *Rice Economy of the Philippines.* Quezon City: University of the Philippines Press, 1974.

Medina, José C. "Land Reform Implementation in the Philippines," *Philippine Economy Bulletin* [Manila], VII, No. 5, May–June 1969, 1–12.

Medina, José C., Jr. "The Philippines Experience with Land Reform since 1972: An Overview." (Paper presented at the Southeast Asia Development Advisory Group, Rural Development Seminar on Land Reform in the Philippines, Baguio, Philippines, April 24–26, 1975. SEADAG Paper, No. 75–3.) New York: SEADAG of the Asia Society (mimeo.).

Montemayor, Jeremias. "Progress and Problems of Philippine Agrarian Reform under Martial Law." (Paper presented at the Southeast Asia Development Advisory Group, Rural Development Seminar on Land Reform in the Philippines, Baguio, Philippines, April 24–26, 1975. SEADAG Paper, No. 75–3.) New York: SEADAG of the Asia Society (mimeo.).

Montgomery, John D. "Land Reform and Popular Participation: Some Possibilities for the Philippines." (Paper presented at the Southeast Asia Development Advisory Group Rural Development Seminar on Land Reform in the Philippines, Baguio, Philippines, April 24–26, 1975.) New York: SEADAG of the Asia Society (mimeo.)

Myint, Hla. *Southeast Asia's Economy: Development Policies in the 1970s.* New York: Praeger, 1972.

National Council of Churches of Christ in the United States. Corporation Information Center. "The Philippines: American Corporations, Martial Law, and Underdevelopment," *IDOC*, No. 57, November 1973.

Nelson, Raymond. *The Philippines.* New York: Walker, 1968.

Noble, Lela Garner. "The National Interest and the National Image: Philippine Policy in Asia," *Asian Survey*, XIII, No. 6, June 1973, 560–576.

Nowak, Thomas C., and Kay A. Snyder. "Economic Concentration and Political Change in the Philippines." Pages 153–242 in Benedict J. Kerkvliet (ed.), *Political Change in the Philippines: Studies of Local Politics Preceding Martial Law.* (Asian Studies at Hawaii, No. 14, Asian Studies Program, University of Hawaii.) Honolulu: University Press of Hawaii, 1974.

Oñate, Burton T. "Estimation of Population and Labor Force in the Philippines," *International Rice Research Institute Journal* [Manila],

No. 43, 1965.

Organization of Economic and Cooperative Development. *Labour Absorption in Philippine Agriculture*. (Employment in Developing Countries Series, No. 6.) Paris: February 1973.

———. *National Accounts in Development Countries of Asia*. (Study Session Organized by Development Centre, Paris, March 1971.) Paris: November 1972.

Overholt, William. "Land Reform in the Philippines." (Report on Southeast Asia Development Advisory Group, Rural Development Panel Seminar on Land Reform in the Philippines, Baguio, Philippines, April 24–26, 1975.) New York: SEADAG of the Asia Society (mimeo.).

Paauw, Douglas S., and John S. H. Fei. *The Transition in Open Dualistic Economies—Theory and Southeast Asian Experience*. New Haven: Yale University Press, 1973.

Paramore, Lee R. "Peak Rice Crop Signals Philippine Agricultural Gains," *Foreign Agriculture*, V, No. 47, November 20, 1967.

Peaslee, Amos. J. (ed.) *Constitutions of Nations*, III. The Hague: Martinus Nijhoff, 1956.

Pelaez, Emmanuel. "Philippine Foreign Policy: The Whole and Its Parts." Pages 480–486 in Jose Veloso Abueva and Raul P. de Guzman (eds.), *Foundations and Dynamics of Filipino Government and Politics*. Manila: Bookmark, 1969.

Phelan, John L. *The Hispanization of the Philippines: Spanish Aims and Filipino Responses, 1565–1700*. Madison: University of Wisconsin Press, 1959.

"Philippine Cotton Trade Faces Depressed Market Conditions," *Foreign Agriculture*, XIII, No. 15, April 14, 1975, 9.

Philippines. *Almanac and Handbook of Facts, 1973*. Quezon City: 1973.

———. *An Interim Study of Commercial Banks in the Philippines, at September 23, 1974*. Manila: Sycip, Gorres, Velayo, October 1974.

Philippines. Central Bank of the Philippines. "Annual Report," *Central Bank Review* [Manila], XXVI, No. 42, October 1974, 24–31.

———. *Central Bank of the Philippines, January 3, 1949–January 3, 1974*. Manila: 1974.

———. *18th Annual Report, 1966*. Manila: 1967.

———. *Twenty-Second Annual Report, 1970*. Manila: 1971.

———. *Twenty-Third Annual Report, 1971*. Manila: 1972.

Philippines. Department of Agrarian Reform. *Eight Years of Land Reform, August 8, 1963 to September 10, 1971: A Terminal Report*. Manila: 1973.

Philippines. Department of Commerce and Industry. Bureau of the Census and Statistics. *Economic Census of the Philippines*. 5 vols. Manila: Department of Commerce and Industry, 1973.

Philippines. Department of National Defense. *1972 National Economic Atlas*. Manila: 1973.

Philippines. Social Security Commission. *Report, 1970*. Manila: 1971.

"Philippines—New Labour Code Adopted," *Social and Labour Bulletin* [Geneva], No. 1, 1974, 3–5.

Power, John H. "The Structure of Protection in the Philippines." Pages 261–289 in Bela A. Balassa (ed.), *The Structure of Protection in Developing Countries*. Baltimore: Johns Hopkins University Press, 1971.

Power, John H., and Gerardo P. Sicat. *The Philippines: Industrialization and Trade Policies*. (Organization for Economic Cooperation and Development Series.) London: Oxford University Press, 1971.

Price Waterhouse. *Doing Business in the Philippines*. (January 1975 Series.) N.pl.: 1975.

Quiazon, Troadio T., Jr. "Philippine Foreign Trade 1974 and Outlook for 1975," *Commerce* [Manila], 71, Nos. 11 and 12, November–December 1974, 7–14.

————. "Review of Philippine Foreign Trade, 1973." Pages 104–112 in Betty Go-Belmonte (ed.), *Fookien Times Yearbook, 1974*. Manila: Fookien Times Yearbook Publishing, 1974.

Ranis, Gustav. "Employment, Equity and Growth: Lessons from the Philippine Employment Mission," *International Labour Review* [Geneva], CX, No. 1, July 1974, 17–28.

Ravenholt, Albert. *The Philippines: A Young Republic on the Move*. (Asia Library Series.) Princeton: Van Hostrand, 1962.

Research for the World Food Crisis. Washington: American Association for the Advancement of Science, 1970.

Romulo, Carlos P. "Philippine Foreign Policy under the New Society." Pages 72 and 76–77 in Betty Go-Belmonte (ed.), *Fookien Times Yearbook, 1974*. Manila: Fookien Times Yearbook Publishing, 1974.

Ronquillo, Bernardino. "Philippines: Second Thoughts," *Far Eastern Economic Review* [Hong Kong], 89, No. 27, July 4, 1975, 26–27.

————. "Special Ties End," *Far Eastern Economic Review* [Hong Kong], 85, No. 26, July 1, 1974, 42–44.

Rosen, George. *Peasant Society in a Changing Economy*. Urbana: University of Illinois Press, 1975.

"Rural Development Panel Seminar on Peasants, Land Reform, and Revolutionary Movements." (Southeast Asia Development Advisory Group Seminar chaired by Donald S. Zagoria, June 4–6, 1974, in Savannah, Georgia.) New York: SEADAG of the Asia Society (mimeo.).

Salonga, Jovito. "Myths and Realities in Philippine Foreign Policy." Pages 496–506 in Jose Veloso Abueva and Raul P. de Guzman (eds.), *Foundations and Dynamics of Filipino Government and Politics*. Manila: Bookmark, 1969.

Savkar, D.S., and Joachim Ahrensdorf. "The Philippines: Stabilizing an Economy," *Finance and Development*, IV, No. 1, March 1967.

Schul, Norman W. "Hacienda Magnitude and Philippine Sugar Cane Production," *Asian Studies* [Manila], V, No. 2, August 1967, 258–273.

Scott, James C. "The Erosion of Patron-Client Bonds and Social Change in Rural Southeast Asia," *Journal of Asian Studies*, XXXII, No. 1, November 1972, 5–37.

Seah, Chee-Meow. "The Muslim Issue and Implications for ASEAN," *Pacific Community* [Tokyo], 6, No. 1, October 1974, 139–160.

Shafie, M. Ghazali bin. "The Neutralization of Southeast Asia," *Pacific Community* [Tokyo], 3, No. 1, October 1971, 110–117.

Shand, Richard T. (ed.) *Agricultural Development in Asia*. Canberra: Australian National University, 1969.

Shoesmith, Denis. "Land Reform in the Philippines: Emancipating or Emaciating the Tenant Farmer?" *Australian Outlook* [Sydney], XXVIII, No. 3, December 1974, 274–289.

Sibley, Willis E. "Social Organization, Economy, and Directed Cultural Change in Two Philippine Barrios," *Human Organization*, 28, No. 2, Summer 1969, 148–154.

Sicat, Gerardo P. *Economic Policy and Philippine Development*. Manila: University of the Philippine Press, 1972.

————. "*July 4, 1974: An End to Special Relations*," Pages 94–96 in Betty Go-Belmonte (ed.), *Fookien Times Yearbook, 1974*. Manila: Fookien Times Yearbook Publishing, 1974.

————. "Philippine Economic Development and Japan in the Future," *Developing Economies*, XI, December 1973, 363–370.

————. "The Philippine Economy and Its Prospects," *Commerce* [Manila], 71, Nos. 11 and 12, November–December 1974, 23–28.

Sicat, Gerardo P. (ed.) *The Philippine Economy in the 1960s*. Quezon City: University of the Philippines, 1964.

Southerland, Daniel. "Philippine Reforms Questioned," *Christian Science Monitor*, 68, No. 7, December 4, 1975, 11.

Spencer, J. E. "The Rise of Maize as a Major Crop Plant in the Philippines," *Journal of Historical Geography*, 1, January 1975, 1–16.

Standard Chartered Bank. "Philippines," *Standard Chartered Review* [London], October 1975, 27.

————. "Philippines," *Standard Chartered Review* [London], November 1975, 26–29.

Standard Chartered Bank Group. *The Philippines: The Businessman's Guide*. London: 1975.

Starner, Frances. "Rice Politics in the Philippines," *Far Eastern Economic Review* [Hong Kong], 75, No. 5, January 29, 1972, 24–25.

Statistical Handbook of the Philippines, 1965. Manila: Central Bank of the Philippines, 1965.

Stockwin, Harvey. "Philamerica: End of a Chapter," *Far Eastern Economic Review* [Hong Kong], 85, No. 26, July 1, 1974, 38–41.

Strauss, Paul "Manila's Mixed Results," *Far Eastern Economic Review* [Hong Kong], 89, No. 39, September 26, 1975, 49–52.

Taylor, George E. "The Challenge of Mutual Security." Pages 67–94 in Frank H. Golay (ed.), *The United States and the Philippines*. (The

American Assembly, Columbia University.) Englewood Cliffs: Prentice-Hall, 1966.

————. *The Philippines and the United States: Problems of Partnership.* New York: Praeger, 1964.

Thompson, W. Scott. "America Renegotiates with the Philippines," *Pacific Community* [Tokyo], 2, No. 4, July 1971, 819–830.

Tōnan Ajia Chōsakai (comp.). *Tōnan Ajia Yōran, 1968* (South Southeast Asia Factbook, 1968). Tokyo: 1968.

————. *Tōnan Ajia Yōran, 1969* (South and Southeast Asia Factbook, 1969). Tokyo: 1969.

————. *Tōnan Ajia Yōran, 1970* (South and Southeast Asia Factbook, 1970). Tokyo: 1970.

————. *Tōnan Ajia Yōran, 1971* (South and Southeast Asia Factbook, 1971). Tokyo: 1971.

————. *Tōnan Ajia Yōran, 1972* (South and Southeast Asia Factbook, 1972). Tokyo: 1972.

————. *Tōnan Ajia Yōran, 1973* (South and Southeast Asia Factbook, 1973). Tokyo: 1973.

————. *Tōnan Ajia Yōran, 1974* (South and Southeast Asia Factbook, 1974). Tokyo: 1974.

————. *Tōnan Ajia Yōran, 1975* (South and Southeast Asia Factbook, 1975). Tokyo: 1975.

Umehara, Hiromitzu. "Philippines Agriculture and Its Problems," *Asian Agriculture* [Tokyo], II, No. 1, January 1971, 45–54.

United Nations. *Economic Survey of Asia and the Far East, 1966.* Bangkok: 1967.

U.S. Congress. 91st, 2d Session. Senate. Committee on Foreign Relations. Subcommittee on United States Security Agreements and Commitments Abroad. *United States Security Agreements and Commitments Abroad,* I. (Pts. 1–4, Hearings.) Washington: GPO, 1971.

U.S. Department of Agriculture. *Agricultural Policies in the Far East and Oceania.* (Foreign Agricultural Economic Report, No. 37.) Washington: GPO, 1967.

U.S. Department of Agriculture. Foreign Agricultural Service. *Philippines: Agricultural Situation (Supplemental).* (No. PH 5003.) Manila: February 5, 1975.

U.S. Department of Commerce, Bureau of Foreign Trade. *Investment in the Philippines.* Washington: GPO, 1955.

————. *Philippines: A Market for U.S. Products.* Washington: GPO, 1965.

U.S. Department of Commerce. Bureau of International Commerce. *Foreign Agricultural Service, Airgrams,* [U.S. Embassy in Manila], December 1969–December 1975.

————. *International Commerce,* LXXIV, No. 4, January 22, 1968.

————. *International Commerce,* LXXIV, No. 10, March 4, 1968.

————. *Marketing in the Philippines.* (Overseas Business Reports, OBR

74–46.) Washington: GPO, October 1974.

U.S. Department of Commerce. Bureau of International Commerce. Domestic and International Business Administration. Bureau of International Commerce. *Foreign Economic Trends and Their Implications for the United States.* (FET–75–064.) Washington: GPO, 1975.

U.S. Department of Commerce. Office of Business Economics. *Survey of Current Business*, XXXVII, No. 9, November 1967.

U.S. Department of the Interior. Bureau of Mines. *The Mineral Industry of the Philippines*, by Robert A. Clifton. (Preprint from the Bureau of Mines *Mineral Yearbook, 1973.*)

U.S. Department of State. Agency for International Development. *Development Assistance Program for the Philippines.* Manila: AID/ Philippines, 1974.

U.S. Department of State. Bureau of Public Affairs. Office of Media Services. *Background Notes: Philippines.* (Department of State Publication 7750.) Washington: GPO, September 1974.

U.S. Export-Import Bank of Washington. *Report to the Congress for the Six Months Ended December 31, 1963.* Washington: GPO, 1964.

U.S. Export-Import Bank of Washington. Foreign Assistance Program. *Annual Report to the Congress Fiscal Year 1966.* Washington: GPO, 1967.

U.S.-Philippines Economic Relations. (Center for Strategic and International Studies, Georgetown University, Special Report Series, No. 12.) Washington: 1971.

Usher, Richard E. "Philippine-American Economic Relations," *Asia*, No. 23, Autumn 1971, 80–88.

Valino, R. "Philippine Farming: The Good Earth and the Barrios," *Modern Asia*, VIII, No. 2, 1974, 25–32.

Villaviega, Raciano C. "Role of Government in Industrial Relations: A Philippine Example," *Labor Review*, I, No. 4, April 1965.

Virata, Cesar. "Philippine Industrialization Strategy and Foreign Investment Policy," *Asia*, No. 23, Autumn 1971, 61–79.

Wernstedt, Frederick L., and J. E. Spencer. *The Philippine Island World: A Physical, Cultural, and Regional Geography.* Berkeley: University of California Press, 1967.

West, J. M. "The Minerals Industry of the Philippines." In *1964 Minerals Yearbook*, IV. Washington: Bureau of Mines, U.S. Department of the Interior, 1966.

———. "The Minerals Industry of the Philippines." In *1965 Minerals Yearbook*, IV. Washington: Bureau of Mines, U.S. Department of the Interior, 1967.

———. "The Minerals Industry of the Philippines." In *1966 Minerals Yearbook*, IV. Washington: Bureau of Mines, U.S. Department of the Interior, 1968.

Wharton, Clifton E., Jr. *Subsistence Agriculture and Economic Development.* Chicago: Aldine, 1969.

Wheelock, Gerald C. "Predicting the Distribution of a Rural Credit Union in the Philippines," *Journal of Developing Areas*, IX, No. 1, October 1974, 69.

The World Bank Group in Asia. Bangkok: United Nations, 1967.

Wurfel, David. "Some Notes on the Political Role of Labor Movements: A Philippine Case Study," *Labor Review*, I, No. 4, April 1965.

Yengoyan, Aram A. "Demographic and Economic Aspects of Poverty in the Rural Philippines," *Comparative Studies in Society and History* [London], 16, No. 1, January 1974, 58–72.

(Various issues of the following periodicals were also used in the preparation of this section: *Asia Research Bulletin* [Singapore], January 1972–November 1975; *Business Asia* [Hong Kong], January 1972–November 1975; *Christian Science Monitor* [Boston], June–December 1975; *Far Eastern Economic Review* [Hong Kong], January 1972–November 1975; and *Philippines Business Day International* [Manila] January 1974–August 1975.)

Wheelock, Lloyd C. "Predicting the Distribution of a Rural Social
Action in the Philippines." Dissertation of the Alumni Association of
the Philippines.

The World Bank Business Asia, Bangkok, Chiang Mai and Songkhla
World, Bank Group, Modernizing Pan Thai, Intercultural Press, Philadelphia
Philippine Case" (paper) Mahbubani, Asia, Tokyo, April 1975.

Yongyuth, Ananda. "The Employment Problems and Aspects of Poverty in
the Rural Philippines." Conference on Survey of Housing and Incomes.
Chulalongkorn University, January 1976. Seoul.

(Various issues of the following periodicals were also used in the
preparation of this section: Asia Week (Hong Kong), February 1, 1977, January
1976, December 1976; Far Eastern Economic Review, January 1976,
November 1976; Counter Statistics Yearbook, Bhutan; Singapore, Saturday
1976; Far Eastern Economic Review, (Hong Kong), January 1976;
Newsweek, Asia Edition; Thailand Business Day, Association of the World
Philippines; The Bangkok Post.)

Section IV. National Security

Adie, W.A.C. "Uneasy Riders: The Role of Military and Paramilitary Elites in China and Some Other Developing Countries," *Asia Quarterly* [Brussels], 2, 1972, 167–188.

Agoncillo, Teodoro A., and Oscar M. Alfonso. *History of the Filipino People.* (Rev. ed.) Quezon City: Malaya Books, 1967.

Amnesty International. *Report on Torture.* London: Gerald Duckworth, 1973.

Averch, Harvey A., Frank H. Denton, and John E. Koehler. *A Crisis of Ambiquity: Political and Economic Development in the Philippines.* (R–473–AID.) Santa Monica: Rand Corporation, January 1970.

Bauer, Ronald G. "Military Professional Socialization in a Developing Country." Unpublished Ph.D. dissertation. Ann Arbor: University of Michigan, 1973.

Bellah, R. H. (ed.) *Religion and Progress in Modern Asia.* New York: Free Press, 1965.

Biemen, Henry (comp.). *The Military and Modernization.* Chicago: Aldine, 1971.

Bixler, Paul H. *Southeast Asia: Bibliographic Directions in a Complex Area.* (Choice Bibliographic Essay Series, No. 2.) Middletown, Connecticut: Wesleyan University Press, for Association of College and Research Libraries, 1974.

Bōei Nenkan (Defense Yearbook.) Manila: N. pub., 1975.

Clinard, Marshall B., and Daniel J. Abbott. *Crime in Developing Countries: A Comparative Perspective.* New York: John Wiley and Sons, 1973.

Concepcion, Roberto. "Legal Aid in the Republic of the Philippines." (Paper presented at Seventh Congress on the Law of the World. Sponsored by World Peace Through Law Center and Others, October 12–17, 1975.) Washington: Seventh Congress on the Law of the World, October 1975 (mimeo.).

Crisol, Jose M. (ed.) *Marcos on the Armed Forces.* Manila: Capitol Publishing House, 1971.

Crozier, Brian (ed.). *Annual of Power and Conflict 1973–74: A Survey of Political Violence and International Influence.* London: Institute for the Study of Conflict, 1974.

Day, Beth. *The Philippines: Scattered Showcase of Democracy in Asia.* New York: M. Evans, 1974.

Del Carmen, Rolando V. "Changes in the Philippine Judiciary under the New Constitution." (Paper presented at the Annual Meeting of the

Midwest Conference on Asian Affairs, at University of Kansas, October 1974.) 1974 (mimeo.).

————. "Philippines 1974: A Holding Pattern—Power Consolidation or Prelude to a Decline?" *Asian Survey*, XV, No. 2, February 1975, 139–147.

Dupuy, Trevor N., and Wendell Blanchard. *The Almanac of World Military Power*. (2d ed.) Dunn Loring, Virginia: T. N. Dupuy Associates, 1972.

Dupuy, Trevor N., Grace Hayes, and John A. C. Andrews (eds.). *The Almanac of World Military Power*. (3d ed.) New York: R. R. Bowker, 1974.

Enrile, Juan Ponce. "Public Order, Integration, and Community Action." Pages 56–58 in Betty Go-Belmonte (ed.), *Fookien Times Yearbook, 1974*. Manila: Fookien Times Yearbook Publishing, 1974.

Espino, Romero C. "Forging Today's Defense Through Our 'Trustees of Tomorrow.'" Pages 60–61 and 66 in Betty Go-Belmonte (ed.), *Fookien Times Yearbook, 1974*. Manila: Fookien Times Yearbook Publishing, 1974.

Far Eastern Economic Review Yearbook, 1970. Hong Kong: FEER, 1969.

Far Eastern Economic Review Yearbook, 1971. Hong Kong: FEER, 1970.

Far Eastern Economic Review Yearbook, 1972. Hong Kong: FEER, 1971.

Far Eastern Economic Review Yearbook, 1973. Hong Kong: FEER, 1972.

Far Eastern Economic Review Yearbook, 1974. Hong Kong: FEER, 1973.

Far Eastern Economic Review Yearbook, 1975. Hong Kong: FEER, 1974.

Fernando, Enrique M. "The Rule of Law Under Martial Law: The Philippine Experience." (Paper presented at Seventh Congress on the Law of the World. Sponsored by World Peace Through Law Center and Others, Octover 12–17, 1975.) Washington: Seventh Congress on the Law of the World, 1975.

Fookien Times Yearbook, 1974. (Ed., Betty Go-Belmonte.) Manila: Fookien Times Yearbook Publishing, 1974.

Funnel, Victor. "South and East Asia." In Brian Crozier (ed.), *Annual of Power and Conflict 1973–74: A Survey of Political Violence and International Influence*, London: Institute for the Study of Conflict, 1974.

Golay, Frank H. (ed.) *The United States and the Philippines*. (The American Assembly, Columbia University.) Englewood Cliffs: Prentice-Hall, 1966.

Hoadley, Stephen J. *Soldiers and Politics in Southeast Asia: Cases and Comparisons in Civil-Military Politics*. Cambridge, Massachusetts:

Schenkman Publishing, 1974.

International Institute for Strategic Studies. *The Military Balance, 1974–75.* London: September 1974.

——. *Strategic Survey, 1969–74.* London: April 1975.

Jane's Fighting Ships, 1975–76. (Ed., John E. Moore.) New York: Franklin Watts, 1975.

Jane's Weapons Systems, 1974–75. (Eds., R. T. Pretty and D. H. R. Archer.) New York: McGraw-Hill, 1974.

Kann, Peter R. "The Philippines Without Democracy," *Foreign Affairs,* 52, No. 3, April 1974, 612–632.

Keesing's Publications. *Treaties and Alliances of the World: An International Survey Covering Treaties in Force and Communities of States.* New York: Charles Scribner's Sons, 1968.

Kemp, Geoffrey. *Arms Traffic and Third World Conflicts.* New York: Carnegie Endowment for International Peace, 1970.

Kerkvliet, Benedict J. "Critique of the Rand Study on the Philippines," *Journal of Asian Studies,* XXXII, No. 3, May 1973, 489–500.

——. "Land Reform in the Philippines since the Marcos Coup," *Pacific Affairs* [Vancouver], 47, No. 3, Fall 1974, 286–304.

Kiefer, Thomas M. *The Tausug: Violence and Law in a Philippines Moslem Society.* (Case Studies in Cultural Anthropology.) New York: Holt, Rinehart and Winston, 1972.

Knapp, Victor (ed.). *International Encyclopedia of Comparative Law.* 8 vols. The Hague: Mouton, 1970.

Kona, Takao. "Ajia Shokoku no Minhei" (The Militia in Asian Countries), *Gunji Kenkyū* [Tokyo], 8, No. 4, April 1973, 42–53.

Landé, Carl H. "The Philippines." In James S. Coleman (ed.), *Education and Political Development.* Princeton: Princeton University Press, 1965.

Larkin, John A. "The Place of Local History in Philippine Historiography," *Journal of Southeast Asian Studies, VIII, No. 2, September 1967.*

Lightfoot, Keith. *The Philippines.* (Nations of the Modern World Series.) New York: Praeger, 1973.

Loveday, Douglas F. *The Role of U. S. Military Bases in the Philippine Economy.* (Rand Corporation Research Memorandum RM–5801–ISA series.) Santa Monica: Rand Corporation, 1971.

Lynch, Frank (ed.). *Four Readings on Philippine Values.* (Institute of Philippine Culture Papers, No. 2.) Quezon City: Ateneo de Manila University Press, 1964.

——. *Sulu's People and Their Art.* (Institute of Philippine Culture Papers, No. 3.) Quezon City: Ateneo de Manila University Press, 1963.

Manglapus, Raul S. *Philippines: The Silenced Democracy.* Maryknoll, New York: Orbis Books, 1975.

Marcos, Ferdinand E. *The Democratic Revolution in the Philippines.* Englewood Cliffs: Prentice-Hall International, 1974.

————. *Notes on the New Society of the Philippines*. Manila: The Marcos Foundation, 1973.

Millar, Thomas Bruce. *The Indian and Pacific Oceans: Some Strategic Considerations*. (Adelphi Papers Series, No. 52.) London: Institute for Strategic Studies, 1969.

Molony, Carol. "La guerre contre les Musulmans au sud des Philippines," *Temps Modernes* [Paris], 29, October 1973, 656–665.

Nelson, Joan. "The Urban Poor: Disruption or Political Integration in Third World Cities," *World Politics*, XXII, No. 3, April 1970, 393–414.

Nolledo, Jose N. *Criminal Law*. Manila: National Book Store, 1968.

Olivas, Prospero A. "The Goal of an Integrated Metropolitan Police Force." Pages 68–70 in Betty Go-Belmonte (ed.), *Fookien Times Yearbook, 1974*. Manila: Fookien Times Yearbook Publishing, 1974.

Padilla, Ambrosio. *Criminal Law: Revised Penal Code Annotated*, I. (11th ed.) Manila: Padilla Publications, November 1974.

Pascual, Crisolito. *The Philippines*. (Lawasia Legal Systems Series.) Sydney: Butterworth, 1970.

Pecache, Guillermo A. "Philippines," *Asian Defence Journal* [Kuala Lumpur], 1971.

————. "Service to the People: Soldier's Duty and Pride." Pages 64–66 in Betty Go-Belmonte (ed.), *Fookien Times Yearbook, 1974*. Manila: Fookien Times Yearbook Publishing, 1974.

Philippines. Laws, Statutes, etc. "Acts of the Congress of the Philippines, RA No. 4864, The Police Acts of 1966," *Decision Law Journal*, XXIII, No. 4, April 30, 1967.

————. *Philippine Annotated Laws: Cumulative Supplement*. Manila: Lawyers Cooperative, 1967.

——. *Philippine Annotated Laws*, XI, Titles 52–68. Manila Lawyers Cooperative, 1957.

Ramos, Fidel V. "The Armed Forces of the Philippines: Home Defence Programme and National Security," *Asian Defence Journal* [Kuala Lumpur], October 1972, 47–51.

————. "Philippine Constabulary: New Horizons." Pages 62–63 in Betty Go-Belmonte (ed.), *Fookien Times Yearbook, 1974*. Manila: Fookien Times Yearbook Publishing, 1974.

Ravenholt, Albert. *The Philippines: A Young Republic on the Move*. (Asia Library Series.) New York: Van Nostrand, 1962.

————. "The Spoils of Nationalism: The Philippines." Pages 178–186 in Kalman H. Silvert (ed.), *Expectant Peoples: Nationalism and Development*. New York: Alfred A. Knopf, 1963.

Revised Rules of Court in the Philippines. Manila: Rex Book Store, 1972.

Reyes, Luis B. *The Revised Penal Code* (6th ed., rev.) Manila: Philaw, 1965.

Romulo, Carlos P. *Report to the President on the Two SEATO Ministerial Council Meetings: Canberra, Australia 27–28 June 1972, London, U. K. 27–28 April 1971*. Manila: Department of Foreign Affairs,

Philippines, 1972.

Santos, Vincente Abad. "The Conduct of Justice under the New Society." Pages 280–283 and 293 in Betty Go-Belmonte (ed.), *Fookien Times Yearbook, 1974*. Manila: Fookien Times Yearbook Publishing, 1974.

Sellers, Robert C. *Armed Forces of the World: A Reference Handbook.* (3d ed.) New York: Praeger, 1975.

Senoren, Cleto B. "Philippine Police System," *International Police Academy Review*, 6, No. 3, July 1972, 1–3.

———. "Philippine Police System Manual," *International Police Academy Review*, 7, No. 4, October 1973, 6–8.

Shaplen, Robert. *Time Out of Hand: Revolution and Reaction in Southeast Asia.* (Rev. ed.) (Harper Colophon Books Series.) New York: Harper and Row, 1970.

Smith, Robert M. (ed.) *Southeast Asia: Documents of Political Development and Change.* Ithaca: Cornell University Press, 1974.

Sternberg, David T. "The Philippines: Contour and Perspective," *Foreign Affairs*, XL, No. 3, April 1966.

Stockholm International Peace Research Institute. *The Arms Trade Registers: The Arms Trade with the Third World.* Cambridge: MIT Press, 1975.

Stowe, Judith. "Philippines: The Need for a New Society," *Conflict Studies* [London], No. 37, August 1973, 3–7.

Tadiar, A. F. "Administration of Criminal Justice in the Philippines," *Philippine Law Journal* [Manila], 47, Spring 1972, 547–602.

Tanham, G. K. "Some Insurgency Lessons from Southeast Asia," *Orbis*, XVI, No. 3, Autumn 1972, 646–659.

Taprell, Dorling H. *Ribbons and Medals: The World's Military and Civil Awards.* Garden City: Doubleday, 1974.

Tate, C. Neal, "Political Development and the Philippine Judiciary," *Asian Forum*, 6, January–March 1974, 32–44.

Tilman, Robert O. "Student Unrest in the Philippines: The View from the South," *Asian Survey*, X, No. 10, October 1970, 900–909.

U. S. Arms Control and Disarmament Agency. *World Military Expenditures and Arms Trade, 1963–1973.* (ACDA Publication No. 74.) Washington: GPO, 1975.

U. S. Congress, 91st. 2d Session. Senate Committee on Foreign Relations. Subcommittee on United States Security Agreements and Commitments Abroad. *United States Security Agreements and Commitments Abroad*, I. (Pts. 1–4 Hearings.) Washington: GPO, 1971.

U. S. Congress. 93d. 1st Session. Senate. Committee on Foreign Relations. *Korea and the Philippines, November 1972: A Staff Report Prepared for the Use of the Committee on Foreign Relations.* Washington: GPO, 1972.

U. S. Congress. 93d. House of Representatives. Committee on Foreign Affairs. *The Narcotics Situation in Southeast Asia: Report of a*

Special Study Mission. Washinton: GPO, July 26, 1973.

U. S. Congress. 93d. 2d Session. House of Representatives. Committee on Foreign Affairs. Subcommittee on Asian and Pacific Affairs. *Political Prisoners in South Vietnam and the Philippines* (May 1 and June 5, 1974). Washington: GPO, 1974.

U. S. Congress. 94th. 1st Session. House of Representatives. Committee on International Relations. Subcommittee on International Organizations. *Human Rights in South Korea and the Philippines: Implications for U. S. Policy*. Washington: GPO, 1975.

U. S. Department of Defense. Navy. CINCPAC Representatives, Philippines. *A Country Law Study for the Republic of the Philippines*. (CINCPACREPPHIL P-5830.) San Francisco: FPO, Department of Navy, U. S. Naval Forces Philippines, 1967.

U. S. Department of Defense. Security Assistance Agency. Comptroller. *Foreign Military Sales and Military Assistance Facts, April 1974*. Washington: 1974.

U. S. Department of State. Agency for International Development. *Agency for International Development (AID) Economic Data Book for East Asia*. Washington: U. S. Department of Commerce, National Technical Information Service, 1973.

U. S. Department of State. Agency for International Development. Office of Public Safety. *Drug Abuse Education/Rehabilitation for Republic of Philippines*. Washington: November 1972.

———. *Survey of Philippine Law Enforcement*. Washington: GPO, 1966.

———. *Termination Phase-out Study: Public Safety Project, Philippines*. (No. 492–11–710–231.) Washington: May 1974.

———. *Traffic Survey Report of the Makati Police Department, Philippines*. Washington: April 1973.

U.S. Department of State. Agency for International Development. Statistics and Reports Division. *U.S. Overseas Loans and Grants: Preliminary Fiscal Year 1974 Data, Obligations and Authorizations July 1, 1973–June 30, 1974*. Washington: February 1975.

U.S. General Accounting Office. *Military Assistance and Commitments in the Philippines*. (Report to the Congress, B-133359.) Washington: GPO, April 12, 1973.

Utrecht, Ernst. "The Separatist Movement in the Southern Philippines," *Race and Class* [London], 16, No. 4, April 1975, 387–417.

Van der Kroef, Justus M. "ASEAN's Security Needs and Policies," *Pacific Affairs* [Vancouver], 47, No. 2, Summer 1974, 154–170.

———. "Communism and Reform in the Philippines," *Pacific Affairs* [Vancouver], 46, No. 1, Spring 1973, 29–58.

———. "Communist Fronts in the Philippines," *Problems of Communism*, XIV, No. 2, March–April 1967, 65–75.

———. "Patterns of Cultural Conflict in Philippine Life," *Pacific Affairs* [Vancouver], XXXIX, Nos. 3 and 4, 1966–67.

———. "Philippine Communism and the Chinese," *China Quarterly* [London], No. 30, April–June 1967, 115–148.

———. "Philippine Communist Theory and Practice: A New Departure?" *Pacific Affairs* [Vancouver], 48, No. 2, Summer 1975, 181–198.

———. "The Philippine Maoists," *Orbis*, 16, Winter 1973.

Villegas, Antonio J. "Criminality, Government, and Citizenry." Pages 87–90 in Jose Veloso Abueva and Raul P. de Guzman (eds.), *Foundations and Dynamics of Filipino Government and Politics*. Manila: Bookmark, 1969.

Wilson, Richard Garratt. *The Neutralization of Southeast Asia*. New York: Praeger, 1975.

Wurfel, David. "The Philippines." Pages 523–534 in Roger M. Smith (ed.), *Southeast Asia: Documents of Political Development and Change*. Ithaca: Cornell University Press, 1974.

———. "The Philippines." Pages 679–777 in George McTurnan Kahin (ed.), *Governments and Politics of Southeast Asia*. (2d ed.) Ithaca: Cornell University Press, 1964.

(Various issues of the following periodicals were also used in the preparation of this section: *Ang Tala: AFP Command and Information Bulletin* [Quezon City], December 1973–September 1975; *Asian Defence Journal* [Kuala Lumpur], January 1971–December 1972; *Asia Research Bulletin* [Singapore]; December 1974–August 1975; *Bulletin Today* [Manila], January–December 1975; *Christian Science Monitor* [Boston], June–December 1975; *The Constable* [Quezon City], June–December 1972 and November–December 1972; *Far Eastern Economic Review* [Hong Kong], February 1974 to September 1975; *Fookien Times* [Manila], 1969 and 1974; *The National Security Review* [Rizal], September 1973 and December 1973; *New Philippines* [Manila]; April 1974 to November 1974; *News Release* [Manila], January–August 22, 1975; *News Review on Japan, South East Asia, and Australia* [New Delhi], January 1972–December 1974; *New York Times*, January 1969 to October 1975; and *Weekly Government Bulletins* [Manila], May–November 1975.)

GLOSSARY

AFP—Armed Forces of the Philippines; includes army, navy, air force, and police.

barangay—Orginally the name given to communal settlements of the indigenous Philippine people at the time of the Spanish arrival. After 1973 the term was used to denote the citizens' assemblies established in each *barrio (q.v.)*; after mid-1974 replaced *barrio* as the lowest political subdivision of the Philippines.

barrio—Village. Principal settlement form of the country. A *barrio* usually consists of a primary hamlet and several satellite hamlets. Also, until renamed *barangay (q.v.)* in mid-1974, the lowest political subdivision of the municipality *(q.v.)* and municipal district *(q.v.)*.

cacique—One of an elite of wealthy landowners.

compadrazgo—The relationship between godparents and their god-child's parents.

CPP—Communist Party of the Philippines, usually referred to as PKP *(q.v.)*.

datus—Local leaders in pre-Spanish Philippine communities; also term used to denote Moro *(q.v.)* leaders.

fiscal year (FY)—The Philippine fiscal year extends from July 1 through June 30; beginning in 1977 the fiscal year is to correspond to the calendar year, January 1 through December 31.

GDP—Gross domestic product. Equals GNP *(q.v.)* at market prices less income from foreign investments and possessions owned abroad.

GNP—Gross national product. The value at market prices of all goods and services produced in the country during a given period, plus interest, profits, and dividends received from abroad.

hiya—A feeling of shame; having a sense of social propriety.

Huk—Short form of Hukbalahap *(q.v.)*.

Hukbalahap—Abbreviated form of the Tagalog *(q.v.)* name for the guerrilla force, established in 1942, known as the Hukbong Bayan Laban sa Hapon (People's Anti-Japanese Army); in 1946 renamed Hukbong Mapagpalaya ng Bayan (People's Liberation Army).

Igorots—Unassimilated pagan tribal peoples of central and northern Luzon mountains; popularly known for their spectacularly built rice terraces and past history of headhunting.

lider—A political broker between the voters and candidates in electoral politics before 1972.

mestizo—The offspring of Filipino and non-Filipino marriages; includes those of Spanish-Filipino parentage (Spanish mestizos) and Chinese-

Filipino parentage (Chinese mestizos).

MNLF—Moro National Liberation Front. Militant guerrilla organization striving for greater Moro *(q.v.)* autonomy.

Moro—Name given by Spanish to Muslim Filipinos and still used. Moros mostly inhabit southern and western Mindanao, the Sulu Archipelago, and Palawan and have not become assimilated into the mainstream of Philippine society.

municipal district—Administrative unit organized in an area inhabited for the most part by non-Christians. Roughly equivalent to a municipality *(q.v.)*.

municipality—Administrative unit equivalent to a county.

NDP—Net domestic product. The value at market prices of goods and services produced in the country in a given time. Does not include income from foreign investments and possessions owned abroad. Equals GDP *(q.v.)* at market prices less depreciation.

NPA—New People's Army. A militant Marxist-Leninist guerrilla group, operating principally in central Luzon.

peso (₱)—The monetary unit of the Philippines, composed of 100 centavos. Before 1962 the official exchange rate was US$1 equals ₱2.00. In 1962 the peso was devalued and stabilized at US$1 equals ₱3.90. This rate became the par value in 1965 and continued as such until 1970. The exchange rate was adjusted in 1970 through a major devaluation in which the peso was allowed to float in relation to other currencies. Since 1970 the peso has floated downward from a 1971 value of ₱6.50 per US$1 to ₱7.50 per US$1 in 1975.

Pilipino—A modified form of Tagalog *(q.v.)*. Adopted in 1939 as the national language.

PKP—Partido Komunista ng Pilipinas (Communist Party of the Philippines). Sometimes referred to as CPP *(q.v.)*.

población—The government seat of a municipality *(q.v.)*.

Samahong Nayon—The component of an agricultural cooperative at the *barrio (q.v.)* level created as part of the agrarian reform program.

sari-sari—Local general store.

sitio—A hamlet; part of a *barrio (q.v.)*.

Tagalog—Lowland Christian group located principally in Luzon and centered in Manila; also their language.

tao—The common man.

utang na loob—Literally, a debt inside oneself; the name for a system of reciprocal obligations that emphasizes interdependence.

INDEX

stitutional, 1, 191, 197, 210, 224, 225, 227, 348; and religion, 184

Babuyan islands: 11, 12
Baguio (city): 17, 18, 121
Balagtas, Francisco: 146
balance of payments (*see also* economy; trade): 252, 268, 269; deficit, 269, 301; problems, 256, 257, 258, 302, 303, 306, 331
Bangladesh: 244
Bangsa Moro Army: 358, 379
banks and banking (*see also* Asian Development Bank; economy): ix, 260, 263–264, 291; Central Bank, 255, 263; commercial, 264; Bank of the Philippines (DBP), 264, 303, 310; Land Banks, 292, 293; Philippine National Bank (PNB), 264, 283; rural, 283
Barangay Theater Guild: 150
barangays (*see also* government, local): 5, 23, 44, 45, 48, 78–79, 104, 143, 198, 203–204, 205, 222–225, 228, 230; formation of, 223, 224; under martial law, 209.
Barrio Charter Law: 205
Barrio Education Movement: 156
barrios (see also barangays; government, local): 23, 30, 101, 102, 103, 104, 112, 131, 134, 284, 338; high schools, 163; and land use, 293, 294, 295; and patronage, 213; and religious festivities, 176; self-defense units, 365
Basic Industries Act: 302–303
Basilan island: 12, 17, 309, 379
bastenero: 103
Bataan Peninsula: 12, 13; battle of, 65, 349
Batan islands: 11, 12
Batangas (town): 344
Bell Act. *See* Philippine Trade Act of 1946
Benguet Consolidated: 315
Biak na Bato (town): 57
Bilibid Prison: 392
Bicol Peninsula: 30, 275, 377
Bikolano group: 75, 77, 81, 82, 84, 88
bill of rights: 193, 195
birth control. *See* family planning
Board of Investments (BOI): 297, 306–308, 310, 311
Bohol island: 12, 13, 20, 277, 314
Bonifacio, Andrés: 56, 58
books and libraries: 167
Borneo (*see also* Sabah): 71, 242
budget (*see also* economy): 7, 267; campaign spending, 215–216, 252, 253; deficits, 269; education, 160; expenditures, 259, 262, 265, 267; family planning, 34; health, 132; military, 356–357, 371

Bukidnon-Lanao Highlands: 16
Bulacan airport: 345
Bulosan, Carlos: 148
Bureau of Industrial Coordination: 308
Bureau of Industrial Information and Programs: 308
Bureau of Plant Industries (BPI): 276
Burma: 234, 244

cabinet (*see also* departments): 191, 199
Cagayan de Oro (city): 120
Cagayan River: 11, 14, 21
Cagayan Valley: 11–12, 19, 21, 275, 344
Cambodia. *See* Khmer Republic
Canada: 32, 41, 264; and trade, 325, 334
Career Executive Service Development Program: 207
Castro, Servando: 182
Cavite Province: 30
Cebu (city): 120; and trade, 339
Cebu island: 12, 13, 20, 22, 30, 46, 277, 306, 314, 344; copper, 316
Cebuano group: 75, 77, 80, 81, 82, 83, 86
censorship. *See* freedom of expression
census: 27–28
Central Luzon Plain: 10, 13, 19, 21–22, 30, 83
Ceylon. *See* Sri Lanka
Charles I of Spain: 46
chiefs (*datus*): 44, 45, 48, 89, 284
children: 107, 111, 112, 113, 117, 137; and church rituals, 177
China: and nineteenth-century trade, 322, 338
China, People's Republic of (PRC): xiv, 7–8, 228, 232, 233, 235, 242, 246–247, 249, 329, 358, 378; and Sino-American détente, 231, 348; and trade, 337
China, Republic of (Nationalist China): xiv, 72, 234, 246, 247, 337
Chinese population: vii, 9, 45, 50, 53, 62, 71–72, 75, 76, 78, 79, 82, 92–94, 99, 282; early trade with, 45; and industrial control, 300; massacre of, 92; mestizos, 46, 49, 50, 51, 52, 53, 78, 80, 92, 106, 282, 285; religion of, 93; and the Spanish, 50, 92
Chou En-lai: 246
Christians (*see also* missionaries; Protestants; religion; Roman Catholic Church): viii, 10, 43, 47, 75, 76, 79, 80, 86, 87, 88, 90, 91; Chinese, 50; and drama, 148, 149; and education, 155; and indigenous religion, 171; Lowland Christians, 75, 76, 80, 81, 82–85, 91, 94, 95; minor groups, 85; and Moros, 87–88, 149; Muslim conflict, 287, 378, 380; and Spain, 48

chromite: 22, 313, 314, 315; and chromium, 298

cities and towns (*see also* Manila; urban society): 23, 24, 25, 30, 120–122, 136, 198; and crime, 382; government, 203, 204–205; problems of, 120–122; squatters, 107, 119, 121–122, 123

citizenship: 195; for Chinese, 94; and the United States, 196–197

Civil Intelligence and Security Agency: 383–384

civil rights (*see also* freedom of expression): 375; bill of rights, 193, 389; judicial, 389; loss of, 374

civil service: 64, 156, 205–207; prestige of, 206; purge of, 228

Civil Service Commission: 201–202

Clark Air Base: 349, 352, 362

Clave, Jacobo C.: 197

climate (*see also* droughts; earthquakes; floods; rainfall; typhoons): 9, 10, 17–19, 272–273

clothing (*see also* industry): 128–129; national costume, 128; during Spanish rule, 54

coal: 313, 314, 315

coconut: viii, 20, 274, 275, 279, 280, 283, 331

Command for the Administration of Detainees: 386

commerce (*see also* trade): 266

Commission on Audit: 201–202

Commission on Elections (COMELEC): 201–202, 207

Commission on National Integration: 80

Commission on Small and Medium Industries: 308

Common Market: 337

Commonwealth of the Philippines: 61, 63–64

communications, mass (*see also* books and libraries; freedom of expression; motion pictures; newspapers; periodicals; press; telecommunications; telephones; television): viii, 166–170, 345; word-of-mouth, 168

communist countries (*see also* China, People's Republic of; Soviet Union): 231, 235, 244, 245–248; Romania, 235, 246; Southeast Asia, 244–245; and trade, 321, 329, 337; Yugoslavia, 235, 246

communists and communism (*see also* insurgency; violence): x, 1, 44, 191, 217, 219, 221, 231–232, 238, 244, 245–248, 380; defense against, 249, 351; Maoists, 4, 373, 375, 377–378

Community Relations Unit: 356

compadrazgo: 110, 113

conscription: 357, 359, 360, 364, 365–366; of reserves, 364

constabulary. *See* Philippine Constabulary

Constabulary Offshore Anticrime Battalion: 386

Constitution of 1935: 19, 192, 193, 210, 211, 212, 221; and industry, 254

Constitution of 1973: 2, 41, 107, 191–192, 194–195, 199, 201, 207, 208, 222–223, 224, 385, 389; church and state, 172; constitutional commissions, 201–202; provisions of, 194–195

constitutions: viii, 57, 68, 192–197; bill of rights, 193–195; and the United States Constitution, 193

construction industry: 122, 298, 318–319; materials available, 313; plans, 266; urban, 318–319

cooperatives (*see also* Samahong Nayon): farm, 102, 103, 284, 292

copper (*see also* resources): 22, 261, 313, 314, 315, 316

Cordillera Central: 11, 13, 14

corn: viii, ix, 19, 20, 274, 275, 276, 279, 280, 282, 283, 291, 292

Corregidor: battle of, 65, 349

Cotabato Lowland: 16, 19, 379

cottage industry: 309; 317–318; handicrafts, 317

Council of the Indies (*see also* Spain): 47, 51

courts (*see also* judges; judicial branch; jury system; Sandiganbayan): viii, 200–201, 388–389; and agrarian reform, 293, 294 civil, 388–389; Court of Appeals, viii, 198, 201, 388; criminal procedure, 390–392; delays of, 387–389; military tribunals, 200, 370, 374, 388–389; Muslim, 89; New Rules of Court, 390, 391; Supreme Court, viii, 60, 191, 195, 198, 201, 388, 389, 390, 391

crafts: 143, 153–154; handicraft industry, 317, 318

crime (*see also* death penalty; insurgency; judicial branch; penal code; security, internal): 1, 2, 119, 222, 373–375, 381–383; criminal procedure, 390–392; detection and investigation, 384; urban, 374, 382

crops (*see also* abaca; coconut; corn; exports; fruits; rice; sugarcane): viii, 16, 20, 44, 49, 272, 273, 274, 275, 279, 280; cacao, 274, 280; coffee, 274, 280; commercial, 271, 273, 291; food, 271, 273, 282; production, 279; subsidies, 283

Cruz, Andrés Cristobal: 148

Cuba: 246

Cultural Center of the Philippines: 150
cultural life (*see also* artistic expression): 141, 142–154; heterogeneity of, 86; homogeneity of, 75, 79, 81, 99; traditional, 141.
currency (*see also* peso): ix, 325
curriculum (*see also* education): 158, 163

dairy products: 280, 281
dance (*see also* artistic expression): 143, 150, 151–152, 153; folk, 151, 152; *tinikling*, 152
datus. See chiefs
Davao (city): 16, 18, 19, 343; and trade, 339
Davao-Agusan Trough: 16
de las Llagas, Ciriaco: 182
de los Reyes, Isabelo: 181
de los Reyes, Jr., Isabelo: 183
death penalty: 381–382, 390, 391
debt *(see also* economy): external, 252–253, 259, 269; foreign, 269
defense. *See* security
democracy: 209, 210, 211, 215, 216, 217, 230; and the *barangays*, 223; failure of, 373–374
departments (*see also* cabinet; executive branch): agrarian reform, 199, 292, 293, 294; agriculture, 199, 282; education and culture, 159–160; finance, 199; foreign affairs, 199; health, 129, 132, 133, 135; industry, 199, 308; justice, 384; labor, 41, 299; local government and community development, 199, 202, 204; national defense, x, 347, 354, 359, 385, 387; natural resources, 199; public highways, 199; public information, 199; public works, transportation, and communications, 38, 199; social welfare, 199; tourism, 199; trade, 199
Design Center Philippines, 318
Development Academy of the Philippines, 207
Dewey, Commodore George: 57
diet and nutrition (*see also* health): 125–128; corn, 127; fish, 127; of infants and children, 127; rice, 127, 128; sweet potato, 127
Diokno, José W.: 219, 221
discrimination: against Chinese, 92, 93–94; during Spanish rule, 54, 174
disease (*see also* gastroenteritis; malaria; malnutrition; pneumonia; tuberculosis): vii, 125, 126, 135–136; bubonic plague, 129; cholera, 129, 135; control, 135; dysentery, 129; epidemics, 130; filariasis, 136; leprosy, 129; smallpox, 129; viral, 135; xerophthalmia, 127
dissidence. *See* insurgency

Diuata Mountains: 14, 16
divorce: 114, 186; and the church, 172
doctors: 134
Domingo, Damian: 154
drainage: 21–22, 273, 275, 276; erosion, 273
dress. *See* clothing
droughts: 18–19, 220, 272, 331
drugs: 382, 386

earthquakes: 10
economy (*see also* agriculture; balance of payments; banks and banking; budget; debt; exports; foreign exchange; gross national product; imports; income; industry; inflation; investments; National Economic Council; net domestic product; peso; tariffs; taxation; trade; underemployment; unemployment; United States): viii, 5–6, 68, 251–270; balanced growth of, 265–266; deficiencies of, 258; diverse foreign economic policy, 328–329; early development, 53, 253, 255; government role, 251, 254, 255, 262; growth of, 251, 252, 257, 266; and natural disasters, 260; planning, 256, 260, 264–267; private free enterprise; 193–194, 251, 254, 309, 316; reforms of, 252, 259, 260, 270, 297; during United States occupation, 62
education (*see also* curriculum; schools; students; teachers; universities and colleges; vocational and technical training): vii–viii, 95, 141, 142, 155–170; adult, 161; enrollments, 156, 163, 164; examinations, 158; government agencies, 160; of professionals, 156; reforms, 157–159; and the social structure, 100, 106; student fees, 160, 163; textbooks, 161, 163; during United States occupation, 60
Educational Decree of 1863: 155
Educational Development Decree of 1972: 157
elections. *See* voting
electoral system. *See* voting
electricity: 319, 320; hydroelectric sources, 319, 320
elite (*see also ilustrados; principalia;* upper class): 2, 3–4, 6, 44, 46, 52–53, 54, 55, 80, 99, 104, 105, 291; cultural, 141, 144; education of, 156; and the government, 59, 61, 67, 74; industrial, 301, 304–305; and the media, 167; military, 348; monopolies, 100; and politics, 215, 216–217; and World War II, 65, 66
Emergency Employment Administration: 36–37

employment (*see also* underemployment; unemployment): 258, 261, 268, 269; and agriculture, 271; of graduates, 165; and industry, 298, 303, 305, 309–310

encomiendas (*see also* landownership): 49, 284; and labor service, 51

energy: 337; crisis, 267, 315; resources, 319

Enrile, Juan Ponce: 228–229

Estrella, Conrado F.: 292–293

ethnic groups (*see also* pagan groups): 75–97; homogeneity of, 75, 76, 81–82

Europe, Western: 325, 326, 337

European Economic Community (EEC): 337

executive branch (*see also* cabinet; departments; Marcos, Ferdinand; presidency; prime minister): 67, 192, 197–199; staff units, 197

Export Incentives Act of 1970: 298, 306; and foreign enterprises, 329

Export Processing Zone Authority: 309

exports (*see also* crops): ix, 256–257, 297, 309, 321, 324–325; in colonial period, 255, 300; and the economy, 253–254, 255, 259, 261; major, 331, 332; of manufactured goods, 330; and primary products, 330, 332, 333; trends, 329–337; to the United States, 322–323, 328, 330

family life (*see also* social values): 3–4; 101, 102, 107, 108, 109, 110, 111, 112, 113, 114, 118; Chinese, 93; and crime, 381; and domestic trade, 339; extended family, 107, 108, 109–110; godparenthood, 110; nuclear family, 104, 108; solidarity of, 108–109

family planning: 11, 33–35, 111, 260, 267; and the church, 172; contributing organizations, 34

farms and farming (*see also* agriculture; irrigation; landownership; peasantry; tenants; rural society): 32, 38, 105, 286, 289, 291, 293, 295–296; credit, 283; and the New Society, 227; owner-cultivators, 287–288; subsistence, 287, 296

Federation of Free Farmers: 105

fertilizer: 20, 276, 278, 295

Fertilizer Industry Authority: 282

fiestas: 48, 111, 138

firearms: confiscation of, 221–222

fish and fishing: ix, 9, 17, 23, 38, 272, 277, 279, 281; and the economy, 251

floods: 272, 273; control of, 278

Flor Mata, Angel: 182

Food and Nutrition Research Center: 126

food industry: 308, 310, 312; beverages, 310, 312; coconuts, 325; cottage industry, 317

Food Production Corps: 359

food supply (*see also* crops; diet and nutrition): 126, 267–268; imports, 325

Ford Motor Company: 309

foreign exchange: 253, 257, 259, 269, 328; earners, 315, 332; shortage, 302

foreign relations (*see also* Asia; third world; United States): 7–8, 231–250

forests and forestry: ix, 15, 20–21, 38, 272, 277, 278–279, 281; and the economy, 251; mahogany, 20, 281; mangrove, 21; teak, 21

Four Year Development Plan: 251, 265, 266, 268, 299, 318; and construction, 319

France: 233

freedom of expression (*see also* civil rights): 375; and the bill of rights, 193; and censorship, 169, 170; international, 249; and the media, 2, 142, 168–170, 211; in the New Society, 209, 211; during United States occupation, 60

fruits: viii, 20, 272, 274, 280

Garcia, Carlos P. 71, 240

Garcia Villa, José: 147

gastroenteritis: 135

General Agreement on Tariffs and Trade (GATT): 329

Germany, Federal Republic of (West Germany): ix; and trade, 317–318, 334, 337

godparenthood: 110, 111

gold (*see also* resources, mineral): 22, 313, 314, 315

Gonzalez, N. V. M., 148

government, local (*see also* barangays; barrios; cities and towns; governors; *liders*; *poblaciónes*; provinces; voting): viii, 4–5, 198, 202–205; finance, 203, 204; Manila, 224–225; Muslim, 88–89; Spanish colonial, 48; during United States occupation, 60

government, national (*see also* executive branch; judicial branch; legislative branch; Marcos, Ferdinand; martial law; reforms; voting): viii, 67, 69–70, 191–202; checks and balances, 209, 211; commissions, 201–202; corruption, 207, 214, 215, 222, 228; Muslim, 88–89; before 1972, 210–211; Spanish colonial, 48; unitary, 193; during United States occupation, 60, 211; Western inspired, 211, 213

Government Service Insurance: 124, 137

governors: 204

governors general: 61

Great Britain (*see also* United Kingdom): 23; and the North Borneo Company, 242–243

gross national product (GNP): 27, 252, 256,

257, 259–260, 262, 263, 265, 269–270, 302, 315, 356
guerrilla warfare *(see also* Huks): 70; Maoists, 377; Moros, 86, 88

harbors: 10, 13, 17, 322, 339, 342, 344
Harrison, Francis B.: 61
headhunting: 91
health *(see also* diet and nutrition; disease; medical care): vii, 125, 126, 129–136; government agencies, 132, 133; and the school system, 131–132
higher education. *See* universities and colleges; vocational and technical training
Highway Patrol Group: 386
Hindus: 45
holidays: 138–139; Christmas, 176; other religious rituals, 138–139; 176–177
Home Defense Forces Group: 360–361
Home Defense Program: 348, 355–356, 357, 358, 365, 387; in agriculture, 356; civic programs, 355–356, 359; and the economy, 357
Hong Kong: 334
hospitals: 132, 133; Protestant, 189
housing: vii, 32, 120–121, 122–124; government programs, 123–124; low-cost, 319
Huks (Hukbalahap) *(see also* insurgency): 65–66, 69, 173, 184, 284, 293, 356, 373; and armed forces, 350, 355; remnants of 377

Ifugao group: 145, 154
Iglesia ni Kristo *(see also* religion): 171, 180, 183–184; and politics, 183, 184
Igorots *(see also* pagan groups): 43, 47, 78, 90–92, 95, 174
Iloilo (city): trade, 339, 344
Iloilo island: 30
Ilokano group: 75, 76, 77, 81, 83–84, 86, 88, 109, 287
Ilongo group: 77, 84, 85
ilustrados (see also elite; *principalía;* upper class): 53, 54, 55–56, 57, 59, 67
imports *(see also* industry): ix, 256–257, 321, 324, 325, 330, 333; chief, 334; during colonial period, 255, 300; consumer goods, 331, 334; controls, 256, 257, 264, 325; dependence on, 302; and the economy, 259, 268, 269, 303; producer goods, 331; trends, 333–334
income: distribution, 119, 125, 256, 258, 259, 263, 268, 269, 271; national, 7, 262; personal, 124, 125, 252; rural, 271, 288, 295
independence: 44, 57, 63, 64, 66, 72, 231
Independence Day: 57, 72, 139

Independent Philippine Evangelical Church *(see also* religion): 182
India: 233
Indonesia: xiv, 88, 233, 234, 241, 242, 337, 352; early trade with, 45; people from, 78
industry *(see also* agriculture; construction; cottage industry; economy; food; labor force; manufacturing; mining; power; textiles; tourism): ix, 6, 297–320; clothing, 311, 317; colonial, 253; and consumer goods, 301–302, 310, 321; and government, 254, 255, 301, 303–304; growth of, 306; and import-substitution, 301, 302, 303, 311; "military-industrial complex," 357; paper, 311, 312; and producer goods, 321
infant mortality: 135
inflation *(see also* economy): viii, ix, 7, 124, 125, 216, 260, 267, 268, 333, 338; during 1969 election, 259
infrastructure: and the armed forces, 357; improvements, 298, 318, 319, 341, 343
Institute of National Language: 95, 96
insurgency *(see also* Aglipayan movement; communists and communism; crime; guerilla warfare; land reform; peasantry; security; subversion; violence): x, 1, 2, 44, 202, 225, 355, 358, 359, 371, 373, 375–381, 383; agrarian, 288; and armed forces, 354, 355, 358, 359, 371; communist, 348, 377–378; and government action, 377–378; in Luzon, 348, 359, 373, 377; in Mindanao, 347, 355, 358, 359, 373, 375, 378, 379; Muslim, 1, 2, 219–220, 222, 225, 243–244, 245, 287, 358, 359, 366, 374, 375; in Sulu Archipelago, 347, 355, 359, 363, 373, 378, 379; during Spanish rule, 52; during United States occupation, 63
Integrated Civil Home Defense Forces: 364–365
Integrated National Police (INP): 374, 383, 385
interest groups: 5, 214
International Bank for Reconstruction and Development (IBRD): 34, 260, 307, 310, 330
International Monetary Fund (IMF): 252, 330
International Rice Research Institute (IRRI): 73, 166, 276
Investment Incentives Act: 306
investments *(see also* Board of Investments; economy): 252, 254, 255–256, 261, 265, 306; and agriculture, 271; American, 305, 327; foreign, 7, 253, 265, 300, 301, 305, 311, 329, 339; public, 252; in transportation, 341

101, 142; Tagalog, vii, 3, 45, 75, 77, 83, 96–97
Pius X, Pope: 175
pneumonia: vii, 135
poblaciónes: 24, 30, 102, 103, 104, 131; government of, 205
police (*see also* Philippine Constabulary; security): ix–x, 373, 374, 377, 387
political parties: 4, 66, 67, 211–216, 376; Communist Party of the Philippines (Partido Komunista ng Pilipinas—PKP), 220, 377, 378; Federal Party, 211; Liberal Party, 66, 72, 212, 213, 218, 219, 220–221; Partido Democrata (Democratic Party), 212; Partido Nacionalista (Nationalist Party), 66, 70, 211–212, 213, 215–216, 218; patronage, 58
political philosophies. *See* authoritarianism; communists and communism; nationalism
political systems (*see also* Marcos; martial law; New Society): 209–230; checks and balances, 209, 211; values, 213
political values: 229–230; loyalties, 210, 213; and reform, 229, 230
pollution: 136
polygamy: 89, 186
population (*see also* family planning): vii, 2–3, 24–35; density, 17, 28, 30; growth, 10–11, 28, 66–67, 257, 267, 270, 287, 295; homogeneity of, 3, 75, 76, 78, 99; lack of statistics, 27, 30; and land use, 295; youth, 28
Population Commission (POPCOM): 33–34
ports: 10, 13, 17, 322, 339, 342, 344
poverty: 1, 6–7, 167; and Protestantism, 172
power industry (*see also* oil): 319–320; electric, 319, 320; thermal, 319, 320
Pramot, Khukrit: 244
presidency (*see also* executive branch; Marcos): 67, 82, 191, 192, 193, 196, 197–199, 211, 212; and armed forces, 353; and national security, 383; redefinition of, 195, 196; since independence, 121; succession of, 199, 222, 227
Presidential Arm for National Minorities (PANAMIN): 80
Presidential Economic Staff (PES): 264
press (*see also* freedom of expression; newspapers): viii, 142, 168, 169, 211, 376
prices (*see also* inflation): 124–125; controls, 125
prime minister (*see also* executive branch; Marcos): 191, 198, 201–202; and armed forces, 353
principalía (*see also* elite; *ilustrados*; upper

class): 48, 50, 52
prisons and jails: 392
Propaganda Movement: 56
Protestants (*see also* Christians; missionaries; religion): 62–63, 171, 187–189; denominations, 187–188; and dissent, 376; National Council of Churches, 188, 189, 376; Protestant Episcopal Church, 183; schisms, 188; schools, 187–188
Proto-Malay people: 44
provinces: 23, 25, 198; government of, 203; population of, 31, 32; and the Spanish, 48

Qudhaafi, Muammar al: 380
Quezon City: vii, 10, 376
Quezon, Manuel L.: 61, 63, 64, 65, 96, 211–212, 349; and Social Justice program, 64
Quirino, Elpidio: 69, 70, 233

radio: 149, 150, 166, 167, 168, 170; and martial law, 221
railroads: ix, 341, 342, 343–344; of sugar mills, 343
rainfall (*see also* typhoons): 10, 18, 19, 272–273; monsoons, 18
rebellion. *See* Philippine Revolution; violence
recession: worldwide, 297, 299, 332, 333
reforms: 221, 222; land, 222; political, 217, 228, 230; social, 219
religion (*see also* Christians; Islam; missionaries; Muslims; pagan groups; Protestants; Roman Catholic Church): 91, 171–189; indigenous, 138–139; 172–173, 175; minor sects, 185; polytheism, 173; revivals, 172–173; rituals, 138–139, 176–177
Reserve Officers Training Corps (ROTC): 364, 365, 366, 367
resources, mineral (*see also* chromite; coal; copper; gold; iron; manganese; mining; nickel): 3, 22–23, 313–317
resources, natural: ix, 3, 46, 60, 68, 91, 193, 194, 257, 278, 298, 316; human, 270
Retail Trade Nationalization Law of 1954: 338
Revised United States-Philippine Trade Agreement of 1955 (Laurel-Langley Agreement): ix, 71, 236, 237, 253, 321, 325–328
Revolution of 1896–1899 (*see also* Katipunan society): 55–57, 149
rice (*see also* agriculture): viii, ix, 18, 19, 275, 276, 277, 279, 280, 282–283, 286, 291, 292; black market, 283; marketing, 282–283,

341; "miracle rice," 73, 166, 276; palay, 274, 278, 282; wet rice agriculture, 79, 91
Rice Share Tenancy Act of 1933: 288–289
rivers: 21–22
Rizal, José B.: 55–56, 174; writings of, 146–147
Rizal Province: 30, 32, 318
roads and highways: ix, 10, 278, 341–343; and Japanese aid, 240; Pan-Philippine Highway, 343; rural, 278
Roman Catholic Church (see also Christians; holidays; religion): 11, 43, 45, 46, 54, 62, 75, 76, 79, 87, 101, 110, 113, 171, 173–179, 181, 184; abuses, 174; Church of the Indies, 47; and death, 178; and dissent, 375–376; and education, 155, 172, 175; and family planning, 33, 35; festivals and rituals, 176–177; friars, 46, 47, 52, 54, 55, 61, 171, 180; and indigenous beliefs, 144, 172; and landownership, 49, 61–62, 285; organization, 178–179; and politics, 226; reforms, 175, 179; religious orders, 174; and social action, 179
Romulo, Carlos P.: 147–148, 232, 239, 241, 247
Roosevelt, Franklin D.: 236, 349
Roxas, Manuel A.: 66, 68–69, 212; and armed forces, 349–350
rural health units: 132–133, 134
rural society (see also barrios; farms and farming; lower class; peasantry; sitios): viii, 3, 35, 37, 55, 101–105, 214; and communication, 167–168; cooperative work, 102, 103; and health, 131, 132, 133; housing, 123; incomes, 124, 125; and politics, 214

Sabah: xiv, 11, 17, 23, 74, 242–244, 348–349; insurgency in, 348, 380
Sakdal group: 173; uprising, 63, 64
Samahong Nayon (see also cooperatives): 292, 293, 295
Samal group: 77, 85, 86
Samar island: 12, 13, 22, 277, 314
San Miguel Corporation: 310
Sandiganbayan (see also courts): 200, 388
Sangguniang Bayans: 198, 203–204, 210
sanitation: vii, 135–136
Sarawak: 242–243
Saudi Arabia: ix, 248, 334, 335, 336, 337; and Muslim rebellion, 381
School of Reserve Commissions (see also armed forces): 367–368
schools (see also education; universities and colleges; vocational and technical training): accreditation, 158–159; elementary, 155, 156, 161–163; and health programs, 131–132; and martial law, 221; military, 359, 362, 364, 365, 366–367; nursery, 161; parochial, 175, 178, 187, 189; private, 156, 159–160, 164; secondary, 163–164, 364
science: 165–166; agencies, 165–166; publications, 165
sculpture: 154
security, internal (see also communists and communism; courts; crime; insurgency; Muslims; police; subversion; violence): ix–x, 227, 347, 373–392; agencies, 383–384; and handguns, 375, 380, 381–382; and identification cards, 383; and private armies, 375, 381
security, national (see also armed forces): ix, 347–371; policy, 347, 351, 370; and the United States, 348, 350, 351, 352
service industries: 258; plans, 266
settlement patterns: 44, 45; and isolation, 46
shantytowns: 32
ships and shipping: ix, 13, 341, 344
Sierra Madre: 11, 13
sinakulo: 148–149
Singapore: xiv, 234, 244, 351, 352
Sison, José Maria: 221
sitios: 101, 102–103, 104, 112
slavery: 44, 186; and Moros, 87, 89–90
smuggling: 384, 386
snakes: 23
Social Security System: 41, 124, 137
social structure (see also elite; family life; ilustrados; kinship; lower class; middle class; peasants; principalía; tao group; upper class): 3, 99–118; early, 44–45; hierarchical, 99; mobility of, 100, 106, 108
social values (see also family life; political values): 114–118; acceptance and approval, 117; and civil service, 206; family loyalty, 107, 108, 109, 111, 112, 114, 210, 227, 229; hiya, 116; manner of speech, 118; personal honor, 117–118; sense of obligation, 101, 102, 104, 114–115, 116; utang na loob, 114, 115, 116
Social Welfare Administration: 136–137
soil: 10, 13, 16, 19–21, 272, 273, 275; fertilization, 20, 276, 278, 295
Southeast Asia. See Asia, Southeast
Southeast Asia Treaty Organization (SEATO): 71, 233, 244, 249, 250, 351–352
Soviet Union: 8, 232, 234, 245, 246, 247–248, 249, 329
Spain (see also Audiencia; Council of the Indies; encomiendas; judicial branch;

landownership; Roman Catholic Church): vii, 9, 23, 32, 80, 86, 92, 322; and bureaucratic corruption, 54; colonial administration, 46, 48, 49, 50, 53, 54
Spanish Orient Lodge of Freemasonry: 175, 181
Spanish-American War: 43, 57; treaty, 57
Special Science Fund: 166
sports: 139
squatters: rural, 278; urban, 107, 119, 121–122, 123
Sri Lanka: 233, 234, 244
students (*see also* education): 161; activism, 219, 376, 377, 384; demonstrations, 1, 74; dissent, 157, 375
Sturtevant, David R.: 173
Subic Bay: naval base, 352, 362
subversion (*see also* insurgency; violence): 358, 375, 377, 391; and the church, 376
sugarcane: viii, 19, 68, 274, 276, 277, 280, 282, 285, 291, 328; industry, 310, 315, 325, 332, 354; marketing, 283; and the world market, 328
Suharto: 234
Sukarno: 241, 242
sultanates: 88, 89
Sulu Archipelago (*see also* insurgency): 7, 11, 12, 17, 19, 44, 52, 85, 174, 387
Sulu region: 45, 88
Sulu Sea: 16

Tabila: 97
Taft, William Howard: 59, 60, 181
Tagalog group (*see also* Pilipino language): 80, 82–83, 287
tagnawa: 102, 103
Tanaka, Kakuei: 241
tao group: 70
tariffs: 257, 260, 263, 326; import duties, 326; and independence, 323, 325; protective, 334; reforms, 263; and the United States, 328, 334
Taruc, Luis: 69
Tasaday group: 10
Tausug group: 77, 85, 86, 379
Tawitawi island: 17, 379
taxation: 260, 262, 263, 267; of cottage industries, 317; and investments, 252, 306; reforms, 263; incentives, 297, 301, 302, 303, 306, 307, 309, 317
teachers (*see also* education): 163, 164, 165, 375, 384; prestige of, 103, 132
technical training. *See* vocational and technical training
Telangtan Bros. and Sons: 310

telecommunications: 345
telephones: 345
television: 149, 166–167, 170; and martial law, 221
tenants (*see also* farms and farming; landlords; peasantry): 55, 59, 60, 62, 68, 72, 100, 278, 283, 285, 286–288, 289, 290, 291, 292, 293, 294, 295; leaseholders, 290, 291, 292; sharecropping, 285
textiles industry: ix, 308, 310, 311, 312; cottage industry, 317
Thailand: 71, 233, 234, 244, 249–250, 352
third world: 248
Toledo: 22
Tondo district. *See* Manila
topography: vii, 10, 11, 13, 14, 15, 16; mountains, 9, 10, 11, 13, 14, 15–16, 17, 18, 19; volcanoes, 13, 16
tourism: 139, 298–299
trade, domestic (*see also* marketing): 321, 338–341; barter, 338; department stores, 340; government role, 338; peddlers, 340; *sari-sari* stores, 340; trading houses, 340
trade, foreign (*see also* balance of payments; economy; exports; imports; industry; investments; Japan; Saudi Arabia; tariffs; United States): ix, 71, 253, 257, 269, 321–337; agreements with United States, 71, 236, 253, 255; deficit, 256, 269, 300–301, 329, 331, 332; early, 45, 321–322; entrepôt trade, 46, 50; surplus, 253; trends, 329–337
Trade Reform Act of 1973: 328
transportation (*see also* air transportation; railroads; roads and highways; ships and shipping; waterways): ix, 338, 339, 341–345; plans, 266; water, 338
Treaty of Friendship, Commerce, and Navigation (*see also* Japan): 240–241, 329
tuberculosis: vii, 135
Tun Mustapha: 243–244
Tydings-Koscialkowski Act of 1939: 64
Tydings-McDuffie Act. *See* Philippine Independence Act
typhoons (*see also* rainfall)): vii, 10, 19, 123, 220, 273

underemployment: ix, 1, 36, 252, 268–269; 309; rural, 288
unemployment: ix, 1, 36, 37, 252, 258, 265, 268–269, 309; rural, 288
United Kingdom (*see also* Great Britain): 233, 325, 334, 337, 351
United Nations: 232, 244, 248–249
United Nations Command: 350
United Nations Development Program: 34

PUBLISHED AREA HANDBOOKS

550–47	Syria	550–97	Uruguay
550–62	Tanzania	550–71	Venezuela
550–53	Thailand	550–57	Vietnam, North
550–178	Trinidad and Tobago	550–55	Vietnam, South
550–89	Tunisia	550–99	Yugoslavia
550–80	Turkey	550–75	Zambia
550–74	Uganda		

☆ U.S. GOVERNMENT PRINTING OFFICE : 1976—O–211–451/18